ref
tea

in high

2nd ed

To renew, find us online at:
https://capitadiscovery.co.uk/bromley

Please note: Items from the adult library
may also accrue overdue charges when
borrowed on children's tickets.

In partnership with

BE**TT**ER
the feel good place

reflective teaching

in higher education

2nd edition

Paul Ashwin
and
David Boud, Susanna Calkins, Kelly Coate, Fiona Hallett,
Gregory Light, Kathy Luckett, Iain MacLaren, Katarina Mårtensson,
Jan McArthur, Velda McCune, Monica McLean and Michelle Tooher

BLOOMSBURY ACADEMIC

LONDON • NEW YORK • OXFORD • NEW DELHI • SYDNEY

BLOOMSBURY ACADEMIC
Bloomsbury Publishing Plc
50 Bedford Square, London, WC1B 3DP, UK
1385 Broadway, New York, NY 10018, USA

BLOOMSBURY, BLOOMSBURY ACADEMIC and the Diana logo are trademarks of
Bloomsbury Publishing Plc

First published in Great Britain 2015
This edition published 2020

Cover design: Adriana Brioso
Cover images © iStock (skynesher, D76MasahiroIKEDA, Jovanmandic, South_agency,
Wavebreakmedia, monkeybusinessimages, Rawpixel, lisafx)

A catalogue record for this book is available from the British Library.

A catalog record for this book is available from the Library of Congress.

ISBN: HB: 978-1-3500-8467-4
       PB: 978-1-3500-8466-7
       ePDF: 978-1-3500-8469-8
       eBook: 978-1-3500-8468-1

Series: Reflective Teaching

Typeset by RefineCatch Limited, Bungay, Suffolk
Printed and bound in Great Britain

To find out more about our authors and books visit www.bloomsbury.com
and sign up for our newsletters.

*In memory of our colleague and friend Brenda Leibowitz,
an inspirational educator who dedicated her life to
enhancing social justice.*

Contents

Part four Reflecting on consequences

Part five Deepening understanding

Introduction

Teaching in Higher Education is a creative and intellectually demanding process. It can be exciting and inspiring when things go well and difficult and disheartening when things just don't seem to work. An important part of becoming a reflective teacher is recognizing that all teachers experience these highs and lows and they are an integral part of being a teacher rather than a reflection of individual brilliance or incompetence.

This book is designed for all of those working in higher education who are interested in further developing their approaches to teaching, whether they are new to teaching or wish to reflect on an activity in which they have been engaged for many years. It offers both ready access to material to help you deal with the immediate demands of teaching in higher education and ideas that will allow you to reflect on your teaching and your students' learning in a deeper and more sustainable way over the course of your career. Throughout the book, we argue for a reflective approach to teaching in higher education.

WHY REFLECTIVE TEACHING IN HIGHER EDUCATION?

The basic idea of reflective teaching is to systematically re-evaluate our teaching experiences in order to improve our future teaching practices. Being reflective is of central importance to our practices as teachers in higher education because it:

- underpins our professional judgements;
- provides a vehicle for learning and professional development and thereby promotes our independence and integrity as teachers in higher education;
- is a means to improve our teaching, to enhance our students' learning and to further develop the quality of higher education.

Underlying the notion of reflective teaching in this book are four key messages. The first is that it *is* possible to identify teaching strategies which are more effective than others in most circumstances. Teachers in higher education therefore have to be able to develop, improve, promote and defend their expertise by marshalling evidence and by embedding enquiry and evaluation within their day-to-day practices. Second, all evidence has to be interpreted – and we do this by 'making sense'. In other words, as well as inform-ation about effective strategies we need to be able to discern the underlying principles of learning and teaching to which specific findings relate – we need to *understand* what is going on in this complex aspect of our academic lives. Third, we need to draw on this understanding to change our practices so that reflection is more than simply 'thinking' about our teaching. Finally, that our work as reflective teachers in higher education is connected to the future of our societies and to the life-chances of the students with whom we work. Therefore, our values and sense of the 'good society' are implicated in this work.

A PRINCIPLED APPROACH

So what are the underlying principles of learning and teaching? In this book, we draw on ten principles that encourage a deeper understanding of teaching practices in higher educa-tion. These are based on international research findings about effective learning, teaching and assessment in higher education, including the outcomes of a major UK research and development programme, the Teaching and Learning Research Programme (TLRP). The principles in brief are:

1 Effective teaching and learning demands consistent policy frameworks, with support for learning for diverse students as their main focus.

2 Effective teaching and learning depends on the scholarship and learning of all those educators who teach and research to support the learning of others.

3 Effective teaching and learning recognizes the significance of informal learning to developing specific expertise.

4 Effective teaching and learning fosters both individual and social processes and outcomes.

5 Effective teaching and learning promotes the active engagement of the student as learner.

6 Effective teaching and learning needs assessment to be congruent with learning.

7 Effective teaching and learning requires learning to be systematically developed.

8 Effective teaching and learning recognizes the importance of prior or concurrent experience and learning.

9 Effective teaching and learning engages with expertise and valued forms of knowledge in disciplines and subjects.

10 Effective teaching and learning equips learners for life in its broadest sense.

These principles are used to frame each chapter, although we do not discuss them in detail until Chapter 4. This is because we need to have a sense of who we are as teachers and who our students are (Chapter 1), how our students learn (Chapter 2) and how we can develop a reflective approach to teaching (Chapter 3) before we can productively engage with principles that can help to guide our reflective practices.

A PRACTICAL APPROACH

This book deliberately brings together these ten principles for effective teaching, learning and assessment in higher education with the discussion of practical examples in the form of case studies and reflective activities. Because the ways in which we teach are influenced by who we teach, what we teach, and where we teach, these examples and activities are from a broad range of the disciplines and areas of professional practice levels, and institutional settings that make up contemporary, global higher education. In addition, because taking a research-informed approach is a key element of reflective teaching, the book also contains 25 Research Briefings which provide an introduction to the substantial body of research into teaching, learning and assessment in higher education that can usefully inform our ways of teaching.

In the next section, we outline the structure of the book and indicate which of the principles listed above each chapter covers. In general, all of the principles are each covered equally across the book. However, there is one exception. Whilst nine of the principles are each covered in three or four chapters, Principle 2, on the scholarship and learning of educators, is covered in six chapters. This is because the central aim of this book is to inform our learning as teachers in higher education.

A COLLECTIVE AND INTERNATIONAL APPROACH

As we argue throughout this book, teaching is more of a collective endeavour than an individual one. The same is true of this book. It has been collectively written by an international team of experts in teaching, learning and assessment in higher education, whose details are provided at the end of the book. Whilst this was true of the first edition, this second edition is based even more strongly on a collective understanding of teaching in higher education. We have had new members join the team and existing members of the team led on different chapters than they did in the first edition in order to encourage us to further develop our collective account of university teaching. The task of the members of the second-edition team was to update the chapters in terms of new issues, ideas and research findings that have arisen since the publication of the first edition. This writing process means that all of the chapters have been worked on by at least four members of the teams for the first and second edition, although particular authors led the revision of particular chapters in this edition (the Acknowledgements on p.404 provide further detail on the authors who led the revision of each chapter).

In working collectively, we have sought to bring together the latest knowledge and understanding of teaching, learning and assessment in higher education in this second edition. We have integrated this knowledge with practical examples and attempted to show the importance of making active judgements about how to use this knowledge in particular situations. We hope you find this book helpful in developing and sustaining your approach to reflective teaching over the course of your academic career.

Using this book

This book contains a number of features to support teachers in higher education, whether they are new to teaching or have many years' experience of teaching. In developing a greater understanding of teaching, it helps to 'stand back' as well as engaging in the detail of educational issues – the structure of the book will help in this.

Within each chapter

Each chapter introduces and explores key issues using a combination of experiences of teaching and contemporary research. Additionally, you will find:

Reflective Activities Reflective activities are designed to support you in developing your thinking about teaching further. Each Reflective Activity comes with a full explanation of its aims, methods and follow-up required, and can be carried out individually or with colleagues.

Research Briefings In order to support research-informed approaches to teaching, we provide summaries of important research studies that convey their intentions, key findings and practical implications.

TLRP Principles

Experienced teachers get used to policies and practices which come and go – however, there are enduring features of effective teaching and learning on which most practitioners and researchers can agree. At the start of each chapter, these boxed features invite consideration of some of these 'principles' of teaching, as identified by a large UK research programme, TLRP.

Case Studies provide examples of particular situations and initiatives found in higher education, and explore their educational implications.

At the end of each chapter

Key Readings Each chapter ends with a review of available resources for follow up study, directing you to a selection of useful texts which will help further your learning.

Online

This icon shows where related material can be found online, including on the book's dedicated website reflectiveteaching.co.uk/books-and-resources/rthe2, which offers many free resources to support this book:

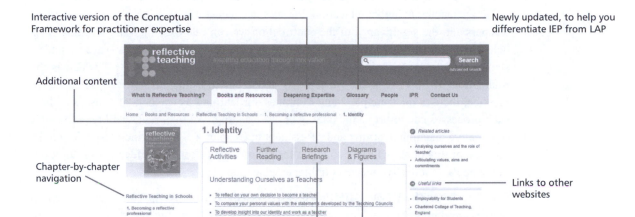

Interactive version of the Conceptual Framework for practitioner expertise

Newly updated, to help you differentiate IEP from LAP

Additional content

Chapter-by-chapter navigation

Links to other websites

Downloadable versions of items from the book

A summary of the book

PART 1: BECOMING REFLECTIVE introduces and structures the activity of becoming a reflective teacher in higher education. We start in Chapter 1 with a focus on who we are as teachers and the significance of the contribution we can make through our teaching. This helps to illustrate Principles 2 and 10. Then comes an introduction to ways of understanding students' 'learning' (Chapter 2 examining Principles 3 and 8) – which is the foundation of how we make judgements about our teaching. Chapter 3, on reflective practice, focuses on Principle 2 and examines our learning as teachers and discusses how such processes can improve the quality of our teaching. We then review all ten principles of effective teaching, learning and assessment in Chapter 4. These principles underpin the purpose of this book, which is to argue for the methodical use of evidence to inform our judgements as reflective teachers in higher education.

PART 2: CREATING CONDITIONS FOR LEARNING concerns the construction of environments to support high-quality teaching and learning. We begin by considering the range of contexts that help to shape teaching and learning in higher education (Chapter 5, Principles 1 and 3) – and we note the ways in which people contribute to and challenge the impact of such contexts. We then move to the heart of teaching and learning environments with a focus on the relationships between students and teachers in higher education (Chapter 6, Principles 3 and 4). Because such relationships are so crucial for students' success, this is an extremely important chapter. Chapter 7 (Principles 2 and 9) builds further and considers how we make disciplinary knowledge accessible to our students by engaging deeply with our teaching. Finally, we consider a range of learning spaces in higher education and beyond (Chapter 8, Principles 4 and 5) and the ways they can help students to engage in high-quality learning.

PART 3: TEACHING FOR UNDERSTANDING supports the development of practice across the three classic dimensions of teaching – curriculum, teaching and assessment. Chapter 9 (Principles 6, 7 and 9) first examines the ways in which disciplinary knowledge is transformed into curriculum before examining how we might design curricula. 'Planning' (Chapter 10, Principles 5, 6 and 7) puts these ideas into action. It is more practically orientated and starts at the level of the individual session before considering module and then programme planning. Chapter 11 (Principles 2, 4, 5, 8 and 9) offers ways of understanding the art, craft and science of teaching – and examines how we can focus our teaching on student understanding. 'Communication' (Chapter 12, Principles 4 and 5) extends this with an introduction to the role of dialogue across the curriculum, which highlights the importance of engaging our students in discussions about their learning. Finally, this part concludes by examining how assessment makes a contribution to students' learning and how we can make decisions about the design of assessment (Chapter 13, Principle 6). In short, this part of the book examines how we can support students in developing an understanding of disciplinary knowledge and professional practices through the careful design of our curricula, teaching and assessment practices.

PART 4: REFLECTING ON CONSEQUENCES examines how we can make sense of the effects of our teaching. Chapter 14 (Principles 2 and 7) considers important practical issues of how we monitor and improve the quality of our teaching. 'Inclusion' (Chapter 15, Principles 1, 8 and 10) highlights various dimensions of difference and the ways in which unreflective teaching can unfairly differentiate between different groups of people and inadvertently disadvantage some. It examines the positive role of difference in teaching and learning and how to build more inclusive university communities.

PART 5: DEEPENING UNDERSTANDING is the final, synoptic part of the book. It integrates major themes through an examination of teacher expertise and professionalism. 'Expertise' (Chapter 16, Principles 2 and 3) focuses on how we can bring together reflective teaching and the scholarship of teaching and learning in order to develop expert teaching. The chapter returns to the ten principles outlined in Chapter 4 and considers how we might develop these through our teaching. Chapter 17 on 'Professionalism' (Principles 1 and 10) considers the role that teaching in higher education plays within our societies and suggests how it might contribute to societal change.

Part one

Becoming reflective

Part 1 introduces the activity of becoming a reflective teacher in higher education. We start in Chapter 1 with a focus on identities, who we are as teachers and who are our students. Then comes an introduction to ways of understanding students' 'learning' (Chapter 2) – which is the foundation of how we make judgements about our teaching. The chapter on reflective practice (Chapter 3) examines our learning as teachers and discusses how such processes can improve the quality of our teaching. We then review the ten principles of effective teaching, learning and assessment in Chapter 4. These principles underpin the purpose of this book, which is to argue for the methodical use of evidence to inform our judgements as reflective teachers in higher education.

Chapter 1
Identities
Who we are as teachers and who are our students?

INTRODUCTION

Why does it matter who we are as teachers in higher education? Why does it matter that we think about who we are? Why does it matter who our students are, and why does it matter what we think about them? Why does it matter how our students think about themselves as learners?

These questions all concern matters of identity, which lie at the heart of what it means to be a reflective teacher in higher education. This is because the ways in which we see ourselves as human beings, as academics and as teachers, play a vital role in how we teach. Likewise, how our students see themselves as learners is crucial to how well they will be able to engage with the learning experiences we share with them. Understanding matters of identity helps us to navigate our careers and helps us to orientate ourselves towards our students, and to help them to learn.

Our identities can be attributed to us and our students, as white, black, female, LGBT+, working class, middle class, disabled, as members of particular disciplines or fields of study, as 'home' or international students or staff. Our identities are constructed through the work we do and the practices that we engage in. They are also a matter of affiliation, in that we may choose to identify with a particular group, but we do not have full control over matters of our identity. What is certain is that an understanding of matters of identity, our own identities and those of our students, enhances our sense of agency, efficacy and ability to influence our teaching and learning in many ways.

Being a teacher and being a student are interrelated processes and so our own identities as scholars and learners can help us to understand our students' identities. Simply because as teachers we are not learning the same things as our students, it does not mean that we stop learning. On the contrary, our learning should be ever deepening and broadening as we move through our careers as reflective teachers in higher education.

See Chapter 4

TLRP Principles

Two principles are of particular relevance to this chapter on identity:

Principle 2: Effective teaching and learning depends on the scholarship and learning of all those educators who teach and research to support the learning of others. The need for lecturers, teachers and trainers to learn through doing research to improve their knowledge, expertise and skills for teaching should be recognized and supported.

Principle 10: Effective teaching and learning equips learners for life in its broadest sense. Learning should help individuals develop the intellectual, personal and social resources that will enable them to participate as active citizens, contribute to economic, social or community development, and flourish as individuals in a diverse and changing society. This means adopting a broad conception of worthwhile learning outcomes and taking seriously issues of equity and social justice for all.

This chapter discusses the significance of identities for teachers, covering issues such as sense of direction, values, attitude towards students, narrative and biography, shared assumptions, and the role of emotions. In relation to students' identities, it considers: their perceptions of themselves, their views of each other and their attitudes towards their teachers. The chapter concludes with a restatement of the importance of coming to terms with the role of identity in reflective teaching.

In this chapter, some of the examples we draw upon come from South Africa. South African higher education remains influenced by the vestiges of its apartheid past, and its university teachers often need to grapple with ongoing tensions and opportunities in relation to group and individual identities. Whilst these issues may be more immediately striking in the South African context, they are issues that we all face as reflective teachers. Other examples in this chapter come from research conducted in the UK into how academics understand themselves as teachers and how students from different backgrounds see themselves as learners. Wherever we are located, these cases can help us to think through what 'identities' might mean in contexts of diversity and change, which are increasingly present in higher education globally.

To aid this process, Research Briefing 1.1 examines the different meanings of identities and how these relate to agency.

RESEARCH BRIEFING 1.1 Identities and agency

It is quite common when writing about how academics and students see themselves to use the word 'identities'. This plural form is used to signal that how we understand ourselves is a complex dance over time between: stories we tell about ourselves; stories others tell about us; our values; and our sense of connection with or exclusion from different groups and communities (for recent explorations of academic identities see Evans and Nixon 2015; Brew et al. 2018; McAlpine and Amundsen 2018; Ursin et al. 2018).

It can be helpful to think of our identities as a set of stories about us which are created and recreated over time through social, cultural and historical processes (Sfard and Prusak 2005; McAlpine and Amundsen 2018). The consistent storylines we use over time can give us motivation and drive particular ways of being (Archer 2000; Taylor 2008). Margaret Archer suggests identities can be relatively stable by the time one reaches adulthood. For professionals, identities are strongly influenced by one's life projects and commitments (Archer 2000).

This stability can help to underpin a sense of agency and shape the choices we make as academics. Agency refers to the ways in which an individual is able to engage in autonomous or self-defined action which is meaningful for them (Jääskelä et al. 2017). How we decide what is meaningful is greatly shaped by our identities. Agency can be understood as action in particular contexts at particular times rather than being a fixed capacity of individuals that they can enact equally anywhere.

The approaches described above typically see identities and agency as constructed within particular social, political and historical contexts. They also see identities as influenced by power and privilege. The suggested readings at the end of this chapter will be helpful for those who wish to explore identities in education in more detail.

KNOWING OURSELVES AS TEACHERS

Case Study 1.1 Reggie's privilege

. . . it's a huge privilege [working as an academic], I feel so lucky and people who work at institutions like ours are lucky, lucky. Yes, I complain but I don't like it when I hear people moaning and complaining and feeling hard done by. I want to say 'Then go and find another job. Where basically you can do what you love to do; come and go just as you please; be exposed to young people all the time; have technology just provided for you! Find another job like that!'

Reggie is an example of a lecturer whose identity is bound up positively with his role as an academic. A professor of psychology at a medium-size research-intensive university, he enjoys his work as an academic, even though at times he is critical of his conditions. This allows him to see what he does as a 'privilege'. Enjoying what he does encourages him to teach better. It also encourages him to see himself as a good teacher, and to take risks in his teaching.

Reggie was willing to become Head of Department when it was his turn, but he also took a risk by joining a group of academics who began an inter-institutional collaborative curriculum design project on anti-racism with students in Psychology, Social Work and Occupational Therapy. The project involved investing many hours in collaboration with academics from several departments at his own and a nearby university. Reggie was willing to do this, because he sees himself as someone who supports innovation, change and development. He invests a lot in his teaching, working extra hours and his whole sense of who he is – his identity – is bound up with his teaching. If he did not enjoy teaching, he says he should have looked for something else to do. Reggie is lucky that his sense of identity is affirmed by his teaching. It is something we all need to consider: is our identity as a teacher affirmed by what we do, and if not, what can we do about it?

What we can do

Reggie, cited in Case Study 1.1, illustrates how professional identity is often based on a sense of competence and fulfilment. In a seminal article, Wenger (2010) argued that learning transforms us and what we can do, and thus our sense of our own identities. He argued that when we become fully-fledged participants in a particular community, for example as academics in a particular department, we can have more creativity, autonomy and independence. When we feel we are competent at something, for example teaching or conducting research, we behave in a certain way, with confidence or a sense of entitlement, which might prompt us to take on more of that kind of work, and be seen by others as a leader or as excellent in that area. Our students should also know that we feel comfortable with teaching and with the disciplinary knowledge and practices that we share with them. So we may need to seek out opportunities which help us to develop our sense of confidence as teachers in order to be able to identify positively with the idea of ourselves as teachers. If our local academic community of practice is not so supportive of teaching, we might want to find additional communities to be part of which affirm our identities as teachers.

Where we are going

McAlpine and Amundsen (2018) examine what they term the 'identity trajectories' of early career researchers. Where we see ourselves going relative to our research, teaching or wider communities are important aspects of our identities. Our commitments and concerns prompt us to reach our goals, even to go against problems and challenges that face us in the workplace. It is our sense of agency that prompts us to face these challenges in order to realize our goals. An important issue we should be aware of as reflective teachers, is our thoughts about our careers as academics, and the various roles involved: teaching, research, community engagement and administration. If we are serious about actively navigating our careers, we might have to take a hard, cold look at what we do, how much time we spend on these activities, and what the long-term benefits are. This kind of strategic approach should be accompanied by another aspect of professional identity: values. We return to the issue of values later in the chapter. Case Study 1.2 explores how understanding our own identities makes it easier for us to negotiate our career trajectories in the complex and fast-changing world of higher education.

Case Study 1.2 Eugenia's dilemma

Eugenia, in her late thirties, has returned to work in a research-intensive university in the South of England after a five-year stint in a non-governmental organization dedicated to adult literacy in Glasgow, Scotland. She now has a post as a junior lecturer where she teaches and counsels students on a widening participation project. She applied for this post in order to accompany her husband to the university, where he could complete his PhD in Polymer Science. She had always imagined that she would return to the field of literacy and public activism once her husband was firmly established as an academic. She is becoming increasingly fascinated with theories on language and literacy acquisition amongst adults. She also realizes that she could benefit by earning more, to support her family. To satisfy both her interest in the field of language and education, and her need to become better qualified so as ultimately to earn more, she will need to embark upon a PhD. She finds it difficult to commit to this new project. It contradicts her image of herself as a practice-oriented person, who works directly for the good of others in the community. She is not sure she is capable of theorizing and conducting research. For two years she cannot decide to go forward. Finally, she realizes she is already starting to think like an academic, and to engage in academic practices such as theorizing and writing conference papers. She also realizes that if she undertakes the PhD, she will learn more that she can use to inform her teaching, and thus benefit her students. She surmises that her future identity as a 'Dr' might give her a stronger sense of her own voice in the classroom and staffroom. Her emerging sense of herself as an academic makes it easier for her finally to take the plunge and register to do the PhD.

Who we are going there with

Identification with others plays a key role in how we structure our reflection and planning as academics. If, for example, a historian is comfortable with being a member of that community, there is more chance that she will go to history association conferences, read articles on history and wish to share some of the rules of the game – some of the excitement shared with colleagues – with her students. Of course it would help to see oneself as a teacher, and identify with the group of people who are teaching undergraduates or postgraduates. It would be even better to establish a sense of identification with the students as well.

Eugenia, from the case study above, starts to seek out and engage in conversation with other teachers who have embarked on further study. Reggie, who is a recipient of a teaching excellence award, says that for him, the most significant thing he does to improve his teaching is to engage in research and report on this at public forums. When he goes to psychology conferences and hears what other researchers are doing, he gets an overview of his subject, to distil the essence. He is able to 'tell the wood from the trees'. Roxå and Mårtensson (2009) describe these kinds of processes in terms of the 'significant conversations and networks' that help us to develop our thinking about our teaching. We explore the importance of dialogue in developing reflective approaches to teaching further in Chapter 3.

What our values are

Lygo-Baker (2017) explores the role of values in academic careers. As we explore in more depth in Chapter 17, reflecting on our values can provide us with a sense of inner purpose and resolve. This can be useful when we face challenges and dilemmas in professional practices. Academic work has intensified in many countries in recent years (Kenny 2017) and we are often pulled between different stakeholders with quite different values underpinning what is asked of us. What we do is increasingly audited and measured and competition between individuals and institutions can be fierce (Broucker et al. 2018). In these kinds of contexts, we will often have to make tough decisions about how we use our time and it is reflecting on our values which will help us make these choices. Case Study 1.3 is a good example of having strong positive values relating to teaching even in a context which might not entirely support those values.

Case Study 1.3 Moira the educator

Moira is an experienced professor in a research-intensive university. In these kinds of institutions, it can sometimes be difficult to establish identities where caring about students' learning is central. There are strong competing pressures on academics' time and the cultures and reward processes of these institutions tend to value research most highly. While research-teaching linkages are often discussed as an important advantage of research-intensive institutions, it is increasingly the case that the ways in which research is measured and valued can pull people away from engaging deeply with education. Moira, however, has managed to develop a strong sense of herself as an educator, and strong values relating to teaching, while being highly successful in a research-intensive context. So even if you feel that it is a real challenge to stay deeply engaged with education and your students' learning, do remember that it is possible.

> I suppose that is what research-led teaching is, it's you're bringing the other part of your academic life into the classroom but doing it in a way that is relevant and not just because you want to talk about your project [. . .] I will strongly identify myself as an educator, not as a researcher. I happen to do research and the research educates me and others but I would see myself and identify myself professionally as an educator, rather as a researcher, which isn't always the case, I don't think? [. . .] the job isn't worth doing without the educational aspect. [. . .] And I would always have been very strongly of the position that as an educator, that as a professional educator, it was my job to design curricula.

Karien and Marcus, in Case Study 1.4, focus more explicitly on the moral underpinnings of their values relating to teaching.

Case Study 1.4 Karien and Marcus's values

Karien, an associate Professor in Mathematics, has a strong sense of the moral obligation of being a teacher. This strengthens her resolve to teach to the best of her ability, as well as to undertake research in her discipline:

> I guess my point of departure, especially when it comes to the teaching–research connection, would be that as a mathematician it would be quite hedonistic to be involved in pure research and not have a commitment to teaching, especially in an African context, and at the University of Stellenbosch. I really enjoy teaching, but that aside, I do feel what I suppose you can call a kind of moral obligation; that if I have been entrusted with a certain level of knowledge and skill I should share that.

Sometimes the values informing our teaching can be a general sense of obligation, as with Karien, but for others, it is a specific set of social values and experiences, which drive one's teaching. This is the case with Markus, a Geography methods lecturer who grew up in a rural village in South Africa:

> I grew up in very difficult circumstances in a poor and impoverished rural village, Wolsely, and if I think back today, in that whole class that were with me in primary school in Wolseley I think I am the only one who got out of that situation. I never forget those who were with me and especially if I go back to my family and I see the people who were with me at primary school, I do realise how happy I am and how blessed I am, so I need to do something in small ways also on their behalf. . . . And those are the things that drive what I am doing.

Markus's values inform his desire to see better teaching in schools, so that more young people can realize their dreams.

How our identities interact with our institutions, academic disciplines and work groups

Our institutions influence how we see ourselves as teachers and how we teach. One aspect of an institutional culture is the identities and backgrounds of the students. Another is the history of the university itself. Then there is how the institution is understood: research-led or teaching focused? Liberal arts or vocational and professional? The choices and dilemmas about what kind of university to work in, or how to orientate oneself to the institution, are for many of us influenced by the changing idea of 'the university'. Chris Brink (2018) explores the changing role of the university in society and argues that we need to have a clear sense of what universities are good for as well as what they are good at. What we understand to be the purposes of a university will strongly interact with our identities as teachers.

Our identities as teachers are also influenced by the disciplines in which we teach, the contexts within which we develop our teaching, and the paradigms we adhere to. Our disciplines influence how we see knowledge, the social value we attach to this knowledge, and how we teach, assess and design programmes. The tacit assumptions, norms and values about teaching and learning – which pervade our disciplines, work groups and departments – can strongly influence our identities and practices as teachers (Trowler, P. 2019). These can be important sources of inspiration for excellent teaching but may also constrain us from seeing other valuable possibilities. We explore some of these issues further in Chapter 5 when we examine contexts.

The role of narrative and autobiography

Who we come to be as teachers is informed by our pasts: our abilities, our aspirations and the capacities we develop at school, at home, at work and in wider society. These are our biographies, and they help shape what we are today. But these are not given, determining our sense of self and our identities in an absolute way. As we discussed earlier, identities can be seen as the stories which we as individuals tell about ourselves. The stories might change shape depending on how we feel now, and how we reshape these stories about our pasts. Similarly, how we tell these stories about ourselves and our pasts, feeds back to us how we understand ourselves, who we feel we are, and very significantly, what we feel we are capable of doing.

Engaging in thinking about these stories can encourage greater awareness and agency (McAlpine and Amundsen 2018), which is why Markus speaks of his memories of his impoverished rural past, memories that 'drive' what he does now as a teacher. It can also help us to identify some aspects of our lives that are painful and limit what we do, even if we cannot have a full understanding of these factors and how they impact on our lives.

How we understand and engage with our students

Our professional identities are also informed by our engagement with our students. For instance, if our students enjoy our classes, we become encouraged and want to improve our teaching. If they respond negatively, either by their actions or as expressed in student feedback response forms, we might respond in one of two ways: we might become despondent and neglect our teaching, focus more on research and administration; or we might rise to the challenge and try out new ways to enhance our teaching. We examine this further in Chapter 3 when we look at the role of dissatisfaction in reflective teaching.

If we see students as capable active participants in the learning process then our teaching identities might involve seeing ourselves more as a guide or facilitator rather than an authority figure. If we see students as important in their own right, as human beings who are grappling with the world and positioning themselves in relation to their own important futures, we will also invest more in our teaching. We see from Case Study 1.5 how we can work reflexively with our identification, or lack thereof, with students from backgrounds different to our own.

Case Study 1.5 Shafiek 're-curriculates'

Shafiek, an English-speaking Muslim lecturer from a working-class background and working-class university, finds himself relocated to a South African university with predominantly Christian middle- and working-class white students speaking mainly Afrikaans (see **theconversation.com/more-than-an-oppressors-language-reclaiming-the-hidden-history-of-afrikaans-71838** for a discussion of Afrikaans in the South African context):

When I stand in front of my undergraduate classes [which can be up to 95% white students] the affective disconnect is so enormous that I begin to feel it on my skin for the first time in my life. It's not racism. But I feel the gap between what I am trying to do in my class and suddenly there is something here that I had thought was not so important. . . . So I was completely thrown [by being in front of these classes]. How do I teach? How do I organise my courses? How do I engage with language issues? I can speak Afrikaans but some of my students told me I should perhaps not speak Afrikaans because of my inability to speak it properly! These are the kinds of things that students tell you! So what do you do? You have a responsibility to these kids. Many of them are Afrikaaners, they are not the English urban/suburban types that my kids bring home from school; they come from a reference field that I have no idea about.

In my first year I floundered. I tried to tell them this is how you understand the world, this is how theorists like Bourdieu and Bernstein theorise the kinds of things we are experiencing. Come the student evaluations – they are not crass – but students have a way of telling you 'this made no sense'. It was not that they don't want to hear what you are saying, it was more about 'we've got other pre-occupations in life, what the hell are you doing teaching us these things? This means nothing to us; it's just too weird'. It's not only about differently raced kids not being able to hear what one's trying to get across. They just said 'you are talking about stuff that just doesn't touch sides with us'.

Shafiek responded to this difference by what he called 're-curriculation', in other words, teaching his students in a way that what he has to say made sense to them. For him one of the first tasks he had to undertake was to translate his own disciplinary interests and research into a language and format that would connect with the worldviews of his students. He tried various other strategies to connect with the group, for example to make attendance compulsory, to speak the language of the majority of the students, and to use an in-depth system of interviews to find out from students in more detail about their views and responses. From the student feedback he found that he tried too hard to meet the majority students' worldviews, thereby excluding some of the other students with identities which were marginalized in that context. He had to recalibrate his style once again:

I even became aware how my humour (rugby jokes, for example) excluded woman students and the African males. In other words, I developed a keen sense of who they are and how they access learning, as well as how one can disrupt that but also build on it.

KNOWING OUR STUDENTS AS LEARNERS

Knowing our students has become an even greater priority in relation to reflective teaching, because of the changes affecting student groups entering higher education. Internationalization and the call to increase access to education amongst broader and more diverse groups of students are key trends accounting for the diversification of student groups. For example, in the UK in 1960 there were less than 200,000 students in higher education, whereas in 2016–17 there were over 2 million students, over 400,000 of whom were from outside of the UK.

Students' views of themselves as learners

Case Study 1.6 Lungi the tutor

Lungi was one of the top maths and science students at his under-resourced urban school in Cape Town, South Africa. Given the vast disparities informing education in post-apartheid South Africa, the fact that he was one of the best students at his school did not stop him from feeling vastly underprepared on his first day studying at university, where he was a different ethnicity from the majority of the other students and he felt that his schooling was inferior to theirs. He impulsively decided to leave, after the very first science lecture. On his way to the station, he noticed the science lecturer come running after him, saying 'I noticed in the lecture that you were very down-hearted.' By the time they had reached the end of the long building, the lecturer had convinced him to stay on. Despite all the effort of this and the other lecturers on the programme, he and his three friends consistently obtained mediocre scores. This persisted until the third year, when the same lecturers implemented a programme in which Lungi and his peers could become tutors of the new first-year cohort. They were given intensive training, and were told that they were now the experts, and role models to the first-year students. The tutoring work gave him more opportunity to engage with the core concepts in science, he felt the responsibility to behave like an expert and his self-esteem grew by leaps and bounds. By the end of that year he had moved from mediocre to top-performing. Fifteen years later Lungi had become a professor at a nearby research-intensive university, with several PhD students of his own and collaborative research relationships in the field of nuclear physics in Eastern Europe. He was appointed Deputy Dean in charge of teaching and learning in his faculty and decided it was once again time to 'give back' and began several teaching and learning initiatives to encourage the development of uncertain first-year students.

Students' identities as learners can have a significant influence on their performance at university, as we see in the case of Lungi above. When Lungi's stories about himself changed, from seeing himself as a weaker student to seeing himself as an expert, it had a profound effect on his engagement with his studies and on his academic performance. The same principles apply as for teachers, namely that if students identify positively with the idea of being a student, an academic or a professional in a specific field and feel competent to achieve that, this should have a beneficial effect on their academic performance. If they feel that they can perform the functions expected of them and they are expected to do well, then this can encourage them to do better. This is not to underestimate the very real challenges facing students but rather to emphasize the importance of students feeling that their teachers believe in them.

Another example of the importance of students' identities for their learning comes from the Enhancing Teaching-Learning Environments in Undergraduate Courses (ETL) Project in the UK. Amongst other groups, the researchers spoke with biological sciences students who had been involved in authentic learning experiences which helped them shift their identities from feeling like students to feeling like scientists or professionals. These experiences included a research scientist coming to their classes to discuss interpretations of some of their raw research data and also some of the students going on research work placements. There seemed to be a strong beneficial interaction between students seeing themselves as scientists or professionals and their feeling able to engage critically and deeply with the scientific literature. Case Study 1.7, drawn from McCune (2009), illustrates the differences.

Case Study 1.7 Feeling like a scientist? Mark and Sean

Mark had felt a real shift in his identity during a work placement and was now able to see himself as a scientist who was deeply engaged with his studies:

> I think it was the work placement [. . .] [Before the placement] it was a bit of a farce! [. . .] I didn't go to as many lectures, and this year I've been to everything. [Without the placement] I wouldn't have known anything really about the whole background of science. I'd be like, 'Oh, here are the facts that we've been given', but I wouldn't have a clue about how people went around doing it [. . .] You've gone up a level, you're not a student anymore. [. . .]

Sean, on the other hand, still felt very much like a student and that affected his confidence to engage critical with academic readings:

> It's difficult to question things that you read in journals sometimes, I think because we're just undergraduates.

Gee (2017) makes a compelling case for the ways in which learners entering new academic cultures need to be able to explore and take on new identities. He also emphasizes that learners need to be able to imagine themselves into the future identities which might be associated with their studies, if they are to feel motivated to learn. To be actively engaged in authentic enquiry in a science classroom, for example, a student will need to be able to see themselves as a certain kind of problem solver or thinker. They will also need to be able to imagine that being a scientist is a possible future identity for them. Where students can't identify in these ways, or hold other identities which clash with the ways of being needed in the classroom, they will be at a disadvantage. A student who is strongly identified with their family as not being the kind of person who engages with science, for example, is more likely to struggle in a science classroom. Gee suggests that where students do not yet have some of the forms of identification they need then they must be induced to *try*, even if he or she already has good grounds to be afraid to try. The student must also be enticed to *put in lots of effort* even if he or she begins with little motivation to do so. Finally, the student must *achieve some meaningful success* when he or she has expended this effort.

There are a number of other ways to encourage students to identify with their disciplines and to develop their identification with their future careers. For example: 'service learning', where students go into practice, often in community settings, during their undergraduate studies (Dolgon et al. 2017); authentic learning, where students are given tasks where the outcomes of the tasks are useable in the real world (Herrington et al. 2014); and research-rich teaching, where students are encouraged to perform like researchers in their chosen disciplines (Healey et al. 2014). These approaches are examined in more detail in Chapter 8 on Spaces and Chapter 9 on Curriculum.

Students' identities and their experiences of university

Like us, our students have multiple identities which interact in different ways in different contexts. Some identities, such as feeling like an expert or a professional, may really help students to feel comfortable at university. In other cases there may be tensions. If a student feels that their peers and teachers have very different identities and ways of being than their own, then it might be harder for them to develop the sense of social and academic integration which is so important to persistence and success at university (Mayhew et al. 2016).

This is not a simple picture, however, as we can see from the work of Diane Reay and her colleagues. Reay interviewed working-class students studying in an 'elite' university in the UK where they were very much in the minority in terms of their social class. Whilst this did cause tensions and crises of confidence for the students, and they did distance themselves from some aspects of university life, there were also positive experiences. The students often felt that university was the first time they had peers who were as interested in and committed to studying as they were and this could be a good experience. So in this one sense at least they felt more able to be authentic in the university environment than in their prior education. The stories they included in their identities often involve emphasizing the resilience and self-reliance they had developed through learning in contexts where being studious was not the norm. Being in such a novel environment also led the students to be much more reflective on their developing selves and how they could move between different cultural worlds, a process which could bring important learning for their later lives (Reay et al. 2009).

Hazel Marzetti from the UK writes about the experiences in higher education of Lesbian, Gay, Bisexual, Transgender and other students who resist traditional gender norms (LGBT+ students) (Marzetti 2018). Marzetti raises concerns about how the absence of data on these students can lead to their being rendered invisible and their perspectives not being taken into account by their teachers. We need to take care as teachers to see, understand and respect the diverse perspectives of all of our students and may need to find creative ways to do so if institutional support is not available. Marzetti notes that while students and staff are often welcoming to LGBT+ students, these students still often experience prejudice. Marzetti argues powerfully that as teachers we need to challenge the unreflective assumptions about genders and sexualities in our curriculum choices wherever possible. We also need to be ready to challenge any discrimination against LGBT+ students that might arise in our classrooms.

Student mental health has been a significant topic of conversation across higher education recently in the UK and elsewhere. This is very much a matter of identities as students may struggle with feelings of stigma that can be unfairly attached to experiences of mental illness. Further, where students' identities are not supported in their learning cultures this may contribute to feelings of stress and isolation which can exacerbate mental ill health. There are some excellent resources developed by the Charlie Waller Memorial Trust (learning.cwmt.org.uk) which advise on how we can support students with mental health concerns in higher education. Good listening can go a long way in making a student feel welcomed and reducing stigma. Another possibility in some subject areas would be to include in our curricula excellent work done by academics who have experienced mental illness. It is important in such instances to take care to focus on the quality of the academic work rather than giving any sense that this academic is somehow 'other' or unusual.

Student identities are central to our attempts to use teaching approaches that promote engagement, such as collaborative learning or peer feedback. Social and peer mediated approaches to learning require students to collaborate and learn from each other, not just from the teacher. For this to occur, students must see themselves and other students as having valid perspectives to contribute to learning. This requires giving greater attention to the inclusion of diverse identities and the valuing of students' ideas and experiences. Case Study 1.8 illustrates how students' perceptions of one another can derail the learning process if we do not take care to help students value one another's perspectives.

Case Study 1.8 Student feedback in Susanna's module

In a learning environment where students are encouraged to learn from each other, and in particular, to learn through social activity, matters of identity and perception play an important role. Here is an example: in Susanna's module on research methods in teaching health science education, students were required to form pairs and provide each other with peer feedback on their assignments and provide a written report on the experience to Susanna. For most of the pairs this process worked well and students provided each other with supportive, but critical, comment. But for Martine and Paula the process was fraught with difficulty: Martine felt that Paula was not an English first-language speaker and her work was not very good. She reported that Paula had not had the privileged schooling she had had, and she was tense about sharing her observations of Paula's work with her. Paula sensed this tension, and did not enjoy the experience. She experienced Martine as stiff and disapproving. It was only after examining the students' feedback about the peer learning experience that Susanna was able to ascertain how matters of identity and difference were informing the learning experience, so that she could devise an appropriate response.

Our assumptions about our students

One of the greatest challenges associated with diversity and widening participation is the need for us to ascertain when assumptions, values or references are widely shared, and when they are only shared by individuals with particular backgrounds, experiences or identities. It is precisely because values and assumptions are tacitly acquired and held, that we find it difficult to know which these are in any particular circumstance. In research on how tutors select students for graphics design foundation degrees in the UK, Penny Jane Burke (2012) describes how tutors are unaware of how their selection of students is influenced by hidden class-based criteria, such as taste in music or what they are currently reading. She points out that the dominant assumptions that the tutors have not uncovered are those of 'hegemonic and privileged groups' (2012: 133). In this case, 'hegemonic' means belonging to the socially dominant class, the class that sets the dominant tone and discourse in society or an institution. Failure to identify these hidden values and assumptions can at worst make those who do not share them feel isolated, or leave them feeling disconnected from course content. It can deprive the teacher of the opportunity to make connections with the students' frames of references, their aspirations and their points of identification, as it did in the case of Shafiek, until he engaged in explorations of how his students think and feel.

Reflective Activity 1.1 Finding tacit assumptions and socially exclusive examples

This activity works best if you do it with academics from varied social and disciplinary backgrounds.

Preparation: choose a key passage that you have prepared as part of a course handbook, a lecture outline or assignment that deals with an important aspect of being a student in your discipline.

Read through the passage carefully, highlighting any word, activity or example that assumes values, points of reference or cultural practices which may be foreign to any students in your class because of their socio-cultural backgrounds. Suggest alternatives or ways to explain these. Share your reflections in pairs.

Share this in a larger group of teachers. Allow other teachers to point out items that you had not even considered might exclude certain students. Ask them to suggest alternative words or explanations.

Students' perceptions of their teachers' identities

Students are just as capable of attributing identity positions to their teachers, or of having stereotyped conceptions of their teachers, as the other way around. It is important to understand this and, if possible, to provide students with the opportunity to have their preconceptions of their teachers challenged. In this way, a difficult situation can have the potential to inform students' learning. Students' preconceived ideas about their teachers can be particularly damaging where there is mistrust and fear. For example, if a black student feels they get low marks on an assignment because of their white teacher's racist thinking. These are difficult issues to address and need to be handled with care. The model of reflective teaching discussed in Chapter 3 highlights how we need to think about such issues in dialogue with our colleagues rather than feeling that we should handle them on our own.

Responding to individual students' identities and their needs

It is not easy, especially when teaching large classes, to respond to individual students' identity-based needs. There are four key considerations for responding to students' needs. The first is the need to communicate an open and caring approach to students, such that they feel free to talk to you about their needs. This is dealt with in more detail in Chapter 6 on Relationships.

The second, and most important, is to be a reflective, evidence-informed teacher. It is worth garnering information from a variety of sources about the students in your class, for example if your university provides biographical detail about students, such as their age, previous school or degrees. You could also ask students to provide this information at the beginning of a course, in the form of a quick questionnaire. An example of this kind of research is provided in **Reflective Activity 1.2**, although it is important to be clear that this will not give you full access to all aspects of your students' identities.

This leads to a related, third consideration: the importance of designing a course with student diversity in mind. Once you have an idea of the composition of a particular class of students, you can plan in advance, so that many of the needs will have been factored into the design of the course. Concepts such as flexibility and choice become important. This is well dealt with in the literature on Universal Design (Burgstahler 2010) that anticipates diversity of needs and we explore these issues further in Chapter 15. However, it is also important to be aware that students' identities and their impacts on their studying are unpredictable. Thus this is an issue that we need to return to in our teaching rather than being something that can be ticked off once-and-for-all.

This leads to the fourth consideration: we should not make assumptions based on our perceptions of students' identities. We should not essentialize student identities or reify them. For example, because a student is from a particular privileged or marginalized group, we should not assume that he or she can or cannot perform a particular function; simply because a student is a member of a particular religious affiliation we should not assume that he or she will feel comfortable or uncomfortable with a particular idea about society or the world. Students coming from particular backgrounds do not always share the same learning profiles, or clusters of strengths and weaknesses.

Interesting research has been conducted in the United States on the kinds of strengths students from apparently marginalized groups display in educational settings. Yosso and

Burciaga (2016) challenge the notion of deficit for students of colour, and suggest that in contrast to their suffering from a lack of cultural capital, they enjoy other assets such as 'aspirational capital', 'resistant capital' or 'familial capital'. They refer to these as forms of Community Cultural Wealth and argue that academics should restructure their teaching to be able to capitalize on the strengths and assets these students bring to the learning situation. The need to avoid assumptions of student deficit is discussed in more detail in Chapter 15 on inclusion.

Reflective Activity 1.2 Getting students to talk about their needs

1 One way of getting to know your students is to ask them to fill out a short survey.
2 Another is to get them to interview each other, according to a semi-structured and preset schedule, with questions about their prior learning, their fears and expectations for the course, the strengths and resources they can draw upon and their anticipated needs. They can write short reports, and if possible, hand these in as a short assignment which is marked.
3 A third method is to ask students to draw 'maps' of their communities, showing the supportive and constraining factors in their previous experiences that have impacted on their studies. They should share what they draw in groups of three to six, and debrief thereafter in a plenary session.

Activities 2 and 3 can be used as practice data-gathering activities in a research methods course. Here are some examples of community maps drawn by students from various countries in Africa and Asia, beginning an MPhil for Health Science Education

course in South Africa. The data from the interviews and community maps were used by the students themselves to write research reports on the influence of prior learning in an educational setting. In the debriefing, they mentioned having particular as well as common issues. Two issues that stood out for them as influences on the success of their studies that they have in common, were the potential significance of time, and material and financial resources.

THINKING ABOUT IDENTITIES WITH OUR STUDENTS

Being a reflective teacher entails an element of reciprocity or symmetry, where we should explore how we experience the processes that we ask students to engage in. If we would like students to become more conscious about the impact of their identities, we should have experienced exploring our own identities. This is particularly important as we are often in a position of power relative to our students and should not expect them to make themselves vulnerable in a learning environment if we are not prepared to do the same.

An example of a group of teachers undergoing the same processes involving risk and vulnerability in order to explore talking to the 'other' in the South African context, is documented in Leibowitz et al. (2010). While a group of teachers were conducting an innovative project in which students were encouraged to talk to each other about issues of identity and difference across race and class and across boundaries of institutions, the teachers realized that they should undergo a similar process. This they found to be a deeply engaging and fruitful learning experience: both gratifying and at the same time, threatening, in much the same way that the students found the experience to be both intense and difficult.

Reflective Activity 1.3 Doing identity work as teachers

You should try this activity with a group of teachers who would like to engage with issues of difference and identity, but do not all have the same identities, experiences or backgrounds. Consider having a facilitator.

1 Get together in a group and share instructions.
2 Using a sheet of flipchart paper or newsprint and coloured crayons or pens, each member of the group should draw your educational river of life, showing the critical incidents (high and low moments), the supports and hindrances along the way, culminating at the point that you are at now.
3 In as diverse groups as possible of between three and six individuals, share your stories.
4 Debrief in the larger group, discussing difference, commonalities, themes and trends which might require action or further discussion in your university setting, either in terms of how you interact and support each other, or in terms of how you interact with students.

Variation: you could decide to feature somewhere in the drawing, the values or ideas which were particularly influential in your academic career. If you do not have a group of colleagues at your institution, you could consider trying this activity with colleagues from other institutions by constructing your river in a form that can be shared by email or in an online environment.

Further related activities are provided in Chapter 15 on Inclusion (see **Reflective Activity 15.2**).

CONCLUSION

In this chapter, we have considered the importance of exploring our own identities as teachers and investigating how to work productively with the identities of our students in developing reflective approaches to teaching. Matters of identity are social and involve issues of power and distribution. This is the case in society in general, as well as inside the classroom, as Case Studies 1.5 and 1.8 involving Shafiek and Susanna's students demonstrated.

Exploring matters of identity, on our own, in groups or with our students, is not simply a self-indulgent exercise. On the contrary, it involves elements of risk taking and exposure to vulnerability. It requires honesty, openness and rigorous, critical thinking. On the other hand, the benefits accrue in the form of a greater engagement in teaching and learning by both teachers and students and a greater insight into our role as teachers.

How we see ourselves, as human beings, as academics and teachers, plays a vital role in how we teach. As we explore further in Chapter 3, reflection plays a central role in our understanding of our own identities, those of our students and in how we encourage students to work productively with their emerging identities as students and future profes-sionals. There is no clear recipe or set of tips on how to work with our own identities and how to work with students' identities. It is far more about an approach: of openness, care and reflection. What remains essential is to plan and to design the curriculum, so as to anticipate students' identities and their needs. It is equally necessary to consider and plan our own career trajectories, so as to fulfil our obligations, as well as our dreams and aspirations.

KEY READINGS

On student and academic identities in higher education, see:

Arday, J. and Mirza, H. (eds) (2018) *Dismantling Race in Higher Education: Racism, Whiteness and Decolonising the Academy*. Cham, Switzerland: Palgrave Macmillan.

Burke, P., Crozier, G. and Misiaszek, L. (2016) *Changing Pedagogical Spaces in Higher Education: Diversity, Inequalities and Misrecognition*. London: Routledge.

Evans, L. and Nixon, J. (eds) (2015) *Academic Identities in Higher Education: The Changing European Landscape*. London: Bloomsbury Publishing.

McAlpine, L. and Amundsen, C. (2018) *Identity-Trajectories of Early Career Researchers*. London: Palgrave Macmillan.

Smith, J., Rattray, J., Peseta, T. and Loads, D. (eds) (2016) *Identity Work in the Contemporary University: Exploring an Uneasy Profession*. Rotterdam: Sense Publishers.

Chapter 2
Learning
How do students develop their understanding?

INTRODUCTION

What do we mean when we talk about 'student learning'? What impact do the ways in which students approach their learning have on the quality of their learning? What factors appear to shape whether or not students are successful in their learning? What can we do as teachers to help our students to learn?

In this chapter, we examine different ways of conceiving of learning in higher education and different ways we can think about our students as learners. It might seem surprising at first to place so much emphasis on how we understand students and their learning. After all, students in higher education have successfully obtained their place at university or college. We may therefore think it is mostly a matter of us teaching effectively and students putting in enough effort. As we look at the literature on student learning, however, we will find important insights to inform our teaching practices. There is considerable debate about the nature of learning, and where we stand on these matters will make a real difference to what we see as effective teaching. For example, constructivist perspectives on learning can help us to see the importance of focusing on the ways that students actively engage with course content rather than seeing students as passive receivers of information.

The literature on students as learners is full of interesting insights into what students may bring to the learning process which can affect the quality of their learning. There is strong evidence that students vary in their core beliefs about learning, how they manage their learning, and in the learning processes that they follow and use. In addition, there is increasing research on both the different types of learning outcome which students might achieve and the best ways and methods for measuring the learning gains they achieve with respect to those outcomes. Importantly, the literature also suggests that it is possible for us as teachers to have a positive influence on all of these aspects of students' learning in higher education.

See Chapter 4

TLRP Principles

Two principles are of particular relevance to this chapter on learning:

Principle 3: Effective teaching and learning recognizes the significance of informal learning to developing specific expertise. Learning with friends, families, peer groups and professionals should be recognized as significant, and be valued and used in formal processes in higher education.

Principle 8: Effective teaching and learning recognizes the importance of prior or concurrent experience and learning. Teaching and learning should take account of what the student as learner knows already to plan strategies for the future. This includes building on prior learning but also taking account of the emerging concurrent learning in context, and the personal and cultural experiences of different groups of students as learners.

In this chapter, we first examine different ways of thinking about how students learn in higher education. We then consider the factors that have been found to impact the quality of students' learning in higher education. The chapter concludes by emphasizing that our understanding of our students' learning is always provisional and argues that it is this that makes teaching such an intellectually challenging and engaging activity.

HOW CAN WE THINK ABOUT HOW STUDENTS LEARN IN HIGHER EDUCATION?

In this section, we examine different ways of understanding our students' learning. In examining these ideas, it is important to bear in mind that learning is **relational** (Marton 2014). There are two crucial aspects to this. First, learning is the learning of something; there is always an object of learning. Often discussions of learning in higher education can be focused around *generic* concepts which obscures the idea that our students are always learning *particular* concepts, arguments, theories or ways of engaging in practices. We need to remember that what students are learning plays an important role in how they experience learning. Second, our students are always learning in a particular time and space. Generic discussions of 'learners' often hides the fact that, as we discussed in Chapter 1, our students have embodied identities. How students engage with the learning of their courses is shaped by the understanding of the contexts in which they are learning, their background, beliefs, motivations and prior experience of learning, as well as their understandings of what is expected of them in those contexts (see Chapter 5).

As we examine different ways of thinking about students' learning in the rest of this section and chapter, one way of focusing on these two relational aspects of learning is to connect the discussions in this chapter to our own experiences of learning and to the experience of students' learning on courses that we have taught. Approaching the chapter in this way can help us to think about the implications of the ideas and arguments for our day-to-day teaching. We explore this further in Reflective Activity 2.1.

Reflective Activity 2.1 Reflecting on our own learning

Think about something important that you have learned recently, that you deliberately intended to learn. Develop an account of this but responding to the following questions:

- What did you learn?
- Why was it important for you to learn it?
- How did you go about learning it?
- What context did you learn it in?
- What aspects of this context helped you to learn?
- What aspects of this context seemed to get in the way of your learning?
- How would you describe the overall experience of learning?
- In what ways is this experience similar and different to the experiences of the students whom you teach?

Learning as acquisition and participation

In making sense of the rich array of perspectives on learning in higher education, one distinction it can be helpful to consider is the extent to which the metaphors of 'acquisition' and 'participation' can be usefully applied to make sense of what it means to learn (Sfard 2009, 2015). The idea that learning involves 'acquisition' of new knowledge, skills or understanding is common both in our day-to-day ways of speaking about learning and also throughout much of the educational literature. Different theoretical perspectives may indicate that the acquisition happens in different ways – from reproduction to active construction of knowledge – but the broad idea is that an individual, the student, comes to know something new or to understand things in a different way. Whilst the individual acquisition metaphor is widespread, one of the challenges to seeing learning as simply individual acquisition is the real difficulty that students can have in making use of what they know in situations different from the context in which their learning occurred (Hattie and Donoghue 2016). If learning is the acquisition of facts, concepts or ways of thinking which reside within the individual student, why is the transfer of that learning to other contexts so often challenging?

The second metaphor, where learning is seen as 'participation', reveals why the transfer of learning can be problematic. Theorists who see learning as participation suggest that learning is acquisition of knowledge within the practices of a particular community rather than a matter of the student simply gaining 'knowledge' (Sfard 2015). Learning is seen as a process in which the student, the process of knowing and the community within which the learning is situated are inextricably intertwined. So a student may come to have greater facility in enacting the practices associated with a particular knowledge community while they are situated within that context. The nature of the context is also seen as dependent on the students who contribute to the community. Learning is then more a matter of 'becoming' or 'being' a biologist, economist, designer or musician in context than it is about owning distinct pieces of knowledge and skills which can just be transferred to quite different contexts. Viewing learning as 'participation' can be valuable in explaining why students who seem skilled and knowledgeable in one context may struggle to engage effectively at first when they transition to another setting, even where what they know might be expected to be relevant (for an examination of this issue in relation to medical education, see Engeström 2018). Overly narrow interpretations of participation metaphors can, however, make it more difficult to account for the ways in which students clearly do carry some of what they have learned previously into new situations even when they have not yet been fully engaged in the new context.

Following Sfard (2015), this chapter argues that both the acquisition and participation metaphors for learning have value for making sense of student learning in higher education, but that taking either to an extreme can be unhelpful. In the rest of this section, we explore the distinction between acquisition and participation through some examples from the literature.

Learning as acquisition through active construction

Constructivist perspectives on learning have been highly influential in making sense of how students learn in higher education (Biggs 2014). Constructivism brings together a range of theoretical perspectives with varying emphases. A common thread within these is to see the acquisition of knowledge and the development of conceptual understanding as involving active constructive processes rather than simply passive transfer (Hoidn 2016).

Constructivist perspectives commonly emphasize how students' prior knowledge and understanding shape their interactions with new learning and the understandings which they construct (Hoidn 2016). There is a large body of research which illustrates how students can come to build qualitatively different understandings within the same context which may vary markedly from what the teacher had intended. Constructivist perspectives often vary in the extent to which they emphasize active knowledge construction as an individual student process as opposed to more social and collaborative processes (Hoidn 2016).

Particularly rich examples of how students can enhance their conceptual understanding through active dialogue and engagement (questioning, discussing, explaining) can be found in the research on 'peer instruction' in physics and engineering (Kalman 2017; Zhang et al. 2017). Peer instruction is an effective technique for encouraging active engagement with key concepts in large lecture classes. It involves, first, posing conceptual questions to students in the lecture, often in a multiple-choice format (although other formats are possible). Students then give an individual answer to the conceptual question using, for example, an electronic voting system such as 'clickers'. The next step is that neighbouring students are asked to try to convince one another of the correctness of their own answer to the question. The students then give an individual answer to the question again, which may have changed based on the peer discussion. Finally the teacher explains the correct answer to the class. Crouch, Mazur and their colleagues have provided strong evidence that peer instruction leads to improvement in students' conceptual understanding across a range of measures, as compared with more traditional lecturing (Crouch et al. 2007; Watkins and Mazur 2013). Interviews with students who have experienced peer instruction suggest that being asked the test question prompts them to construct their own understanding of the problem as a first step, then discussion with their peers exposes them to differing interpretations and involves them in a process of critically evaluating these competing perspectives in a way which enhances their own understanding. There is also strong evidence that 'learning as acquisition through active construction' can be used in similarly structured but 'teacherless' peer environments outside the classroom. In Research Briefing 2.1 overleaf, we explore the findings of a ten-year project funded in the US by both the Mellon Foundation and the National Science Foundation.

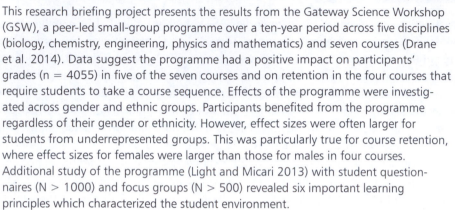

RESEARCH BRIEFING 2.1 Peer learning: Six principles for improving learning in higher education

This research briefing project presents the results from the Gateway Science Workshop (GSW), a peer-led small-group programme over a ten-year period across five disciplines (biology, chemistry, engineering, physics and mathematics) and seven courses (Drane et al. 2014). Data suggest the programme had a positive impact on participants' grades (n = 4055) in five of the seven courses and on retention in the four courses that require students to take a course sequence. Effects of the programme were investigated across gender and ethnic groups. Participants benefited from the programme regardless of their gender or ethnicity. However, effect sizes were often larger for students from underrepresented groups. This was particularly true for course retention, where effect sizes for females were larger than those for males in four courses. Additional study of the programme (Light and Micari 2013) with student questionnaires (N > 1000) and focus groups (N > 500) revealed six important learning principles which characterized the student environment.

1 Learning deeply: learning as active construction of knowledge in which the learner becomes increasingly autonomous, independent and learns how to learn.
2 Engaging problems: learning prompted by interesting, meaningful, challenging and relevant problems which help identify misunderstandings, but also challenge, stimulate and illuminate understanding of core concepts and ideas.
3 Connecting peers: co-learning with like-minded, independent peers in functional collaborative groups allowing respectful participation of all members.
4 Mentoring learning: learning aided by peer mentors who have gone before and can be emotional as well as intellectual guides to new learners.
5 Creating community: learning within a broader multi-layered community with norms and practices with which students can increasingly identify and in which the student is increasingly empowered.
6 Doing research: learning as original research in which students identify the problem, experience the research context, practices and participants, and learn a series of research skills.

The principles of learning revealed in the study of the GSW programme, outlined in **Research Briefing 1.1**, essentially describe the kind of learning and the kind of learning environments in which the best science is conducted. It describes a way of learning that, for the most part, characterizes the work of university teachers in their own research and scholarship. This section has examined the first three of these principles, active construction of knowledge, engaging problems and connecting peers. Drawing on additional research, the sections below examine the three additional principles.

Learning as legitimate peripheral participation

Lave and Wenger (1991) use the notion of 'legitimate peripheral participation' to emphasize the ways in which learning and knowing always take place through participation within particular communities. In this perspective, learning is understood as developing greater mastery of the contextualized knowledge, understanding and 'ways of being' required for full participation within a particular community (Wenger 2010). Learning has meaning for the student by virtue of the ways in which it enhances their capacity to participate effectively and gain a sense of legitimacy in valued contexts (Wenger 2010). Learning is thus seen as a profoundly social and relational enterprise which engages the student's values and sense of self. Under this approach, even apparently abstract or general knowledge only has meaning when it can be made relevant within a particular context at a given time because knowledge can only be gained in the first place within specific contexts where such knowledge is valued and shared.

In relation to higher education, this would suggest that what is learned is not simply discrete knowledge or academic tasks which can easily be made explicit, but rather a shared experience of practising an academic subject area in which what is learned is partly tacit. The use of legitimate peripheral participation as a heuristic to make sense of learning in higher education focuses attention on those experiences where our students might get the closest experience of *being* a biologist, historian or economist. This picture is rendered more complex when we acknowledge that the majority of students studying in higher education will not enter the same community of practice as the academic staff who teach them and/or other more senior students in the community who may assist or even mentor them. This then suggests the importance of close attention to how we can work with students to achieve learning which they experience as meaningful, despite not having full membership of our disciplinary communities. Students may also not have a rich understanding of their future communities of practice against which to establish the meaning of what they are learning, or to find the common frames of reference which are so important for effective communication (Anderson and McCune 2013).

Wenger's work (Wenger et al. 2009) draws attention to the need to see learning as occurring across multiple overlapping and permeable communities in a way that emphasizes the kinds of challenges which may be faced by students in higher education as they seek to make sense of their learning. One area for reflection this presents for us as teachers in higher education, is that conceptualizing learning as legitimate peripheral participation argues against the idea that students who have been successful in their prior learning experiences at school or elsewhere will quickly make sense of what is meant by high-quality learning in a particular subject area at university provided they are taught clearly and put in sufficient effort. Rather it would be more plausible to expect gradual processes of acculturation with considerable effort to achieve shared understanding on the part of teachers and students (McCune and Hounsell 2005; Anderson and McCune 2013). Thus, a common expectation of the ideal student as an independent or autonomous learner, who is fully prepared for university study is called into question. Given that even the most experienced of us develop our work within communities of practice – which offer a wide spectrum of learning experiences from informal conversations to peer review of publications – the idea of wholly 'independent' learners has clear limitations.

Learning in different subject areas

Whether we see learning more as acquisition or more as participation, our academic subject areas are fundamental to our understanding of what makes for high-quality learning and to shaping our practices as teachers in higher education (Trowler et al. 2012). It is worth thinking about what we expect within our particular subject area in order to say that a piece of work by a colleague or a student is genuinely of high quality. Our own understanding of what constitutes good work will have developed gradually over many years and may be something that is difficult to articulate. This can present real challenges when we are trying to support and guide students who produce weaker work and are struggling to grasp our notion of quality.

These issues of how to articulate what might make for high-quality learning within particular academic contexts were an important part of the focus of the Enhancing Teaching-Learning Environments in Undergraduate Courses (ETL) Project. Whilst this project is over ten years old, it led to the development of two key ideas that are still of great relevance to contemporary higher education. For this reason, an overview of the wider findings from this project is provided in **Research Briefing 2.1** and we further explore the two key ideas from this project below: *ways of thinking and practising* (WTPs) and *threshold concepts*.

The idea of *ways of thinking and practising* (WTPs) of an academic discipline was used in the ETL project to encapsulate the rich complexity of what students might come to understand and how they might develop and progress in their thinking as they engaged with an academic discipline across their undergraduate studies (McCune and Hounsell 2005; Hounsell and Anderson 2009). Focusing on WTPs draws attention to exploring students' capacity to think and act in ways which are closer to the ways that we might think and act as academics within our own subject area. As students come to grasp the WTPs of a subject area we might hope that they have a better understanding of how new knowledge and understanding are developed in our field, as well as having a good knowledge base, relevant skills and high levels of conceptual understanding. The ways in which WTPs differ between subject areas is illustrated by Anderson and Hounsell (2007, p. 466) based on their research with staff and students in history and the biosciences. In history, for example, there would often be an emphasis on 'appreciation of history as socially constructed and contested' and 'sensitivity to the "strangeness of the past"'. Whereas in the biosciences critical thinking would take different forms focusing, for example, on sound understanding of experimental design and the interpretation of experimental research evidence. WTPs have more recently been examined as a way of thinking about curriculum in higher education (Barradell et al. 2018).

RESEARCH BRIEFING 2.2 Enhancing Teaching-Learning Environments (ETL) in Undergraduate Courses: The influence of subjects and settings

The ETL project (Entwistle and Hounsell 2007) focused on a cross-section of subjects – electronic engineering, biological sciences, economics and history – and course units from nineteen departments in seven teaching-focused and twelve research-focused universities in England, Scotland and Wales. Focusing generally on one first-year and one final-year module in each university, they interviewed collaborating staff (N = 90) and had questionnaires completed by students (N = 6,488) at the beginning and end of each selected course unit. They also interviewed small groups of students about their experiences of the teaching (N = 668). Course teams were involved in reviewing the strengths and limitations of their unit or module, drawing on evidence collected by the research team, and in modifying the unit in order to enhance student learning. These modifications were then monitored to measure their impact. The key findings were as follows:

- Underlying what students learned in specific course units was a developing grasp of how to think and go about the subject like an expert, what they called 'ways of thinking and practising in the disciplines'.
- There was an inescapable disciplinary dimension not only to what students learned but also to how they were taught and assessed in undergraduate courses.
- Although most courses worked well as environments that supported learning, students were often dissatisfied with the guidance and feedback on course work.
- Conceptually focused research evidence about students' experiences of their courses helped staff to fine-tune teaching and learning environments.

As teachers then, we need to think carefully about how students will come to grasp the particular ways of thinking of our subject areas. One good starting point is to think about where our students commonly get into difficulties. We can think, for example, about particular aspects of completing assignments which seem challenging. If many of our students struggle with providing good evidence to underpin the arguments they make in their essay writing, what misunderstandings may they be holding about how evidence is used in our subject area? If our students find it challenging to design their research projects, what aspects can be clearly set out for them and what might they need to learn through gradual apprenticeship and discussion? When do these opportunities for apprenticeship occur?

New students cannot come to understand a subject area simply through being presented with relevant content or arguments. In order to make full sense of what they hear in lectures or read in textbooks, students need to experience and have a good grasp of the values and histories of debate in their subject area which they may well not yet possess. Northedge and McArthur (2009) suggested that one good way to help students in this position to make more sense of the subject area is to focus on accessible examples such as case studies and to connect it to the students' current understanding through peer discussion. So there is a sense of working together to achieve at least partially shared understanding rather than assuming this could occur simply through clear exposition.

Another way to help students connect with our subject areas is to identify key *threshold concepts* and reflect on how we can help our students grasp these concepts. *Threshold concepts* are those key concepts in a given subject area and associated community of practice which, when they are understood, provide students access to a transformed way of understanding their subject area (Meyer and Land 2005; Land 2011; Land et al. 2016). These concepts tend to be 'troublesome' for students to grasp but provide opportunities for substantive shifts in their perspectives on their subject areas and world views. Making sense of a threshold concept may give a more integrated understanding of a subject area and perhaps an irreversible change in perspective, meaning that once a student has 'stepped through' a threshold, they are less likely to return to their prior level of under- standing. Making sense of a threshold concept tends also to give students better capacity to communicate like more experienced practitioners of the subject area (Baillie et al. 2013). Grasping threshold concepts can be highly significant for students' success in their studies and for their sense of self as a learner or practitioner of the subject. This does not necessarily come about through a single 'ah hah' moment; it may involve a longer struggle.

Examples of threshold concepts may include 'depreciation' in Accounting, 'the central limit theorem' in Statistics and 'entropy' in Physics (Meyer and Land 2005). They have been explored in a wide range of disciplines including medical education (Randall et al. 2018). A very useful website provides a database of studies using threshold concepts in a wide range of subjects and disciplines: ee.ucl.ac.uk/~mflanaga/thresholds.html

If we find there are certain concepts in our subject areas which seem to be important thresholds for our students, this suggests giving particular care and attention to how these are learned. This might involve, for example, considering how and when students' under- standing of these concepts is assessed and what opportunities there are for formative feedback to address misunderstanding. Attention to the variations in understanding of threshold concepts within our classes may also prove fruitful. In a similar vein, it can be important to consider how to give students good opportunities to experience varied examples of the application of threshold concepts and to develop their capacity to discern and reflect on variation to enhance their understanding (Baillie et al. 2013). This is likely to be particularly important in subject areas that require a particular understanding before being able to proceed to the next stage. Meyer and Land (2005) caution, however, against assuming that the challenges students face in grasping threshold concepts can be resolved simply by better organized curricula or more well-aligned learning environments. There is a need to be sensitive to students' experiences of engaging with uncertainty and 'stuckness' and the impact of such experiences on how they feel about themselves and their learning. This kind of sensitivity can be gained through considering how students develop their 'academic literacies'.

Learning as situated discourse practice and the development of academic literacies

Seeing learning as 'situated discourse practice' retains the focus outlined earlier in this chapter on how what is understood to be high-quality learning is situated within, and shaped by, the particular social contexts within which learning occurs. An emphasis on situated discourse practice does, however, bring to the fore elements which are less central in the literature on legitimate peripheral participation in communities of practice. One strand of criticism of the work on communities of practice has suggested that greater attention should be paid to explicitly exploring power relations, as this dimension is acknowledged but perhaps not foregrounded in the work of Lave and Wenger (Tight 2015). Research focusing on situated discourse practice brings questions of power more to the forefront and considers more closely the interplay between students' senses of self and the particular ways of being, making meaning and using language which are available and valued in academic contexts (Lillis et al. 2016), which have been termed 'academic literacies'.

An emphasis on discourse practice and academic literacies implies that we should consider how talking and writing are: bound up in particular social contexts and draw on the available ways of communicating which are used in that context; can become habitual and tacit practices; are connected with and shape social structures (Lillis et al. 2016). This then draws attention to which communicative practices are dominant in particular settings and how this may affect students' capacity to make meaning in ways which sit comfortably with their wider selves. In this vein, Lillis et al. (2016) emphasize that learning to write well at University is not simply a matter of students developing a set of generic communicative skills which would be seen as good communication in any setting, but rather involves students engaging with particular practices and a set of views of what good writing is. These are shaped by the histories and cultures of our academic disciplines and institutions, and which privilege the forms of writing which are valued by those with power within these contexts.

Pursuing these themes of power and social structure, Sheridan (2011) suggests that universities have tended to respond to increasing student diversity by expecting that students will conform to the existing norms of literacy practice established in those contexts. Through analysing interviews with 'non-traditional' students – students who are not middle-class white men – and examining samples of their writing and related documentation, Lillis (2003) illuminates how the power of academics and institutions to shape student writing can affect the quality of students' engagement. For example, 'Mary' received comments on her essay indicating that the marker viewed some elements as irrelevant. Mary's interview reveals, however, that the points she made in the essay were very relevant to her life experiences. Comparing her experience as a black working-class woman to that of a white middle-class male student taking the same course Mary comments, 'He doesn't have to make a switch. It's him you see. Whereas when I'm writing I don't know who it is (*laughs*). It's not me. And that's why I think it's awful' (Lillis 2003,

p. 202). Her ability to identify with the community is severely undermined by her perception that her experience is less relevant. Mary further explained that texts in her sociology course seem to focus only on negative perspectives of black people, such as the disadvantage they suffer, rather than their positive contributions. While Mary's remarks exemplify some of the potential negative consequences of students' experiences of their subject areas (Lillis 2003), it is important to also consider how changing our ways of thinking and teaching to include a more diverse range of material can empower all of our students to gain access to new deeper ways of engaging and thinking through academic study (Anderson and McCune 2013).

The possibilities for us to respond to these themes, as academics teaching in increasingly diverse higher education contexts, vary from straightforward suggestions to more radical questions about the extent to which particular forms of communication and assessment are valued in higher education. More simple possibilities could include efforts to ensure that curriculum content is as relevant as possible to the experiences of diverse student groups and that course texts do not give students a sense that their culture or background are being cast in a negative light. Making space within our teaching for genuine dialogue around the interconnections among students' wider lives and what they are studying can be an important step. The literature on 'co-creation of learning' is relevant here, as work in this area emphasizes the value of genuinely involving students in the design of teaching and curricula (Bovill et al. 2016).

Looking at assessment (which we explore in depth in Chapter 13), we might consider how to better value the perspectives students bring from their personal experiences. Academic assessment often weights arguments based on particular kinds of published sources more heavily, but less experienced students may struggle to express what is most personally relevant when engaging with these challenging texts. Yet for many students, their personal life experiences may have shaped their initial interest in a subject area. As we discuss in Chapter 12, this highlights the importance of teaching processes that engage students in dialogue and help them better make meaningful connections between the academic discourse of published texts and aspects of their wider lives. Another possibility is that we engage in more negotiated and participative forms of assessment, such as giving students a say in assessment criteria (Falchikov 2005). Lillis et al. (2016) suggest that rather than giving feedback as closed commentary on students' finished texts, more discursive engagement with students' texts in development would be a more inclusive approach.

One area for further exploration here is the possibilities offered by online resources, including blogs and wikis, which may allow writing to be a more ongoing developmental process of shared reflection rather than an emphasis on a final product. These spaces may also provide opportunities to value forms of expression which are more personal, visual and sometimes less linear, and we explore them further in Chapter 8 on Spaces.

HOW CAN WE UNDERSTAND OUR STUDENTS AS LEARNERS IN HIGHER EDUCATION?

Figure 2.1 sets out a simplified model of students' learning in higher education that is made up of three elements: *presage*, those factors which exist prior to the student entering the teaching and learning context; students' experiences of teaching and learning *processes*, and the *products* or outcomes of learning. This model is useful because it highlights a number of crucial elements of students' learning. First, that students come to higher education with prior experiences and understandings that help to shape what sense they make of the teaching and learning context in higher education. Clearly, this understanding is also based on the course and department learning context, and the community of practice they enter into. Second, these understandings lead them to *perceive* the teaching and learning context in particular ways, which informs the ways in which they approach and regulate their learning. Finally, these ways of approaching and regulating their learning help to shape their learning outcomes both in terms of the quality of their learning and how much they learn.

In this section, we describe some of the research that shows how each of these elements affect students' experiences of learning in higher education. Much of the research we examine comes from studies of students' *approaches to learning* over the past forty years. This literature suggests that students go about their learning in quite different ways and that this is related to their reasons for studying, their beliefs about learning and their perceptions of how they are taught and assessed (Entwistle 2018). However, as with all conceptual models, there are aspects of students' engagement with higher education that are not highlighted.

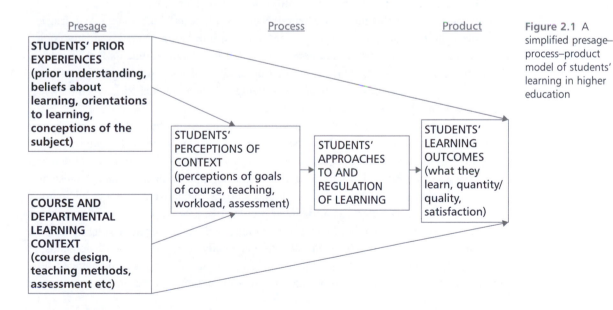

Figure 2.1 A simplified presage–process–product model of students' learning in higher education

Presage: Students' prior experiences of studying

Prior understanding

How students understand a discipline or subject, prior to their entry into higher education, is a crucial factor in shaping their experience of learning in universities. Prior academic achievement was among the first factors identified as being a strong predictor of learning outcome (Ausubel et al. 1978), and it has since been found to be one of the most powerful features for determining students' academic performance at college and university (Cassidy 2012). Thus, as we will examine in Chapter 11 on teaching, taking account of what our students already know is a crucial element in deciding how we approach our teaching.

Students' reasons for studying

In their classic study, Beaty et al. (1997) identified four broad sets of motivations which students have for learning in higher education which he refers to as learning orientations. These are *vocational orientation* focused on gaining effective training and qualifications for a future career; *academic orientation* concerned with academic learning and achievement; *personal orientation* related to personal achievement and development, and finally *social orientation* focused on the opportunities studying presents for an active social life and the benefit of their learning to their community. Traditionally, each of these orientations has been viewed as either *intrinsic* for interest or satisfaction in the activity itself, or *extrinsic* for a separate outcome. And it is common for students to hold multiple learning orientations and for their orientations to change over time.

Research suggests that much of what people do is not described by a simple extrinsic–intrinsic dichotomy but rather there is a continuum of motivations between the two poles characterized by the degree of autonomy and self-determination students feel they have (Vansteenkiste et al. 2018). This is revealed in heightened levels of student persistence, creativity, performance, self-esteem and well-being, which is often lacking when they feel they are externally controlled and with little choice.

At one end of the continuum, a student may not engage in study at all if they see no value in an activity or expect to fail. They feel they have zero control. The student might feel some minimum sense of choice to engage but simply to satisfy an external demand like an attendance rule for a particular class or a parental demand to take a particular programme. Further along the continuum the student might want to meet an internal demand such as doing better than a friend, or proving one's worth or avoiding the guilt and anxiety of failure. On the other hand, a student may feel a sense of increasing autonomy, engaging in study because, for example, she personally identifies with the demands of being an excellent student who gets high grades. A sense of even more heightened self-autonomy may accompany personal feelings of satisfaction and freedom in studying a particular subject or engaging in a type of activity which assist them in achieving a goal to be a doctor or go to graduate school. As strong and valid as these motivations are, particularly those that enhance the students' sense of self-regulation and autonomy, they are, nevertheless, part of an extrinsic continuum because the study is undertaken for a separate outcome, other than the excitement and pleasure of the study itself. Most students will engage for extrinsic motivations such as these, the point is where along the continuum of autonomy and self-determination they will do so.

These different orientations for studying and the degree of autonomy students feel they have in their study can all impact how students approach their studies at university (see also Zusho 2017) and are something we need to be aware of as reflective teachers in higher education.

Students' beliefs about learning and knowledge

As well as students' reasons for studying, the ways in which students approach their studies are shaped by their beliefs about learning, including the ways in which they understand intelligence and the nature of knowledge and learning.

Carol Dweck (2013) outlines two broad ways in which students understand their abilities. Those with an 'entity theory' of intelligence see ability as innate, fixed and stable. It cannot be changed by learning. Those with an 'incremental theory' view intelligence as something that can be cultivated through learning. These are often referred to, respectively, as the 'fixed' and 'growth' mindsets. Based on empirical studies, Dweck argues that students who hold an 'entity theory' of intelligence are more likely to lack persistence when they find things difficult because they will put the difficulty down to their own lack of ability. In this respect, Dweck's ideas relate to notions of *self-efficacy*, the strength of students' belief in their abilities to complete their study. And the amount of belief that students have in their own abilities have been consistently found to relate to the quality of their learning outcomes (Cassidy 2012; Zusho and Edwards 2011).

Dweck's findings resonate with research in higher education about students' perspectives on the meaning of learning and understanding, and the nature of knowledge and knowing. For example, there is evidence that some students in higher education subscribe to the view that there is one correct way of understanding a given topic and that we, the teacher, can be seen as the authority to provide this correct version for them to receive and reproduce in their assessed work (Hofer and Sinatra 2010). Where a student holds this position, they are unlikely to respond positively to peer feedback or group learning experiences as they may worry that they will not get the 'correct' perspective from their peers. By contrast, a student who believes that learning is a process of actively constructing a personal understanding through a process of critical evaluation may well see their peers as a useful source of alternative viewpoints. Researchers who have investigated the ways in which students' views about learning and knowledge may develop over time have noted that shifts in students' viewpoints can be challenging and/or upsetting for students and may provoke disengagement from the learning situation, at least for a time (van Rossum and Hamer 2010).

Over many years research has also examined students' views of the nature of knowledge and how these change over the time of study in higher education (Perry 1999; Baxter Magolda 2004b; Hofer and Pintrich 2002; van Rossum and Hamer 2010). In general, this research suggests a shift from a view of knowledge as a set of fixed facts, to a view of knowledge as being created in particular contexts and open to challenge and change. This involves a conceptual shift in the students from seeing knowledge as separate from themselves to understanding that knowledge involves the development of personal commitment.

Similarly, students' view of what learning involves can differ and change over the course of their studies. Seminal research by Säljö (1979) and Marton et al. (1993) describe five different student conceptions of learning – seeing learning as: (a) an increase in knowledge; (b) memorizing; (c) acquisition of facts, procedures, etc., which can be retained and/or utilized in practice; (d) abstraction of meaning; (e) an interpretive process aimed at the understanding of reality. A sixth conception: (f) changing as a person, was reported by Marton et al. (1993) who also describe learning in the first three conceptions as primarily reproducing, and the last three as primarily seeking meaning. Van Rossum and Hamer (2010) found that these conceptions develop over the course of a university degree but that most students did not develop a view of learning beyond that of the acquisition of facts.

Finally, research has examined differences in students' understanding of the disciplines they are studying. Ashwin et al. (2014, 2016, 2017) examined the differences in sociology students' accounts of sociology as a discipline and how these changed over the three years of their degree. They found that these ranged from seeing sociology as a way of developing their *opinions*, to seeing sociology as the *course* they were studying, to seeing sociology as offering a number of different ways to study the relations between people and society, each of which offers a different and partial picture of these relations. Similar studies have been conducted in Mathematics, Accountancy, Geography, Geoscience, Music and Law (see Ashwin et al. 2014 for a summary).

What is important about all of these different ways of viewing intelligence, knowledge, learning and disciplines is that they inform the ways in which students make sense of what is going on when they engage with their studies at university. Vermunt and Donche (2017) show how the ways in which we teach at university need to take account of the extent to which students are able to regulate their own learning. If the levels of self-regulation that are expected of students are too distant from students' current levels, then students are likely to experience a 'destructive friction' in which they withdraw from the task ahead. On the other hand, if they are just slightly in advance of the students' self-regulation then they will result in a 'constructive friction' in which students are positively challenged to develop their levels of self-regulation. This idea of constructive and destructive friction (Vermunt and Verloop 1999) can also be extended to students' understanding of the knowledge and of the teaching and learning processes they experience in higher education. As teachers, we can explicitly plan how we will enable them to develop this understanding so that it is aligned with what is expected on the modules that we teach. We explore this issue further in Reflective Activity 2.2.

Reflective Activity 2.2 Understanding different types of destructive friction

Look at the two quotations below from students who were interviewed about their experiences of tutorials for the study reported in Ashwin (2005). They both show evidence of students experiencing a form of 'destructive friction' with their learning environment because the students express dissatisfaction with the way in which it is supporting their learning.

- How would you describe the differences between the kinds of dissatisfaction that the students are experiencing?
- What do you think are the causes of their dissatisfaction?
- If you were tutoring these students, how would you seek to improve their experiences and the quality of their learning?

Some tutors, their tutorials are like a lecture, you come away with very organized notes, adding *a lot* to the information you didn't know before, which is very useful. Other times you leave the tutorial not feeling like you've gained a lot from it because some tutors will discuss ideas. Very often those ideas I haven't written about I won't remember, which means the tutorial isn't perhaps as useful as it could be . . . I like dealing with facts whereas other people will write about how this is possibly true because of all these theories and possibilities and so on, and I need the anchoring of facts, whereas other people don't seem to need them as much. (Humanities Student)

The tutorials I had at the beginning of this term were wonderful but I've found progressively that you feel like you are doing it just to learn facts and to reinforce your lectures. It would be nice if you could explore something different rather than this fact after fact after fact after fact . . . Maybe your tutor could email you saying 'I recommend you read this journal which has just come out and states that this guy had this theory' and you could say whether you agreed with it or disagreed and why, and what other questions would stem from it, because a question always breeds a question. I think it would be more interesting, would motivate me more and inspire me more, whereas this just gets you bogged down and there's not much you can get excited about. (Medical Sciences Student)

Process: Students' perceptions of the teaching and learning context

Whilst students' prior experiences of studying help them to make sense of the contexts that they experience in higher education, how they approach their studies is also influenced by those teaching and learning contexts. The quality of their learning is likely to be higher where students *perceive* that:

- the goals and aims are clear;
- the quality of teaching is good;
- their level of workload is appropriate;

- the ways in which they are assessed require them to demonstrate understanding rather than the recall of facts or procedures. (Entwistle 2018)

This is important for us as academic staff teaching in higher education as it indicates that even in this relatively late stage in their learning careers, how students are taught can still make a difference to the quality of their learning. This is because the way in which they perceive their teaching and learning environment informs them about what kind of approach to learning is appropriate in higher education.

Students' approaches to and regulation of learning

The origins of research into students' approaches to learning lie in studies carried out in Gothenburg which looked, initially, at students reading an academic article provided by the researchers. The researchers found qualitative differences in the quality of the students' understanding of the article they were given to read. These differences in understanding appeared to be related in systematic ways to differences in the ways in which students went about reading (Marton and Säljö 1997).

Since these early studies, students' approaches to learning research has consistently found differences between students who adopt a 'deep' approach to learning and those who take a 'surface' approach to learning. A deep approach involves a student having an intention to understand what they are learning, coupled with particular learning processes which are involved in achieving understanding. Students taking a deep approach typically also indicate active interest in what they are learning. A surface approach, by contrast, comprises an intention to cope minimally with course requirements, combined with unreflective studying and routine memorization of facts and procedures (Entwistle 2018). While the details of how the approaches are described varies somewhat between different studies, the broad distinction between deep and surface has proved robust across different methodologies, subject areas, research teams and countries (Entwistle 2018). Numerous studies have shown that students' perceptions of supportive learning contexts and the adoption of deep approaches to learning are strongly related to higher quality academic achievement (Trigwell et al. 2013).

Students' approaches can show some stability over time and they may prefer a particular approach (Entwistle and McCune 2013). However, they are also open to change. Importantly, students' perceptions of the teaching and learning context outlined above have been found to be consistently related to whether students adopt a deep or a surface approach to learning (Entwistle 2018).

The research into *self-regulation* also provides useful insights into how students can be supported to learn more effectively. Self-regulation activities include the student planning what is to be learned, monitoring the extent to which learning is occurring, adjusting the plan in relation to the outcomes of monitoring, and evaluating and reflecting on the extent to which learning outcomes have been successfully achieved. Vermunt and Donche (2017) summarize the literature on self-regulation as showing differences in the ways that students steer their learning processes, which vary from a lack of regulation to a focus on the teacher regulating learning as an external agent, to a focus on self-regulation.

RESEARCH BRIEFING 2.3 Students' learning patterns

Vermunt and his colleagues argue that orientations to learning, conceptions of learning, learning processes and regulation strategies often come together in four overall learning patterns for students in higher education. These are an undirected, reproducing-directed, application-directed and meaning-directed learning pattern (Vermunt 2007; Martínez-Fernández and Vermunt 2013; Vermunt and Donche 2017).

Students with an *undirected-learning pattern* tend to attempt to focus on everything in their courses and do so in a way that is unregulated. They are very likely to struggle on their courses because they are unable to discern what the important elements of their courses are.

Students with a *reproduction-directed learning pattern* tend to study the material thoroughly with a focus on remembering the important elements of the course. They are guided strongly by their teachers because they see learning as a process in which knowledge is transferred from their teachers and books into their heads so that it can be reproduced for assessment purposes.

Students with an *application-directed learning pattern* focus on the relations between what they are learning and the outside world. They tend to focus on how the knowledge from their courses can be applied to the outside world and are mainly interested in how they can use this knowledge in their future careers. These students tend to be both self-regulated and externally regulated.

Students with a *meaning-directed learning pattern* focus on finding relations between the different elements of their courses in order to build structures and to critically engage with the ideas and arguments that they are studying. They tend to set their own goals and monitor their own progress and see learning as a process in which they are responsible for constructing their own understanding.

While students may follow different but consistent learning patterns in different courses with different teachers, Vermunt (2007) also reports that some students have 'dissonant' learning patterns. They do not adopt a consistent learning pattern. Often it is these students who struggle the most because they lack a systematic way of approaching their studies and therefore can approach them with incompatible learning strategies.

Reflective Activity 2.3 Understanding learning patterns in your subject

Read the summaries of learning patterns in Research Briefing 2.3.

Think about students you have taught:

- Which patterns fit with your experiences of teaching?
- How might you respond to students who adopt an undirected learning pattern? What about those adopting the other patterns?
- How might you extend or change these patterns in order to give a richer account of these students' learning patterns in your subject area?
- What aspects of your students' experiences are not being considered in these learning patterns?

Product: Student learning outcomes and learning gains

The third element of the student learning model we have been looking at concerns the product or outcomes of learning. In its simplest formulation learning outcomes consist of the knowledge, skills and values which a student has achieved and can reliably demonstrate on the completion of a course of study. Long the domain of teachers and their educational programmes, in the past few decades there has been broad international interest in learning outcomes. In the United States, for example, the Spellings Commission (2006) called for universities and colleges to 'measure and report meaningful student learning outcomes', initiating a process which has grown substantially in the past decade (Neuman 2017). And the European framework of higher education qualifications for European countries adopted through the Bologna Process characterizes qualifications in terms of learning outcomes.

Types of learning outcomes

At the individual programme level, much of the discussion concerns the determination, teaching and assessment of specific learning outcomes for particular courses and modules. These will be discussed in other chapters (see, for example, Chapters 9, 11 and 13). We are concerned here to look at the product of learning in terms of the research on more general types of learning outcomes.

Two of the most widely used frameworks of learning outcomes in higher education are Bloom's (1956) classic *Taxonomy of Educational Objectives*, updated by Anderson et al. (2001) and Biggs' (2003) *Structure of Observed Learning Outcomes (SOLO) taxonomy*. While the two taxonomies were developed very differently – Bloom drew on the expertise of psychologists and education experts and Biggs primarily drew on research with students – they can be useful mapped against each other (Light et al. 2009).

In Bloom's case, there are six categories of thinking which increase in quality and complexity. Subsequent categories of thinking appear to subsume the thinking in the categories that come before (see Figure 2.2). Thus, understanding a concept requires remembering information about the concept; and further along the taxonomy the ability to generate new ideas about a subject requires the ability to understand, analyse and evaluate old ideas about a subject.

Significantly, Bloom's taxonomy has been criticized for dividing these thinking outcomes into a discrete and isolated set of six mental behaviours without any epistemological analysis or justification (Pring 2008). Teachers and curriculum designers have often interpreted these thinking processes as distinct outcomes which students engage separately or must work their way through starting with the mere recall of facts. One often hears teachers say, for example, that students must learn facts before they can engage in deeper thinking – a claim for which there is no evidence. Indeed, research shows that engaging

Learning outcome type	Description
Remembering	Recalling information
Understanding	Explaining ideas or concepts
Applying	Using information in another familiar situation
Analysing	Breaking information into parts to explore relationships
Evaluating	Justifying a decision or course of action
Creating	Generating new ideas, products or ways of viewing things

Figure 2.2 Bloom's Taxonomy of Educational Objectives (adapted from Bloom, 1956)

students in higher order thinking processes is more effective even for lower level recall type outcomes than engaging students in simple remembering activities (Agarwal 2019). Bloom's taxonomy is better regarded as describing a hierarchically related set of learning outcomes in which a focus on higher order outcomes will, as a matter of course, help student achieve lower level outcomes.

Biggs' (2003) SOLO taxonomy avoids the problem and confusion of Bloom's taxonomy, as it describes outcomes in terms of the increasingly complex structure of the thinking involved (see Figure 2.3). Indeed, it includes a pre-structural outcome in which there is essentially no learning, and learning outcomes are then described in terms of a qualitative enhancement in student thinking abilities. The higher-order abilities of the 'extended abstract' learning outcome, for example, assume the abilities of the previous categories of learning outcome.

While very different in their development and design, these two widely used taxonomies are, nevertheless, similar in their division of learning outcomes into more basic and higher learning outcomes. They describe a range of outcomes with which, as we have seen, different student perspectives, approaches and conceptions closely align. Understanding and planning for student learning ought actually to begin with outcomes – particularly the higher-order levels of learning – which can then help us to reflect back on how we can assist students to achieve the deeper approaches and levels of learning described above.

Learning outcome type	Description
Pre-structural	Misses the point
Uni-structural	Identify; do simple procedures
Multi-structural	Enumerate, describe, list, combine, do algorithms
Relational	Compare/contrast, explain, analyse, relate, apply
Extended abstract	Theorize, generalize, reflect, hypothesize

Figure 2.3 Biggs' Structure of Observed Learning Outcomes (SOLO) Taxonomy (adapted from Biggs, 2003)

Learning gain

Closely related to the idea of learning outcomes is the concept of learning gain (which we also examine in our discussion of quality in Chapter 14). However, learning outcomes and learning gain are not the same. The demonstration of a learning outcome does not mean it was a learning gain. A student might demonstrate higher levels of learning achievement at the end of a course, but perhaps he or she started at that level. How do we in fact know that they gained anything? In a report on learning gain in higher education, McGrath et al. (2015) define learning gain as the 'the difference between the skills, competencies, content knowledge and personal development demonstrated by students at two points in time. This allows for a comparison of academic abilities and how participation in higher education has contributed to such intellectual development' (p. xi) – in other words, the difference between two sets of assessed learning outcomes at two points in time. It is important to recognize that while learning outcomes can be used by educators in the design of modules, courses and programmes (see Chapters 10, 11 and 13), learning gain is the product of assessment of actual student performance.

Learning gain data can be obtained using a wide range of different methods. McGrath et al. (2015) describe five groups or types of methods by which learning gain data can be gathered: 'grades, surveys, standardised tests, qualitative methods and other mixed methods' (p. 21).

These methods provide data and information on learning which can be used for both formative and summative purposes on a range of different levels. In the former, learning gain data can be used as feedback to teacher and student for the improvement of student learning, for enhancing teaching development, and for the design of courses and programmes. It can also be used to review and improve academic policies, processes and procedures for teaching and learning at broader departmental and institutional levels. And on a summative level, learning gain can be used to extend the accountability of students, teachers, departments and institutions – although critics have also cautioned about the sole or over use of the data. Boud (2018) argues, for example, that learning gain may be valuable for assessing students but the 'assessments need to be directly related to explicitly articulated course/programme learning outcomes, not unit or module outcomes' (p. 56). McGrath et al. (2015) raise concerns about assessing higher education institutions that 'serve different missions according to a similar standard' (p. 12). Drawing on increasing interest in the assessment of critical thinking (Neuman 2017), Research Briefing 2.4 describes a method for gathering data on critical thinking – the Critical Thinking Assessment Test (CAT) which is often used to assess student learning gain. Importantly, the CAT requires students to engage in the higher levels of thinking and learning of the kind described by Bloom's and Biggs' taxonomies (see above).

RESEARCH BRIEFING 2.4 Critical Thinking Assessment Test (CAT)

The CAT project was supported by three separate National Science Foundation TUES (formerly CCLI) Program under grants 0404911, 0717654, and 1022789, and has now been used in over 250 institutions across the United States. It has also been used in Canada, Australia, China, Japan and Palestine. The test is a 15-item, short answer essay test that takes students about one hour to complete. It is designed to assess critical thinking skills in science, technology, maths and engineering (STEM) disciplines across four domains: (a) evaluation of information; (b) creative thinking; (c) learning and problem solving; and (d) communication of ideas. (See specific critical thinking skills in Table 2.3 below.)

National Science Foundation (NSF) supported research reveals that the CAT:

- is valid and reliable and appropriate for college students across all levels;
- has been shown to have face validity and criterion validity: in addition CAT scores are moderately correlated with general measures of academic performance;
- is sensitive to differences between courses;
- is internally consistent (Cronbach's alpha = 0.695) suggesting that items are measuring the same general construct;
- is culturally fair – in regression analyses, after controlling for previous academic achievement, neither gender, ethnic background nor racial group were found to be statistically significant predictors of overall CAT performance. (Stein et al. 2006, 2007)

Evaluating information	• Separate factual information from inferences. • Interpret numerical relationships in graphs. • Understand the limitations of correlative data. • Identify inappropriate conclusions.
Creative thinking	• Identify and evaluate evidence for a theory. • Identify new information that might support or contradict a hypothesis. • Explain how new information can change a problem.
Learning and problem solving	• Separate relevant information from irrelevant information. • Integrate information to solve problems. • Learn and apply new information. • Use mathematical skills to solve real-world problems.
Communication	• Communicate ideas effectively.

Figure 2.4 Critical thinking skills assessed by the CAT

The CAT can be used to assess learning gain over a course, module or programme, or even over a full undergraduate course of study and discipline-specific analogue questions can be developed.

Reflective Activity 2.4 Understanding critical thinking in your teaching

Look at the categories of critical thinking skills in Figure 3.4 above.

Think about your teaching:

- Which specific critical thinking skills are important for your students to learn?
- What activities are you having your students do to achieve these skills?
- How might you extend or change the activities to help students achieve these skills?
- How are you measuring whether or not they are achieving these skills?
- What methods might you use to measure the actual gain in their learning of these skills?

CONCLUSION

In this chapter, we examined different ways of thinking about learning in higher education as well as the different ways in which students approach their learning. Learning is an immensely complex topic and this chapter has simply touched the surface of some of the many issues which are involved. In one sense, perhaps the provisional nature of our understanding is no bad thing, because, if we knew it all, then one of the greatest sources of fascination and fulfilment in teaching would be diminished. Teaching in higher education will always include this element of intellectual challenge as we seek to understand who our students are, what they understand, and then how to provide them with support to further develop their deeper understanding. But all too often, teachers do not perceive this challenge as appropriate for their students. This raises an interesting, if rather insidious, division or rift in the way in which learning is understood in higher education (Light and Calkins 2015). Meaningful learning, whether it is the student's learning or the teacher-scholar-researcher's learning, is after all the primary idea at the heart of the university and it needs to be cohesively and consistently understood and pursued as such across all of our academic work. In the next chapter, we examine a model of reflective practice that can help us to respond to this challenge by drawing on our experiences in a structured, discursive and powerful manner.

KEY READINGS

For thought-provoking studies of students' experiences of learning in a range of contexts, see:

Case, J. (2013) *Researching Student Learning in Higher Education: A Social Realist Account.* London: Routledge.

Light, G. and Micari, M. (2013) *Making Scientists: Six Principles for Effective College Teaching*. Cambridge, MA: Harvard University Press.

McLean, M., Abbas, A. and Ashwin, P. (2018) *How Powerful Knowledge Disrupts Inequality: Reconceptualising Quality in Undergraduate Education*. London: Bloomsbury.

For helpful summaries of research on how students are affected by higher education, see:

Entwistle, N. (2018) *Student Learning and Academic Understanding: A Research Perspective with Implications for Teaching*. London: Academic Press.

Mayhew, M., Pascarella, E., Bowman, N., Rockenbach, A., Seifert, T., Terenzini, P. and Wolniak, G. (2016) *How College Affects Students: 21st Century Evidence that Higher Education Works* (Vol. 3). San Francisco, CA: John Wiley & Sons.

For a discussion of designing assessments for critical thinking, see:

Haynes, A., Lisic, E., Harris, K., Leming, K., Shanks, K. and Stein B. (2015) 'Using the Critical Thinking Assessment Test (CAT) as a model for designing within-course assessments', *Inquiry: Critical Thinking Across the Disciplines*, 30(3), 38–48.

Chapter 3
Reflection

How can we develop the quality of our teaching?

INTRODUCTION

Teaching in higher education is a challenging process. The ideas we work with are demanding, the students we meet are diverse and come with huge variations in knowledge and experience, and we are increasingly being held to account for what our students do. We often gained our positions because of expertise in things other than teaching, but organizing learning opportunities for our students is what we do, and need to do well. We can gain professional expertise in teaching in many ways, through participating in courses, through reading, and through observing and sharing experience with colleagues who are particularly accomplished at what we aspire to. But, no matter how much we learn, we will always be confronted with situations that challenge us. It is in these contexts that we resort to what is commonly called reflection or reflective practice. If we knew what to do, or could look it up or just consult with a colleague, then we wouldn't need to go down the path of reflection, we could just get on and do it. The purpose of this chapter is to understand what reflection involves, apply it to teaching and use it for our continuing learning. In the process, we will also be able to design it into our teaching so that students can understand and benefit from it as well.

See Chapter 4

TLRP Principles

One principle is of particular relevance to this chapter on reflective practice for the improvement of teaching:

Principle 2: Effective teaching and learning depends on the scholarship and learning of all those educators who teach and research to support the learning of others. The need for lecturers, teachers and trainers to learn through doing research to improve their knowledge, expertise and skills for teaching should be recognized and supported.

WHY BOTHER WITH REFLECTION IN HIGHER EDUCATION?

As teachers in higher education, we are faced with a range of competing demands and agendas. How can we manage our teaching effectively, when we have other tasks that need completing and perhaps the need to establish ourselves in a new institution and in a new role? How do we balance competing priorities? While we have considerable expertise in some areas, we may well be teaching in others in which we are less accomplished and we do not have a repertoire of understandings about student learning and approaches to teaching that a trained and experienced teacher would have.

Figure 3.1 presents some of the dilemmas and challenges that we may face as university teachers. Engaging with these requires us to use our judgement to assess the most

Area of practice	Potential dilemma		
View of knowledge	Disciplinary	↔	Vocational
Course quality	Disciplinary view	↔	Institutional view
Student retention	Meeting standards	↔	Retaining students
Supporting students	Focus on typical students	↔	Recognize diversity
Student outcomes	Focus on student understanding	↔	Focus on pass rate

Figure 3.1
Common dilemmas faced by university teachers

appropriate course of action in any particular situation. This is why reflective practice matters because it helps us to develop informed actions and develop a rationale for our practices (see Brookfield 2017).

Reflective Activity 3.1 Reviewing dilemmas that you have experienced

Think about your own situation and experiences. Look carefully at Figure 3.1 and see whether any of the identified dilemmas provide a realistic reflection of those you are experiencing. Are there other dilemmas that relate to your specific context?

Having carried out this exercise, try to identify the three most pressing dilemmas that you are facing. Think carefully about each of these and consider whether there are any measures that you might take to help mitigate them (for example, discussions with relevant colleagues about developing approaches to assessment; researching how students approach seminars in order to have the evidence for curriculum developments).

The important point here is to start with one dilemma and consider what evidence you need to be able to address it effectively, and where that evidence might come from. Progress will often be slow and incremental, but such professional development has powerful potential for change.

Note that this reflective activity may well lead to a more formalized piece of practice-based research.

WHAT IS THE MEANING OF REFLECTION?

Before focusing on how reflective teaching might be applied in our own context, we need to first look at the notion of reflection and what it has come to mean in professional practice. In modern times, the concept of reflection stems from John Dewey (1933) who contrasted 'routine action' with 'reflective action'. According to Dewey, routine action is guided by factors such as tradition, habit and authority, and by institutional definitions and expectations. By implication, it is relatively static and is thus unresponsive to changing priorities and circumstances. Reflective action, on the other hand, is prompted by changing circumstances and challenges. It involves a willingness to engage in continuing self-appraisal and development. Among other things, it implies flexibility, systematic analysis and awareness of our social and material context.

Reflective action, in Dewey's view, involves the active, persistent and careful consideration of any belief or supposed form of knowledge in the light of the grounds that support it. It is precipitated by a state of perplexity, hesitation and doubt (Dewey 1933). Teachers who are unreflective about their teaching tend to accept the *status quo* and simply 'concentrate on finding the most efficient means to solve problems that have largely been defined for them' by others (Zeichner and Liston 1996, p. 9). Of course, routine action based on ongoing assumptions is necessary, but Dewey argued that it is insufficient on its own. In Dewey's view, reflection 'enables us to direct our actions with foresight' (1933, p. 17). Mezirow (1991) took this further and emphasized the role of critical reflection in helping us to become aware of and challenging what we take for granted.

Donald Schön (1983; 1987) extended Dewey's ideas in analysing the actions of many different professional occupations – medicine, law, engineering, management, etc. Schön emphasized that most professionals face unique situations that require the use of knowledge and experience to inform action. This is an active, experimental and transactional process which Schön called 'professional artistry'. It is the 'kind of professional competence which practitioners display in unique, uncertain and conflicted situations of practice' (1987, p. 22) – a form of 'knowing-in-action'. Schön thus came to distinguish between 'reflection-on-action', which looks back to evaluate, and 'reflection-in-action', which enables immediate action. Both contribute to the capabilities of a reflective teacher.

Reflection has been taken up in the context of complex, often messy situations, which do not allow for a simple, rational analysis drawing upon readily available and well-established evidence to solve problems. Mezirow (1991) has referred to such situations as disorienting dilemmas and Brookfield (1987) as inner discomforts. While reflection is often taken to be synonymous with analysis or even just thinking, there is increasing recognition that more than thinking needs to be taken into account. Boud, Keogh and Walker (1985) drew attention to the importance of a focus on feelings and the role that emotions have in inhibiting and enhancing learning. They argued that feelings often create an emotional barrier which occludes our ability to clearly see a problem for what it is and what we might do about it.

Ideas around reflective practice are both challenging and exciting and, in the rest of this section, we review their implications by identifying and discussing eight key characteristics of reflective practices as they might apply in higher education. These are based on work about reflective practice more generally already discussed and others (for example Ghaye 2010; Pollard 2018), but also work that examines reflective practices in higher education (for example Zuber Skerrit et al. 2015; Brookfield 2017; Van Beveren et al. 2018). They are:

1 Reflective practices take shape at a particular time and in a particular context.

2 Reflective practices are sparked by dissatisfaction with existing arrangements and involve a cyclical process of questioning our everyday thoughts, assumptions and feelings.

3   Who we are, emotionally and intellectually, is key to our reflection.

4   The contexts in which reflective practices take place play a critical role in shaping them.

5   Seeking evidence is crucial in reflective practices.

6   Engagement with others is essential in developing reflective practices.

7   Reflective practices are about making judgements at a particular time and place.

8   Reflective practices lead to changes in action.

A process located in time and context

Reflective practices take shape at a particular time and are located in a particular place.

The first characteristic is a general one that is important to bear in mind when thinking about any kind of reflection. Reflective practices like learning are relational: we are always reflecting about something rather than reflecting generally and this process of reflection takes place in a particular time and space. This means that whilst we can discuss general principles and models of reflection, we always need to undertake work to translate these to fit with the particular contexts in which we work – a solution needs to fit a specific situation and needs not to be generalizable (Boud and Walker 1990). Thus reflective teaching practices are about responding to evidence and making judgements rather than following recipes or fixed protocols.

A cyclical process prompted by dissatisfaction

Reflective practices are sparked by dissatisfaction or unease with an existing situation and they involve a cyclical process of questioning that we take for granted.

Based on a conceptual analysis of the meaning of 'reflection' within a wide range of sources, Rogers (2001) argues persuasively that dissatisfaction is central to any notion of reflective practice. It is our sense of dissatisfaction with the status quo and a distrust of easy solutions that drives on the reflective process (Van Beveren et al. 2018; Narey 2019). It is a cyclical process which moves through different stages and questions our everyday assumptions.

The starting point of any reflective process is, as mentioned above, a dilemma which disorients us or a discomfort that won't go away; it is something we feel is just not right. It is often something we sense rather than rationally come to a view about, and it is framed by what we value, what we aspire to do and who we see ourselves to be in our professional role. It is useful to see this initial dissatisfaction as a point of reference in judging when we have resolved the issue: have I lessened or removed the sense of dissatisfaction that initiated the reflective process?

Reflective Activity 3.2 Identifying potential triggers that might initiate a reflective process

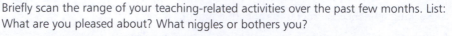

Briefly scan the range of your teaching-related activities over the past few months. List: What are you pleased about? What niggles or bothers you?

In terms of my recent teaching:

What pleases me?	What bothers me?

Taking the second list, sort it into three categories:

1 What is entirely outside my influence and I will need to live with?
2 What is partly within my scope of influence? I might be able to have a modest effect, but not fully resolve it.
3 What is mostly within my own scope of influence? I could conceive of the possibility of dealing with it, even though currently I don't know what I would do.

Of the things that bother me, which are:

Outside my influence?	Partly within my influence?	Mostly within my influence?

Of course, if you can see a solution to one of these niggles as you do this exercise, just tick that item off your list and do what you see is needed.

Finally, taking the items in the third category, set some priorities: which of these is most worth working on?

Ask yourself: 'What is the nature of the problem I have identified?' How can I frame it in such a way that I can start to work on it? Is it related to what someone else does? Is it about my reactions to it? Is it about something that now appears stuck because of what has happened previously?

Don't try to work directly on it; just expose the different facets and dimensions it has. **Reflective Activity 3.3** will give suggestions for how you can work further on it.

A process informed by who we are

Who we are, emotionally and intellectually, is central to our reflective practices

Thinking reflectively about our teaching involves considering who we are and what we are doing: our thoughts, our feelings and our values. Learning is always rooted in our prior experiences and we need to take account of how these shape our understanding of our current situation (Harrison 2018). However, whilst it is our embodied past history that shapes this understanding, our experience of particular contexts *evoke* particular aspects of our prior experiences rather than all of them being present in the moment.

Dewey (1933) emphasizes three key personal attributes that are important in undertaking reflective action: open mindedness, responsibility and whole-heartedness in reflective action. Open-mindedness involves being mindful of the evidence, and thinking about alternative possibilities, and being aware of our own fallibility. We need to challenge our assumptions and prejudices as well as those of others. Responsibility involves being aware of the consequences of our actions and taking ownership of them. So we need to be aware of whose interests are served by our actions and ensure we act with integrity. Wholeheartedness is about having enthusiasm and energy in focusing our reflection.

Whilst Dewey's (1933) qualities set a challenging agenda, it is important to be aware that they tend to focus on reflection as something that happens in our rational minds. Reflection is also an embodied and emotional process and we need to be aware of the roles these aspects of our identities play in the reflective process (Harrison 2018). Often a strong affective response to a teaching situation can be the original source of a dissatisfaction and, rather than ignoring this or explaining it away, we need to stay with our feelings and seek to understand their meaning. Swan and Bailey (2004) outline a number of different roles that emotions can play in the reflective process. They show how emotions can be the catalyst for reflection, they can be the content of reflection, how reflection itself can generate emotions and regenerate past emotions. However, as Swan and Bailey (2004) recognize, whilst it is important to pay attention to the emotional aspects of reflection, we still need to subject our emotions to critical analysis and discussion. It is not that either our thoughts or our feelings are more important than each other. Rather it is a case of seeking to understand the relations between them. We also need to consider how they relate to the principles that we value.

Reflection and reflective practice are essentially processes of learning from experience. That is the experience we bring to any occasion, and the experience we have when we are engaged in any activity. So, for teaching, it includes our experience of being taught as well as the experience we have when we are teaching others. How we act is often a result of both of these experiences modified by the particular context in which we find ourselves. Reflection starts with experience and moves forward from it. Boud and Walker (1990) examined this process and developed a model that focuses on how reflection operates when confronted with a new experience (see Figure 3.2).

Figure 3.2 Model of reflection in learning from experience (adapted from Boud and Walker, 1990)

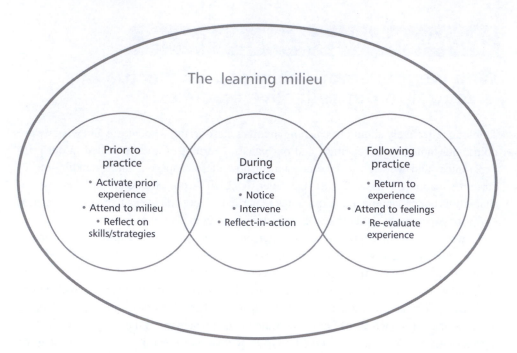

We can consider the implications of this model for reflecting on university teaching. The starting point is the overall milieu in which we operate: our department, our colleagues, the institutional rules and process that influence what we do, and the everyday assumptions about 'how we do things here'. The latter includes such things as how we teach and interact with students and what kinds of assessment are normal. We can think about a prompt for reflection as something occurring in anticipation of an event – 'I'm going to meet a student tomorrow and I don't know what I am going to say', during an event itself – 'This module doesn't seem to be going the way I want', or following an event, 'I don't want that to ever happen again'. Depending on the timing, we can enter the model at any one of these occasions.

Before practice involves:

- *Bringing prior experience to the fore* – what do we know and can do that will help us in the new situation?

- *Considering the milieu* or context in which we are operating – what can and can't we do? What is enabled and what is constrained?

- *Reflecting on skills and strategies* that we can deploy to help us once we get started – how can we find space to notice and reflect on our actions when we are in the midst of them?

During practice involves:

- *Noticing* carefully what is occurring – the people, the interactions, our responses, trying not to prematurely interpret what is happening, and findings ways to note or record salient features.

- *Intervening* not according to some pre-set plan but in accordance with what is appropriate to what we have noticed. How should we act, how should we refrain from acting?
- *Reflecting-in-action*, continually noticing and intervening appropriately to meet our goals in ways that respond to the immediate circumstances.

Following practice involves:

- *Returning to the experience*, recapturing as much of it as possible without premature interpretations and with awareness of the assumptions we are making.
- *Attending to feelings*, both positive and negative – how are these getting in the way, or assisting, our making sense of the occurrence, identifying how we can avoid being limited by them.
- *Re-evaluating the experience*, in the light of our reflections and the knowledge we have gained by looking to our personal responses and those of others.

Reflective Activity 3.3 Reflecting on a specific event

This activity focuses on how we can approach any dissatisfaction we have to begin to explore it, make sense of it and lead to a useful outcome. It focuses on the third circle of the model of learning from experience above. It can be helpful throughout to make notes of key features. Consider:

1 Which specific aspect of your teaching most bothers you currently? Identify specific instances that have given rise to your concern.
2 Work through a reflective process. Take one particular instance where you have experienced a disquiet or concern about what is occurring.

   a *Return to the experience*. Review in detail what occurred without trying to interpret the situation or draw conclusions. Stick with a description of events: What makes you focus on this occurrence? How was it manifest? Who said what to whom? How did it unfold? What did you do at the time? What did students or others do?

   b *Attend to feelings*. What were you feeling? Did you experience negative or positive emotions? Did some of them get in the way of you acting appropriately? If you find yourself identifying any strong emotions, stay with them because moving to a rational analysis without addressing them first will lead to a distorted outcome. You may wish to have a chat with a colleague or friend whom you trust to express what you are feeling.

   c *Identify what else you need to do to resolve the issue*. Do you need to find out more about the student perspective? Do you need to source ideas about strategies and interventions you can use? Can you do this informally by asking students or colleagues, or do you need to collect evidence more systematically through polling students or searching the literature? What types of evidence are pertinent and would be convincing to you? How can you can generate them?

    d   *Following your exploration, set the evidence out and see what conclusions you can draw.* Some of these will involve clarifying the problem, others will involve making plans which you can try out and test in a new situation.

    d   *Re-evaluate the experience.* Go back to the instance that prompted your reflection and see how it is illuminated by the process you have gone through and the evidence you have assembled. Would you do the same again? If not, what would you change? It may not involve a different strategy, but the way you raise it, apply it, or explain it may differ. Alternatively, you may wish to do something completely differently.

3 Apply the outcomes. This process may seem rather formal, and it is only worth doing if the solution to the problem you face is not apparent or can be simply resolved by asking a colleague or checking out a strategy. They are all things to consider about any situation in which you are faced with a challenge or a dilemma or something tricky to resolve. Issues of implementation will be picked up later in this chapter.

A process that is shaped by a wide range of contexts

The contexts in which reflective practices take place play a critical role in shaping them.

The fourth characteristic of reflective teaching is that it is profoundly shaped by the contexts in which it takes place. This picks up from the first characteristic but in this case the emphasis is on the range of contexts that shape our reflective teaching practices, including institutional cultures, disciplinary cultures and the teaching and learning contexts in which we teach. As we discuss further in Chapter 5, a useful way of thinking about these contexts is in terms of the way that they are woven into our reflective teaching practices (Cole 1996). So rather than simply seeing our teaching practices as being 'contained' in a range of contexts, the focus is on understanding how in particular interactions these contexts come together to shape our experiences. For example, this means examining how aspects of institutional cultures become visible in teaching and learning interactions rather than seeing these cultures as completely separate from these interactions.

Case Study 3.1
Maria confronts a new teaching context

Maria has a few years of experience as a lecturer, but when she is allocated to a new course, she finds she is being asked to move one of her modules to blended learning. The number of face-to-face meetings with students is halved, lecturing as information-giving is severely reduced and she is expected to prepare online activities for students. The subject matter and learning outcomes are little changed from what she was doing before, but the context has shifted radically for her.

Maria is told that there will be a briefing session about blended learning from colleagues who have used it, and some training sessions available to help her design online tasks for students, but that is it. If you were Maria, what would you do to prepare yourself for your new role? What would you need to understand about the new context? What would you need to take into account?

A process in which evidence is key

Evidence is crucial in reflective teaching practices.

As reflective teachers, we need to reflect on our experiences but also relate these to evidence in order to make sense of them. Figure 3.3 sets out Pollard's (2018) model of reflective teaching which shows how it starts with a problem and moves through a series of stages in which the use of evidence is key, until it reaches a point of judgement. Pollard (2018) argues that this process is evident in the thinking of Dewey and Schön but that the specific conception of a classroom-based, reflexive process derives from the teacher-based, action–research movement in schools of which Lawrence Stenhouse was a key figure. Stenhouse (1975) argued that teachers should act as 'researchers' of their own practice and should develop the curriculum through practical enquiry. Central to this model is a concern with self-monitoring and reflection.

Pollard's model emphasizes that, as university teachers, we are principally expected to plan, make provision and act, and, as reflective teachers, we also need to monitor, observe and generate data on our own, and our students', intentions, actions and feelings. This evidence then needs to be critically analysed and evaluated so that it can be shared,

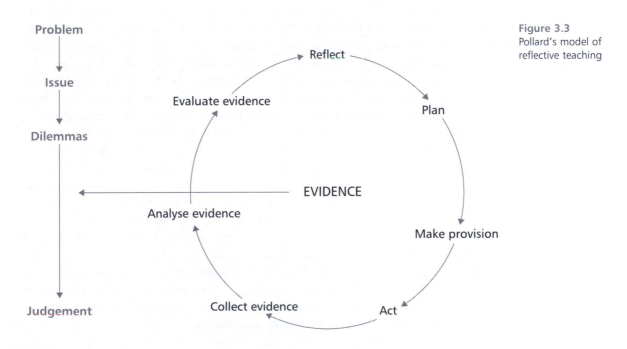

Figure 3.3
Pollard's model of reflective teaching

judgements made and decisions taken. Finally, this may lead us to revise our policies, plans and provision before beginning the process again. It is a dynamic process which is intended to lead through successive cycles, or through a spiralling process, towards higher-quality ways of teaching.

As teachers in higher education, there is a range of evidence we can draw on. As this is evidence which speaks to the problems we face, it will not necessarily meet the strict requirements of evidence for a journal or other scientific publication. Data directly related to our own teaching already exists. This includes students' performance on our modules as well as their feedback on our teaching. It also includes observations of our teaching carried out by colleagues. As indicated above, we can also find evidence from the research literature into higher education. As this book seeks to demonstrate, there is a rich body of research into all aspects of teaching and learning in higher education.

A third source of experiential evidence is data that we generate for ourselves by looking at our own experience of key events, as **Reflective Activity 3.3** explored in more detail. In generating new data, we need to think about what sources of data we have relating to what we and our students actually do and what data we have about how they perceive and experience our teaching practices and what data we have about our own emotional experiences related to what we encounter. It is important to draw on all these kinds of data in order to build on a sound foundation for actions we take.

Figure 3.3 summarizes the relationship between teaching practices and enquiry. It suggests that a practical *problem* in our teaching can helpfully be considered in terms of the *issues* which might underlie it. As we saw above, this foregrounds an appreciation of teaching *dilemmas* – the challenge of deciding what to do when there are a number of competing possibilities. The essence of professional expertise in teaching is being able to make high quality practical *judgements* (Heilbronn 2010). Figure 3.3 shows how evidence from our own enquiries and other research sources can enhance such judgements. For example, students' lack of engagement in a seminar discussion might result in an exhortation to them to do the necessary reading and participate more. However, later reflection might promote consideration of a number of possible longer-term issues. Why are the students not interested in engaging in discussion in the seminar? Do they understand their roles? Do they know the ground rules for the discussion? Have I created a safe enough climate for some of them to participate? (See Chapters 11 and 12 for further discussions of this particular issue.) Each of these topics, and others, could merit further investigation through classroom enquiry.

The sources of evidence we have reviewed – using existing data, interpreting research into higher education and our own enquiries – actually complement each other. As reflective university teachers we can draw on, or contribute to, many sources of evidence, and use them to inform our teaching practices. However, such evidence must always be critically evaluated. This is because it is tempting for it to be taken at face value and any difficult aspects ignored. For example, Hammersley-Fletcher and Orsmond (2015) show how, in some situations, the evidence from the observations of teaching can be used superficially to focus on tips and techniques rather than to think deeply about how teaching can be developed further by relating them to theories and research evidence. They found that amongst the lecturers they interviewed, reflection had become something that was uncomplicated and un-contentious, and potentially unproductive.

Further, because education is imbued with values, it would also be inappropriate to base educational decisions entirely on evidence. This is the reason why the term 'evidence-informed' is preferred over 'evidence-based'. It shares the assertion of the importance of evidence in decision making, but does not make inappropriate claims for precedence. Judgement remains essential for teachers in higher education, just as it is necessary for managers and policy makers. This is explored in more detail in Case Study 3.2.

Case Study 3.2 Mohan's dilemma

Mohan teaches a module for final-year undergraduate students. Many aspects of it are going well in his view, but he is concerned about a particular problem. There seems to be a dissonance between his desire to extend student understanding of the subject beyond the assessment requirements and what he perceives to be the instrumental interpretation of assessment requirements by colleagues. By encouraging his students to think about the moral and ethical implications of human impact upon the environment they often produce work that other tutors are not looking for when marking exam papers in this field. This increasingly results in him receiving comments that question why his students are considering aspects of the course that do not align with the module learning outcomes. This continues despite the fact that the students have covered, and demonstrated achievement of, assignment specific criteria. This misunderstanding produces complaints from students who are confused by the relationship between module content and the information they are getting from markers.

He generates evidence on the impact of his module in three ways. First, he collects student evaluations at the end of the module covering module content and the effectiveness of learning activities. He finds this form of evaluation superficial due to the fact that the students cannot always articulate the impact of teaching activities at this stage in the teaching and learning cycle. The second form of evidence he collects are records of retention and achievement levels across each cohort. His retention rates are good but achievement levels can vary depending upon who is marking the final examination.

How should Mohan handle the tension between what he thinks is valuable in his module and the views of his colleagues? Is the evidence he presently has at his disposal relevant for what he needs to do? Are there ways of dealing with the students' concerns without teaching the subject in a way that he does not agree with?

Case Study 3.2 offers an example of the intersection between tutor beliefs and module assessment and student outcomes. Figure 3.3 usefully indicates the way in which reflective evaluation of evidence might serve to resolve dilemmas. In the case of Mohan, the 'problem' stems from the grading of exams by colleagues. From this, the 'issue' relates to his aim to extend student understanding of his subject beyond the assessment requirements for final-year undergraduate students and the degree to which such aims are shared by colleagues. This presents Mohan with a 'dilemma'; should he mark all exam scripts himself? In order to make an informed judgement about this dilemma, Mohan can engage in the 'reflection on evidence' cycle suggested in Figure 3.3. Such models can help us to view challenges from a more reasoned position. However, the reflective cycle alone does not show us the full picture of how evidence-informed reflection might lead to improvements in practice. One crucial aspect that is not emphasized is the importance of discussing our analysis of the evidence with supportive colleagues.

A process that requires dialogue

Dialogue is essential in developing reflective practices.

As we discussed above, individual contemplation or evidence on its own is not enough for reflective practices. The evidence needs to be interpreted and transformed so that we can use it to challenge our everyday assumptions about teaching. In undertaking this transformation, dialogue is crucial. This dialogue can be both internal and external. As we discussed in Chapter 1, Margaret Archer (2003) uses the term the 'internal conversation' to refer to the dialogues that we have with ourselves in order to develop self-knowledge. She emphasizes the way in which we move from being the subject to seeing ourselves as an object and thus we speak and listen to ourselves. She argues that such conversations are crucial if we are to exercise agency and be more than at the whim of social structures.

However, dialogues with others are also crucial because, when we have a conversation with ourselves, we are able to leave many aspects of that conversation implicit. Discussing our reflections with others means that we need to be more explicit about our thoughts and feelings. This discussion is important because it offers the opportunity for critique and alternative explanations that can move us from 'descriptive reflection' to 'dialogic reflection'. It enables us to gain a 'critical distance' on our own experience and see it through the eyes of others. Other people can help us see what we may be overlooking, or help us frame the problem in ways more susceptible to a solution. If this discussion can help us to analyse our reflection from multiple perspectives and think about the socio-political and cultural influences on our practices, then it can move us towards 'critical reflection' (Brookfield 2017).

In engaging in dialogue with others, an important feature to consider is trust. Do I trust the other person enough for me to be able to reveal my uncertainties and otherwise unvoiced opinions to them without negative consequence? A feature of trust is that trusting begets trust. This means that it can be useful to cultivate a number of colleagues with whom you can reflect and know that what you say will go no further, and that they will listen well and not attempt to press their views on you when you just need space to explore for yourself.

Creating the conditions for collective reflection, that is a group or team engaging in reflection together, is more challenging still and we explore it further in Chapters 11 and 12. Boud and Walker (1998) argue that for such communities to work effectively they need to develop clear ground rules and acknowledge the influence of power within the community. This can allow us to develop a common language to collectively share our experiences. Such collective dialogues are crucial in gaining access to the different ways in which people can experience the same context and thus open these contexts up to multiple readings. These multiple readings are important if our reflective practices are not to become mechanistic and unchallenging. We explore these issues further when we look at barriers to reflective practice in the next section. In developing such multiple readings, we also need to be aware that evidence needs to play a crucial role. Otherwise, there is a danger that experiences can go unchallenged because there is seen to be an inherent truth to the way that they are experienced. In this way, collective dialogues also offer us the opportunity to learn to account for ourselves and justify what we are doing in our teaching (Ghaye 2010). This also involves justifying our interpretation of the evidence we are using to develop our teaching practices and opening this up to scrutiny by supportive others.

For some, collective dialogue is such an important aspect of reflection that it is central to the reflective process. Cressey et al. (2006) argue that productive reflection needs to be considered as a collective activity with an organizational intent rather than an individual process. Thus it needs to involve multiple stakeholders in order for us to have access to multiple perspectives for the reflection to be generative and developmental. Whether or not we agree that reflection needs to be collective, there is no doubt that discussion with others plays a crucial role in developing our reflective practices.

A process that depends on our judgement

Reflective teaching practices are about making judgements at a particular time and place.

Schön's (1983) work offers a helpful way of thinking about the kinds of judgements that we make as reflective teachers in higher education. He contrasted technical professional work, such as laboratory science, with human-oriented professional work, such as education. He called the former 'high hard ground' and saw it as supported by quantitative and 'objective' evidence. On the other hand, the 'swampy lowlands' of the human professions necessarily involve more interpersonal areas and qualitative issues. Schön argues that these complex 'lowlands' can become 'confusing messes' of intuitive action. Whilst these 'messes' are key to our practices, they are not easily amenable to technical analysis because they draw, as we have seen, on a type of knowledge-in-action. It is spontaneous, intuitive, tacit and intangible, but it 'works' in practice. Of course, there will always be scraps of harder evidence available – student grades, opinion surveys, etc. – but we need to be careful not to privilege that information which is easy to come by.

Schön's ideas have received powerful empirical support in recent years, with the sophistication of teachers' classroom thinking and 'craft knowledge' being increasingly recognized and understood by researchers in both schools and policy organizations (for example, see Mead 2019). It is clear that effective teachers make use of judgements all the time, as they adapt their teaching to the ever-changing learning challenges which their circumstances and students present to them. In school education, there has also been much greater recognition of the role of intuition in the work of experienced teachers (Atkinson and Claxton 2000) and decision-making. Of course, reflective teachers need to recognize potential bias in their judgements as a result of their diverse experiences, and this again emphasizes the need for open-mindedness and dialogue.

A process that leads to changes in our teaching practices

Reflective practices lead to changes in action.

Unless the processes we go through end up changing what we do, then they are hard to justify. As discussed earlier, reflection is a response to situations in which we cannot readily find an answer and a way forward by consulting what is readily available to us. It points to the need to look to ourselves and our own experiences and our emotional reactions to them, to look for evidence both formal and informal and to make judgements on the basis of them. If we are to make a difference to our students, we must then put them into action. What happens when we put into practice our best conclusions based on our analysis? We hope that the issues that prompted us in the first place get readily resolved. More likely though, we will have made some progress but recognize that more needs to occur. Reflection thus is an iterative process. The outcomes of one cycle of reflection lead to the next steps which prompt a further cycle with new evidence, hopefully new insights and further improvements. At some stage, we conclude enough has been done with regard to one set of issues and move on to another. Reflection is not something we do at one stage of our career and move on. It is a process which continues to be available to us to deploy as needed.

BARRIERS TO REFLECTIVE TEACHING IN HIGHER EDUCATION

In this section, we consider what gets in the way of our reflection on teaching. These barriers can be considered in terms of personal and contextual barriers, although as we will see there are clear overlaps between them.

Personal barriers to reflection

Even when we are genuinely committed to reflective teaching practices, there are a number of personal barriers that can prevent such practices being successful.

First, our notions of what reflection involves might act as a barrier. As Boud and Walker (1998) suggest, this can happen when we try to follow recipes of reflective practice. Thus, rather than thinking deeply about our teaching we focus on a series of steps in an uncritical way without engaging with the uncertainties of the teaching process or the ways that our emotions, power dynamics and contexts impact on our practices.

Second, as McAlpine and Weston (2000) argue, a lack of knowledge about teaching and learning can hinder our abilities to interpret evidence about our teaching and form plans for alternative ways of approaching our teaching. An aspect of this is if we focus overly on our teaching performance or the content of our teaching rather than how our students are learning then we are likely to overlook key evidence about the quality of our teaching. We can only be effective if we can see what we do from the perspective of learners.

A third barrier is a gap between our reflections on our practices and our ability to take action on the basis of these reflections (Mälkki and Lindblom-Ylänne 2012). Whilst some of the causes of this gap may be contextual, some of them are of a more personal kind. For example, whilst dissatisfaction is often the driver for reflective practices, it does depend on the kind of dissatisfaction that we experience. If we are dissatisfied with the effectiveness of our current teaching practices, this is very different from being dissatisfied with ourselves. Mälkki and Lindblom-Ylänne (2012) argue that whilst some teachers in higher education experience reflective practices as joyful and pleasurable, others experience dissatisfaction with themselves for being unable to live up to the image of the effective teacher. This highlights again the importance of taking account of our emotions in reflective teaching and not just seeing it as an intellectual exercise. It also highlights the importance of understanding reflective teaching as being focused on improving our existing practices rather than trying to aim for an unrealizable perfection. It is never about criticizing ourselves as people but in focusing on particular actions we take and the effects of them. We generally improve our teaching through progressive improvements over time, not huge changes over short periods. We need to be careful not to develop unrealistic expectations, which can end up leaving us demotivated and demoralized. We can always do better than we are doing now, but that 'better' will rarely be a transformation.

Finally, McAlpine and Weston (2000) highlight the way in which reflective teaching practices can be blocked by the temptation to explain away any issues with our teaching in terms of the environment in which we are working. As we shall see in the next section, these contextual barriers may be real, but they do not render us powerless. Mälkki and Lindblom-Ylänne (2012) identify a similar tendency in terms of the temptation to focus reflection on making our daily lives bearable rather than as a way of critically engaging with our teaching. Starting with that might be a good initial survival strategy, but it leads nowhere beyond that. We may feel that it is too risky to attempt to engage in more critically reflective practices. If that is the case, then we need to build our resilience to move into more challenging questioning of our assumptions.

There are no simple or fail-safe solutions to any of these personal barriers to reflective teaching. Rather, they highlight the complex and challenging processes that are involved in adopting such an approach. Sometimes our reflective teaching practices may be more or less engaged or effective. The key is to maintain a focus on how we can enable our students to develop an understanding of our disciplines and meet the learning outcomes we have set, rather than becoming overly focused on whether we have been reflective in exactly the right way.

Contextual barriers to reflective teaching

The previous section highlighted personal barriers to reflective teaching and in doing so emphasized the challenging nature of engaging in critical reflective teaching practices.

Given this, it is important to be aware of contextual barriers that exist in developing these practices.

Boud and Walker (1998) are clear that we need to think about how the different contexts in which our practices are situated impact on our reflective teaching practices. We explored a number of these contexts on page 000 and explore them further in Chapter 5. In this section we focus on barriers relating to our institutional contexts but it is worth thinking about the impact of the other contexts we discussed earlier.

The first contextual barrier we explore is that in some institutions the dominant notions of reflection can discourage critically reflective engagement with our teaching (Thompson and Thompson 2018). We mentioned earlier how Hammersley-Fletcher and Orsmond (2005) found that uncritical use of the outcomes of teaching observations limited their potential to challenge lecturers' teaching practices. This appeared to be based on the collective definition of reflection that had developed amongst this group of lecturers. Similarly, Kreber and Cranton (2000) suggest that lecturers tend to focus on the technical subject-matter aspects of teaching rather than critically examining their curricula and pedagogical knowledge in developing their academic practices. Thus, we need to consider whether the ways in which reflection is positioned in our institutions and departments are supportive of a critical engagement with teaching. Unfortunately, reflective tasks set for students are sometimes little more than thinking and analysis exercises and do not touch on the range of reflective practices we have discussed earlier.

Research into approaches to teaching shows that the context in which we teach can have a strong influence on the ways in which we approach our teaching (Entwistle 2018), and similar arguments have been made in relation to the ways in which the context can impact on reflective teaching practices (Thompson and Thompson 2018). Thus we are more likely to engage in reflective teaching when we have control over what and how we teach; our workload is not too high so as to prevent us from engaging in such practices and we feel that our students are sufficiently prepared to engage with our teaching. Finally, we need to feel that our department and institution are supportive of such practices and see teaching as an important element of being an academic. This may be related to how teaching is positioned in the disciplines that we teach: is it generally seen as the simple transfer of knowledge or something more complex and challenging?

This point links to a final contextual barrier: the absence of a supportive group who can help us to develop our reflective teaching practices. As we have seen, collective dialogue is crucial to the development of such practices and so it is important to find a group of people with whom we feel we can discuss our teaching in a constructively critical manner. Given the importance of trust and respect in developing such groups, they are something to be highly valued and cared for when we do establish them. We explore the processes of establishing such groups in more detail in Chapters 11 and 12.

It is important to be clear that none of these contextual barriers would make reflective teaching impossible to engage in. Rather, the challenge is to consider how we would go about mitigating their effects. We explore this further in Reflective Activity 3.4.

Reflective Activity 3.4 Responding to contextual barriers to reflective teaching

The following table lists a number of contextual barriers to the development of reflective teaching. In each case, draw on the discussions in this chapter to develop a response that would allow you to address these barriers. Your response could be to challenge the assumptions underlying the potential barrier or to suggest a way of limiting its impact. For example, you might challenge the notion that students are not suitable for higher education or, in relation to the lack of a supportive group, you could suggest joining or developing an online discussion group with people from outside your institution.

Potential barrier	Potential response
Uncritical dominant notion of reflection in your institution	
Lack of control of what and how you teach	
Very large cohorts	
Very high workload	
Students not well prepared for study	
Teaching not valued in your faculty or department	
The lack of a supportive group of colleagues	

CONCLUSION

In this chapter we have examined the reasons for adopting reflective teaching practices, explored seven principles of reflective teaching practices in higher education and looked at some contextual and individual barriers to reflective teaching.

In this conclusion, we consider the notion of reflective teaching in higher education from another perspective. **Research Briefing 3.1** outlines the 'university oath' that Watson (2014) developed for contemporary higher education. This provides another expression of values that can underpin our reflective teaching practices in higher education. The point of introducing an alternative set of principles at the end of this chapter is to emphasize that it is not necessarily the particular approach to reflective teaching in higher education that matters. As we explore in **Reflective Activity 3.5**, rather it is the taking of a principled approach to our teaching that is based on using available evidence to make sense of our experiences of teaching and helping our students to develop better understandings of the disciplines that we teach. In Chapter 16, we examine the development of teaching expertise over this career in more detail.

RESEARCH BRIEFING 3.1 The university oath

Watson (2014, pp. 89–97) sets out ten elements of an oath for contemporary higher education. These 'ten commandments' are focused at the level of higher education institutions but can equally be applied to our practices as reflective teachers in higher education:

1 *Strive to tell the truth* – a key element of academic freedom is following the truth wherever it leads us.
2 *Take care in establishing the truth* – we should subject our thinking to rigorous analysis and critique.
3 *Be fair* – we should treat people with respect and be aware of our responsibilities in terms of equality and diversity.
4 *Always be ready to explain* – we should always be prepared to explain our actions and should resist the temptation to make pronouncements on things that we know little about.
5 *Do no harm* – we should not exploit our students, our colleagues or our environments and should be careful to anticipate the potentially negative impacts of our practices.
6 *Keep your promises* – we should do what we have agreed to do and not make unrealistic claims in promoting ourselves to others.
7 *Respect your colleagues, your students and especially your opponents* – we should listen to others, always try to understand their point of view and ensure that discussion is not prevented by competitiveness, prejudice, egotism or bullying.
8 *Sustain the community* – we should all work to sustain higher education as a whole rather than simply in the interests of individual institutions or disciplines.
9 *Guard your treasure* – we need to look after the long-term sustainability of the knowledge and teaching-and-learning communities in which we engage.
10 *Never be satisfied* – we should always strive to improve the practices that we are engaged in.

Reflective Activity 3.5 Developing your own oath as a reflective teacher in higher education

Look at Watson's (2014) list of elements of a university oath in **Research Briefing 3.1**.

What do you think and feel about this list of elements?

Are there any items in Watson's list that seem relatively unimportant to your practices as a reflective teacher in higher education?

Do they help you to think about how you might help your students to engage with the knowledge that you teach?

Are there any key principles or values missing that you see as central to your identity as a reflective teacher?

Rewrite the list to reflect your own principles and discuss your 'university oath' with supportive colleagues.

What would they change or add?

What is your sense of the reasons for any differences you have in what you would position as important in reflective teaching in higher education?

KEY READINGS

A classic work by Dewey which has strongly influenced the development of reflective practice is:

Dewey, J. (1933) *How We Think: A Restatement of the Relation of Reflective Thinking to the Educative Process.* Chicago, IL: Henry Regnery.

For analyses on the nature of professional knowledge and its potential to enhance learning, see:

Schön, D. (1983) *The Reflective Practitioner: How Professionals Think in Action.* London: Temple Smith.

For a useful guide for reflecting on one's teaching:

Brookfield, S. (2017) *Becoming a Critically Reflective Teacher.* 2nd edn. San Francisco, CA: John Wiley & Sons.

For discussions of the role of reflection in learning, see:

Boud, D., Keogh, K. and Walker D. (eds) (1985) *Reflection: Turning Experience into Learning.* London: Routledge.

For a review of the purposes of reflective practice see:

Van Beveren, L., Roets, G., Buysse, A. and Rutten, K. (2018) 'We all reflect, but why? A systematic review of the purposes of reflection in higher education in social and behavioral sciences', *Educational Research Review*, 24, 1–9.

Chapter 4
Principles

What are the foundations of effective teaching and learning?

INTRODUCTION

This chapter is focused on ten 'evidence-informed educational principles', which have been specifically identified to support the development of university teachers' professional judgement. Whilst the previous chapter focused on the *process* of reflective teaching, this chapter highlights some of the *enduring substantive issues* with which teaching and learning are concerned.

The ten principles were initially conceptualized by the UK's Teaching and Learning Research Programme (TLRP) (2000–12) by reviewing the outcomes of its many research projects, consulting with UK practitioners in each major educational sector, and comparing these findings with other research from around the world (see James and Pollard 2012). The TLRP was the UK's largest ever coordinated programme of educational research (Pollard 2007). Spread over a decade, the programme involved over 100 projects and other initiatives. In higher education this included seven projects on higher education practice, focusing on undergraduate students' learning and teacher education, and seven projects on widening participation in higher education. Together these projects on teaching and learning covered sixty UK higher education institutions, including some specialist colleges for music and education.

Whilst the TLRP was UK focused, both the programme as a whole and the findings from the individual projects have been significant internationally (see James and Pollard 2012). The ten principles have relevance for teaching and learning in universities globally and are consistent with other sets of principles and accounts of high-quality teaching and learning in higher education that have been developed over the past thirty years (Chickering and Gamson 1987; Kuh 2008; Ambrose et al. 2010; Gibbs 2010; Laurillard 2012; Entwistle 2018). Whilst the teaching and learning contexts in which these approaches have been applied have changed over time, the principles of good learning and teaching have been found to be remarkably robust. The challenge for us as reflective teachers is to carefully consider how we can draw on these principles in the particular contexts in which we are working.

EVIDENCE-INFORMED PRINCIPLES

Each of the ten principles which are described in this chapter has an extensive research base – they are 'evidence-informed'. They do not, however, seek to tell us as university teachers what to do. Indeed, each principle is expressed at a level of generality which calls for us to interpret them in relation to our knowledge of the educational needs of our students and the particular higher education setting in which we work. The principles are thus intended as a guide and support for us in making the professional judgements which we are uniquely positioned, and required, to make.

The identification of principles in this way avoids oversimplified claims for the certainty of 'evidence-*based* decision making' which, as we discussed in Chapter 3, cannot always be justified. Rather, this approach promotes contextualized, evidence-*informed* judgement, as has been argued by Darling Hammond:

> Bureaucratic solutions to problems of practice will always fail because effective teaching is not routine, students are not passive, and questions of practice are not simple, predictable, or standardized. Consequently, instructional decisions cannot be formulated on high then packaged and handed down to teachers. (Darling-Hammond 2007)

The ten principles are an attempt to pick out prominent patterns from the complexity of teaching and learning, and to shed light on them. They are statements of what we think we understand, at this point in time. The evidence-informed principles offer reference points, thus making it easier to take stock and review progress in educationally sound ways. But when particular dilemmas arise, the principles will not actually determine a specific decision, for that is the job of the reflective university teacher.

The principles begin with a focus on what conditions are needed to enable success in policy and practice. A second group then highlights the personal and social processes that underpin teaching and learning. There is a cluster of principles on knowledge, curriculum, teaching, learning and assessment that take us to the heart of expert teaching. Finally, Principle 10 is concerned with the bigger picture in terms of the most enduring objectives and moral purposes of education.

In the following section, we introduce and illustrate each of the ten principles. The ten principles are also used to frame the other sixteen chapters of the book (as indicated in Figure 4.1). We return synoptically to them in Chapter 16 when discussing our ongoing development of expertise in teaching. Figure 4.1 represents the ten principles holistically.

Policy frameworks

Effective teaching and learning demands consistent policy frameworks, with support for learning for diverse students as their main focus. Policies at government, system, institutional and organizational level need to recognize the fundamental importance of learning for individual, team, organizational, institutional, national and system success. Policies should be designed to create effective and equitable learning environments for all students to benefit socially and economically.

As we explore in more detail in Chapter 5, teaching and learning in higher education institutions are partly shaped by policy frameworks. This means that it is important for policy frameworks to be clear about the kinds of teaching and learning that they seek to promote and for policies to be consistent in the messages they send.

There are four key elements to this principle. First, it is important to be clear that policies operate at different levels. There are international policies such as the Bologna

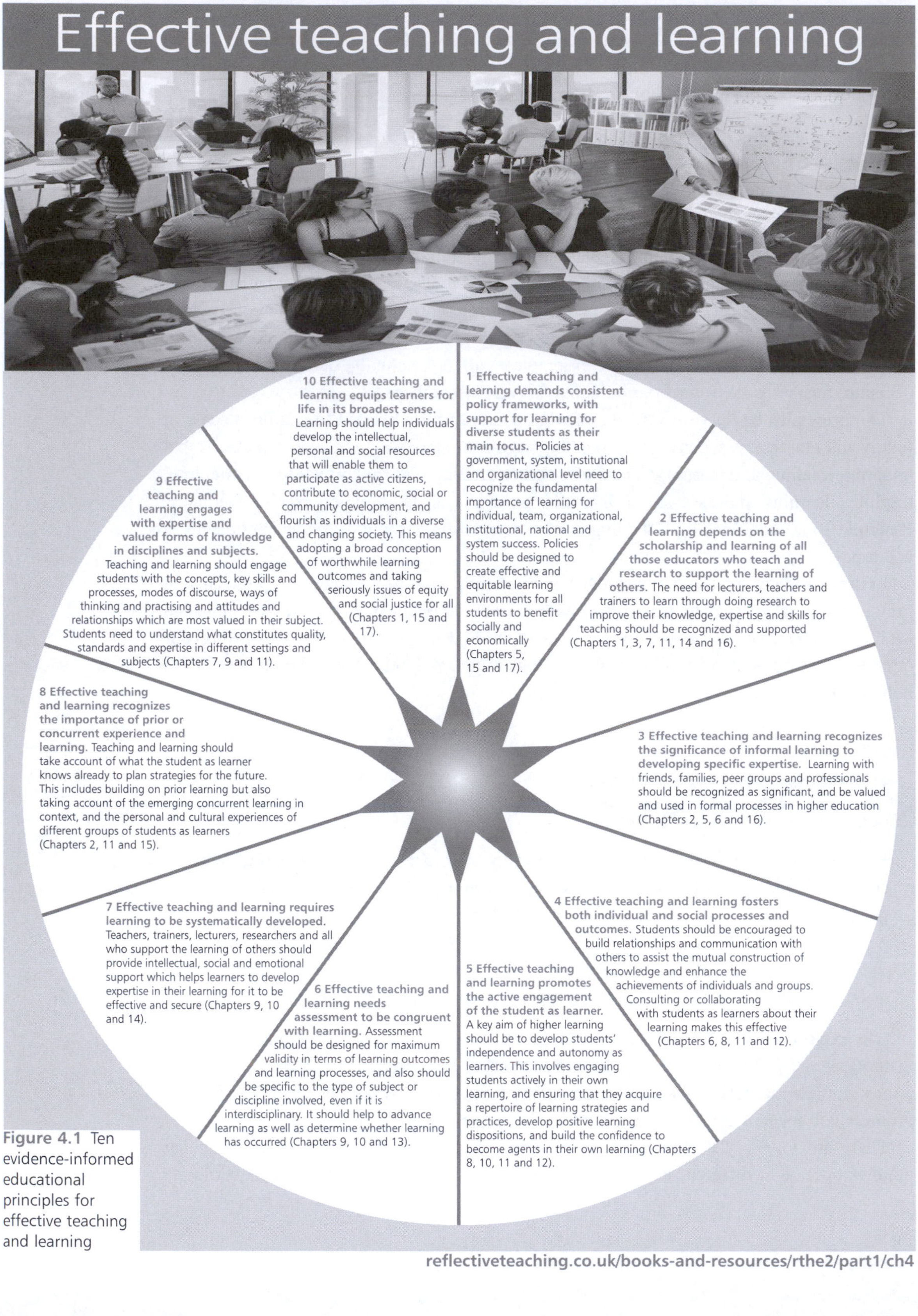

Effective teaching and learning

10 Effective teaching and learning equips learners for life in its broadest sense. Learning should help individuals develop the intellectual, personal and social resources that will enable them to participate as active citizens, contribute to economic, social or community development, and flourish as individuals in a diverse and changing society. This means adopting a broad conception of worthwhile learning outcomes and taking seriously issues of equity and social justice for all (Chapters 1, 15 and 17).

1 Effective teaching and learning demands consistent policy frameworks, with support for learning for diverse students as their main focus. Policies at government, system, institutional and organizational level need to recognize the fundamental importance of learning for individual, team, organizational, institutional, national and system success. Policies should be designed to create effective and equitable learning environments for all students to benefit socially and economically (Chapters 5, 15 and 17).

9 Effective teaching and learning engages with expertise and valued forms of knowledge in disciplines and subjects. Teaching and learning should engage students with the concepts, key skills and processes, modes of discourse, ways of thinking and practising and attitudes and relationships which are most valued in their subject. Students need to understand what constitutes quality, standards and expertise in different settings and subjects (Chapters 7, 9 and 11).

2 Effective teaching and learning depends on the scholarship and learning of all those educators who teach and research to support the learning of others. The need for lecturers, teachers and trainers to learn through doing research to improve their knowledge, expertise and skills for teaching should be recognized and supported (Chapters 1, 3, 7, 11, 14 and 16).

8 Effective teaching and learning recognizes the importance of prior or concurrent experience and learning. Teaching and learning should take account of what the student as learner knows already to plan strategies for the future. This includes building on prior learning but also taking account of the emerging concurrent learning in context, and the personal and cultural experiences of different groups of students as learners (Chapters 2, 11 and 15).

3 Effective teaching and learning recognizes the significance of informal learning to developing specific expertise. Learning with friends, families, peer groups and professionals should be recognized as significant, and be valued and used in formal processes in higher education (Chapters 2, 5, 6 and 16).

7 Effective teaching and learning requires learning to be systematically developed. Teachers, trainers, lecturers, researchers and all who support the learning of others should provide intellectual, social and emotional support which helps learners to develop expertise in their learning for it to be effective and secure (Chapters 9, 10 and 14).

6 Effective teaching and learning needs assessment to be congruent with learning. Assessment should be designed for maximum validity in terms of learning outcomes and learning processes, and also should be specific to the type of subject or discipline involved, even if it is interdisciplinary. It should help to advance learning as well as determine whether learning has occurred (Chapters 9, 10 and 13).

5 Effective teaching and learning promotes the active engagement of the student as learner. A key aim of higher learning should be to develop students' independence and autonomy as learners. This involves engaging students actively in their own learning, and ensuring that they acquire a repertoire of learning strategies and practices, develop positive learning dispositions, and build the confidence to become agents in their own learning (Chapters 8, 10, 11 and 12).

4 Effective teaching and learning fosters both individual and social processes and outcomes. Students should be encouraged to build relationships and communication with others to assist the mutual construction of knowledge and enhance the achievements of individuals and groups. Consulting or collaborating with students as learners about their learning makes this effective (Chapters 6, 8, 11 and 12).

Figure 4.1 Ten evidence-informed educational principles for effective teaching and learning

process, which, as we will explore in Chapter 9, has helped to shape the nature of higher education curricula in Europe and beyond. There are national policies, for example the introduction of tuition fees in England or higher education's key role in supporting the transformation of South African society, that help to shape who has access to higher education (see Ashwin and Case 2018 for a discussion of access to, student experiences of and outcomes from South African higher education). There are institutional policies such as admission policies and assessment frameworks. There are also departmental policies on, for example, the way in which the observation of teaching is approached in a particular department. Thus one important aspect of understanding policy frameworks is being aware of how policies at these different levels interact, support and contradict each other.

Second, even policies located at the same level can push in different directions. For example, one of the criticisms of policies to enhance teaching and learning internationally is that they often take no account of the way in which the quality of research is assessed in universities. When research is prioritized by institutions, for both financial and reputational reasons, this can undermine policies that seek to promote the development of teaching in universities.

Third, whilst policies can be seen to originate at a particular level, they have effects at other levels that are complex. This is because institutions and departments and individual academics may interpret national policies in a number of ways and thus understand their meaning differently. Thus national policies can be seen as being *refracted* differently in different contexts and their meaning changes as they move through contexts (Ashwin 2009). We explore this idea further in Chapter 5. This means that the impact of a particular policy in a particular context cannot be easily predicted.

Fourth, whilst the meaning of policies can change as they move through systems of higher education, it still makes sense to explore the *theory of change* of particular policies (Saunders et al. 2005). This means thinking about the ways in which a particular policy is intended to lead to improvements in teaching and learning in higher education. In many cases policies can lack a sense of how they will lead to wide-scale improvements (for example, see Trowler et al. 2014). One attempt to develop a more coherent approach to teaching enhancement is examined in Case Study 4.1.

Case Study 4.1 The Scottish approach to teaching enhancement

In Scotland, the Quality Enhancement Framework (QEF) attempts to bring together Quality Assurance (QA), the monitoring of quality, and Quality Enhancement (QE), the improvement of quality, in an integrated way. It draws on a number of elements:

- reviews of institutions that are focused on enhancement;
- institutions' internal review processes;
- the active involvement of students in quality processes;

- a focus on particularly targeted areas for enhancement across the sector (for example, employability and the student experience);
- new ways of communicating to the public about the quality of universities.

This complex policy instrument is designed to create a culture that is focused on improving teaching practices across the sector and is built on a sustained partnership between the funding council, the student body (NUS Scotland) and the quality assurance agency (the Scottish QAA). There are some issues with the QAA's dual role as reviewer and agent of enhancement and the same tension between teaching and research discussed earlier (Land and Gordon 2013). However, the QEF represents the bringing together of a coherent strategy for enhancement across an entire higher education system that has a unified change theory and involves a commitment to changing institutional teaching and learning cultures through consensual development (Saunders 2014).

Reflective Activity 4.1 Policy and your teaching practices

Select an institutional policy that in some way helps to shape your teaching practices. For example, this could be a teaching and learning strategy or a policy about assessment procedures.

Examine the text of this policy and identify the way in which it depicts the process of teaching and learning. What assumptions does it make about the relationship between teaching and learning? How does it depict students and teachers?

Thinking about your own teaching practices, examine the extent to which they are aligned to or contradict the depiction in the policy.

What reasons can you see for the alignment and/or contradiction between the policy and your practice?

What are the implications of this for both your teaching practices and the policy?

Teacher learning

Effective teaching and learning depends on the scholarship and learning of all those educators who teach and research to support the learning of others. The need for lecturers, teachers and trainers to learn through doing research to improve their knowledge, expertise and skills for teaching should be recognized and supported.

This principle provides the rationale for this book as a whole – we need to be reflective, and thus commit to our own learning, because this enhances our effectiveness in supporting the learning of our students. Teacher learning is concerned with both what we do and how we think, so that developing more effective forms of teaching depend on our changing our teaching practices, engaging with new knowledge about teaching and learning, but also on developing our values. Working with colleagues in developing our teaching is particularly important in teacher learning, as we explore in more detail in Chapters 11 and 12.

Some of the findings from the Teaching and Learning Research Project about teaching both within and beyond higher education give a sense of the importance and nature of teacher learning (James 2005). Here they are adapted for higher education:

1 Learning involves the acquisition of knowledge and skills *and* participation in social processes. Thus the development of supportive professional cultures is vitally important if we are to successfully develop our teaching.

2 We are most ready to accept ideas for change if they resonate with our existing or previous beliefs and experience. However, this does not necessarily make them 'right' or appropriate. We need to develop knowledge and skills to evaluate evidence and the confidence to challenge taken-for-granted assumptions in our teaching, including our own. This is difficult and it is often helpful to involve outsiders, perhaps members of other departments or institutions, to help us to do this. We need to feel assured that it is acceptable and often fruitful to take risks – so a culture of trust and openness is crucial.

3 Evidence from research about effective practice is not always sufficiently accessible for us to use it as the basis for action. Findings often need to be transformed into practical and concrete strategies that can be tried out. This may involve the production of concise and user-friendly materials, although ideas are often mediated best by talk and personal contacts with other teachers who have had some success in using them.

The Enhancing Teaching-Learning Environments research project, which we examined in Chapter 2, involved researchers working with university teachers to help them to fine-tune the design of effective teaching and learning environments for students (see Entwistle 2018). The researchers used research-informed concepts about students' learning to generate and analyse data about the students' learning experience on seventeen courses in five subject areas. These were brought together with the subject knowledge of the university teachers in order to develop new insights into students' experiences of learning at university. As we saw in Chapter 2, this project was particularly effective in developing new ways of thinking about students learning at university through the development of two major new concepts: 'ways of thinking and practising' (WTPs) and threshold concepts. This shows how partnerships between researchers and university teachers can not only enhance our understanding of the teaching and learning process in universities but also help to improve the quality of teaching and learning in universities. In Chapter 16, we examine ways of engaging in research and the scholarship of teaching in order to maintain a career-long fascination with teaching in higher education.

Reflective Activity 4.2 Your expertise as a teacher

Which areas do you consider yourself to be an expert in? For example, this could include:

- The subject matter you are teaching?
- The ways in which you teach your students?
- The ways in which you assess your students?

Which areas would you like to develop your expertise in further?

How do you plan to further develop your expertise?

Informal learning

Effective teaching and learning recognizes the significance of informal learning to developing specific expertise. Learning with friends, families, peer groups and professionals should be recognized as significant, and be valued and used in formal processes in higher education.

This principle draws attention to the boundaries of the formal aspects of higher education programmes and emphasizes the importance of experiences beyond these boundaries in helping students to develop their knowledge and expertise. In doing so, this principle draws attention to the way that our students in higher education are more than simply 'learners'; they have lives outside of higher education that play an important role in helping them to make sense of their experiences in higher education.

These aspects of students' lives include not only their relationships with friends, families and peer groups but also their experiences in professional and working contexts. The *Learning Lives* project (see Biesta et al. 2010) emphasized the way in which learning can be seen as a process of constructing a narrative identity. Making sense of the relations between our personal, professional and working contexts is an important aspect of this process of construction. It is worth noting that this way of thinking about the importance of informal learning contexts is seen as controversial by some. Furedi (2013) suggests that being concerned with the personal lives of our students infantilizes them and argues that tutors should simply focus on the intellectual development of students. The position taken here is that, whilst we need to be clear that students enter higher education to study, we do need to have a sense of how their engagement with their discipline is shaped by contexts outside of the university.

The boundaries between formal and informal learning tend to vary between disciplines. For example, Nespor (1994), in a classic ethnographic study of undergraduate degrees in physics and management, contrasts the very course-focused experiences of physics students with the more socially focused interactions of management students. The physics students spent their time studying with the same physics students in formal and informal settings. These groups were largely created by their degree programme. In management, students' groups were formed by independent student networks that connected them to the world of work and changed regularly over the course of their degrees. Thus, for the physics students their informal learning contexts were much more strongly shaped by their formal learning contexts.

This principle highlights the need to think about how to make productive use of students' formal and informal learning experiences. This is important because, as Ivanič et al. (2009) show, transferring knowledge between the personal, academic and professional contexts is very challenging, and helping students to do this is an important part of our role as university teachers. Again, we also need to recognize that this might play out differently in different disciplinary settings. For example, in Sociology, Jenkins et al. (2017) explore how student understanding can be developed by juxtaposing abstract sociological knowledge with everyday problems that students face in their lives. In Medicine, Tai et al. (2016) examine how peer assisted learning can help students to develop evaluative judgement in clinical settings. In Chapter 8 on learning spaces, we examine a range of spaces beyond the traditional formal settings of higher education in which students can develop their knowledge, such as Service Learning which bring together academic courses and more informal learning contexts.

Reflective Activity 4.3 Engaging with our students' lives

Think about elements of a module you teach that could make greater use of students' experiences in informal learning contexts.

Is this something that fits with your sense of how students develop knowledge in your discipline?

How might you encourage them to draw on these experiences in this module?

What might be the differences between students' conceptions of knowledge in their everyday lives and the conceptions of knowledge that are important in your subject area?

Do you have any concerns about taking this kind of approach?

Social relationships

Effective teaching and learning fosters both individual and social processes and outcomes. Students should be encouraged to build relationships and communication with others to assist the mutual construction of knowledge and enhance the achievements of individuals and groups. Consulting or collaborating with students as learners about their learning makes this effective.

Learning is a social as well as an individual activity. The learning of our students flourishes when the conditions are right for them to engage in the mutual construction of knowledge with other students. Good relations between teachers and students are central to supporting such conditions.

The importance of supportive social processes in supporting the learning of our students is highlighted by research into collaborative and peer learning (Hanson et al. 2016). Innovations in which students support each other's learning are frequently found to improve the quality of learning processes and outcomes in a wide range of disciplines and teaching and learning settings in higher education. In education, De Backer et al. (2012) found that peer learning helped students to develop their regulation of their learning and it has also been found to be helpful to PhD students in developing scholarly skills and disciplinary knowledge (Meschitti 2019). Similarly, forms of peer assessment can help students to be able to better assess their own work (Reinholz 2016) and peer learning processes are seen as an integral part of effective e-learning (Broadbent and Poon 2015).

Central to these processes of peer support is the way in which working with their peers offers students the opportunity to discuss ideas and to gain an insight into the way other students understand these ideas. However, such supportive social relationships are unlikely to develop spontaneously. They also do not develop in isolation from the rest of the course that students are studying. For example, there is clear evidence that forms of peer support are influenced by the teaching and learning context in which they are situated and in particular by the ways in which students are assessed (Ashwin 2003; Berghmanns et al. 2013). This means that we cannot see forms of peer support as way of reducing our responsibilities as teachers. They work best when they are an integral part of our design of our courses and when we have a clear sense of what we intend them to achieve.

Another aspect of this principle is the importance of consulting and collaborating with students in developing their learning. Case Study 4.2 highlights one example of this at the University of Exeter where students were employed as change agents. This case study also highlights issues of student engagement that we explore in the next principle.

Case Study 4.2 Students as change agents at the University of Exeter

Dunne and Zandstra (2011) outlined how, at the University of Exeter, students from across the university carried out a series of research projects aimed at developing their learning and teaching environments. Responding to issues identified by student–staff liaison committees, students drew on the knowledge of research they have gained on their course to generate data on the issues and presented the results and their recommendations for change to a staff–student conference. This initiative led to the development of new policies and practices within the university, whilst giving the students involved the opportunity to develop their research, project management and communication skills. It also helped students to integrate their theoretical knowledge with practical know-how.

Student engagement

Effective teaching and learning promotes the active engagement of the student as learner. A key aim of higher learning should be to develop students' independence and autonomy as learners. This involves engaging students actively in their own learning, and ensuring that they acquire a repertoire of learning strategies and practices, develop positive learning dispositions, and build the confidence to become agents in their own learning.

Student engagement has become a buzz word in the literature on learning and teaching in higher education (Trowler 2010; Ashwin and McVitty 2015). Its attraction is that it offers a fairly obvious explanation of the teaching and learning process: the more students are involved in their learning, the more they are likely to gain from it. The idea of involvement highlights students' participation in their education both inside and outside formal educational settings. As we saw in Case Study 4.2, it can include engagement in the development of the teaching and learning environment as well as engagement in the ideas and process of their courses. Based on an extensive review of the literature, Trowler (2010) argues that engagement has been found to be positively associated with nine outcomes:

1 Students' general abilities and critical thinking;

2 Students' practice competence and ability to transfer skills across contexts;

3 Students' level of cognitive development;

4 Students' self-esteem and identity formation;

5 Students' moral and ethical development;

6 Students' levels of satisfaction with their course;

7 Students' development of social capital;

8 Students' academic performance;

9 Levels of student retention.

However, student engagement does not simply happen. A key part of our task as reflective teachers is to work out how to engage students in their learning. As Ashwin and McVitty (2015) argue, we need to be clear what we are trying to engage students with. Trowler (2010) identifies five objects of engagement: student engagement with learning processes; learning design; particular teaching tools; extra-curricular activities; and institutional governance. Whilst this list is an accurate reflection of the mainstream literature, one element that is missing is students' engagement with knowledge. Ashwin et al. (2014; 2016) argue that this is central to the transformative potential of higher education because it involves a change in the ways in which students see themselves, the world and the disciplinary knowledge that they are studying. This way of conceptualizing engagement draws on the three dimensions of engagement that Jary and Lebeau (2009) develop from Dubet's (2000) work: 'personal project', which reflects students' view of the value and usefulness of what they are studying; students' level of social integration into university life; and students' level of intellectual engagement with their studies. This conceptualization is helpful because it highlights the importance of students' identities and sense of fit with their institutions in developing their engagement with knowledge. However, we need to take care in applying these ideas to different educational contexts, as Ashwin and Komljenovic (2018) found when they examined these ideas in relation to South African higher education and found that personal projects, social integration and intellectual engagement took on different meanings in this context.

Another way of thinking about student engagement is to consider their engagement with particular educational practices. In the United States, a body of work has developed examining 'high impact' educational practices, which are examined in Research Briefing 4.1.

RESEARCH BRIEFING 4.1 Educational practices that have a high impact on student engagement

In the United States, a set of educational practices have been found to be effective for students from a diverse range of backgrounds (Kuh 2008) and have the potential to increase student engagement and retention. These have been endorsed by the Association of American Colleges and Universities. These practices include:

- collaborative assignments and projects;
- undergraduate research;
- ePortfolios;
- service learning, community-based learning;
- internships;
- Capstone courses and projects.
        (For the full list see: **aacu.org/sites/default/files/files/LEAP/hip_tables.pdf**)

Kuh (2008) argues that these educational practices are successful because they require students to engage with the ideas on their courses, their peers and their university teachers. In their longitudinal study of a review of students from seventeen US institutions, Kilgo et al. (2015) found that two of the practices, active and collaborative learning and undergraduate research, were particularly beneficial to students and were consistently positive predictors of educational outcomes including critical thinking and students' commitment to lifelong learning.

Assessment for learning

Effective teaching and learning needs assessment to be congruent with learning. Assessment should be designed for maximum validity in terms of learning outcomes and learning processes, and also should be specific to the type of subject or discipline involved, even if it is interdisciplinary. It should help to advance learning as well as determine whether learning has occurred.

As Entwistle (2018) makes clear, the ways in which students are assessed has a profound influence on the ways in which they approach their learning. The ways in which we assess their achievements on modules and courses inform them of the kinds of learning that we expect them to engage with. The importance of assessment often makes it a pressure point for both teachers and students, with students unhappy about the lack of clarity of the ways in which they are assessed and the meaning of their feedback and teachers disappointed with the use that students make of the feedback they are provided with.

Discussions of assessment often distinguish between summative and formative assessment. Summative assessment provides information on how students have performed at a particular moment in time and is used to give students academic credit for their performance, whilst formative assessment is intended to help students improve their performance (Yorke 2008). As the same tasks can have both summative and formative elements, they are best seen as different purposes of assessment rather than different types of assessment. Our focus on assessment should also go beyond the short-term considerations of the particular programme that they are studying if it is to be sustainable (Boud and Soler 2016). This means we need to prepare students for the learning that they will engage with through the rest of their lives and help them to be able to effectively assess their own performance on an ongoing basis.

Based on her extensive review of research into formative assessment in higher education, Evans (2013) generates six key elements of feedback. First, it needs to be integrated into assessment in an ongoing way by being a central part of the teaching and learning process that is aligned with the learning objectives and provided in a timely manner. Second, students need to be given explicit guidance on the assessment requirements and helped to understand what a high-quality performance would entail. Third, that greater emphasis is given to how formative assessment can be used to improve performance (feed-forward) rather than simply assessing performance. Fourth, that students need to be centrally involved in feedback processes and the design of assessment so that they can develop the capacity for self-assessment. Fifth, that feedback focuses specifically on how well students have engaged with the task and how to improve, rather than simply indicating whether it is correct or not. Sixth, that part of the design of assessment provides opportunities for both teachers and students to learn how to give and use formative assessment.

These elements highlight the ways in which assessment, whether formative or summative, needs to encourage and enable students to engage with the kinds of learning that our programmes and modules are designed to promote. This means that assessment should not be shrouded in mystery for students but rather should be addressed from the early stages in which they are studying with us. If students are orientated towards assessment, then this is only a problem if the forms of assessment we use are not designed to assess the learning outcomes that we wish our students to achieve. As Yorke (2008) argues, students' performance in relation to assessment tasks also gives us invaluable information about the success of our teaching. We examine the effective design of assessment in Chapter 13.

> ### Reflective Activity 4.4 Reviewing your assessment practices
>
> Consider a module or course that you have taught recently.
>
> What was the most important thing that you wanted students to gain through studying this module?
>
> Now consider the assessment for this module or course.
>
> To what extent did the assessment require students to demonstrate that they had gained this most important thing?
>
> How might the assessment be changed to better encourage students to gain this most important thing?
>
> What barriers might prevent you from making this change?

Teaching as design

Effective teaching and learning requires learning to be systematically developed. Teachers, trainers, lecturers, researchers and all who support the learning of others should provide intellectual, social and emotional support which helps learners to develop expertise in their learning for it to be effective and secure.

There is nothing haphazard about effective teaching and learning. The curricula of the modules and programmes that we teach need to be explicitly designed to engage our students with valuable knowledge. The assessment of these programmes and modules needs to be designed to assess students' understanding of this knowledge. The sessions and teaching spaces in which we engage with students need to be designed to bring particular kinds of learning about. There will still be unexpected learning outcomes and interactions that develop in unexpected ways but as reflective teachers in higher education we need to know what we expect students to gain from our teaching and how we have designed our teaching to achieve this. In Chapter 9, we explore notions of 'congruence' (Hounsell and Hounsell 2007) and 'constructive alignment' (Biggs and Tang 2011) to conceptualize the way in which all aspects of a degree programme come together to help students to develop particular kinds of understanding.

The issues relating to 'teaching as design' are central to this book and explored in far greater detail in Chapters 7 to 13. It involves a relationship between knowledge and design. As we explore below, we need to know who our students are and their current levels of understanding. We need to know our disciplines and understand the knowledge we are teaching. However, we also need to know how to make this knowledge accessible to the students we are teaching and, based on this, be able to design curricula and programmes that support them to develop understanding of this knowledge. Shulman (1987, p. 8) calls this 'pedagogical content knowledge' and argues that it is 'that special amalgam of content and pedagogy that is uniquely the province of teachers, their own special form of professional understanding'.

It is important to be clear that we do not engage in such processes on our own. Higher education curricula are collectively designed by academics, external examiners, employers, educational developers and students. In this way, they involve disagreements and struggles over the version of the programme that will be enacted (Bernstein 2000). The collective nature of these processes makes them more challenging but also more rewarding to engage in.

As we discussed in Chapter 3 and explore further in Chapter 11, our teaching is never perfect. Rather it is always a work-in-progress. There are always new ways that we can find to more effectively develop our students' learning. Reflective Activity 4.5 invites you to think about the basis on which your modules or courses are designed.

Reflective Activity 4.5 Reviewing the design of your modules or courses 1

Consider a module or course that you have taught recently.

1 On what basis was the knowledge selected for inclusion in this course? Who had a say in selecting this knowledge?
2 What new things were students able to do because they engaged with this knowledge?
3 How and why did you expect students' engagement with knowledge to lead to these new ways of thinking and doing for the students?

Review your responses to these three questions and consider what changes you might make to your module or course based on them. We will examine this further in **Reflective Activity 4.6** overleaf.

Prior experience

Effective teaching and learning recognizes the importance of prior or concurrent experience and learning. Teaching and learning should take account of what the student as learner knows already to plan strategies for the future. This includes building on prior learning but also taking account of the emerging concurrent learning in context, and the personal and cultural experiences of different groups of students as learners.

In line with the previous one, this principle emphasizes the need for us to know our students, who they are and what they know, both in terms of their prior experiences and learning and their current experiences. We explored students' identities in Chapter 1 and the impact of their prior experiences on students' learning in Chapter 2. There are three critical elements relating to how we understand our students' prior experiences.

First, students make sense of their current experiences based on their previous experiences. This is because their previous experiences help them to understand higher education as a particular kind of experience, as Case et al. (2018) found. This is also informed by what students want to get out of higher education or, in Dubet's (2000) terms that we explored earlier, what their personal project is and how they see higher education helping them to achieve this. This has an impact on how students engage with their courses, how they see the role of their teachers and how they relate to other students.

Second, whilst it is important that we have a sense of who are students are, it is important that we do not make assumptions about their identities and experiences based on unhelpful generalizations about particular kinds of students. For example, Abes and Wallace (2018) show how students with disabilities are often seen as an objectified disability rather than as people with many facets to their identities. Rather than making assumptions about students and their needs, we need to listen to what these students need to fully participate in our courses and modules. We should also recognize that often any changes we make will benefit all students. Similarly, whilst students value teaching that recognizes their academic and social identities and addresses their individual learning needs, Vicki Trowler (2019) argues that the dominant notions of 'traditional' and 'non-traditional' students create simplistic understandings of students. This can limit the development of inclusive and engaging teaching. We examine these issues further in Chapter 15.

Third, it is important not to see our students' identities as fixed. A key element of higher education is that students engage in transformative relations with knowledge that changes their sense of who they are. As we saw in Chapter 2, the notion of 'threshold concepts' (Meyer and Land 2005) highlights the ways that students' engagement with particular concepts transforms their view of the world. Thus, whilst we need to understand students' prior experiences, we also need to recognize that a 'higher' education is about a transformation in students' identities. These life-changing processes can be a source of anxiety for students and we need to recognize this in our teaching. We consider this further in Reflective Activity 4.6.

Reflective Activity 4.6 Reviewing the design of your modules or courses 2

Consider the same module or course that you examined in **Reflective Activity 4.5**.

What account was taken of who the students were and what they knew in designing this module or course?

What evidence did you have for this view of the students?

How was the module or course designed to support these particular students to change in the ways you described in Activity 4.5?

Review your responses to these questions and consider what changes you might make to your module or course based on them.

Valued knowledge

Effective teaching and learning engages with expertise and valued forms of knowledge in disciplines and subjects. Teaching and learning should engage students with the concepts, key skills and processes, modes of discourse, ways of thinking and practising, and attitudes and relationships which are most valued in their subject. Students need to understand what constitutes quality, standards and expertise in different settings and subjects.

Under the previous principle we discussed the transformation of student identities and, as we argued in relation to student engagement, it is students' engagement with knowledge that is key to these transformations. This means that we need to think seriously about which aspects of our disciplinary knowledge are made available to students in our curricula. As Bernstein (2000) makes clear, the arrangement of this knowledge into a curriculum is itself a process of transformation. There are debates and arguments between, for example, academics, students, educational developers, professional bodies and employer representatives over:

- what constitutes valued knowledge in a subject or field;
- what a curriculum should consist of;
- how it should be organized;
- how it should be represented and communicated to students;
- how students' knowledge, understanding and skills can be identified and evaluated.

The outcomes of such debates partly reflect the capacity of particular stakeholders to promote their views and means that the logic of a curriculum will not be the same as the logic of a discipline (Bernstein 2000). At a policy level, Ashwin et al. (2015) show how debates about what constitutes a high-quality undergraduate education play out between different national and international actors.

As teachers in higher education, our power to shape the curriculum will vary at different times and in different institutional locations. Sometimes we will have the opportunity to design a new curriculum for an entire programme and at other times we will simply be given a part of a module. In Chapter 9, we explore this difference in terms of top-down and bottom-up curriculum design.

As well as introducing our students to transformative knowledge, as we explored in **Reflective Activities 4.5** and **4.6**, we need to have a sense of how it will transform them and what it will allow them to do. This is challenging and difficult work. Research Briefing 4.2 overleaf outlines a project in South Africa that examined these issues in relation to professional education. It illustrates that, rather than being an individual or technical process, this kind of work is collective and raises important issues about our values and our view of what constitutes a good society.

RESEARCH BRIEFING 4.2 Developing public-good professionals in South Africa

Walker and McLean (2013) explored professional education in three South African universities. They examined programmes in Engineering, Law, Public Health, Social Work and Theology. They interviewed students, alumni, lecturers, Heads of Department and Faculty Deans about what kinds of professionals were needed to transform South Africa and what kind of university education was needed to develop these professionals. Based on this, they developed a concept of 'public-good professionals' who:

- will recognize the dignity of all people;
- act for social transformation and to reduce injustice;
- make sound, knowledgeable, thoughtful and imaginative professional judgements;
- work with others to increase the capabilities of those living in poverty.

They developed these capabilities into educational goals and identified the institutional and teaching and learning environments needed to achieve them. Finally, they analysed the obstacles to achieving these goals in the South African context, whilst arguing that their concept of the public-good professional is equally applicable to other national higher education contexts.

Education for life

Effective teaching and learning equips learners for life in its broadest sense.
Learning should help individuals develop the intellectual, personal and social resources that will enable them to participate as active citizens, contribute to economic, social or community development, and flourish as individuals in a diverse and changing society. This means adopting a broad conception of worthwhile learning outcomes and taking seriously issues of equity and social justice for all, across social, economic, ethnic and gender differences.

This principle emphasizes the long-standing commitment to broad, rich and inclusive forms of education. **Research Briefing 4.2** conveys a good sense of how effective teaching and learning in higher education prepares people to be active citizens and also highlights how education is informed by personal and political values. It is not a neutral activity. Higher education outcomes should play a role in promoting social justice.

This principle also highlights that, whilst students engage with higher education at particular moments in their lives, we also need to be clear about how it prepares them for their lives after they leave higher education. In a classic text, Bowden and Marton (1998) argued for a university education that can prepare students for an unknown future. This is because the professional contexts in which students will eventually end up are unknown. Even in contexts related directly to their degrees, if students are dependent on the information they learn at university then this will quickly become obsolete. Thus students need to be able to:

- develop the ability to identify the key aspects in any situation;
- relate this to what they know;

- define the issues in the situation;
- design a process to address it;
- follow this solution through in partnership with others.

Baillie et al. (2013) set out how these ideas can be applied to what is learned, how it is learned and what is assessed.

Finally, this principle raises questions about the overall purposes of higher education. As we discussed earlier this is not a value-neutral issue. Thinking about purposes brings us back to our first principle, the need for supportive policy contexts. We still need to think about how we prepare our students for the world even when the policy context is one that is hostile to the values that we hold. We explore this issue further in Reflective Activity 4.7.

Reflective Activity 4.7 The aims of higher education policies and our practices

Read the following extract from the Foreword to the 2016 White Paper on Higher Education in England 'Success as a Knowledge Economy: Teaching Excellence, Social Mobility and Student Choice' and then consider the questions that follow:

> Our universities rank among our most valuable national assets, underpinning both a strong economy and a flourishing society. Powerhouses of intellectual and social capital, they create the knowledge, capability and expertise that drive competitiveness and nurture the values that sustain our open democracy. Access to higher education can be life changing for individuals and, by ending student number controls, we have made the possibility of participation in it a reality for more people than ever before. The skills that great higher education provides – the ability to think critically and to assess and present evidence – last a lifetime and will be increasingly in demand as the number and proportion of high-skilled jobs rises. If we are to continue to succeed as a knowledge economy, however, we cannot stand still, nor take for granted our universities' enviable global reputation and position at the top of league tables. We must ensure that the system is also fulfilling its potential and delivering good value for students, for employers and for the taxpayers who underwrite it.

What view of the purposes of higher education is presented in this extract?

How does this view of higher education relate to your sense of the purposes of higher education?

How does this relate to the ten principles that we have discussed in this chapter?

How does your view of the purposes of higher education inform your approach to teaching in higher education?

Are there ways that you could develop your practices to reflect your values more strongly?

What constraints and support is there in your institution for you to do this?

CONCLUSION

In this chapter we have reviewed ten evidence-informed principles that can support our judgements as we work towards developing high-quality teaching and learning. Each principle focuses attention onto particular dimensions of teaching and learning. However, the principles should be seen as being interconnected and it is helpful to consider their inter-relationships. The salience of particular principles may change in relation to the specific circumstances or issues which we face, but none of them is likely to recede entirely.

We use the ten principles to structure reflection within this book because they tap into the enduring issues which we must face as university teachers. At various points within the book, the text thus draws attention to particular principles in relation to the issues under consideration. The principles offer a framework for our understanding and they have a particular cutting edge when used to evaluate or review actual policy or practice. When that is done, there is often a gap between aspiration and achievement. This gives pause for thought, and can lead to new insights and developments. It can be helpful to apply the principles to review a policy in your institution, as we did in **Reflective Activity 4.1**, or to interrogate a government policy document, as we did in **Reflective Activity 4.7**, or to explore a dimension of your teaching practice that has been concerning you.

We conclude this chapter with a statement about the role of evidence-informed, principled judgement. Whilst this statement was made in relation to schools, it is equally relevant to teaching in higher education:

> Teachers use expert judgement to recognise and resolve the dilemmas in teaching and learning which they face every day in the classroom. At their best, teachers are able to reflect on and evaluate their practices, and to make rationally and ethically defensible judgements that go beyond compliance, pragmatic constraints or ideological preferences. (Bartley 2010, p. 2)

This book is designed to support the development of such judgement and the ten principles are intended to aid this process.

KEY READINGS

For an extended academic review of the principles and international commentaries, see:

James, M. and Pollard, A. (2012) *Principles for Effective Pedagogy. International Responses to Evidence from the UK Teaching and Learning Research Programme.* London: Routledge.

An attempt to summarize the implications deriving from what is known about learning from across the world is:

OECD (2011) *The Nature of Learning. Using Research to Inspire Practice.* Paris: OECD.

For an examination of how higher education systems as a whole can contribute to the public good, see:

Ashwin, P. and Case, J. (eds) (2018) *Higher Education Pathways: South African Undergraduate Education and the Public Good.* Cape Town: African Minds.

For further information about High Impact Educational Practices, see the website of the American Association of Colleges and Universities: **aacu.org/resources/high-impact-practices**

For further ideas about peer learning and assessment in higher education, see:

Reinholz, D. (2016) 'The assessment cycle: A model for learning through peer assessment', *Assessment & Evaluation in Higher Education*, 41(2), 301–15.

Tai, J., Canny, B., Haines, T. and Molloy, E. K. (2016). 'The role of peer-assisted learning in building evaluative judgement: Opportunities in clinical medical education', *Advances in Health Sciences Education*, 21(3), 659–76.

Meschitti, V. (2019) 'Can peer learning support doctoral education? Evidence from an ethnography of a research team', *Studies in Higher Education*, 44(7), 1209–21.

For further discussion of the development of public-good professionals see:

Walker, M. and McLean, M. (2013) *Professional Education, Capabilities and the Public Good: The Role of Universities in Promoting Human Development.* London: Routledge.

Part two

Creating conditions for learning

Part 2 concerns the construction of environments to support high-quality teaching and learning. We begin by considering the range of contexts that help to shape teaching and learning in higher education (Chapter 5) – and we note the ways in which people contribute to and challenge the impact of such contexts. We then move to the heart of teaching and learning environments with a focus on the relationships between students and teachers in higher education (Chapter 6). Because such relationships are so crucial for students' success, this is an extremely important chapter. Chapter 7 builds further and considers how we make disciplinary knowledge accessible to our students by engaging deeply with our teaching. Finally, we consider a range of learning spaces in higher education and beyond (Chapter 8) and the ways in which they can help students to engage in high-quality learning.

Chapter 5
Contexts

How do they shape us and how do we shape them?

INTRODUCTION

Why is it important to understand the contexts that shape our experiences of teaching and our students' experiences of learning? When we teach, we are producing written and spoken texts for our students to engage with. However, as Michael Halliday (1994), the founder of functional linguistics claimed, the meanings of these texts do not simply reside within texts, but rather, in the relationship between texts and their contexts: 'Every text – that is, everything that is said or written – unfolds in some context of use' (Halliday 1994, p. xiii). He went on to explain that texts work when readers and writers, speakers and listeners know how to interpret not only the text but also its contexts. We therefore need to know how our teaching is shaped by contexts and to understand the contexts from which our students are speaking and writing.

In this chapter, we will discuss the interweaving of a range of contexts that impact on our teaching, such as the skewed and unequal system of global knowledge production; government, institutional and departmental policies and cultures, and of course the nature of our disciplines and classrooms. In addition, we need to understand how who we are as lecturers, where we have come from and who our students are and where they come from, shape the ways in which we can teach and learn together.

This chapter is concerned with relations between the contexts that shape the teaching and learning practices of students and academics. The central argument of the chapter is that while the influences of such contexts pervade everything we do in higher education and shape our experiences, they do not *determine* our actions. Rather, we have choices about how we take these political and socio-cultural contexts into account in our teaching practices, even if our degrees of choice vary according to our roles and the constraints and opportunities of each situation. This means that developing an awareness of the impact of such contexts, and how to function within them in principled ways, is an important aspect of developing our approach to reflective teaching. Reflexive teachers need to be able to name and understand how the various contexts we find ourselves in influence what we can and cannot do with our students and to what extent we can change this. This chapter offers a number of different ways of thinking about these multiple contexts, which are intended to support critical reflection on how the relations between contexts and our teaching practices work.

In addressing this issue, this chapter is deliberately structured into two parts. The first, 'aspects of socio-political contexts', emphasizes the different aspects of the contexts that *structure* action in various ways. The second part, 'people, agency and interactions', is concerned with the factors which, in various senses, *enable* our actions and those of our students. In taking this approach, this chapter attempts to highlight the mutually shaping relationships between people and their socio-political contexts and how contexts both enable and constrain what actions we can take as individual teachers and learners.

See Chapter 4

TLRP Principles

Two principles are of particular relevance to this chapter on the contexts in which teaching and learning take place:

Principle 1: Effective teaching and learning demands consistent policy frameworks, with support for learning for diverse students as their main focus. Policies at government, system, institutional and organizational level need to recognize the fundamental importance of learning for individual, team, organizational, institutional, national and system success. Policies should be designed to create effective and equitable learning environments for all students to benefit socially and economically.

Principle 3: Effective teaching and learning recognizes the significance of informal learning to developing specific expertise. Learning with friends, families, peer groups and professionals should be recognized as significant, and be valued and used in formal processes in higher education.

ASPECTS OF SOCIO-POLITICAL CONTEXTS

As we discussed in Chapter 3, in thinking about the ways in which contexts shape our day-to-day activities, Cole (1996) argues that a context can either be seen as a 'container' or as a 'weaving' together of factors. In the container view, teaching and learning activities are positioned as taking place within a context but this context is not an integral part of the activities. The alternative way of thinking about context, which informs this chapter, is to understand that particular interactions involve the weaving together of different factors that may be local, such as the nature of the people involved, or may be more global, such as the discipline of the course being studied. As we noted in the Introduction above, it is the relations between contexts and particular interactions – the texts and practices produced in those contexts – that are significant for meaning-making. Contexts 'get into' our communicative interactions rather than simply providing the container in which they take place. This approach emphasizes that different contexts will construe different meanings for the same factor or variable. For example, the same national language policy will be interpreted differently and have different effects at institutional level depending on the composition of a university's staff and student populations and the extent to which they are native speakers of the prescribed language(s). In this section, we examine five context types: the global political-economy of higher education, national policy contexts, institutional cultures, disciplinary cultures, and teaching and learning contexts at the level of individual departments or programme teams.

The global political-economy of higher education

The marketization of higher education

Historically, higher education has been viewed as both an individual private and a collective public good, with public funding for higher education dependent on it being perceived as a public good (Carnoy et al. 2014). Since the 1980s, the dominance of political and economic ideologies linked to a neo-liberal market paradigm has led to an erosion of the idea of higher education as a public good and instead emphasized higher education as a private good – usually defined in terms of employability and economic and social benefits. These ideas have been used to justify transferring the costs of higher education onto individual students (Naidoo and Williams 2015).

Naidoo and Williams (2015) describe how in England, the marketization of higher education has allowed government to champion student consumer rights and set up contractual relationships between students and universities. This has undermined the historic role of universities as autonomous and critical institutions. 'Marketization' means that universities increasingly have to compete for students, positioned as consumers who require reliable information about the quality of the 'product' they are purchasing (Collini 2012). The pressure to run universities as businesses has also led to a new wave of what is called the 'internationalization' of higher education. In many countries, universities, supported by national governments, are partnering with private companies to buy and sell their products on a global market.

Carnoy et al. (2014) in their study of trends in BRIC (Brazil, Russia, India and China) countries show that, through globalization, these same neo-liberal ideas, plus a sustained 'private rate of return' on investment in higher education, have been used by the governments of these four countries to justify decreasing the public funding of higher education. This rolling back of public funding has been compounded by a simultaneous increase in the differentiation of institutional types in higher education in these countries. The increased private costs of higher education means that many disadvantaged students end up attending low-status, low-quality public institutions, while the wealthy elites pay for high-quality private education, often exported from the global North through partnership arrangements (Carnoy et al. 2014).

Another recent related form of the market logic currently driving the provision of higher education is that of 'unbundling'. This occurs when the three main functions of a university – research, teaching and community engagement – are disaggregated; the work of academics gets portioned out to various sub-contracted para-academics; while students, as consumers, are offered personalized choices regarding which units of curricula they can purchase. In many cases, this 'no frills' approach, promoted by the for-profit sector, allows affordable access to higher education services to the poor. A consequence is that the more costly, full-time, high-quality, integrated experience of studying at research universities may become reserved for privileged elites who can afford it (McCowan 2017).

The political-economy of knowledge production

We live in an era of globalization which on the one hand has democratized access to higher education, but on the other serves to exacerbate economic and social inequality and reinforce the ideological and cultural dominance of the global North. The 'internationaliz-ation' and 'unbundling' of higher education mentioned above are examples of this. Driven by business models, universities based in the global North are setting up satellite campuses and online platforms in the global South to which they export their curricula and expertise – leading to neo-colonial North–South relations and greater inequality within Southern nations (Burke et al. 2018).

Furthermore, as decolonial theorists have pointed out, the unequal relations of the global political-economy are mirrored in the production and circulation of knowledge (Mignolo 2010). Decolonial theorists argue that current knowledge formations that control the production and circulation of knowledge on a global scale have emerged from histories of colonialism and empire. In the context of a global market, the processes and products of intellectual labour are commodified and circulate within a very unequal global division of labour (Connell et al. 2018). All of this means that we should be critically aware of how the global knowledge economy places power and control over what counts as knowledge, 'excellence' or 'best practice' in our universities in the hands of editorial boards, publishing houses, donors, development agencies, universities, researchers and academics located in the global North in ways that often just seem natural. Intellectuals in the South have questioned these relations of academic dependency (Houtondji 1997) whereby, for example, researchers in the South work as 'local experts' providing data for research projects funded and controlled by academics in the North. Instead decolonial theorists advocate the recognition and inclusion of previously ignored indigenous forms of knowledge production in formal knowledge formations and education systems.

Decolonial theorists are critical not only of the ways in which knowledge gets produced and circulated, but also of the fundamental ways in which we think about knowledge and research (epistemology and methodology). They oppose the notion of an autonomous, universal, fully rational knower, instead emphasizing that all knowledge is situated, embodied and produced within specific social relations – including the histories and legacies of empire (Mignolo 2010). The decolonialists are critical of the ways in which modern European ways of thinking have been institutionalized and universalized as the only legitimate forms of knowledge through the Western university system, the modern disciplines and the five ex-colonial European languages (Grosfoguel 2013). In turn, they argue, the universalization of the European path to modernization has led to a widespread assumption that all nations will and should develop along the same trajectory.

Our insistence in this book that teaching and learning are social practices, shaped by specific contexts, means that we should be wary of unquestioningly adopting imported norms and notions of 'excellence' and 'best practice'. Particularly in Southern contexts, we should be suspicious of developmental paradigms that set up universal norms for all higher education contexts, often positioning people in the South as falling short of global standards. For example, empirical research, using comparative and statistical methods, is often used to legitimate policy, development projects or quality assurance interventions for improvement projects in the South geared towards globalized norms.

While some anti-colonial theorists promote unhelpful dualistic, anti-modern positions that advocate replacing Northern or European knowledge with that from the South, most offer more nuanced arguments for critically inclusive, diverse and deconstructive approaches (for example, Mbembe 2016).

Decolonial arguments raise important questions for universities in the global North. Case Study 5.1 outlines how these ideas have been taken forward by the Students' Union at University College, London. We also explore how these debates have developed in South Africa later in this chapter in **Research Briefing 5.3** and explore the implications for teaching in **Reflective Activity 5.2**.

Case Study 5.1 Decolonizing University College London

At University College, London (UCL) the Students' Union has developed a campaign to decolonize the institution. This has three elements:

1 Decolonize Education – which seeks to promote the review of the curriculum at UCL so that it is more inclusive of knowledge from across the world and less dominated by male, white voices.
2 Decolonize the Mind – which seeks to promote greater cultural understanding in the delivery of university support services to create a more inclusive campus.
3 Decolonize the Institution – which seeks to ensure that staff and students are committed to challenging racism at UCL.

(See **studentsunionucl.org/make-change/what-were-working-on-0/decolonise-ucl**)

National policy contexts

Shifts at global level, and particularly the dominance of neo-liberal market logics, impact on higher education at national and local levels, often through state policies. For example, the massification and privatization of higher education and increases in fees globally have led to a more intense focus by national governments on the 'quality' of higher education. The auditing of institutions, accreditation of programmes, appraisal of academics and national student experience surveys by quality assurance agencies allows governments to regulate private provision and hold public universities to account for state funding. National approaches to measuring the quality of higher education have a direct impact on teaching and learning in universities.

In the UK for example, the framing of students as customers who need reliable information about the quality of their higher education product sets up competition for students
between institutions. The use of the National Student Survey in the UK as a performance
indicator has directly shaped the way in which institutions have approached different
aspects of the student experience of higher education (see Gibbs 2012).

Since 1994, state policy interventions in South African higher education have focused
on improving access and the efficiency of the system by using planning, funding and
quality assurance as mechanisms to steer the system. But the neo-liberal framing of these
new policies – which focuses on employability and economic growth – has led to a failure
to adequately address the social and cultural legacies of the apartheid regime at the level
of institutional cultures. This may well have contributed to recent student protests (Lange
2018).

As teachers in higher education, we may not be able to directly influence structures,
policies and practices that operate at global and national levels, but we can reflect on how
they impact on our practices, on the students we teach, our relationships with our students,
the kinds of curriculum knowledge that we teach and our own sense of status and
authority.

Institutional cultures

Higher education institutions are differentiated by type and history; they have to serve a
range of purposes but prioritize these differently. These differences have an impact on an
institution's culture (for example, see Tierney, 1988 for a classic framework of organizational cultures) which have been found to have an impact on teaching and learning
processes. The research briefing below sets out the findings of one project that sought to
understand how such institutional differences impact on students' learning.

RESEARCH BRIEFING 5.1 The Social and Organisational Mediation of University Learning (SOMUL) Project

The SOMUL Project (Brennan et al. 2010) explored the relationships between three
kinds of diversity – of universities, of students, and of what students learn while at
university. The study examined students' experiences in three academic subjects:
biosciences, business studies and sociology. The project developed a typology based on
two dimensions: the diversity of the student population and whether students had a
predominately collective or individualized experience. These dimensions define three
types of contexts for student learning. In a Type A context, a diverse group of students
came together to share a largely common experience during their time at university.
This provided opportunities for 'learning from difference' and appeared to be linked to
the promotion of social integration and cohesion. In a Type B context, broadly similar

---

kinds of students came together to share a largely common experience. This appeared to be associated with the maintenance of existing differences, reinforcement of existing identities and the promotion of status confirmation and legitimization. In a Type C context, students had only limited contact with other students, so the diversity of the group was not particularly significant. These are the students who typically had demanding outside commitments, whether domestic- or employment-related. Their time for study was limited and even more so was their time for other aspects of university life. For such students, university may be more about living with difference, and maintaining and constructing multiple identities, at university, home and work. It was possible for individual students to have a Type C experience in a Type A or B setting.

Whilst there were some subject differences, the different types of settings appeared to relate to different kinds of university experience. For example: Students from Type B university settings developed strong loyalties towards their universities which were not shared to the same extent by students in the other two types. They generally emphasize the importance of the people they have met at university, their ability to get on with a wide range of people and their commitment to maintaining contact with them after university.

Type A students shared the commitments of Type B students to friends made at university but lacked their loyalty to the university itself. They were the students who seem to be most committed to their subjects and their studies, in some cases evidenced by a strong commitment to postgraduate study. They were less likely than other students to feel that their time at university had changed the way they see the world.

Students from Type C settings differed from other students in a number of respects. They reported lower gains in self-confidence and were much less likely to expect to retain university friendships after graduation. They were more likely to feel that they 'never fitted in' and very much more likely to feel that the 'qualification was the main thing'. They tended to report that life outside university remained the most important aspect of their lives. They were more likely than other students to have a clearer view of the future than when they commenced their course.

The project's findings challenge those who uncritically accept existing reputations as being the key to the understanding of the effects and consequences of diversity. The project identified many commonalities to the experiences and outcomes of university study, almost irrespective of where and what one studies. And where differences did exist they did not automatically match the institution's reputations.

There are many ways in which institutional cultures impact on teaching and learning in universities. Here we examine four. First, institutional cultures inform who can legitimately become a student and a lecturer within particular programmes within particular institutions. The requirements as to who is eligible to become a student or a lecturer differ between institutions both in terms of formal qualifications and experiences that are required. Both as students and lecturers, we tend to choose universities in which we feel comfortable, recognized and 'at home' (Smith 2017; Wainwright and Watts 2019). However, given its elitist history, higher education tends to uncritically accept the norms and values of the national middle class. For example, well-intentioned equity programmes often misrecognize their students by framing them as 'at risk' – leading to a negating of their identities by placing them in marginal, remedial programmes (Burke et al. 2018). With regard to staff, what is valued by an institution's culture is likely to be reflected in its appraisal, promotion and reward criteria. These criteria affect how academic staff approach and what they prioritize in their careers (Smith 2017). For example, at research-intensive universities, the promotion and status of academics will be linked to research outputs rather than excellence in teaching.

Second, institutional cultures also impact on the range of disciplines taught in a university and the particular version of a discipline that is taught. For example, McLean et al. (2018) show clear differences in the way that Sociology was presented in different kinds of higher education institution. Equally, the level of autonomy that we have as teachers in deciding what and how we teach varies between institutions, although there are no straightforward relationships between the level of autonomy of an institution and the level of autonomy experienced by staff at that institution (Carvalho and Diogo 2018).

Third, the ways in which the development of teaching is approached varies between institutions. There is evidence that there are different approaches to educational and staff development in different institutions, with the strategic priorities and relative wealth of an institution important factors in shaping the extent to which such development is valued (Leibowitz et al. 2015).

Finally, the types of spaces in which teaching and learning interactions take place can differ between institutions. The ways in which both time and space are constituted by different institutions is a function of their relative wealth. For example, poorly resourced institutions are likely to cram large numbers of students into crowded lecture halls and tight timetables to compensate for low fees, whereas better resourced institutions with high-fee-paying students will have higher staff–student ratios and less tightly packed classrooms and timetables. Burke et al. (2017) describe the impact of pervasive neoliberal conceptions of time on student learning practices. They suggest that individualized notions of productivity and performativity within tight timetables and rigid deadlines get reduced to developing 'time management' skills in students, in ways that fail to account for the complex, uncertain and precarious lives that many students must manage. In addition, these notions of time put pressure on academics in ways that take time away from teaching and caring for students.

These differences highlight the ways in which institutional types and cultures shape teaching and learning. As we noted above, some of the more radical critiques come from decolonial theorists who point out how modernist assumptions and values in Western university cultures work to exclude and devalue other ways of knowing and being (Gordon 2014). Whether we agree with them or not, as teachers it is important to recognize the implicit as well as the explicit ways in which our institutions influence our own identities, discourses and practices – especially how we teach and relate to students. We should be careful not to unreflectively take up the collective ways of thinking and institutional norms of our contexts without questioning how these affect our teaching and learning practices.

Disciplinary cultures

As university teachers, it is common to believe that the way in which we teach is shaped by the subject matter we are teaching. Becher (1989) argues that these disciplinary differences in teaching are related to both the structures of knowledge and the social structures within disciplines that are often also reflected in departmental cultures (see Tight 2015a for analysis of how these ideas have developed over time). The concept of 'ways of thinking and practising in the disciplines', which we discussed in Chapter 2, attempts to capture the ways in which both the processes and outcomes of learning vary between disciplines, as students engage with different kinds of knowledge (see Entwistle 2018).

Paul Trowler (2019) argues that much of the work on disciplinary knowledge practices has been informed by 'epistemological essentialism', the notion that disciplinary knowledge practices *determine* teaching-learning processes. He argues that this overstates the power of disciplinary knowledge practices to shape teaching and learning. This is partly because disciplinary practices are refracted through other factors such as the identities of academics and institutional cultures, but also because, in the words of Becher and Trowler (2001, pp. 29–30), the knowledge domain of a discipline is more like 'a badly made patchwork quilt' than 'a seamless cloak'. This view is supported by research examining the experiences of research and teaching-learning processes in particular disciplines. For example, in a classic examination of the discipline of English, Evans (1993) argued English is more of an archipelago than a landmass and suggests that it is only when different disciplines are compared that they appear to be coherent and solid.

Thus, while disciplinary cultures do have an impact on teaching and learning, it is important to be clear that disciplines are expressed differently in different institutional settings and that they are not the only factor that shapes teaching and learning. Drawing on the work of the sociologist Basil Bernstein, Ashwin (2014) argued that there are differences between knowledge when it is involved in research (knowledge-as-research), when it is situated in a curriculum (knowledge-as-curriculum) and when it is learned by students (knowledge-as-student-understanding) *even when this involves apparently the same idea or concept.* For example, Hay and colleagues (2013) examined the differences in the drawings of a brain cell by undergraduates, PhD students and postdoctoral researchers, and leading neuroscience researchers in a single university. The differences in the drawings of the three groups reflected very different ways of understanding the same concept. The research leaders' drawings appeared to present a research concept whereas the undergraduate students mainly produced textbook-style diagrams of brain cells. The drawings by PhD students and postdoctoral researchers varied the most and were the most likely to be seen as 'non-expert' by the other two groups. This research gives a clear sense of how a specific concept means different things in different research contexts as well as in undergraduate contexts.

As we discussed in Chapter 4, Bernstein's (2000) approach emphasizes the transformation of knowledge as it moves between research, curriculum and teaching contexts. It also highlights the ways in which this transformation can be a site of struggle between different groups. For example, how particular concepts are positioned in a curriculum can be the outcome of contestations and negotiations between academics, institutional approval mechanisms, external examiners, professional societies or national standards. The outcomes of these negotiations vary across different contexts, meaning that relations between research knowledge and curriculum knowledge are contingent and unstable, often the result of power relations and ideologically charged contestations than epistemic or pedagogic concerns.

In Southern contexts, the disciplines, especially the Social Sciences, are sometimes critiqued as institutions of power and gate-keeping rather than custodians of knowledge. Decolonial critics point out that the social sciences emerged during the European colonial and imperial eras, meaning that their understandings of knowledge (epistemology) and reality (ontology) were marked by gendered and racial nationalism based on biological essentialism. The modern Social Sciences thus operate as paradoxical sites of knowledge (re)production – promoting humanist and enlightenment values such as equality, justice and democracy but also carrying the historical baggage of injustice and exclusion. We need to exercise vigilance and high levels of reflexivity, allowing others space to interrogate our disciplinary ways of seeing and being and to challenge and re-imagine our processes of knowledge production.

This sociological understanding of the impact of disciplinary cultures does not imply that disciplinary knowledge is unimportant in shaping teaching and learning. However, it does emphasize that it is just one factor among many that shapes the ways in which we engage with students. When teaching, it is useful to question the extent to which our teaching practices are really helping students to understand and question disciplinary knowledge or whether this is simply how this knowledge has always been taught in our discipline.

Teaching and learning contexts

As we have discussed, the global knowledge production system, national policies, institutional and disciplinary cultures all have a role in shaping teaching and learning processes. These different contexts create 'social imaginaries' (Rizvi 2006), the sets of values, rules and institutions that provide a normative backdrop to our everyday practices. Rizvi (2006) argues that, increasingly, the social imaginaries of our students are global, hybrid and culturally diverse and go beyond particular national settings. These insights are important for thinking about how we relate to diverse groups of students.

However, there are also cultures that operate at the level of individual departments or programme teams within universities. Paul Trowler (2019) calls these 'Teaching and Learning Regimes' (TLRs). These are defined as:

> A constellation of rules, assumptions, practices and relationships related to teaching and learning issues in higher education . . . In deploying the term 'regime' we draw attention to social relationships and recurrent practices, the technologies that instantiate them (room layouts and pedagogic techniques) and the ideologies, values, and attitudes that underpin them. (Trowler and Cooper 2002, p. 224)

The concept of Teaching and Learning Regimes captures the ways in which global systems, national policies and institutional and disciplinary cultures are mediated by other factors at play in the academic departments or programme teams in which we operate. For example, educational initiatives are seen to play out differently because they are filtered through different cultural 'moments' (Trowler, P. 2020). These moments include:

- 'Recurrent practices' – the ways in which things are done around here.
- 'Tacit assumptions' – the un-discussed shared and collective views about, for example, the 'true nature' of the discipline.
- 'Implicit theories of teaching and learning' – for example, whether students have innate ability and so should be left to sink or swim or whether students' abilities are related to their past educational experiences, in which case they should be supported in their learning.
- 'Discursive repertories' – ways of talking about teaching and learning that are derived from wider social imaginaries. For example, the extent to which students are seen as 'consumers', 'customers', 'co-constructors' or disembodied 'learners' all impact on the ways we relate to them.
- 'Conventions of appropriateness' – what kinds of behaviours are considered appropriate in teaching and learning and what kinds are not.
- 'Power relations' – who is seen as powerful within discussions of teaching and learning in a work team? Whose opinions carry most weight and why? For example, are students' views seen as important or is the smooth running of courses felt to be a more important consideration? How are these two issues related?
- 'Subjectivities in interaction' – how different people in the department or workgroup are positioned relative to each other in relation to particular issues. Are some people in your team meetings seen to be the experts in particular areas? Do your opinions carry more weight on some issues than others?
- 'Codes of signification' – the meanings of particular objects or signs in a group.

The concept of TLRs gives us tools to think about how global knowledge systems, national policies and institutional and disciplinary cultures are refracted through the ways in which particular programme teams or groups of academics work together on a curriculum. As reflective teachers, this concept can help us to think through critically the ways in which our teaching practices are simply the effects of these contexts and influences and the extent to which we can reshape them to have a positive effect on student learning.

Reflective Activity 5.1 Thinking about the impact of contexts on teaching and learning practices

This activity works as a bridge between this section on contexts and teaching and learning regimes and the next which considers agency. An interesting way of approaching the interaction between contexts and agency is to think back on your own educational biography through the lens of these concepts. For this activity we suggest that you find a colleague with whom you feel secure. You might draw on your work from **Reflective Activity 1.3** in Chapter 1 to do this. Taking turns, take time to provide a narrative of how you moved through your education, learning from different teachers, growing up, finding some learning difficult but succeeding in others. Identify and focus on some key episodes or turning points where you experienced difficulties, setbacks or disappointments. Think about what contextual constraints you faced as well as what enabled you to recover and move on. Explore if you can the key actions you took and the encouragement or support you received from others.

Does consideration of such narratives and key moments enable you to see the constraints and affordances of your contexts and the significance of agency, in the form of your own determination to succeed and the support you received from others who believed in you?

You could think about one or two of your own students. To what extent are they able to exercise agency in relation to their contexts and goals, and in what ways might you support and encourage them?

PEOPLE, AGENCY AND INTERACTIONS

We now turn to the individual and personal factors which are the second element in the dialectical model that underpins this book. As well as understanding something of the historical, cultural and institutional factors affecting the socio-political contexts of teaching and learning, we also need to consider how, along with our students, we respond to and help to create, recreate or disrupt these contexts and their meanings. This is the exercise of agency and voice – and involves understanding that our subjectivities are not simply effects of our histories and cultures, nor are our actions simply determined by our circumstances. That said, as reflexive teachers, we need to develop a sense of social and self-critique that allows us to see how racial, class, cultural and gendered stereotypes get assigned to us and 'others' in arbitrary, unproductive ways. We will not become 'critical professionals' (Walker 2001) with capacity to act for social change if we don't first introspect and reflect. We need to first understand how the ways in which we think and speak about ourselves, our communities and others and our assumptions about cultural difference, social authority and political power, might work to rationalize and perpetuate relations of domination (Soudien 2012).

In this section, we look at the ways in which our identities as academics and the identities of our students are the product of our ongoing engagement with education processes as well as our experiences outside education. In this way, we highlight how our identities as teachers, and those of our students, emerge from our personal identities, our social identities, our roles and experiences within particular institutions and our previous histories of teaching and learning. We also discuss the ways in which these identities come together in particular teaching and learning interactions.

Academics

As we discussed in Chapter 1, our identities as teachers in higher education are shaped by our individual histories, the institutions and disciplines in which we have taught, as well as other roles we have played in higher education (Smith 2017; Van Lankveld et al. 2017). Furthermore, there is ample evidence to show that our global location, gender, class and race impact on how we construct our personal identities and how our social identities as academics and teachers are assigned (for example, see Morley 2016; Behari-Leak 2017; Arday and Mirza 2018). Also, different institutions position our teaching, research and administrative careers in different ways, offering different opportunities, time and constraints for the development of teaching careers (Behari-Leak 2017; Whitchurch and Gordon 2017; Smith 2017). Disciplinary identities also play a role in shaping our teaching identities (Janice et al. 2018) although Brew (2008) qualifies this, suggesting that, depending on the relation between our institutional careers and personal identities, we can experience the same discipline in different ways and these experiences can change over time.

The contexts and influences mentioned in the first section of this chapter such as the audit culture, the rise of managerialism and performativity are widely understood to constrain academics' sense of autonomy and agency (Leibowitz and Holgate 2012). Holding both perspectives together – our potential as academics to contribute to society through teaching and research – and the increased control and surveillance over academics' work – suggests that we work in conditions of 'duality' in which we face both constraints and opportunities (McLean 2006). In this way, who we are as university teachers is shaped by our contexts, our previous and current experiences as well as where we see ourselves going in the future. This means that our sense of our teaching careers is dynamic and changing rather than something fixed.

In order to reflexively and creatively generate a sense of agency and professionalism under conditions of duality, we suggest taking up Walker's (2001) concept of 'critical professionalism' developed through an action research project at Glasgow University and closely related to Nixon's (2001) idea of the 'new professional'. Leibowitz and Holgate (2012) point out the irony that while academics are expected to produce critical and creative graduates, institutions often fail to encourage the same attributes in their teaching staff. Pulling together Walker's (2001) and Nixon's (2001) definitions, we suggest that a critical professional academic would be someone who has a strong commitment to learning; a strong sense of public service and responsibility towards students, colleagues and the wider community; and finally someone who wishes to challenge institutional power and domination and work for change.

Taking this further, advocates of critical or engaged pedagogy argue that we should encourage our students to move beyond their common sense realities and experiences by getting them to engage with critical, multiple perspectives and counter narratives from the periphery or global South (Subreenduth 2012).

Students

There is extensive evidence that the intersections of students' age, disabilities, ethnicities, genders, sexualities, social class and whether they are studying in their home countries impact on their experiences of higher education (for example, see Jones 2017; Waller et al. 2017; Case et al. 2018; Arday and Mirza 2018; Howell 2018; Ngabaza et al. 2018; Walker 2018). In addition, students' sense of agency and, ultimately, their academic performance, is affected by the extent to which they feel that they belong and can participate in learning events (Soudien 2012). Other factors include students' previous experiences in education (Entwistle 2018) and the time they have available to study (see Callender and Dougherty 2018). It is important to emphasize that such factors do not operate in a deterministic or uniform manner; for example, there is no single working-class or middle-class identity and no single experience of being an international student (see Jones 2017). Rather, it is the complex ways that these factors both enable and constrain students' potential and how they work with their situations individually and collectively to forge personal and social agency that requires analysis. This suggests that analyses that assume that our universities are meritocracies and thus attribute students' success or failure to inherent individual attributes are simplistic.

The ways in which students' experiences of higher education develop over time is related to the factors that we examined earlier: the global system of knowledge production, national policies, institutional cultures, disciplinary cultures and teaching and learning regimes. The institutional setting can impact on students' experiences. For example, how the role of student is seen can differ institutionally, for example the extent to which students are seen as 'consumers' (Tomlinson 2017). Likewise, a study on the impact of the Scottish Quality Assurance Agency's enhancement theme on 'student voice' (Trowler et al. 2018) shows that while quality assurance systems do provide opportunities for students to give feedback to institutions, this is not always taken up in visible and constructive ways. Institutional responses to student feedback partly depend on what role the institution gives to students – the student as consumer, representative, partner or agent.

Similarly, there is some evidence that different disciplines involve quite different paths for students over their time in higher education. For example, in a classic study, Nespor (1994) gives a clear sense of how differences in the way time and space are constituted in physics and management offer students different kinds of learning careers in these disciplines.

The research briefing below illustrates the ways in which students from different social classes draw on different kinds of resources and have different expectations of higher education. It also highlights the way in which studying at university is a time of challenge and change for students in which they forge their identities.

RESEARCH BRIEFING 5.2 The socio-cultural and learning experiences of underrepresented students in higher education

Case et al. (2018), who conducted a longitudinal study in South Africa, found that, while all first-generation students in their study who succeeded in higher education showed high levels of agency and reflexivity, social class, race and gender continue to be key factors in constraining access to and success at university. Also writing from a Southern context, Fataar (2018) argues for the need to better theorize the nature of underclass students' 'emerging agency' in ways that view students' 'educational becoming' as a journey that includes factors such as mobility, space, time, scale and the body. On this journey, students move through precarity and ontological uncertainty as they cross over from the family/community/school divide into the shadows of main-stream university culture. Not only do underclass students have to deal daily with the social pathologies of their communities, but they develop informal cognitive, affective and strategic mediating practices to cope with middle-class university environments that continue to misrecognize who they are. Furthermore, Bangeni and Kapp (2017) show how these students' transitions to university are 'unhoming' in that being at university alienates them from their home communities, while simultaneously they find themselves ill-equipped to participate and feel 'at home' in the university community. As they develop agency and 'educational becoming', some of the informal learning strategies widely used by students in Southern contexts include strict learning routines and peer-learning groups – the latter make use of social media and trans-languaging modes of communication to help each other learn (Norodien-Fataar 2018). As reflexive teachers we would do well to think about how to legitimate and build on our students' informal learning strategies by bringing them into the formal teaching and learning frame.

Interactions between students and academics

Our identities as teachers and our students' identities as learners do not develop in isolation from each other. In specific teaching and learning interactions there are many factors that contribute to the identity positions that we and our students take up and assign to one another as we relate to each other. Thus, in responding to each other, we may perceive that different positions are or are not available to us depending on our past experiences, social positions and institutional roles. Within a particular interaction, different aspects of our identities will be foregrounded while other aspects will be backgrounded – for both teacher and learner. Sometimes our race or gender, or that of some of our students, might feel central to the interaction (Bhopal 2002), but at other times disciplinary identities come to the fore. This means that those aspects of our identities that help us to make sense of an interaction can shift in the process of engagement. Thus teaching and learning interactions are both dynamic and changing, but also based on teaching and learning careers that seem relatively stable and have developed over many years (Ashwin 2009).

There are two important points to be made when thinking about these interactions between ourselves as teachers and our students. First, the institutional forms of teaching and learning that are very familiar to us as teachers may be far less familiar to our students. Thus they may be uncertain about their roles within these interactions and how to fulfil them, even at postgraduate level.

Second, it is important to be clear that although we are interacting with our students, this does not mean that we are focused on the same objects as our students. Sarah Mann (2003) conducted individual interviews with a university teacher and some students who had been involved in a seminar that had been video recorded. In separate interviews with each participant, she played back the video and asked them to explain what was going on in the seminar. The very different meanings the teacher and students ascribed to the interaction and their completely different interpretations of what was going on at particular moments of the seminar offer a really important insight into how different teachers' and students' experiences and understandings of apparently shared interactions can be.

So in our interactions with students there are two different things going on. First, students play a very important role in shaping the meaning that we make from those interactions and similarly, as teachers, we play a very significant role in the meaning our students take from these interactions. However, this does not mean that we and our students will have *shared meanings* of these interactions. Understanding what we share and what we don't and the tension between the two is one of the biggest challenges in developing a reflective approach to teaching. Equally, a reflective approach to teaching is crucial for developing an understanding of this fascinating aspect of teaching and learning in higher education. We explore this further in Research Briefing 5.3.

RESEARCH BRIEFING 5.3 Decolonizing the curriculum in a southern context

A research project conducted recently in the context of the student protests in South Africa (2015–17) illustrates well the lack of intersubjectivity and shared meanings between staff and students at one historically white institution (Luckett et al. 2019). In the wake of students' demand for a decolonized curriculum 'linked to social justice and the experiences of black people' (RMF 2015), staff were interviewed about how they were responding to this call with regard to their curriculum and teaching. Overwhelmingly, the data showed that academics viewed curriculum reform as reform of content. Most thought that adding more 'blackness' to curriculum content was what was required. The wider structures of power were not questioned, while some academics felt that their autonomy was being threatened. The data gathered for this project suggests that academics were foregrounding the content of their curricula, while its norms and cultural and ontological assumptions (the hidden curriculum) remained taken-for-granted and thus opaque to them. Whereas for (black) students it was the other way around – they could clearly see the hidden curriculum (its norms and linguistic, cultural and ontological assumptions – which they experienced as excluding and alienating), while the formal curriculum content remained opaque to them, inaccessible and hard to grasp due to wrong assumptions by many academics about their levels of English language proficiency and prior learning.

Reflective Activity 5.2 Pedagogic agency

This activity involves working with a colleague. First spend some time on your own, noting your answers to the questions below. Then interview each other using the questions below. Once you have listened to each other's responses, spend some time discussing the opportunities and challenges that you each face with regard to your teaching contexts.

1 How do you articulate for your students your own social and intellectual position – from where you speak when teaching?

2 To what extent does your teaching avoid compelling all students to become assimilated into dominant practices, dispositions and Western culture? What can you do in your classroom to facilitate inclusion without assuming assimilation?

3 What proportion of your class comes from subordinated groups? How does your teaching recognize and affirm their agency and legitimate and respect their experiences and cultures?

4 How do you build a learning community in your classroom where students feel 'at home', learn actively from one another and draw on their own knowledge sources?

CONCLUSION

In this chapter, we have examined the relations between the socio-political contexts that structure teaching and learning in higher education and our experiences as teachers in higher education. In this way, it has examined the relationship between society as a whole and the actors involved in higher education.

This is important because the courses and programmes we teach on and our daily teaching practices are influenced by the social circumstances within which they occur. However, it has also been argued that we can have an impact on future social change, although the degree of our influence ebbs and flows depending on the institutional roles we occupy, our social identities and what is happening in the institutions in which we teach.

This kind of perspective is important for reflective teaching because it establishes the principle that we can all 'make a difference' within our society. Critical professional commitment is therefore very important, and we should not accept that our role as teachers in higher education is simply to respond to the external demands of our institutions, our students and wider society. The development of excellent teaching in higher education is enhanced when our social- and self-awareness complements our teaching expertise, and when we take our teaching responsibilities seriously.

This fundamental belief in the commitment, professionalism and constructive role of teachers in higher education underpins this book. Developing excellent and transformative higher education experiences for students depends on the expertise of those who teach in higher education.

KEY READINGS

On the impacts of contexts generally, see:

Trowler, P. (2020) *Accomplishing Change in Teaching and Learning Regimes: Higher Education and the Practice Sensibility.* Oxford: Oxford University Press.

On decolonizing the university, see:

Bhambra, G., Gebrial D. and Nisancioglu, K. (2018) *Decolonising the University.* London: Pluto Press.

Mbembe, A. (2016) 'Decolonizing the university: New directions', *Arts & Humanities in Higher Education*, 15(1), 29–45.

Mignolo W. and Escobar, A. (eds) (2010) *Globalization and the Decolonial Option.* New York: Routledge.

On the impact of high levels of participation on higher education systems, see:

Cantwell, B., Marginson, S. and Smolentseva, A. (eds) (2018) *High Participation Systems of Higher Education*. Oxford: Oxford University Press.

On the impact of disciplines, see:

Trowler, P., Saunders, M. and Bamber, V. (eds) (2012) *Tribes and Territories in the 21st-Century: Rethinking the Significance of Disciplines in Higher Education.* Abingdon: Routledge.

Chapter 6
Relationships

How are we getting on together?

INTRODUCTION

From the perspective of the critical theorist Jurgen Habermas (1987), educating people concerns the human lifeworld: society, culture and individual identity. For this reason, education is a 'communicatively structured' and collective endeavour (see Chapter 11). For higher education teaching, academics come to agreements with each other, with students and with managers about what constitutes a good course, good teaching and good learning. In this way, teaching and learning are socially, culturally and historically mediated; they are also influenced both positively and negatively by emotional responses, so attending to the quality of human relationships and interactions is important.

This book stresses the social as well as the psychological nature of teaching and learning. Chapter 1 demonstrates how matters of identity formation influence learning; Chapters 5 and 11 highlight the social context in which learning takes place; Chapter 12 discusses the role of communication and dialogue in learning, as well as how matters of power and authority impact on learning; and Chapter 15 considers how an inclusive environment consolidates opportunities for effective teaching and learning. Given this focus on the social, a logical step for the reflective teacher is to consider how to manage the teaching process so that relationships between teacher and student, student and student, student and other significant peers including peer tutors, friends and members of the family and broader community, all support learning.

This chapter is in three sections and provides a focus on the role of the teacher and the student separately, before bringing them together with a focus on their interrelationship and on how they co-exist within the institution. The first section begins with the role of the teacher in creating positive relationships and then moves to the role of the teacher in distributed learning and virtual or electronic environments, where creating sustaining and collaborative relationships might be more complex but equally important. The second section considers the role of the student in relationships and also argues that the role of emotions in teaching relationships is a neglected area in higher education research and development. The conclusion draws attention to how important the institutional environment is to good relationships and summarizes the main points from the chapter.

See Chapter 4

TLRP Principles

Two principles are of particular relevance to this chapter on relationships:

Principle 3: Effective teaching and learning recognizes the significance of informal learning to developing specific expertise. Learning with friends, families, peer groups and professionals should be recognized as significant, and be valued and used in formal processes in higher education.

Principle 4: Effective teaching and learning fosters both individual and social processes and outcomes. Students should be encouraged to build relationships and communication with others to assist the mutual construction of knowledge and enhance the achievements of individuals and groups. Consulting or collaborating with students as learners about their learning makes this effective.

THE ROLE OF THE TEACHER

The importance of the teacher's role in developing relationships cannot be over-emphasized. A report (Mountford-Zimdars et al. 2015) on the causes of differential outcomes in higher education identified four explanatory factors of which two were about relationships: 'a sense of belonging' and 'the extent to which students feel supported and encouraged in their daily interactions within their institutions and with staff members' (p. iii).

Relationships and the teacher in traditional teaching sessions

Case Study 6.1 Cathy establishes a relationship with first-year students

Cathy Humane taught first-year Law students for several decades before being promoted to the position of Dean of the Faculty of Law. During this time she achieved several teaching excellence awards and was twice nominated by the top thirty first-year students at her university as the teacher who had the highest impact on their academic achievement. Cathy was interviewed by researchers at her university, who were interested to find out why she thought she might be viewed by others as a good teacher. Her reply demonstrates the significance of good relations between teacher and students, especially first-year students.

Making connections with first-years

I think the first thing is that I'm fortunate because I teach what I love, I really do love the first-year subjects, and so it is very easy to get enthusiastic about that. It is the kind of subject where you are in a position to discuss law, but also to relate that to real life issues. Maybe because I came to study law at a later stage in my life, I think I understood the value of a teacher who is in a position to really describe difficult work in a simple way, and I think that maybe also makes life a bit easier, I hope it makes life a bit easier for the first-year students as well.

I go to a lot of trouble to understand the minds of, especially, first-year students, I try and read a lot, I try and stay up-to-date with the latest music developments and TV programmes, and games. Another thing that I have attempted to do is to stay away from hi-tech things, because I still believe that one needs to look at body language, and make eye contact, and if you do that, I think you can manage a situation in class.

Those are the kinds of things that students pick up on. Learn their names. First years are so surprised the first time you say 'Miriam Ormingo'. Or if you go through the name list and you for example see their date of birth, and you see it is one student's birthday in class, you just sometimes go into class and you say, 'Congratulations

Mark Boshoff, I see it is your birthday.' When it works, there is such a positive reaction from them that you also feed off that positive reaction as well, and it is just so nice.

You can never assume knowledge on their side. You need to be aware that you are helping them with their dreams, they will get hurt along the way, but you should not simply take away their dreams.

Being direct

I am just honest with students. If I feel that they've underperformed I would tell them that in a diplomatic way, but if necessary I'll tell them straight away. Take for example as happened the other day, a student with a mark of something like 20% for a test, was sitting in my office. I said to him, 'What happened that led you to only get a mark of 20%? Is it the place where you live, do you have a problem with the language, or whatever?' and his mood changed just like that. So now he comes to see me on a regular basis and he is a totally different young man.

How I have developed

Maybe making contact with students is one's personality to a certain extent, but if it is not part of your personality that is something that you consciously have to work at.

I think I have changed over the years in the sense that now I have a much greater awareness of the person behind the student, and of how to manage the person. If you can do that, then I think you'll have a better student. It's also as a result of chatting to students after they completed their first year, as senior students they walk around and I'd go and fetch a cup of tea and sometimes they will say something about the private law – that it was nice, or it was a bit difficult, so I get feedback from them and I get feedback from colleagues.

(Account based on research described in Leibowitz et al. 2009)

This account by Cathy Humane depicts a caring teacher who establishes strong rapport with her first-year students. Some of the attributes that enable her to develop such a good relationship with her students are: her passion for her discipline; that she studied late and thus has insight into finding academia difficult and unfamiliar; that she cares for the students and their aspirations; that she has an intuitive sense, supported by her years of experience, of 'what works'; that she is honest or direct with students; that she invests time and effort into her relationships with students; and, that she engages in various forms of reflection in order to improve her relationships. The accolades for her teaching imply that her investment in relationships has paid off.

Cathy Humane's success is predictable. Over time, research aimed to establish principles for good or 'excellent' teaching – such as those on which this book is based – invariably confirms the importance of establishing good relationships with students (for other sets of principles in the higher education context, see: Chickering and Gamson 1987; Kuh 2008; Ambrose et al. 2010; Gibbs 2010; Laurillard 2012; Entwistle 2018).

Taken together, the teacher characteristics that are emphasized are: being personally available to students and developing a rapport by showing care, kindness and patience; knowing and respecting students; concern about students' learning; encouraging reciprocity and cooperation among students; and being inspiring. For reflective teaching, first we need to be convinced that the quality of our relationships with students (as well as with colleagues with whom we teach) helps to shape the quality of learning. Second, we need to think about what it takes to develop good relationships with students in lectures, seminars and tutorials, as well as through individual encounters and as the tone of our comments on assignments.

For example, Kincaid and Pecorino (2004) distinguish between different models for relationships with students. They propose discarding the 'code' model based on mediaeval conceptions of the guild with an emphasis on other members of the guild (academics), ceremony, and written and unwritten rules to uphold the craft. This model grants autonomy to academics but lacks a sense of accountability to those outside the guild, namely students and broader society. Similarly, they argue for putting aside the 'contractual' model, which assumes a contract between equal parties but is motivated by self-interest and is assured through legalistic approaches, limiting consideration of professional ethics and obligation. Rather, they propose the 'covenant' model based on the promise of caring about the intellectual development of the students. When this model is successful, teachers are aware of their own privilege and their responsibility both to students and to the structures and systems that support education.

While 'teaching models' offer a way of thinking about the basis of a teaching relationship with students, the concept of 'teaching persona' is how the individual teacher conveys impressions of him or herself to students. Parini (2005) parallels the use of masks in theatre to what a teacher does. He does not see it as inauthentic to decide what mask or persona will encourage students, rather it is a matter of choice of what to reveal and emphasize. In his case, it is as someone strongly attached to his discipline of literature, modelling commitment to the students; and as someone who is keen to interact with students in and out of class. Deciding on a teaching persona takes conscious reflection.

RESEARCH BRIEFING 6.1 Relationships for encouraging independent study

A comparative and longitudinal research project called 'Quality and Inequality in Undergraduate Degrees' (McLean et al. 2018) explored the curriculum and teaching practices of four sociology degrees in universities of different reputation and status in England: two 'lower status' and two 'higher status'. The researchers argued that, while students from relatively disadvantaged backgrounds are already disrupting social hierarchy by gaining access to university, in a stratified higher education system, how they are taught can disrupt it further. If teachers can make what is expected explicit and visible to the students and, simultaneously, encourage them to study, then students are more likely to understand and be transformed by the discipline they are studying. The research revealed that for students the three aspects of teaching which were most important were: relationships with the lecturers; the nature and quality of seminar interactions; and support to study independently. These three aspects were intimately interrelated. Students wanted lecturers to be friendly, to take an interest in their academic progress, and to be available for questioning and dialogue. Markedly more informal, open and supportive relationships with lecturers were reported in the two lower-status universities: students commented on the lack of hierarchy and the respect the lecturers showed for them; felt entitled to time with lecturers and to knock on their office door with an appointment; and they talked with them about when they saw them outside class. It is important to note that, for most students, good relationships were for improving work, rather than for enjoyment or counselling: students wanted to feel confident enough to ask lecturers to clarify aspects of feedback on assignments for assessment.

The quality of relationships played out in the quality of seminar discussion. Students much preferred seminars to lecturers in the following conditions: when everyone was prepared; when they felt confident to speak; when everyone else spoke freely; when their ideas were discussed and challenged by other students and the lecturer; and when the discussion was enjoyable. These conditions seemed difficult to achieve. However, from the students' perspective they were more likely to want to prepare and to have the confidence to speak when they related to them as academic peers whose opinion they were interested in and valued.

Finally, the researchers found how important it is that students are supported to be committed, to make efforts and undertake many hours of productive, independent study. The students at the lower-status universities reported doing less, saying they found the solitariness of reading and writing difficult. Although they knew that their lecturers wanted them to work hard, some students wanted to be explicitly pushed to work. Understandably, academics resisted because they did not conceptualize their students as school pupils whom they must control; however, the researchers concluded that the students required something akin to what a caring parent does: scaffolding for independence.

The kind of relationships we establish with our students is informed by how we understand what we are doing when we teach and by our values and goals. Based on the discussion so far, the reflective activity below asks you to reflect about how you conceptualize your teaching role and how you conceptualize students as learners; and then, what kind of teaching persona you might want to develop and how you might do that.

Reflective Activity 6.1 What kind of relationships with students matter to you?

Participating in this reflective activity in a group might be more fun and any differences of opinion can encourage depth of reflection. The point of this exercise is to see the connections between your conception of yourself as a teacher; your conceptions of students-as-learners and what you actually 'do' in the classroom. These connections help you to reflect on what kind of relationship with your students will support their learning. It might be easier, for the purposes of this exercise, to choose one class you teach rather than all your teaching responsibilities. Now answer the following questions.

1 How do you conceptualize your role as a teacher or, put another way, what persona do you convey?
   Kincaid and Pecorino (2004) identified eight self-concepts that can be a starting point:
   ● Paternalistic – authoritarian, deciding for students and neglecting to develop their autonomy.
   ● Therapist – focused on curing students' learning weaknesses and vulnerabilities.
   ● Priestly – the teacher as infallible guide.
   ● Employee – servicing students.
   ● Collegial – democratic, making decisions about what is to be learned together with the students.
   ● Contractual – based on the idea of a contract in which interested parties agree on what is to be accomplished.
   ● Edutainer – focusing on entertaining students.
   ● Convenential – the educator has a promise and debt to society and uses his/her knowledge to honour this.
   Name the concepts you think you adopt, but for the purposes of the exercise, no more than three. Or create other conceptions that more closely characterize your view of your role as a teacher. If you make up an additional conception, give it a name and describe it.

2 How do you conceptualize your students as learners?
   Here your choices might be influenced by the eight conceptions you considered above. Feel free to make other choices or select more than one below, but try not to name more than three.
   ● Recipients of your professional decisions and choices.
   ● Learners with areas of weakness for modification.
   ● Learners to accept your views and practices on faith.
   ● They pay, so they make the choices about what to learn and how.
   ● As equals, they make the choices in collaboration with you.
   ● As equal parties to a contract.
   ● They will only learn if they are engaged by being entertained.
   ● As potentially committed to the learning process and to being transformed via learning your discipline/field.

3 What kind of teaching persona are you interested in presenting to students?
   Consider your conceptualizations of academic-as-teacher and student-as learner. Now decide what kind of teaching persona you now present to your students.
   ● Does your teaching persona align with your conceptions or are there contradictions?

- Is there anything that you would like to change in your conceptions and/or teaching persona?
- What teaching persona do you want to present to students? (The one you now present or another?)
- Can you provide examples of the teaching behaviours of your preferred teaching persona in and out of class?
- What do you believe are or might be the effects of your preferred teaching persona on your students' learning?

Relationships in distributed learning environments

So far in this chapter on relationships, we have focused on the teacher in traditional settings where interactions are face to face. We now move on to approaches to teaching and learning where contact is 'virtual' and teaching and learning is viewed concurrently as 'distributed', 'connected' and 'spatially spread out' (issues to which we return in Chapter 8 on Learning spaces). A distributed environment requires a different consideration of how conducive relationships can be fostered.

A classic definition of 'distributed learning' is as 'networks of learning in which learners take up opportunities in a variety of ways without necessary involvement from teachers or supervisors' (Boud and Lee 2005, p. 503). This definition implies that there are various role players in the environment, one of the most significant being peer learners, but also others who potentially influence students' learning, including parents, siblings or other role models in the media. Viewing a student within a broader ecology allows us to consider not only our own relationships as teachers with students, but also their relationships with their peers and with significant others in their broader environment. A useful question to bear in mind when planning your modules or courses is: 'How can I structure this module so that students can benefit from productive relationships with their peers within the class and in other classes, and other significant role-players in their lives?'

The learning context can also be viewed as 'connected', in the sense that we learn informally as well as formally, in a variety of different environments and stages of our lives. This learning is fostered by access to various electronic media. Over fifteen years ago Siemens (2004) popularized the notion of 'connectivism', which he characterized using the following principles:

- Learning and knowledge rests in diversity of opinions.
- Learning is a process of connecting specialized nodes or information sources.
- Learning may reside in non-human appliances.
- Capacity to know more is more critical than what is currently known.
- Nurturing and maintaining connections to facilitate continual learning.
- Ability to see connections between fields, ideas, and concepts is a core skill.

- Currency (accurate, up-to-date knowledge) is the intent of all connectivist learning activities.
- Decision-making is itself a learning process.

The implication of living in a connected world is that teachers are not the sole sources of expertise, knowledge and learning. Learning environments can be designed so that students can learn from significant others, in their classes and off campus. And students can form relationships whereby they can learn from each other. This potential requires more pedagogic attention to fostering such student dispositions as willingness to take risks, ability to work in groups, humility to learn from others and preparedness to share with others (see Chapter 9 for a fuller discussion of these dispositions as graduate attributes). A connectivist approach to learning in a technologically mediated environment allows for caring relationships to emerge in which individual students are considered and where students can customize their learning environment (Bozalek 2017).

A further element of the distributed environment is that students can be geographically more separated from the teacher and from each other. This is obviously the case when courses are offered purely online, but it is also the case for residential courses, which are increasingly mixed face to face and online, or 'blended'. There is an assumption that online learning is automatically more impersonal, but this is not necessarily the case. With discussion forums and blogs, there is much opportunity to encourage students to engage in dialogue with each other, to work in groups and to collaborate. Rourke et al. (2001) suggest three ways in which teachers and students use language to build 'social presence' in online asynchronous communication: 'affective indicators' (personal expressions of emotions, beliefs, values, humour and self-disclosure); 'cohesive indicators' that build a sense of community (for example, greetings, referring to people in the group as 'us', reflecting on the course and sharing of information not relevant to the course) and 'interactive indicators', indicating acknowledgement, agreement, approval, invitation and personal advice. This is a useful framework for reflecting on how we design distributed courses and frame teaching when students are online.

THE ROLE OF THE STUDENT

A crucial role-player in the learning process is, of course, the student, who is primarily responsible for his or her own learning, and to some extent, for supporting the learning of others. There is a great deal we can do as teachers to make students aware of this responsibility and to extend to them a sense of agency or self-efficacy so that they believe they can achieve their goals. It is also important to create a productive, inclusive and supportive learning climate. How to do so is discussed in Chapter 15 on inclusion and in **Reflective Activity 6.2**. Cathy Humane, the Law Professor in **Case Study 6.1**, communicated her high expectations of her students, her care and interest in their achievement, and her expectation that they exercise the responsibility to learn. The student is in an unequal power relation to the lecturer. *We* decide the type of relationships to be fostered with students and even between students, however democratic we try to be.

What kind of relationship do we want to foster? One in which no student or teacher inhibits the right to learn from another, but which is actually 'each person for themselves'? One in which students and teachers support each other in a general way, in the belief that every student has the same chance to succeed, if they exercise their will? Or one which is based on an acknowledgement that students have not all had equal life chances, that biographies and socialization predisposes students to react to higher education learning in different ways? This latter version of relationships is based on the view that there are hidden power relationships and forms of privilege, which constrain and enable individuals in different ways in teaching and learning situations. If we adopt this latter view, we may find managing relationships with and between relationships more complex and demanding. First, we must consider the hidden and taken for granted norms which privilege some students over others and, if possible, do something about this – without conveying the impression that this privilege or inequality is someone's 'fault', especially someone else in the classroom.

Case Study 6.2 A 'Respect Contract'

At 'Diversity University' in the UK (which has a high proportion of students from working-class and ethnic-minority backgrounds) the lecturers in the Sociology Department worked hard to build positive and supportive relationships with their students. They were available and friendly and encouraged high levels of participation in class. The discussion in seminars and workshops was lively and noisy, but it was often uninformed, and some students complained in formal evaluations and informally:

> The seminar is limited in its usefulness 'cos they try and make them student oriented and we just don't prepare well enough. We would get an awful lot more out of them if we did and I'll put my own hand up there. I just haven't read enough and so it's going to be of limited value. (Lloyd, Year 3)

> The problem with the seminars is not actually the lecturers [. . .] it's the people that are part of the seminar with you. Because they don't do their reading, they don't know what they're talking about – you can see that because they ask things that [make you think] 'If you'd done your reading you'd know what that means'. (Lauren, Year 3)

In addition, students arrived late without apology; talked over each other; and were on their mobile phones. This behaviour compromised the students. So the staff decided to address the problem of lack of discipline not by exerting authority, which they were reluctant to do, but by during the first seminar of each semester agreeing with students a set of ground rules for behaviour in seminars (including preparation so that what was said was worth listening to). This was focused on respect to reformulate the relationships between lecturers and students and students with each other. It was called the 'Respect Contract' and the lecturers reported that it made a significant positive difference to the quality of seminars and workshops.

(Based on research reported in McLean et al. 2018)

Some universities and departments have courses for first-year students which foster their understanding of what it means to be a student and how to study effectively. Some teachers develop specific exercises to encourage their students' self-awareness as learners, or include questions designed to foster students' awareness of their roles as learners in course evaluation forms. A choice for some is to assess and give grades to seminar participation and/or activities designed to foster student responsibility for their own learning or for the effective functioning of a group. The argument for making this choice is that giving credit that 'counts' sends a strong message to students about how important it is to be self-aware about their own roles and responsibilities. The counter argument is that assessing everything is an extrinsic form of motivation which encourages a performance or surface approach, rather than the student internalizing the values which teachers are modelling and promoting (for example, respect for others and commitment to thinking critically about a discipline or field). These are dilemmas that as a reflective teacher we can think through on our own or with our colleagues, and make decisions which suit our particular contexts.

Reflective Activity 6.2 The students' responsibilities

This activity is designed to encourage students to think consciously both about the kinds of relationships with teachers and with other students that would enhance learning and about their own responsibility for these relationships. This activity could be assessed – this would depend on the kinds of outcomes set for the course. Students can work on their own or in groups. The final list could be pasted on a wall or an electronic site.

Instructions to students

Discuss and write down the kind of relationships that would ensure that this class is conducive to learning for all students. (Five bulleted points.)

Discuss these ideas in plenary and devise a composite description of these relationships.

Write down a set of behaviours for what you would expect to see that would demonstrate that these relationships are being upheld by:

- the teacher;
- the student – towards others; and
- the student – in relation to own learning.

THE INTERRELATIONSHIP BETWEEN TEACHER AND STUDENT: CREATING DIALOGUE

In *Clueless in Academe*, Gerald Graff (2003) argued that the goal of university education is to make it possible for students to enter conversation with an intellectual community. However, rather than achieving this goal, this education generally 'obscures the life of the mind' because 'Academicspeak' (the language of lecturers) and ordinary speech don't coincide: bringing them together is the task of education. Arguably, dialogue or discussion between teacher and students and between students is a core activity of higher education, alongside the solitary activities of reading and writing. Again, there are many resources for thinking about creating dialogue with students. For example, Burbules (1993) clarified that dialogue is different from other communication because it is directed towards new understandings and discovery. Teaching can be underpinned by understanding the different forms it can take (inquiry, debate, instruction and conversation) and about how it can fail and be improved. And for Mezirow (2009) whose interest is in how education can be transformative, dialogue is the 'essential medium' (p. 9); he invokes Habermas's 'discourse ethics' to remind teachers that there 'ideal conditions' (p. 9) for discussion which emanate from the quality of pedagogical relationships: for example, freedom from coercion; openness to alternative views; concern about how others think and feel; awareness of context; equal opportunities to participate; and willingness to seek understanding and come to agreements.

These 'ideal conditions' might seem far from the daily work of teaching, but Habermas has pointed out that the 'learning processes' of universities reflect the learning process necessary for a functioning democracy (Habermas and Blazek 1987). But to bring the discussion closer to everyday life teaching, Pollard (1982) describes the interrelationship between teachers and students at school as one in which 'working consensus' is aimed for. This applies to higher education as well (see Ashwin 2009). Students and teachers adapt to each other's demands, reaching a working consensus, which over time becomes more established. The implications of this habituation to each other are, first, for us to consider the expectations and norms that students have acquired in previous years of schooling or university. If we suggest radically different norms or ways of operating, or norms that will take students out of their comfort zones, we need to consider how to convince students that what we are suggesting is of value to them. Second, we need to be wary of accommodating students as an easy 'way out'. For example, it can become exhausting to constantly give low marks or insist on standards that might make us unpopular, so accommodation to students' expectations can become attractive. Third, we need to be aware, as Pollard (1982) reminds us, that students have different educational biographies and so their orientations and expectations at the onset of our relationship with them are a rich source for exploration.

Reflective Activity 6.3 Academic conversations with students

The final reflective activity in this chapter is designed to inform our thinking about what might constrain and enable the dialogue we would like with our students about our disciplines or fields. Graff (2003) identified six university education mindsets which prevent students from taking part in academic conversation. His context is teaching literature in the USA – see if it relates at all to your own experience. Either on your own or with others from the same or different disciplines think about whether you recognize them, whether you agree with them (and can you think of others) and, if so, what you think might be solutions in your interactions with students (you can find Graff's solutions in his book).

1 *Taking academic discourse for granted*. Academic jargon is foreign to students when they start university. More than this, they don't understand how and the way

that problems are formulated (it is an oddity that academics make problems out of everything).

2   *The volleyball effect.* Academic intellectual culture is contentious and conflicted. Students expect coherence (which they usually experienced at school) and become confused by what they experience as mixed messages, rather than academic disagreements, which actually masks much agreement (common ground and shared assumptions). They cope by trying to give teachers what they appear to want, so they feel batted about between what can seem to be incommensurate demands. Examples are: a student taking a joint degree in sociology and psychology which have different conventions; or more generally, the message 'Be yourself, but do it the way we want it done'.

3   *The overrating of fact.* The belief that <u>before</u> students can engage in higher-order thinking they must acquire a foundation of information. But trying to learn information before it makes sense has been shown to be ineffectual because storing and recalling information is usually tied to interests and purpose. It is, anyway, difficult to 'deprogramme' students who think learning is knowing decontextualized facts.

4   *The mystification of research.* Students don't know when their teachers are researchers and can be alienated from the culture of research. For students to grasp what an academic discipline or field is about, it is helpful to come close to how knowledge is produced in that discipline or field.

5   *Anti-intellectualism.* The belief that what Graff calls 'Arguespeak' is Western-centric, white, male and middle class. Current forms of being rational and searching for truth, associated with the Enlightenment in the West, is imposing a repressive dominant culture on marginal or disempowered people. The question is: How can disadvantaged students be supported to channel their debating and reasoning abilities into academic work? (This question connects strongly to the discussion about decolonization in Chapters 5 and 9.)

6   *The contrast of academia and popular culture.* Setting academic culture against popular culture and the media: the former is complex, abstract and accessible only to specialists while the latter is everyday, concrete and accessible to everyone. The problem though is how to encourage students to argue, analyse and talk about everything in intellectual ways.

We conclude this section by considering the role emotion plays in interrelationships. While a fair amount of literature about teaching in higher education promotes student-centredness and positive, empathetic relationships, comparatively little focuses on emotions and how relationships play into them. Yet, we know that university students who come from relatively disadvantaged backgrounds can feel anxious about not understanding expectations so that navigating the learning environment is difficult for them. They can also feel lonely and out of place in an unrelentingly middle-class and affluent environment (see, for example, Wilson-Strydom 2015; Bathmaker et al. 2016; Hanley 2016; Calitz 2018). So societal inequalities and differences affect not only access to knowledge, but also dispositions and management of emotions. Boler (1999) shows how emotions are both located in individuals and have strong class and cultural influences. This affects how individuals might react in educational settings, which the reflective teacher would be alert to in her or his dealings with students.

More generally, over thirty-five years ago the psychoanalysts Salzberger-Wittenberg et al. (1983) discussed the emotional factors intrinsic to the processes of learning and teaching. In their view, the teacher–student relationship evokes the dependency of infancy, and:

> It is the quality of this relationship which deeply influences the hopefulness required to remain curious and open to new experiences, the capacity to see connections and to discover their meaning. Affective and cognitive aspects of learning are therefore closely linked and inter-dependent. (Salzberger-Wittenberg et al. 1983, p. ix)

Emotion is evident. Teachers aspire, for example, to pass on knowledge, to enable students to succeed, to foster personal development; they fear criticism, hostility or losing control; and can be angry with students for many reasons. Students can feel anxiety, stress, panic and despair (and some report that they increasingly do) or are afraid to ask questions and speak up, or envy others who appear to do well. They can also feel excitement, admiration, gratitude and joy at horizons broadening; the world opening up; and being transformed.

A book which addresses the gap in literature about the emotion of learning and teaching in higher education is *How Higher Education Feels*, edited by Kathleen Quinlan (2016) who commissioned poems about aspects of higher education which are accompanied by 'expert commentaries' by educationalists. It can make a wonderful resource for the reflective higher education teacher because it invites us into the hidden nooks and crannies of teaching and is an antidote to the dubious certainties of 'best practice'. The poems and commentaries often deal with teaching and learning difficult topics – genocide, racism, death, trauma, colonization and war – and they show and discuss the powerful emotions that are inevitably evoked by such topics (for example, shock, disgust, shame or sadness). Zembylas (2008) discusses such 'difficult' or 'discomforting' knowledge arguing for paying explicit pedagogical attention to emotional responses. Yet, this does not mean only imagining how the students might feel but also supporting them to be critical because the emotions are often evoked by having beliefs and assumptions challenged. Zembylas (2008) uses the term 'critical emotional praxis' to suggests the kind of work undertaken to understand how emotions can lock us in to defensive positions in which we exclude the 'other', and how we can use emotions like anger to mobilize ourselves to action for social justice.

Calls for decolonization of curriculum and teaching (discussed in Chapters 5 and 9) invite joint attention on the part of both teachers and students to difficult emotions and critical understandings of knowledge. Waghid (2010) writes about the emotional aspects of extending democracy and citizenship in South Africa in a post-apartheid period, including: 'belligerence, deliberation and belonging', 'compassionate imagining', 'respect and forgiveness' and 'sceptical encounter with the other'. Emotions in difficult educational contexts give rise both to challenge, argumentation and confrontation, and to peaceful, understanding, kind interactions and relationships.

Keep in mind, though, that difficult knowledge capable of evoking strong feelings does not relate only to traumatic topics or challenging contexts or to the humanities and social sciences. A section in *How Higher Education Feels* is about teaching sciences and it identifies, for example, the mismatch between a lecturer who is passionate about mathematics and has always found it easy and students who find it difficult and anxiety-provoking.

Moreover, it is in assessment and feedback that emotions can run most high. Providing and receiving feedback is influenced by socio-cultural factors such as prior education (Paul et al. 2013), and by emotions such as anxiety and fear (Molloy et al. 2013). Carless (2013) advocates a key role for trust in the feedback process and provides the definition: 'One's willingness to be vulnerable based on an investment of faith that the other is open, reliable, honest, benevolent and competent' (p. 91). Unless students feel that their teachers possess these attributes, they are unlikely to take critical feedback. It is hard not to feel humiliated by critical judgements, and teachers can help make it as positive as possible. If we wish to extend agency and autonomy to our students, and to see them as essential components in the teaching and learning process, trust appears to be one of the most crucial emotions. Trust in ourselves and our students is also crucial if we wish to be creative and take risks in the classroom (for example, engaging in peer feedback).

CONCLUSION

This chapter has tried to show that good relationships between higher education teachers and their students and between students is integral to the educational endeavour of drawing students into (inter)disciplinary and professional ways of thinking and being. Yet, there is also a more overarching responsibility that lies with the policy-makers – as discussed in Chapter 5 on Contexts – and with the institutions in which we teach. A useful concept for thinking about the institution versus the individual is the feminist concept of a 'political ethics of care'. For Tronto (2010) caring is not the responsibility of the individual alone, but of institutions which can be explicit about how they undertake their obligations to care for students. Nevertheless, as Pollard (1982) argues, the teacher is the 'intervening variable' between the macro culture of the institution and the culture at the micro level of students' lives. If this is so, then we have a responsibility to interpret the values and norms of the institution for our students.

However, it is important to guard against becoming subsumed within the caring relationship because we are part of a larger societal process. This means it is important to ask when to show care to a group or individual students, and when it would be more productive to invest energy in supporting change at a policy or more managerial level. The responsibility for conducive relationships is broad and sometimes it is necessary to lobby for conducive learning environments at the institutional level. Collaborative classroom relationships are not only based on kindness and generosity, but also require us to inter-rogate unstated norms and power relations, and to participate in robust dialogue.

This chapter has not provided a series of tips on how to foster productive working relationships. It has stressed as key ingredients some of the key themes of this book: reflection, self-awareness, dialogue and being critical. While some teachers may naturally have a warm or charismatic disposition and may effortlessly communicate a caring relationship to students, most of us will require some conscious and overt attention to our own development and ability to generate these relationships. The chapter has demonstrated that positive relationships are not one-way where the teacher communicates to the student: in the current connected and networked world, relationships are multi-dimensional and multi-directional. They require conscious attention to how the learning environment is constructed, and the processes that are set in motion.

KEY READINGS

On how to create an environment in which students feel they belong, see:

Thomas, L. (2012) *Building Student Engagement and Belonging in Higher Education at a Time of Change: Final Report from the What Works? Student Retention & Success Programme*. London: Paul Hamlyn Foundation. heacademy.ac.uk/system/files/what_works_final_report.pdf

Kay, J., Dunne, L. and Hutchinson, J. (2010) *Rethinking the Values of Higher Education: Students as Change Agents?* Gloucester: Quality Assurance Agency. dera.ioe.ac.uk/1193

On relationships and feedback, see:

Boud, D. and Molloy, E. (2013) *Feedback in Higher and Professional Education: Understanding It and Doing It Well*. London: Routledge.

On 'Crafting a Teaching Persona', see:

Lang, R. (2006) 'Crafting a teaching persona', *The Higher Education Chronicle*, 6 February. chronicle.com/article/Crafting-a-Teaching-Persona/46671

For examples of teacher–student contracts, see:

home.snu.edu/~hculbert/contract.htm

courses.nus.edu.sg/course/elltankw/history/contract.htm

teachingcenter.wustl.edu/resources/inclusive-teaching-learning/establishing-ground-rules

Chapter 7
Engagement

How does our engagement with teaching influence student learning?

INTRODUCTION

The 'fourth wall' is a well-known term used in the theatre, which describes the invisible 'wall' that stands between the audience and the performers on stage. The fourth wall places the audience in a passive mode, and the performers on stage play out their roles as though the audience does not exist. To what extent can we (still) see the existence of the fourth wall in university teaching, and what would it mean to break down the fourth wall so that teachers engage in ways that support student learning? Breaking down the fourth wall requires interest in and knowledge about student learning, and a corresponding commitment to teaching well. While there is a lot of literature on 'good teaching', there is far less on how each of us as academics gets to that point of teaching well (Leibowitz et al. 2012).

See Chapter 4

TLRP Principles

Two principles are of particular relevance to this chapter on engagement:

Principle 2: Effective teaching and learning depends on the scholarship and learning of all those educators who teach and research to support the learning of others. The need for lecturers, teachers and trainers to learn through doing research to improve their knowledge, expertise and skills for teaching should be recognized and supported.

Principle 9: Effective teaching and learning engages with expertise and valued forms of knowledge in disciplines and subjects. Teaching and learning should engage students with the concepts, key skills and processes, modes of discourse, ways of thinking and practising, and attitudes and relationships that are most valued in their subject. Students need to understand what constitutes quality, standards and expertise in different settings and subjects.

Traditionally, the role of teaching in higher education has been part of a broader academic role including research, academic service (e.g. administration, committee work) and in recent times public engagement (particularly in the sciences). Unlike nearly every other formal area of teaching, teachers within higher education often come to this role tangentially, accidentally, or even reluctantly. Our education background is unlikely to have been in the area of 'teaching' and, even once taking up the role, expectations about what it means to teach within higher education can be conflicted and confusing. Often academics are recruited on the basis of research output rather than teaching ability, and teaching is sometimes seen as merely a distraction from the 'real' work of research. Even at institutions which promote themselves as focused on teaching, heavy teaching loads and high administrative requirements can make teaching a procedural activity, rather than a creative one focused on student–teacher interrelationships and interactions.

A traditional solution to this issue of balancing roles has been to consider them separately. Hence, teaching is considered as a distinct and separate part of the broader academic role, with few if any links to our research roles. Indeed, many early career academics in particular often find that the subjects they teach have little direct relevance to their research specialisms. Teaching within higher education often seems a paradoxical part of our role:

> Academic work could be characterised as a hybrid of different activities which are difficult to fit together. The esteem of the academic community and the career development of the individual are still firmly based on research, but everyday life is more and more dominated by teaching, planning, administration and development activities. (Jauhiainen et al. 2009, p. 421)

In addition, the way in which we learn to be teachers is therefore also considered separately from other aspects of our role as academics (Åkerlind 2011).

The separation of research and teaching roles can create tensions for academics when they come to engage with teaching, particularly in research-intensive departments. There is also an increasing body of evidence to suggest that academic labour can be divided along gender lines, with academic women tending to do more of the teaching and pastoral support of students than male academics, who tend to spend more time on research (Heijstra et al. 2017). For many universities, teaching activities generate a large amount of income and constitute the 'bread and butter' work of the organization, and yet for individual academics it is often the pursuit of research that generates rewards and progression. Pursuing a research career is often seen as more prestigious than a teaching career, which is an aspect of the academic role that some women academics find problematic because they place high value on their teaching (Kandiko Howson et al. 2018).

There can therefore be pressures on academics to make choices about how they orient their time and energies. Often, focusing on either teaching or research is felt to be done at the expense of one or the other. Yet it is possible (and probably prudent) to come to a view of teaching and research as intricately intertwined. For example, teaching can offer the opportunity for our research to come alive as we bring it to our students in the classroom. Also, the rewards of engaging with our teaching and doing it well are sometimes less tangible than the rewards and prestige of doing research really well, but fostering a love of learning a subject in students is in itself a highly engaging and deeply satisfactory experience. Finally, our own engagement with teaching is intertwined with our students' engagement with their learning. To be committed and engaged in teaching, and enabling students to see the passion we have for both research and teaching, can help foster a sense of joy in learning in our students.

RELATIONS BETWEEN TEACHING AND RESEARCH

Understanding the commonalities between teaching and research

In Kandiko Howson et al.'s (2018) research, a number of academics described how they valued their contributions to teaching and student learning, but felt that the institutional structures tended to value and recognize research rather than teaching. Within this context, teaching and research can feel as though they are in tension with each other. Åkerlind (2011) observed that academics often find their own way through these tensions, and that 'there is not a simple linear relationship between the two phenomena, with a range of combinations of different ways of understanding or experiencing being found' (p. 189).

There are a number of possibly complex combinations and manifestations of the relationships between teaching and research (Coate et al. 2001). Doctoral supervision, for example, is often viewed as falling somewhere between teaching and research. Some academics teach their research through the textbook that they have written; others use their teaching on a specialist module to help the development of their research monograph. Social media increasingly offers opportunities for academics to share their research with wider audiences, including their students.

It is important to remember that a unifying thread that runs through both activities is learning itself. As Rowland et al. (1998) explain:

> [T]eaching and research are both about learning: our learning, our students' learning. Both require a spirit of enquiry, reflection, critique and, most of all, of passion. They are also both fundamentally social activities. Without a context in which we face the challenge of presenting ideas through teaching, our ideas become sterile, out of touch with ordinary life, and inward looking. Teaching which is not accompanied by our own enquiry, reflection and passion for a subject matter in which we are wholly engaged, becomes merely a technical service to customers, the purpose of which is no concern of ours. (p. 134)

Understanding the separation between teaching and research

Whilst we argue that engagement in teaching and in research are fundamentally related, it is still important to understand that institutional pressures can work to separate them. A particular challenge for teaching is that the vital signposts of rewards and recognition understood in the research environment may be harder to recognize when assessing teaching quality. Research achievements are recorded in terms of published papers, research grants, books and conferences. But what are the markers of teaching success? How do we know we are engaging with the role in a helpful way?

In recent years, many universities have developed much more sophisticated promotions criteria to reward success and/or leadership in teaching. It is now possible, even in some research-intensive universities, to be promoted to full Professorship on the basis of education leadership (Fung and Gordon 2016). For a number of universities that have traditionally focused on research, the need to assert the parity of esteem between education and research is helping to ensure education enhancements and improvements to the student experience (especially in a context of high tuition fees) are prioritized. There are therefore opportunities for those committed to education to focus their careers on building a profile as an education leader.

However, there is still a discernible separation between teaching and research, and academics may struggle to find ways of making connections between them. Part of the problem may be that we still lack the same conventions about discussing our teaching as we do with our research. Teaching in many disciplines still occurs behind closed doors. Peer observation schemes are well established in some institutions but strongly resisted in others.

In this extract, an academic describes how she managed to alienate her colleagues by talking about her teaching:

> I think a lot of people don't want to talk about teaching partly because I think they find it very threatening, so if I was bouncing around the common room going 'Oh aren't they [my students] wonderful, they've just been so nice and I've done this exercise and it worked!' and I think there was quite a lot of hostility and quite a lot of naivety on my part about talking in that way, about teaching and being enthusiastic about it because it's not part of the research culture of a research university to be that enthusiastic about the teaching and the ideas that you see in the students. (McArthur et al. 2004, p. 52)

So far we have discussed how engagement with teaching is not without challenges, but that such engagement can benefit from considering our teaching within a holistic sense of our academic role and identity (this is equally true whether we are on 'lecturer' or 'teaching fellow' contracts). In the next sections, we move on to consider some of the practical manifestations of engagement with teaching. What do we bring to this role? How do we understand our relationship to our students' learning? How does engagement develop in practice; that is, how is it formed by the experience of actually teaching and working with students? How do we sustain ourselves as teachers in higher education while there is so much change and challenge all around?

The rest of this chapter explores how engagement with teaching is formed and re-formed. These include: students' relationship to specialist disciplinary knowledge and community membership; and the importance of our relationships with students to our engagement as teachers (and hence to their engagement as learners). In emphasizing the shifting, evolving and dynamic nature of engagement, and situating it in the reality of actual teaching and real students, we seek to avoid approaching teaching as a dull, procedural or unfulfilling part of our academic role. Instead, we stress the benefits of personalization, academic challenge and critical reflection.

THE ROLE OF KNOWLEDGE IN ENGAGING WITH TEACHING

It has been argued that a defining feature of higher education is the nature of knowledge engaged with, generated and critiqued within this sector (McArthur 2013). This knowledge is largely based, or grounded within, specialist disciplinary areas that encourage knowledge to be critically examined in dynamic and robust ways. Even where academics are based within an interdisciplinary area, this too requires the rigorous base of the disciplines that feed into it (Rowland 2003; McArthur 2010). Thus, one of the most important things we bring to our teaching is this disciplinary expertise.

New academic staff can face particular challenges when bringing their disciplinary expertise to their teaching practice. As recent postgraduate or doctoral students, researchers or professionals in another sector, their disciplinary or professional experience is likely to be highly specialized and focused. In contrast, new academics are often given more general teaching, perhaps in lower undergraduate years. Sometimes these staff are used to fill gaps in the teaching provision and slotted in to vacancies, regardless of any links to their particular specialism. For these reasons, our disciplinary expertise is important to our teaching engagement, but the linkages are by no means always easy or obvious. However, it is important to avoid simply adding teaching skills onto existing disciplinary knowledge, as if the two are unconnected. As Rowland et al. (1998, p. 135) argue:

> We will not turn an academic historian into a history teacher merely by making her attend a course in teaching skills. What is required, is to understand the connection between the methods and field of enquiry (say, history) and the means by which we can entice others (our students) into this.

In this section we consider five ways in which our subject specialist knowledge intertwines and influences our engagement with teaching. We suggest that key aspects of the role of teacher in higher education include: making knowledge accessible to students; ensuring that even simplified forms of that knowledge retain accuracy and disciplinary integrity; establishing the credibility of the disciplinary area, in part by relating it to the broader social world; orchestrating different moments, or stages, as students engage with a discipline, for example, initial exposure to a disciplinary area through to more complex levels; and finally, how the way students experience our discipline enables us to reflect on our engagement with teaching that discipline. Running throughout each of these aspects is an ongoing theme of how we balance our role and that of our students. Are we there as a detached facilitator as they navigate the unfamiliar disciplinary territory, or should we be more interventionist, even in the name of self-directed learning?

Making knowledge accessible

The notion of the disciplinary specialist may seem at odds with notions of self-directed learning or student-focused teaching. If the students are to be free to direct, shape and pursue their own learning, then surely the role of teaching becomes subordinate, peripheral even? In this chapter, we suggest a more complex interaction between being student-focused and how disciplinary expertise is used within teaching. The choice is not between a teacher-focused form of didactic lecturing *at* students and a supposedly student-friendly approach of standing back to become facilitators on the boundary.

In a series of works, Northedge (2003a; Northedge, 2003b; Northedge and McArthur 2009) has explored in detail how an academic can share their highly specialized knowledge with students, who are students because they do not yet share that knowledge. His view on engagement with the role of teacher has been formed over many years of experience with adult students at the Open University (OU). He writes:

> Early on I found that adult students strongly resisted the notion of my hovering in the background, gently facilitating. Some pointed out that they were paying good money to be 'taught'. They wanted to use their hard won study hours learning what educated people know, not 'exploring' collaboratively with 'uneducated' peers . . . Adult OU students, many with chequered educational backgrounds, tend to be studying in order to catch up; to put themselves on an equal footing with graduate colleagues and friends. They want to be able to read the same books and articles as them, and join in their discussions. They want to work their way into a relevant knowledge community and be accepted as legitimate participants. To this end, they want their teachers to take the initiative in helping them get there and they do not want them to hold back from using their expertise. (Northedge 2003a, p. 170)

In contrast, several academics interviewed by Ashwin (2006) in a study of tutorials at Oxford University, made comments suggesting tutors there take a much more background role. For example:

> In the tutorial I try to facilitate the discussion and fade into the background as much as I can, again it's one of those things that depends on the students but I normally try to fade into the background and facilitate something, to give it a purpose and this is what we are thinking about. I bring the conversation back on course if it strays too far away from the basic structure. (Ashwin 2006)

In the differences between the quoted perceptions in Northedge's and Ashwin's research about the nature of engagement with teaching, several broad issues are illuminated. First, Northedge is discussing large and/or long-distance learning contexts, while the Oxford tutorial is noted as one based on a very small number of students. Second, Northedge is explicitly dealing with a course taken largely by adult learners (i.e. not straight from school). Third, the student intake of the Open University and Oxford University tend to be quite different. Oxford tends to recruit high-achieving school leavers, while in Northedge's own words, the Open University attracts people who want to 'catch up' or get on an 'equal footing' with peers and graduates. These are people with 'chequered educational backgrounds'.

There is, however, also common ground between the two approaches, and this lies in the importance of discussion to students' meaning making. Yet it appears to be what students bring to these discussions that most highlights the differences between the two approaches. In the Oxford examples, the focus is on the ideas that the students bring:

> Their role is really to be able to communicate what they've read, I ask them to summarise what are the three key points they have made in their essay. (Ashwin 2006, p. 658)

In these accounts, the focus is mainly on students communicating what they have read, and critically analysing it. But the idea that such communication might be foreign to the students is not mentioned – it may not be relevant in this context perhaps. In Northedge's view, such situations can be hard going because we assume too much of our students, in the name of being student-centred:

> If HE [Higher Education] is to offer genuine opportunities to diverse student audiences, we cannot persist with models of teaching as 'knowledge transmission', nor rely on unfocused student-centred approaches that leave the students floundering within everyday discourse. (Northedge 2003b, p. 31)

Another reason for the apparent difference in Northedge's approach to the role of teacher and that of the Oxford tutors may revolve around the degree of experience of the students. In a sense, the two examples highlight potentially different moments in the process by which a student comes to engage with an unfamiliar discipline. Northedge's (2003a) work is a particular insight into the role teachers have in supporting students' transition from the unknown to the known, the unfamiliar to the familiar. The Oxford tutors are largely picking up the story further on, after initial engagement and when the focus turns to the nature of engagement.

Northedge's work is interesting because he places a great deal of emphasis on the beginnings of students coming to know a specialist discipline. His discussion of teaching starts with the very first act, so even before we start to share meanings, we must capture the attention of students whose knowledge of the disciplinary subject is limited, or drawn largely from popular culture and images of it. The role of the teacher is to find ways to link what the students might already be familiar with to the specialist subject matter of higher education. One way to begin this is to consider the differences between certain words and how they are used in everyday conversation as compared within disciplinary discourses. For example, *precedent* means something particular in the discipline of law, and something more general in everyday conversation. The same is true of *context* in archaeology, *catalyst* in chemistry, and many other examples across all of higher education's disciplines of an everyday word also having a specialist meaning. It may be the case that a student's prior understanding of the meaning of a word clouds their ability to make sense of the meaning it has within a disciplinary context, and care may need to be taken to help them learn the new meaning.

Ambrose et al. (2010) provide comprehensive examples of the challenges that students face when learning disciplinary knowledge, and offers advice for supporting their learning. We have discussed a number of sets of principles of effective teaching and learning in higher education in Chapters 4 and 6. Ambrose et al. (2010) set out Seven Principles of Learning, each of which includes different disciplinary examples of how and where students might get 'stuck'. The Principles are:

1 Students' prior knowledge can help or hinder learning.

2 How students organize knowledge influences how they learn and apply what they know.

3 Students' motivation determines, directs, and sustains what they do to learn.

4 To develop mastery, students must acquire component skills, practise integrating them, and know when to apply what they have learned.

5 Goal-directed practice coupled with targeted feedback enhances the quality of students' learning.

6 Students' current level of development interacts with the social, emotional and intellectual climate of the course to impact learning.

7 To become self-directed learners, students must learn to monitor and adjust their approaches to learning.

One easily understandable example that is covered in the book is the commonly used concept of 'negative reinforcement' in Psychology. Many students will associate the term 'negative' with something bad, such as a punishment. The concept of 'negative reinforcement' is usually a positive process, however, intended to encourage positive behaviour change. The example given in the book is a mother who promises to stop nagging her son if he cleans his room: a rather different proposition from punishing an untidy child. For some students, however, their prior knowledge of the term 'negative' will trigger the wrong associations and will distort their ability to learn the disciplinary meaning of the term.

Reflective Activity 7.1 Enabling student engagement with unfamiliar knowledge

Consider an example from your own subject area of a particularly fundamental or important idea, theory, concept or example.

What sort of 'bridge' could you provide to help students unfamiliar with this idea to move towards greater familiarity? Is there an idea from popular culture or popular science that could act as an interim form of understanding, or a staging post?

How can you ensure that students have confidently moved over to engage upon this unfamiliar territory?

Balancing the complexity and accessibility of knowledge

Undergraduate, and especially early-year teaching, may require a simplification of our disciplinary knowledge, but this needs to be done in ways that are not misleading. Looking from the student perspective, we fail in our duty as teachers if we provide a false impression of the discipline and its knowledge, and justify this in terms of 'they are only first years'. The problem with this is that if students are given a false sense of the discipline in first year, at what point are they then ready for the 'real thing'.

Stevenson (2011) emphasises the difference between simplifying knowledge (while retaining accuracy) and misrepresenting it. Figure 7.1 shows two different representations of the structure of the atom. The representation on the left illustrates a very simple model for the structure of the atom, i.e. that the atom has a central nucleus surrounded by electrons moving within prescribed volumes. This simple model can subsequently be used as a starting framework to construct a more complex understanding as a student progresses. The representation on the right, on the other hand, is a common misrepresentation of the structure of the atom. It was named 'the plum pudding' model of the atom as its central idea is of electrons randomly distributed in a sphere of positive charge, rather like dried fruit randomly distributed in a sphere of pudding. If the starting model is a misrepresentation, as in the representation on the right, students are unable to use it to construct more complex understandings. The challenge in teaching, therefore, is to retain accuracy and to avoid misrepresentation when simplifying knowledge.

An important aspect of complexity is also to be open with students about the debates, arguments and controversies around the subject knowledge. They may not be able to fully understand this, but it is vital to know that such debates occur. If we present knowledge as fixed and uncontested, we cannot then despair that students lack critical thinking.

Figure 7.1
Representations of the structure of an atom

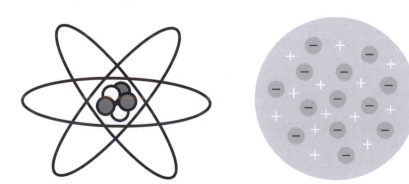

> ### Reflective Activity 7.2 Enabling complex engagement
>
> Think of a very complex idea from your own subject area that you need students to understand.
>
> How do you currently enable students to understand this?
>
> To what extent does this approach achieve both accessibility and complexity?
>
> Can you think of any other ways of enabling understanding of this complex idea?

Credibility: why students need to know that knowledge matters

While it can be hard to share specialist knowledge and practices with the novice student, this expertise is also an important basis for the role of university teacher because it provides one of the greatest motivations to learn. It is through this expertise that our credibility as teachers is established (Strang et al. 2016). Students value this, so if we can engage in our teaching in a way that communicates this expertise and credibility, our students will benefit in terms of their own engagement. This is particularly true in some clinical and professional disciplines: students value highly the experiences of people who have done what they aspire to do.

As the previous section explored, subject expertise alone cannot provide a solid foundation for engagement with teaching or learning. A teacher must also have what Rowland (2005) describes as a love of subject and a love of sharing one's subject knowledge (Rowland 2005; McArthur 2009; Craig 2019).

A love and respect for your own subject matter is essential to establish the credibility of what students are expected to learn. It is essential to establishing a sense of 'why does this matter?' Without this students are, rightly, reluctant to engage with a subject. Students are able to pick up when a lecturer is disengaged from their own subject matter. Consider this vignette from a Professor of Economics:

> I remember going to a[n economics] lecture by my friend and he asked me to come along and listen to him. He didn't do very well on the teaching evaluations and as soon as he opened his mouth I could see why he didn't do very well because he thought economics was useless. His whole thing was, it wasn't as if he was ranting about it, he was fairly laid back, temperate type of personality but on and on he went, it was all negative and it was astonishing. (Jones 2011, pp. 114–15)

In contrast, in a classic study of highly respected teachers by Andrews et al. (1996), they found that a respect for knowledge sat alongside other forms of respect such as for the activity of teaching itself and respect for students. In addition, a 'respect for self' was critical: evidence of their belief 'they had something to offer and that they perceived themselves as being there primarily to help students succeed' (p. 88). They also found that there was a tendency to emphasize the importance of learning as meaningful to students in terms of the ways in which they found it useful in their own lives. This approach appeared to make students more likely to take responsibility for their own learning.

This suggests something more than simply discrete bits of knowledge, but rather a broader sense of the nature of disciplinary knowledge. As Kreber (2001) observes: 'at a time of rapid social, political and technological changes ... the content or factual knowledge presently taught may not be sufficient, let alone useful, throughout one's lifetime' (p. 218). For this reason, she argues that students require critical thinking and self-direction so that they can apply and assess knowledge in a changing world.

Situating students' experiences within disciplinary communities

Some academics find it particularly challenging to work with students who are completely new to a subject area. This is not only because of the challenge of the unfamiliar knowledge, but due to perceptions about the way in which such students approach learning. It is one thing to try to share, accurately and credibly, unfamiliar subject knowledge with students; it is another thing to have to combine this with leading them into new and unfamiliar ways to approach that learning. However, genuine engagement always has to be understood in terms of both the nature of knowledge being learned and how students approach their learning.

Northedge (2003b) outlines the sort of orchestration that a teacher must engage with when faced with a diverse student population. In part, this can be between students with different experiences, as well as different levels of subject knowledge:

> by presenting a strong narrative with a variety of detail and an emphasis on human experience, it enables a broad student audience to follow a single flow of discourse, each engaging with it according to their own level of experience and understanding.

This ties with the notion of enabling, or orchestrating, opportunities for students' academic growth within a subject area, but taking account that this will differ between students. In the study by Andrews et al. (1996), the academics they interviewed specifically mentioned the ways in which they could encourage student growth:

> They spoke of encouraging independent thought (e.g. through the use of discussions and other interactive strategies), and of creating an awareness of the alternatives and choices that students had. In doing so, they attempted to create a degree of excitement in the students.

Kreber (2001) suggests that case studies provide a particularly useful way of enabling such academic growth within a specialist knowledge area. She argues that the strength of a case study approach is the ways in which 'concrete experience (examples) and abstract conceptualization (concepts)' can be combined with active or experiential learning.

As we discuss in Chapters 9 and 10, a clear aspect of situating students' learning experiences comes through the design of the courses or programmes within which this is to occur. However, many academics, especially people reasonably new to teaching, do not feel that they are part of the design process because this is the responsibility of another colleague or has already been done. But good course design is never static; it is always part of an evolving process. Hence, all teachers should be active within a course to enable the design and delivery to enable the development of self-directed learning.

Reflecting back: how sharing our disciplinary knowledge helps us to understand teaching and learning

From our perspectives as academics, the process of looking at our specialist knowledge through the eyes of someone new to the field can be useful to our own broader practice. Rowland et al. (1998) suggest that to enable the unfamiliar subject to become 'more transparent to the relative newcomer to the field of study . . . academics should not see themselves as setting aside their enquiry into their field, but rather as broadening it, deepening it, or transforming it, so that it can engage the interests of students' (p. 135).

While many academics remain sceptical about teaching as something to be learned, there are now many compelling examples of how academics can change their approach through engagement with both experience and scholarship. For example, Macmillan and McLean (2005) provide a useful example of how their experience of teaching led them to believe that things could be done better. It was this experience combined with engagement with the educational literature that really led them to rethink how they engaged in teaching:

> despite having used a range of 'active learning' approaches, for example students working on various exercises in a combination of small and large groups, the feeling that more could be done to develop active learning in tutorials remained. It was, however, the relationship drawn in the theoretical, pedagogic literature between student learning and the assessment regime that was especially thought-provoking.

One challenge in practice is when the way we believe we should engage seems at odds with what we are actually doing. Indeed, it is a challenge alone to be aware when this is happening. This can sometimes happen if practice becomes too routine or repetitive. Structuring all educational experiences in the same way may lead us to miss when that structure does not fit with the backgrounds, assumptions or preferences of our students. This is where Brookfield's (2017) critical reflection using four lenses, outlined in Chapter 3, can be so useful in picking up on mismatches between our beliefs on teaching and what is happening in practice as illustrated in Case Study 7.1.

Case Study 7.1 Alan – Archaeology Lecturer

An archaeology lecturer, Alan, was asked to give a series of lectures to students on a forensic course. Here the challenge was taking knowledge from one disciplinary area and applying it in another. Despite carefully planned, and seemingly clear lectures – with lots of examples of archaeology in a forensic context – Alan was dismayed when he came to mark the students' exams. What he had said, and what they had heard, were very different.

The exam question asked students to consider a principle from archaeology in a forensic context. To his dismay, Alan found that the majority of students supported the archaeological principle with an example from Roman Britain. He had never talked about Romans, but it would appear that when he talked about archaeology, the students seemed to interpret this in terms of familiar contexts – i.e. archaeology equated with Roman history.

(From McArthur, 2009)

ENGAGEMENT WITH OUR STUDENTS

In this final section, the focus is to more explicitly consider the interconnections between how we engage in teaching and how our students engage with their own learning experiences. A particular emphasis is on how the concept of student engagement is facilitating new forms of co-partnerships with students, enabling them to more directly shape their learning experiences. The second part of this section will draw on aspects discussed so far: the personal qualities and attitudes that shape how we teach and interact with students.

Students at the educational interface

The concept of student engagement in higher education emerged in the US in the 1980s, when Astin (1984) proposed a link between levels of student 'involvement' ('the amount of physical and psychological energy that the student devotes to the academic experience' 1984: 518) and student success. Subsequently, national surveys were developed in the US and Australia to measure the extent to which students were participating in formal and extra-curricular learning opportunities during their time at university. The presumption of this early work, which largely remains with us, is that students who show high levels of engagement in 'educationally purposeful activities' have more successful outcomes and improved satisfaction levels. This premise – that student learning is enhanced if it is a 'joint proposition' between the students and the institution – is intuitively sensible and provides enough rationale for many teachers and institutions to invest resources and effort into improving the levels of engagement of students.

However, the multidimensional nature of learning experiences presents challenges for researchers who are hoping to find straightforward correlations between high levels of engagement and positive learning outcomes. Ultimately, the success of student engagement initiatives is dependent on the complex interplay of factors within what has been termed by Kahu and Nelson (2018) as the 'educational interface'. The education interface is a dynamic, psychosocial space which recognizes the agency of students in helping to shape their experiences. It acknowledges that the ways in which students engage with their education experience involves a range of factors including their prior learning experiences; personality; perceptions of workload; and a range of institutional factors that influence student behaviours in different ways. The practices of teachers, and students' perceptions of these practices, are clearly a very important part of the educational interface, which is why we will go on to discuss attitudes to teaching in the next section.

Student engagement initiatives can raise interesting and challenging questions about who has power and authority in determining the student learning experience. However, the main drivers are to ensure that students become active participants in their learning, as well as deeper and more reflective learners. Some institutions have implemented university-wide partnership projects with their students, as we explore in Case Study 7.2. Yet there are many other ways in which teachers can create co-partnership opportunities with students, particularly through curriculum design (Bovill, Cook-Sather and Felten 2011).

Case Study 7.2 Bryn Mawr Students as Learners and Teachers

One of the longest-standing partnerships between students and academic staff is the Students as Learners and Teachers (SaLT) initiative at Bryn Mawr and Haverford Colleges in the US. Established in 2006 in the Teaching and Learning Institute, SaLT pairs undergraduate students, who are employed as pedagogical consultants, with academic staff who bring their disciplinary expertise. As described by one of the founders of SaLT, Alison Cook-Sather: 'These pairs work in semester-long partnerships through which they explore, affirm, and, where appropriate, revise teaching practices in an effort to create welcoming and productively challenging learning environments' (Cook-Sather 2015, p. 4). Partnerships have explored such issues as inclusive pedagogies and inclusive practices, with students observing their academic staff partner in the classroom, taking notes, and then sharing the notes afterwards. The dialogues that are opened up through these partnership discussions are focused on enhancing education practices. Reflective practice is a key element of the programme (Cook-Sather 2015).

(Based on Cook-Sather and Des-Ogugua, 2019)

Some criticisms of student engagement have emerged that suggest there can be a tendency to focus on short-term, somewhat performative conceptualizations of student engagement, which arguably undermines the longer-term goals of enabling students to thrive as productive citizens in life (e.g. Barnacle and Dall'Alba 2017; Zepke 2018). Barnacle and

Dall-Alba (2017) have extended the scope of our understandings of student engagement by suggesting that it is underpinned by the concept of 'care', and a sense of care for the students. They explore the idea of care, particularly as developed through the works of philosophers Heidegger and Nel Noddings, to suggest that educators need to look beyond the short-term considerations of student engagement surveys, given that: 'Narrow approaches to student engagement overlook broader issues addressed by care, such as what education contributes to who students are becoming and their freedom to become in multiple ways' (Barnacle and Dall'Alba 2017).

What might an approach to student engagement, underpinned by a commitment to care, look like? If we take the example in the Case Study of Bryn Mawr, where student consultants work side by side with a member of academic staff, it might mean that both the teacher and the student approach each other with empathy and responsibility for the relationship. Both of the partners might feel challenged by each other, but both are able to grow and learn through their dialogue. Approaching teaching in this way is certainly a far cry from the 'sage on the stage', or the performer behind the fourth wall. It may seem unrealistic or idealistic in an age of mass higher education systems, but the underpinning ethos is hopefully one that could inform our encounters with each other. We will, in the final section, consider what other values might underpin our approaches to teaching.

Understanding ourselves and our students

It is hopefully clear by now that our personal qualities and attitudes cannot be understood in isolation from other factors such as our backgrounds and specialist knowledge. Nowhere is this link more clearly made than in Rowland's (2005) concept of intellectual love – a love of enquiry and discovery that fuels both teaching and research. Here he uses the example of a lecturer in Dentistry:

> Thus, for our academic dentist, the more his love of dentistry is enhanced by his own enquiries into dentistry, the greater will be the intellectual love which inspires his teaching. This is not to suggest that teachers should teach students their particular specialism, but that their teaching is fuelled by the love that motives their specialist research.

For Rowland, one of the key dispositions of a university teacher is to try to share or engender this form of intellectual love in his or her students. Whilst we may not all be comfortable thinking about teaching in terms of love, it does further reinforce that a focus on our students is a vital part of a disposition to teach within higher education. There is a transformational moment when we think of our subject matter not simply in terms of what we know, but what our students need to learn. Here is how one academic described this moment:

> And another thing that really stuck, that I thought was great, was the idea that this isn't about you and what you know; it's about the student experience, and it's about what they learn rather than what you teach. (quoted in Kahn 2009, p. 201)

Nixon (2001) describes this moment as shift in 'moral bases' of the academic. It represents a reconceptualizing of the role of university teacher. He explains:

> The choice, however, is not between a hopelessly compromised and over-managed professionalism, on the one hand, and the return to the grand old days of 'amateurism', on the other. Rather, the choice is between different versions of professionalism that represent different values and priorities and that constitute different moral bases.

Here again the idea that teaching should be more than a procedural adherence to institutional requirements is emphasized. We can extend this by considering scholarship on teaching and learning that looks at teaching from the perspectives of explicit values (as we have touched on already), such as care, virtue, hope and kindness (Nixon 2008; Clegg and Rowland 2010; Barnacle and Dall'Alba 2017). This is far removed from any notion of the teacher as impartial transmitter of knowledge. Here the relationship with students is foregrounded in the formation of the disposition to teach. Clegg and Rowland (2010) argue that kindness is not a new idea or practice in teaching, but that it is under threat within the context of greater managerialism and commodification in higher education. They argue that we must celebrate it as an aspect of teaching more explicitly and openly. Further, they recognize the differences between teaching in higher education and other formal settings. Assumptions that all teachers 'care' become more complex in higher education, according to Clegg and Rowland, because of the pull of other influences, notably disciplinary loyalties and research priorities.

The multi-faceted nature of the academic role can encourage a sidelining of care and caring (Lynch et al. 2009). In these circumstances, care can be passed around within an academic community, often in highly gendered ways. Even attempts to provide greater pastoral support to students can artificially divide the pastoral and academic. In contrast, a study of six academics in mathematics who were regarded by colleagues as 'outstanding' demonstrated the links between caring and students' well-being, and their attitudes to teaching and learning. In this study, academics shared 'expressions of concern, interest, and affection for students' (Weston and McAlpine 1998, p. 147). Examples included:

> 'Be gentle about expectations of how fast they can learn.'
> 'It is how much you care rather than how much you know; caring is very significant.'
> 'Care for, respect, love students.'
> 'Talk to, get to know students as individuals.'
> 'Build their confidence.'

In another study, 'strong and respectful' student–teacher relationships 'were seen by all of the participants to be the foundation for excellent teaching' (Andrews et al. 1996, p. 87). The authors explain:

> It would be very difficult for good teaching to occur in the absence of good relationships. Relationship development included clarifying roles and responsibilities, encouraging student discussion and interaction, and being available. Consistent with the caveat noted above with respect to self-revelation, the relationship was defined from an intellectual context. Although some talked of personal relationships, the common theme across all

participants was that the bond that is established between professor and student is first and foremost an intellectual one, focusing on concepts and ideas.

This study also emphasized students and teachers as occupying different, but equal, academic roles. Emphasis was placed on respecting the integrity of students. However, such shared respect is perhaps sometimes harder in practice than we might like to admit. Gordon (2005, p. 427) discusses this in terms of his own experience as a Jew, with progressive views, within a Mormon university in Utah. He describes the ongoing struggle between his commitment to his students, and his knowledge that their beliefs clash so fundamentally with his own:

> I don't hate the Mormons. But I do hate the Mormons. At least sometimes. I haven't *really* gotten over, or beyond, my anti-Mormonism. I, and every progressive faculty member I know, struggles with it constantly, and not always valiantly or successfully . . . But you can't hate your students and teach them. Not if you're me. So every semester, every month, every week, every day, I fight a little struggle. (p. 427)

This is a rare piece of teaching and learning scholarship that openly admits that sometimes we do not find our students very likeable – and yet we also know that this is a very precarious basis for a teaching–learning relationship. On the other side of the coin, Clegg and Rowland (2010) suggest 'that speaking (or writing) about kindness in the context of higher education brings about embarrassment' (p. 721).

Care, kindness and respect can be lost in our understandings of teaching when the focus is solely on students' performance, or outcomes (Clegg and Rowland 2010; Barnacle and Dall-Alba 2017), and not on the processes and experiences along the way. Another problem lies in confusing kindness with a lack of academic rigour. However, as Clegg and Rowland (2010) explained, kindness is an academic virtue:

> Kindness as a public virtue, built upon a commitment to social justice, embraces critique. In educational research the term 'critical friend' is used by action researchers to describe the relationship between co-enquirers (be they researchers or students) who share a commitment to social justice. It combines the kindness of friendship with the critique of the educator. (p. 723)

It is important, however, not to confuse such kindness with leniency. As Clegg and Rowland (2010) also explained:

> In wanting a kind teacher, the student may be confusing this with one who will be lenient, soft, prepared to overlook errors and shallowness of thought. In wanting to be kind, a teacher might not be motivated by the learner's needs but simply avoiding responsibility for the student's confrontation with the inevitable pain of learning. The confusion with leniency rests on seeing kindness as emotion. (p. 274)

Just as Andrews et al. (1996) noted that respect should include respect for self as a teacher in higher education, so too would we extend the notion of kindness to being kind to oneself. Teaching in higher education, with numerous pressures and a balancing of roles, can be very stressful. It is important to be aware that fear or anxiety about teaching can be a very disabling experience (Rowland et al. 1998). On the other hand, as academics become more comfortable teaching, the process becomes less of an effort (Ăkerlind 2011).

Another common problem in practice, once we are actually teaching students, is to discover that it is harder, or at least even more complicated, than we imagined. Some academics approach teaching with an assumption that 'their purposes and good intentions would be communicated by their general attitude and approach with students' (Wilcox 1996, p. 172). However, Wilcox goes on to argue that this approach leaves the teacher with little room to move in the classroom: with no explicit strategy they have little to reflect on and consider in terms of how they might do things differently.

Another difficulty in practice is the actual sharing of control necessary for this type of teaching–learning interaction. As Wilcox (1996) explained:

> Self-directed learning includes, by definition, some aspects of learner control over the instructional process. Instructors who do not share important course decisions with students are indicating through their actions that they are not committed to self-directed learning. These instructors may expect students to take responsibility for their learning, yet at the same time limit the students' ability to do so by retaining their institutionalised right to hold final decision-making power in their own hands.

In this way, a commitment to students' self-directed learning may actually post unexpected challenges for us as teachers. For example, it can challenge the sense of autonomy that, as discussed earlier, academics greatly prize. Here again we return to the issue that the ways in which we enable student engagement with learning is intertwined with our own approach to engagement with our role of university teacher. In particular, it requires a responsiveness in how we approach teaching. This includes a capacity to change normal practices in the face of individual student differences (Cassidy 2011).

The intertwined understanding of our engagement as teachers and our students' engagements as learners, as outlined in this chapter, goes beyond procedural understandings of student learning and instead emphasizes the relationships between students, teachers and the knowledge both examine, learn and critique within higher education and interact within the educational interface. As such, this approach resonates with that of Mann (2001), who suggests transcending understandings of student learning simply in terms of deep or surface learning, and focusing instead on the more social aspects of alienation and engagement.

CONCLUSION

This chapter has considered our engagement as teachers within higher education in terms of this being a process over time and a relationship with both our students and our subject knowledge. As a process of time, the foundations of our engagement lie in our previous experiences, both personal and academic. We have tried to stress that it is legitimate and important to allow our engagement to be shaped by who we are as individuals. However, in also stressing the relational aspects of engagement we have sought to place this personal dimension in a more dynamic context. Here we consider how it can, and should, be challenged and shaped by the experiences of those who are different to us, and who occupy different places in the learning and teaching context. Clearly, this refers particularly to our students. It is not possible to separate our engagement as teachers with our students' engagement with their own learning. The two exist in a state of symbiosis, and this inter-dependent state is therefore something to understand, cherish and protect as part of our broader reflective practice.

KEY READINGS

For a personal discussion of developing a sustaining career, see:

Craig, C. (2019). 'Sustaining self and others in the teaching profession: A personal perspective'. In J. Murray, A. Swennen and C. Kosnik (eds), *International Research, Policy and Practice in Teacher Education* (pp. 79–91). Cham: Springer

For further explorations of student engagement, see:

Cook-Sather, A. (2015) 'Dialogue across differences of position, perspective, and identity: Reflective practice in/on a student-faculty pedagogical partnership program', *Teachers College Record*, 117(2).

Barnacle, R. and Dall'Alba, G. (2017) 'Committed to learn: Student engagement and care in higher education', *Higher Education Research & Development*, 36(7), 1326–38.

Kahu, E. and Nelson, K. (2018) 'Student engagement in the educational interface: Understanding the mechanisms of student success', *Higher Education Research & Development*, 37(1), 58–71.

On kindness in relationships of students and teachers, see:

Clegg, S. and Rowland, S. (2010) 'Kindness in pedagogical practice and academic life', *British Journal of Sociology of Education*, 31(6), 719–35.

Chapter 8
Spaces
How are we creating environments for learning?

INTRODUCTION

In reflecting on our teaching practices, we should remember that our actions are situated in physical space – our teaching, and students' learning, takes place in specific locations, usually built for that purpose, such as lecture theatres and laboratories – but these are often pre-configured according to traditional expectations. Or, in the case of online programmes, space is often 'commandeered', whether in an office, a bedroom, a library, or even a cafe, to enable us to connect and enter a pre-built *virtual* learning environment.

In so many other areas of life and work, the interplay between behaviour and environment is recognized as a legitimate area for investigation and research, so why should teaching and learning be any different? Many of us take for granted the teaching spaces which we have been allocated, some of which may be more flexible and adaptable than others, but how often do we get the opportunity to probe the implicit models of education underpinning this architecture? If we had scope to design our 'ideal' teaching environment how might we go about it? For those teaching in online or virtual spaces, the questions are the same, and indeed the relationship of the virtual to the physical spaces surely is fundamental to the design of *blended learning* courses.

In this chapter we will examine key considerations on the spaces we use for teaching and learning, taking the opportunity to reflect on the extent to which our campuses, our workplaces and our online tools meet, or perhaps conflict with, our educational goals. An underlying question to consider is the extent to which we feel we are (at one extreme) subjects of 'architectural determinism' or (at the other) free agents empowered to reshape our environment on our own terms.

See Chapter 4

TLRP Principles

Two principles are of particular relevance to this chapter on learning spaces in higher education:

Principle 4: Effective teaching and learning fosters both individual and social processes and outcomes. Students should be encouraged to build relationships and communication with others to assist the mutual construction of knowledge and enhance the achievements of individuals and groups. Consulting or collaborating with students as learners about their learning makes this effective.

Principle 5: Effective teaching and learning promotes the active engagement of the student as learner. A key aim of higher learning should be to develop students' independence and autonomy as learners. This involves engaging students actively in their own learning, and ensuring that they acquire a repertoire of learning strategies and practices, develop positive learning dispositions, and build the confidence to become agents in their own learning.

UNDERSTANDING TEACHING–LEARNING SPACES

Scheduled classes on a university campus usually take place in physical spaces which have been designed and constructed according to an architectural expectation of the needs of the student and the teacher. Most long-established institutions have a considerable estate of traditional (tiered rows of seating, lectern at the front) lecture theatres, smaller classrooms and laboratories. The design of these spaces has largely been based on the notion that information is transmitted by the lecturer to the anonymous rows of recipient students, pen in hand, or that recipe-driven experiments are conducted in synchrony, bench to bench, students in pairs, passing equipment to one another and scribbling down results for consideration later (if at all!). The design of the physical and virtual spaces in which we teach, to a large extent, signals to us what approaches to teaching we should be using (Jamieson 2003; Temple 2008; Duggan 2011; Bligh and Crook 2017). If we enter a lecture theatre at the front, we find a lectern facing the audience, with a microphone in front of us, almost commanding us (and us alone) to speak, to deliver. If we enter at the back or at the sides, we are a student and have to file along rows of seating to find our place. There's no microphone for us, no spotlight, and our seats are all fixed to the floor facing in one direction, line of sight forced forwards, straight to the lecturer.

How then, if we are inspired by research and by the educational principles which form much of the discussion in this book, are we to react to such spaces? Can we realistically subvert them to encourage active forms of learning, and if we were seeking change, what would teaching and learning spaces that embraced active learning look like? And what of technology? What is its role and how can it be co-opted to serve effective teaching practices rather than also push us into the deliver-transmit-broadcast mode? To what extent might it lead to the creation of new forms of space, a virtual realm that parallels or intersects with the physical?

Thus far we have spoken only about the spaces in which teaching takes place, but what about the spaces beyond the classroom in which students try to learn? Scheduled lectures, after all, only constitute a minority of the hours in the week, and students are expected to read, to gather information, to build notes, to practise, to complete assignments, or to work on projects either individually or in groups. Where is all that to happen? Do we have, on our campuses, adequate facilities, or indeed do we even have enough seating for our student population, and where is that to be found? In the library, throughout the campus, in the coffee shops, or student residences? And in our consideration of the students' experience of the environments in which they learn, do we take into account commuter students, those that might spend a significant amount of time travelling back and forth from campus to home; the extent to which there is access to facilities for students who work and study part-time; or whether our campus environment is inclusive to those with disabilities or other particular needs?

When we speak of space, and spaces, we should recognize (and perhaps give a nod of acknowledgement to the science of relativity in doing so!) that space is also deeply connected with time. The sheer complexity of timetabling multiple cohorts of students and courses across an institution has an impact on learning in the sense that classes scheduled first thing in the morning, or late in the day, rarely prove popular with many students or staff, leading potentially to issues of attendance and attention. Nor is it uncommon, in many institutions, to find a room allocation that barely accommodates the numbers of students enrolled in a course, perhaps compounding discomfort with heating, ventilation, seating, lighting or acoustics. However, space is also connected with time in a more subtle and important sense. Maggi Savin-Baden (2008: 2), for example, suggested that 'learning spaces are increasingly absent in academic life', where she means both the space and time for reading, thinking and reflection that is characteristic of the deeper levels of learning expected in higher education. She contended that this is being 'eroded' and lost, with the increasing complexity of the higher education landscape, and the reality of life for many students often involves part-time work, family and social commitments, and many other challenges which were less prominent in the pre-massification era of university education. But this doesn't necessarily mean that time and space for learning has eroded, rather than perhaps evolved to fit into new shapes and patterns.

More than ten years ago, Lomas and Oblinger (2006) proclaimed that students preferred 'learning experiences that are digital, connected, experiential, immediate and social' (p. 52). There is a sense of urgency in this type of pronouncement but it is worth questioning the extent to which it is true for all students in all higher education contexts. What the quotation does usefully highlight is that learning will take place when and where it can, rather than only in those bounded spaces and times of the formal curriculum, and within the walls of the classroom.

These are all important questions that need to form part of a more deliberative approach to the design of our courses and learning activities. By seeking to answer them, we are ensuring that our teaching isn't just based on abstracted principles, but recognizes the challenges that students might face and helps to identify strategies which can overcome these and support student success.

Working with students in effective learning spaces

There are a number of ways in which we might feel constrained by formal learning spaces and unable to achieve our intended objectives, as we discussed earlier. In this section, we will consider some practical ideas for learning activities, which enable us to use learning spaces in different ways and are focused on actively engaging students in their learning. Reflective Activity 8.1 first invites us to consider how we use our learning spaces.

Reflective Activity 8.1 Thinking about our learning spaces

Think about one of the teaching and learning spaces which you frequently use.

- What are some of the challenges of working in this space in relation to the things you would like your students to learn?
- Are there physical constraints (e.g. the furniture and resources in the room)?
- Is the room comfortable or overcrowded; does it get enough light and air?
- Do the students have space to work together in groups?
- Do they have space to work comfortably on laptops or with other resources?
- In relation to your learning objectives, do you feel this space is conducive or restrictive? If it is restrictive, what are some of the practical steps you can take in order to help foster a climate that is conducive for learning?

Please keep in mind the learning objectives you have set: how are you creating spaces that enable the students to gain the kinds of understandings that you intend them to develop?

Although the discussion below focuses on activities designed to encourage engagement with the content, or knowledge, of the curriculum, it is important to recognize that learning activities can and should be designed around the assessment tasks that students are required to undertake. The idea that we design 'assessment for learning', rather than assessment of learning, shifts the emphasis from a summative judgement of a student's performance to a formative process of improving learning (see Chapter 13 for a full discussion of this). This shift in emphasis expands the notion of learning spaces, as it enables us to think about incorporating assessment activities into the learning opportunities we design for the students. As we consider some practical examples below, it is worth bearing in mind that many classroom-based activities can be designed with assessment in mind, either in terms of preparing students by giving them practice on an assessment-related activity, or by designing activities in which they get feedback on their progress (from peers or instructors).

Engaging large groups in learning activities

The formal lecture theatre, which may hold hundreds of students, is often perceived to be a space that is not conducive to active learning. However, many teachers have developed techniques for ensuring that the students in large lecture classes are doing more than just sitting in that space, listening to the speaker at the front.

As we discussed in Chapter 2, one of the most well-known proponents of active learning in the lecture theatre is the Harvard-based physicist Eric Mazur. He has made valuable contributions to science education by publishing extensively on techniques for engaging students in their learning during formal class time, and has collected evidence of improved student performance in the process. One of his first contributions was his work on *peer instruction*, in which he asked students to discuss in pairs the concepts he was teaching in class. He found that by giving students the space to work out problems in class together their understanding improved (Mazur 2009). Just the fairly simple idea of asking students to teach each other improved their results, and helped him to understand what concepts they found particularly difficult.

Mazur then developed the use of personal response systems (or 'clickers') to help him engage the students in peer-to-peer learning activities in large groups. As he explains (Mazur 2009), students can be given preparation tasks to be done in advance of a large group session, such as a set reading. Class time is given over largely to the further exploration of the key concepts which need to be understood by the students. The lecturer can provide some instruction, but then through the use of multiple choice questions that are answered with clickers (or more commonly these days, an equivalent app on a student's phone or laptop), the lecturer gains the ability to judge students' understanding, as well as the opportunity to enable the students to teach each other. Mazur does this by asking the students to discuss their responses in pairs. He has found significant improvement in students' conceptual understanding through this approach. Case Study 8.1 explores another teacher's experiences of attempting to engage students in a large group setting.

Case Study 8.1 Engaging students in a large lecture theatre

The following case study gives an account by a political scientist, Niall Ó Dochartaigh, of how he experimented for the first time with engaging students in a large lecture theatre. He wrote this account as part of the learning journal he produced as he undertook a Postgraduate Certificate in Teaching and Learning in Higher Education at the National University of Ireland, Galway.

An expedition to the back of the lecture theatre

I implemented changes to my first-year large-group teaching this week and the experience was a very positive one overall. The content speaks more directly now to a lot of the issues that students are interested in and concerned with in political life. The material I teach on political institutions is now embedded more firmly in current debates about the political system and public policy.

I began the lecture by getting the students to work on their own, writing down a list of four or five top sources of power in society. When I noted that a few people at the back weren't writing anything I told them that this was stage one of the exercise and that they needed to do this in order to do the next stage. That got them all writing.

I then asked them to form pairs or threes (depending on the numbers around them and what made sense) and to agree on the top two sources of power from the list of four or five sources I had asked them to list on their own. In one sense this went fantastically well as the room was abuzz and huge numbers of the students were engaged in animated discussion. It was fantastic to see the large lecture hall transformed in that way and I felt that I had changed the tone of the lecture in a very positive way. However,

I saw problems. In many cases people came in with one buddy and made no new contacts. This happened even after I went up to two such groups and asked them to work together. Some of those who paired up were clearly not happy to be talking to the person beside them and many of these pairs went silent very quickly. Nonetheless, enough people were lively and engaged to make it worthwhile.

In getting their answers fed back to the class as a whole, I decided to make sure that those at the back were included and I began by asking anyone in the back row to shout out their top answer. Someone did and I then moved down to the second and third from the back – they also answered. I then pointed to other areas of the hall and after doing this a few times I asked if anyone had answers that hadn't yet been mentioned. As we went along I typed the answers and they appeared on the big screen. I felt this exercise really did grab their attention. I was pleased that so many people were willing to shout out answers and that we got a really interesting set of answers that could be connected very directly to the topic. After each answer I talked briefly about why the body/organization mentioned could be considered a source of power and connected them to the topics that we will be covering over the next few weeks. I then asked them to indicate by a show of hands which of these they thought was the most important source of power and did a quick count. Far and away the most popular options were the public followed by the government. I hadn't entirely expected this, which was great. I then linked this to the idea of popular sovereignty and state sovereignty and explained that this is where power is formally vested in a democratic system. The fact that they felt power genuinely resided in these locations provided a measure of the legitimacy of the political system in Ireland, and it might provide part of the explanation for the lack of mass protest or street violence in Ireland in response to austerity measures.

Flipping the classroom

As discussed above, many teachers have been inspired by the abundance of high-quality knowledge content that is now freely available and accessible to students. Technologies have also made it possible for lecturers to make their own content and either publish this in open access formats or to upload it onto their institutional Virtual Learning Environment (VLE) or Learning Management System (LMS). For instance, it is now fairly easy to video record a lecture or short presentation, or capture a 'walkthrough' explanation of a tool or technique using software on your laptop, and upload it onto a video hosting site (YouTube being a public example, but there are also institutional platforms that allow restrictions on who can view). These types of video recordings or webcasts can now be made with little time, expense or difficulty and, increasingly, there is also expectation that students can do similar, submitting digital artefacts for assessment.

As we commented earlier, there is a distinction between 'content' and a course – after all, the provision of a library or a shelf full of books does not by itself ensure that learning will take place. Learning is an active process of constructing understanding, which involves feedback, challenge, testing and progress. If that is the case, then a legitimate question to ask is why do we still place so much emphasis on the use of 'contact time' between students and staff to simply deliver content and expect the difficult tasks, grasping with concepts and problem-solving, to be handled by the students alone, in their own time? Would not a more effective approach be to expect the basic content knowledge (whether in the form of textbook chapters, podcast, video or multimedia materials) to be something that the students can sensibly cover in their own study time and use the scheduled classes as opportunities to explore topics in greater depth, to tackle problems, to raise and answer questions? Surely this is made all the more feasible by the ubiquity of networked technologies, VLEs/LMSs and digital libraries?

This is the basis of the 'flipped classroom' approach (Walvoord and Anderson 2009). There are many examples of flipped approaches and Eric Mazur whom we discussed above has also written about his own experiments with flipping the classroom which are worth reading (Mazur 2009). To give one general example which could be adapted to suit specific subject areas and local contexts, the lecturer could require students to watch a recorded lecture (webcast), listen to a podcast, and/or read a set text prior to the scheduled class time. The class time is then used for activities that explore and develop the students' understanding of the material. Typical tasks would be small group work that might involve students in a problem-solving exercise in which they must utilize the key concepts that they studied prior to class. The tasks they complete during class time can become a type of formative feedback, so students can gauge their progress during the course. Michael Seery (2015) has provided an informative review of flipped teaching/learning implementations. Although ostensibly focused on the teaching of chemistry, the findings and analysis are applicable to many disciplines across higher education.

Case Study 8.2 The flipped classroom

From 2012–17, the Australian Government Office for Teaching and Learning (OLT) funded a project titled *Radical Transformation: Reimagining Engineering Education Through Flipping the Classroom in a Global Learning Partnership* at the University of Queensland. This project developed a number of case studies. One of these was developed by Jason Tangen. He described how he flipped his Science of Everyday Thinking course. Dissatisfied with the traditional lecture format, and motivated to act after hearing someone say 'if you can be replaced by a video, you probably should be', he decided to redesign the course so that the content is delivered outside of the class 'meetings'. In fact he deliberately changed the weekly lecture and tutorial format to a weekly two-hour 'class meeting' in order to create a different mindset about the types of activities that would take place during the scheduled sessions. He video-recorded his lectures and made them available prior to the class meetings along with required readings. The students were quizzed on this material during the first twenty minutes of each class meeting, and the quizzes comprised 50 per cent of the final grade. The rest of the class meeting time was spent on discussions, peer interactions, debates and other activities. Jason felt that this made class time more intellectually exciting and fun. His redesign of the course enabled him to stop 'teaching by telling', and instead create an environment that 'inspires students to learn independently'.

New technologies also make it possible to engage students in large groups in those subject areas that are classroom and laboratory based. Some research has suggested that students are not very motivated by traditional lab sessions in which they follow set instructions to a predicted outcome. In one study, by Mann and Robertson (2009), students rated laboratory sessions as the most boring teaching method they experienced in higher education, and the authors explain that their findings are corroborated with evidence from elsewhere which suggests that controlled experiments are widely perceived to be 'tedious'.

Therefore, many academics have turned to technologies to help create more active learning opportunities for students. Demonstrations of the use of lab equipment or particular laboratory techniques and protocols, for example, can be video recorded and made available to students, thereby freeing up class time for experimenting rather than demonstrating. Computer simulations can also be used in a variety of ways, saving on the physical resources which would otherwise be needed to properly equip a lab (one of the reasons why lab sessions are 'boring' could be because of the constraints of resources). Games and competitions are also increasingly popular. Spaghetti bridge competitions, for example, can be a fun way of engaging students in engineering (students use uncooked pasta to construct free-standing models of bridges). Or even simply looking at ways of linking the experiments and measurements being undertaken by each student (or pair, as is more typical) to a collective, common purpose or enquiry, combining data and analysing as a group. We explore other ways of approaching lab sessions in Chapter 11.

The main point here is that learning spaces should ideally be *active* spaces. If, as teachers in higher education, we feel that the spaces we are given are not helpful in this regard, we possibly need to become a bit creative. There are thousands of ideas for encouraging active learning on the web, so a good start would be a google search on active learning in your subject area.

Designing teaching and learning spaces

As Brown and Long (2006) noted, the design of teaching and learning spaces in contemporary higher education institutions incorporated three specific trends: (a) design based on learning principles, particularly those founded on pedagogies of social and active learning; (b) emphasis on human-centred design, considering the relationship of the users of the space and how to meet their anticipated needs; (c) the increasing availability (and ownership) of mobile technologies and the ubiquity of technologies for communication, engagement and interaction.

In practice, this shaped the design of new buildings, refurbishment programmes, and supported a new focus on the need to provide students with learning spaces that facilitate both group and individual study. The role of university libraries, for example, has shifted to embrace their potential central role as a 'learning commons'. Traditional, tiered lecture theatres have been re-engineered to support 'buzz group' sessions and other forms of student active participation by simply replacing rows of seating with clustered or flexible seating, or reducing the number of tiers to create more space on each level and allowing greater mobility.

Research into student learning, such as that of Wieman (2017) and colleagues (which has extended the work of Mazur and others), has also led to a reconsideration of the requirement for lecture theatres in the first place and there are growing numbers of examples of institutions which have significantly rethought their teaching of STEM subjects in particular (although the principles may also hold true for any discipline) by reducing (or abolishing) lectures and replacing them with problem-solving activities in teaching-learning 'studios' with students seated in groups, guided by a facilitator moving amongst them. Case Study 8.3 provides a fascinating example of a major building project which has taken cognizance of all of these ideas and provides a living laboratory for new pedagogies.

Case Study 8.3 Starting from scratch – building teaching spaces where learning matters

Opened in April 2018, close to the heart of the Clayton campus (in Melbourne), the Learning & Teaching Building (monash.edu/lt-building) provides an example of the principles of learning space design being fully implemented both in terms of the 'teaching' venues and in the provision of a range of formal and informal study and collaborative spaces for students. The building contains sixty-eight teaching rooms, most of which are open to view, via glass walls, and which have a variety of possible configurations with flexible and well-considered furnishing and display panels allowing a variety of lines-of-sight as well as the potential for sharing of presentations from any of the groups of students in the class.

Two of the larger venues effectively subvert the expectation that large classes will meet in lecture theatres, by offering scope for a range of different teaching and learning approaches and removing the notion that the lecturer is at a primary focal point. The 'learning in the round' space has a large circular 'map-table' at its centre in which groups can come together to collaborate, to examine artefacts, or participate in design activities, whilst the entire circumference of the room is a continuous (except for the doors) whiteboard, each segment of which is covered by cameras for capturing and sharing ideas. Two of these map-tables are also installed in another of the large venues, in front of a large multi-projection displays and, once again, seating is clustered around group tables, the surface of which is a horizontal whiteboard on which students are encouraged to develop their ideas and approaches to problem-solving.

What immediately strikes the visitor to the building, however, is the large number and wide variety of seating arrangements for every possible study approach, with more social space on the lower levels (near entrances, stairways, etc.), and the quieter, more individual study spaces as we ascend to the top level. Recognizing basic student needs, there are coffee-docks, sinks, microwave ovens, power sockets, and hot and cold water provision throughout the building. The visitor would also notice, through the glass walls of each room, that much of the teaching which is taking place is indeed participatory and students are actively engaged. There's motion, activity, group presentations – a real sense of 'things happening', rather than the ranks of sleepy students taking lecture notes or browsing phones whilst the lecturer stands pinned in at a lectern, as might be revealed were some of our traditional lecture theatre walls to become transparent! It is also notable that although technology is everywhere, it is clearly used to support rather than dictate the approach to teaching. Much of the time students are in discussion, or jotting ideas on whiteboard surfaces, only flicking to screens when sharing conclusions with the wider class.

The visibility of the teaching and learning, as it is argued, serves a professional development function, allowing colleagues to pick up ideas from one another and to perhaps reflect on practice in the provided, comfortable teachers' lounge.

TEACHING AND LEARNING BEYOND THE CLASSROOM

Much of the current thinking in educational theory promotes the view that *learning is a social activity*, and therefore the most effective learning experiences are often believed to be those that occur through interaction with others. Indeed, the traditional lecture, which encourages a passive response from the students, has been argued to be an ineffective learning environment (Bligh 2000; Wieman 2017). Much of the teaching and learning literature attempts to deal with the 'problem' of lectures partly because they are still such a pervasive feature of higher education. In Chapter 11, we challenge this view and argue that the important issue is to focus on the understanding that we want our students to develop through our teaching and then to consider how lectures can help us to do this. However, it is clear that the lecture is a difficult space in which to encourage social interaction.

What other learning spaces, then, do we offer to students which encourage the type of social interaction that stimulates learning? If we think about it, the experience of studying in higher education can be an intensely social one, and teachers in higher education have been designing innovative learning experiences that encourage learning through interaction for a long time. Within tutorial classes, seminars and laboratory teaching there has always been an emphasis on active engagement, working in groups or pairs, and tackling conceptual problems and issues together.

Many courses and degree programmes have embedded internships, professional placements and other forms of work-based learning (Morley 2018). For some professions such learning beyond the classroom is essential for accreditation, as well as having intrinsic merit. Other disciplines have field-based learning at their core and many universities operate programmes of 'service learning' where students work in partnership with community. Let's look at some examples and suggestions for teaching and learning 'off campus'.

Placements, internships and simulation

The organization of placement programmes is non-trivial, but it is something which is core to many degree programmes in a wide range of disciplines (Morley 2018). In the context of our current discussion, students working in a site of professional practice are inhabiting a quite different space for this period, one which is more associated with the practice rather than designed specifically for learning. The role of the student and the nature of their relationship with their mentors, supervisors or others in the workplace can be complex but crucial for their personal and professional development. Placement programmes are required to have appropriately addressed issues of duty of care, supervisory arrangements, insurance and much else. Inhabiting and negotiating such spaces provides invaluable learning opportunities, as well as exposing students (and their hosts) to risk and challenge.

In some cases, such as nursing, medicine and law, it is not uncommon to develop on-campus simulated environments such as hospital wards and 'moot courts', which help students' professional enculturation as well as skills development (Rooney et al. 2015). The design of such facilities often also incorporates embedded cameras and microphones to record sessions for playback and review. Learning to 'teach' or to facilitate learning in such environments requires not only the specialist knowledge of the discipline, but finely tuned skills of observation, an ability to proffer constructive and effective feedback, and in some cases additional specialist technical support.

Field-based learning

Geology, geography, archaeology, botany, environmental studies and ecology, to give several obvious examples, are subject areas in which field-based learning experiences are seen as central to the programme of study. These may take the forms of field trips, where the learning spaces of these courses are based on 'site', and the students can practise research-oriented tasks (see Chang et al. 2018 for an exploration of such spaces in Geography). Boyle et al. (2007, p. 300) define field trips as 'any component of the curriculum that involves leaving the classroom and learning through firsthand experience'. These field-based learning spaces are seen as necessary as they cannot be replicated in a laboratory setting. They are also highly social learning spaces, as students and teachers may live in close quarters for the duration of the field trip. The social aspect of field-based learning is a valued part of the experience.

There are some concerns that field trips are an expensive form of education and are becoming less prevalent in mass higher education (Boyle et al. 2007). There are now some technological alternatives that can make leaving the classroom less important, and reduce the pressure on academic staff who would otherwise invest significant time into the organization and facilitation of field-based learning opportunities. However, there is widespread agreement amongst academics (and students) who have experienced field-based learning that it is a valuable part of the curriculum and are also increasingly seen as important in supporting students' understanding of sustainability (Kricsfalusy et al. 2018)

Field-based learning has advanced from the traditional forms of observation to more active forms of research. Observation activities can be quite passive and teacher directed, with the students given guidance on what they are observing and instructions on how to record their observations. Notably, even with the wide open space of the 'real world', it is possible to design a passive, teacher-led learning experience for students. In more recent years, however, field-based teachers have become interested in the potential learning opportunities of student-led projects.

For example, an environmental studies course might include a student-designed research project on the impact of the changed use of land, in which students propose hypotheses, select appropriate equipment, conduct experiments and analyse the results. An urban geography course might include a student research project on the quality of life in privately developed suburban housing estates, involving interviews with local residents and council members. These examples (based on 'real' practices) illustrate the range of opportunities that field-based learning can offer, although they do of course have financial and other resource implications. Examples of how students can develop research skills and experience through fieldwork can be found in Nicholson (2011), whilst Morrissey et al. (2013) explore a fascinating example, and the challenges, of the interconnections between fieldwork, research and civic engagement.

Service learning

There are other types of learning spaces that are designed to give students the opportunities to learn in the 'real world' and which are not necessarily specific to any particular disciplines. *Service learning*, for example, is an increasingly popular means of enabling students to learn outside the campus environment through engagement with communities beyond the campus walls (see, for example, Buhl 2010; Dolgon et al. 2017). Although service learning may be most familiar in US higher education, where there is historically much encouragement of students to spend time outside the formal curricula engaging in activities such as volunteering, it is also growing in popularity in Australia, South Africa, the UK, Ireland and elsewhere.

A common form of service learning is the design of learning activities, for academic credit, which provide students the opportunity to give something back to a community group or organization. In that sense, service learning opportunities share similarities with volunteering, but the objective is to enable the students to learn from the experience and assess them against the learning outcomes of the module (some of which will usually be discipline-specific). An example of a typical service learning activity would be one in which engineering students work with a community-based organization for people with physical disabilities in order to design and develop a product that will aid mobility. Another example would be a module requiring Italian students to run an Italian club in a local, socioeconomically disadvantaged school. Academic credit might be obtained by student presentations on their experiences, or through the production of reflective diaries about their experiences, or other academic outputs. Again, these examples are loosely adapted from recent projects in universities and help illustrate the range of possibilities.

Service learning is connected to a broader 'civic engagement' agenda for higher education. In South Africa, this has been important in terms of emphasizing learning *from the community* and not only from the experience of civic engagement. This more critical take on service learning emphasizes the bringing of 'other' forms of knowledge into the university (Bender et al. 2006). In the United States this is probably best represented through the Campus Compact organization (see: compact.org). Campus Compact is a network of 1,200 college and university presidents, and works to embed community service within the curriculum, to develop citizenship skills, and to strengthen community–university partnerships. Whilst many students have benefited from service learning modules, the underlying ideological agenda of the civic engagement movement has proved at times to be counter-productive, given that not all academics perceive their role to be one of fostering civic responsibility or citizenship skills. The problematic assumptions that can underpin some models of service learning have long been recognized. For example, Butin (2006) argued that:

> The service-learning literature is replete with discussions of how students come to better understand themselves, cultural differences, and social justice through service-learning. The overarching assumption is that the students doing the service-learning are white, sheltered, middle-class, single, without children, un-indebted, and between ages 18 and 24. But that is not the demographics of higher education today, and it will be even less so in 20 years. (Butin 2006, p. 481)

We need to be careful, then, about the assumptions we are making when we draw distinctions between the space of the university from the space outside. What characteristics are we ascribing to the university by claiming that the spaces within the campus walls are not fit for purpose for some types of learning? The design of learning experiences that take place outside of the campus are a response to what is perceived to be the artificial and constrained learning spaces within the campus walls. In other words, it is the recognition that some types of learning experiences cannot be recreated in classrooms or laboratories that can lead us, as reflective teachers, to want to utilize spaces in the 'real world' for learning. Of course this raises the question of what is not 'real' about the formal curriculum and the learning spaces within universities.

The traditional spaces of universities in particular have often been characterized as somewhat detached from reality. The term the 'ivory tower', often used as a somewhat disparaging description of the university, suggests that certain intellectual pursuits are disconnected with the practical concerns of everyday life, and the people within universities are somehow not connected with the 'real world'. Is this characterization fair? As reflective teachers, are we concerned with whether our students are learning in an environment which may be disconnected with the 'real world', or do we feel it is necessary for them to have some 'real world' experiences as part of their learning? Are they bringing the 'real world' to us?

Digital technologies and virtual spaces

Students, as we have noted, have the opportunity to learn in a much greater range of spaces than before, although this does depend on their available resources. Many students now effectively have virtual libraries on their laptops or smart phones, making long study sessions in the campus library almost unnecessary. They can watch videos of lectures from universities around the world from wherever they are working. Does the now almost limitless opening up of learning spaces to some students mean that the campus walls, in a symbolic sense, are permeable? What are the implications of these changes for our understandings of 'learning spaces' and the effective design of learning spaces?

One of the challenges of the pervasiveness of digital technologies and the ability of some students to learn anywhere is that much of this learning can take place outside of the control of the lecturer. The types of digital learning spaces that students can access are vast and unstructured, so the students navigate them of their own accord and not through design. Bligh and Crook (2018) develop six different ways of thinking about the relations between students and these spaces.

Students are also increasingly likely to learn in networks and other online communities. Digital technologies enable students to become 'co-constructors' of their learning environments, actively shaping their online experiences (Sharpe et al. 2013). Yet we need to remember that their independent forays into the digital environment may not translate into the learning outcomes we desire. As Laurillard (2012) reminds us, new technologies do not mean that 'students can do it for themselves'. Instead, new technologies make the role of the teacher more vital in terms of scaffolding and structuring students' learning (Laurillard 2012, p. 4). We should also avoid falling into the trap of believing the 'digital natives' trope. All of us, students and academic staff alike, are adept at some technologies, ignorant of others, confident with some, apprehensive of others. A more useful perspective is that of David White and Alison Le Cornu's (2011) 'Visitors and Residents', which also carries through the metaphor of spaces and provides a very useful tool for personal reflection.

Digital technologies, of course, also entangle space with time, just as it is easy to get lost exploring a new space, it is also easy to lose track of time online and either drift from link to link, be distracted by social media or email, or to superficially flick through content which really requires more consideration. Thriving intellectually in a digital environment requires self-discipline, purposeful engagement and retaining a connectedness to real space and real time. Our virtual world is noisy, like wandering through Times Square, perhaps, and we on occasion need to find our way to a quiet corner where we can focus, uninterrupted, when we need to and connect with others when that is necessary also. The importance of good curricular design, particularly the crafting of effective learning outcomes and the estimation of how much time students need to complete the different elements of any course is vital, as is student understanding of such expectations.

Online and virtual spaces

Whether or not 'we are all cyborgs now' (Case 2010), there is no doubt that technology pervades almost every aspect of our professional and personal lives. 'Space' in this new era, is no longer constrained to merely the physical realm. We and our students move through, and between, online and 'real' spaces frequently throughout the day, and the implications of this for learning and teaching merit some consideration.

The types of tools being used, and the nature of the various virtual spaces, are hugely varied in both capabilities and intent, as often too is our *presentation of self*. Those spaces established for social engagement, friendship and family networks, offer not only a distinct set of affordances and constraints, but also scope to build and reflect our own online personalities; whereas those established for learning purposes from the outset manifest quite different individual and collective behaviours, norms of engagement and role expectations.

Social media

The rise of social media tools sparked interest amongst many educators in higher educa-tion in exploring their potential for use in teaching, learning, student support and engagement (Ahern et al. 2016). Facebook groups associated with courses, or institutions, abound, often created and run by students themselves, though frequently for social discourse, chat and gossip, as much as for 'peer-learning'. Transforming these informal social networks into learning spaces in which academic staff were present, however, presents significant challenges in terms of the ways in which interacting with different audiences online can blur the boundaries between professional and personal contexts (boyd 2014; Davis and Jurgenson 2014), which raises key questions about personal space, privacy and identity (see Malesky and Peters 2012). This is particularly the case for those spaces which require identity verification, rather than permitting anonymous accounts. This can limit the ability to separate personal spaces from formal educational (open to assessment, judgement and scrutiny) spaces and requires a sophisticated level of knowledge of security settings and identity management. Those which allow anonymous accounts (such as, at the time of writing, Twitter) alleviate some of these aspects but by themselves also raise issues regarding being in public and the risks associated with inappropriate online behaviour. Finding the balance between the educational benefits and the personal (and reputational) costs is not always easy for either those in a 'teacher' or 'student' role, and we mustn't assume that simply because our students appear comfortable inhabiting such spaces that we should incorporate them into our teaching.

Indeed, as has come to the fore in more recent times, now that such spaces and tools have become firmly embedded on our mobile devices and in the sphere of broader public discourse, we have come to appreciate some of the specific challenges, limitations and indeed dangers associated with their use. Whether it be major data leaks, identity theft and hacking of accounts, addiction, trolling, cyber-bullying, or worse, we owe a professional duty of care to our students when designing our learning activities and selecting the spaces in which they are to occur. There is now a growing focus on issues around 'digital wellbeing' (Beetham 2015) and a more sober consideration of our (particularly young people's) relationships to such technology. Learning in the 'open' of course offers significant potential to collaborate, to share ideas, learn about different cultures and perspectives, build networks of support and mutual interest – but it requires consideration of the risks, agreed standards of behaviour and the development of coping skills. We should also be aware that such spaces offer potential for unethical practices such as plagiarism (indeed, 'contract cheating' mediated through online tools has been a burgeoning new 'spin off' industry worldwide), the subversion of assessment and 'examination security' – aspects which we cannot ignore and which may arise whether or not we, as teachers, elect to use online spaces for our courses.

Virtual Learning Environments/Learning Management Systems (VLE/LMS)

Often derided for their monolithic, hierarchical and surveillance/performance ethos, institutional 'virtual learning environments' (or 'learning management systems'), it has come to be realized, at least offer a closed or private, safe space in which to operate and in which learning can be the primary focus of attention. It may well be that we can learn from the social media experience ways in which we can use such spaces more effectively to engage students, by for example being prepared to develop media-rich content and nurture online debate, polls and student-created resources, rather than simply as a dumping ground for our PowerPoint slides. With additional features such as 'live classrooms' (online video streaming and collaboration) there are opportunities to explore a hybrid space that links the physical classroom with the online both in real time and asynchronously. Developing appropriate *hybrid pedagogy* takes more than just an enthusiasm for technology, indeed it requires consideration of all of the TLRP Principles, and benefits from shared practice and collaboration amongst colleagues. For multi-campus institutions, or for multi-institutional collaboration, the barriers to shared teaching and learning have been considerably reduced by such tools, but in many cases the full potential is perhaps yet to be realized when we note how frequently we speak of 'streaming lectures' (which is effectively one-way broadcasting) from campus to campus, rather than true collaborative engagement.

The conflation of VLE with LMS is sometimes confusing, particularly when considering actual 'virtual environments' or worlds. There has been a renewal of interest recently, in, for example, not just virtual reality but 'augmented reality' in which digital components are overlaid on real-world scenes or locations, viewed through mobile devices or even headsets. Some examples of how technologies related to this meaning of 'virtual' are being used in higher education can be found in Bower et al. (2017).

MOOCs

The MOOC (massive, open, online courses) phenomenon which grabbed the attention of the media and politicians for a number of years, was initially posited as a 'threat' to universities and established higher education institutions, with grandiose claims being made about these new providers replacing universities in the near future and providing access to higher education for all, regardless of financial and geographical circumstances. Ironically, it is many of the MOOC companies which have been 'disrupted'; retrenched to focus on more specific niche areas (such as IT and programming) and have begun to charge fees and restrict access to their resources and materials, or are serving as a means of advertising programme offerings from established universities and providing a channel for public outreach activities.

Nonetheless, the MOOCs raised interesting questions about: (a) the distinction between the 'delivery of content' and the other forms of engagement, tuition and support that characterize the higher education experience; (b) effective versus ineffective uses of technology; and (c) the role of physical versus virtual space in teaching and learning.

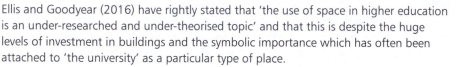

RESEARCH BRIEFING 8.1 Towards an integrated model of learning spaces

Ellis and Goodyear (2016) have rightly stated that 'the use of space in higher education is an under-researched and under-theorised topic' and that this is despite the huge levels of investment in buildings and the symbolic importance which has often been attached to 'the university' as a particular type of place.

By bringing together research in the learning sciences, as well as in resource management and architecture and design, they attempt to piece together a picture of the important factors and influences including identifying the blurring between the physical and the virtual. They recognize the challenges and difficulties faced by those who choose to adopt more engaged modes of teaching and learning, referencing Dillenbourg's (2013) notion of 'classroom orchestration' and the 'mental load' on teachers of monitoring and managing multiple groups and activities – technology in such a context needs to be simple and supportive, rather than adding another layer of complexity.

And, in addition to summarizing a number of active classroom design projects, they also emphasize the crucial importance of the student experience and the need to be cognizant of the diversity of perspectives and needs of learners.

They develop a model which builds on that of Lamb and Shraiky's (2013) 'collaboration-readiness model', factoring in ideas related to the socially-situated nature of learning, knowledge creation, and opportunities to identify observables amenable to evaluation and further research.

CONCLUSION

It is perhaps interesting to note that as we have developed more sophisticated under-standings of effective teaching and learning over the years, many learning spaces on campus have not kept pace. The stuffy large lecture theatres with fixed furniture, and the large, out-of-date and under-resourced labs still dominate many campuses. Often, the places on campus that have the most creative uses of space are modern university libraries. They are university 'flagship' buildings, designed for the entire university community (and often also the wider public), serving as 'learning commons' (see Holmgren 2010), which are focal points for students seeking space to study or to collaborate.

On the other hand, some of the most incredible buildings in the world are university libraries that are centuries old. They are spaces that invoke feelings of reverence for knowledge and learning, where people naturally speak in hushed tones and carefully handle the dusty books on the shelves. Some of our love from learning comes from these types of spaces.

Whilst we can aspire to new buildings and spaces shaped by pedagogical considerations and equipped with all the technologies we need, we shouldn't be entirely downhearted by the reality of many of our legacy theatres, rooms and labs. Whilst they may constrain and limit, we are intelligent, motivated and creative, and there are no shortages of potential means of subverting, if not the structures themselves, at least the message we feel they are implicitly conveying. Learning requires active engagement, participation, feedback, collaboration; all of these can take place anywhere groups of people gather with common purpose. At least, in the moment, perhaps with our passion and commitment we can draw our students into a 'virtual', imagined space where learning and intellectual discovery are enacted and celebrated.

KEY READINGS

For excellent overviews of the various strands of research into learning spaces in higher education, see:

Ellis, R. and Goodyear, P. (2016) 'Models of learning space: Integrating research on space, place and learning in higher education', *Review of Education*, 4(2), 149–91.

Bligh, B. and Crook, C. (2017) 'Learning spaces'. In E. Duval, M. Sharples and R. Sutherland (eds), *Technology Enhanced Learning* (pp. 69–87). Cham: Springer.

For careful, balanced consideration of technology application in higher education, see:

N. Selwyn (2013) *Distrusting Educational Technology: Critical Questions for Changing Times*. Abingdon: Routledge.

Of particular relevance to those in STEM subjects, but also useful to other disciplines which have established curricula:

Wieman, C. (2017) *Improving How Universities Teach Science: Lessons from the Science Education Initiative.* Harvard, CT: Harvard University Press.

A comprehensive (and accessible) overview of the design of teaching and learning spaces, which encompasses design methods, technology selection and integration, and the management of refurbishment and new build projects: **ucisa.ac.uk/learningspace**

For an influential article that argues that teachers and those who work with learning spaces need to develop their understanding of how physical space has an impact on students' learning, see:

Jamieson, P. (2003) 'Designing more effective on-campus teaching and learning spaces: A role for academic developers', *International Journal for Academic Development*, 8(1–2), 119–33.

Part three

Teaching for understanding

Part 3 supports the development of practice across the three classic dimensions of teaching – curriculum, teaching and assessment. Chapter 9 first examines different approaches to producing curricula that underpin many debates about the higher education curriculum. We also consider debates around the 'de-colonizing' of the curriculum. It then considers ideas that inform curriculum design. 'Planning' (Chapter 10) puts these ideas into action. It is more practically orientated and starts at the level of the individual session before considering module and then programme planning. Chapter 11 offers ways of understanding the art, craft and science of teaching – and examines how we can focus our teaching on student understanding. 'Communication' (Chapter 12) extends this with an introduction to the role of dialogue across the curriculum, which highlights the importance of engaging our students in discussions about their learning. Finally, this part concludes by examining how assessment makes a contribution to students' learning and how we can make decisions about the design of assessment (Chapter 13). In short, this part of the book examines how we can support students in developing an understanding of disciplinary knowledge and professional practices through the careful design of our curricula, teaching and assessment practices.

Chapter 9
Curriculum
What is to be taught and learned?

INTRODUCTION

Who is a curriculum for? What should be taught and how; by whom and to whom? The answers to these questions are all highly contested and yet, in higher education, seldom made explicit. One of the most intriguing aspects of higher education is the extent to which higher education curricula are a fundamental aspect of our academic practices but remains so poorly defined and understood. Compared to research into school education, there has been much less focus on curricula in higher education research (Ashwin 2014), and when academics have been asked what they mean by the term 'curriculum' they often discuss rather vague notions around the content, reading list or course outline of a module (Barnett and Coate 2005; Fraser and Bosanquet 2006; Bovill and Woolmer 2019). A curriculum is, however, much more than a course outline. It is a basic organizing principle of the higher education system itself. Different structures of curricula realize particular visions of the purpose of higher education as well as the ways in which the disciplines and professions have been institutionalized in higher education.

Even more intriguing is the extent to which higher education curricula convey implicit, subtle but powerful messages about our social imaginaries – about what is valued with regard to culture and norms – and what is considered to be legitimate knowledge. Decisions about the selection of curriculum content are decisions about what kinds of knowledge 'counts' and, similarly, decisions of exclusion are determinations about what does not count, what is considered to be non-legitimate knowledge (Bernstein 2000). In modern universities, there are also deeply embedded hierarchies of legitimate knowledge, with the most abstracted forms of knowledge being accorded the highest status.

Questions are currently being asked about the legitimacy and 'fitness-for-purpose' of inherited curricula, particularly in relation to the need to be responsive to the new diversity of students and also significant global issues (such as global inequalities, climate change, the economic crisis and post-truth regimes). A number of higher education institutions around the world are reconsidering the role of their curricula in terms of preparing students to rise to the demands of twenty-first-century challenges. We will go on to discuss some of these developments, but it is worth pausing first to better understand what the term 'curriculum' means before we discuss how it might be designed.

Strangely enough, despite contemporary challenges, the higher education curriculum is peculiarly stable: much of the curriculum taught in universities is long-standing in its legitimacy, although academics will often acknowledge that new content is continually brought into the curriculum. As we will see below, even how to explain this consistency and stability of the higher education curriculum is contested. For some it is an effect of the global power relations that uphold the West's idea of the modern university and control of knowledge production; for others it is due to the intrinsic value of the forms of curriculum knowledge themselves.

See Chapter 4

> ## TLRP Principles
>
> Three principles are of particular relevance to this chapter on curriculum in higher education:
>
> **Principle 9: Effective teaching and learning engages with expertise and valued forms of knowledge in disciplines and subjects.** Teaching and learning should engage students with the concepts, key skills and processes, modes of discourse, ways of thinking and practising, and attitudes and relationships which are most valued in their subject. Students need to understand what constitutes quality, standards and expertise in different settings and subjects.
>
> **Principle 7: Effective teaching and learning requires learning to be systematically developed.** Teachers, trainers, lecturers, researchers and all who support the learning of others should provide intellectual, social and emotional support which helps learners to develop expertise in their learning for it to be effective and secure.
>
> **Principle 6: Effective teaching and learning needs assessment to be congruent with learning.** Assessment should be designed for maximum validity in terms of learning outcomes and learning processes, and also should be specific to the type of subject or discipline involved, even if it is interdisciplinary. It should help to advance learning as well as determine whether learning has occurred.

The Latin origins of the word 'curriculum' are variously defined as 'race-course' or 'to run/proceed'. This definition conveys an image of a curriculum as a planned pathway designed and controlled by academics on which students embark towards a clear finish line. Others (for example Blackmore and Kandiko 2012) define curriculum very broadly as a 'social practice' which suggests a more collective process embedded in its social context. Regardless of our definition of curriculum, society still grants enormous power to academics to determine what students must learn and which hoops they must jump through in order to graduate. Our expertise in our disciplines and professional fields is regarded as the most appropriate criteria for according us this role. As reflective teachers we should not take this responsibility for granted but exercise it thoughtfully and with care.

One of the earliest forms of Western modern university curricula was the liberal arts curriculum, established in European medieval universities as the determination of all of the knowledge and skills necessary for the formation of a 'free' (libre) citizen capable of contributing to civic life. The core liberal arts – grammar, rhetoric and logic – called the trivium – were extended to include music, astronomy, arithmetic and geometry – called the quadrivium (Scott 2006). For several hundred years then, the secular liberal arts curriculum was a stable portrayal of all that was considered of value in European university education (but of course it was reserved for the elite – i.e. men from the upper classes or church).

Of course, knowledge production and transmission and the idea of the university is not an exclusively European idea. Knowledge was handed down in Pali, Sanskrit, Devnagari, Chinese, Amharic and Arabic scripts long before it was transmitted in Greek and Latin in

European medieval universities. Al Karaouine (859 AD) a centre of Islamic scholarship in Fez, Morocco is considered by UNESCO to be the oldest continuous university in the world, while Sankora in Timbuktu, home to a student population of 25,000 in the twelfth century, was the largest medieval university of its time (Mamdani 2012).

If we look at the curricula of most higher education institutions today, we will see both an underlying uniformity based on the West's idea of a modern secular university which reflects the legacies of the European Enlightenment and of European colonialism and imperialism of the eighteenth and nineteenth centuries; and a number of shifts. First, there is a greatly expanded curriculum offering related to the massification of higher education since the Second World War and the explosion of knowledge, information and technology in the twentieth century. Second, with regard to knowledge, already in the 1960s the poststructuralists followed by feminists challenged the foundations of Enlightenment epistemology, relativizing long-held notions of truth. As a consequence, Beck (1992) and Giddens (1990) identified a loss of faith in established expertise as a feature of late modernity. Third, in the twenty-first century it is likely that the higher education curriculum will be obliged to respond to a new social challenge – variously termed the 'new scepticism', the post-truth era and the phenomenon of 'alternative facts' – exacerbated by the ubiquity of social media. These contextual factors drive concerns for curriculum reform and relevance.

Curriculum is a broad catch-all phrase for many different activities and practices. The different dimensions of curriculum have been usefully distinguished as the *intended or planned curriculum* (a document such as a course outline and reading list); the *delivered curriculum* (what actually gets taught by the teaching staff and materials); the *understood curriculum* (what students actually learn) and finally the *hidden curriculum* referred to above (the implicit, tacit but powerful messages about what is valued with regard to culture and norms) (Blackmore and Kandiko 2012). These dimensions closely map onto Pollard's model of reflective teaching (see Figure 3.3) presented in Chapter 3. Applying this model to curriculum, we would move through all four of the dimensions mentioned above, and this is precisely how this book is designed – to take you through each of these dimensions of curriculum. For example: **Plan** a programme/course/module (what to teach, the purpose, approach and content of a curriculum – see later in this chapter). **Make provision** (detailed planning and ensuring access to adequate resources [lecturers, tutors, materials, venues, time-tabling, e-platform, etc.] – see Chapter 10). **Act** to deliver the curriculum (how to teach and communicate with students – see Chapters 11 and 12). **Evaluate** (what students have actually learned and understood from the curriculum – see Chapter 13 on assessment and also Part 4, Chapters 14 and 15 for how to collect, analyse and evaluate evidence generated by students).

To recap, this chapter deals with the very first stages of planning a curriculum, its overall orientation or approach and decisions about its purpose, goals, outcomes, content and big-picture design. In the first part of this chapter, we consider what is at stake in the notion of curriculum and then examine four competing discourses that shape the production of higher education curricula in different ways. In the second part of the chapter, we examine issues related to the design of curricula. In Chapter 5, we explored a range of contexts that shape higher education including the global political-economy of higher education, national policy contexts, institutional cultures, disciplinary cultures and teaching and learning contexts at the level of individual departments or programme teams. Each of these contexts generate different and sometimes competing sets of values, norms and discourses that shape and constrain how we imagine, construct and legitimate the curricula we offer to students. The central argument in this chapter is that we need to explicitly and reflexively consider how we construct our curricula in order to give all students the best opportunity to understand the knowledge and knowledge practices that we want them to engage with. In this chapter, we are focused on the strategic issues involved in thinking about curriculum design, whereas Chapter 10 focuses on the more practical issues of implementing curricula. For this reason, the ideas in these two chapters should be considered as strongly informing each other.

THE TRANSFORMATION OF KNOWLEDGE IN THE PRODUCTION OF CURRICULA

As we discussed briefly in Chapter 4, the production of curricula in higher education involves the transformation of knowledge (Bernstein 2000). As we discussed in Chapter 5, knowledge transforms as it moves from knowledge-as-research to knowledge-as-curriculum to knowledge-as-student-understanding (Ashwin et al. 2012b; Ashwin 2014). This process of transformation means that we cannot assume that differences in curricula are based purely on internal disciplinary differences, or in Bernstein's (2000) terms, that the logic of a curriculum will be the same as the logic of a discipline. It involves the selection of particular kinds of knowledge and practices to be included in particular curricula based on considerations of both what society values and thinks is important for students to know, do and become; and also on explicit theories of learning or common sense notions of how we as teachers believe we can best get students to learn and understand what we want them to know. As Bernstein (2000) makes clear, these are matters of disagreement and argument over:

- what constitutes valid knowledge in a subject or field;
- what a curriculum should consist of;
- how it should be organized and sequenced and paced;
- how it should be represented, communicated to students;
- how students' knowledge, understanding and skills should be identified and evaluated.

Such discussions do not simply involve academics. A curriculum is embedded in the social practices of particular societies and so, as we noted in Chapter 5, the ways that knowledge-as-research gets transformed into knowledge-as-curriculum is profoundly shaped by its historical, socio-cultural and institutional contexts, as well as by the identities, subjectivities, norms and worldviews of teachers, which are often shaped by their disciplinary expertise. Depending on national policy, the discipline and institutional norms and practices, these curriculum drivers may include norms and explicit rules relating to what constitutes a legitimate curriculum, the views and requirements of disciplinary or professional bodies, and standards from quality agencies outside of the university (Ashwin 2009). Additionally, curricula are structured and shaped by institutional rules and practices that govern the use of space, time, workloads, class sizes and the provision of teaching staff, technology and resources. If we understand curriculum as a dialogic social practice that is responsive to students, then they will also shape the curriculum in various ways – depending on what levels of agency the curriculum affords them – for example: the student composition in a class or programme, their performance in assessment, their engagement with the teaching process, their formal and informal feedback and the extent to which they are able to participate in the design of the curriculum and teaching activities will all impact its ongoing form and reform.

Debates around knowledge and curriculum often become heated because they implicate people's identities and ideals about society. When the composition of the student body in higher education changes, this usually triggers calls for curriculum change and especially the call for the curriculum to be more relevant to new kinds of students. The outcome of these debates, drivers and contexts reflects the power of particular stakeholders to promote their views and to get them institutionalized and implemented. This process of debate and compromise around curricula means that the ways in which different ideas, discourses and practices come together in a particular curriculum context will transform the knowledge as it moves from knowledge-as-research to knowledge-as-curriculum. Curriculum knowledge is transformed a second time when it is taught and learned as students bring the curriculum into relation with their own identities, cultures and ways of understanding. Being aware of these processes of knowledge transformation are important because they shape both the kinds of knowledge and practices with which students are invited to engage and also determine who a particular curriculum legitimates as the 'right kind of student' (Maton 2014).

In order to make sense of the complex field of curriculum studies in higher education, we outline four discourses or approaches to producing curricula that underpin many contemporary debates around the higher education curriculum. The oldest, and probably most criticized approach, is that of *traditionalism* (Moore and Young 2001). This approach assumes that there are given bodies of authoritative knowledge or canons on which the curriculum should be based. The second, and probably dominant approach, is called *technical-instrumentalism* which fits with the assumption that the higher education curriculum should serve economic needs by producing graduates who will be highly employable and competitive in a global market. The third approach, *curriculum for social change* is an umbrella term for the range of approaches that assume a critical view of society and wish to use the curriculum to promote social justice, undo the inequalities of society and empower students from subordinated groups. The fourth approach, *social realism*, looks carefully at how research communities produce and practice knowledge-making and at their criteria for evaluating and legitimating knowledge. It asserts that forms of curriculum knowledge are not arbitrary and seeks to uncover how and why knowledge is differently structured, in order to inform coherent curriculum design.

Below we outline the key tenets of each approach in more detail and also discuss its critiques and limitations. We include some examples of how these approaches tend to translate into certain curriculum designs and practices; although it must be pointed out that there is no direct relation or tight fit between an approach to curriculum and a set of methods for its design and practice. It is quite possible to adopt a particular curriculum approach and use a range of different methods associated with other approaches. Thereafter we outline some key curriculum design principles that hold across the different approaches. Finally, we look at some of the constraints to designing creative curricula faced by academics.

Traditionalism

This approach to producing a curriculum is held by academics who hold to a traditional hierarchical model of higher education in which academics, as authorities in disciplinary knowledge, are entitled to determine what and how to transmit knowledge to novice students (Henkel 2000). Academics, whose worldviews tend to be shaped by their disciplines, are likely to design curricula with vertical structures that require students to progress up a major or programme in the discipline. While this approach offers disciplinary depth, it focuses on content, that is 'what' academics will teach. Advocates sometimes defend this approach on the basis of a liberal notion of academic freedom – accorded to individual academics to teach who, what and how they choose, free from 'external interference'. It is argued that the academic project needs to be protected from immediate economic and political demands in order to preserve the conditions and specialist practices necessary for the production and transmission of knowledge (Moore 2000).

Applications and examples

Examples of the traditionalist approach to curriculum are everywhere but nowhere. While this approach can be found in the handbooks and course outlines of most research-intensive universities across the globe, it is hard to find it advocated in the literature on higher education, except as something to challenge and critique.

Limitations

Despite its persistence, this approach to curriculum has been under critique since the 1970s (Young 1971). It is critiqued by the technical-instrumentalists for being out of touch, resistant to change; for being inefficient and for failing to address adequately the economic and social needs of society. Traditionalism is also critiqued for subscribing to a naïve view of knowledge and curriculum as neutral and objective; a view that fails to acknowledge that knowledge and curriculum are relative to their historical and social contexts (Moore 2000). Those advocating curriculum for social change are critical of the traditional approach for accepting disciplinary knowledge as given and for not making explicit its values and 'the how' of disciplinary practices. It is argued that this reinforces the power of academics, the disciplines and their canons in ways that simply reproduce the inequalities in society. Further this traditional transmission approach to curriculum is widely critiqued for being blind to the importance of designing curricula that focuses on student learning, often failing to generate student engagement, motivation and emotional investment.

Technical-instrumentalism

In contrast to the traditional approach, which views higher education as an intrinsically worthwhile end in itself, the technical-instrumentalist approach believes that higher education should serve a larger purpose, that of economic growth and development. This approach has dominated the management of higher education since the 1980s and is often articulated by stakeholders other than academics, such as government officials, quality assurance agencies and senior managers. It is argued that higher education should produce highly skilled, trainable, flexible graduates who will participate in the global economy and contribute to national economic growth. This discourse emphasizes productivity, efficiency, useful knowledge and student choice. It has introduced a market logic for managing universities as businesses, the commodification of knowledge and it markets the benefits of higher education to students as a private good for individual advancement within a global corporate economy (Naidoo and Williams 2015). Advocates of this approach make the private benefits of higher education explicit, usually for marketing purposes, for example by promising students distinctive and competitive forms of graduate employ-ability, graduate attributes and generic skills.

When realized in curricula, this approach tends to prioritize the applied sciences, the business sciences, the professions, technology, problem-solving, inter-disciplinarity and breadth rather than depth; leading to a weakening of the status of the formative disciplines, especially the Humanities. Using a rational planning model based on pre-determined learning outcomes and modularization, this approach promotes structural reform and standardization for transferability in a global market via qualifications frameworks and accreditation such as the Bologna Process (Blackmore and Kandiko 2012).

Applications and examples

Qualifications frameworks: the Bologna Process

A number of European universities have undergone reforms as a result of engaging with the Bologna Process (Bologna Declaration 1999). The Bologna Process is a higher educa-tion reform process that began in 1999, when a number of education ministers came together with the agreed aim of creating a European Higher Education Area (EHEA). The EHEA encourages mobility of staff and students both within Europe and internationally, by ensuring Higher Education programmes of signatory countries are easily comparable and compatible, based on a three-cycle structure. The process set in motion the restructuring of (first cycle) Bachelors degree programmes to a standard length of three years (second cycle) Masters programmes of two years, followed by (third cycle) doctorate degrees. In some European countries, for example Spain and Germany where students typically spent much longer in the higher education system, this was quite a significant reform. The structures have been somewhat relaxed in later years, to allow four-year first cycle and one-year second cycle degrees. The process also encourages a focus on quality assurance, the use of learning outcomes, and credit systems to measure student workload required to achieve learning outcomes.

Graduate attributes: 'The twenty-first-century graduate?'

There is strong international focus on curriculum reform at present, questioning the traditional curriculum and whether it is fit for purpose in the twenty-first century. Higher education institutions at organizational rather than disciplinary level are asking big questions about their curricula, their graduates, their graduates' place in society and especially in global markets. Questions also arise as to what it means to be a graduate. Is a graduate someone ready to go out into the world and find employment in the global labour market, or contribute to society using the skills and knowledge they have acquired in their undergraduate studies? Or, is a graduate someone ready to start their professional training, or embark on further specialization through a graduate programme after first having gained a broad undergraduate education? Institutions are answering these questions in different ways through their individual strategic plans and reforms.

In universities across the world, changes to curricula are being informed by the notion of 'graduate attributes'. Some institutions are attempting to make themselves and their students distinctive by defining themselves through statements of what it means to be a graduate of their organization, as opposed to a graduate of one of their disciplines. In addition to the knowledge and practices of their disciplines, institutions are looking to define the additional attributes and qualities their particular programmes, co-curricular activities and institutional cultures can provide to graduates. In particular, institutions are attempting to define those attributes that are considered necessary for a graduate entering employment in a highly competitive graduate world. Considerable resources are being placed in the development of attributes, with varying levels of engagement with them, beyond stating them on institutional websites, promotional materials or prospectuses.

The University of Aberdeen (see abdn.ac.uk/graduateattribute/) used its graduate attributes to inform changes to its curricula to include sets of core modules designed specifically to help cultivate particular graduate attributes. Emphasis was also placed on the co-curriculum and its potential to develop graduate attributes, and measures were put in place to allow students to 'prove' their attainment of graduate attributes. However, we need to engage critically with such claims. For example, what does it mean to be an 'active global citizen' in the abstract? To what extent can anyone claim to be an effective communicator without reference to the particular context in which they are communicating? Without being clear about how the experiences we offer students can be convincingly argued to lead to the development of such attributes, we are in danger of creating a set of vacuous statements of aspirational graduate achievements that are used simply as marketing strategies.

These challenges are reflected in the very different approaches taken to embedding graduate attributes into curricula in Australia. The University of New England, for example, has had the *Attributes of a UNE Graduate* policy since 1998 and in 2003 published a lengthy guide for academics to assist them in embedding these attributes into their disciplines. Others have defined quite vague graduate attributes, which, for the most part, are aspirational and not assessed.

Engaging in the process of defining graduate attributes gives us a chance to question our curricula and the skills and attributes students will acquire through engaging with the curriculum, but we need to be careful not to allow the process to become a repackaging exercise in the name of marketing.

Limitations

The technical-instrumentalist approach is widely resented by academics, especially those adopting a traditionalist approach, for imposing a form of 'managerialism' and 'market logic' on universities that undermines academic autonomy and the conditions necessary for knowledge production (for example, Barnett 2003; Mann 2008). Further, this approach is sometimes couched in the universalist assumptions of neo-liberal discourse which leave academics on the ground with a sense that 'there is no alternative'.

Those who see curriculum as a means of social change are critical of the imposition of instrumental rationality and market values such as competitive individualism and performativity on higher education by university managers and government agencies (Mann 2008; Mbembe 2016). They also note that pre-determined fixed learning outcomes inhibit the possibilities for a curriculum to be flexible and responsive to students' needs. Rigid curriculum specifications lead to a lack of time and space for staff–student engagement, interaction and the kind of sociality in which learning can flourish. When applied on a global scale, these critics of the technical instrumentalist approach suggest that it works in Southern contexts via a developmentalist paradigm that positions institutions and people in the South as deficit and dependent on knowledge production systems in the North (Connell et al. 2018) (see also discussion on the political-economy of knowledge production in Chapter 5).

Social realists (Moore and Young 2001; Moore 2000) point out that the specification of learning outcomes over-prescribes what will be taught and does not guarantee the development of expertise. Furthermore, the causal relation between higher education and economic development has yet to be satisfactorily demonstrated.

Curriculum for social change

Those who advocate curriculum for social change suggest that current curricula have been constructed on arbitrary social and political grounds and should therefore be changed. Advocates of this approach are often critical of the two previous approaches which they claim support the status quo and knowingly or unknowingly reproduce social inequalities through the curriculum. Instead, curriculum for social change is a values-based approach that wants to use the curriculum to change society – for example, to undo social hierarchies, redress socio-economic inequalities and promote social justice. Through curriculum and teaching strategies, this approach hopes to shift power from traditional elites and authorities, including academics, to oppressed groups, especially students from these groups; it hopes to empower such students by making the curriculum relevant to their contexts and experiences (for examples of this approach, see Arthur 2016; Jester 2018; McGregor and Park 2019).

The curriculum for social change approach views curriculum as social practice which has the following kinds of implications for curriculum practice. First, the rationales and contexts in which a curriculum gets produced should be made visible to students for discussion and interrogation. Second, the curriculum should provide opportunities for diverse groups of students to connect the curriculum to their own lived experiences and contexts. Third, it is often suggested that teachers take a dialogical, negotiated or collaborative approach to curriculum activities, including curriculum design and assessment (Weller 2012; Bovill et al. 2016). This third implication falls under the broad heading of student engagement in the curriculum, which we address in more depth below.

Applications and examples

Engaging students in curricula

An emerging and potentially powerful idea around curriculum for social change is that of student engagement within curricula. Essentially, the idea of engagement suggests that students should no longer be passive recipients of the curriculum but should instead be taking an active role in helping to shape the curriculum. For traditionalists, this is a fairly radical idea, given that traditionally the control of the curriculum has been the domain of academics, earned through expertise and disciplinary specialization.

There are various ways in which the idea of student engagement has been incorporated into modules and programmes of study. Some of these are quite radical in terms of the shifts in power and responsibility accorded to students. We will examine some examples of this, starting with those that are less radical and more familiar.

Problem-based learning

Problem-based learning (PBL) is a concept that sounds slightly out of date, yet it still has much currency within higher education institutions as it can be an effective means of enabling students to take responsibility for their learning. PBL involves giving students problems to work on in small groups, guided by a facilitator. The students undertake whatever research is necessary in order to work through the problem. Problem-based learning is widely viewed to be a pioneering example of student-centred learning and was first designed within medical schools (for example, Savin-Baden 2003; Barrett and Moore 2010), but has since been adopted as the basis for designing particular modules in almost any discipline. The basic idea of PBL is that the discovery of knowledge is a much more effective means of learning than the memorization of knowledge. The teacher who uses a PBL approach needs to be prepared to relinquish control of the curriculum, given that it is the students' job to search for the knowledge that is necessary to solve the problems set by the teacher. Students need guidance and feedback as they tackle the set problems, so the role of the teacher changes from lecturer to facilitator. Teachers also need to ensure that there are no important gaps in students' knowledge as they progress through the course or module, but otherwise the students largely take responsibility for their own learning.

Case Study 9.1 The University of Leicester's research-led approach to undergraduate Science

Recognizing that real-world problems require the input and collaboration of many disciplines, the Centre for Interdisciplinary Science at the University of Leicester have created a Natural Sciences programme that is not only interdisciplinary, but also problem-based. Students are presented with interdisciplinary problems from an early stage in their undergraduate education.

The curriculum is devised in a way that interdisciplinary problems are presented from the beginning, and modules are put in place to help students develop their problem-solving skills as they progress. Modules are designed specifically for the interdisciplinary programme. Collaborative areas in the centre allow students and academics to interact outside of the formal timetable. Tutors provide most of the face-to-face teaching and specialist academics then lecture on one or two key areas. Students are given work in order to prepare for the classroom sessions, and the timetable is designed to allow students time to work on their own learning. Students take one module at a time.

First-year modules include: Ecology, Neuroscience and Computation, Solar and Planetary Sciences, and Origins of Science.

(see **www2.le.ac.uk/departments/interdisciplinary-science**)

Enquiry-based learning

Another emerging theme in the student engagement literature, designed to help move teachers out of the traditional transmission approach, is enquiry-based learning. The term enquiry-based learning conveys an approach in which students are asked to embark on a process of enquiry or discovery, much as academics do when they are engaged in research (for example, see Summerlee 2018). Enquiry-based learning is therefore a commonly referenced term within the literature on the enhancement of research-teaching synergies (for example, Healey and Jenkins 2009). The desire to bring teaching and research activities closer together has led some academics to develop methods for bringing their research into their teaching to a much greater extent. A curriculum designed to incorporate research might involve either bringing particular topics of research expertise into the curriculum, or bringing processes of research enquiry more to the fore in the student experience of the curriculum.

Healey (2005) has produced a framework to help us think about the different relationships between teaching and research reproduced in Figure 9.1.

Healey's framework has a continuum from teacher-focused to student-focused initiatives along the one axis, and a continuum from an emphasis on content to an emphasis on process along the other axis.

Student-focused
Students as participants

Research-tutored

Curriculum
emphasizes learning
focused on students
writing and
discussing
papers or essays

Research-based

Curriculum
emphasizes
students
undertaking
inquiry-based
learning

**Emphasis on
research content**

**Emphasis on
research processes
and problems**

Research-led

Curriculum
is structured around
teaching subject
content

Research-oriented

Curriculum
emphasizes
teaching processes
of knowledge
construction in the
subject

Teacher-focused
Students as audiences

Figure 9.1
Curriculum design
and the research-
teaching nexus
(Healey, 2005)

Student-as-producer

Some recent and very innovative approaches to student engagement are the initiatives identified within the 'student-as-producer' movement. For example, at the University of Lincoln, the *Student as Producer* project was rolled out across the institution (see studentasproducer.lincoln.ac.uk). As we saw in Chapter 4, the University of Exeter has also pioneered the student-as-producer model by fostering an ethos in which students are positioned as change agents. As change agents, students are given a voice and an opportunity to enhance their learning through projects they initiate and conduct. The underlying rationale of these projects is to ensure that students are given more responsibility for their learning experiences through collaboration with academic staff.

All of the above projects are innovative variations on the same theme: that of encouraging greater student engagement in and responsibility for their learning, often through an aim to foster learning communities. The perceived benefits of facilitating greater student engagement are that students take more responsibility for their learning experiences, and therefore become more actively involved within their university communities with potentially better learning outcomes. However, there will undoubtedly be concerns, especially from some academics adopting the traditionalist approach, that the value of their subject expertise is being side-lined in favour of giving greater power to students who are not (yet) experts. It is important for academics and course teams to find their own path through these differing views and having a clear understanding of the pedagogic rationale behind their choices.

RESEARCH BRIEFING 9.1 Addressing potential challenges in co-creating learning and teaching

Bovill et al. (2016) undertook a survey of the different meanings of co-creation of the curriculum and pedagogy. They identified three levels of co-creation by students:

1 Student engagement – which focuses on staff developing a curriculum that encourages students' emotional and intellectual investment in their learning.
2 Co-creation – where staff and students work collaboratively with each other to create components of the curriculum or pedagogy.
3 Students-as-partners – which is more radically defined as 'a collaborative reciprocal process through which all participants have the opportunity to contribute equally, although not necessarily in the same ways, to curricula or pedagogical conceptualisation, decision-making, implementation or analysis' (Cook-Sather et al. 2014).

Bovill et al. summarize the claims about the benefits of co-creation as: enhanced student engagement, responsibility and sense of agency as well as improved staff–student relationships. They note that students are afforded different degrees of agency in co-creation projects – from consultant to representative to co-designer to co-researcher. They also note how the role of academics shifts from being disciplinary experts to becoming facilitators and co-learners in shared enquiry. This disrupts traditional power relations and transmission modes of teaching found in the traditional approach to curriculum and instead generates trust, respect, openness and reciprocity between teachers and learners. Bovill et al. note significant challenges to the co-creation movement, for example many academic staff are resistant to the identity shifts, time and vulnerability and risks entailed; many curricula are pre-specified, leaving little scope for innovation; the selection of students can be problematic because those with the most social and cultural capital will be the first to come forward to work in partnerships with staff.

Reflective Activity 9.1 Self-assessing the extent of student engagement in your courses

Choose a session, module, course or programme for which you have some responsibility for curriculum design. Now consider the level of student involvement you have enabled within this particular course (we will use the term 'course' to denote whatever you have chosen to reflect on):

	1	2	3	4	5
	No involvement			Lots of involvement	
1. Input into knowledge content of the curriculum					
2. Input into the design of learning activities in the curriculum					
3. Input into the design of the assessment methods					
4. Input into the production of assessment criteria					
5. Involvement in processes of research or enquiry as part of the course					
6. Involvement in evaluation of the course for future development					
7. Involvement in decisions about the future development of the course					

Looking at your responses above, are there areas in which you would like to increase student input and, if so, how might you do this?

Case Study 9.2 The call to decolonize the curriculum at the University of Cape Town

A recent version of advocating curriculum for social change in a Southern context is the call by student protesters for 'decolonizing the curriculum'. This was triggered by the RhodesMustFall Movement at the University of Cape Town whose manifesto demands 'a curriculum (. . .) linked to social justice and the experiences of black people' (RMF 2015).

As noted in Chapter 5, this call to decolonize the curriculum draws on Latin American decolonial theory which targets the global political-economy of knowledge production and critiques the ways metropolitan Western universities, the modern disciplines and five modern European languages continue to dominate research and curriculum production in the rest of the world (Grosfoguel 2013). This version of decolonial theory insists that the West's claim to 'modernity' has a 'darker side' – that of 'coloniality' – which must be acknowledged and redressed. It thus calls for a shift in knowledge production agendas and power relations to serve the needs of subordinated peoples (Mignolo 2010). It wants to open up disciplinary canons to previously excluded knowledges, cultures and languages (Ndlovu-Gatsheni 2013) – believing that this will empower students from subordinated groups and result in great social and epistemic justice.

In response to the student protests at the University of Cape Town, a Curriculum Change Working Group was established to work with student activists using a students-as-partners approach to 'make sense of the student protests and their critique that the university context is socially unjust and exclusive' (UCT 2018, p. 52). The group tabled a report, the University of Cape Town's Curriculum Change Framework 2018: **news.uct. ac.za/images/userfiles/downloads/reports/ccwg/UCT-Curriculum-Change-Framework.pdf**

Regarding students' role in curriculum production, the CCF asserts that 'students are important stakeholders, they must participate in the academic project without having to be stripped from their identities by colonial narratives' (UCT 2018, p. 62). Taking the view that curriculum is social practice, the CCF asserts that the curriculum must reflect students' cultural capital and 'bring African ways of knowing to the centre' (UCT 2018, p. 62). It goes on to note that curriculum change is not only about content, but also about challenging the tacit practices of the hidden curriculum. For example, the CCF aims to 'resist deficit and assimilationist models based on Anglonormativity and Eurocentricism', claiming that 'Anglonormativity preserves a language hierarchy, it is a mechanism by which race and class are reproduced and black students' cultural capital devalued' (2018, p. 58).

On the nature of curriculum knowledge and the disciplines the CCF states that 'Curriculum change is about contesting power, especially disciplinarity which carries colonial narratives'. Further, 'Colonial authority is sustained by a belief that some people are superior or inferior to others, and that some knowledges are superior or inferior to others. Central to resisting coloniality is defying colonial authority in what constitutes knowledge, how it is produced and who is allowed to claim custodianship. Here there is disruption of the false divide between different subjectivities and knowledge, such that it is no longer possible to claim absolute objectivity and universalism' (2018, p. 54).

There is still much debate at UCT as to how the institution should take the Curriculum Change Framework further towards implementation across the faculties.

Limitations

Depending on their own position or approach to curriculum, people will come up with different kinds of critiques of the curriculum as social change approach. Many academics shy away from this approach because it implies a loss of power and control over what and how they teach. Others are resistant simply because of the intense personal investment and time that this approach demands. Some in the traditionalist camp are likely to believe that this approach adopts a romanticized view of students that overlooks their lack of disciplinary expertise when attempting to co-design a curriculum. Others, probably from the technical-instrumentalist camp, are likely to feel irritated by this approach for its idealism and for not adequately taking into account the pre-specified standards and requirements of external stakeholders such as qualification frameworks, employers and professional bodies. Perhaps the most concerted critique of the curriculum as social change approach comes from the social realists (discussed below) who challenge its theory of knowledge. While accepting that the social identity of knowers is salient to knowledge production and epistemic judgement, social realists argue that social identity on its own is insufficient grounds for making or attributing a knowledge claim (Maton 2014; Moore and Young 2001). The social realists believe it is reductionist to reduce knowledge to the interests of its knowers; that we should not reduce standards and criteria for knowledge and for determining the curriculum to the social interests of certain groups. Furthermore, they argue that relevance and experience are inadequate bases for determining what knowledge should be selected for a curriculum and that curricula that privilege relevance and experience will ultimately short-change students who may not get adequate access to 'powerful knowledge' (Wheelahan 2010).

Social realism

A social realist sociology of education is the fourth approach to curriculum production that we discuss in this chapter. It builds on the work and methods of Basil Bernstein who focused on analysing forms of communication in schools. As we saw above, the social realist school challenges what it views as the relativist and reductionist views of knowledge adopted by many curriculum as social change approaches because in their view this short-changes students' access to 'powerful knowledge' (Moore 2000; Moore and Young 2001). The social realists argue that the debate around curriculum knowledge should focus on the internal properties of knowledge and ensure that curricula give access to the specialized practices of communities of expertise in the disciplines and professions; whereas the social identity of who produces the knowledge is secondary (Moore 2000). The social realists do not deny that knowledge gets produced in and is shaped by particular socio-cultural contexts – and is therefore fallible – but they argue that under certain conditions, knowledge can transcend its context of production and endure across time and space. A key advocate of this approach, Michael Young (2008), uses the concept 'powerful knowledge' to refer to the specialized knowledge, developed and verified by disciplinary communities of enquiry according to transparent epistemic rules. Young's definition locates 'powerful knowledge' firmly in the disciplines; on the assumption that it is this institutionalized knowledge that is the best currently available to humanity and to which, therefore, access should be democratized. Furthermore, this approach believes that it is in the disciplines that we find the best methods, procedures, criteria and social practices (such as blind peer review) for verifying knowledge claims.

Applications and examples

When it comes to actual curriculum production, the social realist approach is seldom used as a driver for new curriculum design or reform. This is probably because to a large extent it endorses the traditional approach of working from within the disciplines and taking a content- or knowledge-driven approach to curriculum. Instead, the social realist approach has made a strong contribution to policy formulation and critique (e.g. Muller 2009) and also to research on already existing curricula. The social realist approach provides concepts and research tools for analysing the nature of different kinds of knowledge structures, focusing on the internal properties of knowledge which can then be used to improve the coherence and integrity of curriculum design. This enables a differentiated view of knowledge that can, for example, inform decisions about the extent to which different curricula might emphasize 'conceptual coherence' or 'contextual coherence' (Muller 2009). Building on the social realist approach, Maton's (2014) Legitimation Code Theory provides further conceptual and methodological tools for analysing knowledge structures in ways that can inform curriculum design – especially with regard to designing curricula that enable the cumulative building of knowledge through sequencing and pedagogic practices to enable students to build conceptual coherence (see Maton et al. 2016). The integrity of a knowledge structure, it is argued, needs to be retained in curriculum design to enable students to build knowledge cumulatively and progress vertically up a curriculum spine. Studies using the social realist approach include Wheelahan (2010) who analysed vocational education in Australia to show how competency-based education short-changes students, failing to give them access to the epistemic rules and powerful ways of thinking in the disciplines. While in South Africa the social realist approach and tools have been used to critique higher education policy and academic planning (Muller 2009; Shay et al. 2016). Other studies that analyse knowledge structures in particular disciplines or professions include African Studies (Luckett 2019); Biology (Kelly-Laubscher and Luckett 2016); Design (Shay and Steyn 2016); Engineering (Wolff and Luckett 2013; Wolmarans 2016; Wolff 2017); Physics (Georgiou 2016); and Sociology (Luckett 2009).

Maton's LCT (Legitimation Code Theory) Centre for Knowledge-Building at the University of Sydney has generated a large number of empirical studies used to analyse in detail different forms of curriculum knowledge and to tease out the implications of the findings for sound curriculum design and pedagogic practice in both higher education and schooling (legitimationcodetheory.com). For example, in Maton, Hood and Shay (2016) one can find applications of LCT to physics, English literature, music, design, vocational education, education and ethnographic methods.

Limitations

The social realist position is critiqued for coming to the defence of the disciplines and for upholding their institutionalized power and elitist practices. Unsurprisingly, the strongest critiques come from the curriculum as social change camp who point out how the assumed universal reach of 'powerful' knowledge excludes other forms of knowledge and knowers and, in post-colonial contexts, perpetuates the power relations of 'coloniality'. The social realists are accused of reinforcing the West's control of symbolic space and of privileging abstract context-independent theory over contextualized practice (Leibowitz 2017). Feminist and decolonial scholars would be critical of the social realist approach for its privileging of epistemology over ontology, mind over body, reason over affect that works to exclude 'others' and other ways of knowing (Alcoff 2011). Similarly, educationists in the curriculum as social change camp argue that the social realists fail to give sufficient attention to how people come to know; that learning is affective, emotional, social and experiential, as well as cognitive (Zipin et al. 2015; Leibowitz 2017).

Reflective Activity 9.2 Thinking about our own curriculum practices

This activity is designed to help you think critically about your own curriculum practice using the four approaches outlined above. Once you have read through Chapter 9 to this point, arrange to meet with a small group of colleagues and share out the set of questions listed below. Then meet to discuss your responses to the questions you were allocated. Keep your discussion focused on what assumptions, values and approaches you assume when working on a curriculum. You are unlikely to find that your position or your curriculum fits neatly into only one of the approaches discussed above. Talk to each other about what currently drives your curriculum decisions and what opportunities exist for change.

Knowledge-as-research

1 How do you view knowledge? To what extent do you think it is a product separate from society?
2 How self-reflexive is your discipline about its historical development, its dominant paradigms and methodologies and what assumptions about knowledge are these based on?
3 What are the debates that you and your colleagues engage in, who do you read and talk to, who comprises your communities of practice? Who are the peers whom you look to who validate your research? What conferences do you attend and where do you publish? To what extent does your discipline regard the global South as a site of theoretical production as opposed to application and sites for data-gathering?
4 What are the absences and silences in your research field, what issues could it address, but does not and why? To what extent does your field undertake research that addresses the problems and complexities of Southern issues?

Knowledge-as-curriculum

1 What principles, norms, values and worldviews inform your selection of knowledge for your curriculum? (Think about absences as well as presences, centres as well as margins.)

2 Does your curriculum articulate clearly for students your own intellectual and social position and that of the authors you prescribe?

3 For whom do you design your curriculum? Who is the ideal/imagined student that you hold in mind and what assumptions do you make about their backgrounds, culture, languages and schooling?

4 How does your curriculum promote epistemic and social justice? To what extent does it historicize and relativize inherited curricula and dominant worldviews?

5 To what extent does your curriculum 'level the playing fields' by requiring traditional middle-class students to acquire intellectual and cultural resources to function effectively in a plural society?

ALIGNMENT AND CONGRUENCE IN CURRICULUM DESIGN

In the second part of this chapter, we examine the principles of alignment and congruence for curriculum design. Regardless of the approach to thinking about curriculum that you adopt, when it comes to the practice of curriculum design, whether you are setting out to design a new curriculum or evaluating an existing one, we urge you to take these principles seriously – at programme, course and module level.

When designing curricula we need to think about how the different elements of the curriculum come together to help students to achieve high-quality learning outcomes. John Biggs' notion of 'constructive alignment' (see Biggs and Tang 2011) is one very visible approach to alignment within the higher education literature. Whilst it has been criticized for emphasizing a particular approach to constructivism (Jervis and Jervis 2005), the basic idea of alignment is simply that the ways in which we teach and assess need to be congruent with what we want students to learn. This is a useful idea and what Biggs importantly highlights is that it needs to be visible from the student perspective, rather than simply obvious to us as teachers (see Gallagher 2017; Higgins et al. 2017; Croy 2018; and Bovill and Woolmer 2019 for recent explorations of the ideas around constructive alignment).

The idea of alignment has been developed further by Hounsell and Hounsell's (2007) notion of 'congruence'. This notion was developed in the Enhancing Teaching-Learning Environments in Undergraduate Courses (ETL project) we discussed in Chapter 2. During the project it was felt that the notion of alignment implied a straightforward link between aims, teaching methods and assessment, whereas congruence emphasizes that these different elements form a complex system of interconnections, which can change over time (Entwistle 2018).

Hounsell and Hounsell (2007) emphasize that learning outcomes need to be congruent with:

- curriculum aims, scope and structure;
- teaching and learning activities;
- learning support;
- students' backgrounds, knowledge and aspirations;
- assessment and feedback;
- course organization and management.

In actively designing our modules and programmes to achieve such congruence, it is important that the intended student experience is central to design decisions. Consider the, unlikely and extreme, example of a student studying mathematics, who learns through lectures but never actually *does* any mathematics. This student is extremely unlikely to become a mathematician. All the different elements in the list above should inform and be congruent with each other. For example, we should assess in a way that adequately and fairly allows students to demonstrate how they have met the learning outcomes by developing their knowledge and practices through engagement with the teaching and learning activities and learning support (see Engelhardt 2016 for an exploration of using these ideas in practice).

Specification of intended learning outcomes

Learning outcomes are statements of what we intend that a learner should know, understand or be able to do at the end of a period of learning (Gosling and Moon 2003).

Learning outcomes focus on the student and are written both *for* and *to* the student, typically taking a form similar to: 'By the end of this course, you should be able to . . .'. Learning outcomes are a shift away from learning objectives, which can read more like statements of teacher intent, what it is we intend to cover over the period of instruction. We are, through learning outcomes, attempting to move away from a focus on teaching, what *we* do, to a focus on learning what the *student* does. Learning outcomes can be considered on a number of levels: programme, module or course level. Crucially, learning outcomes should take account of what students do, their participation, engagement and learning activities, rather than reflect the material that we 'cover' in an individual lecture or seminar. It is important to be aware that their meaning can be seen to change from the perspective of teachers and students (Sweetman 2019) and the quality of learning outcomes is often quite low (Schoepp 2019). This means we need to recognize that writing learning outcomes is a challenging task and we need to think carefully about the extent to which they reflect an understanding of the subject matter that our students would recognize.

Once we have generated the intended learning outcomes for our programme, course or module, we can then consider what activities will best help students achieve them. These activities can be teacher- or student-led. They can take many forms, including what is done in and outside of the lecture hall, classroom, laboratory, tutorial, peer group, library and other learning environments. Both the learning outcomes and the teaching and learning activities will inform the assessment. If students are practising what they are learning, then assessment tasks should be an extension of these learning activities. Assessment that is well designed and adheres to the principles of congruence or constructive alignment will also promote active engagement by students (Rust 2007). **Reflective Activity 9.3** and the associated grid (Figure 9.2) may help you work with this process. The activity and grid encourage us to step back and consider the entire teaching and learning experience in which the students will be engaged. For further discussion on designing teaching and learning activities and assessment, see Chapters 10, 11 and 13.

The process of curriculum design will be a cyclical process. Few of us will manage to design a module or programme that satisfies the principles of congruence or constructive alignment in our first attempt. We should reflect on our design iteratively, asking ourselves what we want to achieve, what we want our students to achieve, how they are responding to our teaching–learning activities and what we can do better to support them to succeed. Student participation, student performance, student evaluations and our own reflections on how the course is progressing will inform future revisions. It is also useful to engage a critical friend who is familiar with the discipline to review your module design. As academics, we are busy, and it can be difficult to find the time and head-space to take a step back from the daily demands of teaching, assessment, administration and so on, to appraise what we are doing and how we are doing it – but it is worth it. In the next sections we consider both top-down and bottom-up design of curricula.

Reflective Activity 9.3 Congruence between learning outcomes, teaching and learning activities and assessment methods

This activity can be undertaken for review of an existing course module or the design of a module that you would like to develop in the future. You may find the grid in Figure 9.2 below helpful for this exercise.

Consider a module for which you have responsibility. Starting with the learning outcomes, write down what it is the student should be able to know and do at the end of the module.

Next consider how you plan to assess these learning outcomes, or in the case of redesign, how you currently assess the learning outcomes?

Finally, write down all planned teaching and learning activities the students will engage in, for example lectures, practical activities, readings.

Taking each learning outcome in turn, map the teaching and learning activities that best support the achievement of that learning outcome and the assessments that will allow students to demonstrate their achievement.

Looking at your completed grid:

- Are all learning outcomes supported by teaching and learning activities, either tutor- or student-led?
- Are all learning outcomes assessed?
- Are any learning outcomes over-assessed?
- Are all learning outcomes, activities and assessments necessary?
- Are you assessing anything not expressed in a learning outcome?

You may find that there are adjustments you can make to the design of your module that will better support the students in their learning, or make space in the curriculum for other activities or learning outcomes.

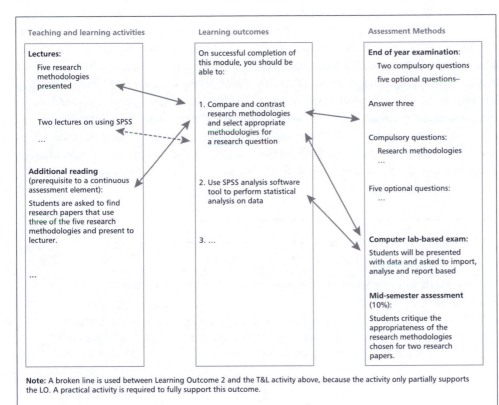

Figure 9.2
Congruence between teaching and learning activities, learning outcomes and assessment methods

Note: A broken line is used between Learning Outcome 2 and the T&L activity above, because the activity only partially supports the LO. A practical activity is required to fully support this outcome.

Check to see if you are:

• over-assessing: Are any of your learning outcomes assessed more than once or twice? Do they need to be assessed multiple times?
• under-assessing? Are any of your learning outcomes not assessed at all? If they are not assessed, are they essential learning outcomes?

Do teaching and learning activities appropriately support all learning outcomes?

Top-down design

Ideally, curriculum design starts at the programme level and is undertaken by the programme team or all those contributing to a programme as opposed to a sole individual. The key question we need to ask is 'What should a graduate of this programme be able to do?' This will involve defining programme outcomes that are informed by both disciplinary and institutional resources.

There are a number of resources available to help inform the design of programme outcomes; for example, in the UK the Quality Assurance Agency (QAA) for Higher Education have set out Subject Benchmark statements, which outline what kind of achievements graduates of a particular discipline should attain at either Honours or Masters degree level (see qaa.ac.uk/quality-code/subject-benchmark-statements). Also, it is worth bearing in mind a number of countries now have national frameworks of qualifications; for example, the Framework for Higher Education Qualifications (FHEQ) in England, Wales and Northern Ireland, the Scottish Credit and Qualifications Framework (SCQF), the National Framework of Qualifications (NFQ) in Ireland and the Australian Qualifications Framework (AQF). These frameworks were developed in order to describe national qualifications in terms of the knowledge, skills and attributes a programme of a certain level will offer. Module outcomes can be identified that will contribute to the attainment of the overall programme outcomes (Figure 9.3). It may be that there is an existing suite of modules that can deliver the outcomes needed to satisfy a programme or it may be that some additional modules will need to be designed.

Reflective Activity 9.4 The relationship between programme and module outcomes

This activity will ideally take place as a group activity with members of the programme team.

Take an existing programme and the contributing modules. Do current programme and module outcomes complement each other? Are all programme outcomes either directly or indirectly capable of being achieved given the current suite of modules?

	Module 1	Module 2	. . .	. . .	Module . . .
Programme Outcome 1	x	x	Outcome 2	x	x
. . .					
. . .			x		
Outcome 8	X	x	x	x	x

Figure 9.3 Mapping relations between module and programme outcomes

Reflective Activity 9.5 Curricular domains

If you are responsible for curriculum design or evaluation, you may find the following schema useful in thinking through the emphasis placed on different domains within the curriculum (Barnett and Coate 2005). The diagram suggests that there are three possible domains within every curriculum which we can identify as the knowledge, action and self domains (or knowing, acting and being domains). You may already be familiar with a version of this schema, as some professional associations and national frameworks stipulate that curricula address key domains such as knowledge, skills and attributes.

In this schema, Barnett and Coate (2005) are encouraging a reflective approach in which consideration is given to the extent to which each domain is emphasized within curricula and how it is expressed. Is the knowledge domain the most significant (has the curriculum been designed on the basis of transmission of knowledge content)? How important are the elements that require acquisition of skills (the doing rather than knowing)? And finally, to what extent is there emphasis on the development of students as human beings, or of their own sense of self?

You may also want to reflect on not just the emphasis placed on each domain but the extent to which they overlap with each other. For instance, in some professional subjects such as nursing studies, the sense of the student's development as a nursing professional (being) overlaps to some extent with the skills they need to acquire. In other words, their professional behaviour may be shaped by the actions that they perform with patients (for instance, learning to calm a patient who is nervous about having blood taken). Students learn technical skills but these may also require appropriate behaviours.

One of the key aspects of this schema is that it encourages reflection, in particular on the 'being' domain which is often a hidden or implicit aspect of a curriculum. Students grow, develop and change during the time they are in higher education, but we often do not take the time to reflect on whether we can articulate within our curricula an understanding of this growth and change. This is partly the reason why it took so long for courses in medical fields to include these types of 'softer skills' of communication or professional behaviour, but it is useful to consider this domain in the wider respect of the development of students as human beings. Can you, within your own curricula, gain a sense of the students' development as human beings? Would you even want to be able to explicitly define this domain, or do you see it as outside your purview?

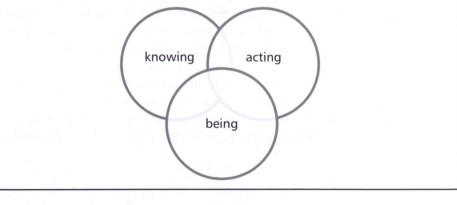

Potential constraints and barriers to innovative curriculum design

Higher education institutions are complex multi-purpose organizations with delegated authority and dispersed power. This means that top-down curriculum change processes run from the centre are seldom successful and may be resisted by academics who are the key curriculum change agents. Blackmore and Kandiko (2012) argue for strategic curriculum change that views higher education institutions as networks, encouraging change through incentives and being responsive to student demands rather than by fiat from top management or external bodies. They suggest that institution-wide curriculum reform is best driven through providing broad frameworks that permit on the ground interpretation. In addition, managers should create organizational environments that encourage and reward innovation and pay attention to the quality of the staff experience (as well as to that of students).

The constraints and processes of curriculum design and reform will be different for different disciplines and professional fields. For example, some such as the Health Sciences and Engineering have professional accrediting bodies that pre-specify learning outcomes, compulsory modules and/or assessment types. These requirements can constrain curriculum innovation. Others would like to redesign their courses but have little scope to do so given the nature of their departmental role and departmental constraints. In such cases, it may be possible to introduce new or innovative ways of teaching and learning while still meeting requirements beyond your control.

More often than not, we find ourselves responsible for one or two modules in a programme, but with little input into the design of the entire programme or other contributing modules. If we are not part of an active programme team, this can make (re-)designing our module problematic, in terms of what to expect of students, their prior learning and the learning taking place in complementary modules. This is likely to limit our scope and expectations for what we can achieve as individuals. In the absence of functional programme teaching teams, well-written module descriptors in terms of learning outcomes, assessment and teaching and learning activities are of benefit, not only to our students, but also to our colleagues.

Other well-known constraints to curriculum innovation are linked to a lack of resources and to having to teach large classes. Both of these factors can limit the type and frequency of assessments and the potential for engaging with and providing feedback to students. We may feel an end-of-year essay-based exam is the only workable solution for a large class. However, there are ways that large classes can be assessed regularly without requiring extensive resources, for example, by involving students in the assessment process, through self and peer assessment (see Falchikov 2005; To and Panadero 2019; Merry and Osmond 2018) which can be very rewarding for both student and teacher. Self and peer assessment highlight the power of involving students in curricular processes.

CONCLUSION

It is easy to think of curriculum knowledge as universal and therefore of the curriculum as static and fixed. We tend to talk more about the actions we can take to adjust our curricula rather than consider how curricula are implicated in changing students and enabling learning. For example, we talk about doing things to the curriculum such as internationalizing it or broadening it. But we have no language to describe what curricula do to students, even though the curriculum is one of the most fundamental aspects of the student experience. This is why working with students and legitimating their contributions in the curriculum development space has become increasingly important.

Thinking about the curriculum as a process rather than a product can help us to design curricula with students' learning in mind (Fraser and Bosanquet 2006; Bovill and Woolmer 2019). Considering the ways in which students can become more involved in all stages of curriculum development, as discussed above, can also help us to view the curriculum as a process which students actively experience and shape throughout their studies. It is no longer possible to view students as passive consumers of curricula; instead we should invite them to respond and help shape it through working together with us as reflective teachers.

KEY READINGS

For a review of the use of learning outcomes in universities, see:

Schoepp, K. (2019) 'The state of course learning outcomes at leading universities', *Studies in Higher Education*, 44(4), 615–27.

For a discussion of how different approaches to curriculum affect the co-creation of the curriculum, see:

Bovill, C. and Woolmer, C. (2019). 'How conceptualisations of curriculum in higher education influence student-staff co-creation in and of the curriculum', *Higher Education*, 78(3), 407–22.

On encouraging student engagement in the curriculum, see:

Bovill, C., Cook-Sather, A., Felten, P., Millard, L. and Moore-Cherry, N. (2016) 'Addressing potential challenges in co-creating learning and teaching', *Higher Education*, 71, 195–208.

For an introduction to different dimensions of curriculum, see:

Barnett, R. and Coate, K. (2005) *Engaging the Curriculum in Higher Education*. Maidenhead: Open University Press and McGraw-Hill Education.

For guidance on writing learning outcomes, see:

Gosling, D. and Moon, J. (2003) *How to Use Learning Outcomes and Assessment Criteria*. 3rd edn. London: SEEC.

Chapter 10
Planning
How are we implementing curricula?

INTRODUCTION

Whilst the previous chapter focused on how we can conceive of and design curricula, this chapter focuses on the practical issues involved in planning and implementing them. Moving from the design of a curriculum to its implementation can often be a challenging process as we are faced with putting our ideas about teaching into practice. For this reason, in this chapter we work from the opposite end of the process that we examined in Chapter 9. We begin by examining the issues related to planning and implementing individual sessions and then examine the implementation of individual modules in terms of the planning of teaching–learning activities, assessment, how to use feedback from our students and how to work collaboratively with colleagues. Finally, we explore the practical aspects of programme planning and review and the issues related to involving students, employers and external examiners in these processes.

This chapter and Chapter 9 have the common aim of ensuring that the design of each level of a course (programme, module and sessions) is congruent with the overall programme goals or 'programme-level outcomes'. However, much of our real exposure to teaching starts from the bottom-up with us being given responsibility for particular classes or modules rather than starting with a complete blank sheet. For this reason, in this chapter, we begin with planning for individual learning sessions before we ascend to the dizzy heights of programme design.

See Chapter 4

TLRP Principles

Three principles are of particular relevance to this chapter on planning in higher education:

Principle 5: Effective teaching and learning promotes the active engagement of the student as learner. A key aim of higher learning should be to develop students' independence and autonomy as learners. This involves engaging students actively in their own learning, and ensuring that they acquire a repertoire of learning strategies and practices, develop positive learning dispositions, and build the confidence to become agents in their own learning.

Principle 6: Effective teaching and learning needs assessment to be congruent with learning. Assessment should be designed for maximum validity in terms of learning outcomes and learning processes, and also should be specific to the type of subject or discipline involved, even if it is interdisciplinary. It should help to advance learning as well as determine whether learning has occurred.

Principle 7: Effective teaching and learning requires learning to be systematically developed. Teachers, trainers, lecturers, researchers and all who support the learning of others should provide intellectual, social and emotional support which helps learners to develop expertise in their learning for it to be effective and secure.

SESSION PLANNING

Teaching approaches and session planning

Those with experience of teaching in schools will be familiar with the idea of session planning and how demanding it can be for new trainee teachers. In those sectors there is often a statutory requirement for each class to be planned in detail and to match national curricula and standards. Fortunately, in higher education we usually have considerably more freedom to shape our own curricula and to select from a wide range of possible approaches to teaching, but we often do not make the most of this freedom. In addition, given that contact time with any particular group of students can be very limited, there is an onus on us to ensure that the time spent in class is productive and as effective as possible – but that certainly does not mean always doing the same as has always been done.

Preparation and planning need not be inflexible. Indeed, quite the opposite is the case when done well. What is key is having an explicit sense of the connection between what we want to achieve and what we – and our students – actually do. Good planning can enhance the spontaneity and sense of dialogue between us and our students, not diminish it. And to step into a lecture or tutorial class with little preparation, little forethought for possible eventualities, is not only a high-risk strategy but one that is likely to frustrate teacher and student alike.

Learning and teaching interactions, including engagement with curricula, are co-constructed by students and us as teachers. Indeed, over recent years far more importance has been ascribed to students' active roles in their own learning, and we return to this later in this chapter. But the logical extension of this is not that our role in these processes is less; simply that it is different. Some see the active involvement of students to construct their own learning experiences as reducing their teachers to facilitators; no longer active teachers but the enablers of independent student learning. But this view goes too far to diminish the important role of the teacher, and the reasons why their planning is so crucial to effective student learning. Indeed, it is time to get beyond the unhelpful binary of teacher-centred or student-centred and focus on the relationship between them, and the different ways this is enacted during different stages in the learning process.

A helpful insight into the relationship between student and teacher in higher education comes from Northedge and McArthur (2009) as they argue for the significance of what the teacher does, even when one is committed to student agency. Figure 10.1 captures different aspect of the teaching–learning process teased apart for further consideration.

The implication of this figure is not that we choose one of the four categories as our own personal teaching approach. Rather, it suggests that at different moments, and in different contexts, the nature of the teaching–learning situation can differ. Each of these four categories is equally legitimate, depending on the purpose of the particular part of the curriculum you are seeking to implement. But understanding that the teaching–learning relationship is dynamic and likely to change according to context and purpose is an important part of good planning.

Figure 10.1
Different ways of
approaching
teaching

	Personal/social learning	Intellectual/cognitive learning
Outer aspects concerning the discipline community, its knowledge, discourses and practices	**Apprentice scholar** approach foregrounds learning how to function as a member of the discipline community, through researching, debating, publishing	**Lecture-centred** approach foregrounds the knowledge produced by the discipline community: how it can be assembled, organized, encapsulated and presented
Inner aspects concerning processes within the mind and social being of the student	**Radical student centeredness** foregrounds development of self, realignment of values, coping with acquiring an identity as a member of a knowledge community	**Constructivism** foregrounds the processes of cognitive reorganization and development entailed with making sense within an unfamiliar field of knowledge

Reflective Activity 10.1 Reflecting on different manifestations of the teaching–learning relationship

Thinking about your own teaching, can you think of an example that fits into each of the four categories in the above table?

How does your role as teacher differ depending on which of these forms of engagement you are seeking to encourage?

Of course, our preparation and performance in class is also shaped by the perspectives we hold on the nature of knowledge in our discipline, and our beliefs as to how students come to know. But taking real consideration of disciplinary issues also requires one to be careful of myths surrounding certain disciplines which can limit the sense in which students are seen as active partners in their own learning. In particular, do we buy in to myths that some disciplines require a purely transmission form of teaching or do we believe all university teaching should enable active forms of learning?

In their classic text, Prosser and Trigwell (1999) argued that approaches to teaching are shaped by both an *intention* and a *strategy*, and the combination of each affects how we shape the curriculum, how we actually teach and the learning experience of the students. In broad terms, there are two general categories of intention: either *Information Transmission* or *Conceptual Change*, where the terms are fairly self-explanatory. Disciplinary knowledge and cultures as well as formal course requirements and institutional practices often shape our own dispositions (Lindblom-Ylänne et al. 2006). Many subject areas such as science or medicine are, of course, considered usually to be very 'content heavy' with curricula determined almost completely in terms of topics to be covered (as hundreds of years of scientific progress are crammed into a three- or four-year programme).

Other disciplines are more obviously open to debating issues, to exploring implications and to re-framing perspectives and this is what is captured in 'Conceptual Change'. However, and this is an important point, these categories are not necessarily inevitable consequences of the discipline. Indeed, many would argue that problems students face with conceptual understanding in sciences are precisely because much teaching and learning focuses on covering content to the detriment of challenging conceptions. Indeed, one can argue that across any discipline, tackling dynamic and contested conceptual knowledge is key to what makes higher education distinctive.

The other dimension highlighted by Prosser and Trigwell (1999), that of strategy, is equally important to consider. Here we can reflect on the table from Northedge and McArthur (2009) and the different forms of the teaching and learning relationship we may aim to nurture in different situations. We should not be afraid to use traditional lectures, for example, when they are designed to serve a particular purpose and enable engagement with knowledge in necessary ways. Again, we come back to moving beyond the simple binary of student or teacher centred and to consider more (a) the nature of the knowledge task and (b) the relationship between student and teacher. Indeed, the phrase 'student centred' is often misunderstood, or misused, to imply 'spoon feeding', but this is not what is meant in this context. In fact, it is the opposite. It is about students taking responsibility for their own learning but with you as teacher, aware of their levels of prior knowledge, anticipating where they are likely to face difficulty and designing learning activities that will help them progress, providing the scaffolding for their learning.

It is also important at this stage to consider the effect of class size on the teaching strategy. Indeed, in this age of high rates of participation in higher education combined with reduced funding, the issue of staff–student ratio is of increasing concern. There is no doubt that there are limits to the level of individual attention and support students can be offered and that this can pose a serious challenge to the quality of the learning experience. The somewhat extreme example of early versions of expository MOOCs (Massive Open Online Courses) demonstrates what a 'course' that is based solely on content delivery might look like (although more recent MOOCs have focused on student participation and interaction). Thousands may enrol, but only a handful of students have the staying power, the determination and the prior educational experience necessary to successfully complete.

So what can we do in practice to not just mitigate class size, but actually make large class sessions more effective? This is discussed further in Chapters 11 and 12, but it is worthwhile noting one interesting finding from some of the studies on approaches to teaching where, in some cases, it wasn't just the actual class size that shaped teaching orientation but also the teacher's perception of the class size as being either 'too large' or 'manageable' (Prosser and Trigwell 1999). For some, the large lecture is something that needs to be endured, got through, material presented, notes taken and perhaps some questions at the end. For others, the situation can be re-framed as more of a 'large group meeting' or 'plenary session', where discussion, debate and activity are regarded as vital. An interesting example of where such re-framing has arisen, within the context of traditionally content-dominated subject disciplines, has been the increasing use of 'clickers' (or personal response systems). In some institutions these have taken hold and when used correctly (i.e. to promote discussion rather than to test knowledge) there is evidence that it improves student understanding and subject confidence (Hubbard and Couch 2018). We explore other ways of engaging large groups such as textwalls (McArthur and Huxham 2013) in Chapter 12.

Planning individual sessions

Preparation and planning can of course be taken to extremes, with too high a level of granularity, of attempts to schedule every minute, of trying to include too many activities or too much content. Striking a balance requires a basic plan but also factoring in possible contingencies, scope for a change of direction, for reiteration or alternative explanations of points that students are struggling with. Good planning is also responsive to what the student brings with them to the encounter (McArthur 2018), which is another reason why it cannot tie things down too tightly. Again, this is about emphasizing teaching and learning interactions as genuine partnerships – and this has to be reflected in the planning.

Sawyer (2011), for example, likens teaching to jazz performance, taking signals from the audience, judging pacing and timing, knowing when to reach beyond and when to recap, each class session being unique and unrepeatable. This is characteristic of an accomplished expert practitioner rather than something which comes easily to the new teacher. However, it is something that we should hope to be able to develop with experience, provided we are open to improvement, able to assess our own strengths and weaknesses, and think reflectively about our teaching in the way that was outlined in Chapter 3. So let's begin to draft our basic jazz score.

Structuring sessions

In thinking about how to structure sessions, it is useful to refer back to Pollard's model of Reflective Teaching in Figure 3.3. What is important about this model is that it embeds evaluation and reflection into our teaching rather than seeing feedback as an additional, external process. Reflective teaching demands continual review and renewal of our approach. Not, of course, to the point of obsession, but at least an alertness to the dynamics of the class; the ready identification of areas for improvement as well as approaches which proved particularly effective.

Clearly we need to be cognizant of the timeframes and the size of the class we are dealing with, as well as their prior knowledge, motivation and how this session fits within their broader studies. Reflective Activity 10.2 provides practical suggestions in the drafting of a provisional session plan.

Reflective Activity 10.2 Developing a session plan

Using the prompts in the table below, develop a session plan for a workshop, tutorial, or even a lecture in your own discipline.

	Suggestions
Specify your aims and goals for the session	You could do this in the form of learning outcomes but also think a little more widely if you can. Value the 'unintended' outcomes, the scope for following different pathways depending on how the session goes.
Identify the constraints under which the session is taking place	'Forewarned is fore-armed', after all. Here, think about issues such as how the session fits into the student timetable, the venue, technology limitations or dependencies, anticipated level of student preparedness, timeframe, resource requirements, etc.
Consider the characteristics of the particular student group	Background knowledge and skills, possible pre-conceptions, levels of preparedness, confidence levels, range and diversity of approaches to learning, other contextual factors
Select teaching methods and learning activities	What is the focus of the session to be in terms of the balance between acquisition of new knowledge or exploration of particular concepts? How can you ensure that there is sufficient opportunity for the students themselves to be active in the class and that any activities you select are appropriate, manageable and credible in the eyes of learners (i.e. not just group activities for the sake of it)?
Outline any preparatory work required by the students	And, importantly, identify how you can ensure that this is likely to have been completed and what your response is going to be where students have not done so and how such a response is likely to ensure better compliance in future rather than lead to greater disengagement. What preparatory work do you have to do?
Plan the session – structure and sequencing	Use a rough schedule of what is to be done at each stage and how to strike a balance between adhering to this and allowing scope for responding to emergent issues, in other words allow for contingencies. Think about how groups (if used) are to be constructed, how the best use is made of the venue and the space, including arrangements of seating, provision of required items (e.g. flipcharts, projectors, markers, etc.), roles and detailed tasks, mix of group and plenary, how to bring things to a conclusion and reinforce the main learning points. Bearing in mind the nature of the class, think about what potential pitfalls there may be and have some basic strategies for coping with such.

Suggestions	
Is the work of the students in this session to be assessed?	What assessment methods do you propose to use, and have you ensured that these align with your proposed learning outcomes and make sense in the context of the activities you've planned? Are the students clear about the assessment requirements and whether it is formative or summative? How quickly are they to receive feedback or a grade?
Think about how to obtain feedback and improve the next session	Perhaps a simple questionnaire is appropriate in some circumstances, such as when running an intensive, specialist workshop, but also we shouldn't underestimate the potential of simply being alert to cues from student behaviour and responses during the session. It is effective practice to keep a teaching journal in which you can, soon after the class, jot down observations that you made on issues that arose (including what are often referred to in professional contexts as 'critical incidents'), ideas that emerged and what your conclusion is about how successful the session was.

Clearly, there is no need to go into extensive detail each time you meet the same group of students and most of the emphasis should be on the selection and sequencing of the activities within the timeframe available. Indeed, this is often one of the trickiest aspects, that of estimating how much time is needed for students to complete particular types of task. We often fail to give students enough time to respond to questions (for example, a few seconds in a hushed lecture theatre seeming like an age), but we must resist the urge to fill the vacuum.

Within workshops and other group work, a considerable amount of time needs to be allocated to keeping groups on task, to moving around and monitoring progress, judging when to intervene, when to step back. This, in a sense, is akin to Schön's (1983) idea of 'reflection in action', maintaining progress, adjusting the steering as necessary. But it is important also for us to spend even just a short time at the end of each class to jot down key points to help us improve, or items to follow up on, maintaining a simple teaching journal. The idea that one teaching session should inform the next is of fundamental importance and needs to be integrated into the ways in which we plan learning events.

Encouraging participation amongst all students

One of the biggest challenges, particularly with large classes, is ensuring that students actively engage with the processes of learning and avoiding the continual tendency to drift into broadcast–receive mode. This is why the selection of tasks is important, why we need to become comfortable with letting go of control, of allowing noise and chatter, of movement and energy. A classic approach to promoting participation is to break the class down into smaller groups of two, three or four and allocating tasks to groups rather than individuals; perhaps with a plenary at the end for group results to be shared. It is far preferable to motivate and encourage by designing authentic and credible activities (although occasionally 'fun' doesn't go amiss either) than it is to adopt extrinsic methods such as awarding marks for participation. However tempting such measures may be, they do little to encourage genuine engagement.

Even in large lecture classes, as we have seen, it is possible to have dynamic, interactive engagement through discussion, peer teaching and debate. The aim of such approaches is to try and get as many students as possible to participate in the activities and to overcome the natural tendency towards passivity whilst sitting in the typical tiered theatre. Breaking into small groups, encouraging 'reporting back' to the wider class, perhaps getting some students to present findings or questions are all possible even in such a context. Or simply pausing and providing space for students to reflect on what they have learned so far, perhaps offering small prompts for reflection which also reinforce the students' engagement with the knowledge under consideration. We explore other ways of doing this in Chapter 12.

In planning our teaching, we need also to ensure that we are aware of the range of students within the cohort. This includes those taking different courses and programmes, whose motivation might be quite different from others specializing in this particular field. We also need to give consideration in particular to aspects which may require sensitivity or additional support. There is more discussion of these issues in Chapter 15, but session planning is where theory meets practice and we are obliged to ensure that we do not, however inadvertently, select tasks that will disadvantage particular students or which create undue stress or even conflict. For those students with particular learning support needs, your institution should have systems in place which will alert you and you need to ensure that you make due and reasonable accommodation to facilitate their achievement of the learning outcomes.

Case Study 10.1 Charter for inclusive teaching and learning

In Ireland, the Higher Education Authority supported AHEAD (Association for Higher Education Access & Development) project has developed a *Charter for Inclusive Teaching and Learning* (**ahead.ie/userfiles/files//documents/Charter_4_Inclusive_Teaching_&_Learning_Online_Version.pdf**) which outlines a number of key commitments for institutions, which can be seen as general principles of effective practice in any teaching and programme design context. These include:

Provide students with access to course materials, including online, before the lecture, where possible, so students can fully engage with the lecture	Staff will use creative and innovative teaching methods	Learning outcomes and assessment approaches are clearly stated for all student courses/ programmes	All staff teach in accessible formats – with institutional support and training provided
Study skills clearly articulated as part of the curriculum for all students, including those with disabilities	Maximum use is made of timely and effective, constructive feedback	Students engage as partners in the learning process	The most appropriate and balanced methods are used to assess learning outcomes
Clear information is provided on assessment methods and marking schemes	Choice of assessment form should be available		

Using student feedback and coping with the unexpected

As we discussed earlier, a teaching session which excludes any form of feedback about our teaching from students (whether formal or informal) is a missed opportunity. There are practical considerations, but there is often far more scope for 'quick and cheap' feedback than we realize. In lectures, 'one minute papers' (for identification of 'muddiest points') are often used, but even, as we have suggested, paying attention to student responses, to non-verbal cues, can be informative. We should particularly avoid the temptation to blame the students if they seem uninspired or unsure about the topic that has been discussed. We need to be prepared to ask ourselves questions such as, are there other ways to try to convey this material?

For any extended session, such as a workshop, a simple questionnaire really can be effective as well as indicating to the students that you respect their opinions. This is further evidence of dialogue: of teaching and learning as a partnership. A long checklist of items is probably not of much value and may simply distract students from the learning task. But a simple three-question format can be very rich, ascertaining what they liked or gained from the session, what wasn't particularly effective, and any suggestions for future sessions. Or you can use the practice of 'boot grit' feedback (discussed further in Chapter 12) developed by Mark Huxham at Edinburgh Napier University (Huxham et al. 2015). Here students are invited at the end of every lecture to write down on a piece of paper any concept they still don't understand. These are anonymous and handed into a box, or old boot, as they leave the lecture. The lecturer then has immediate feedback to gauge if a small or large number of students don't understand key concepts. The answers to the students' queries are then posted on the VLE within a short time period – again ensuring the feedback loop continues. What is clear here is that again the lecturer and the student both benefit from feedback opportunities, as they co-construct the learning event. Furthermore, the end of the lecture is planned to be a rich learning moment in its own right.

But since sessions can sometimes develop in unexpected ways, it is important that we are confident enough to be able to take an alternative path if the class is not proceeding as we'd hoped due to technical problems, unanticipated student difficulties or whatever the cause. Being too rigid about our planning is as unproductive as too little planning. In the context of many contemporary higher education institutions, it isn't easy to simply cancel a class and re-schedule, so there's a responsibility to make best use of the available contact time. A 'plan B' needn't be elaborate but some capability of 'rescuing' a session also demonstrates to the students that you are a committed, experienced teacher and one who can think on their feet. In other words, modelling effective practice and with a real sense of 'presence' rather than only capable of teaching in an uninterrupted, 'broadcast' mode.

MODULE PLANNING

Structuring the module

The structuring of degree programmes into modules, each defined by a formal set of learning outcomes and an associated 'module descriptor' that provides a checklist of elements such as teaching methods and types of assessment, is now widespread across most higher education institutions. Clearly, this is effective administrative practice, which ensures clarity and establishes criteria for quality assessment and comparability.

The issue is, however, the extent to which such documentation and procedures are used as a basic scaffolding for a set of rich teaching and learning experiences which will allow students (and those who teach them) to flourish intellectually and culturally, or whether they are seen as constraining, restrictive and a means to impose uniformity. The balance between the two perceptions is often determined by institutional and departmental culture, but it is important for those of us who seek to be reflective practitioners in our teaching and wider academic practice, to ask the question as to where the balance lies in our context.

We can see this question of balance at play when we consider the role that ideas such as 'constructive alignment' (Biggs and Tang 2011) perform in our planning processes. In Chapter 9, we discussed both constructive alignment and the idea of 'congruence' (Hounsell and Hounsell 2007) to emphasize the importance of having an integrated approach to intended learning outcomes, teaching strategies and assessment methods. In so doing, however, we still need to keep in mind this balance between good planning and affording necessary flexibility. Indeed, Huxham et al. (2015) have critiqued the practice of rigid, procedural adherence to constructive alignment, which misses the original intention of a flexible and dynamic, but integrated, learning space. These authors (three of whom are life science students) share their experience of co-navigation of a module in which uncertainty, risk and challenge are highly valued, as they engage with complex and unpredictable forms of knowledge. The irony is, however, that such uncertainty needs to be allowed for in the planning process: it is about carefully considered opportunities for rich student engagement, not just any mayhem.

But it can seem daunting, and possibly onerous, to consider alternative teaching approaches. In practice, many of us with heavy teaching loads and research responsibilities often find most difficulty in conceiving of alternative methods of teaching or of promoting active student learning. The delivery of traditional lectures, perhaps enhanced somewhat by a degree of in-class discussion, is in many ways the easiest approach to take. It involves minimum risk in that it sticks rigidly with the traditional information transmission model that has long been dominant in much of education and it still remains highly cost-effective in terms of addressing large classes and in preparation time (Bligh 2000). Everything else, we are led to believe, takes considerably more effort with the added uncertainty as to whether students themselves will be prepared to take on a more active role or thank us for introducing an element of risk and uncertainty (for a thorough deconstruction of these myths, see Tagg 2019). Indeed, it has often been remarked that the students that have thus far (i.e. by the time they reach us) been successful educationally, are those who have best adapted to the current system and therefore likely to be highly resistant to change.

However, we do a disservice to our students and our own professional integrity if we don't take the opportunity in designing and planning modules to explore a range of alternative teaching approaches, building on research and scholarship. Diana Laurillard (2002, p. 20) reminds us of the important, almost definitional, characteristic of a 'higher' education:

> What is the difference between a curriculum that teaches what is known and one that teaches how to come to know?
>
> Knowledge, even academic knowledge, is not adequately represented as propositional statements but has a historicity that incorporates individuals' previous experiences, their perceptions of the immediate situation, their intentions, and their experiences of discovery, of recognized tensions, of uncertainties, of ambiguities still unresolved.

Resonant of Laurillard's overview of the purposes of higher education, a useful distinction comes from Hardarson (2017), who differentiates between closed and open aims when planning a course. He gives these examples to demonstrate the difference between closed and open aims:

> Going for a swim this afternoon, painting the kitchen, and going for a walk with one's life partner next Sunday are aims of the first type. Staying healthy, keeping a beautiful home and having a happy marriage are lifelong tasks of the second type. (p. 65)

If we then apply this idea to a discipline such as physics we can see the implications of planning, at least in part, for open rather than purely closed aims:

> Learning to use Newton's inverse square law to calculate the gravitational force between two masses may be understood as a closed aim in this sense, but understanding gravity is better seen as an open aim that cannot be conclusively reached. When has a student

understood gravity? When she has learned to do simple calculations based on Newton's formula? Is able to explain how massive objects affect space-time? Has mastered the concepts used to describe black holes? Knows what the long search for the Higgs boson was all about? Can participate in debates about the differences between gravity and the other fundamental forces of nature? Understanding gravity is an endeavour which, arguably, cannot be completed. (p. 65)

Clearly, good module planning is likely to involve a mixture of closed and open aims, with the former often acting as important building blocks for the latter. But if our goal is to enable students to engage with complex disciplinary knowledge, then we need to keep an eye on those larger, open aims as well – as they are likely to be where the really exciting disciplinary material comes to life.

Reflective Activity 10.3 Reflecting on your context

Ensure you have a copy of the module descriptor for a module you currently, or are planning to, teach. To what extent do you feel that you have freedom to build on what is included in the module descriptor or do you feel a pressure to simply 'deliver instruction'? And for new modules that you are asked to design, does your local descriptor provide an effective template, or does it fail to capture aspects which you'd like to explore?

Is it still dominated by content rather than process?

Are the assessments legitimate and authentic or routine and standardized?

Are the aims open or closed?

For many in higher education, concerns about bureaucratization aside, the design of a new course or new module, actually can be a refreshing opportunity to demonstrate a degree of creativity and to share our passion for our discipline. The module space can provide a landscape within which we as teachers can flourish along with our students. We do have to be cognizant, of course, of overall programme aims and the wider context within which the module is placed (for example, other topics the students will be studying in parallel, before or after). As we discussed in Chapter 9, there may be specific 'graduate attributes' that characterize the overall degree programme which are expected to be addressed and we may also be operating within the context of subject benchmarks or accreditation requirements from professional bodies (although these tend to be considered at the programme level).

The module design process can also be captured by Pollard's reflective teaching cycle from Figure 3.3. It is unlikely that we'll get everything right in the first draft and we need to be prepared to adapt to experience, to ensure feedback and review is embedded. We can't of course, completely rewrite and redesign every module, every year, but we should provide scope for adjustment and consider each module to have an overall fixed lifetime after which it may be eligible for a more substantive overhaul or even replacement.

Many, but not all, institutions work on this basis. A consistent and systematic approach to course development and operation would embed the idea of a 'lifecycle' and aid, at the departmental and institutional level, the distribution of resources, and provide opportunities to refresh offerings.

Practical steps in course and module design

There are many guides that describe practical approaches to course and module design in some considerable detail (for recent examples, see O'Neill 2015; Mackh 2018). A simplified process diagram is shown in Figure 10.2 and is an expansion of 'plan-act-evaluate' from Figure 3.3.

One practical approach to drafting learning outcomes is to consider whether there are *threshold concepts* in our discipline or field. Threshold concepts, which we discussed in Chapter 2, are 'core concepts that, once understood, transform perception of a given subject' (Meyer and Land 2003, p. 417) and are ideas with which we know students struggle and many find 'troublesome' (as they challenge their pre-conceptions), yet must be understood before real progress can be made. Designing courses and modules from this

Figure 10.2 Module Design Process (adapted from University of Brighton, 2012)

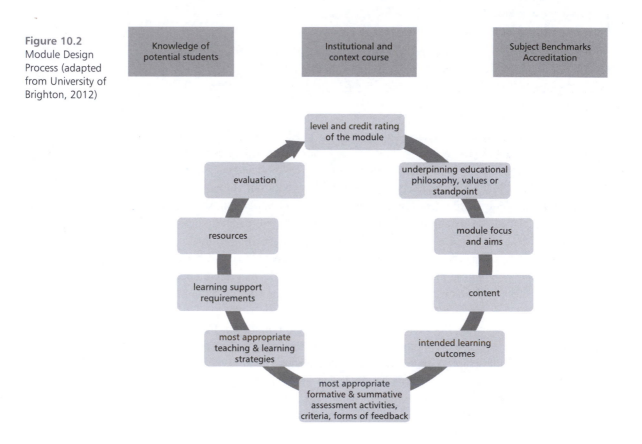

perspective acknowledges to students that we recognize that there are real conceptual barriers and our role is to help them overcome them. Being explicit that advanced learning requires struggle, effort and difficulty (which we have all had to face) also helps to build resilience and learner confidence.

Reflective Activity 10.4 Using threshold concepts to think about module design

Consider your own academic discipline or field and a particular module for which you are responsible.

Can you identify what the threshold concepts are in this subject, at this level? What areas do students traditionally have difficulty with and how do you think you might help them overcome this?

Are there particular teaching approaches (e.g. case studies, project work, practical sessions) that might be appropriate?

What forms of assessment (both formative and summative) might align well with this intention?

What are the typical, traditional methods used in the teaching of this particular topic? To what extent do you feel these are successful and are there any alternative approaches that are both likely to enhance student learning and are manageable within the constraints of the module timeframe and resourcing?

We will explore the related notion of teaching 'troublesome knowledge' in Chapter 11.

Assessment within modules

The subject of assessment in higher education is itself a major sub-discipline with an extensive literature. Here, we'll identify a few of the underlying principles and some practical aspects about assessment within modules. These are discussed more extensively in Chapter 13. Here what we need to focus on is the timing and role of assessment in the planning process. What is particularly important is to challenge the perception of assessment as occurring as that bit on the end of the module, or that bit at the end of the planning process. If we are committed to the principles of assessment for learning, then assessment should be front and centre at the start of the planning process too.

By assessment *for* learning, we refer to the key role assessment has in shaping what and how students learn. Assessment tasks send out powerful messages to students about what matters in a course and how they should engage with knowledge. This means that rather than coming up with a course design and then thinking 'how can we assess this?' you begin with the aims of the course and ask 'what forms of assessment would encourage the learning we are trying to achieve?'.

For academic staff struggling with larger enrolments, reduced resources and an increasing range of demands, the pressure to default to simple summative examinations is a genuine risk. But if the focus is to be on student success, effective learning and indeed a more satisfying mutual engagement between students and staff, then we need to ensure that our approach to assessment and feedback really does meet our educational intent. It is clear that formative feedback can be highly beneficial (Evans 2013; O'Donovan et al. 2016). As Black and Wiliam (1998, p. 61) influentially concluded many years ago:

> The research reported here shows conclusively that formative assessment does improve learning. The gains in achievement appear to be quite considerable, [. . .] among the largest ever reported for educational interventions.

Here, perhaps, is the strongest argument for a rebalancing of teaching away from content delivery to more emphasis, time and resources being spent on iterative feedback and improvement. We must think how we can design our modules for effective understanding and not simply to cover a certain amount of content in a given time.

Closely related to how we plan assessment activities in a course or module is the issue of building in opportunities for genuine formative feedback. But such opportunities need not only be linked to actual assessments tasks. Indeed, McArthur and Huxham (2013, p. 92) make the claim that: 'Shackled to formal assessment, feedback is like great art hung in a dark corner; in contrast, it needs to be illuminated, displayed and discussed.' They even go so far as to say that feedback opportunities can be built in – planned for – starting before the course even begins and going through to after it finishes. This challenges our understanding of feedback and echoes the definition put forward by Carless and Boud (2018, p. 1315), which views feedback 'as a process through which learners make sense of information from various sources and use it to enhance their work or learning strategies'.

So what does it mean to plan for these multiple feedback points? Well, a starting place, before the course begins, is in the course documentation shared with students: to what extent does this make expectations clear? Does it provide the information they need to successfully navigate the course? This reinforces another important point: that good planning is not the same as curriculum design, but rather encompasses the broader sense of the whole student experience and the very many influences upon that.

To reinforce the idea of dialogue and a learning partnership, McArthur and Huxham (2013) argue that these multiple feedback moments in a course must be genuinely two-way. Thus it is just as important for students to feedback to us how things are going, as us to provide them with feedback. In either context the really crucial aspect of feedback, as encapsulated by Carless and Boud (2018) is *use*. Feedback only comes into being in that moment in which it can be used to improve learning and understanding. This clearly then has enormous implications for how we plan feedback moments in a module. In our planning we have to think not simply in terms of when we give 'feedback' but when and how students will be able to use it.

An apparent lack of formative feedback is the single most common complaint from students in institutional and national surveys (see O'Donovan et al. 2016 for a thorough exploration of this problem and possible responses). Some colleagues find this recurring problem confusing and even demoralizing because they feel that they are providing detailed and thorough feedback on students' work. But here again we must stress this notion of use and usefulness. If students receive the feedback after any significant opportunities to apply it to their studies have passed, then they are likely to be dissatisfied. So this is a planning issue, locating and realizing the optimum places for effective feedback.

In practice, this requires a more coherent approach to coursework across the module and beyond, allowing tutors and students alike to access previous work in order to monitor improvement. Nonetheless, from an educational perspective it holds considerable promise in overcoming the classic limitations of highly modularized courses, where knowledge and skills are compartmentalized into discrete blocks. A more holistic, developmental assessment regime is, in principle, more likely to meet the higher-level outcomes and many of the 'graduate attributes' which programmes typically espouse.

Associated with this is mapping out the student workload across the module or semester. Small-scale, relatively low-stakes, assessment spread across the time period are often used to overcome the traditional urge of last-minute cramming for end of semester examinations. Indeed, it could be argued that this learner activity mapping is one of the trickiest aspects of course design and often neglected. Identifying an appropriate overall workload is not easy for those of us who are now subject experts. Coping with the diversity within any given cohort of students can make it even more challenging. Not only do we need to address the workload within our own modules, but agreement between those responsible for each module within a student's programme of study and the development of a shared assessment schedule is ideal and avoids conflicting demands, deadline clashes and is more likely to encourage students to work consistently over the semester. The management of assessment across modules and courses, in other words, whilst much neglected, is an important factor in the design and implementation of effective programmes of study (Yorke 1998).

Reflective Activity 10.5 Thinking about assessment on your modules

Look over your own modules and examine the extent to which your assessment requirements meet the criteria for 'assessment for learning'.

To what extent do you think your students' efforts are strategically focused on the assessment requirements rather than the intended learning outcomes per se?

How might you revise your assessment types, loading and scheduling to better promote learning development?

What realistic methods might enable you to provide effective formative feedback which students can 'feed forward' to subsequent coursework?

Student feedback on modules

Like feedback *to* our students, feedback *from* our students needs to be considered in the planning process as timing is again crucial. However, it remains common to have the only opportunity for student feedback to be an end of module questionnaire, the results of which may or may not be acted on and which may or may not be communicated back to students. Apart from effective practice requiring the 'closing of the feedback loop', it might be argued that there is a missed opportunity in not embedding student feedback as part of the overall learning experience. Standard exit questionnaires provided for every module, every semester, will undoubtedly result in survey fatigue (for both students and staff!) and give the impression that feedback is an afterthought, or is separate from the learning process (see Goos and Salomons 2017 for an exploration of the impact of survey fatigue on the reliability of student evaluations).

A better approach is to take stock at key points across the semester; indeed many lecturers make use of 'one minute tests' or short feedback pieces provided at the end of a lecture to ascertain what areas students are having most difficulty with. Mid-semester evaluations typically would ask students to respond to three basic questions:

- What do they like about the module?
- What do they think needs to be improved (i.e. what don't they like!)?
- What ideas do they have for making it a more valuable learning experience for them?

Feedback at this stage may then allow for some adaptation and give insight on how the students are faring and what their current perceptions are. There is after all a distinction to be made between the curriculum that you think you are offering, and the curriculum that the students feel that they are engaging with. In addition, being seen to act on feedback from students is an important aspect of building a strong and positive relationship: it demonstrates respect for their unique role in the planning process. It is also a clearly enacted form of dialogue between students and their teachers as they co-create the learning experience.

One interesting approach that is taken in some courses, particularly those which are oriented towards particular professions for which 'reflective practice' is a key aspect, is the use of learning journals (Bolton 2014; Bruno and Dell'Aversana 2017). In these, students would collect short notes on their progress through the module, highlighting areas in which they might be experiencing difficulty, or relating concepts learned in class to personal experience or professional practice. These can be done purely for the students' own use but with agreement it can be a valuable document to share with their teachers and a foundation for genuine dialogue to occur. Today we can also make good use of online tools, such as those provided in VLEs, to enable different, perhaps richer, types of feedback on students' responses and reaction to their modules (Martin et al. 2018).

Working with colleagues

Working with colleagues on joint-taught modules presents an excellent opportunity to engage students in more active forms of learning and for a team-based approach to curricular innovation. Within many professions, peer feedback on performance is also recognized as essential for quality assurance and enhancement and we discussed its importance in developing a reflective approach to teaching in Chapter 3. It is ironic that in many higher education courses we often promote peer-supported learning and peer-assessment amongst students whilst not considering the scope for embedding such in our own teaching practice. Peer review, after all, is also lauded as a hallmark of high-quality research and what we do in that domain is considered legitimately under 'public' scrutiny (at least insofar as those who review and read journals and grant applications can be considered a 'public').

Why should the teaching and learning dimension be any different; a closed, private matter between us and our students (even if there are hundreds in our lecture theatre)? In part, the answer may be that we fear learning just how good we actually are at teaching because few of us, historically, received any formal training. Indeed, many academics in traditional institutions, it might be argued, took pride from being professional researchers within their discipline whilst being perfectly content to regard teaching as an amateur, or at any rate, inferior, concern. Times have, fortunately for the student, changed. New staff are often expected to complete at least a certificate programme in teaching and assessment, but again it might be argued that this is in danger of relegating teaching still, in that it implies it can be mastered by a couple of modules of compulsory training at the start of your career. What we are arguing in this book, however, is that effective teaching, i.e. that which leads to real student learning, must be a reflective endeavour. In other words, by its very nature it is ongoing and requires continual development, frequent re-visiting of assumptions, updating and refreshing not just of domain knowledge but also of curricular models, teaching technologies and strategies. This openness to change needs to be informed by the literature, the experience of others, evidence and debate; in short, a professional activity and a scholarly disposition.

Where there is agreement, team-teaching can be highly rewarding and can result in innovation, creativity and personal professional satisfaction. However, of course, we cannot guarantee that those with whom we are partnered to teach a module share the same passion for teaching as we do, but we should still be in a position to make the most out of the situation. At the very least, planning the curriculum and its 'delivery' needs to be a joint activity, agreeing on who covers which aspects and the range of teaching methods, assessment requirements and workload distribution. Within the context of a single module, students need to have some consistency of approach, while allowing for the natural style of individual lecturers. This is a tricky balance to get right, which makes the planning all the more important. We know that students respond well to lecturers who show something of their personality, and don't act like identical automatons. However, we need to balance the scope for individual styles with ensuring that there is a consistent message across the module, and particularly that basic expectations are shared. Students can cope well with two lecturers who have two different styles, but they cannot cope with getting conflicting or fragmentary information.

Shared teaching also provides scope for peer observation of each other's teaching, providing an invaluable alternative perspective from a similarly qualified 'critical friend' (for reviews of approaches to peer observation, see Fletcher 2018; Wingrove et al. 2018). In some institutions, it may be a formal requirement that observation is undertaken regularly, but in others where such is not the case, there is much to be said for encouraging colleagues to participate. Protocols for peer observation are often used to establish trust, to be clear that the aim is developmental rather than judgemental and that the exercise should be carried out by both parties on each other. There is as much (if not more) to learn from observing another as there is in comment on our own performance. We discuss the importance of finding collective ways of developing our teaching further in Chapters 11 and 12. From a planning perspective, it is important to note that such peer observation does not have to take place in a traditional lecture or class, but can be built in at many different stages and include small group teaching, online forums or assessment and feedback practices.

RESEARCH BRIEFING 10.1 A collegial approach to curriculum change

In the hectic world of contemporary higher education, there can often be too strong an emphasis on individual performance at the expense of collective endeavour. The spaces for collegiality, in other words, narrowing and closing off. Yet working collaboratively with colleagues can yield significant benefits, particularly when there is a desire for change, for a renewal or re-energizing of curriculum and organization. Healey et al. (2013) describe such an approach, building on the principles of the 'Change Academy', an initiative of the Leadership Foundation for Higher Education and the Higher Education Academy (now part of Advance HE). This study draws on reflections on experience, interviews, feedback and analysis of change to describe a path towards effecting significant reform of curriculum in localized contexts (i.e. at departmental/discipline level). In this case, the Change Academy is run via an intensive, three-day series of workshops, followed up by telephone and email support. The process involves open discussion, a range of structured exercises and the support and facilitation of subject-expert academic developers and establishes a potentially very effective model that can be used by departments and institutions as part of a longer-term process of curriculum planning and development. The key lesson is that the planning process is enhanced when multiple voices are able to contribute and work together.

PROGRAMME PLANNING

Programme planning and review cycle

There has been a marked shift over the past decade away from some of the more extreme incarnations of modularization which followed the move back in the 1980s from a focus on programmes to modules. The arguments in favour of modularization centred around greater student choice and flexibility. However, some people have increasingly felt that something was lost when the programme level of activity became downgraded. We can note a number of initiatives in which there have been explicit efforts to re-engage the programme level as part of curriculum development and planning processes, and in terms of our understanding of the student experience. For example, graduate attributes take the perspective of the programme as a whole, rather than individual modules in isolation. Similarly, in recent years the idea of curriculum mapping has taken hold, guiding efforts to get that programme-wide perspective on what students learn and how they are assessed. So we can see that over this chapter we have built up from individual teaching sessions, to the modular level and now the programme level. Each of these requires careful planning, and the ability to keep each of these domains in mind when planning at a particular level.

A further challenge at the programme level is that planning will necessarily involve a number of colleagues. We already, in the module section, discussed the benefits and potential pitfalls when having to take account of the interests, styles and preferences of a number of colleagues. But there are rich advantages for the student experience of a programme that 'hangs' together coherently and within which the different elements build clearly upon one another.

Formal requirements

The design of entire degree programmes, their quality assurance and accreditation are all subject to institutional, national and professional requirements. Formal processes for course proposals, for evaluation and for review are well established in all higher education institutions and it is incumbent on staff to be familiar with these regulations and procedures, and to ensure liaison between these formal requirements and less formal aspects of the planning process.

In the UK, the Quality Assurance Agency has extensive literature on many of these aspects on its website, along with guidelines, recommendations and archives of quality reviews. Similarly, Advance HE (incorporating the former Higher Education Academy) has an archive of handbooks, guides and case studies. It is worth spending time to become familiar with some of these if you are to be involved in programme-level planning. In addition, they can help in understanding how an individual module fits into the broader programme.

It is common for programmes to include a diverse range of modules and an array of different activities including optional courses, work placements, international exchanges and, increasingly, co-curricular contributions. This all needs to be planned carefully to ensure good management. We are likely to face some challenges that are beyond our control, such as timetabling and room allocation, along with other responsibilities such as ensuring clear, readily accessible documentation and efficient resource allocation (including staff and tutor deployment). To be successful, it is clear that collegiality and teamwork are vital despite potential conflicting interests and differences in personal, professional goals. The overall quality of the student learning experience depends crucially on coherence and a sense of collective endeavour.

Formal programme boards, with student representation, should be in place to review operations, identify and resolve problems as they arise and periodically undertake more comprehensive reviews of programme offerings. Again, this formal setting is another opportunity to reinforce the sense of mutual endeavour, of co-construction of the curriculum, which we discussed earlier.

Involving students in programme planning

In the next three sections we will consider three key partners that we may work with when planning at programme level. We begin with the involvement of students. Earlier, we considered the important role students play in module planning, and particularly opportunities for feedback about their experiences. There are a number of additional ways in which students can play a role in the programme-level planning. As we discussed in Chapter 9, initiatives such as 'student as producer' deliberately set out to counter the dominant discourse of students as consumers which has come to the fore in those national education systems that charge tuition fees. Thus we need to think of a programme of study as not simply something students buy off the shelf, but something in which they are active partners.

Traditionally, much of the student input towards programme planning and course organization would have been through class representatives, staff–student liaison committees and student representatives on a number of formal boards and committees. More recently there has been a growth in interest in deeper levels of participation and cooperation between academic staff and students even at the level of collaborative design of modules or piloting of learning innovations. The University of Exeter's 'Students as Change Agents', which we discussed in Chapter 4 was an early example of such work. Many institutions have now begun to embrace this notion of partnership, and student teams are increasingly contributing to institutional research, undertaking projects, and conducting interviews and surveys.

In the University of Glasgow, for example, an institution-wide project to determine a set of graduate attributes employed students as 'investigators' to undertake research interviews, compile data and contribute to workshops and reports. This approach linked student participation in shaping graduate attributes, curriculum reform and research–

teaching links and was a key case study in the QAA Scotland, Enhancement Theme on *Graduates for the 21st Century* (enhancementthemes.ac.uk/completed-enhancement-themes/graduates-for-the-21st-century).

Working with employer-partners

The role of employers in implementing the curriculum is contentious in some academic fields, but viewed as utterly essential in others. There is thus considerable disciplinary variation in the nature and extent of employer participation. Whilst we need to be careful to recognize that employers offer a particular perspective on the purposes and contribution of higher education, they are increasingly being seen as an important partner in curriculum design and implementation. Many students also wish to be assured that their studies will improve their career prospects whether or not they choose a vocational subject. Such concerns should not be dismissed as utilitarian or necessarily contrary to a perspective on learning as something to be valued in its own right. But economic wellbeing is essential to broader social wellbeing and is thus a legitimate goal. However, we can have a broad sense of the economic sphere when we bring employers and professional groups into our planning processes and see them as providing one set of voices among others.

Many programmes now have explicitly embedded career development modules, emphasize 'transferable skills' and offer internships or work placements. A number of institutions 'self-brand' as responsive to the needs of the wider economy or focused on regional development. Thus we need to think of institutional context when deciding what role these employment issues play in your curriculum implementation; however, there are few institutions now, regardless of type, which do not give a strong focus on employability and/or graduate attributes.

In the postgraduate and research domains, there have been increased levels of engagement between industry and universities (Ankrah and Omar 2015). 'Industrial liaison offices' which historically may have explored options for student placement or part-time study have transformed themselves into 'Technology Transfer Offices' looking to capitalize on the institution's research output, translating it into potential products in the marketplace, seeking joint funding for research and development, or exploring options for the development of specialist, bespoke Masters programmes.

Each institution will have its own particular structures for engaging with employers and other external 'stakeholders' and it is important that such are coordinated at an institutional level rather than built on a collection of ad hoc arrangements. Formalizing the relationship around effective mechanisms and appropriate terms of engagement will also help to build trust and minimize duplication and hopefully go part of the way to overcome that perennial problem in academic institutions of death by a thousand committees.

Working with external examiners

In some higher education systems, the external examiner is seen as crucial to quality assurance, providing benchmarking between comparable programmes and institutions (see Bloxham et al. 2015 for an evaluation of the effectiveness of this approach and a discussion of alternative approaches). The UK is one in which the external examiner is seen as playing an important role. However, the system received considerable criticism from a Parliamentary Select Committee on students and universities. This resulted in a major review by a number of statutory agencies and sectorial bodies which ultimately resulted in a renewed Code of Practice (QAA 2011) and a handbook was produced by the Higher Education Academy (HEA 2012), which outlines the roles and responsibilities of external examiners and the host institutions and also provides a set of useful case studies that probe some real-world situations that may be faced by the external examiner. This handbook describes the role of external examiners in the following terms:

> External examiners are experienced higher education teachers who offer an independent assessment of academic standards and the quality of assessment to the appointing institution. Acting as an external examiner generally involves the review of a selection of exam scripts, assignments and dissertations followed by informal engagement with staff to discuss the assessed work and the formal meeting of the examination board.

> The aspects of the role around scrutiny and inspection [. . .] have increasingly been based around collegiate discussion and interaction. The critical friend approach is now more or less universal with the expectation that the external examiner will identify strengths, weaknesses and good practice of the provision and play a role in quality enhancement. (HEA 2012, p. 5)

The Codes of Practice at national and institutional levels spell out in some considerable detail the expectations of the system and the need to ensure that it is robust and transparent. Such codes typically include criteria for the selection of examiners, their terms of office and level of involvement in quality assurance.

The external examiner, therefore, plays not just an important formal role in assuring standards, but also is an invaluable resource for programme development. When it works well the external examiner is a critical friend to the programme, offering insights and advice from a different perspective than those directly teaching on the programme. External examiner reports are produced annually and issues raised should be acted upon and any resulting changes documented. In addition, if a programme anticipates making major or significant changes to their provision then they are well advised to consult the external examiner as part of the process, and in some institutions this will be a formal requirement.

CONCLUSION

In this chapter, we have highlighted the importance of taking a systematic, planned approach to implementing programmes, modules and teaching sessions. We have argued that effective courses are those in which evaluation and feedback are regarded as essential components rather than simply statutory obligations. The old model of a single lecturer engaged in a private conversation behind closed doors is no longer tenable and we have greater scope for successful outcomes and personal, professional satisfaction if we can take a team-based, collaborative approach with colleagues, students and others. To co-ordinate these different facets, however, requires careful planning at a number of stages and at different levels of the curriculum and beyond.

KEY READINGS

For overviews of some of the key issues in planning and designing courses, see:

Mackh, B. (2018) *Higher Education by Design: Best Practices for Curricular Planning and Instruction*. Abingdon: Routledge.

O'Neill, G. (2015). *Curriculum Design in Higher Education: Theory to Practice*. Dublin: UCD Teaching & Learning. **researchrepository.ucd.ie/handle/10197/713**

On the myths that underpin many of approaches to planning and how to change them, see:

Tagg, J. (2019). *The Instruction Myth: Why Higher Education is Hard to Change, and How to Change It*. New Brunswick: Rutgers University Press.

For more on the difference between open and closed aims, and how these relate to planning at all levels, see:

Hardarson, A. (2017) 'Aims of education: How to resist the temptation of technocratic models', *Journal of Philosophy of Education*, 51(1), 59–72.

For more on learning journals, see:

Bolton, G. (2014) *Reflective Practice: Writing and Professional Development*. 4th edn. London: Sage Publications.

Chapter 11
Teaching

How can we develop strategies focused on student understanding?

INTRODUCTION

Teaching can be engaging and rewarding, yet it is also uncertain and complex. This chapter discusses some of the intellectual and practical challenges of teaching so that students understand the disciplines and professional fields they are studying. It might seem obvious that higher education teachers' main aim is to help students understand what is taught. Sometimes, though, understanding is confused with attainment. The reflection that passing an assignment might not involve in-depth learning is uncomfortable. We can train our students to pass assignments, but are we sure that they have understood? (See Chapter 13 for a further discussion of these tensions in relation to 'assessment for learning' and 'assessment for certification'.) So, a key focus for reflection is what teaching for understanding demands and the extent to which students achieve it.

The chapter has two main sections. It starts by offering six bases for thinking about teaching for understanding. The second section offers ideas for teaching for understanding in different typical modes. This section is framed by a relational view of teaching whereby the educational effects of teaching modes are conceptualized and analysed in relation to other modes and whole programmes of study, courses or modules.

See Chapter 4

TLRP Principles

Five principles are of relevance to this chapter on teaching in higher education:

Principle 2: Effective teaching and learning depend on the scholarship and learning of all those educators who teach and research to support the learning of others. The need for lecturers, teachers and trainers to learn through doing research to improve their knowledge, expertise and skills for teaching should be recognized and supported.

Principle 4: Effective teaching and learning foster both individual and social processes and outcomes. Students should be encouraged to build relationships and communication with others to assist the mutual construction of knowledge and enhance the achievements of individuals and groups. Consulting or collaborating with students as learners about their learning makes this effective.

Principle 5: Effective teaching and learning promote the active engagement of the student as learner. A key aim of higher learning should be to develop students' independence and autonomy as learners. This involves engaging students actively in their own learning, and ensuring that they acquire a repertoire of learning strategies and practices, develop positive learning dispositions, and build the confidence to become agents in their own learning,

Principle 8: Effective teaching and learning recognize the importance of prior and concurrent experience and learning. Teaching and learning should take account of what the student as learner knows already to plan strategies for the future. This includes building on prior learning but also taking account of the emerging concurrent learning in context, and the personal and cultural experiences of different groups of students as learners.

> **Principle 9: Effective teaching and learning engage with expertise and valued forms of knowledge in disciplines and subjects.** Teaching and learning should engage students with the concepts, key skills and processes, modes of discourse, ways of thinking and practising, and attitudes and relationships which are most valued in their subject. Students need to understand what constitutes quality, standards and expertise in different settings and subjects.

BASES FOR THINKING ABOUT TEACHING FOR UNDERSTANDING

This section discusses six bases for thinking about teaching that generates students' interest in what they don't know and supports their understanding of their disciplines of fields. The narrative about teaching which connects the sub-sections is that good quality teaching is not instinctive, rather there are resources for reflective learning in three forms: personal teaching experience; working with others; and scholarly educational literature. Such learning about teaching generates the following insights: teaching for understanding involves knowledge about how to relate disciplinary and professional field curriculum content to teaching practices; it is educationally sound for teachers to take responsibility for encouraging students' efforts to understand; teaching is a moral activity involving the reproduction of students' lifeworld; and good quality teaching results from collaboration. The chapter carries the message that the quality of thinking about teaching is as significant as practical skill and expertise: as higher education teachers, we must make judgements and know why we decide to teach as we do.

Learning to teach

As suggested by Chapter 1, when we are new to teaching (ideally) we think about what we are trying to do when we teach; gleaning ideas from different contexts and resources; and trying things out with students and colleagues. These activities constitute a gradual process of forming a teaching identity which feels authentic. Some believe that being a good teacher results from natural talent and is ineffable – we all recognize a great teacher when we meet one, particularly a charismatic lecturer. We refute this belief. Certainly, some people appear to teach well instinctively, and some are more comfortable with the performance of a lecture than others, but most people can learn to become good teachers. This book proposes that the fundamental factor is being reflective. Chapter 3 offers an extended discussion and the book contains many resources that stimulate reflection. At its simplest, reflection is about what appears to 'work', that is, what appears to help the students understand or enjoy what we try to teach them. But this approach is limited, particularly if the main source of evidence for what works is student satisfaction. It is not unusual for new teachers to try something, find it doesn't elicit the response they had hoped for and so despondently fall back on what they had experienced from teachers when they were students.

As an alternative way of thinking about acquiring knowledge about how to teach, Rowland (2000) offers a model of three contexts for learning about teaching: the 'personal context' of one's own experience; the 'shared context' of colleagues and students; and the 'public context' of educational theory. The contexts generate resources for learning and none are privileged because resources arising from one context are examined in the light of those arising in another. The aim of using these resources to learn about teaching is to build what Brookfield (2017) calls a 'critical rationale' (p. 83), a set of assumptions and beliefs about the essential forms and fundamental purposes of teaching.

Making use of educational theory and research

While this book reflects how teaching knowledge emanates from the three contexts, here we make a strong case for the 'public context'. Higher education teachers can usefully bring theoretical resources or lenses to bear on their observations and thoughts about everyday teaching and the students' responses. It is sometimes stated that educational theory irritates or overwhelms new teachers. Yet, as in other disciplines, theories offer high ground and alternative ways of viewing; and can underpin teachers' judgements about curriculum and teaching. Having educational knowledge furnishes teachers with a language for justifying and, if necessary, defending what they decide to do. Moreover, learning to teach can be the re-discovery of being a novice learner and by intellectualizing it rather than thinking of it as a practical-technical activity only, understanding of teaching can deepen and hold a teacher's interest over a long career, just as research does (McLean 2006).

Education is a multidisciplinary field, that is, theory and research from a range of disciplines have advanced thinking: for example, psychology, sociology, history and philosophy. Kurt Lewin, an American social psychologist, pronounced that 'there is nothing so practical as a good theory' (Lewin 1951) because a good theory can stimulate systematic thinking about practical matters. Here the thinking that is stimulated is about how to teach for student understanding. The caveats are: while a theory can illuminate an aspect of practice, it cannot illuminate all aspects; and educational theories are always provisional and open to adjustment in the light of everyday practices.

The multidisciplinary nature of higher education teaching theory and research makes it difficult to characterize as a field (see Tight 2013). Arguably, what is most useful to a new teacher is understanding how students learn. Examples of research which shed light on student learning are: socio-cultural theories such as 'academic literacies' (discussed in Chapter 2); research about teaching for students' 'criticality' based on Ron Barnett's (1997) philosophical ideas (Johnston et al. 2012); research based on 'phenomenography' which is a qualitative methodology that explores variations in how students learn (for example, Prosser and Trigwell 1999); and research which applies the constructivist principle that human learning is constructed through how they make experience meaningful (Entwistle 2018).

Taken together, the field of higher education research presents evidence and advances arguments about generic principles for good teaching (as this book does – see also

Chickering and Gamson 1987; Kuh 2008; Ambrose et al. 2010; Gibbs 2010; Laurillard 2012; Entwistle 2018). Most consistently, we find a distinction being made between teacher-centred and student-centred teaching. As Åkerlind (2008, pp. 633–34, emphasis in the original) argues:

> With a *teacher-centred* understanding, academics' attention is focused on what they, as the teacher, are doing in any teaching–learning situation; what is happening for the students is taken-for-granted and not explicitly attended to. Conversely, with a *student-centred* understanding, academics' attention is focused on what the students are experiencing in any teaching–learning situation and the potential impact of the teacher's actions upon the students' experience.

When we focus solely on our own performance as teachers, we ignore how students experience teaching and how they grapple with the ideas and concepts of the curriculum. Research tells us that the most important task of the teacher is to understand the student's experience and perspective, which does not mean making the students satisfied but rather understanding their misconceptions and difficulties and thinking about how to make them feel that knowing and understanding is worthwhile. In student-centred teaching the focus is on knowing whether students are understanding what we are teaching and exploring how to help them understand.

Ways to help students understand can be found in other consistent findings about what encourages students:

- Coherent course design: Chapter 9 on Curriculum discusses the importance of congruence or alignment of teaching, the curriculum and assessment.

- Making content interesting and relevant: this depends on the discipline or field and the students; for example, sometimes it is possible to make connections to students' everyday lives, or to draw analogies that make sense to them.

- Varied teaching methods: using varied methods is not for the students' entertainment, but rather because different educational goals require different methods. For example, if students are to learn how to speak fluently about their discipline, they need practice doing so; or grasping a difficult concept could involve getting the students to make a representation of it (for example, diagrams or drawings). Using varied methods includes thinking creatively about how to encourage the students to undertake activities that further their understanding.

- Authentic and varied assessment: see Chapter 13 on Assessment.

- Feedback for improving student understanding: see Chapter 13.

- Supportive and accessible teachers: see Chapter 6 on Relationships.

- Being inspiring and taking responsibility for students' understanding of your discipline or field: sometimes higher education teachers think students will be inspired by revealing their own commitment to and passion for their discipline or field, but, while it is necessary for students to see why what they are studying matters to their teachers, it is insufficient. Thoughtful, creative teaching strategies are also necessary.

Good teaching is discipline or field specific

Offering pedagogical ways for students to understand what it means to be critical in their own disciplines or fields is central to the 'craft practices of teaching' (Clegg 2009). While much can be learned about teaching from applying generic principles and reflecting on the effect, what is powerful for students is becoming adept in their own discipline or field. Bass (2012, p. 28) highlights the possibilities of students becoming experts:

> Learning to 'speak from a position of authority' is an idea rooted in expert practice. It is no more a 'soft skill' than are the other dimensions of learning that we are coming to value explicitly and systematically as outcomes of higher education – dimensions such as making discerning judgments based on practical reasoning, acting reflectively, taking risks, engaging in civil if difficult discourse, and proceeding with confidence in the face of uncertainty.

This quotation prompts thinking about what we intend students to be and do as a result of our teaching. Do we want them to be able to speak from a position of authority? If so, what kind of authority can students be and how do courses and teaching help them become authoritative? Do we want them to make discerning judgements based on reasoning and proceed with confidence in the face of uncertainty? If so, how do specific disciplines and fields enable them to do so?

As discussed in Chapters 5 and 9, the extent to which academic disciplines or fields structure approaches to teaching is a matter of disagreement and debate. Andresen (2000) reflects the position of many within this debate by arguing that what is taught is one of three features of scholarly teachers who are proficient in:

- *What* they teach – their discipline, their field, their subject matter.
- *How* they teach – their pedagogy.
- *Why* they teach – ranging from their own aims to their knowledge of the aims of higher education generally (2000, p. 142).

Lee Shulman (1987) encompasses these three aspects in the concept of 'pedagogical content knowledge', which describes the necessary knowledge for teachers to make content or expert practice knowledge accessible. In this concept, content/expert knowledge and pedagogical knowledge are equally essential and closely related. While Shulman acknowledges the usefulness of generic research about teaching, he describes the absence of reference to subject matter a 'missing paradigm' (1987, p. 7). Achieving pedagogical content knowledge entails first being:

> Not only capable of defining for students the accepted truths in a domain. [But] also able to explain why a particular proposition is deemed warranted, why it is worth knowing and how it relates to other propositions, both within the discipline and without, both in theory and in practice. (Shulman 1987, p. 9)

These capabilities require the broad and deep disciplinary or professional field under-standings characteristic of higher education teachers. Second, pedagogical content knowledge requires knowledge about 'ways of representing and formulating the subject that makes it comprehensible' (Shulman 1987, p. 9). Examples of questions raised for reflection by pedagogical content knowledge are: How do we decide what to teach? How do we introduce what is contested and contestable in our discipline or field? What are students' common preconceptions and misconceptions about the discipline or field? How can material be reorganized to take account of them? What makes specific topics difficult? What are the sources for metaphors, examples, demonstrations and re-phrasings powerful enough for advancing understanding of subject matter? Ignoring *either* the teacher's content knowledge *or* her pedagogical knowledge side-lines these questions.

In Chapter 2 on Learning, we examined the research around 'ways of thinking and practising in the disciplines' and 'threshold concepts' that emphasize the challenges that students can face in engaging with disciplinary or field knowledge. In the same vein, in the US there is work on 'bottle necks' in specific disciplines (Middendorf and Pace 2004). Evidently, understanding what the students find difficult is a vital aspect of good teaching. In Research Briefing 11.1, we examine five different types of what Perkins (2006) calls 'troublesome knowledge'.

RESEARCH BRIEFING 11.1 Types of troublesome knowledge

Perkins (2006) uses the concept of 'troublesome knowledge' to highlight aspects of subject knowledge that students tend to find difficult to grasp. He highlights five kinds of troublesome knowledge and suggests ways of addressing them in our teaching:

Ritual knowledge – which has a routine and meaningless character, such as learning specific rules or dates. Perkins suggests that ritual knowledge can be given meaning by placing it in a wider context.

Inert knowledge – which is used in specific contexts, separate from everyday contexts, and rarely applied. Perkins suggests helping students to make connections between abstract concepts and their own lives.

Conceptually difficult knowledge – which usually challenges the knowledge that students have acquired from everyday experience. Perkins suggests asking students to undertake investigations that bring them face to face with the contradictions between their prior understanding and the new difficult knowledge; and providing fora to discuss competing understandings and explanations.

Foreign or alien knowledge – which arises from a perspective other than the students' own. Perkins suggests getting students to identify and elaborate different perspectives of the same thing, so that they can experience the differences between these perspectives.

Tacit knowledge – this is knowledge possessed by the students of which they are unaware or largely unconscious. Perkins suggests 'surfacing' and discussing tacit knowledge.

Reflective Activity 11.1 Teaching troublesome knowledge

Think about some concepts or ideas in your own discipline or field that students find difficult to grasp.

- Does it fit with one of the types of troublesome knowledge outlined in **Research Briefing 11.1**?
- How can you help students to get to grips with this troublesome knowledge?
- Do Perkins' (2006) suggestions give you any ideas about how to do this?

In thinking about how students might acquire powerful disciplinary or professional knowledge, a consideration of the curriculum is essential. In Chapter 9, we discussed different ways of organizing a curriculum, such as inquiry-based learning, which enculturate students into their disciplines and fields. The concept of 'signature pedagogies', which are aligned with disciplinary or field ways of thinking, implies fixed cultures (Gurung et al. 2009), yet the discussion of decolonization in Chapters 5 and 9 clarifies for students and teachers that academic knowledge and the way it is taught is always open to challenge and intellectual scrutiny.

Encouraging students to study independently

There is a view that students are entirely responsible for choosing the amount of effort they put into their study. Higher education teachers want their students to work hard and independently, but they are often disappointed. Of course, finally it is what the students do that influences the extent to which they study and understand their disciplines or fields: we can't understand *for* anyone. However, we can teach in ways that are more likely to give students what Wally Morrow (2009) called 'epistemological access' and encourage independent study.

We use the term 'independent study' to capture the usually solitary work that students do away from formal teaching and learning modes such as reading, taking notes, completing problem sheets and essay writing. Yet it is a confusing term because the studying might be legitimately conducted in groups and the outcomes drawn upon in formal teaching and learning modes. Moreover, consciously or not, teachers determine what it is that students do outside formal teaching sessions Thus, it is unclear exactly how and when higher education studying is 'independent'. Nevertheless, it can be said that the expectation for each student is that she comes to think independently about her discipline or field; and understanding is a prerequisite of independent, critical thinking.

Studying outside formal sessions, often alone, is central to students' experience of learning. At the simplest level, it often takes up more hours than formal teaching. A national survey in the UK states: 'The total amount of work put in is more important for predicting learning gain than the number of contact hours, so it is vital to take into account private study hours and other forms of independent learning' (Soilemetzidis et al. 2014, p. 8). Yet for students unprepared by their schooling for what is expected at university, it is possible to put in long hours of unproductive study (for example, memorizing without understanding). So we need to consider how we can structure and encourage independent study by designing independent study tasks with clear goals in mind; making visible to the students what it is they are expected to do and why; and recognizing that different students will engage in these tasks in different ways depending on how they perceive them and that some students find long, solitary hours studying difficult. We can also send the message that we care about whether these tasks are done: McLean et al. (2018) found students discouraged when they were asked to do reading which was not discussed in seminars. We illustrate these issues with reference to three aspects of independent study: reading, essay writing and problem solving.

Chapter 2 showed how different students experience the academic tasks of reading and writing when they enter university. Mann (2000) reveals how students experience reading differently based upon their understanding of what they are reading for and their understanding of what it means to be a student. She points out that for some students reading for pleasure is experienced as a purely private activity, while reading for academic purposes is experienced as public because it is used to make judgements about students through essays, seminar discussions and examinations. This experience shifts reading from being pleasurable and engaging to being risky and threatening. Viewing reading as within the personal and biographical context of the student and within the socio-cultural context of higher education can help teachers understand the challenges that students face.

Academic essay writing too can be experienced and understood in different ways by different students. Based on interviews with history students, Hounsell (1997) argues that for some students an essay is simply the arrangement of material; for some it gives a viewpoint on a topic; and for some the purpose is to make an argument that critically draws on the available evidence. Clearly, there is a hierarchy of understanding here and the hope is for all students to hold the third understanding of essay writing. Added to these categories is that some students hold back from presenting their views or opinions, through lack of confidence or through a belief that lectures will penalize views with which they do not agree (Read et al. 2003). There is evidence that making the conventions of essays in different disciplines and fields explicit to students contributes to a more sophisticated understanding of their purpose and better realizations (Goldman et al. 2016; Clarence and McKenna 2017). The process of making explicit has been shown to work well when students are organized to work collaboratively (Daddow 2016).

In science subjects, students' way of tackling problems is shaped by how problems are presented (Laurillard 1997; Hattie 2015). When the students in Laurillard's (1997) study were asked to manipulate mathematical objects but not to interpret them, their response was to focus on completing the calculations rather than think about the meaning of the problem. In other words, they tended to take a surface rather than a deep approach to learning (see Chapter 2 for a discussion of this distinction). Laurillard (1997) argues that any task that students can solve by following a standard procedure rather than thinking does not deserve to be called 'problem solving'.

In general, when students work independently, it is helpful to give them opportunities to understand why they are doing it. We can reveal our awareness that there are different ways of understanding academic tasks; probe students' misunderstandings; and explain what is expected. Finally, students want to feel that their teachers are concerned about whether they are studying. One way of knowing that students are studying is by making use of what they have done in formal teaching sessions.

An element of the notion that students are entirely responsible for their own learning is that, if they have problems studying, they can seek specialist help. The risk with study support provision is that it can encourage the view that, as teachers, we are solely responsible for content delivery and students are responsible for acquiring the skills to understand the content elsewhere. Systems of study support are usually separated from students' programmes or courses, which places limitations on what they can do; nevertheless, they can help students to find ways of understanding their course materials and academic practices.

In Chapter 2, we examined the concept of 'academic literacies', the idea that students must understand the particular meaning of academic practices in universities. These ideas are often misinterpreted in study support context in terms of students 'learning to learn' (Wingate 2007), implying that academic literacies are generic rather than highlighting how literacies vary between academic disciplines and fields of study (Daddow 2016; Clarence and McKenna 2017). As discussed above, good teaching is discipline specific, so, while we might encourage our students to make use of central services, we need to be aware of the ways in which study support is separate from our own teaching of disciplinary knowledge. The question is how generic help with study skills is related to what and how we teach.

Teaching is a moral endeavour

Teaching is not a value-free or technical activity, rather it is what Jurgen Habermas (1987) calls a 'moral-practical' area of human activity because being educated concerns individual fulfilment and transformation and being a citizen as well as preparation for work. Teaching is the core activity in higher education which creates and recreates culture, society and personal identity, sometimes as a force for social mobility and change and sometimes reproducing existing hierarchies. This book promotes the idea of teaching as a moral endeavour in its discussions of the role of relationships in Chapter 6, critical pedagogy in Chapters 12 and 17, and decolonization of the curriculum in Chapter 9.

We argue here for 'socially-just pedagogy' defined as teaching which gives diverse students access to knowledge and understanding which gives them power in their lives (Walker and Wilson-Strydom 2017; McLean et al. 2018). Pring (2001, p. 112) captures what teaching must do for students to gain this power:

> [Teaching mediates a] transaction between the impersonal world of ideas embodied
> within particular texts and artefacts and the personal world of the [student] as he or she

struggles to make sense, searches for value, engages in discovery, finds ideals worth striving for, encounters ideas.

What is not visible in this quotation is the diversity of students and their different levels of understanding. What is called 'inclusive teaching' is to consider these differences when we teach without compromising the power of the knowledge and understanding we want the students to gain. The following case study examines issues related to student diversity and teaching in higher education.

Case Study 11.1 Celia and her colleagues design a socially just course

In 'Diversity University' (UK) the course team led by Celia were preparing for revalidation of the sociology degree course. They wanted to adapt the curriculum and teaching in ways which transformed the lives of their students who were largely working class, and half were Asian (just as when they were students they had been transformed by sociological thinking). They were determined to avoid 'dumbing down' the course. As they set about redesigning the curriculum and thinking about pedagogic principles, they felt disconnected from students because of the wide chasm between their own cultural capital and that of the students and because, it seemed to them, students had become more instrumental, only interested in getting right answers. In terms of curriculum content, the team decided to pursue sociological interests (for example, social class, race, gender and sexual orientation) by making the students' identities and cultures the objects of their (the students') sociological analysis and critique. The new course built on students' own interests by engaging them in iterative research from the first year, culminating in a dissertation in the final year (those conducting the revalidation thought the dissertation would be better dropped because it was too demanding; the team fought to keep it). The aim was to help students to challenge the taken-for-grantedness of their everyday lives and see it through the lens of sociological thought.

Examples of the principles the team pursue are: (1) from the beginning of the course, inviting the students to revaluate their understandings of their own experiences in the light of sociological concepts or theories (previously they had found teaching theory confrontational); (2) telling students about their own research; (3) making explicit what is expected of a sociology undergraduate student; (4) not teaching too much content but rather teaching it thoroughly, returning to theories and concepts in increasingly complex ways; (5) making workshops as dialogic and collaborative as part of inclusive pedagogy; (6) attending constantly to processes of abstraction, conceptualization and theorization; (7) using a wide variety of teaching and assessment methods; (8) making efforts to show students that they care about their academic progress and respect them.

In the course team's view, despite anxiety earlier in the course, by the final year most students appreciate the challenges set for them and emerge from the fusion of socio-logical and self-understanding with new critical identities which allow them to locate power and social process in their life experiences.

(Summarized and adapted from Jenkins et al. 2017)

Reflective Activity 11.2 Reflecting on how to change your course or module

Think about the efforts of Celia's course team at Diversity. If you wanted to make a more determined effort to get students to understand how your discipline or field can transform the ways they see the world, how might such changes appear in your own course or modules? How might the curriculum content change? How might you change teaching methods and practices and what you ask students to do? How might assessment change?

There are many resources for thinking about making curriculum and teaching more inclusive. For example, in **Research Briefing 5.1**, in Chapter 5, we outlined the findings from the Social and Organisational Mediation of University Learning (SOMUL) Project (Brennan et al. 2010) which raises questions about dealing with student diversity within a single institution. They found that to cope with increasing student diversity, some institutions were effectively running 'parallel universities' for different types of students. They argue for universities thinking hard about whether it is fair to target different kinds of curriculum and teaching to different kinds of students, which risks 'dumbing down' for some students. McLean et al. (2018) use the theories of Basil Bernstein to explore whether relatively disadvantaged students in lower-status universities receive lower quality education than more privileged students in higher status universities. A starting point for socially just and inclusive teaching is to be clear about the purpose and justifications of our selection of different content, learning activities and teaching methods for different students. Can we explain how all students will be given the opportunity to attain the same level of disciplinary or professional field understanding?

Teaching is a collective enterprise

Rowland's 'shared context' for learning about teaching challenges the belief that teaching is an individual enterprise (as awards for teaching might lead us to believe). Throughout the book you will find an emphasis on dialogue, working together and relationships (see Chapters 2, 3 and 6). Teaching for understanding does not take place in isolation. Given that university education comprises courses made up of curriculum and teaching designed by many, we are required to work with academic colleagues and students as well as others from both within and outside our institutions. There is evidence that we tend to make teaching congruent with the departments or workgroups in which we work (Trowler, P. 2020). Conceptualizing teaching as collective rather than individual is likely to produce better courses, which is the level that most influences student learning.

Cressey et al. (2006) coined the term 'productive reflection' in relation to situations in which there is a collective rather than an individual orientation to reflection (see also Boud 2010). The focus in productive reflection is on organizational issues, for example a course team building a sustained approach to teaching for understanding (as do Celia and her team in **Case Study 11.1**). In discussing how to think together about understanding student learning, we can draw on ideas about creating communities of practice, which we explored in Chapter 2. 'Productive reflection' is often not easy to pursue. Cressey et al. (2006) list factors that prevent it: for example, if problems are pre-defined or unilaterally defined, or if members have set ideas and are not open to alternatives or insist that they know the correct way to proceed rather than allowing exploration of the issues of the whole group. Versions of these factors are probably recognizable to us all. Although degree validation procedures or student and staff consultative committees is collective work, for them to be genuinely productive might entail new approaches.

Two principles can help us. First, we need to work out whether solutions to problems come from outside the course or module. Colleagues, curricula and other regulatory requirements change in often unpredictable and unsatisfactory ways, which require us to think and act beyond the course and into the arena of institutional practices. Second, we can draw on multiple perspectives to find ways of gaining access to what teaching for understanding means to academic colleagues, students and others, both inside (for example, those who work in academic development and study support) and outside (for example, professional bodies) our organizations (Cressey et al. 2006; Boud 2010). We can strive to make connections between these groups recognizing that they have different concerns and interests.

So, like teaching itself, working collectively is a work in progress that has degrees of success rather than being wholly effective all the time. Good quality teaching and learning can only be sustainable if it is 'owned' collectively rather than being the preserve of individual university teachers.

TEACHING IN DIFFERENT MODES

Having established bases for thinking about teaching in the first section of the chapter, in this section we analyse how we might focus on teaching for understanding within different modes that are typical of higher education: lectures; small group modes; laboratory and fieldwork; supervision; online teaching and learning. While, in this section, we focus on specific teaching modes separately, this separation should not detract from the desirability of considering the modes in the context of all the elements of the modules and/or programmes in which they are located. In Chapter 2, we discussed the relational nature of students' learning and the same is true for teaching. How we teach will shift according to our perceptions of our students; what they are required to learn and module assessment; of the resources and spaces in which we teach. How different students experience teaching modes differently is explored in Research Briefing 11.2 overleaf.

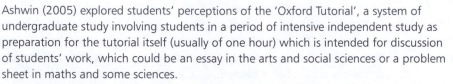

RESEARCH BRIEFING 11.2 Students' perceptions of tutorials

Ashwin (2005) explored students' perceptions of the 'Oxford Tutorial', a system of undergraduate study involving students in a period of intensive independent study as preparation for the tutorial itself (usually of one hour) which is intended for discussion of students' work, which could be an essay in the arts and social sciences or a problem sheet in maths and some sciences.

While some students saw tutorials as a way in which students and tutors could exchange ideas and come to new understandings, others saw them as an intimate lecture. Compare these ways that history students saw the tutorial:

> It varies very much between tutor and tutor, some tutors' tutorials are like a lecture, you come away with very organised notes, adding **a lot** to the information you didn't know before, which is very useful. Other times you leave the tutorial not feeling like you've gained a lot from it.

> The apogee of the tutorial is where you don't know, the tutor doesn't know, but between the two of you you're going to analyse this thing. I love it when you're in with someone like Professor X and he's just whacking books off the shelf, getting maps out. He's there on his hands and knees and between the two of you, you manage to clarify something and that's a tremendous experience.

Ashwin (2006) found similar differences in how tutors experienced tutorials at Oxford. This research shows how both teachers and students can experience the same teaching and learning method differently. It highlights that there is nothing intrinsic within specific methods that determine how we conceptualize and experience them; rather it is a case of reflective teachers making a conscious choice about how they wish to use particular teaching methods to assist their students' understanding of disciplinary knowledge.

Any teaching mode is shaped by its relationship to the rest of the programme and other elements of students' experiences. Figure 11.1 sets out a model of teaching and learning, from the Enhancing Teaching-Learning Environments Project discussed in Chapter 2. The model represents the relational nature of teaching. At the centre are students' ways of thinking and conceptual understanding. The model shows how students' understanding is informed by the design and implementation of the teaching and learning environment, which in turn is shaped by our understanding of our subjects and our beliefs about teaching and learning as well as the departmental and disciplinary norms. Equally, students' perceptions of teaching are influenced by their backgrounds, their approaches to learning and their peers.

Despite the inter-relatedness of modes, we talk of 'lecturing' or 'tutoring' or 'giving seminars' or 'running a workshop' or 'having a lab'. Nevertheless, the questions for teaching in each of these modes are broadly similar:

- What role does each mode play in the module and programme as a whole?
- What do we want our students to achieve in this mode and how does this relate to, and is different from, what we want to be achieved in other modes?

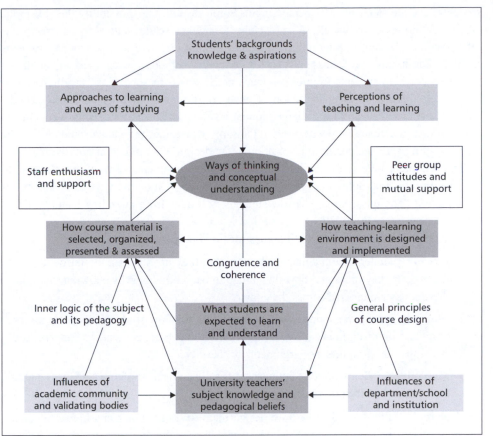

Figure 11.1 A model of teaching and learning (from David, 2009)

- How will we evaluate whether students have achieved what we want them to?
- How does students' work in this mode relate to the assessment of the module or programme?

Moreover, whatever the mode, teaching for understanding is never about simply presenting content to students. It involves being aware of how the selected content, teaching mode and learning activities contribute to students' an understanding of disciplinary or field ideas and concepts.

Lectures

As we saw in Chapter 8 on Spaces, lectures are at the centre of our concept of teaching in higher education. In some contexts, it has been estimated that students spend 80 per cent of their contact time listening to lectures (Armbruster 2000). While we can all remember examples of good and bad lectures, the question for reflective teachers is how they can help students to understand what is being taught. Some dispute that possibility. For example, Bligh's (2000) review of the efficacy of lectures found that, while lectures are as effective as other methods for transmitting information, they are not effective for encouraging students to think. Can it really be the case that such a dominant method of teaching in higher education does not help students to think? Perhaps not, for two reasons. First, as Bligh (2000) recognizes, there is no clear definition of what constitutes a 'traditional lecture' and the difference between a lecture and a large seminar is often unclear. Second, Bligh's conclusion assumes that the lecture is always used in the same way rather than understanding that the meaning of a lecture comes from its position in the design of a module or programme.

The argument here is for thinking about the understandings we want our students to achieve through a module or programme and then thinking about how we can use lectures to achieve it. The question is what the students will gain from attending lectures that is different from other modes?

In Mathematics, Pritchard (2010) argues for three purposes for the lecture:

1 Providing students with a map of the area that they are studying by introducing them to the key ideas and how they relate to each other and by showing them how these ideas are tackled across the course.

2 Modelling problem solving and expert thinking to show students how they might grapple with disciplinary ideas, think beyond the subject content, and analyse the strengths and limitations of arguments or theories.

3 Motivating students through enthusiasm for the subject, showing students what is at stake in the discipline and why that matters.

For lectures to fulfil these purposes, we design them to do so. For many higher education teachers, rethinking the purposes of lectures results in changing how they use the mode to be more effective in promoting student understanding. For example, Tormey and Henchy (2008) sought to reimagine lectures for around 300 students so that students could discuss the ideas and concepts presented in the lecture. They showed 10–15-minute videos introducing students to ideas with the rest of the time divided between individual and small group activities when students worked with the ideas and a final whole group discussion. Students' reactions to the innovation were mixed with many students valuing the approach and others feeling that traditional lectures were a better preparation for exams. Their reactions illustrate how new ways of using lectures will be perceived in different ways. They also identify that, while it is important to evaluate how students are experiencing lectures, student satisfaction is not the goal: new approaches can make students anxious, but this reaction does not justify abandoning principled ways of teaching. It might be more productive to focus on evaluating what has been understood, which can be done quite simply. For example, by ending a little early and asking the students one or two general questions to write down and hand in: 'What do you think were the main points of today's lecture?' or 'What point or example in today's lecture would you like reviewed or clarified?' The answers can be enlightening about what the students have understood or misunderstood: it is worth trying. Further examples of alternative ways of using the lecture mode can be found in other chapters. In Chapters 2 and 8, the discussion of 'flipping the classroom' offers an alternative way of approaching lectures, while Chapter 12 on Communication offers suggestions for generating dialogue in lectures.

Small group modes

Small group modes, such as seminars, tutorials and workshops, are often seen as the space where students can discuss and think about material that has been presented in lectures. There is evidence that small group modes can enhance higher order thinking; transfer of learning between contexts as well as the acquisition of skills and attitudes (Pai et al. 2015; Skinner et al. 2016; Swanson et al. 2019) and are also important in online settings (Sun and Chen 2016). Brookfield and Preskill (2005) list fifteen benefits of discussion, including: the opportunity to explore a diversity of perspectives and have assumptions challenged; increased awareness of tolerance and ambiguity; and greater interest in the topic under discussion. It appears therefore that understanding occurs naturally in such modes.

However, as we saw in **Research Briefing 11.2**, students can understand small group modes in different ways and, as we discuss in more detail in Chapter 12, our experiences of small group modes can often be disappointing. Similarly, students can be disappointed by other students' silence or lack of preparation (McLean et al. 2018). Brookfield and Preskill (2005) offer a number of reasons for poor discussions. First, teachers' unrealistic expectation of scintillating exchanges to simply blossom. This expectation is often connected to a failure to properly prepare students for discussion by sharing with them our view of a good discussion and why we want them. We often do not discuss the ground rules of discussions with our students and agree collectively how all students will have an equal chance to participate (see **Case Study 6.2** for an example). These discussions can also appear unrelated to assessment and so students see them as a poor investment of their time. Finally, we fail to model the kind of participation we seek from students.

Once again this shows that teaching for understanding in small groups is a matter of pedagogic design. Creating a climate in which groups of students participate in high-quality discussion is generally not a one-off event, it is often a long, hard haul and depends on good, friendly relationships (see Chapter 6). The conditions for high-quality discussion are: that all students are prepared to speak; they are confident enough to speak freely and not fearful of saying the wrong thing; they can be challenged and challenge others; and there is a sense of enjoyment. McLean et al. (2018) found that sociology students recognized that the quality of discussion depended on the quality of their own preparation and their capacity and confidence to make contributions. They felt they improved as contributors to seminars: when the teacher explicitly pushed for them to prepare; when the teacher relaxed boundaries, relating to them as academic peers and encouraging and valuing their opinions; when there were specific smaller group activities; when the teacher offered examples, illustrations and stories; and when the teacher didn't lapse into giving a 'mini' lecture. Finally, it is useful to reflect upon the tacit messages we send to students about what is expected of them in the small group modes, for example ticking off names in a register sets up the seminar as a teacher-controlled rather than a discursive space. We explore these issues in more depth in Chapter 12 on Communication.

Reflective Activity 11.3 Silent seminars

The following is adapted from an account written by Heidi Yeandle and found at **salt.swan.ac.uk/silent-seminars**. Think about what kind of exchanges between students were produced and whether you would want to adapt the idea for your groups.

I decided to pilot a 'silent seminar' whereby students use written communication rather than spoken communication to respond to questions in a seminar environment. Students were asked to read some Emily Dickenson poetry and given some questions to think about in preparation for the seminar. In the class, students were divided into small groups and each group was given one of the poems, printed on A3 paper in a large font. They were asked to annotate the poems in relation to themes, language, and poetic techniques (in line with the questions). After 5 minutes, the poems rotated, so each group had a sheet of A3 paper with a different poem on, with the previous group's comments and interpretations. Students were asked to continue to annotate the poems, to read the other annotations and add to them, thinking about alternative interpretations, or whether a comparison or contrast could be made in relation to another Dickinson poem, thereby encouraging students to interact with other students in the class without speaking. The poems continued to move between groups until students were reunited with the first poem they annotated, giving them the opportunity to see how the rest of the groups responded to that poem and their reading of it.

Laboratories and fieldwork

In laboratories (labs) and fieldwork, students can learn together in groups; help each other through peer learning; and learn inquiry skills in 'real-world' contexts. Again, these teaching and learning modes can be effective in helping students' understanding but they will not do so unless they are designed to do so.

Edward (2002) argues that labs offer students the opportunity both to learn and to test new theory and in many disciplines they are seen as the vehicle for students to understand the relations between observations and theories and practise scientific reasoning. However, this potential is by no means always realized (Hofstein and Lunetta 2004). Experiments often take a recipe-following approach in which the teacher defines the topic to be investigated and tells the students what to do. The results students achieve in the lab are then compared to the expected result. Such approaches do not enhance students' understanding because they do not require them to think about the concepts at stake in the experiment, but rather try to follow the recipe in the right way (Domin 1999). There are problem-based approaches that require students to reformulate problems and grapple with concepts (see Chapter 9).

The challenge of designing labs that are both scientifically and educationally sound informed the Advancing Science and Engineering through Laboratory Learning (ASELL) project in Australia (see Barrie et al. 2015; Yeung et al. 2019), which set out to improve the quality of labs. The project has a website providing a database of experiments tested for whether they promote student understanding. The literature on labs highlights two issues. First, it emphasizes the difference between the potential and the actual educational effects. Unless labs are designed with a clear sense of how they help students to understand identified concepts, they are unlikely to be effective. Second, it highlights thinking about courses and teaching in relation to wider disciplines. The case of ASELL highlights how designing and evaluating laboratories collectively is more effective and results in a better quality than doing so individually. There is still work to be done in adapting resources to our own teaching and learning contexts, including our students, but there is no need to design experiments from scratch. Many of the same issues arise in relation to the successful design of fieldwork activities for students and we examined some of these in Chapter 8 on Spaces (Chang et al. 2018). Kent et al. (1997) argued that fieldwork design be based on students' current levels of academic and practical knowledge; fit with the design of the rest of the course; and take account of time and budgetary constraints. They also emphasized preparing students for fieldwork and being clear about the work students are expected to produce based on the fieldwork, and about how the fieldwork and the subsequent written work is related to understanding aspects of the discipline. Leydon and Turner (2013) outlined their design of a large field trip for 120 geography students that moved students away from simple observation of the field towards analysing their surroundings and practising fieldwork techniques. This change gave students a richer sense of what it meant to be a geographer.

Supervision

Supervision, whether it is of undergraduate projects, Masters dissertations or PhDs, and whether it takes place in an office, coffee shop or online, is focused on students undertaking research that they have initiated, suggesting that it is comparatively straightforward to focus on students' understanding, but in supervisory modes student understanding must be of a depth and breadth to underpin original and creative thinking.

There is a large literature on supervision pedagogies, mainly PhD supervision, which can be roughly divided into three categories. First, there is 'how to supervise' literature on which new supervisors can draw for ideas about 'good practice' (for example, Peelo 2011; Walker and Thomson 2010; Wisker 2012). Second, there is research literature which presents models and typologies of supervision based on empirical data, of which Research Briefing 11.3 overleaf is an example.

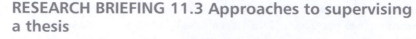

RESEARCH BRIEFING 11.3 Approaches to supervising a thesis

Lee (2008) found that different supervisors focus on five different aspects of the processes of producing a dissertation or thesis.

1 Functional supervision, in which supervisors focus on project management. This can maintain focus on the project but can also cause difficulties if the students' findings take them away from the clearly defined limits of the project.

2 Enculturation-orientated supervision, in which supervisors involve the student becoming a member of their discipline. This can help students to participate in the discipline but can be intolerant of student identities which do not conform to those in the discipline.

3 Critical thinking-focused supervision, which encourages the student to become critical of their own work and the work of others. This can help students to produce logical and robust work but can stifle their creativity and leave them feeling inadequate.

4 Emancipation-focused supervision, in which the supervisor focuses on students' personal growth. This can also put the supervisor in an inappropriately powerful position because the focus of the relationship is the student's identity.

5 Relationship development-focused supervision, where the supervisor is concerned about a high-quality working relationship. This can enhance the student's self-esteem but has the potential for the student to feel harassed or rejected.

Lee points out that many supervisors draw on more than one of these approaches at any one time and that the approach is likely to change over the course of a student's PhD.

Within the models and typologies literature, the quality of the supervisory relationship emerges as pivotal to the student producing good work (for example, Adkins 2009; Bastalich 2017). However, a third small category of literature problematizes both the 'how to' and the models and typologies literature by drawing attention to the unpredictable and emotionally traumatic character of the experience of producing a thesis or dissertation. For example, Hendersen (2018), poised between completing her PhD and becoming a supervisor, employs autoethnography to challenge literature which proposes that supervisors can create safe spaces for students, arguing that the identity work involved in producing a thesis makes emotional upheaval unavoidable, even when the relationship with the supervisor is positive. Bastalich (2017) undertook a critical review of twenty years' research about improving supervisory practices and found most perspectives to be over psychologized and decontextualized with the good supervisor characterized as 'all-responsible and all-knowing' (p. 1154). Literature in the third category is therefore rare in its emphasis on the psychosocial nature of supervision (Grant 2003, 2008, 2010; Petersen 2007).

Supervision is high stakes for the student who must acquire specific discipline, methodological, theoretical knowledge; be proficient at academic writing and research practices;

become familiar with research cultures and gain access to research networks. And supervision is complex for us, we might reflect about why we supervise as we do by making use of the three contexts of personal experience, what others do and research literature. Moreover, supervision is usually seen as an individual task, but, as Bastalich (2017) proposes, we might be helped by an institutional research culture which understands supervision as part of a collaborative educational project, allowing us to articulate our own limits in knowledge and capacity.

Online teaching and learning

We examine the use of digital learning spaces in Chapter 8. Mason and Rennie (2006) point out that, while for some observers the potential of Massive Open Online Courses (MOOCs) challenges the nature of higher education, we have been here before: there was a time when it was argued that the new technology of television would render lectures irrelevant. New technologies include Virtual Learning Environments (VLEs), other forms of remote learning and a range of social media. The challenge for reflective teachers in higher education is to think creatively about how they can be employed to promote students' understanding of disciplinary knowledge.

Those who advocate online learning argue that it offers 'more creative opportunities to present knowledge content at various levels and in different temporal zones' (Bach et al. 2007, p. 127). However, the argument in this chapter, in relation to all teaching and learning modes, is that teaching for understanding demands more than presenting knowledge content. Laurillard (2012) emphasized that we need to design online teaching with the same care as when it is face-to-face or, as Mazur (2009, p. 51) put it, 'it is not the technology that matters but the pedagogy'.

Natriello (2005) warned that lecturers with little experience of online learning tend to transfer traditional approaches to the online classroom and perpetuate approaches that have been proven to be ineffective in the face-to-face classroom. The pedagogical issue at stake is how different media allow different kinds of learning processes. McConnell (2006) argues that there are three broad models of online e-learning: those based solely on transmission of information to students; those in which transmission is followed by the opportunity for students to discuss ideas; and those which are focused on the building of a learning community. The focus on learning communities has given rise to the notion of networked learning which emphasizes designing online environments for interactions between students to be at the centre of the learning process, with some arguing that digital technologies are so integral to educational activities we are now at the stage of 'post-digital' education (Hodgson and McConnell 2019). Decisions about the extent to which our teaching supports students to network connects to Laurillard's (2012) proposal to think about where the locus of control lies in the online environments that we create: where do we give students more and less control and why. We also need to consider the extent to which our students' 'digital literacies' support their engagement in such networks (Reyna et al. 2018).

Central to being clear about whether online environments are enhancing understanding is, once again, guarding against conflating the educational potential of online spaces for what happens in practice. Developing effective discussions in online environments is a challenging task (Thomas and Thorpe 2019) and we further explore issues relating to online dialogues in Chapter 12. So, while new technologies offer exciting opportunities to have exchanges with students across larger geographical distances and to enhance learning that occurs in more traditional spaces, the potential will not be realized without thought about how to design online spaces and activities to deepen students' understanding of disciplinary knowledge.

CONCLUSION

This chapter is framed by encouraging the reader to think about how teaching can advance students' understanding of disciplinary or field knowledge. In the first section, the bases for thinking was evidence that this endeavour is worthwhile and possible for all higher education teachers. The pedagogical routes to providing students with an education that opens horizons for them are many and are to be found in the selection of curriculum content; in teaching modes and methods; and in learning activities and assessment. The second part of the chapter provided a few examples. Decisions about what to teach and how will depend on individual teachers, groups of teachers and disciplinary cultures.

A main message of the chapter is that teaching is a complicated matter and that it helps to have theories about what engages students' interest and deepens their understanding based on experience, discussion and reading. We promote the idea of theory-building about teaching, provided the theory is constantly appraised and refined in the light of practice. The interplay of theory and practice can be powerful and guard against higher education teachers being buffeted by educational fashion and directives which might not be educationally sound.

KEY READINGS

For further discussions of teaching for understanding, see:

Entwistle, N. (2018) *Student Learning and Academic Understanding: A Research Perspective with Implications for Teaching*. San Diego, CA: Academic Press.

Entwistle, N. (2009) *Teaching for Understanding at University*. Houndmills, Basingstoke: Palgrave Macmillan.

On developing socially just approaches to teaching, see:

Walker, M. and Wilson-Strydom, M. (eds) (2017) *Socially Just Pedagogies, Capabilities and Quality in Higher Education*. London: Palgrave Macmillan.

For the concept of pedagogical subject knowledge, see:

Shulman, L. (1987) 'Knowledge and teaching: Foundations of the new reform', *Harvard Educational Review*, 57(1), 1–23.

For a database of Laboratory Learning in Science and Engineering: **asell.org**.

For an examination of how to use learning technologies in a principled manner, see:

Laurillard, D. (2012) *Teaching as a Design Science: Building Pedagogical Patterns for Learning and Technology*. Abingdon: Routledge.

For a review of the literature on PhD supervision, see:

Bastalich, W. (2017) 'Content and context in knowledge production: A critical review of doctoral supervision literature', *Studies in Higher Education*, 42(7), 1145–57.

Chapter 12
Communication

How can we support learning through dialogue?

INTRODUCTION

In this chapter we examine the importance of communication in supporting students' learning. We propose that communication for learning be understood as a dialogue and its importance for developing a reflective approach to our practice recognized, as introduced in Chapter 3. In everyday contexts, dialogue is generally understood as a conversation between two or more people. It includes a sense of genuine listening and understanding. From this everyday context we can draw out certain principles about dialogue that are important in a learning context. These include notions of exchange, responsiveness and respect. We can also extend the notion of dialogue and use it to explore a range of interactions within the teaching–learning context to include an exchange of ideas that may or may not take place through talking.

See Chapter 4

TLRP Principles

Two principles are of particular relevance to this chapter on communication in teaching–learning settings in higher education:

Principle 4: Effective teaching and learning fosters both individual and social processes and outcomes. Students should be encouraged to build relationships and communication with others to assist the mutual construction of knowledge and enhance the achievements of individuals and groups. Consulting or collaborating with students as learners about their learning makes this effective.

Principle 5: Effective teaching and learning promotes the active engagement of the student as learner. A key aim of higher learning should be to develop students' independence and autonomy as learners. This involves engaging students actively in their own learning, and ensuring that they acquire a repertoire of learning strategies and practices, develop positive learning dispositions, and build the confidence to become agents in their own learning.

The notion of 'dialogue' thus captures the ways in which the links between communication and learning are best understood on many levels. On one level it is a clear and simple relationship: taking a simplified view, some might say teaching is about communicating new ideas, knowledge or skills to students. But do students receive the communications simply as given – the information has been transferred, therefore it is to be learned – or do they enter into dialogue with the information, interpreting, reconstructing, or even challenging as a natural part of the process?

This introduces a more complex aspect between communication and learning, the idea that communication is both an active and two-way set of processes – as is learning. The notion of dialogue goes hand in hand with understanding learning as a dynamic and social process. Dialogue is the avenue through which meaning is made by the social interaction with other people and the ideas of other people. Hence there must be more to communication *for learning* than simply the telling, passing over or sharing of information. In earlier chapters we touched on transmission-focused modes of teaching, based on assumptions (often implicit) that we can simply hand over or transfer information, and thus knowledge, to students. Knowledge is treated rather like a parcel; we hand it over to students and they hand it back to us through assessments. There is no sense in this transmission-focused model of the student interacting with what we tell them or that they might take apart what we tell them and reconstruct it in their own minds, through the lenses of their own experiences. As we know, students learn best through more active approaches to learning. And, there is no sense of the diverse backgrounds, cultures and experiences that students bring to this process. Thus, transmission is about passive and static communication: communication without dialogue.

The aim of this chapter is to consider communication in teaching–learning interactions, while stressing the dialogical nature of learning. Dialogue cannot occur without mutual respect and consideration of other views. Nor should dialogue and communication occur without consideration of the diversity of our institutional communities. As we saw in Chapter 1, we cannot safely assume that our students will have shared identities, values and expectations. This is particularly important to the theme of communication as students come to this act of dialogue from many different discursive contexts, be they based on language, culture, class or other contextual factors. This means that there are issues of social justice at stake in how we communicate with our students. Issues of critical pedagogy and social justice are further explored in Chapter 17.

The remainder of the chapter is divided into three main sections. The first section explores communication within learning and teaching contexts, and the implications of these for student–teacher relationship. The second section looks at dialogue in different teaching and learning settings. We explore how to facilitate and develop dialogue in settings with differing numbers of people, from the self to peers, educators and decision makers within the institution. The third section looks at what we do as educators. We consider the nature of disciplinary knowledge and discourses within higher education. This includes the issue of how to achieve dialogical and active communication within the realms of highly specialized, and often unfamiliar to students, disciplinary subject areas. We also consider how we as educators communicate with students and colleagues, the impact this might have on the student experience and how we can engage in dialogue to enhance our own professional development.

RESEARCH BRIEFING 12.1 Dialogical teaching

Research on dialogue, and its relationship with teaching has, to date, predominantly been at the level of school teaching. A number of concepts have been proposed, most drawing on Bakhtin's theoretical work (Bakhtin 1981), on the dialogic nature of language, and Freire's on the importance of dialogue to human nature: 'dialogue imposes itself as the way by which they [people] achieve significance as human being. Dialogue is thus an existential necessity' (Freire 1996, p. 69). Freire's conception of dialogue was firmly based on the idea of critical dialogue: dialogue that seeks to unearth meanings, challenge and consider ideas through new eyes. Such dialogue in the context of a learning–teaching environment cannot be imposed on students, nor can it be based on assumptions that only students have anything to learn. Speaking as a teacher, Friere asks: 'How can I dialogue if I always project ignorance onto others and never perceive my own?' (p. 71). In earlier work and expressed in interview with Shor (Shor and Freire 1987), Freire describes the dialogical method of teaching, and the many potential educational and social outcomes of such an approach.

Skidmore (2006) usefully summarizes research on three concepts of dialogue and teaching in the classroom: dialogic instruction (Nystrand 1997), moving away from monologic discourse (coined by Bakhtin), a predominantly teacher-led transmission approach to teaching and learning, based on remembering and recitation sometimes with the pretence of dialogue but insincere in purpose and execution, and moving instead to dialogic discourse, where students are asked to think, ask questions and modify topics; dialogic inquiry (Wells 2001), which focuses on group work with true collaboration and peer assistance, where knowledge is co-constructed through activities; and dialogic teaching, which is purposeful and collective, focusing on students' growing understanding and knowledge (see Skidmore and Murakami 2016).

All concepts under the umbrella of dialogue and teaching, while presented at the school level, have something to offer higher education and resonate with the efforts to move away from the persistence of information transmission with an expectation of high-level engagement and subsequent ability to dialogue and discourse despite lack of opportunity to develop this, to more active learning, encouraging students to bring their voices to the classroom, engage and co-create knowledge and learning.

However, classroom communication does not necessarily lead to true dialogue. Boyd and Markarian (2011) explore how 'talk structures', impact discourse within the classroom. They explore not only what is said, but how it is said and how we are predisposed to hear it. This works in both directions, from teacher to student and student to teacher. Therefore, closed questions may still lead to meaningful dialogue, and more open perhaps considered 'authentic' questions can still lead to silence.

LEARNING RELATIONSHIPS AND APPROACHES TO COMMUNICATION

The roles of students and teachers, and the nature of their relationships, is formed by and reflected in the communication that takes place within the learning environment. In the traditional lecture, the communication appears to be one-way from the lecturer at the front to the students, all in rows facing forward. Underpinning this form of communication are implicit assumptions about the nature of knowledge, which we will return to later. There may also be assumptions about roles, power, authority and legitimacy: in this situation the teacher's power may be symbolically reinforced by the spatial situation and by the one-way nature of communication. The teacher is expert, delivering, passing or transmitting knowledge to the passive and inexpert students.

In contrast, some teachers favour encouraging a more dialogical approach by rearranging the traditional setting into, for example, roundtable or circle style seating. Here the authority of the lecturer appears diminished, a circle challenges the notion of hierarchical power and the face-to-face aspect of all participants supposedly encourages greater interaction. However, both such scenarios are stereotypes. Each one has an element of truth, but neither fully reflects the potential complexity and nuance of dialogue within a teaching context. As Brookfield (2017) has observed, it is rather too easy to think that putting chairs in a circle ensures a democratic space within the classroom. Similarly, Shaw et al. (2008) argue that 'organising desks in a U-shape does not transform a space into a "tutorial". It requires work by the tutors and students to achieve this' (p. 711). If our aim is to create a learning relationship with our students, a dialogical form of communication, then we have to think beyond the physical settings. This is not to deny that physical space influences the creation of these relationships; the point is simply that we cannot rely on it in isolation as either a cure or an excuse for poor communication.

Dialogue is not simply essential to the teaching–learning relationship but to be educative, the relationship needs to be dialogical. And the implications of this are far wider than how classrooms are arranged or whether learning–teaching interactions are labelled lecture, seminar or tutorial. Dialogue implies a sharing of authority – not necessarily a sameness but a recognition of equally legitimate roles. In a dialogue both parties make a contribution and both parties are potential learners, gaining something through the interaction with others. There are three key aspects to dialogue within teaching–learning interactions:

- a recognition of legitimately different roles between students and teachers;
- a rethinking of authority and power relationships between students and teachers;
- an understanding of all parties in a dialogue as potential learners.

Students are students because they do not yet know (Northedge and McArthur 2009) and this right to not yet know is an essential aspect of student identity. Indeed, the difference between students and teachers is as important to an educative dialogue as the aspects of common ground.

It does not help students to pretend that they already know everything that there is to be known, nor to underestimate the value of what a teacher brings to their learning. It is important to recognize this given the recent emphasis on students as partners (Matthews et al. 2019) and this point was emphasized by early critical theorist, Theodor Adorno, during a discussion on education. Adorno made clear that the fact that a teacher hopefully has greater subject expertise than his/her students is not something we should easily forget (Adorno and Becker 1999). However, this should not imply the teacher deserves a more important role in the creation of dialogue in the teaching–learning situation. Dialogue is inherent within the teacher–student relationship, even when lying inert or unfulfilled. The authority for dialogue is not teacher-given (for example, by the arrangement of chairs or by attempts at surface negotiation): it is already there – waiting for fulfilment through that relationship.

Stephen Rowland's (2000) idea of 'surface negotiation' is a powerful way of understanding the implications of rethinking authority and power with the teaching setting. Rowland describes how teachers often ask questions ('What shall we do today?', or 'Would you like to look at Hamlet in this session?') about which they assume a compliant answer. They never have any intention of deviating from the path they have decided on for the class, but ask the question as a type of good form or student-friendly face. Surface negotiation is far more damaging than no negotiation because it creates an illusion of dialogue where none actually exists. As such it distorts the teaching–learning relationship by its falseness and dishonesty.

Recognizing the legitimate differences between students and teachers means that, as academics, we sometimes make the decisions, based on our prior experience, greater subject knowledge or deeper understanding of the assessment tasks. In such situations it is important to clearly communicate the reasons for our decisions, rather than to pretend we are not making them. A useful example of this comes from Shor's (1996) account of trying to share power with students. As part of this initiative, Shor offered his students 'protest rights', by which he aimed to encourage public and transparent questioning and criticism of the course, and his teaching, as the students were experiencing it. A particular focus for students' criticisms, in the example discussed, was a seemingly unintelligible and irrelevant reading they were required to do. Shor gave the students the space to express their frustrations with the reading and their reasons for opposing its use. However, this did not mean he changed the reading – though he considered doing so. Instead, he took steps to more clearly communicate to the students his reasons for choosing it and what he believed it would contribute to their learning. This follow-up communication reinforces his commitment to partnership in learning and respect for the students.

If a dialogue is genuine, then all parties must be open to learn through it. As academics we can and should learn through the very inexperience of our students. Seeing the discipline through their eyes forces us to reconsider the tacit assumptions informing our practices, the taken-for-granted aspects: it enables a reflection and re-engagement with our own learning of the subject.

Reflective Activity 12.1 How dialogue can shape our professional practice

Consider your responses to the following questions:

- In what ways do you believe a teacher's role is also to be a learner?
- What have you learned from your students, or through the act of teaching?
- Do you ever communicate this learning back to your students?

DIALOGUE IN DIFFERENT TEACHING–LEARNING SETTINGS

Dialogue is partly about an interaction between people, but more fundamentally for learning it is also about a certain relationship to knowledge and to the act of learning (and teaching). This means that there is a need to approach learning as dialogue in all teaching–learning contexts, not just the obvious ones such as tutorials or one-to-one supervision. To highlight this, the following examples will gradually expand the number of participants with which we consider dialogue in the learning process, beginning with the lone student and ending with the potential of social media and other online opportunities. It is important to stress that these contexts are best not understood in isolation, or as alternatives, but as different facets within a broader approach of learning as/through dialogue. Ashwin (2006) observes that 'different academics approach similar teaching methods differently, depending on the ways in which they think about those teaching methods' (p. 663). We should consider the pedagogic aim of our approaches to encourage dialogue. Different interactions can lead to very different pedagogic effects, perhaps contrary to those planned. As we know, the planned curriculum is not always the experienced curriculum. The aim in this section is to consider the importance of learning through dialogue in any teaching situation, while exploring the different ways in which it can be enacted in different contexts and the implications of this for learning.

Reflective Activity 12.2 Opportunities for students to engage in dialogue

Using the example of a course on which you teach, consider the opportunities you currently provide for students to engage with these different types of 'dialogue'. We will ask you to return to this exercise at the end of this section, to encourage you to consider further ways in which you can enable learning through dialogue in your course.

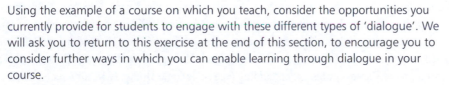

Dialogue with the **course content/subject knowledge**	Dialogue with the **teacher**
Dialogue with **peers**	Dialogue with **self/own learning**

Encouraging a dialogue with one's own learning

There is considerable literature on the notion of the self-directed learner, much of it in the wake of Knowles' (1975) seminal work. This literature considers the learner who is able to take control of his/her learning in a broad and integrated sense. Thus, this is more than simply organizing their time (for example, homework and revision), though that is also important. But beyond this form of organization is a self-directed capacity to check and shape what they are learning in an ongoing way. Baxter Magolda (2004a; 2016) describes this in terms of students being able to 'self-author' their own learning.

Key to being self-directed, or to achieving self-authorship, is to be in dialogue with oneself and one's own learning. To reflect and ask questions: Do I understand this? What alternative explanations might there be? Have I supported my arguments? How can I improve? This is a sort of self-dialogue that is essential in reflective teaching and learning. While this is an individual and independent act, teachers can construct opportunities to encourage students to develop these self-dialogues and to integrate them into their practices as learners. Critical here is that self-dialogue is not just something for when students are alone in the library or at home: it should be occurring at the same time as other forms of communication, such as within a lecture or tutorial. For example, questions can be used at the start of a session to encourage students to reflect on what relevant knowledge they have already acquired and can draw on in developing further understanding.

Encouraging this sort of self-dialogue is important. It can be done through question and answer sessions, although there are limits on the extent to which this successfully fosters self-dialogue within all students; instead the risk is it can become a teacher-led session. Some use technology such as 'clickers', electronic voting systems, which allow for multiple-choice answers. However, there is a difference between having a go at the right answer, reflecting on one's own learning, and possible gaps within it. Mazur (1997) details how he uses such systems to engage students in peer learning for conceptual understanding which, well designed, will first involve dialogue with one's own learning followed by peer dialogue and an opportunity to self-assess one's understanding (see Schell and Butler 2018 for a recent review).

A method that tries to encourage genuine self-dialogue and to enable this to be student- rather than teacher-led is that which Mark Huxham has named 'boot grit' feedback (see McArthur et al. 2011; McArthur and Huxham 2013; Huxham et al. 2015). Imagine a piece of grit caught on a person's boot. While it initially does no harm, over time it can fester and cause problems. This metaphor can be applied to the important concepts that students might not quite grasp, but still be able to seemingly carry on with a subject. Eventually, however, such misunderstandings cause problems – often discovered too late for the student to be able to do anything about it. In the 'boot grit' approach, students are introduced to the idea of checking their own learning at the end of every lecture. A box (or old boot) is left near the door and students can anonymously ask for clarification of any key concepts or ideas as they leave. The lecturer then posts a response on the virtual learning environment within a couple of hours. Students can see what other students have not understood (which can be encouraging) without anyone publicly admitting to uncertainty. Variations on this approach are to ask students at particular points during or after a lecture to note down the 'muddiest and clearest points' from the materials just covered. These notes can be stuck to the wall during a break or passed to the lecturer. During longer classes, there may be a chance for the lecturer to scan the responses and respond within the class while the students are still present and those points are still fresh in their heads. This not only allows students to take stock of their learning, it presents an opportunity for lecturers to take stock of what is happening within the lecture, and add this to their own self-dialogue, reflecting on what they are doing, what the students are doing and whether the planned curriculum is aligning with the experienced curriculum. Using these techniques, we offer students the opportunity for a safe dialogue with unnamed peers, the educator and with their learning experiences. We open up the possibilities for continued dialogue and communicate to students that we value their learning, their self-efficacy and ability to monitor their learning.

In Chapter 13, we are introduced to the idea that feedback on assessment should be seen as a dialogic process. As noted by Nicol (2010), for feedback to be useful, we need to move away from the transmission view of feedback, an 'impoverished dialogue', given from expert to novice and instead move to a process that involves two-way communication between the recipient and the reviewer, with interaction between student–teacher, peers and active learner engagement. Analysing students' reasons for not engaging with feedback, Winstone et al. (2017) report that understanding of feedback, lacking motivation or enthusiasm, not knowing what to do with feedback or how to act on it, or not feeling sufficiently equipped to act on feedback are common barriers. Assuming these barriers are in place, not only are students not encouraged to enter into dialogue with the feedback on their learning, such barriers can discourage students from reflecting and engaging. In order to overcome these challenges, a dialogue between educator and student needs to occur before students can themselves enter into a dialogue with their own learning, and the feedback on their learning, provided by reviewers. Further propelling the argument for promoting feedback as a dialogic process, Ajjawi and Boud (2018) report that feedback dialogue not only enhances student engagement in learning beyond the initial task, but also results in learning for the assessor. What can we learn from what the students have not learned? Feedback, therefore, should not be seen as something that concludes an assessment piece; rather it is a starting point for development of their learning, our teaching, and dialogue with self and peers. To further enhance self-dialogue via assessment and feedback we can look towards peer review. Nicol et al. (2014) report that through the process of peer review students benefit through engaging in 'multiple acts of evaluative judgement'. The comparative process students enter into when reviewing a peer's work immediately triggers reflection on their own performance versus the work under review. Students are as a result better equipped to engage in self-review and reflection.

Such initiatives introduce a culture of dialogue within a course, not simply between students and lecturers but the students with themselves and their own learning. Actually walking out of a lecture itself becomes a key learning/dialogue event: What have I understood or not understood over the past fifty minutes? After an in-class peer review of work: What am I doing that I could do better? How is my work meeting the criteria more than others or less than others? How did our work differ? Am I understanding the assessment task and criteria as well as I could or should?

Silent dialogues

The above examples of dialogue with one's own learning may or may not be silent. In contrast, consider the case of the 'quiet student' in a class. Many tutors will talk of the frustration trying to get some students to engage in class discussion (explored further in the next section). While there are clearly many advantages to encouraging all students to participate in class discussions, as Chanock (2010) observes, we must also sometimes recognize the 'right to reticence' among our students. Students from some cultural backgrounds may have different conventions of behaviour within a classroom, but we should avoid equating silence with passivity. Silence fits uncomfortably with traditional approaches to teaching, particularly in Western contexts (Yan 2013). As Yan, argues, there is a strong sense of associating silence with a lack of engagement. Carless (2011) has provided sensitive and new insights into the richness of other learning cultures – such as the Confucian-Heritage – which are often misunderstood within Western contexts, despite the very large number of students from such backgrounds studying in Western universities.

Thus, being quiet does not mean being unengaged. The quiet student may be engaged in a rich dialogue about the subject and with the ideas of others. The emphasis here is again on understanding as essentially a dialogical act: an exchange between two minds. And it may be a very quiet act.

Dialogue in group settings

Small or large, group settings can present challenges for both students and teachers. When students have timetables filled with different teaching formats (lecture, tutorial, lab session) they are not simply being asked to move between rooms, or contexts of different group sizes. They are moving between different social contexts with different attendant power/authority relationships and different discursive practices. The authority of the traditional lecture can hang heavy in the air of the tutorials and seminars that often go hand in hand with them. As such, the success of group settings may lie in thinking not of small versus large, tutorial versus lecture, but all group settings as a place for communication and learning as dialogue.

There can be a misconception that engaging small groups is easier, but small group settings can be a great source of disappointment for both students and teachers. The problem of long silences, punctuated only by the voice of the tutor or a small group of students who always have something to say, appears to be an enduring one. Depending on the discipline and session type (tutorial, seminar, language class) students may be asked to prepare for such interactions, perhaps by advance reading or homework, so that discussion can be informed and a sense of progression through the subject matter be established. This can suffer from problems of engagement with the materials or fear of exposure in a group setting.

However, small group settings are regarded as serving an important role in students learning the knowledge about how to learn within higher education (Hockings et al. 2018). Thus if things go wrong in small group settings, this is a problem that can extend to other teaching–learning contexts and influence a student's overall learning experience.

Case Study 12.1 Sonia's struggle with seminars

Sonia is a seminar tutor on a large first-year course. When she began she did not have much experience teaching, but she was enthusiastic and committed to the task. She believed that preparation was vital to ensuring a successful seminar discussion and discussions were, to her mind, what seminars were all about. So each week she read the set text for the seminar over and over so that she felt completely familiar with it – she could practically recite sections off by heart. Then she compiled her list of questions, systematically ensuring that all parts of the text were covered. The initial seminars went well, she thought, because she felt really on top of the subject material and when students didn't seem to know the answers to questions she could explain it to them. The students seemed happy enough with this. However, as the semester went on, Sonia started to think that the students should be able to answer more of the questions themselves. So she stopped being quite so quick to fill the silences if no-one answered. Somehow the seminars never quite matched her expectations of a fun and informal exchange of ideas, despite her preparation. So she began trying different techniques. She would single a student out for an answer, but she wasn't altogether happy doing this as it often ended up with her telling them off for not doing the reading. She tried to introduce 'thinking time' to let them form answers before being asked to share with the group. By the end of the semester she has found she could save time and prepare less, and the seminars would run pretty much the same despite this. As the semester came to a close Sonia was still full of enthusiasm. She *loved* her students. They were all *so nice*. But she also realized that as a teacher she could only do so much. Unless the students did their bit, there was nothing more she could do to improve the quality of seminar discussions. She was an enthusiastic teacher – the students had to be enthusiastic too. She should, perhaps, not be so idealistic next time. Maybe lower her expectations just a bit.

It can be easy to assume, as Sonia initially does, that a seminar is an obvious and easy place in which dialogue occurs. However, the traditional image, of a seminar in which the tutor has a list of questions which she works through expecting students to answer, is rarely dialogical. Despite the apparent informality of the seminar space, compared with the lecture, such a situation can be every bit as teacher-driven as a traditional lecture. Indeed, it is worse, because the gaps left (by the teacher) for student input are often contrived and uncomfortable. The communication remains severely dictated by the teacher. Participation is an assumed duty or good, but connections to other learning moments may be weak.

In Sonia's case, her best efforts contributed to the very opposite situation to that which she intended. There are three main ways in which Sonia could have approached the tutorials differently. First, the diligence of her preparation contrasted with that of many of her students. The real problem here was her apparent assumption that students would be able to prepare for the seminar in a similar fashion to how she approached it. However, being able to read an academic text is a skill that needs to be supported and developed over time. To this end, Sonia's early attempts to get a discussion going could have focused on the students' experiences of reading, rather than the content itself. This would better support development of their reading skills, but it is also something that relates directly to the students. Second, Sonia has fallen into the common trap of mistaking questions and answers for dialogue. Natural dialogue does not take the form of a question and answer session. Sonia needed to allow the students to find their own spaces in which to speak. Techniques such as 'snowballing' allow students gradually to build up to larger group discussions, starting with individual input in small groups (two or more participants) and slowly building confidence through merging groups and attempting consensus of opinion. Third, Sonia's reaction at the end of the semester is to lower her expectations. She reduces her amount of preparation: she seems never to think about changing the nature of that preparation. While she rightly believes students share the responsibility to make a discussion work in the seminar, she provides them with little control or say in how that might happen. By thinking about what her students need, Sonia might be able to adapt her plans to facilitate these needs.

The assumed informality of smaller groups can mean they are in fact more complex. The informality of these settings can impose a weight of expectation – of easy communication – that is self-defeating. As Shaw et al. (2008) emphasize, the creation of rich dialogue requires considerable thought and effort. They provide an example from a philosophy tutorial in which the tutor juxtaposes a serious and less serious story, so that the latter provides a path for each student to the former: 'By linking the stories via a common theme, the tutor allows for the possibility that if a student feels they can talk about the second story, they may very well, by extension, realize that they have something to say about the first' (Shaw et al. 2008, p. 710).

An extension of this idea is to think about developing the skills of communication and dialogue by using materials that may already mean something to the students, perhaps more contemporary texts, popular music, 'real world' or student-generated data. Students may already have a relationship to these materials from which they can more readily springboard into dialogue. Focusing on developing the skills required, as opposed to the content in the first instance, may help students break through an initial reticence to engage in more public dialogue.

Student participation within small group settings is a learned experience. However, students, particularly in early undergraduate years, can fall into a Catch-22 because to develop the skills of participation and discussion requires participation and discussion:

> Making contributions in a tutorial – through raising points, providing information, asking and answering questions, seeking clarification, co-operating in group work, etc. – requires skills on the part of the contributor. These can only be learnt by attending classes and by becoming familiar with a set of informal rules governing how to take part. (Shaw et al. 2008, p. 704)

Understanding the reticence of some students to enter into particular forms of public but informal discussion requires more from the tutor than mere 'facilitation'. Sometimes the tutor needs to act as conduit between the individual and the group. In another example from Shaw et al. (2008), they describe the physical movement of a tutor between more and less confident members of a group; as the less confident student begins to talk the tutor moves to make eye contact with them, drawing them into a seemingly safer one-to-one conversation, but one which is then shared with the class as a whole.

This approach can bring some of the benefits of the 'ideal-type' of the small Oxford tutorials (Ashwin 2006) to the larger settings many academics and students have to engage with at the majority of higher education institutions. The tutor is able to forge moments of one-to-one dialogue, alongside the potential benefits of many diverse voices all being heard. However, to really achieve the full potential of this as a learning situation we need to appreciate the different levels of 'learning as dialogue' going on here. One of the benefits of the Oxford tutorial is the scope 'to engage in dialogue that demands more sophisticated levels of understanding, and suggests new conceptions of learning' (Ashwin 2006, p. 653). This is as much about dialogue with one's own learning as dialogue with a tutor or classmate. While this may be arguably easier to achieve within the intimate context of the Oxford model, there is no reason students cannot achieve this within larger formats if they understand the processes required of them to engage fully in this learning context. This again emphasizes Shaw et al.'s (2008) point that we need to learn how to learn within small group settings.

Lectures occupy a strange place within higher education today. On the one hand they are sometimes regarded as old-fashioned and out-of-date; dominated by transmission theories of learning. On the other hand, lectures remain firmly entrenched within many courses at a great many of our universities.

Many of us accept a necessity of lectures – due to large student numbers and financial constraints – and hope that this can be balanced out through learning experiences in other contexts. However, given the entrenched place that lectures have, and are likely to continue to have, particularly within large teaching contexts, we can do better. We can consider the positive potential offered by such large classes: the idea that they offer a different form of dialogue, and hence learning, rather than simply a poorer one. As a social space, the sheer numbers of people in a lecture can open new opportunities rather than only being viewed in negative terms. Indeed, we can go so far as to suggest that lectures 'offer a breadth of alternative experiences for students in a safe and accessible way' (McArthur and Huxham 2013, p. 99).

What is suggested here is something more than token moments of 'interaction' within a lecture just for the sake of it. Or a ritualized changing of pace every twenty minutes based upon Biggs' (2003) influential observation about attention spans. Caution is advised of the idea that all students have the same attention span under the same circumstances, potentially leading to a way of thinking that just doing anything a little different every so often is a good thing. So-called interactive moments in lectures can be filled with the same uncomfortable silences as seminars. By really thinking through the potential for a lecture as a place of dialogical learning we can go beyond this rather negative approach. The lecture can provide a critical mass for the expression of many diverse viewpoints and experiences. Thesen (2009) describes lectures as 'sites of intense co-presence' (p. 391). Thesen's interviews with students about lectures also indicates the very positive experiences that some associate with lectures. She reports descriptions of some lecturers in terms of 'would not want to miss', 'lively', 'makes us feel at home', 'passionate about what she does', and 'entertaining' (p. 394). These examples show 'the lecture as a contact zone, where multiple meanings were brought together, "to the point of combustion" (in the words of one of the lecturers in the study)' (p. 394).

If we look out at large lectures, we find that many students are engaged – just not always necessarily with what the lecturer is saying. The prevalence of mobile phones and other devices in lectures creates a sort of underground hum of activity: numerous forms of social exchange and dialogue actively racing around the room. Some successfully harness this potential, rather than ignore it. Using a textwall or digital post-it note applications (through which students post anonymous messages that are then projected onto the lecture screen) offers both safety and public exchange with all the dynamism and challenge involved in the latter. The safety enables students to take part in ways they may not otherwise do. Here the largeness of the lecture is a positive advantage. As Game and Metcalfe (2009) observe, a large class can form a challenging and dynamic environment in which 'students learn to appreciate and respect their own possibilities when they are surprised by hearing their shy and private inklings enunciated by others' (p. 50). Similarly, the example from Mazur (1997) in using voting systems allows anonymity within large settings but engages self and peer dialogue.

'Flipping' the classroom, introduced in Chapter 8, is becoming an increasingly popular approach to breaking down the assumed transmission-only mode of the traditional lecture setting and turning these sessions into active and collaborative learning environments. By providing materials which students will engage with outside the classroom, time within the classroom can be used for more active approaches to learning. Such approaches can work even within very large lectures. The risk of student disengagement is admittedly high, and the opportunities for dialogue appear limited. Rather than simply abandoning the lectures, and without the resources to put on more lectures, academics at a New Zealand university sought other ways around the problem. They found that structured exercises that did not have any reliance on the physical presence of the lecturer – instead were based on activities in a common course handbook – could bridge some of the distance even within large overflow lectures (Exeter et al. 2010). The sense of participation in a dialogue with the rest of the class, and the teachers, comes as much from working on a common activity as anything else. Students are able to talk amongst themselves for support and ideas, but in avoiding the necessity of organized group work or discussions in such a large environment, this approach appears to skilfully make the most of its apparent drawback. Here there is the potential for dialogue on many levels: first, between the theory and practice; second between students, and third, when the 'traditional' lecture resumes, a different dialogue between the students and their own learning. Not just engagement, but *involvement*: linking their learning to the wider social world.

Dialogical spaces beyond the academy: social media and students

Greater opportunities to exchange ideas with a greater number of people do not necessarily mean more genuine dialogue. While social media and online resources offer many exciting possibilities for dialogue and for learning – they by no means guarantee these any more than other contexts. Many teachers have conscientiously put discussion boards on their local virtual learning environment only to find these seriously under-utilized by students. Rather than being a source of discussion of ideas, they become procedural forums for information about assessments and the like. Even here, the use can be limited, because many of the questions students want to ask about assessment they prefer to ask through the more private means of a direct email. Further, the so-called discussion tends to be tutor-led, stifling the possibilities for dialogue even before it begins.

In a project that sought to share control for course design and delivery with students, McArthur and Huxham (2011) discovered that students felt uncomfortable within the formal confines of the official university virtual learning environment and preferred to communicate through the medium of Facebook. This led to a series of ethical challenges in terms of privacy and setting boundaries, along with the teachers' Facebook illiteracy. However, the discussions became clearly student-led and demonstrated a dynamic and engaged exchange of ideas. This resonates with McArthur and Huxham's work on 'boot-grit' feedback and textwalls which found a marked difference in the vocabulary and level of formality of students depending on whether their questions were hand-written or via texts (McArthur et al. 2011; McArthur and Huxham 2013; Huxham et al. 2015).

Before opting straight to social media as a means to engage, we need to ask ourselves of the pedagogical purpose of using it in the first instance. In some cases, such as online or blended learning, social media spaces offer the potential of building a learning community, alleviating isolation and facilitating dialogue with others. The language learning classroom, for example, can benefit from widening the learning circle to students in other countries and social media presents excellent opportunities for such. However, simply adding a discussion board to the virtual learning environment or mandating students to post one thing on 'Twitter' once a week, can yield little educational gain and may become an arduous tick box, a teacher-led activity, with little true dialogue. A key to successful dialogue in an online environment is a strong sense of purpose. Under-use of online discussion boards is sometimes simply down to there being no apparent purpose other than that of simply posting a message, as demonstrated in the case study below.

Case Study 12.2 Mary's engagement with online communication

Mary is Course Organizer of a second-year, undergraduate course which she inherited and has been running for many years. The course is a mixture of traditional lectures and seminars with a final essay examination at the end. During the course, students are required to post three formative, small pieces of writing on a discussion board, and each time respond to the postings of two other students. The aims of these exercises are threefold: to provide small, manageable academic writing tasks to help students develop their academic writing skills; to encourage deeper engagement with key issues in the course; and finally, to encourage them to engage with the ideas of their peers and be able to provide constructive and relevant feedback. Engagement was deemed to be compulsory, although it was never part of the formal summative assessment.

When Mary took over as Course Organizer she left these formative exercises in place, assuming their continued use was a sign that they were an important part of the course.

However, she discovered that practice did not reflect her assumptions and expectations. Student engagement with the tasks was uneven, and those who did post did so largely out of a sense of compulsion. Mary found herself overwhelmed with requests for extensions or information on how to post, but none at all about the actual subject matter or the issue of how to write in an academic way.

In looking at posts online, Mary found that initial student contributions seemed muddled, with little sense of purpose, and little engagement with proper academic writing conventions. The postings responding to other students were even more disappointing, largely superficial and formulaic (for example, 'You make some good points here'). When marking the final essay, Mary also found that most students had not understood the basic principles of academic writing, or of referencing. They seemed unsure how to get the right pitch between description and opinion and the required academic style of informed analysis. They also had trouble linking ideas from theory to their own practice (which was meant to be the basis for peer discussions).

There were two main problems with Mary's approach to encouraging dialogue online. First, there was no apparent reason why the set task needed to be done online. It may have been more convenient in some ways, but there was no 'added value' from using an online forum. Second, one relatively small task was carrying the burden of a lot of competing purposes. Taking these two ideas together led Mary to rethink both the tasks and what and why any element should be online. She began by separating the academic writing element and putting this within a face-to-face setting – students needed to get certain basic aspects right before progressing further in the course, requiring more direct communication with the teacher, rather than trying this out amongst themselves. She then sought to tackle the lack of engagement by asking 'Why should students do these tasks?' This led to a more explicit connection between each task and the final assessment. Each task had a much more focused purpose, and students could see the link between participation and their final assessed work. Finally, she asked 'What could we do online that we couldn't easily do face-to-face?' Here, she was particularly interested in how to have a more cohesive course experience, despite the large number of students.

Mary believed that an online form of communication offered particular opportunities to challenge the primacy of the teacher in any so-called dialogue, but only if the online discussions did not simply mimic what could be done face-to-face. This led to two new opportunities for dialogue in the course. First, wikis replaced two of the discussion board tasks. Wikis enable something that is very hard to achieve in a face-to-face classroom, and that is multiple voices being heard and understood at once. Students challenged and supported one another within the wiki to develop their critical analysis skills in the context of a specific question. Changes had to be justified, and where necessary debated. Then, Mary tried to link the virtual world and the face-to-face world. This was in sharp contrast to the previous approach in which the online discussions had stood to the side of the main activities in lectures and tutorials.

In Mary's case study, we have a coming together of multiple forms of dialogue, each with the potential to enhance the other. Rather than working in groups and presenting to a tutorial (as had previously been the case), students prepared online presentations which were then shared before the face-to-face seminars. The purpose of the seminars changed from listening to presentations, and making a few cursory comments, to active debate of what had been done in the online format. Similarly, a textwall used in lectures could provide the content for an ongoing wiki on a central course theme, which could feed into tutorials, seminars and online collaborations.

Dialogue for student engagement: within and beyond the curriculum

Returning to our opening comments on dialogue and the principles of exchange, responsiveness and respect, leads us to consider how we help students to develop an understanding of these principles and indeed how we further embed these principles within higher education settings. Should we only be concerned with how students develop such skills within the formal curriculum? Do we respect student contributions in the form of evaluation and feedback on teaching for example? How do we communicate this to students, so that they in turn will treat opportunities for giving feedback and engaging in dialogue on the student experience with respect?

There is a growing movement to better empowering students in defining their student experience through more active participation in all aspects of their higher education journey (Trowler et al. 2018). Student partnerships in Quality Scotland (sparqs, see: sparqs.ac.uk), in operation since 2003, seek to support students and institutions to build partnerships between staff and students in all aspects of higher education. It aims to ensure students are involved in decision making and development across the institution. A similar initiative in Ireland, the National Student Engagement Programme (NStEP, see studentengagement.ie), seeks to dispel the notion of students as mere consumers of education and promote students as partners in decision making within higher education institutions. Both of these initiatives are centred on the belief that student engagement does not start and end with the curriculum. If we expect students to be responsible for their own learning, why not allow them to also share responsibility at the level of decision making within their institution? Valuing student contribution and engagement should include valuing it across the institution. To do this, the institution also needs to promote and model the principles of exchange, responsiveness and respect.

As practitioners, we can promote engagement at the most basic level by encouraging dialogue not just on student learning but also on our teaching. By giving students a voice to express how we can better help them achieve their learning goals, respecting their voice, listening and responding to their voice, we show them that what they have to say is valued. Requiring more preparation and planning, we can consider student partnerships in curriculum and assessment design, research-led teaching, and staff–student projects to name but a few. By encouraging student contribution across the academy, we might confidently expect that students will more readily enter into dialogue in those settings where heretofore they were reticent.

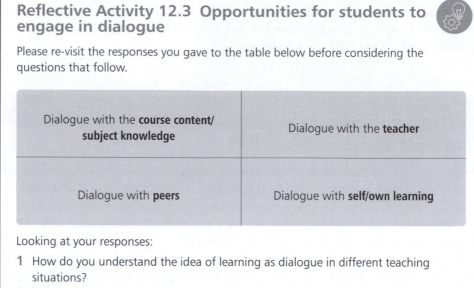

Reflective Activity 12.3 Opportunities for students to engage in dialogue

Please re-visit the responses you gave to the table below before considering the questions that follow.

Dialogue with the **course content/ subject knowledge**	Dialogue with the **teacher**
Dialogue with **peers**	Dialogue with **self/own learning**

Looking at your responses:

1   How do you understand the idea of learning as dialogue in different teaching situations?
2   Pick a quadrant from the above figure and plan ways in which you might better introduce the idea of *dialogue as learning* into one of your courses?
3   What potential barriers are there to effective dialogue in your teaching and learning settings?
4   How might you overcome these barriers?

COMMUNICATION AS EDUCATORS

We have considered the reasons why and possibilities for enhancing and supporting student dialogue. It is also worth considering how we, ourselves, communicate both with and within our practice, with our students and our colleagues. How do we communicate the disciplinary knowledge with which we are so familiar and embedded within? What impact can communication have on our professional development as educators? How can our communication with colleagues have an impact on the student experience?

Disciplinary knowledge and communication

Earlier in this chapter, we discussed transmission models of learning in which knowledge is treated as something to be simply passed over to students. Critiques of these models rightly highlight the far more active role that students play in their own learning – considering, reshaping, constructing knowledge for themselves (through a series of dialogical processes). A further critique lies in what transmission approaches imply about the nature of the knowledge in question. There is an assumption here of knowledge easily known, uncontested and static that can be *transferred* from one person to another. Indeed, in the terms of Brown and Duguid (2000), transmission applies more to information than to knowledge. Brown and Duguid (2000, pp. 119–20) outline three key distinctions between, in their terms, knowledge and information:

1 'Knowledge usually entails a knower' compared with information which is more self-sufficient. As a result, knowledge doesn't simply lie 'around waiting to be picked up'.

2 'Given this personal attachment, knowledge appears harder to detach than information. . . . Knowledge . . . doesn't take as kindly to ideas of shipping, receiving, and quantification. It is hard to pick up and hard to transfer.'

3 'One reason knowledge may be so hard to give and receive is that knowledge seems to require more by way of assimilation. Knowledge is something we digest rather than merely hold.'

In considering communication within teaching–learning settings, the key is not simply 'how' to communicate knowledge, but to understand the nature of knowledge itself as a dialogical and communicative act. As such, in thinking about knowledge we need to think about people: 'what they know, how they come to know it, and how they differ' (Brown and Duguid 2000: p. 121).

This sense of knowledge and dialogue has particularly important implications for our practice in the early undergraduate years. It can be tempting, and to some extent under-standable, to think that we need to first *give* students enough knowledge to let them go on to critically engage with the knowledge. The curriculum in the early years of university may contain relatively uncontested material that is best taught as 'fact' and hence largely through transmission. The problem with this approach is that encouraging passivity in students is an ineffective way of encouraging activity later. Research on student engagement and early attrition tells us that such approaches are disengaging (for example, see Thomas 2012). Students want to be active in the curriculum from early on. They want to start developing the requisite skills for higher education and their discipline from the early weeks of their higher education experience. This is not to deny the importance of a basic grounding when learning within a new discipline, course or topic. Colleagues will often stress the importance of certain established 'facts' when learning in their area. However, we should see these as the beginning of dialogue, rather than an alternative to it. We are in an age whereby the basic facts and information are easily accessible to most. What can we do to help students process this information and turn it into knowledge? Do we assume students know how to engage with information, evaluate it, sort the valid from the less valid, the proven from the assumed? Students can also be encouraged to engage back in time, to understand the debates, theories, myths and disagreements that frequently lie behind the 'established facts' of today. Thus, even established knowledge is understood as part of a dynamic process, and one with which students can be in active dialogue.

The aim is to enable students to be both outsider to the knowledge community and active participant within it (Airey and Larsson 2018). The acts of learning can thus 'be charac-terized as coming to experience disciplinary ways of knowing as they are represented by the disciplinary discourse through participation' (Airey and Linder 2009, p. 28). There is an added challenge here for many international students for whom the disciplinary discourse is unfamiliar, but so too is the language (English) in which it is conveyed (Heron 2019). Many international students have a sense that 'their discourse knowledge is seen as deficient' (Ryan and Viete 2009, p. 303) because of a common conflation of an idealized view of the English of 'native' speakers and competence at disciplinary discourses. This in turn can further disadvantage international students, despite having little foundation in reality.

An important part of this process is for all students to appreciate that the disciplinary forms of communication are not simply 'jargon' that seeks to exclude and/or make the insiders look clever. Of course, poorly used, this may be the case. However, at its heart disciplinary forms of communication are important portals into disciplinary knowledge and practices. The same language that underpins our very identities as academics, and our day-to-day practices, can be remote, odd or unfamiliar to our students. As Woodward-Kron (2008, p. 246) explained:

> Lay people may dismiss the specialist language of a discipline or profession as jargon. However, the specialist language of a discipline is intrinsic to students' learning of disciplinary knowledge; students need to show their understanding of concepts, phenomena, relations between phenomena etc. by incorporating the specialist language and terminology of their discipline into their writing accurately. They also need to adopt the specialist language in order to make meaning and engage with disciplinary knowledge.

Reflective Activity 12.4 Communicating disciplinary knowledge

precedent discourse diagnosis stratigraphy pedagogy social opportunity context theory sustainability validity class postmodernism evidence pathology critical materials cost taphonomy ontology

Consider some of the essential concepts, theories or definitions in your own disciplinary area (examples above):

a Try to recall a situation (for example, conference, journal article or discussion) in which you use these terms with disciplinary colleagues.

b Now consider how you may need to adapt this usage when talking with students.

c How can you find a way to describe/define/use these terms with students which is accessible to them (as disciplinary outsiders) and yet still true to the integrity of the disciplinary knowledge?

Teaching complex knowledge needs to be a process of engagement. In so doing, we and our students construct and reconstruct understandings in our own ways, and often using our own terms. For teachers this requires an understanding of the framework within which one should communicate such knowledge to students. This is likely to be related to our disciplinary research context – and we argue that such a relationship is important – however, it is not the same thing.

The distinction being suggested here, in terms of how we communicate disciplinary knowledge to students and how we enable them to engage in dialogue with this knowledge, is a subtle one – but very important. For example, in mathematics, this can be thought of as the difference between a research mathematician's need to use a formula to represent a vast array of complex material and a student or teacher's need to unpack it of all those elements to understand it (Ball and Bass 2000). The maths teacher may have a bundle of connected knowledge – expertise – but teaching needs to allow room for students' tentative and experimental engagement with the knowledge – with initially looking at formulae and other concepts differently as part of the discourse towards understanding them in established disciplinary terms (Ball and Bass 2000). Writing in the context of school maths education, Davis and Renert (2013, p. 247) discuss the problem of teachers' 'inert' understanding or usage of mathematical concepts:

> The distinction between fundamental and emergent is not a subtle one. It often seems that school mathematics – and, correspondingly, teacher knowledge of mathematics – is regarded as limited, straightforward, and static. . . . Rather than think of this knowledge as a discrete body of foundational knowledge held by individuals, then, we offer that it may be more productive to view it as a flexible, vibrant category of knowing that is distributed across a body of professionals. We thus frame mathematics knowledge for teaching in terms of a learnable participatory disposition within an evolving knowledge domain.

It is important, therefore, to think about how students can develop a dialogue with disciplinary knowledge that will gradually, and over time, start to resemble that which we might have with our discipline, and in later stages of higher education may form the basis of established research activity. However, this does not mean that it would involve a lesser form of disciplinary knowledge. The different contexts for communication within higher education (private study, small group setting, lecture, online) should be understood in terms of the different opportunities for dialogue that they offer. Indeed the different contexts can enable us to 'live through' the multi-faceted and complex nature of knowledge within higher education. We need to think about where students are starting from, the journey they will take through the discipline, and the threshold concepts they will encounter. As teachers we need to provide different modes of disciplinary discourse which can offer different ways of demonstrating disciplinary knowledge (Airey and Linder 2009; Airey and Larsson 2018).

Airey and Linder (2009, p. 31) provide a useful example of this in terms of how an engineering student comes to understand Ohm's law, which refers to the conduction of electricity between different points:

> A student may experience facets of Ohm's law via a number of different modes, for example, current-voltage relational representation through the use of: circuit diagrams, oral descriptions, written descriptions, demonstrations, hands-on activities (with batteries, wires, and bulbs), a table of voltages and currents for a given circuit, the mathematical formula V1/4IR and its graphical illustration. Each of these modes potentially brings certain facets of Ohm's law to the fore, whilst others remain in the background or simply are not present. It is thus only through combining a number of these modes that a holistic experience of the disciplinary way of knowing what we call Ohms law can be constituted (analogous to viewing a physical object from different angles). Thus, typically a disciplinary way of knowing may only be partially represented by one particular mode of disciplinary discourse (or even more than one in certain cases).

The multi-faceted approach to disciplinary discourse relates to thinking in terms of longer-term goals and the ways in which students may go on to participate in future communications within the subject area. This involves a 'kind of continued practice which eventually leads to discursive fluency in a number of modes' (Airey and Linder 2009, p. 34). Students learn through a combination of repetition, repeated application and different forms of application in different contexts. As Airey and Linder (2009) argue, it is not sufficient to expose students to various forms of disciplinary discourse; what they need is 'practice in using disciplinary discourse to make meaning for themselves' (p. 41). Such opportunities must provide scope for the diversity of the student population, not understood simply in broad national or cultural terms, but at the individual level too.

Communication for professional development

As we discussed in Chapters 3 and 11, communication with colleagues and internal dialogues for reflective practice are important for our professional development. Yet it is often neglected. To become a more reflective practitioner, looking at ways we can enhance our practice with positive outcomes for us and our students, requires us to enter into a dialogue with our practice. As well as encouraging students' internal dialogue with their learning, we should also not discount the importance of dialogue with our colleagues and the role it can play in our professional development. Thomson and Trigwell (2018) explore the value of informal conversations with colleagues on professional development in university teaching. The small-scale study focused on mid-career academics with reported outcomes from informal conversations as transforming teaching, problem-solving and reassurance. Admittedly an under explored area of professional development, informal learning and its potential impact on professional development has become a feature in frameworks for recognizing professional development in teaching and learning, for example the Irish National Professional Development Framework encourages us to reflect on both formal and informal professional development moments. This framework also specifically identifies 'Professional Communication and Dialogue in Teaching and Learning' as a professional development domain (National Forum for Enhancing Teaching and Learning in Higher Education 2016). Other frameworks are introduced in Chapter 16.

A National Forum for the Enhancement of Teaching and Learning in Higher Education (Ireland) project, Crannóg (see crannog-he.ie), which sought to enhance the professional development of middle and senior management in the areas of teaching and learning in Irish higher education institutions, found that these time-pressed individuals particularly valued the informal spaces created for them via the project in which to discuss relevant themes, and share challenges and solutions, without the presence of a formal agenda (Tooher and MacLaren 2019). While these roles may aspire to include strategic thinking and planning for the enhancement of teaching and learning, the lived reality is that the operational day-to-day responsibilities of the role leave little time to think about teaching and learning enhancement of individuals, departments, schools or faculty. Making space to engage in dialogue with colleagues across the academy is hugely beneficial to teaching and learning development. Chapter 16 furthers the discussion on how we can usefully link individual components of our day-to-day practice for professional development.

Communication for the student experience

Our continuing professional development has direct and indirect consequences for the student experience. So too will how we communicate in our practice with our students and colleagues on a day-to-day basis. In our communications with students and others, we need to be mindful of modelling professional practice – what norms, as experts in our discipline and professions, are we portraying to students? Are we modelling the disciplinary and professional ways of being and acting? In creating spaces for dialogue with and among students, our own actions and interactions are important. As we work with students in their development to becoming professionals in their chosen fields, how we communicate with our students can impact their learned ways of being and acting within the discipline. The idea of modelling professional practice may immediately resonate with those who work within disciplines for which professional practice is an integral part of the curriculum. In such disciplines, for example nursing, values and processes which can impact patient care will be taught within the theoretical and modelled in the clinical placement settings. In other disciplines, this modelling may be less explicit, but is worth bearing in mind as we facilitate students' development in ways of knowing, acting and being within our disciplines.

A slightly tangential point worth noting is the impact on the student experience of our communication or lack thereof across disciplinary or programme teams. Referring back to the importance of 'congruence' in curriculum design (Chapter 9), it can be all too apparent that there has been little or no communication across programme teams, when students are faced with a timetable of seemingly discrete modules in a programme that bear little relevance to each other or appear to overlap significantly, whose assessment points compete with each other and where little thought has been given to the coherence of the student experience over the course of a semester, academic year or programme. Consider, for example, two modules in a Year 1, Semester 1 programme; one has multiple opportunities for formative feedback on low stakes assessment tasks, while the other has a mid-semester essay which will not receive feedback prior to the end of semester exam. Such an experience can have multiple negative consequences for student engagement and the early experience of third-level education. Students who are attempting to develop their academic literacies, negotiate a sense of belonging in higher education, and understand the rules of the game are in fact instead faced with multiple competing games. These issues are especially problematic in the early years where students need sturdier scaffolding, support and guidance with time management and integrating their learning, to guide them towards autonomous and independent learning (Bovill et al. 2011). We ask students to engage in dialogue with their learning, with their peers and with us, and yet it may be difficult for students to see how we are ourselves engaging in dialogue for good of the student experience.

Reflective Activity 12.5 How dialogue can shape our professional practice

Returning to your answers in **Reflective Activity 12.1**, how can you extend what you are already doing to enhance your professional development in teaching and learning?

CONCLUSION

This chapter has looked at many aspects of communication in teaching and learning, with the particular approach of thinking about communication as dialogue – an exchange with our learning, other people or other ideas, underpinned by principles of respect and responsiveness. Dialogue can occur between people or between the known and the unknown. Where learning fails to materialize, despite our best efforts as teachers, it can often be a problem of dialogue. Such a problem is, however, not just about talking or explaining again. Has the student comprehended the difference between what they understand and our intentions? Such a reflection is an act of dialogue. Have we comprehended the context or perspective from which the student is trying to understand? How might this distort the process of learning and communication? Key to the notion of learning as dialogue is the dynamic nature of understanding and the agency of both students and teachers to enable learning to occur (or to prevent it). Learning from dialogue is not just confined to the student. We also need to think about the dialogues we have and how they impact on ourselves, our learning, our students' learning, their engagement and the student experience.

KEY READINGS

For a text focusing explicitly on language and dialogue central to negotiating meaning and co-constructing knowledge as part of the learning process, see:

Skidmore, D. and Murakami, K. (eds) (2016) *Dialogic Pedagogy: The Importance of Dialogue in Teaching and Learning*. Bristol: Channel View Publications.

For accounts of how to enable students to breach the gap between being outside a disciplinary community and needing to understand the knowledge of that discipline, see:

Airey, J. and Larsson, J. (2018) 'Developing Students' Disciplinary Literacy? The Case of University Physics'. In K.-S. Tang and K. Danielsson (eds), *Global Developments in Literacy Research for Science Education* (pp. 357–76). Cham: Springer.

Shor, I. (1996). *When Students Have Power*. Chicago, IL and London: University of Chicago Press.

For ideas on how to create a democratic classroom, of any size, using discussion as a mode of teaching, see:

Brookfield, S. and Preskill, S. (2005) *Discussion as a Way of Teaching: Tools and Techniques for University Teachers*. 2nd edn. San Francisco, CA: Jossey Bass.

Brookfield, S. and Preskill, S. (2016). *The Discussion Book: 50 Great Ways to Get People Talking*. San Francisco, CA: Jossey Bass.

Chapter 13
Assessment
How does it make a contribution to learning?

INTRODUCTION

Assessment can seem a burden, both to students and to ourselves. It often takes place after the interesting parts of a course have passed. It requires intensive effort of marking, particularly when student numbers are high. It frequently occurs when it is too late to deal with the misunderstandings and problems uncovered. And it is policed by the institution more thoroughly than other parts of our work. It is not surprising then, that many academics feel that assessment is largely beyond their control and a part of our role that offers few choices. While this is true about some aspects, it is very important to understand the many ways we can influence assessment, and the decisions we can make to enhance learning through assessment. When done well, we can design and implement assessment in ways that improve learning, make the experience more satisfying for us and our students and yet not involve additional expenditure of effort.

In reading this chapter, it is worth asking the following questions: What would good assessment look like? If I did assessment well, how could I tell? If I have limited time, where should I spend it in assessment to have most effect? What are the consequences for student learning of the assessment tasks I set? A strong theme running through this chapter is that if we make the right assessment choices this can have the dual benefits of supporting student learning and lessening some of the more burdensome aspects of our workloads.

The answers to the above questions are all dependent on the context in which we operate – the discipline, the class size, the department, the institution. However, there are ways of thinking about assessment, which this chapter will introduce, that can illuminate these questions and lead to a better experience for all concerned.

See Chapter 4

> ## TLRP Principles
>
> One principle is of particular relevance to this chapter on assessment in higher education:
>
> **Principle 6: Effective teaching and learning needs assessment to be congruent with learning.** Assessment should be designed for maximum validity in terms of learning outcomes and learning processes, and also should be specific to the type of subject or discipline involved, even if it is interdisciplinary. It should help to advance learning as well as determine whether learning has occurred.

What this chapter seeks to do is to shift the focus of assessment from what has been conventionally thought of as most important in assessment to what has the greatest impact on improving student learning (Gibbs 2006). These conventional concerns, for example, marking fairly and consistently, are important but a focus on marking alone focuses attention away from ways in which assessment can most make a difference to student learning. Instead we should focus a significant amount of our attention on the role assessment plays in how and what students study.

We wish in this chapter to provide the basis for doing assessment well. But to do so, it is necessary to question what assessment seeks to do and treat many of the taken-for-granted practices of assessment as problematic. We will examine what part it plays in courses and explore how it can be used to work positively for learning as well as judging whether learning has taken place. What is assessment for? Why should we do it in particular ways? How can we ensure that convention doesn't govern all assessment decisions? And how can we avoid it undermining the good things we do in the rest of the course?

We will find that there are many competing demands on assessment, and managing the different and sometimes contradictory purposes it has to serve is a major challenge (Bloxham and Boyd 2007). Assessment necessarily serves different ends and each needs to be given consideration. It is not realistic to treat them as if they are equivalent. We will see that assessment is driven by what it seeks to do and that designing good assessment practices to meet the needs of student learning is at the heart of any course.

The emphasis in this chapter is on deliberate design of assessment as an overall part of a course. The creation of good assessment is a process of design and management of a number of different elements. Some of the bigger picture design decisions occur far ahead of teaching and sometimes are out of our hands, but the overwhelming number of them – from the choice of task, the positioning of assessment activities, the forms of feedback used and the ways of communicating to students – are within the direct influence of those teaching. Even as a tutor operating within a prescribed course, there are decisions to be made about the type and form of comments made to students about their work. A key principle is that each part of assessment needs to be seen in relation to the course as a whole and to each aspect of an overall design that encompasses all the assessment events within a given programme. We do not operate in isolation from our colleagues and their influence is transmitted through the attitudes and actions students take in relation to assessment.

Before getting into particularities of how to act, we need to have a shared view of what assessment is and what it seeks to do. This is usually taken for granted. The unreflective view of what assessment is is the first issue we have to confront if we are to do it well.

WHAT IS ASSESSMENT?

The starting point for any exploration of assessment is to question what it does. Assessment is so commonplace that it is easy to think that this is obvious. But, what is it? The view taken here is that assessment is an activity that involves students undertaking tasks, the outcomes of which enable judgements to be made about what they have learned. These judgements may be used by students themselves to influence their study, by their teachers to influence the course and by others to certify achievement. While conventionally, assessment is represented in tests, examinations and assignments of various kinds, almost any activity in which students do something and reveal what they have done can potentially be used for assessment purposes. The variety of forms and methods of assessment is very large indeed. The fact that only a few are typically used in any given course is more a result of disciplinary and institutional convention, than because of research which shows that some approaches to or methods of assessment are intrinsically superior to others. This is not to say that there is not a considerable body of research on assessment in higher education, some of which addresses what might be appropriate in a given context, but that this research is neither complete enough nor strong enough in favour of particular assessment practices to enable our choices to be grounded in it. We should instead always think in terms of the purposes of a given assessment task when making decisions about its suitability.

The concept of 'fitness for purpose' is helpful here (for example, see Bryan and Clegg 2019). That is, assessment should consist of whatever mix of activities meets the outcomes required. A brief informal quiz in a lecture can meet the purpose of enabling the lecturer (and indeed the students themselves) to judge whether a certain key idea has been understood by the class. Such a quiz might not be suitable for grading that counted for final marks because the items used may not have been aligned with the overall learning outcomes for the course. It might not be suitable for enabling students to address their misconceptions. However, the quiz fits the purpose for which it was designed: to help the lecturer decide whether to move on or devote more time to the conceptions in question. Fitness for purpose also enables us to judge more substantial assessment events. For example, a carefully designed examination conducted at the end of the first semester might be unfit for the purpose of judging students' readiness for graduation because what has been learned may have been superseded by students' work in later courses.

What is assessment for?

This brings us to the purpose of assessment. Why do we assess? To what ends is assessment used? The answer to this question is multifaceted. Assessment can and is used for many different purposes. These include, among others:

1 judging whether students are ready to study particular subject matter;
2 enabling students to judge whether they need to study further in a particular area;
3 determining who should progress to an advanced course;
4 providing information to enable students to improve their performance;
5 generating marks and grades that are weighted to contribute to a final assessment;
6 ensuring that all students have met minimum standards;
7 diagnosing particular student difficulties;
8 helping students track their overall performance;
9 demonstrating to students what really counts;
10 building student's confidence that they are being successful in their studies;

11 developing students' capacity to make judgements about their own learning;

12 developing students' skills in applying appropriate standards and criteria to their own work.

Which of these would apply in the courses with which you are familiar? Which of these features would it be appropriate to incorporate in these courses? Are there other purposes required in the special situation of your courses? While it is very unlikely that all these purposes would be pursued in any given context, it is entirely normal for assessment to be pursued for many different ends in any given course.

While the purposes range widely, there are three main categories of purpose that can be discerned from this list. The first of these is assessment that contributes directly or indirectly to students' successful graduation from the course, called here 'assessment for certification' (for example, Items 3, 5, 6, 8). These include all activities that result in the generation of marks and grades that form some role in a student's official record of performance. They are recorded in a formal institutional repository from which transcripts and decisions about graduation are generated. When a particular episode of assessment counts highly towards final grades, that is widely recognized as a high-stakes event, having implications for both student progression and their future lives. The term summative assessment is often used for this purpose of assessment: it is a summation of students' achievement over a particular period.

The second category of purpose relates to improving students' learning (for example, Items 1, 2, 4, 7, 10). While improved learning outcomes should ultimately translate into certification, this set of purposes is low stakes because the consequences do not translate necessarily into a mark or grade or decision about pass or fail. It is assessment to influence students' study behaviour and enhance the possibility of students meeting learning outcomes. The terms 'formative assessment' and 'assessment for learning' are commonly used for this purpose: it is assessment that helps form students' capabilities (see Samball et al. 2012).

For the sake of completeness, we should include a third category of purpose, that of assessment for longer-term learning (for example, Items 2, 10, 11, 12). While this could be included in the second category, as it is clearly formative, there is value in separating it out as formative assessment typically has a very short-term timescale. It helps students with present learning tasks, and does not directly help them with work that is beyond the scope of the course. If it is dealing with matters beyond the immediate learning outcomes, why should we bother with this at all? The reason is a profound one, but is often overlooked: students need to be able to judge their own work because without this they can't be effective learners now and they will be forever dependent on the efforts of others to form judgements. This has enormous implications for the roles students go on to take after graduation. Dependency on others to judge one's performance occurs infrequently in the contemporary workplace as this kind of close supervision is no longer a feature of work. Employees who can't work out what needs to be done without continual provision of detailed criteria and standards are not seen as capable employees and won't be able to retain their jobs. Similarly in the world of education, opportunities for feedback are very limited, so most development is the responsibility of the individual learner together with their peers. The term sustainable assessment is used to describe this purpose of fostering learning in the longer term (Boud 2000). Sustainable assessment is that which helps students build their capacity to learn and make judgements beyond the immediate situation. Features of sustainable assessment can be incorporated into any task. An illustration of sustainable assessment is provided by activities in which students have to identify and apply appropriate criteria to their work without these being supplied to them. (See also assessmentfutures.com).

Sometimes these categories get mixed a little. For example, when an early assessment task in a course is used both to generate grades and prompt teaching staff to provide useful information to students to assist them to subsequently perform better as part of a feedback process. While this is a frequent occurrence, we should keep in mind that the context of the course may lead students to pay much more attention to one of these ends (marks) than to the other (useful information for learning). Indeed, creating a context in which students are not solely governed by a short-term desire to maximize marks, regardless of their actual learning, is the major challenge of course and assessment design.

The tensions between these sets of purposes are worth exploring in more detail. Different purposes not only involve different approaches to assessment, but they have a different logic to them. Let us, as an instance, explore the different kinds of information needed for different purposes. Assessment for certification requires summary information that can be collated across tasks and courses. Different units of information need to be combined to give an overall indication of performance. Marks and grades are commonplace in assessment for certification as they summarize complex judgements in simple forms that can be readily collated. Some information – indeed, rather a lot – is of course lost during this process, but when gross indicators are all that is required, then this loss of information is acceptable. The logic of assessment for learning is quite different. Students need information that will enable them to alter the ways they think about their work and change their own practices. For this, they need quite detailed and specific information about particular aspects of their work. They need knowledge of what they are doing well and not so well with respect to the particularities of their work. They also need to be actively engaged in the process as participants in a dialogue about the nature of their work. Summary information is not at all useful for this. For example, knowing that their work is graded as a 'C' tells them nothing about what they might need to do to get an 'A' for their next assignment. What they need to know is what specifically were the features of their work that led to the 'C', how they might do things differently, and what good work of an 'A-like' character might look like. So, for certification, summarized data is fit for purpose, but for assessment for learning it is unfit. The irony, which we have to address, is that traditionally a lot of time and effort has been spent adding extra information (e.g. detailed feedback) to assessment for certification/summative assessment but little has been spent on the formative phases. This is the wrong way around.

Similarly, timing needs to be considered in relation to purpose. Assessment for certification requires knowledge of what students end up being able to do once they have completed their learning process. For certification purposes the fact that at one point in time students knew little and by the end they knew a great deal is not normally relevant. For this purpose, what is important is that a student ends up being able to show what they can do. This suggests that assessment for certification should be loaded very substantially towards the end of periods of study. The converse applies to assessment for learning. If assessment is to contribute to subsequent learning, it needs to occur during the learning period, and certainly before the next related episode of assessment takes place. Information for students needs to be prompt as well as detailed, and assessment tasks need to be carefully scheduled so that students can usefully build on knowledge of outcomes from each assessment event. In general, assessment for learning needs to be strongly loaded towards the earlier parts of any given course unit.

Taking another tack, there are also tensions between the second and third categories. Assessment for immediate learning requires information about the execution of the present task, whereas for the longer term, emphasis is needed on helping students work out what counts as appropriate standards and criteria and how to discern features of these in their own work, rather than being given criteria and having the solutions to problems immediately drawn to their attention.

It can be seen then that there are contradictions between the logics of certification and learning. Each prioritizes different features and some of the key features are not compatible with each other. Assessment designs cannot identically meet the requirements of different purposes. Choices need to be made about which purpose will dominate in any given situation. These choices need to take account of the inclination of students towards responding to the contingencies of grades rather than learning as such. If a given assessment task is seen by the teacher as having equal value for both certification and learning, it is the certification feature that may well capture the attention of the student!

It would be comforting if the contradictions could be resolved and elegant solutions devised to ensure that all ends were equally well addressed. Unfortunately, this is not possible. Decisions between the two will always involve, often messy, compromises between different ends. The challenge for us as teachers is to ensure that the end of certification does not always dominate, because this is self-defeating if we are concerned with learning. Indeed there is something of a high stakes–low stakes paradox (McArthur 2018) because we clearly at some point need assessment for certification, but rich learning occurs through low stakes activities.

KEY ELEMENTS IN THINKING ABOUT ASSESSMENT

We have established so far that assessment can serve different purposes and that we must be clear of the intended purposes of any assessment task, but also that the reconciliation of different tasks is likely to be messy and involve compromise. Clearly then, our role in assessment involves much more than simply thinking up questions to pose to students. Rather, our engagement with assessment is multi-faceted. We need to think clearly about the purpose of assessment and ensure that it has the effects that it needs to have within the context of a course. That is, to provide students with useful information about their progress and what they can do to be more effective in their learning, and/or it needs to generate credible and defensible information for purposes of certification. For both these ends it needs to take into account not only the subject matter of the module in question and the learning outcomes from study, but its overall context within a course or programme and the ways different parts of assessment interact with each other.

These different facets to consider regarding assessment include the following, and each will be outlined in more detail in this section: assessment tasks, learning outcomes, appropriate standards, criteria for making judgements, assessment methods, assessment roles, assessment-related activities, marks and grades (if appropriate), institutional requirements. They need not be taken in the order listed here but each needs to be compatible with and support the other elements. As discussed in Chapter 9, this means that there needs to be 'congruence' or 'alignment' in the final assessment design.

Assessment tasks

An assessment task is an activity in which a student is expected to engage as part of their course in which they demonstrate what they can do. It may be a sequence of short items, as in a test, or a single whole task that may encompass different elements, like an assignment. The task is important as it governs the kind of work that students are obliged to engage with, and it frames for them the nature of the subject they are studying. Unlike other teaching and learning activities which may be optional, there is normally no choice but for a student to complete an assessment task if they want to stay enrolled. There may well be scope for variation of some particulars of the task – they could choose one topic over another or negotiate an alternative activity – but this must occur within the limits of ensuring that the desired learning outcomes are addressed.

What are the features of good assessment tasks?

How would we judge a good assessment task? What should such a task be able to generate? Some features relate to the essential requirements for a task, others (the latter two below) have more of the character of desirability:

1 It must provide a means of determining if the desired learning outcomes for the module have been met, that is, it must allow for these to be demonstrated as part of the task.

2 The task should be engaging and interesting and a worthwhile use of students time in its own right.

3 It should be doable in the light of the opportunities that students have had to study and practice (though it need not necessarily be on a topic about which they have had direct instruction).

4 The task must encourage students to engage in desirable study activities in preparation for and conduct of the task. For example, it shouldn't encourage short-term memorization of information that will be soon forgotten.

5 It should not place an unrealistic burden of work on students to complete; the load should take into account the typical loads of tasks in the wider programme of study.

6 It must be seen by students as realistic and a valid representation of what they are learning. It may in many circumstances be needed to be seen as authentic, that is, it has some identifiable relationship with the kind of task that students may face on graduation, rather than something only seen within the confines of an educational institution.

Conversely, poor tasks are the opposite of these. They do not relate well to learning outcomes, they are seen by students as a chore, they include material which it wouldn't be realistic to assume students had studied in the way required, they prompt bad study habits, and so on. In addition, poor tasks have other undesirable characteristics:

- They inadvertently allow for plagiarism through repeating topics or questions used before or which can be found on the Internet without the need for further processing.

- They involve 'busy-work' that does not engage students in thinking deeply about what they are doing or reworking material from other sources.

- They over-sample some learning outcomes at the expense of covering all.

There may also be local and disciplinary requirements for good tasks. What are these in your own context?

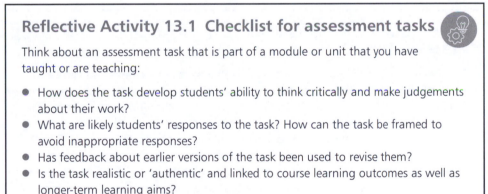

Reflective Activity 13.1 Checklist for assessment tasks

Think about an assessment task that is part of a module or unit that you have taught or are teaching:

- How does the task develop students' ability to think critically and make judgements about their work?
- What are likely students' responses to the task? How can the task be framed to avoid inappropriate responses?
- Has feedback about earlier versions of the task been used to revise them?
- Is the task realistic or 'authentic' and linked to course learning outcomes as well as longer-term learning aims?
- Does the task encourage students to position themselves as active learners?
- Is the task a learning activity in its own right and not just a compliance requirement?
- What particular capacities does the task help build in students?
- Does the task encourage students to work productively with others (as distinct from colluding with them)?

- Have students had sufficient practice in some of the key areas being assessed (for example, through activities that are not formally assessed) for it to be a realistic task for them?
- Will the task focus students' attention on productive learning activities and lead them away from 'cramming' and plagiarism?
- How does the task develop students' capacity to assess
  - their own work?
  - the work of others?
- Is feedback used to help students calibrate their own judgements about their work?
- Is feedback from both peers and staff used, and are tasks scheduled so that students are able to utilize comments from others to improve their work?
- How will the assessment task have a longer-term effect on students beyond the immediate period of assessment?

(adapted from **uts.edu.au/research-and-teaching/teaching-and-learning/ assessment-futures/designing-and-redesigning-1**)

Learning outcomes

The most basic representations of what should result from any course or course module are the desired learning outcomes. This term is often shortened as simply, learning outcomes, which were discussed in Chapters 9 and 10. Thinking about assessment involves thinking about the design of the whole course. Case Study 13.1 examines how the Re-engineering Assessment Practices Project worked to implement new models of assessment practices, whilst Reflective Activity 13.2 considers the relations between learning outcomes and assessment.

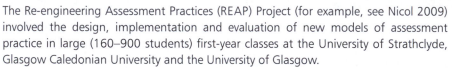

Case Study 13.1 The Re-engineering Assessment Practices Project

The Re-engineering Assessment Practices (REAP) Project (for example, see Nicol 2009) involved the design, implementation and evaluation of new models of assessment practice in large (160–900 students) first-year classes at the University of Strathclyde, Glasgow Caledonian University and the University of Glasgow.

The project involved the redesign of assessment in a range of disciplines including the sciences, engineering, arts, education and social sciences. This redesign was based on explicit principles of formative assessment (Nicol and Macfarlane-Dick 2006). The aim of the project was to use technologies to give students a more active role in assessment in order to support their development as self-directed learners. It showed that if assessment design and e-learning tools are thought about in relation to each other, then technology can improve students' learning in large classes without large increases in staff workload.

Although the project ended in 2007, the project website contains a number of helpful resources and case studies. See **reap.ac.uk**

Reflective Activity 13.2 Checklist for those involved in programmes and courses

Think about the assessment across a whole course or programme that you have been involved in:

- Does the overall balance of assessment activities across tasks fairly reflect the balance of learning outcomes for the programme/course?
- Are assessment activities in alignment with learning outcomes and teaching and learning activities and do they together promote a virtuous cycle of achievement? Is such alignment visible to students?
- Do learning outcomes incorporate features such as building capacity for learning beyond the course, development of students' capacity to make judgements about their own work and that of others?
- Do the assessment tasks within a course/unit adequately reflect the main learning outcomes?
- Do they contribute to the overall graduate attributes of the programme?
- Are all assessment tasks judged according to standards made specific to the task rather than generic standards?
- Are marks given and recorded in no finer detail than is appropriate for the accuracy of grading of the task (for example, it is not possible to reliably mark essays and reports to percentage accuracy)?
- Are assessments across units coordinated to (a) avoid repetition of type of task, (b) avoid overloading students at particular times, and (c) ensure appropriate coverage of learning outcomes?
- Are all staff aware of the assessment tasks required of students in other units/ courses across the programme and within the semester?
- Is assessment normally discussed in all course, programme and assessment meetings primarily in terms of impact on learning, and secondarily in terms of fairness, consistency, etc.?
- Is timing of feedback relative to opportunities for students to utilize feedback considered regularly?
- Do course and programme teams regularly consider information about students' responses to assessment as part of quality assurance deliberations?
- Is the overall assessment in a course or programme such that it can be plausibly concluded that it will build the capacities of students to continue their own learning and assessment after graduation?

(From **uts.edu.au/research-and-teaching/teaching-and-learning/ assessment-futures/designing-and-redesigning-0**)

Appropriate standards

It is possible to engage in long debates about what academic standards are and how they are assessed. What though is needed for assessment design? How do assessment tasks enable us to judge whether students have met an appropriate standard of work? We need to be clear about what is meant by 'standards' in the assessment context.

It should be noted that some familiar and well-used approaches to assessment are so badly constructed in terms of enabling standards to be judged that they need to be rejected. The most common category of such archaic approaches is what is often called norm-referenced testing, or in North America 'grading on the curve'. This involves assessment in which students are compared with other students and grades allocated accordingly. The obvious drawback of such approaches is that they assume that one cohort of students is equivalent to the next. If they are not, then what occurs is that students are either advantaged or disadvantaged according to the overall abilities of the students in the same class. It is intrinsically impossible to judge if students have met a particular standard, because the determination is not made according to a standard (particular quality of work), but to a variable (performance of other students). Grading on the curve also misses the fact that students have already been highly selected and so represent a group skewed towards higher achievement. Having invariant numbers reaching particular grades irrespective of how well they have met standards is a way of undermining those very standards.

An academic standard is a benchmark that represents the type and quality of work to be required from a particular course. There may be a single standard which can be achieved or not achieved or there may be various standards to be achieved beyond an acceptable minimal. However, to be meaningful, these higher standards must be represented with respect to the features of the particular work being judged, not an impenetrable term such as good or excellent. Grade descriptors, which indicate the boundaries that distinguish one grade from another, are necessary in a standards-based approach to assessment. These provide criteria to determine whether a particular grade (standard) has been met. Such grade descriptors need to be module-specific as standards are not meaningfully independent of the objects to which they are applied.

How many standards there should be in any given situation, and their degree of specificity changes from place to place. Too few standards, the more difficult it is to work out criteria for judgement as too many different things are being collapsed. Too many standards and it is impossible for them to be meaningfully sampled without creating an overload of assessment. Generally, standards are not written in operational forms. Turning them into operational form involves determining specific criteria for particular work.

Standards are relatively easy to identify in professional courses and are often documented in statements by professional bodies. In less vocational areas they have been less commonly documented, but this is changing with the publication of the UK disciplinary benchmark standards and the Australian threshold standards that have been developed across the disciplines. Threshold standards are taking on increasing importance as it is through a focus on these that comparability across courses and across nations is being promoted. Even without these pressures, the threshold standards for a course are important as it is only by reference to whether a student has met all standards at at least a minimum level that judgements about graduation can be validly made.

Criteria for making judgements

While learning outcomes and appropriate standards need to be decided upon, they do not fully determine what would count as good work. To these need to be added the criteria for making judgements. To judge any assessment task, what are needed are the standards to be applied not only to the learning outcomes, but also to the particular criteria that will be used to identify whether a particular aspect of the work has or has not met the standard for any given learning outcome. Criteria provide the means for operational translation of standards to actual work produced. Depending on the nature of the assessment task, these criteria may be used as part of a model answer and marking scheme, a rubric or an assignment attachment sheet which also includes a commentary on the extent to which standards and outcomes have been met. Such criteria also ensure we don't rely on 'instinct' or a 'feeling' when evaluating a work to be of a certain standard. Some academics say that with experience they can simply 'tell' what is an 'A' or 'D' piece of work. But this is a dangerous position to adopt and can lead to inconsistencies, mistakes and unfairness.

Transparency is also an important feature of standards and learning outcomes: it is unreasonable to disguise what is being aimed for, even though these might not be fully understood by students at the start. Similarly for criteria. It is important to know how work will be judged. After all, unless the student possesses a clear notion of what is good work, how can such work be produced? Ideally, students will be given some opportunity, for example peer assessment or sample marking, to enable them to actively engage with the criteria. The best way to understand marking criteria is to actually have to apply them oneself.

Assessment methods

Many assessment texts spend many pages discussing the pros and cons of different assessment methods. An assessment method is simply the form in which assessment tasks are presented. For example, unseen examination, multiple choice test, take-home assignment, etc. It may seem that that the intrinsic qualities of an assessment method are one of the most important considerations in assessment design, however the picture is more complicated. While it is true that some kinds of method may allow for some kinds of outcomes to be revealed more clearly or involve more straightforward processing than others, these alone are not the most important considerations. As we argued in relation to teaching methods in Chapter 11, it is also important to consider the advantages and disadvantages of different methods in the context in which they are used. Students will respond to a particular task not because of the intrinsic qualities of the assessment method used but in the light of their personal expectations and experiences about what is involved. In other words, students do not engage with a particular method in a vacuum, but bring their own understandings of assessment and experiences to their engagement. It is no good therefore to have a very well-designed multiple-choice test that is intended to judge higher order thinking if students' expectations of such tests are that they are best approached through memorization!

Assessment roles

Once it may have seemed obvious what roles one had to play in assessment, with the teacher setting questions and then marking a lab report, essay or exam and the student obviously doing whatever task was set. But actually there are numerous assessment roles, each of which requires a broader understanding of assessment practices and purposes.

Obviously we are all more familiar with the processes involved in setting and marking assessments within our own modules. But what about when we are called upon to mark on behalf of a colleague, such as in a system of moderation or second marking, as is increasingly required by our quality assurance mechanisms? In such cases, we may not know the module and what it covers as well as we know those on which we teach. Therefore, to do this role well requires some familiarization with the module and very careful attention to the marking criteria. There is a tricky balance here between liaising with the module convenor to ensure you fully understand what the students have experienced and remaining that external arbiter of standards. This is even more the case when taking on the role of external examiner for a programme at another institution.

It is, however, students who perhaps have the broadest range of roles when it comes to assessment. Most obviously, they do the actual assessment tasks set. But it is now well recognized that this is not as straightforward as was once thought. In particular, there is a strong sense that students must develop a sense of *assessment literacy* in order to do an assessment well, and for it to contribute positively to their learning. Research has demonstrated that rather than simply telling students about an assessment, a far more effective way for them to learn the rules and expectations is by active engagement (O'Donovan et al. 2008). Thus self and peer assessment are rich opportunities to learn how to apply assessment criteria to a piece of work. Knowing how criteria are applied then greatly strengthens students' abilities to ensure their own work matches such criteria. It is the old adage of learning by doing. In addition, students can learn more about assessment by working in partnership with their teachers. One way of doing this is through the use of annotated exemplars of real student work (Sadler 1987, 2010; Carless et al. 2018). Such exemplars are not model answers but real work, ideally of different standards. The teacher then annotates to demonstrate to other students where the strengths and weaknesses lie, particularly as they relate to the marking criteria. In so doing, a sort of asynchronous dialogue is established, with the exemplar as the common focus, between students and their teacher. Even better, argues Sadler, is when class time is set aside for the activity of jointly working through the annotated exemplars. Indeed, there are a range of ways of building in opportunities for students to engage with the assessment processes, as demonstrated by research undertaken by O'Donovan et al. (2008, 2016). Their research suggests that student achievement can be enhanced considerably when they are able to engage actively with standards and other parts of the assessment process.

RESEARCH BRIEFING 13.1 How can students appreciate standards?

Students cannot produce good work, or meet any expectations of what is required of them, without an understanding of standards. This must be based not on an abstract view of how standards are defined, but be grounded in the types of work they are expected to produce. What are the qualities required of what students produce to meet the desired learning outcome?

O'Donovan et al. (2008) developed and investigated a range of strategies to introduce students to standards in large classes. While their application was in the context of business courses, the basic approach can be applied in any discipline.

Their starting point was recognition of the ineffective nature of the device they originally used to communicate standards to students. It took the form of what is now called an assessment rubric, a grid that provided descriptors for each grade against each criterion used for assessment for each piece of undergraduate work. This provided students and markers with specific information about the standards to be applied with respect to each criterion. However, students did not refer to it, did not know how to interpret it, nor did they use it.

O'Donovan et al.'s first intervention, evaluated over three years of classes, was called the social-constructivist approach. Students took an optional 90-minute pre-assessment workshop in which they engaged in the marking of exemplar assignments and small group discussion. This demonstrated a significant improvement in performance compared to those who did not undertake the workshop, an improvement that was maintained over a year later.

Their second intervention was called a cultivated community of practice for sharing assessment standards. It involved three elements:

a Developing hospitable learning spaces in which social interaction can take place – these combine social activities, learning activities and facilitative technology and were fostered by user-friendly out-of-class working environments (physical and virtual).

b Emphasizing within courses more formalized social learning and collaborative assessment practices such as peer review – these involve seeding activities in which students worked together through the provision of tasks and strategies to discuss and review each other's work.

c Facilitating 'pedagogical intelligence' within learners – this involves not only the familiar process of introducing students to the discourse of the discipline, but also to the discourse of teaching and learning: how do they learn how to learn and make judgements about themselves and the course they are undertaking.

Through these various features, students were positioned in much more active roles than conventional courses. They were expected to take the initiative to intervene in their own learning processes as well as the formal proceedings of the course. Standards were not simply provided, but were actively worked with and applied.

So we can see that the role of the student is not to simply memorize some information and recount it back for an assessment task. To begin with, it isn't a well-designed task if that is all the student is required to do. But beyond this, we have to see that students gain the required assessment literacy by their participation in both sides of the assessment process. It really is very difficult to imagine a better way for students to learn how assessment is done, than doing it themselves, either with their own work or that of a peer. Just as students should not be the passive recipients of information as in purely transmission modes of teaching (as discussed in Chapter 10), so too they should not passively undertake assessment, as though the task is wholly managed elsewhere. The more assessment literate students become, the more they enter the assessment arena as active agents of their own destiny.

Assessment-related activities

It is convenient to discuss assessment tasks as if they were separate activities isolated from all else that occurs in teaching and learning. This is far from the case. If assessment for learning is to be successful, then it is the learning activities that accompany tasks that are vital. Some of these will be formally structured (for example, set problems to work through in advance), some will be fully controlled by students (for example, informal study sets, or discussions about assignments). There is more involved in assessing students than simply setting a task. Assessment-related activities might include exercises on identifying appropriate standards from the literature, practice in discerning differences between good and poor work in similar tasks, the analysis of models and exemplars to ascertain features of successful applications of knowledge, practice in giving comments to peers, etc. Study can be transformed through the use of complementary activities linked to assessment. Indeed, for sustainable assessment the use of such features is invaluable. Case Study 13.2 provides an example of how students can be actively involved in feedback across a module.

Case Study 13.2 An example of the active role of students in feedback (for example, typical written assignments)

This is a worked example of how students can be given an active role in feedback across a module. The following features should be noted: a strong expectation for students having an active role in learning and assessment is set at the start of the semester; students are oriented to the need to be proactive in seeking comments not just being content with what is given; comparisons are made explicit and students record actions which they can come back to later; the second assessment task includes some aspects that will have benefited from the round of feedback on the first task. The steps are as follows:

1 Orientation of students to the kind of task, the standards required and the feedback process (for example, Week 3).
2 Assessment task 1 completed (Week 5).
3 Student makes own frank appraisal about their work on Assessment Task 1. Student requests specific kind of comments from peer (Week 5).
4 Student compares own judgements with comments from peer.
5 Revises assignment, hands it in with request for specific kind of comments from tutor (Week 6).
6 Marked work returned (Week 7).
7 Student compares comments and judgement of tutor with own views. Makes a record of what they need to do to prepare better for next assignment (Week 7).
8 Assessment task 2 completed (Week 8).

Marks and grades

We often treat marks and grades as if they had some existence independent of the work they are attached to. However, they are simply summaries of a number of complex judgements made about a piece of work, or of a series of activities by students. They are convenient because, unlike complex judgements, they can be added and mathematically manipulated, so that judgements over a number of pieces of work can be aggregated. In doing this, we should be mindful that the trade-off for convenience is loss of information and, much more importantly, disconnection with learning outcomes. Every act of marking or grading reduces the amount of useful information available. This may be acceptable when dealing with overall certification but, as we have referred to earlier, it is not acceptable for purposes of assessment for learning. What is important for this is what the marks or grades specifically signify, that is, what data they convey to the student. In this process it is important that they do not contain false information. This typically occurs when, say, a written assignment is allocated a mark out of 100. This conveys a false degree of accuracy as decades of research since Hartog and Rhodes pioneering work in the 1930s (1935, 1936) show that the normal variation among markers and between markers could not generate a figure so precise. It is better to use a scale with the number of categories that can be justified by the degree of precision attached to the type of work being assessed. In some cases this is no more than acceptable/unacceptable and rarely more than three or four passing grades. Just because grades can be easily added to produce a more detailed scale does not mean that it is legitimate to do so, despite many decades of tradition.

When assessment is based on standards, it should convey information (when disaggregated) about whether standards and learning outcomes have been met, and perhaps the extent to which they have been met. However, when students seek to produce better work they need more information. Such information needs minimally to include what they have done acceptably and what they have not done to the given standard. It may also need to illustrate and explain problems and issues that have been manifest in the work generated, and perhaps draw attention to examples of work completed well. Information about what is necessary to meet the standard required is vital.

Institutional requirements

Finally, it is important to become familiar with the policies of one's own institution regarding assessment. In recent times, policies have become less a set of rules to follow, more a set of principles that need to inform practice. Whatever the guidelines may be, they need to be taken into account in order to ensure that the final design for assessment is acceptable. It should be realized though that policies are always subject to interpretation, and it is not uncommon to find the same policy interpreted in one way in one faculty, but in a different way in another. Most higher education institutions now have requirements that assessment must be standards-based (though some may formulate this in the earlier terminology of criterion-referenced). This means that despite sometimes distracting rules about grade distributions, all judgements need to be made on the basis of whether students have met a standard, not how well they have done vis-à-vis other students.

Having examined the key elements in thinking about assessment, in the next section we extend our consideration of assessment from the perspective of students and discuss other factors that we should bring to bear on our assessment decisions.

FEEDBACK: AN INTEGRAL PART OF GOOD ASSESSMENT

Feedback is one of the key processes that contribute to assessment for learning. It is of such great importance that, in the UK, the Osney Grange Group produced an agenda for change in the use of feedback in higher education (see brookes.ac.uk/WorkArea/DownloadAsset. aspx?id=2147552220). This agenda, amongst other things, argued for a focus on the process of feedback rather than the product, and that feedback should be seen as a dialogic process that is an integral part of teaching and learning. Importantly, what this notion of dialogue reinforces is that assessment is not something that is done to students, but is a set of activities in which they should have an active part.

The Osney Grange Agenda highlights that feedback is important because it provides information external to the student that is used to assist in the learning process and thus helps the student produce better work. It resonates with the understanding of feedback given by Game and Metcalfe (2009), which states that the role of feedback should be to enable 'participants to have thoughts they could not have had on their own, yet to recognize these thoughts as developments of their own thinking' (Game and Metcalfe 2009, p. 45). As the agenda suggests, it is important to note that, despite everyday language to the contrary, feedback is not just the information provided but refers to the whole process of eliciting and using information for improvement (Boud and Molloy 2013a; Carless and Boud 2018). Feedback should be judged *primarily* in terms of its effects, not on the inputs made to achieve these effects. Feedback only works when students want it to work, as they have to take the initiative to do something useful with the information provided. Only students can do the learning! When such information is either uncollected or unread, then no matter how diligent teachers have been in providing it, it is impossible to claim that feedback has taken place. All that has happened is that assignment-specific information has been made available. The structuring and location of assessment tasks, and their associated activities, to allow for feedback is therefore one of the most important aspects of assessment design.

Successful feedback

Feedback is a mechanism that enables students to benefit from the views of other people about their work. Unlike popular belief, it is not the act of teachers providing unsolicited comments to students about their assignments, though the input of teachers in feedback is vital. It is helpful to distinguish between specific feedback information provided to students and overall feedback processes. Inadequacies in feedback constitute one of the single greatest criticisms of students in opinion surveys across institutions and across countries. This ongoing criticism from students about the quality of the feedback they receive hints at the lingering misconceptions and misunderstandings among academics about feedback. Feedback can be done well, but only so long as it is understood as a process and not an occasion of comment.

The following series of questions outline the main features of feedback processes (Boud and Molloy 2013b). Not all elements may be deployed in any given instance, though all will need to be considered if feedback is to be done well.

What information is needed?

The essence of feedback information is that it is useful to students in improving their work. To have this effect, the information needs to be sufficiently rich and detailed for students to appreciate what they can do, and timed such that they have the opportunity to do something with it before the course moves on to something entirely different.

Hattie and Timperley (2007) have categorized four types of provision of feedback information in terms of the levels at which they operate on students and discussed what research literature suggests are most effective. Should information be focused on the specific task required to be completed (task-focused), should it emphasise the nature of the processes underpinning the conduct of the task (process-focused), should it concentrate on how students think about such tasks and the self-monitoring processes they need to engage in (self-regulation-focused) and finally, should it be directed at the characteristics of the student themselves (personal-focused). Hattie and Timperly's review (2007) shows that the first three have a valuable place, with a particular value in the third of these (self-regulation focused). However, focus on the student rather than the task or their problem-solving processes is normally counterproductive and should be avoided.

In what form is it provided?

The most common form is through written text, though the form depends on the nature of the product being considered and what a student might need to do. Skills might need to be demonstrated, or visual information presented in graphical form. To personalize information, an audio or video file could be provided. In many situations, it can be less time-consuming, and be better received by students to provide audio or video comments rather than to write text.

When is it provided?

Many institutions have policies that require information to be provided to students within two or three weeks of submission, and clearly these maxima should be adhered to. However, there are many circumstances in which feedback needs to operate on a much shorter cycle if it is to have an effect. Part of assessment design is to create realistic deadlines for both students and tutors and so set tasks that enable feedback loops to always be completed. Feedback processes have not been enhanced just because everyone meets the institutional deadline if the overall timing of the feedback occurs after it is likely to be most useful to the student, as is the case in much of the feedback on summative work. Boud and Molloy (2013b) call this 'hopefully useful information'. Information not used is a waste of the time and effort of those providing it, so great attention needs to be paid to providing it in a form and at a time when it has most effect on improving learning. Elimination of comment generation that has little likelihood of being taken up by students can release time for much more useful teaching activities.

By whom is it provided?

While it is commonly assumed that feedback is the responsibility of teachers, other parties can make very useful contributions. Clearly, in placement situations, practitioners have an important role. However, a major under-utilized resource for feedback are students' peers. In almost all circumstances the amount and type of information provided by those with teaching roles will be far less than is needed, so mobilization of peers – for feedback, not for marking – is needed. This has the additional benefit that students learn a great deal by providing feedback, as well as receiving it.

How can students take a more active role in feedback?

If the only feedback processes that students experience are those in which all the decisions are taken by others, they will not nurture an effective student. Students need an active role, and not just in responding to information that others think is important. They can be active in identifying what information they need as well as using it to improve their work. Students need practice in identifying what is most useful to them, and this can further contribute to the sense of dialogue identified by the Osney Grange Group as so important.

How can effective feedback processes be designed?

Feedback design is an essential part of good course design. It should not be something decided at the time of marking. The planning of feedback loops needs to occur at the earliest stage of scheduling the activities of the course unit for the semester. How many cycles can be fitted in to the unit? What does that imply for when topics and assignments are introduced, when deadlines for tasks are set? Which of these will end up with work that will be formally marked and recorded, which for feedback alone? Are the feedback cycles coordinated so that what a student learns from comments on one task can be utilized in time for the next? See Figure 13.1.

How do we know if feedback has been successful?

The simple answer to this is: student work improves in the areas where feedback has operated. While there are steps prior to this – that the tasks have been well timed, information provided when needed in a form that can be used, students have had opportunities to utilize the information – in the end, the consequence for learning is all that really counts. Successful feedback loops for students also provide essential information for teachers about how well they have communicated key ideas and fostered learning in teaching activities.

Successful feedback and the sequencing of assessment tasks

If all tasks are independent of each other, then feedback processes will have minimal effect. Students can be persuaded to take feedback seriously when they see a direct benefit to themselves. One way to do this is to arrange assessment tasks with some degree of overlap of learning outcomes and criteria during a given course unit. Nested assessment tasks enable feedback to be effective (see Figure 13.1).

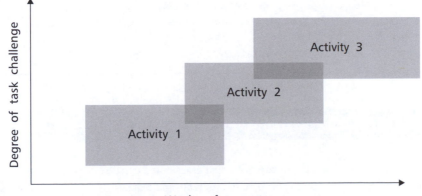

Figure 13.1 Overlap of learning outcomes addressed in subsequent assignments in a course unit (adapted from Molloy and Boud, 2013)

Reflective Activity 13.3 Some ideas to provoke reflection on assessment and feedback

Which of the following might be used to promote students' judgement of their work? What other strategies might be suitable in your context?

The five-minute paper

Just before the end of a session, ask students to write for five minutes on a given topic, what they have learned, or what they need to do to prepare for the next activity.

Instant response mechanisms in class

In large groups, pose questions to which students can respond either after discussion with a neighbour, or just for themselves. To display responses from the whole group use simple technology in which students use their mobile phones to dial a number responding to the appropriate answer on the screen (there is no charge to the student and you need no additional equipment other than internet access or your own computer).

Assessment when they are ready

Students don't need to wait for a test or exam to check their understanding. Provide regular online multi-choice quizzes with discussion of better and worse answers displayed when students have committed to an answer.

Do it again task

Not all set tasks need to differ from the previous one. Set the same writing task again, and again, providing comments in between cycles so that all students can appreciate that they can produce really good work.

Don't mark all tasks

Use peer feedback selectively. Students gain practice in giving and receiving feedback comments. Point out that the person gaining the most from the exercise is the giver, not the receiver as they get practice in rehearsing their understanding and communicating it to others.

What counts as good work?

Use a structured class exercise prior to any substantial new task to engage students in consideration of 'what would a really good example of this assignment look like?' Students identify criteria for themselves and gain an appreciation of what needs to be taken into account in doing the task.

STUDENT EXPERIENCES OF ASSESSMENT

We began this chapter with the observation that assessment can be one of the most stressful parts of the higher education experience for students and teachers. In this section we spend a little more time considering the implications of this. It is important to consider this affective dimension of assessment because it is one of the contextual factors that helps shape how a student engages with an assessment task and what they learn in the process. If students respond negatively to an assessment, if it induces a sense of fear or panic, then they are unlikely to perform well, no matter the set purposes of the task. Moreover, there is an issue of social justice here to consider alongside the more familiar ones of validity and reliability. Is a particular assessment approach just? Both in its implications for the students concerned and in terms of broader social justice.

We have already discussed the importance of assessment to student learning; now we look at this from another dimension and consider the importance of assessment to student well-being. In fact, at stake here is the importance of assessment to students' very sense of self-worth. Indeed, Boud and Falchikov (2007) make this point starkly when they write: 'Assessment affects people's lives. The future directions and careers of students depend on it' (p. 3). The authors go on to explore the ways in which assessment can build or crush students' confidence, and this has both short- and long-term consequences. In this way, Knight (1995) describes assessment as a 'moral activity' (p. 13) because it rests so much on judgements about what we do and do not value. Even where an assessment task might be aimed at a short-term evaluation of student learning, it can have long-term effects on self-confidence and self-worth. Succeeding within the assessment sphere of higher education shapes the ways in which students see themselves as fitting into society and the contributions they can make.

We raise this aspect of assessment not to make it even more stressful and precarious for us as teachers to try to navigate, but rather because it is necessary to understand this dimension of assessment in order to do assessment well and effectively. We can map different social justice considerations against each of the three purposes of assessment outlined earlier in this chapter. Regarding assessment for certification, just assessment involves all students being treated fairly and having equivalent opportunities to demonstrate their learning, knowledge and competencies. Assessment for learning directs our attention to the processes of learning enabled, or disabled, by assessment. Coping with extreme stress, for example, might be a skill necessary for assessment for certification in some disciplines such as medicine, but it is unlikely to nurture a good learning experience where that is our aim. Finally, for the long term, students need to be able to connect what they do within assessment tasks with later roles they will play within society, making a useful contribution and being recognized for doing so.

This focus on justice goes beyond the notion of fairness which is often associated with assessment. Fairness is, of course, important, but the idea of justice encompasses more and highlights the multitude of ways in which we need to think about the impact and the effects of assessment. McArthur's (2016, 2018) concept of *assessment for social justice* seeks to convey this broader aim and significance. It rests on a rejection of thinking of justice in purely procedural terms to instead consider the outcomes and capabilities which are afforded by particular actions, such as assessment tasks.

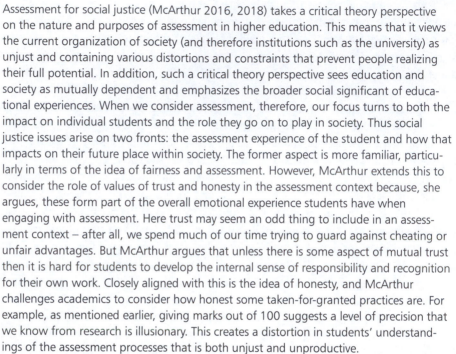

RESEARCH BRIEFING 13.2 Assessment for social justice

Assessment for social justice (McArthur 2016, 2018) takes a critical theory perspective on the nature and purposes of assessment in higher education. This means that it views the current organization of society (and therefore institutions such as the university) as unjust and containing various distortions and constraints that prevent people realizing their full potential. In addition, such a critical theory perspective sees education and society as mutually dependent and emphasizes the broader social significant of educational experiences. When we consider assessment, therefore, our focus turns to both the impact on individual students and the role they go on to play in society. Thus social justice issues arise on two fronts: the assessment experience of the student and how that impacts on their future place within society. The former aspect is more familiar, particularly in terms of the idea of fairness and assessment. However, McArthur extends this to consider the role of values of trust and honesty in the assessment context because, she argues, these form part of the overall emotional experience students have when engaging with assessment. Here trust may seem an odd thing to include in an assessment context – after all, we spend much of our time trying to guard against cheating or unfair advantages. But McArthur argues that unless there is some aspect of mutual trust then it is hard for students to develop the internal sense of responsibility and recognition for their own work. Closely aligned with this is the idea of honesty, and McArthur challenges academics to consider how honest some taken-for-granted practices are. For example, as mentioned earlier, giving marks out of 100 suggests a level of precision that we know from research is illusionary. This creates a distortion in students' understandings of the assessment processes that is both unjust and unproductive.

The second dimension of assessment for social justice, focusing on the impact of assessment on broader society, considers the skills and attributes which students develop that enable them to be fully productive members of that society. Such a situation is one of mutuality, for it is both in individual students' interests and in that of society for them to make such a positive contribution. This idea goes beyond simply employability, though that may be an element, to consider the social world in the whole, not just certain aspects of economic life. The argument proposed is that if assessment shapes how and what students learn, then it has a significant role in shaping the future citizens in our society. What is important is not only for students to develop dispositions, knowledge and skills with which to make this positive contribution, but for them to be able to recognize this in themselves. Thus a form of social empowerment and purpose underpins greater social justice.

The tenets of assessment for social justice can be applied to our assessment planning and practices in a number of ways. First, it reminds us of the profound impact assessment has on students' lives and senses of self-worth: we have a responsibility to think carefully about how and why we assess students. Second, it requires us to think of the inter-personal relationships that lie as a foundation upon which assessment occurs and to ensure these are fair, constructive and just. Finally, it reinforces the fact that what matters about higher education in the end is what it enables students to be and do within society, and that the links between assessment and the wider social world need to be carefully considered.

CONCLUSION

Assessment is probably the most powerful influence on what students do, so it is important that it is carefully designed to have desirable effects on student learning and effectively portray what students can do. This involves making decisions about assessment at a very early stage of course design and ensuring that feedback processes are built in from the start and can operate effectively.

Assessment is also one of the most conservative features of higher education courses and some conventional practices are no longer fit for purpose. This creates challenges for those who want to make it more effective: taken-for-granted assumptions about what assessment should be are disguised as local rules about what should and should not be done. Indeed, within many institutions you will find a number of *phantom* regulations that are used to constrain or direct assessment activities.

Finally, assessment in practice involves making compromises between competing purposes, balancing the needs of learning against those of providing suitable information for certification. While it is relatively easy to privilege certification, in the long term it is the goal of enhancing learning that has the greatest pay-off for students and teachers.

KEY READINGS

For an accessible introduction to innovative assessment, see:

Bryan, C. and Clegg, K. (eds) (2019) *Innovative Assessment in Higher Education: A Handbook for Academic Practitioners*. London: Routledge.

For a focus on what feedback is really about: making a difference to student learning and discussions of key issues in designing courses to effectively utilize feedback processes, see:

Boud, D. and Molloy, E. (eds) (2013) *Feedback in Higher and Professional Education: Understanding It and Doing It Well*. London: Routledge.

For examples of ways of incorporating assessment for learning into courses, see:

Samball, K., McDowell, E. and Montgomery, C. (2012) *Assessment for Learning in Higher Education*. London: Routledge.

For further discussion of assessment for social justice, see:

McArthur, J. (2018) *Assessment for Social Justice*. London: Bloomsbury.

Part four

Reflecting on consequences

Part 4 examines how we can make sense of the impact of our teaching. Chapter 14 considers important practical issues of how we monitor and improve the quality of our teaching. 'Inclusion' (Chapter 15) highlights various dimensions of difference and the ways in which unreflective teaching can unfairly differentiate between different groups of people and inadvertently disadvantage some. It examines the positive role of difference in teaching and learning and how to build more inclusive university communities.

Chapter 14
Quality

How are we monitoring and enhancing the quality of teaching and learning?

INTRODUCTION

How do we know that our teaching has been effective in promoting student learning? How do we generate evidence about our practice that we can reflect on and use to improve the quality of our teaching? How do we change our practices based on this reflection? This chapter presents research-based ideas and strategies for evaluating quality in our teaching practices.

See Chapter 4

> ### TLRP Principles
>
> Two principles are of particular relevance to this chapter on enhancing the quality of teaching and learning in higher education:
>
> **Principle 2: Effective teaching and learning depends on the scholarship and learning of all those educators who teach and research to support the learning of others.** The need for lecturers, teachers and trainers to learn through doing research to improve their knowledge, expertise and skills for teaching should be recognized and supported.
>
> **Principle 7: Effective teaching and learning requires learning to be systematically developed.** Teachers, trainers, lecturers, researchers and all who support the learning of others should provide intellectual, social and emotional support which helps learners to develop expertise in their learning for it to be effective and secure.

As we saw in Chapter 3, key to being a reflective practitioner in higher education is the capacity to reflect on and provide evidence of the quality of our practices and the impact of our teaching on the quality of student learning and outcomes. Professional Standards from a number of countries emphasize the importance of learning from evaluations of teaching practice. Yet measuring teaching quality is not a straightforward task, and can be approached from a variety of angles. For example, is it the capabilities and effectiveness of individual lecturers that will determine quality? Is it the quality of the course, module or programme design that needs to be evaluated? Or can we assess teaching quality at an institutional level? All of these approaches are used, and often for very different purposes. It is therefore important to begin any evaluative process with a clear idea of the purpose and the intended audience (e.g. institutional managers, individual lecturers, employers, government).

The indicators or proxies that are used to assess quality in higher education have been the subject of debate for many years. Individual lecturers' performance is usually measured through student evaluations of teaching. Another common indicator of teaching quality is the use of student satisfaction surveys, which has also become part of the Teaching Excellence and Student Outcomes Framework (TEF) exercise in the UK higher education sector. Student outcomes, as a proxy for quality, are typically assessed by indicators such as the number of students who have graduated and moved to full-time employment or to full-time graduate study (Ashwin 2017; Gunn 2018).

The OECD AHELO (Assessment of Higher Education Learning Outcomes) project investigated the feasibility, utility and validity of applying standardized exit tests to examine a set of agreed learning outcomes within disciplines (see Ashwin 2015 for a critical review). The project was discontinued as it failed to gain agreement from member states. The Tuning project, currently being deployed in Europe, South and North America, is a further example of a cross-national approach to establishing consensus regarding descriptors for intended learning outcomes in undergraduate degrees (see Booth and Ludvigsson 2017). In the United States, the Collegiate Learning Assessment is another tool designed to measure an institution's contribution to the development of students' key higher order competencies. Students' written responses to a set of problems are evaluated to assess their abilities to think critically, reason analytically, solve problems and communicate clearly (see Aloisi and Callaghan 2018).

More recently in the UK, attention has turned to whether measurements can be made of the learning that students gain through the course of their degree programme (as we discussed in Chapter 2). The term learning gain has attracted some currency even though the outcomes of a number of pilot projects have not assured those within the sector that learning gain can be easily measured (Kandiko Howson 2018). These examples of recent initiatives to assess student learning outcomes highlight the intense international interest in this field.

Across the developed world, the quality of teaching and the broader student experience in higher education is a priority for institutions and governments alike (Henard and Roseveare 2012). In a market-driven, massified system, universities thrive or fail based on their capacity to demonstrate that they are delivering outcomes, not only in research but also in the areas of quality teaching, enhanced student experiences and measurable student learning outcomes. An institution's ability to provide robust evidence of quality that is embedded across the university and within disciplinary contexts requires the engagement of individual academic staff who are able to demonstrate how they and their programme teams individually and collectively are making a contribution to the quality of learning, teaching and the student experience (O'Donoghue et al. 2010).

Whilst the focus of this chapter is on the practical issues for evaluating quality, it is important to be clear that the notion of quality is a contested one. It is also the case that, over the years, there have been fairly robust contestations over most indicators of teaching quality (Blackmore 2009; Bedggood and Donovan 2012; Webster 2012). Research Briefing 14.1 overleaf outlines a recent project that challenged the ideas of quality highlighted in university league tables.

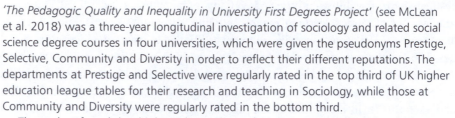

RESEARCH BRIEFING 14.1 Quality and Inequality in undergraduate courses

'The Pedagogic Quality and Inequality in University First Degrees Project' (see McLean et al. 2018) was a three-year longitudinal investigation of sociology and related social science degree courses in four universities, which were given the pseudonyms Prestige, Selective, Community and Diversity in order to reflect their different reputations. The departments at Prestige and Selective were regularly rated in the top third of UK higher education league tables for their research and teaching in Sociology, while those at Community and Diversity were regularly rated in the bottom third.

The project found that high-quality undergraduate courses are those in which students engaged with academic knowledge in transformative ways. When this notion of quality was used to rank the four universities, their ranking was very different from that in national higher education league tables for Sociology.

In this way, this project questioned the status of national higher education league tables as valid measures of the quality of undergraduate courses. This is because such tables misleadingly oversimplify the complexity of a high-quality undergraduate education and because they offer no indication of students' engagement with academic knowledge. The outcomes of the project suggest that, by using measures that largely reflect historical reputation and financial advantage, national higher education league tables are likely to reinforce social inequality by suggesting incorrectly that students who have been to higher status institutions have received a higher quality education and are likely to have developed greater knowledge and skills.

This chapter examines ways of monitoring, evaluating and improving the quality of teaching at an individual, module, programme and institutional level. It starts with a focus on the increased use of data on quality of teaching and employment outcomes to provide information to the public about the performance of institutions and degree programmes. The chapter then presents some practical approaches to gathering and documenting feedback on teaching quality. Approaches for monitoring student learning outcomes are considered next, along with a discussion of implications for using these data to review and renew academic programmes. Throughout the chapter we include case studies and practical examples to demonstrate ways to apply some of the key principles in your teaching practices.

MONITORING TEACHING QUALITY AND STUDENT LEARNING OUTCOMES IN HIGHER EDUCATION

Monitoring and assuring the quality of teaching and student learning outcomes in universities are important mechanisms of accountability, particularly in relation to key stakeholders in higher education. In a number of countries, more data about the quality of higher education provision are made publicly available with the intention of enabling prospective students, employers and the government to gain an understanding of the relative performance of universities and degree programmes. Data such as student satisfaction, league table performance and graduate outcomes are commonly now compiled and published.

In English higher education, for example, where the cost of a university education has risen for fee-paying students over recent years, the government has looked for ways to provide prospective students with information about the quality and outcomes of degree programmes. From September 2012, the UniStats website (unistats.ac.uk) began publishing Key Information Sets, which provide information on a range of different aspects of under-graduate degree programmes, including student satisfaction, graduate outcomes, learning and teaching activities, assessment methods, and professional accreditation. The purpose of the searchable database is to enable prospective students to compare university degree programmes. Although it is not very clear the extent to which prospective students rely on data about quality and outcomes when making choices, the government added another data-gathering exercise in the form of the Teaching Excellence and Student Outcomes Framework (TEF), which awards institutions either a Bronze, Silver or Gold award based on a combination of metrics and institutional information. The TEF rankings and associated data are also intended to inform applicants of the quality of the degrees to which they are considering applying (see Ashwin 2017; Gunn 2018).

Whilst it may seem appropriate for data about the quality of degree programmes to be publicly available, there is not a straightforward 'measure' of quality in higher education. Metrics that purport to provide an assessment of quality are often contentious, and most attempts to provide new measures encounter significant criticism and doubt. The TEF, for example, has been under significant pressure regarding the ways in which the metrics are used, with many commentators doubting that it facilitates meaningful comparisons between institutions on the basis of teaching quality (e.g. Ashwin 2017; Gunn 2018). Nevertheless, it seems likely that the amount of data gathered that purports to provide information on institutional performance will continue to increase.

A proposal for a new measurement of performance, called learning gain (which we discussed in Chapter 2), suggests that the value of a programme of study could be measured by making an assessment of the 'distance travelled' by the students. The idea is that some types of measurements (e.g. standardized tests) could be undertaken at the beginning and end of a programme of study, and the difference in scores would give an indication of the 'value added' of the degree. Assessments could be made of gains in the skills, competencies, content knowledge and personal development demonstrated by students over the time spent in higher education. As a measure of the quality of a degree, the concept of learning gain seems to be a sensible proposal, but it has been harder to implement than initially thought.

In the UK, the former Higher Education Funding Council for England funded thirteen learning gain pilot projects which involved over seventy higher education institutions (Kandiko Howson 2018). There were three aspects of learning gain that were investigated: cognitive gain, soft skills development, and employability and career readiness. There were a variety of methodologies used to try to capture learning gain, including question-naires, grade trajectories, student records and self-assessment activities. If done well, learning gain measurements could be used to provide prospective students with information; and to provide institutions with benchmarking information or data that informs strategic decisions and enhancement activities. There have been suggestions in the past that the TEF should include learning gain measurements.

Some of the challenges that were encountered within the pilots have raised questions as to whether a national exercise such as TEF could include measures of learning gain. Importantly, the pilots provided evidence that there is no 'silver bullet' metric that could be used to allow comparisons across all subject areas and institution types (Kandiko Howson 2018: 7). The challenges of measuring learning gain included a lack of student engagement, data protection issues and methodological complexities. Although there are doubts about the usefulness or practicalities of measuring learning gain, it is unlikely to disappear from the agenda altogether.

Case Study 14.1 Quality indicators for learning and teaching in Australia

The Australian Department for Education and Training has now launched the Quality Indicators for Learning and Teaching (QILT) website (**qilt.edu.au**), which is similar to the UK's UniStats website. It aims to provide transparent information for prospective students on:

- the student experience;
- graduate employment;
- graduate satisfaction; and
- employer satisfaction.

The employer satisfaction measure provides a different lens on teaching quality, by surveying employers of graduates for feedback about the graduates' skills and 'work readiness'. The employers are identified by the graduates themselves, and approximately 4,000 employers of graduates took part in the survey in 2017. The indicators of employer satisfaction are:

- overall satisfaction;
- foundation skills;
- adaptive skills;
- collaborative skills;
- technical skills; and
- employability skills.

There are clearly an increasing number of methods for gathering data that provide a range of different insights into the quality of the student experience and employment outcomes. The extent to which this public-facing information is valued by prospective students is not yet clear, but what is clear is that a larger number of measures of teaching quality are now part of the general higher education landscape.

While most universities have some form of quality framework for teaching and learning, not all academic staff engage positively with the monitoring of teaching quality in their institution (Blackmore 2009). In part this resistance comes from a heightened perception of 'managerialism' in universities (e.g. increased mechanisms of accountability), but also because quality assurance is often equated with the marketization of universities and a focus on the instrumental value of universities (e.g. graduate employment outcomes).

Anderson (2006) interviewed academic staff in ten Australian universities and found considerable scepticism about the notion of quality. Many interviewees reported that their institutions seemed to spend more time developing quality assurance frameworks than actually assuring quality. Anderson found evidence of staff resistance to quality assurance mechanisms which they perceived to be undermining the idea of quality as excellence, instead replacing it with 'instrumental, minimalist' (p. 171) notions of quality. The study concludes that there appears to be misalignment between university managers' views of quality assurance systems and those of academic staff in the disciplines. The latter typically perceived these systems as being ineffective in assuring quality in practical ways. In adopting any quality framework, it is essential to engage academic staff, particularly when it relates to curriculum design, delivery and evaluation in disciplinary settings (Aamodt et al. 2018).

Monitoring and evaluating the quality of teaching in higher education

While there is much discussion and debate about *how* to monitor the quality of teaching in higher education, there seems little disagreement about the importance of using evidence to reflect on how successful our teaching has been. This section builds on the discussion of evidence in Chapter 3 and highlights the importance of expanding our views about the range of sources that might be used to demonstrate the quality of our teaching. Research Briefing 14.2 overleaf reports on a study by Bamber and Anderson (2012) which highlights a range of ways in which academic staff at one UK university evaluate their teaching.

RESEARCH BRIEFING 14.2 Evaluating the quality of teaching

Bamber and Anderson (2012) surveyed 200 academic staff in one UK institution to find out more about their perceptions and practices relating to monitoring and evaluating the quality of their teaching.

In relation to how academic staff evaluated their work, Bamber and Anderson note that the responses revealed an unexpectedly broad range of activities. These were, ordered by the higher number of responses:

- ad hoc discussions with students;
- reflection on their own practices;
- assessment results;
- in-class feedback;
- questionnaires, whether their own or one from their university or department;
- peer observation;
- peer review of teaching materials;
- other forms of student and peer feedback;
- learning and teaching research; and
- mentoring.

When asked 'What could improve the way that you evaluate your learning and teaching practice?', some respondents were not entirely satisfied with their relative autonomy. While a number of staff wanted more team (6) or self-driven approaches (6), there was also a call for more systemic support, for centrally organized evaluation and enhancement activities such as peer observation (5) or mentoring (3).

Nonetheless, while many staff wished for 'more regular and structured processes of evaluation', they did not want bureaucratic systems, but 'a more creative approach as well as the standard approaches', and encouragement not to be so 'set in my ways'.

The next question asked: 'How are you evaluated? In other words, how do your department, institution, line manager or others get information about how your learning and teaching is going?' A number of respondents mentioned specific mechanisms, such as:

- informal student comment (11);
- informal peer feedback (11);
- module evaluations (10);
- student staff committees (8);
- appraisal (8);
- review within team (6);
- assessment results (4); and
- performance (3).

Others felt that their line managers did not receive information about their learning and teaching activity: 'I don't honestly feel that I am specifically evaluated. I think people would only notice something "going wrong" if a large number of students either failed summative assignments or complained via Personal Tutors' (pp. 10–11).

The respondents in this study acknowledged the desirability of evaluation, but they also emphasized the importance of acting on and engaging with the data; in other words, avoid collecting data for the sake of it. They also highlighted the importance of evaluation of teaching that did not require prohibitively large investments of time and effort.

Bamber and Anderson (2012) conclude that there are tensions between institutional evaluative needs and individual evaluative practices: 'The individuals wish to evaluate their learning and teaching, and institutions need to demonstrate the value of their work, but the two activities may not be aligned. Academics' intrinsic desire to do their teaching well and to demonstrate that they are doing so may be untapped in processes that overlook academic cultures and values' (p. 15).

The authors emphasize the importance of evaluation that is grounded in disciplinary contexts and is respectful of academic practices and cultures, rather than solely 'focused on institutional performativity'.

Documenting teaching achievements

One of the most common questions raised by early career academic staff is 'How do I document my teaching achievements?' We have become well acquainted with research metrics such as publications in refereed journals, but what are the equivalent metrics for teaching?

As a starting point, an evidence base may include: subject matter expertise; skills in curriculum and assessment design; skills in classroom teaching/lecturing and student advising; management and organizational skills; mentoring and supervision of colleagues, graduate students and students in practical or professional workplace settings; personal and professional development intended to enhance your teaching practice; departmental development that enhances teaching policies and practices at department level; and contribution to the wider community through teaching and sharing of expertise beyond the university (adapted from McAlpine and Harris 2002).

Having gathered information on the quality of your teaching and on the outcomes of student learning, it is important to document these data methodically over time. We examine how to do this in **Reflective Activity 16.6** in Chapter 16, where we examine the development of expertise in more detail.

Gathering student views of teaching quality

As we make decisions about how to monitor and evaluate our teaching, it is important to take account of the complexity of the task and the importance of considering multiple approaches. The construct of teaching is multidimensional and highly complex. Notwithstanding the many forms of data available, universities and governments continue to rely heavily on standard student evaluations of teaching as the primary source of data to demonstrate evidence of teaching quality. This section explores the use of surveys as a form of student feedback. Other ways of gathering student views will be examined later in the chapter.

Marsh (2007) analysed several thousand studies of student evaluations of teaching. He identified nine factors in the educational quality instruments he analysed. These factors were used to develop the Student Evaluation of Educational Quality (SEEQ) instrument. The items are: the enthusiasm of the teacher; the breadth of coverage; clarity of the organization of the course; the relevance and value of the course readings; the value that students assigned to what they were learning; the appropriateness and fairness of the assessment; the quality of the group interaction; the rapport the teacher has with the students and the appropriateness of the workload and difficulty of the course.

Another instrument to capture the multidimensional nature of teaching is The Course Experience Questionnaire (CEQ) (Ramsden 1991), which captures students' perceptions of their teaching and learning context that we discussed in Chapter 2. The Good Teaching Scale of the CEQ assesses the degree to which graduates feel that the teaching staff of their course provided students with feedback on their progress, explained course material clearly, made the course interesting, motivated students, and demonstrated an understanding of students' problems.

The six items in the scale are listed below:

1 The teaching staff of this course motivated me to do my best work.

2 The staff put a lot of time into commenting on my work.

3 The staff made a real effort to understand difficulties I might be having with my work.

4 The teaching staff normally gave me helpful feedback on how I was going.

5 My lecturers were extremely good at explaining things.

6 The teaching staff worked hard to make their subjects interesting.

The different dimensions of these instruments are important, because as Marsh (2007) argues, any global or overall rating cannot adequately represent the multidimensionality of teaching.

These measures of quality focus on the course rather than the individual teacher. This is important because when evaluations focus on the individual teacher there is evidence of gender bias in student ratings and comments about their teachers (MacNell et al. 2015; Boring et al. 2016). One analysis (Mitchell and Martin 2018) found that female professors are evaluated on different criteria than male professors. The authors state: 'women are evaluated more on personality and appearance', and also that (in line with research elsewhere) women tend to perform less well on student evaluations than their male counterparts (Mitchell and Martin 2018: 648).

The emerging research evidence of bias in student evaluations of teaching needs to be taken seriously, particularly if the evaluations are being used for decisions about promotion. However, as we have noted, the bias that has been found tends to occur within the types of student evaluations that ask specific questions about individual teachers and there are many other questions that can be asked about the learning experience which deflect attention away from the individual. It is also worth noting that evaluations that ask students for comments about learning experiences more broadly, such as the NSS which asks students to reflect on their entire degree programme, are unlikely to be influenced by bias towards individual lecturers.

Engaging the university community in teaching quality improvement through peer review of teaching

Peer review of research is a long-established process of ensuring the standard of research outputs are appropriate. Peer review of teaching is less common, but is increasingly used in universities to complement the use of student feedback on teaching quality. Case Study 14.2 highlights how Flinders University in Australia and Vanderbilt University in the USA provide information on peer review, whilst Case Studies 14.3 and 14.4 offer examples of implementing of peer review schemes.

Case Study 14.2 Peer review of teaching at Flinders University, Australia and Vanderbilt University, USA

Flinders University in Australia is one of many universities introducing peer review of teaching as an integral component of the institution's commitment to monitoring and enhancing the quality of teaching using methods other than student surveys (see **flinders.edu.au/teaching/quality/evaluation/peer-review**).

The University uses the term 'peer evaluation' and defines it as follows:

Peer evaluation is a process of collegial feedback on quality of teaching. It is a purposeful process of gathering information and evidence about the effectiveness of teaching processes and the educational environment with a view to subjecting it to constructive critical scrutiny. It usually begins with people identifying what areas they would like feedback on, and works best where the process is reciprocal between peers. A key component of peer evaluation is peer review of current practice often based on peer observation of teaching interactions. It should always be viewed as an opportunity not a threat for both parties.

An example of the University's commitment to peer review is the fact that it is embedded in their university policy on Evaluation, Monitoring and Review of Academic Programmes and Teaching. All teaching staff are required to undergo regular peer evaluation of their teaching. The webpage contains links to resources for both peer evaluators as well as those whose teaching is being evaluated. It includes Observation Record forms for undertaking the evaluation activities and more general information on peer evaluation.

Vanderbilt University's Centre for Teaching has an extensive website of support materials for teaching staff, including a detailed guide on the purposes, processes and outcomes of peer review (see **cft.vanderbilt.edu/guides-sub-pages/peer-review-of-teaching/**).

The University defines peer review of teaching as 'the prime means for ensuring that scholarship is of the highest quality, and from it flows consequential assessments that shape careers, disciplines, and entire institutions'.

Peer review is distinguished from peer observation of teaching, as it is a broader mechanism for assessing a 'portfolio of information' about a teacher. The portfolio can include:

- a lecturer's CV;
- student feedback;
- self-evaluation statements;
- student coursework;
- peer observations; and
- examples of curriculum and assessment materials.

A formative process of peer review is a valuable way of facilitating the development of teaching through collaboration between teaching staff, and reduces the reliance on student evaluations of teaching, and can form part of a process of mentoring. One of the biggest drawbacks is the time and effort required to embed peer review processes in the collegial work of the department, but when it is done well it can greatly enhance the overall teaching quality.

This section has explored various strategies for gathering and documenting evidence of teaching quality. There are many other approaches available. We explore these further in Chapter 16 when we examine the development of a teaching portfolio. A number of valuable teaching portfolio resources are available online; see, for example, Vanderbilt University Centre for Teaching (**cft.vanderbilt.edu/teaching-guides/reflecting/teaching-portfolios/#samples**).

Case Study 14.3 An example of the implementation of peer review of teaching

This case study offers one example of the implementation of a scheme for the peer review of teaching. It is presented in the form of the responses to key questions by the implementers of the peer review scheme.

1. What led you to implement peer review in your institution?

Two members of the department undertook a postgraduate teaching qualification, run internally by the university. Peer review of their teaching was intrinsic to the educational programme of this postgraduate certificate and both members of staff were convinced of the value of such an approach. The head of department, who participated in this educational process as an adviser to one of the members of staff, could see the value in peer review. It was at his suggestion that the possibility of initiating an ongoing peer review programme was investigated.

2. How did you get the programme started?

The department set aside time at its annual planning day to discuss whether or not to adopt a peer review programme, and if the answer was yes, what form it would take. An expert in peer review from the university was invited to this event to 'facilitate' the process. The various permutations as to how peer review might be initiated and then run in an ongoing fashion were presented to departmental staff and a unanimous vote led to its adoption. During this planning session, with the help of the facilitator, staff also decided upon the various parameters that would constitute our peer review programme.

3. Key features of the approach you have taken

The time demands are small; a maximum of two hours over and above the normal workload per semester. The programme is relatively informal and not linked to the performance development framework or promotion process in our department. However, individuals may opt to have their peers write reports/reviews of their teaching for inclusion in promotion applications. The only formalities in the process are that a set of guidelines is provided for staff members to follow; and that the department manager maintains a spreadsheet documenting who observed whom, doing what (i.e. lecture/tute/clinical teaching, etc.), where, and when. There is no hierarchical approach to the pairings and within five years all staff will have observed each other's teaching.

4. What is working well?

The informality of the process is non-threatening, thus participation has been undemanding on the individual and has probably led to the programme being well adhered to thus far. A number of staff have elected to have more formal reports written against their future promotion applications. The level of seniority appears not to have been a problem. There seems to have been an increase in the sharing of good teaching practices as a result of the pairings varying every semester, with innovative teaching approaches becoming more apparent across the department. Finally, it would be nice to think that as the Quality Of Teaching scores for the department have steadily increased over the period (becoming amongst the best in the faculty last semester), the 'osmosis' of improved teaching practices through the peer review programme has contributed to this.

5. What challenges remain?

To maintain the interest and commitment to the programme when the workload of this department ramps up . . . to keep the process fresh, once every staff member has observed every other staff member within the next two years or so; it is anticipated a full review of our programme will be required, followed by a collective restatement of our desired outcomes from the programme. Initially, just academic staff participated in the programme, but post-doctoral research staff with larger teaching loads have become involved of late, and it will soon be necessary to review whether the programme should also include our casual teachers, postgraduate student demonstrators, and clinical teachers.

6. What advice would you give to someone planning to implement a programme of peer review of teaching?

Get the entire organization/department/group to agree on an appropriate format for the programme; in our experience, collective ownership appears to be important to compliance. Involve someone with expertise in peer review to facilitate the establishment of clearly defined boundaries for their peer review programme. Do not formally link the programme to the promotion or PDF process; I speculate that acceptance of the programme might be an issue and that certain benefits of the programme would be lost. Even if the programme is informal, there still needs to be some documentation of the 'who, when, what, and where' for administration purposes. Plan to review the progress of the programme in the short and medium term.

For more information on sample peer review of teaching templates, see *Peer Review of Teaching in Australian Higher Education: A Handbook to Support Institutions in Developing Effective Policies and Practices*, Section 3 (pp. 27–56) (available online: **melbourne-cshe.unimelb.edu.au/__data/assets/pdf_file/0007/2297320/PeerReview Handbook_eVersion.pdf**).

Case Study 14.4 An example of the implementation of peer review of online teaching

Penn State University in the US has developed guidelines for enabling staff to undertake peer review in the context of online and distance learning, called the Faculty Peer Review of Online Teaching. Given that the amount of online teaching in the sector is increasing, and this is a trend that is unlikely to change, it is important that teachers who undertake online teaching are able to have their teaching reviewed in a similar way to those teaching face to face.

Penn State base their scheme on the 'Seven Principles for Good Practice in Undergraduate Teaching', as proposed by Chickering and Gamson in 1987. These are:

- encourages contact between students and academic staff;
- develops reciprocity and cooperation among students;
- encourages active learning;
- gives prompt feedback;
- emphasizes time on task;
- communicates high expectations; and
- respects diverse talents and ways of learning.

Interestingly, Chickering and Gamson proposed these principles some time before online education as it exists today was a possibility, but the principles have stood the test of time. The process of online peer review used by Penn State involves the standard partnership approach of one peer reviewer assigned to work with the online educator under review. The online educator completes an 'input form' which provides some contextual information, and the reviewer then works through the online materials, addressing each of the seven principles. The resulting documentation can be submitted as part of promotions and tenure processes, and/or used by the reviewer for developmental purposes.

Further information about that scheme can be found here: **facdev.e-education.psu. edu/evaluate-revise/peerreviewonline**

MONITORING STUDENT LEARNING OUTCOMES

As we discussed in Chapter 3, in reflecting on our teaching practices, we can think about the strategies we use to determine whether our students have achieved the outcomes we have articulated in, for example, programme or module guides. Typically, individuals and universities rely on the outcomes of assessment as a key indicator of student learning outcomes. Other outcome indicators might include the proportion of students who have been retained from the first to the final year of a degree programme, feedback from employers about the quality and work-readiness of graduates. Feedback from peers and professional bodies through external examination, benchmarking and accreditation is commonly used to provide impartial assessments of outcomes achieved. Self-reports from students through surveys and focus group feedback are another useful way to monitor student learning outcomes. In order to gather rich data, a range of sources is best. This section highlights several ways in which student learning outcomes can be monitored and documented.

Tools for gathering student feedback on learning

The previous section examined the use of surveys to gather student feedback on input measures such as the quality of teaching. Student surveys are also useful as a way of gathering feedback on their perceptions of the outcomes of their university learning experience. In many cases, surveys combine student evaluations of teaching with scales that invite students to reflect on how teachers have assisted them with their learning. Figure 14.1 summarizes some of the main instruments designed to gather data on students' learning experiences in different contexts and for a range of purposes.

For a more detailed discussion of types and purposes of student surveys and how they might be used to enhance the quality of learning and teaching, see Krause (2011) and Klemenčič and Chirikov (2015).

Much has been written about the limitations of student surveys (for example see Burgess et al. 2018; Spence 2019; Langan and Harris 2019), yet these forms of feedback can be useful, particularly when the feedback is part of a process in which students are made aware of how their responses are being used to improve teaching quality. Students need to see evidence that their feedback is taken seriously through a 'closing the loop' process in which the responses to student feedback are made clear to students (or explanations are given as to why certain issues cannot be easily addressed). 'Closing the loop' may be done in a range of ways, including in module outlines, on module websites or in face-to-face classes and lectures (see Chapter 12 for further ideas for doing this).

To supplement the quantitative data gathered in student surveys, some academic staff use qualitative methods such as student focus groups to gather feedback. If you use this approach, it is prudent to check on whether you need ethics approval within your institution. Depending on the kinds of questions you intend to explore, it may be desirable to invite a colleague or a research assistant to conduct interviews and focus groups with your students. You may also gather feedback from students via other staff, such as tutors or teaching assistants, who are teaching with you. This is particularly relevant in large undergraduate modules where you may have large teaching teams.

Figure 14.1
Student survey
types, purposes,
examples and
typical levels of
application
(adapted from
Krause 2011,
p. 64)

Survey type	Purpose	Example	Typical levels of application
Student evaluation of a module	To gain a summative student evaluation of a subject or unit, which focuses on the day-to-day experiences of a particular teacher or teaching team. These are usually conducted at the end of a teaching session. Formative instruments that have been developed locally are also used to supplement summative data.	Module evaluation questionnaire	Individual, teaching team, subject
Student evaluation of a whole degree programme	To gain students' retrospective evaluation of their whole-of-programme experiences.	The Course Experience Questionnaire (CEQ)	Degree programme within or across departments and faculties
Student satisfaction surveys	To gain students' evaluation of their overall experience of higher education, including extra-curricular dimensions of this experience. Institutionally developed satisfaction surveys can also be used to target specific issues, for example students' levels of satisfaction with IT provision or student services.	The National Student Survey (NSS) in the UK (see thestudent-survey.com)	Institutional, national
Targeted student experience and engagement surveys	To gain students' accounts of their experiences within and beyond the formal curriculum and the amount of time spent on study-related and other activities, such as paid work.	The National Survey of Student Engagement in the USA (see nsse.indiana.edu/html/about.cfm) The Student Experience in the Research University Survey in the USA (cshe.berkeley.edu/seru)	Institutional, national, international

Academic peer review of learning outcomes and standards

While student feedback is useful, it needs to be complemented by other forms of evidence to demonstrate the impact of students' learning experiences on their outcomes. Outcome and impact measures are among the most important forms of evidence for universities. They are of value to external stakeholders like government, employers and funding bodies, as well as to students, parents and communities.

Reflective Activity 14.1 Peer review of student outcomes with colleagues in another university

The following peer feedback form was used in the inter-university peer review project to monitor and assure final year module/subject and programme achievement standards. Consider how you might use this to expand your repertoire of evidence regarding student learning in your module or programme.

PEER FEEDBACK FORM

SECTION A: YOUR FEEDBACK ON THE MODULE/SUBJECT OUTLINE

In reviewing the module/subject outline:

1 To what extent does the module/subject outline cover all that, in your view, a final-year undergraduate module on this topic should cover? (Please circle the number that best represents your view.)

Not at all	Somewhat	Adequately	Very Well	Completely
1	2	3	4	5

Please list up to three reasons for making this rating:

_____

_____

_____

_____

2a To what extent does the module/subject outline guide explain how the assessment tasks relate to the unit learning outcomes? (Please circle.)

Not at all	Somewhat	Adequately	Very Well	Completely
1	2	3	4	5

2b To what extent does the module/subject outline explain how the assessment tasks relate to the overall graduate outcomes of the degree programme? (Please circle.)

Not at all	Somewhat	Adequately	Very Well	Completely
1	2	3	4	5

3 To what extent does the module/subject outline explain clearly (preferably with examples) the requirements for achieving at various grade levels (e.g. what is required to achieve a credit, distinction etc.)? (Please circle.)

Not at all	Somewhat	Adequately	Very Well	Completely
1	2	3	4	5

Comments

_____

_____

_____

Please use additional pages for comments if needed.

4 What, briefly, are the **best aspects** of the module/subject outline?

_____

_____

_____

5 Do you have any suggestions for **further enhancing** the module/subject outline?

_____

_____

_____

Continued over page. Please use additional pages for comments if needed.

SECTION B: YOUR FEEDBACK ON THE GRADING GUIDELINES

In reviewing the assessment grading guidelines provided for the sample assessment task/s that you are reviewing:

1 To what extent is it clear how student work will be awarded grades at different levels for that assessment task?

2

Not at all	Somewhat	Adequately	Very Well	Completely
1	2	3	4	5

Please elaborate on your response:

_____

_____

_____

3 To what extent are the grading criteria at an appropriate level for final-year undergraduate module/subject in this field of education?

4

Not at all	Somewhat	Adequately	Very Well	Completely
1	2	3	4	5

Please elaborate on your response:

_____

_____

_____

SECTION C: YOUR FEEDBACK ON ASSESSMENT TASK/S

In reviewing the list of assessment tasks which students have to complete in the module/subject outline:

1 To what extent is the range of assessment tasks suited to assessing the key learning objectives listed in the module/subject outline?

Not at all	Somewhat	Adequately	Very Well	Completely
1	2	3	4	5

Please elaborate on your response:

_____

_____

_____

_____

**Many thanks for your valuable input. Use additional pages if needed.**

As you think about how you monitor and assure the quality of student learning outcomes in your university, you may consider a multi-tiered approach to assessing student learning outcomes such as the one presented in Figure 14.2 below.

Level 1 (department and unit level) focuses on assuring learning standards through the use of moderation and calibration activities among marking teams (e.g. among teams of sessional staff at the unit level) prior to marking, and during or after marking, moderation activities. This should take place every time a unit is offered. At this level, the purpose is to assure the validity and reliability of assessment practices through ongoing calibration of markers at the unit/subject level.

At Level 2, external checks take place on a cyclical basis as a way to benchmark learning outcomes. Meeting the requirements of accreditation and professional bodies may be included in this level. The purpose at Level 2 is to benchmark processes and outcomes and to address external accreditation requirements.

Level 3 involves inter-university peer review and verification of grades and standards using an external assessor approach. The identity of the external assessor is known, no effort is made to engage in blind peer review, and graded assessment items are shared for verification purposes (i.e. the external assessor either agrees or disagrees with the grade allocated). At Level 3, the purpose is to verify learning outcomes across institutions by agreeing/disagreeing with grades allocated to final-year assessment items.

Level 4 involves blind peer review where two external peer reviewers receive anonymized unit materials and ungraded assessment items (i.e. the identity of the institution and the unit is not divulged). The two reviewers grade assessment items using criteria provided by the home institution. Feedback and graded items are returned to the home institution via a third party (project officer). The home institution receives feedback from two partners to inform practice. The identity of partners may be divulged by mutual agreement to enable further discussion. The purpose at Level 4 is to provide 'arm's length' assurance of learning standards across institutions through blind peer review and grading of final-year assessment items.

Traversing each of these levels are the discipline-based approaches to calibrating academic staff which need to continue. Calibrating staff during the assessment process is important for ensuring that staff have a shared approach to monitoring and assuring standards as they make judgements about learning outcomes. A practical approach for engaging in this calibration process at the discipline level is outlined in Case Study 14.5 facing.

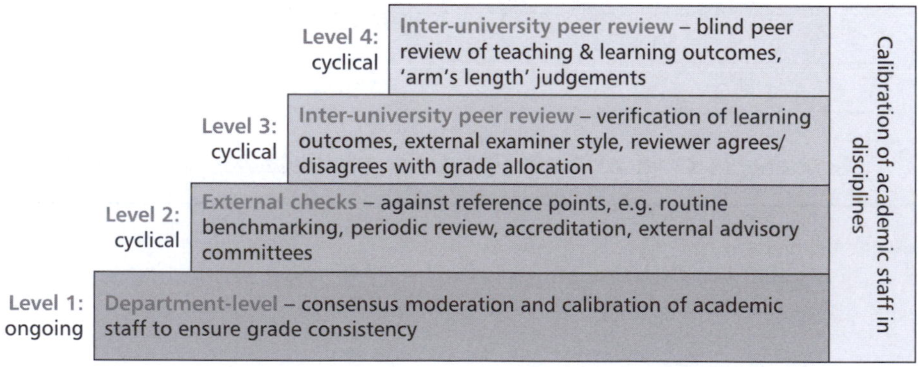

Figure 14.2 Learning Outcomes Framework (adapted from Deane and Krause, 2013)

Case Study 14.5 Calibrating learning standards

(See: **achievementmatters.com.au/overview/about-the-project**)

The Achievement Matters project developed a model for assuring stakeholders that graduates in Accounting met the new learning standards by relying on peer review of assessment design and students' assessed work. The model differs from standardized testing, using anonymous, calibrated external peer review of student learning outcomes. This promotes diversity among institutions and courses, incorporates practitioner and academic views, supports professional development, and reduces employer expectation gaps. Importantly, it also minimizes the potential consequences of standardized tests – such as teaching to the test – and places greater emphasis on the development of soft skills.

The development and assessment of accounting learning standards has considerably influenced thinking about accounting higher education. Steps in the process are summarized in Figure 14.3 below.

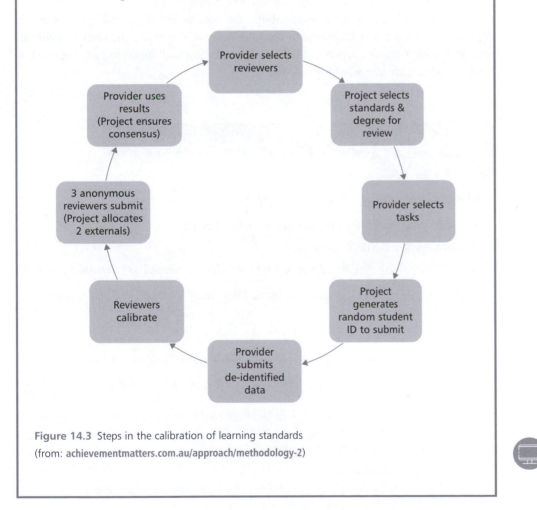

Figure 14.3 Steps in the calibration of learning standards
(from: **achievementmatters.com.au/approach/methodology-2**)

IMPLICATIONS FOR PROGRAMME DEVELOPMENT

The programme review process is critical for improving and maintaining the high quality of academic programmes. Your university probably already has a robust approach to programme review which may include five-yearly cycles with external reviewers, the use of external examiners, accreditation processes, and internal cyclical reviews at the module, programme and faculty/department levels.

Programme reviews tend to focus on whether current programme offerings are meeting the needs and interests of students and of the relevant industry, community and professional stakeholder groups. These reviews gather evidence to assist universities to determine which programmes should be continued, which should be expanded or streamlined, and which should be revised or discontinued. They also help to identify new programme offerings that might be developed in the near future.

While we will not all have responsibility for conducting large-scale programme or department reviews, it is important to consider how we might use the sorts of evidence discussed earlier in this chapter as the basis for renewing and improving our approach to module and programme design and delivery.

Programme review and improvement strategies

Academic programme reviews involve a process of:

1 identifying the review purpose, scope and audience;

2 identifying the criteria to be used;

3 collecting, analysing and documenting the evidence needed to inform the review.

Most programme reviews use similar criteria; Case Study 14.6 sets out one example.

Case Study 14.6 Elements of programme review

This case study is based on the work of Dickeson (2010) and underpins the evaluation process at the University of Regina in Canada. This involves seven elements that are considered when reviewing a programme.

1 Programme relevance.
  Goal: Assess relevance of the Department's programmes to student needs, and their responsiveness to changing needs.

---

2 Programme demand.
   Goal: Assess demand for Department's programmes.

3 Capacity to deliver.
   Goal: Assess the extent to which the Department has the capacity to deliver programmes to effectively address current and expected student needs.

4 Financial impact.
   Goal: Determine the contribution the Department makes to the overall fiscal affairs of the University.

5 Learning and research outcomes.
   Goal: Determine the Department's relative effectiveness in teaching, research and creative contributions.

6 Wider benefits.
   Goal: Determine the overall benefits and value of the Department to the University and the public.

7 Future opportunities.
   Goal: Identify innovative ideas of value to the Department's and the University's future.

Whilst Case Study 14.6 provides an example of the elements that can be focused on in programme review, it does not provide a rubric for evaluating modules and programmes. Reflective Activity 14.2 provides a more detailed group of issues to think about when reviewing a module or programme.

Reflective Activity 14.2 Evaluating your modules and programmes

Consider the following programme evaluation rubric. How would you use or adapt this for your module and/or programme? Using this rubric as a guide, conduct a mini self-review and analyse the strengths of your current module/programme, along with areas for improvement.

Sample Rubric for Evaluating Academic Programmes

1 Stated goals and outcomes for the programme:
   _____ Programme has developed a set of specific goals that are clearly identified.
   _____ Programme has developed a set of measureable outcomes that are linked to programme goals.
   _____ Programme has explained the purpose/significance and the linkages between goals and outcomes.
   _____ Programme has described the processes used for establishing its goals and outcomes.

Comments:

Explicit connection between the programme and institution's mission, vision, values and diversity statements

_____ Programme has specific mission, vision and values statements.

_____ Programme has explained its commitment to diversity and inclusion.

_____ Programme indicates how its mission, vision, values and diversity/inclusion efforts are both derived from and aligned with those of the school and campus.

Comments:

3 Evidence of programme effectiveness, with a particular emphasis on assessment of student learning outcomes.

_____ Programme identifies specific learning outcomes for students.

_____ Programme has a documented process for assessing learning outcomes.

_____ Programme provides evidence of its effectiveness, including student learning outcomes, using a variety of measures (relevant, direct, indirect, quantitative and qualitative).

_____ Programme incorporates findings from its assessment process in ongoing continuous improvement efforts.

Comments:

4 Critical questions to which the programme is seeking answers or guidance from its programme reviewers.

_____ Programme has developed specific questions for its programme reviewers.

_____ Programme explains how these questions will facilitate improvement and planning efforts.

_____ Programme questions are related to, and draw from, information contained in the self-study document.

_____ Programme questions are written in a manner that can be understood and answered by members of the programme review team.

Comments:

5 Overall assessment of the programme's strengths, areas for improvement, and plans for the future.

_____ Programme identifies and describes its strengths.

_____ Programme identifies and describes its areas for improvement.

_____ Programme identifies and describes its plans for the future.

_____ Programme establishes a linkage between information contained in the self-study document and its strengths, areas for improvement and plans for the future.

Comments:

6 Evidence-based information organized in a logical, well-written manner.

_____ Programme provides appropriate evidence to substantiate claims made in the self-study.

_____ Programme uses appropriate evidence in describing activities and accomplishments.

_____ Programme self-study is organized in a logical manner.
_____ Programme self-study is written in a manner free from major spelling, grammar and organization errors.

Comments:

(from: **planning.iupui.edu/accreditation/program-review.html** Guidelines for Academic Programme Review at Indiana University-Purdue University Indianapolis)

CONCLUSION

This chapter has presented several strategies for monitoring, evaluating and improving the quality of teaching at an individual, module, programme and institutional level. It highlights the importance of a whole-of-institution approach to quality that emphasizes the shared responsibility of all members of the university community for achieving high-quality outcomes. Several practical approaches for gathering and documenting feedback on teaching quality have been explored. We have considered the value of student surveys, along with the use of self- and peer-review approaches which represent practical ways for improving teaching quality. The chapter has also examined approaches for monitoring student learning outcomes, including the use of inter-institutional peer review of learning outcomes as part of the suite of strategies that individuals and institutions might consider.

KEY READINGS

For discussions of understanding and measuring educational quality, see:

McLean, M. and Ashwin, P. (2016) 'The quality of learning, teaching, and curriculum'. In P. Scott, J. Gallacher and G. Parry (eds), *New Languages and Landscapes of Higher Education*. Oxford: Oxford University Press, pp. 84–102.

Krause, K. (2011) 'Whole-of-university strategies for evaluating the student experience'. In M. Saunders, P. Trowler and V. Bamber (eds), *Reconceptualising Evaluative Practices in Higher Education*. London: Open University Press, pp. 139–44.

Gibbs, G., (2010). *Dimensions of Quality*. York: Higher Education Academy, (and online at **heacademy.ac.uk/assets/documents/evidence_informed_practice/Dimensions_of_Quality.pdf**).

For discussion of the tensions between academic judgement and metrics, see:

Spence, C. (2019) '"Judgement" versus "metrics" in higher education management', *Higher Education*, 77(5), 761–75.

For students perspectives on quality, see:

Jungblut, J., Vukasovic, M. and Stensaker, B. (2015) 'Student perspectives on quality in higher education', *European Journal of Higher Education*, 5(2), 157–80.

For the conceptual foundations of an approach to assuring academic achievement standards whose aims are to achieve comparability of standards across institutions and stability of standards over time, see:

Sadler, D. R. (2012) 'Assuring academic achievement standards: From moderation to calibration', *Assessment in Education: Principles, Policy and Practice*, 20(1), 5–19.

Chapter 15
Inclusion
How are we enabling opportunities?

INTRODUCTION

How do we develop and implement accessible, equitable and inclusive approaches to teaching? Considering this question is an important aspect of taking social justice seriously in our teaching practices. The United Nations Sustainable Development Goal for Education calls for the international community to 'ensure inclusive and equitable quality education and promote lifelong learning opportunities for all' within key pillars of access, equity and inclusion (United Nations 2015). The targets informing the Education Goal cover all levels of education. Of particular relevance to higher education are the need to:

- By 2030, ensure equal access for all women and men to affordable and quality technical, vocational and tertiary education, including university (SDG 4.3).

- By 2030, eliminate gender disparities in education and ensure equal access to all levels of education and vocational training for the vulnerable, including persons with disabilities, indigenous peoples and children in vulnerable situations (SDG 4.5).

In addition, commitment is made to:

- Build and upgrade education facilities that are child, disability and gender sensitive and provide safe, non-violent, inclusive and effective learning environments for all (4a).

- By 2020, substantially expand globally the number of scholarships available to developing countries, in particular the least developed countries, small island developing States and African countries, for enrolment in higher education, including vocational training and information and communications technology, technical, engineering and scientific programmes, in developed countries and other developing countries (4b).

- By 2030, substantially increase the supply of qualified teachers, including through international cooperation for teacher training in developing countries, especially least developed countries and small island developing States (4c).

(United Nations 2015, p. 17)

These goals are reflected in three of the Principles that are explored in this book.

See Chapter 4

TLRP Principles

Three principles are of particular relevance to this chapter on inclusion in teaching and learning in higher education:

Principle 1: Effective teaching and learning demands consistent policy frameworks, with support for learning for diverse students as their main focus. Policies at government, system, institutional and organizational level need to recognize the fundamental importance of learning for individual, team, organizational, institutional, national and system success. Policies should be designed to create effective and equitable learning environments for all students to benefit socially and economically.

Principle 8: Effective teaching and learning recognizes the importance of prior or concurrent experience and learning. Teaching and learning should take account of what the student as learner knows already to plan strategies for the future. This includes building on prior learning but also taking account of the emerging concurrent learning in context, and the personal and cultural experiences of different groups of students as learners.

Principle 10: Effective teaching and learning equips learners for life in its broadest sense. Learning should help individuals develop the intellectual, personal and social resources that will enable them to participate as active citizens, contribute to economic, social or community development, and flourish as individuals in a diverse and changing society. This means adopting a broad conception of worthwhile learning outcomes and taking seriously issues of equity and social justice for all.

By framing this chapter within the United Nations' key pillar of *access*, *equality* and *inclusion*, the aim is to offer opportunities to explore the unconscious biases that may shape our teaching and learning practices. The first section of this chapter examines access to, and the accessibility of, higher education in order to highlight the importance of equity issues in teaching and learning. From this, the second section of this chapter considers issues of equality in higher education focusing on the degree to which education can, and cannot, compensate for inequalities in society. Finally, the third section of this chapter explores what we mean by inclusive pedagogy and how this can be operationalized in real-world teaching and learning situations.

ACCESS

Accessing higher education

In terms of accessing higher education, there are two broad approaches that are taken to widening participation in higher education to include students from socially disadvantaged groups. The first is a deficit approach, in which any issues that arise are viewed as being the 'fault' of the student. Higher education structures and processes originally developed with the perceived needs of the 'traditional' student in mind, i.e. the relatively unencumbered young, most likely middle-class, person who likely lives on campus, has no significant family or external duties or responsibilities, does not work part-time, does not have a disability and is of the majority ethnic group (Thomas 2014, 2019; Trowler, V. 2019).

The 'non-traditional student' in this context is seen as a problem and it is assumed that he/she must adapt and change in order to fit in with the institution. The underlying assumption is of the superiority of the majority and/or dominant group which takes little account of the United Nations' commitment to provide inclusive and effective learning environments for all. The deficit approach can be contrasted with a social approach that does not view any one group as superior but rather appreciates differences between groups, values all equally and focuses on the advantages associated with a diverse body of people. It also recognizes that resources are unequally distributed between different groups (as identified in sections 4b and 4c of the United Nations General Assembly 2030 Agenda for Sustainable Development). This points to the necessity of institutional adaptation in order to respond to the diverse needs of its students. This does not constitute a lowering of standards, it may merely mean *different* methods and modes of learning and teaching. Indeed, changes to learning, teaching and assessment, based on a student-centred philosophy, should benefit all students and enrich learning experiences.

These two broad approaches to responding to widening participation can be seen in a number of models in higher education (for example, see Richardson and Skinner 1991; Banks 2002; Thomas 2005, 2019; Tapp 2015; Trowler, V. 2019), which are set out in Figure 15.1. An initial stage consists of acknowledging the under-representation of certain groups and increasing their recruitment. Subsequent early stages focus on exploring the assumed different needs of these groups and putting in place measures to bring 'up to standard' their knowledge and skills through the provision of support, usually in a peripheral, 'bolted-on' fashion. During these early stages, falling standards and 'dumbing down' are connoted with widening participation; the 'quality' of students is blamed and some students are seen as incapable of coping with the critical challenges of conventional higher education (see Hutchings 2014; Solbrekke and Helstad 2016). New types of students can be seen as weaker and in need of remediation; and generic academic support courses are provided, while the conventional nature and goals of higher education learning remain unchallenged (Murray and Nalaya 2016; Buyl 2017). Next may come an effort to acknowledge key aspects of the minority culture, albeit in a superficial manner. Here, there may be a perception that conventional teaching methods need to be improved, and new teaching technologies need to be developed, but there can be a lack of focus on interrogating deeper assumptions about the aims and values of higher education. The next stage involves a paradigmatic shift where it is recognized that previous responses have been deficit in nature. Subsequent stages are underpinned by the assumption that there is a need for structural and institutional adaptation, including at the level of teaching, to afford a more pluralistic appreciation of various cultures and traditions and a recognition of the need to ensure equality of access to tertiary education for all (as articulated in Sustainable Development Goal 4.3, United Nations 2015). While the provision of academic support may still be seen as required, it is recognized that such an approach, by itself, is inadequate (Trowler, V. 2019). Haggis (2006) argues that this stage involves problematizing conventional higher education goals and the perceived elitist, exclusionary and narrow assumptions underpinning conventional teaching and assessment practices. As she notes, this inevitably raises difficult questions about the aims and purposes of higher education which are reflected in Figure 15.1.

1. Under-representation noted – focus on recruitment

2. Concern about erosion of standards – blames 'quality' of students

3. Attempt to remediate the 'problem' (the 'weak' student). Provision of generic 'support' re. student needs in a 'bolted-on' manner

4. Acknowledgment of some aspects of 'minority' culture – superficial approach

5. Adapting teaching, assessment, and other aspects of institutional provision

6. Developing inclusive teaching – including examining assumptions underpinning traditional teaching.

> Deficit: Integration and assimilation of students into system

> Transformational: Institutional and teacher adaptation

The ongoing tendency to connect widening participation with falling standards (see Thomas and May 2010; Gourley 2015), and apparent resistance to changing practice, suggests that our current positioning remains in the early stages of the models outlined above.

The fear that admitting students with 'non-traditional' academic qualifications or lower grades negatively affects the 'quality' of students and thus lowers standards is based on unproblematized meritocratic beliefs about the relationship between achievement, 'ability', and various socio-demographic factors (Gillborn 2008) and the political problematization of student failure (Percy 2014). Clearly, a range of factors impinge on a student's capacity to perform to their abilities and we must be careful not to conflate prior academic attainment and someone's potential future abilities. The imperfect relationship between entry qualification and degree performance must also be considered, along with research which suggests that 'non-traditional' students (including those entering via 'special' entry routes) perform at least as well as their 'traditional' counterparts (for example, see Delaney et al. 2010; Keane 2011, 2013). Findings from institutional research studies have also found that those entering higher education via access or other 'non-traditional' routes in Ireland perform 'at least as well' as their 'traditional' counterparts (Kenny et al. 2010; UCCPLUS+, 2011; Share and Carroll 2013). In addition, differences in the degree classifications awarded to students from different ethnic backgrounds have been found, with white students found to achieve more highly than those from other ethnic backgrounds (see Richardson 2015; Cotton 2016), but it is unclear how these differences relate to entry qualifications.

The picture painted above highlights some of the difficulties that students might experience in making the transition to higher education, particularly as it constitutes a significant contrast to students' school (or pre-higher education) experiences. Research has found that students frequently have unrealistic expectations about workload and class size, find standards to be higher than expected and this academic 'culture shock' produces anxiety and other emotional reactions (Lowe and Cook 2003; Bennett and Kottasz 2006; Christie et al. 2008). Further, students can experience difficulty adapting to independent learning

(Thomas and Quinn 2007; Christie et al. 2008) and becoming conversant with, and proficient in, academic discourse (Hutchings 2014; Lillis and Tuck 2016).

In all, an important message for us, as higher education teachers, is that recognizing and deconstructing elitism does not imply lowering standards. Changing the way in which standards are *accessed*, by adapting higher education practices and processes, allows us to maintain high standards while making them more accessible in order to ensure inclusive and equitable quality education and promote lifelong learning opportunities for all (United Nations 2015).

Accessibility in higher education

The design (in terms of accessibility) of resources and course materials, for example, handouts, slides, notes etc., is also vitally important in inclusive teaching. Consider the format of resources; can you design some which are not solely text-based? For students with certain disabilities or learning difficulties, and for some students for whom their first language is other than English, over-reliance on text-type materials can be challenging.

Could you audio- or video-record your lectures and make them available to students on your institution's Virtual Learning Environment? Where text-based materials are created, use sans-serif fonts (e.g. Arial), as serif fonts cause difficulty for students with dyslexia. Making your lecture 'notes'/slides available to *all* students, especially in advance of the session, is recommended, so they can bring them in hard copy to the session and add their own notes. The provision of lecture notes remains a contentious issue and an essential support for many students with a disability, but also other students (see Fuller et al. 2009). Trinity College Dublin in Ireland has developed 'Accessible Information' guidelines, as part of their Inclusive Curriculum Project. The guidelines are available at tcd.ie/CAPSL/TIC/accessible-info and provide important information and support for academics in designing and formatting documents in Word and pdf, PowerPoint presentations, webpages, and even writing emails. Whilst recommendations of this nature might be viewed as somewhat basic by many academics, the fact that equality of access to higher education for vulnerable members of society, including those with disabilities, forms one of the UN Sustainable Goals (SDG 4.5, United Nations 2015) highlights the need for continued work in this area.

Similarly, while most of the suggestions throughout this chapter are relevant to all academic disciplines, at times, additional issues will arise due to the particular nature of specific subjects. In subjects which involve field work (for example, Geography, Archaeology), there may be additional issues of physical accessibility for students with certain disabilities. The selection of particular sites and related transport arrangements may need to be reconsidered depending on the profile of a student group from year to year. We need to consider if *any* of the required activities on site present difficulties for any student in the particular group and, if they do, we need to ascertain what alternative arrangements can be put in place. Similarly, in subjects involving extensive laboratory-related work, such as Chemistry, Biology, Physics and Engineering, we need to consider what barriers may be present for certain students, and how these might be addressed, preferably at the initial planning stage. Further, in some professionally oriented programmes (such as Initial Teacher Education or Nursing, for example), certain 'fitness to practice' standards need consideration, particularly in relation to disabled students. This is emerging as a complex and potentially litigious area, and it is generally the case that programmes have to demonstrate that they have employed reasonable accommodations to ensure that the particular student has an opportunity to demonstrate that he/she has achieved certain core competences. This leads us to a wider debate of examining the sorts of competences which are regarded as 'core', and how these are interpreted, and applied, in relation to other students. Such considerations should form part of discussions at the planning stage.

Research has found that both the 'hidden' and overt curriculum can marginalize some students while advantaging others, with respect to disability, ethnicity, gender, sexuality and social class (see Cheng and Yang 2015; Phipps and Young 2015; Cotton et al. 2016; Bunbury 2018). The 'hidden' curriculum refers to the unintended outcomes of the curriculum; what students actually learn through their experience of the way the course is designed, implemented and represented (see Chapter 9 on decisions about curriculum).

Reflective Activity 15.1 Curriculum audit of module

In terms of the 'overt' curriculum, it would be useful to undertake an audit of the content and resources in one of your modules. Consider to what extent the selected content and resources may be privileging or disadvantaging certain students along the various dimensions of difference amongst students considered earlier and think about what adaptations you could make.

Ask yourself:

1 Who is represented in the curriculum? Who is absent?
2 In what ways are people/groups re/presented?
3 Which topics are included? Excluded? What perspectives and arguments are presented? Left out?
4 Are multiple views represented?
5 Where relevant, in what way(s) are the experiences of different groups of people represented? How were the specific resources/materials selected? Who is represented and not represented amongst the authors of readings, for example? Representing what and whose perspectives? Can the content be adapted to make it 'speak to' more students?

Remember that we are not talking about 'watering down' content to make it less demanding; instead we are considering what we might do to the presentation of the content, to make it more inclusive, whilst maintaining the appropriate intellectual standard. What can you do to better link to and include the interests and experiences of your diverse student group? (for an example, see Jenkins et al. 2017).

EQUALITY

While education cannot compensate for inequalities in society (Bernstein 1970), it remains deeply implicated in the reproduction of the many inequalities which exist. Bell and Adams (2016) argue that teachers can still play an important role by contributing to social movements aimed at the transformation of society's inequities. In thinking about our approach to inclusive teaching, we need to ask whether, as individual teachers in higher education, we can really make a difference. Tapp (2015) explores how this can be approached in practice.

The ability to develop a critical understanding of our own position with respect to different aspects of our identities, such as social class, ethnicity and gender, lies at the heart of the United Nations' key pillar of *access*, *equality* and *inclusion* and is an important step in becoming an inclusive reflective practitioner in higher education. Through critical reflection upon, and interrogation of, the various aspects of our identities, we can begin to see the frames that different aspects of our identities put on our thinking, on our perception of the world, and on how we see, understand and interpret others', including our students', behaviours. Engaging in this work helps us to avoid 'othering' students from different groups and with different backgrounds, experiences and expectations. hooks (2003, p. 147) claims that 'there can be no intervention that challenges the status quo if we are not willing to interrogate the way our presentation of self as well as our pedagogical process is often shaped by middle-class norms'. Engaging in this work also assists us in seeing that our students' perceptions of us, as well as our own reactions to some subject material, may depend on our socio-demographic position. Bell et al. (2003, p. 465) give the example of 'Jerry' who becomes conscious of his 'blend' of social identities in the classroom:

> Even though I come into the classroom as a professional teacher, I do not leave my social identities at the door. I am a blend of such identities, for example, white, male, Jewish heterosexual, beyond middle age, working-class background, now middle class. Especially when I am conducting anti-Semitism courses, I am constantly reminded of my conflicts about being at the same time a member of a group that is targeted by anti-semitism and a member of the dominant white, male group in this society, with all of the inequities and privileges associated with each status.

Reflective Activity 15.2 builds on the reflective activities in Chapter 1 by asking you to think, and write, about your identity.

Reflective Activity 15.2 Identity, values and beliefs, expectations and practices

Reflect upon and write about:

1 Your identity (consider sex, age, profession, ethnicity, social class, family role, strengths, weaknesses, interests etc.).
2 Your educational biography*, consider in particular:
   - the educational background of your parents/guardians and grandparents/other/ extended family members;
   - your educational journey, including how you were able to progress to higher education;
   - the socio-demographic compositions (e.g. but not limited to, the ethnic and social class compositions) of the schools and other educational institutions you attended, and the community(ies) in which you have lived; and
   - why you performed in school as you did.
   - Consider also the main factors to which you attribute your educational success since/overall.
3 Your impressions of why individuals and different social groups fail and succeed in school, and in education more widely, and why you feel you have these beliefs.
4 Your views about how your beliefs and past and present experiences may be impacting upon your understandings of widening participation, student diversity, and your current professional practice/s in that context. For example, consider your expectations of and for different students in your classes.

*Some items are based, in part, on Mueller and O'Connor (2007).

In response to activities such as Reflective Activity 15.2, there can be a tendency to rationalize inequality and to cling to the principles of meritocracy in explaining our own achievement. Typical comments include 'I worked hard, that's why I did well' (see Mueller and O'Connor 2007). When considering adapting their professional practice, a common initial reaction is to focus on treating everyone the same. However, the Aristotelian dictum: 'Injustice results just as much from treating unequals equally as it does from treating equals unequally' helps us to understand that to treat students fairly does not mean treating them all the same or expecting them all to conform to a traditional model. It allows us to consider the possibility of differentiating our practice, of adapting structures, modes and processes, and that this can be done in ways which do not undermine academic standards. Reflective Activity 15.2 is a powerful exercise because it requires us to make explicit, not only our beliefs about diversity and achievement, but also to trace the potential origin of those beliefs. From the perspective of an adult, and based on our professional experience and development, we can much more critically reflect on our past educational experiences and their impact on our current practice. Understanding our socio-demographic position is a key step in developing inclusive teaching. In the next section we focus on implementing our approach to teaching for inclusion.

INCLUSION

Dimensions of student difference

Students traditionally under-represented in higher education include those from disadvantaged socio-economic groups, mature students, students with disabilities, those from minority ethnic backgrounds, part-time students, international students, and those who have vocational and other 'non-traditional' qualifications (Thomas and May 2010; Hutchings 2014; United Nations 2015). Further dimensions of difference include different faith backgrounds/religions and differences in relation to gender and sexual orientation.

Terminology used to describe traditionally under-represented groups has included 'non-traditional', 'non-standard', 'alternative-entry', 'first-generation', 'disadvantaged', 'minority', 'widening participation', 'special-admissions'. It is increasingly recognized that such terminology implies a deficit on the part of these groups and is less than inclusive. For this reason, the term 'under-represented groups' is more frequently used. In particular, Hockings (2010, pp. 2–3) argues that we should be wary of the general distinction between 'traditional' and 'non-traditional' groups:

> First, while there is some overlap between the groups considered to be non-traditional, it does not mean that all these groups are necessarily disadvantaged, although the evidence suggests that many are. Second, an individual may identify with both non-traditional and traditional groups. for example, a Black 22 year old female student from a working class family background, with A levels, a vocational qualification, and the second in the family to go to university would not 'fit' neatly into either non-traditional or traditional categories.

Thomas and May (2010) suggest that differences amongst students can be considered across a number of *dimensions*, which are set out in Figure 15.2.

Figure 15.2
Dimensions of student difference (adapted from Thomas and May, 2010)

Diversity dimensions	Examples
Educational	Level/type of entry qualifications; skills; ability; knowledge; educational experience; life and work experience; learning approaches.
Dispositional	Identity; self-esteem; confidence; motivation; aspirations; expectations; preferences; attitudes; assumptions; beliefs; emotional intelligence; maturity; learning styles; perspectives; interests; self-awareness; gender; sexuality.
Circumstantial	Age; disability; paid/voluntary employment; caring responsibilities; geographical location; access to IT and transport services; flexibility; time available; entitlements; financial background and means; marital status.
Cultural	Language; values; cultural capital; religion and belief; country of origin/residence; ethnicity/race; social background.

Therefore, rather than focusing on specific single-characteristic groups (such as mature students, or ethnic minority students, for example) a more inclusive approach involves acknowledging the wide range of differences which may impact upon any individual student's learning. As Hockings (2010), Griffiths (2010) and Solbrekke and Helstad (2016) emphasize, this does not imply that inequities related to particular groups no longer exist, but rather that each individual student has potentially multiple identities within a given context, and needs to be considered as such, rather than being approached in a certain way because he/she 'belongs' to a particular group. May and Bridger (2010, p. 6) argued that this involves moving away from the traditional approach of 'supporting specific student groups through a discrete set of policies or time-bound interventions' towards a more integrated approach through which 'equity considerations . . . [are] embedded within all functions of the institution and treated as an ongoing process of quality enhancement'.

A rationale for inclusive teaching

What, then, might we mean by the term 'inclusive teaching'? Inclusive teaching can be thought of as a way of teaching that maximizes the outcomes of learning for all learners. It is respectful of individual differences and plans for diversity by default. Bartolomé (1994) explains the need to develop what she termed a 'humanizing pedagogy' rather than a 'methods fetish', thus avoiding focusing on gathering a 'teaching bag of tricks' with regard to student diversity. We discuss humanizing pedagogies further in Chapter 17.

This brings us to an important point with regard to inclusion and higher education. In the context of high student numbers, declining resources and increasing workloads, it is understandable that we may at first seek 'the bottom line' and push to ascertain what 'trick' or strategy will address the 'problem' which presents itself. However, in most cases, there is no single 'trick' or set of 'tricks' that we can unreflexively and uncritically employ which will guarantee an inclusive approach. Rather, as discussed in Chapter 1, in order to develop inclusive teaching, important first steps involve thinking about our own identities as both learners and teachers, making explicit our core values and beliefs about learning, teaching and student diversity, developing an understanding of social justice, equality, inclusion and diversity issues in education, and especially the relationships between socio-demographic variables, educational experiences, teacher expectations and practices, and student achievement. When this work is done, it provides a very solid ground upon which we, as individual university teachers, can devise our own approach to inclusive teaching that aims to support all students in an appropriate and discipline-specific manner.

Implementing inclusive teaching

Familiarizing ourselves with the arguments and research outlined in the previous section is an important start and serves as the basis for developing our individual inclusive teaching philosophy. The next step is to reflect upon our personal educational trajectories and the various impacting factors, as well as our beliefs, values and expectations with respect to education, and the implications for our professional practice.

The way in which we implement teaching for inclusion at the individual level is inevitably tied to institutional policy and practice with respect to inclusion. Indeed, significant commitment to inclusive policies and practices by senior management in higher education is an important factor (see May and Bridger 2010; Thomas and May 2010). Irrespective of the approach taken by our institutions, as individual teachers in higher education, we can employ numerous strategies to make our approach to teaching more inclusive. We might begin by locating and reflecting on our institution's strategy or mission statement. Does inclusion appear? In what way? What language is used? How does the stated mission compare to actual practice?

The next step involves thinking about where, and in what way(s), we personally could be more inclusive in the various aspects of our professional practice. We need to think about programme and course design, learning outcomes, curriculum, planning and preparation, learning and teaching methodologies, content and resources, assessment, interactions and relationships with students, and student support. Reflective Activity 15.3 invites you to consider the various aspects of your professional practice in relation to one module and to explore opportunities for inclusivity. We will revisit this activity later in this chapter.

Reflective Activity 15.3 Opportunities for inclusivity

Choose one module/course/unit for which you have responsibility. (If you do not have responsibility for a full module, then choose one that you contribute to.) With respect to that module, consider each aspect of professional practice noted below (and you can also include any others that you feel are relevant) and explore opportunities for approaching that element in an inclusive fashion. You can include examples of inclusivity in terms of what you are already doing, as well as further opportunities which you come up with during the exercise.

Aspect of Professional Practice	Opportunities for Inclusive Practice	Potential Constraints/ Considerations
Module Design		
Preparation and Planning		
Learning Outcomes		
Curriculum, Content and Resources		
Learning and Teaching Methodologies		
Assessment		
Relationships		
Student Support		
Other?		

Course design, planning and awareness

Inclusive teaching involves catering for diversity as a core activity and involves designing our programmes and teaching to be inclusive from the start, as part of our everyday planning and preparation. Rather than making adaptations to a curriculum in a retrospective fashion, the application of Universal Design principles at programme and module design stages helps to ensure that individual differences, which may be apparent or hidden, are anticipated and catered for and are thus integrated, in a flexible fashion, in the curriculum from the outset.

The Universal Design approach emanated from the field of architecture and has been applied to inclusive higher education teaching, including in online settings (for examples, see Lanterman 2010; Capp 2017; Rogers-Shaw et al. 2018). In relation to programme or module design, it involves thinking about the potential barriers different students may experience and building in solutions to the design of the programme or module. For example, you might offer a range and a choice of assessments within your module from the start, enabling students with different styles, strengths and backgrounds to select an assessment which enables them to best demonstrate achievement of the learning outcomes. We will return to the topic of assessment later in this section. The key idea in our planning is that we anticipate and cater for differences amongst our students with respect to issues which impact on their learning in order to take account of disparities that may hinder educational attainment (United Nations 2015).

While Universal Design principles assist us in catering for individual differences which may be apparent or hidden, we can also help ourselves by building our awareness of who our students are. As individual teachers in higher education, it is a worthwhile exercise for us to reflect upon the diversity dimensions of the student populations we teach, and the student population in our institutions more broadly. To what extent do you think members of under-represented groups are members of your classes? What about at your institution and how does this compare to other institutions? How do you know? How can you find out? We cannot assume we know who our students are. If we do, we can lead to them feeling that they are not recognized within their educational setting (Abes and Wallace 2018), and we can leave them feeling either overwhelmed or under-challenged (Hockings 2010). Inclusive teaching approaches involve taking account of students' diverse interests, needs, backgrounds and prior learning. Similarly, Solbrekke and Helstad (2016) emphasize the centrality of teacher attitude to student identity formation. Thus, it is imperative to build our own awareness and knowledge about the students participating in our courses in terms of their backgrounds, cultures, experiences, entitlements, interests, prior learning and aspirations.

Certainly, it is more challenging to get to know our student groups if we teach large numbers, but it is still possible to get a broad idea of who they are. For example, if you have a class of several hundred students, you might like to send around a brief paper- or online-based, anonymous (unless a student specifically wishes to identify him/herself) 'get-to-know-you' questionnaire (you can also do this, of course, with smaller groups, but you might be able to approach it in a different way with smaller numbers). An example is provided through the case study below, which illustrates a lecturer's attempt to get to know her students in a large, lecture-based, Initial Teacher Education programme at postgraduate level.

Case Study 15.1 Getting to know your students in a large lecture-based module

Elaine Keane – National University of Ireland, Galway

In my work with student teachers (220+) in a lecture-based module on Education, Diversity and Social Justice, I send a request to all students before they commence the programme, with a Survey Monkey link, to inquire about specific issues. I emphasize that the purpose of the questionnaire is for me to get to know them a little and I stress that participation is voluntary and anonymous, unless they wish to self-identify. Because of the nature of the programme upon which they are embarking, I include questions about any past formal or informal teaching or youth work experience. However, I also include a range of questions relating to their sex, age, first language (and other language competence/s), disability, higher education entry route (e.g. whether they completed a pre-entry access course or entered higher education via some other 'non-traditional' route), ethnicity, and their caring responsibilities. I include a question on their under-graduate programme, including the institution in which they completed their primary degree. I also ask about their undergraduate subjects. This allows me to get a feel for their level of prior learning in terms of my discipline (Sociology of Education). I also ask them to contact me if there is anything else they feel I ought to know at any time. I am explicit that if they have a particular need, they should contact me about it to let me know. Survey Monkey does most of the analysis for me and allows me to see the profile of this large class group at a glance, and I spend a bit of time getting to know my students in this way. It is also very interesting to me to track the socio-demographic composition of this programme group over time. I put the key findings on some slides and share these with my colleagues, but also with my students in my first lecture of the module. I embed it in a discussion of the socio-demographic constitution of our teaching populations nationally and internationally, and why that matters. Each year, my students are intrigued to see who they are as a group, and how they compare to national and international profiles. It really engages them. I also use this exercise as an opportunity to ask the students to get to know each other a little, by giving them five minutes in the lecture to introduce themselves to people either side of them and by encouraging graduates from my institution to introduce themselves to graduates from other institu-tions to help them to get to know their way around.

In this exercise, despite its anonymous nature, it is important to remember that some students still may not disclose an issue (often a disability). Therefore, I am very careful to be clear about the purpose(s) of the survey, in case students worry about disclosing something (even anonymously) which they worry may work against them in the future.

In order to respond to a particular entitlement a student may have (for example, a student with dyslexia who is entitled to certain accommodations), you need to know *who* that student is. It is important to check your particular institution's approach for informing you about students with specific entitlements, and depending on what the approach is, you may also need to tell your students to inform you specifically. This latter situation is far from ideal, however, as it puts the onus on the individual student to inform each of their lecturers and to negotiate the same accommodation multiple times.

Completing activities like those outlined in Case Study 15.1 will mean that we have significant information about the profile of our students. This kind of information can assist us in planning how best to design and plan courses that have the potential to include all. It may also be necessary to consult relevant policies and guidelines at local, institutional and national level to develop your response in relation to their requirements. When planning, we need to remember to think broadly about inclusivity; it involves more than catering for specific entitlements. It is about interrogating each aspect of our professional practice and exploring possibilities to be more inclusive.

A key aspect of our planning includes the identification of programme/module aims and learning outcomes. Think about your aims and learning outcomes. How might these impact upon different students? Think about the learning outcomes you set in relation to skills, competencies and knowledge. What is essential and what can you be flexible about? Within various professional fields, we may also need to consider and make provision for 'fitness to practise' standards.

Clarity with respect to outcomes, expectations and everyday procedures and processes is a very important aspect of inclusive teaching; we need to ensure that students clearly understand what is expected. At the planning stage, keep in mind the need to be flexible and to employ variety in relation to teaching, assessment and the creation of materials. Remember that varying teaching and assessment methods benefits all students, not just those from traditionally under-represented groups (Tapp 2015; Buyl 2017). Consider also potential issues relating to facilities, timetabling and scheduling for certain students as well as how you will make online environments accessible (Rogers-Shaw et al. 2018).

Inclusive learning and teaching

It is important for us to acknowledge that there is no one 'correct' inclusive approach to learning and teaching. Understanding and trying to connect with our students' diverse prior knowledge, interests and aspirations is fundamental to good teaching. As we discussed in Chapter 11 on Teaching, to do this we need to know who our students are (hence the activity in Case Study 15.1), rather than making assumptions and basing our approach to teaching and learning upon those assumptions. In addition, we need to be aware of potential barriers to learning such as the need to 'eliminate gender disparities in education and ensure equal access to all levels of education and vocational training for the vulnerable, including persons with disabilities, indigenous peoples and children in vulnerable situations' (United Nations 2015, SDG 4.5).

Ensuring that learning outcomes are inclusive, employing flexible and varied methods, using a range of teaching materials, being very clear in all aspects of what we do, carefully preparing accessible materials and resources and making them available in a timely fashion, taking care over our language, and making efforts to involve students as much as possible are all basic elements of good teaching which take on added significance when aiming to be an inclusive teacher.

The literature regarding inclusive teaching tends to highlight approaches to learning and teaching which are active, student-centred, collaborative, co-operative and 'connectionist' (see, for example, Gourley 2015; as well as Chapters 11 and 12). Such approaches can be less didactic and more engaging for all learners, as well as providing important opportunities for students from diverse groups to work together in collaborative ways on meaningful academic tasks. Approaches such as co-operative learning can be inclusive when they are carefully planned and involve setting important socio-relational, and skills-based, as well as cognitive, learning outcomes, thus facilitating relationship building between students from diverse backgrounds. Nonetheless, as teachers in higher education, it is important for us to be aware that those from under-represented groups may reject, or at least under-participate in, extra-curricular activities and the broader social aspects of higher education (for example, see Keane 2011a, 2012; Gourley 2015).

While it may seem, at first glance, that students' social and extra-curricular engagement may not be important considerations for us as individual higher education teachers, research has found that engaging with the extra-curriculum and building peer relationships impact upon student retention in higher education and their future success in the labour market (Thomas and Quinn 2007; Thomas and May 2010). However, Thomas and May (2010) also caution that collaborative approaches do not work well for *all* students. For example, some students may not feel comfortable working closely with other students. To be an effective reflective practitioner, we have to critically reflect on the specific context in which we are proposing to employ a particular strategy, as there is no 'one-size-fits-all' approach in terms of an inclusive teaching strategy. Each and every situation needs to be carefully considered.

Assuming diverse levels of prior learning, we cannot assume a common starting point amongst our students. In this way, Northedge (2003b, p. 19) encourages us to move away from traditional conceptualizations of teaching which focus on content and knowledge. He explains:

> Any theorisation that represents teaching as presenting 'items' of knowledge to be internalised raises the same difficulty. With a diverse student body, no fixed start or end point can be assumed and, consequently, no selection of items can be appropriate to the needs of all. The challenges of diversity demand a more fluid conception of teaching.

Instead, the move from 'transmission', knowledge and content-focused approaches to modes of 'collective inquiry' creates learning environments where there are 'optimal degrees of freedom' (see Buckridge and Guest 2007; Gourley 2015) and supportive 'knowledge communities' (Northedge 2003a). Such approaches stress making explicit and modelling aspects of disciplinary practice without 'spoon-feeding' (Haggis 2006; Lanterman 2010). This, it has been argued, gives students the opportunity to actively participate in knowledge communities at different levels (Northedge 2003a), and encourages teachers to design learning environments that are open enough to allow different students to reach for and attain different levels, whilst appropriate levels of initial support are provided (see Buckridge and Guest 2007; Hutchings 2014). Thus, in order to create richer forms of engagement, the traditional approach of generic 'study skills' courses and focusing on individual problems moves instead towards 'a detailed investigation of discourses and power in specific disciplinary contexts' (Haggis 2006, p. 526) in order to reconsider pedagogic priorities (Hathaway 2015).

In summary, there is general agreement that we need to focus less on how we might adapt content and knowledge, and more on processes and practices that make that knowledge accessible to students within our specific disciplinary contexts. The notion of *being explicit* about processes and practices is key and Reflective Activity 15.4 has been designed in order to enable some exploration of thinking, doing and being within a discipline impacts upon the processes and practices in the classroom.

Reflective Activity 15.4 Thinking, doing and being in your discipline

1 Think about the typical *ways of thinking*, *doing and being* in your academic discipline. Generate a list of these and write a few sentences to describe them.

2 For each way of thinking, doing and being, try to articulate what precisely are you 'doing' when you do 'x' in your discipline? What steps are involved? Why do you do it that way?

3 From your professional experiences, how do think your students make sense of practices and processes in your discipline?

4 How might you make explicit, and model, these processes and practices in your discipline for your students to observe?

It may, at first, be somewhat difficult to articulate these processes, partly because they have become so 'normalized' within our specific disciplines. However, identifying and articulating them is a necessary precursor to modelling them, and making them explicit, to our students. This is not about giving students 'sample/model answers', but instead it involves, for example, clearly explaining to our students what is meant by (for example) 'critically discuss' and working through an exercise so that they can see our thought processes and the practices in which we engage when working through the exercise. Having modelled the approach and made the process explicit, it becomes possible to design learning situations in which students have an opportunity to demonstrate their engagement in an aspect of disciplinary practice, to observe others doing so, and to reflect on this, and for us to provide feedback. In this sort of collective inquiry approach, students still have the responsibility for reading in and thinking about the topic. The teacher, then, has the responsibility to create learning situations in which students have a chance to develop and compare their interpretations of the topic. It is important for us to remember that making process explicit is not about 'dumbing down' standards. It is about facilitating access to processes and practices in your discipline, whilst maintaining the same level of intellectual demand. Rather than depressing standards, clarity and explicitness with respect to disciplinary practices and processes will likely lead to all students achieving more highly. While considering these issues, you may be able to identify specific processes and practices in your discipline which present challenges, as well as opportunities, with respect to inclusion.

A relatively common concern is the apparent reluctance of some students to actively participate in group sessions (on this, see also Chapter 12, on Communication). It is important to understand that, for some students, the reason for not participating may be due to a lack of confidence in language skills and/or being accustomed to a significantly different academic culture; we need to be patient and explicit about values if the latter is the case. Of course, as was discussed in Chapter 12, we cannot and should not assume that students who appear to be silent and passive are not engaged.

In addition, a lack of confidence can also manifest itself as over-engagement in some respects – for example, with some students appearing to be 'very demanding' in terms of asking additional questions or seeking multiple rounds of feedback. This can be related to the very high stress levels experienced by some students, particularly with respect to assessment tasks. We can support these students by being explicit in our feedback on assessment tasks about what was done well, what could be improved, and how. We must also reflect upon our own interactions with students, including our questioning strategies (see also Chapter 6, on Relationships). For example, in group settings, who do you call on to answer questions? Who tends to answer and who tends not to answer? Is the participation of some students favoured (however unconsciously) over others? Might we be unconsciously showing preference for some groups or some students over others (Griffiths 2010)?

Being aware of the language we use, both in terms of English language for those for whom their first language is other than English and of disciplinary language, is also vital. Speaking clearly, explaining meanings and terminology clearly, taking care with our choice of words, avoiding colloquialisms, improves the learning environment for all of our students. One way of helping our students to build a mental structure of the topic we are teaching and its link to, and position in, the module overall, is by commencing the session with an explicit explanation of the link to the previous session, and then telling students the key aims of the particular session. Then, we flag or signpost each aspect as we go through the session parts, and sum up the key points at the end, before linking to the next session. Where possible, after class, we might wait behind for a few minutes (and tell students we are doing so) for anyone who might like to ask a question in person rather than in front of the class.

Maintaining and exhibiting high expectations of all students is another basic, but fundamental, aspect of effective teaching. In the area of inclusion, we must continually guard against viewing students from under-represented groups as being 'problematic' and/or as inevitably needing additional support. As has been argued, working-class students, for example, have been found to be extremely resilient and committed, often in the face of very significant additional challenges (see Crozier et al. 2008). However, expecting all students to be successful 'independent learners', particularly in the early stages at undergraduate level, and especially for those viewed as 'under-prepared', may be unrealistic. Crozier et al. (2010) argue that for working-class students who may be seen as under-prepared, more controlled learning environments, with higher levels of support, explicitness, monitoring and encouragement, can be especially useful in the first year.

An important theme running through the literature on inclusive teaching is the need to create a safe and respectful space for student involvement, discussion and collaboration so that they feel supported, appropriately challenged, respected and valued with regard to their diverse life, educational and cultural experiences (see Hockings 2010; Hutchings 2014; Percy 2014). The ways in which we interact with our students in the classroom, through questioning, listening, explaining, involving, directing, inviting comment, allowing discussion, organizing, and so forth, all impact on how the classroom climate is perceived and experienced by different students (see also Chapter 6 on Relationships and Chapter 12 on Communication). Indeed, Hockings (2010, p. 32) draws on a number of studies which suggest that 'teacher identity, teaching approaches and methods of questioning, facilitating and chairing discussions are key factors influencing who speaks and who remains silent in class, who is included and who is excluded'.

While many of the recommendations discussed throughout this chapter are relevant irrespective of the type of learning environment in question, some additional issues may require our consideration with regard to online learning environments. In an online learning environment, we need to ensure that the website or Virtual Learning Environment (VLE) is as accessible and user-friendly as possible. To address this, you might consider sending some brief and clear guidelines on accessing and navigating the relevant site/ VLE, well in advance of when students need to engage with the medium. Clarity, consistency, and good organization are just as important – if not more so – in an online learning environment as they are in face-to-face contexts. Considering the format of documents available on the VLE or website is also important – for example, pdf, html, rtf, etc. In this regard, it would be useful to request that your institution's Disability Service (and other relevant Student Services offices, depending on who your students are) test the site to examine its accessibility. For instance, certain types of software (such as those students with a disability may need to use) may not be compatible with the particular VLE or website you are using. In addition, while an online learning environment can be more inclusive in allowing us to include students who might not be able to participate in person, we also need to guard against the isolation which can sometimes arise for some individuals studying in this way. We also need to be careful to build in opportunities for meaningful student interaction, preferably through collaborative work. Where you deem it appropriate and useful for students, consider the interaction and collaboration which chat facilities, discussion fora and web cams might afford. Our earlier discussion of perceptions of student passivity and engagement are also relevant here. Due to the nature of the online environment, there are additional challenges for the university teacher in ascertaining the extent to which students are engaging and actively participating.

Dealing with sensitive material

A common concern expressed by teachers in higher education (and in other sectors) relates to the challenges inherent in handling sensitive material and situations which can potentially involve some level of conflict (see Bowl 2005). This may arise whether or not the material being studied is seen to be 'sensitive'. If we feel un/under-prepared, it is understandable that we might shy away from either the specific issues, opportunities to discuss these issues, or both, in the classroom context. This is where **Reflective Activity 15.2**, on exploring our socio-demographic identity and positionality, can play a vital role. Becoming more open to, and skilled at, handling potentially sensitive issues starts with self-understanding with respect to our own dimensions of difference, the identification of our beliefs with respect to diversity, and a consideration of the implications of these beliefs for our practice.

Reflective Activity 15.5 Uncovering concerns about dealing with sensitive issues

Think about a situation which has arisen (or might arise) for you which involved a sensitive issue, sensitive material, and/or some level of conflict in the classroom. Imagine you are there now, and in the moment. Briefly outline the specifics of the situation. Then describe in detail what is going on, both for you and the others involved. Describe how you are feeling. If you are feeling uncomfortable, try to articulate how and why. What is making your heart beat that little bit faster? What precisely are you nervous/worried/concerned about? Be explicit to yourself about your concerns. Write as much as you can.

When you have finished, perform a 'content analysis' of what you have written. To do this, read through it a few times, and underline key words and phrases. Identify key ideas which may be articulated in different ways, and keep an eye out for repetition, common themes, but also contradictions. Write a summary of the key aspects of your reflection, with the aim of uncovering your main concern in this situation. Next, think about how you might address this/these main concern/s. What do you need to do? Read some literature about a specific topic or about how to go about doing something? Update your skills in relation to some aspect of your practice? Consult a colleague or adviser? After a little bit of work, construct an action plan which allows you to approach the situation in an inclusive way that allows you to feel more comfortable.

Assessment

Chapter 13 explored the issues of assessment and feedback in detail, as well as assessment for social justice. *Inclusive* assessment refers to 'the design and use of fair and effective assessment methods and practices that enable all students to demonstrate what they know, understand and can do' (Hockings 2010, p. 34). In this context, traditional assessment modes and methods are frequently critiqued with respect to their underlying assumptions, particularly in terms of notions of 'objectivity' (see Sadler 2009), and are sometimes regarded as being potentially unfair to students from traditionally under-represented groups (see Read et al. 2005; Hounsell 2007; Hutchings 2014). Research on the attainment gap for disadvantaged students suggests that multiple factors contribute to differential degree classifications including: social class; engagement in paid work; family history of higher education; and experience of marginalization, resulting in a complex situation marked by the intersectionality of disadvantage and discrimination (Richardson 2015; Cotton et al. 2016; Jones 2018).

As with aspects of curriculum and teaching, it is essential to critically consider and adjust the core assessment system from the outset, rather than making special provision for specific groups in a retrospective fashion. Thus, our aim is to consider all assessment approaches that a student will experience at both programme and module levels and, where necessary, to consider how to diversify and make a range of equivalent assessment options available, rather than relying on one or two methods which may consistently privilege, or disadvantage, certain groups. In higher education, there has been a general tendency to over-rely on terminal written papers and/or examinations. When speaking from the perspective of students with a disability, Florian (2015) questions whether formal, written, timed, previously unseen examinations are really necessary in order to test the required skill and knowledge within a particular discipline for *any* student. A central recommend-ation is to be *flexible*, where possible, with regard to mode and format. Given this, it is important to question how flexible our assessment methods are. Could we offer the possi-bility of students demonstrating learning in another format? Could we be flexible with deadlines for students who may be experiencing additional challenges? Could we allow students to choose an assessment option from a range of options? The Inclusive Curriculum Project at Trinity College Dublin offers an interesting case study on the topic of choice in assessment in the BSc in Occupational Therapy programme. The lecturers involved discuss their experiences of designing the approach used at this link: **tcd.ie/CAPSL/TIC/ guidelines/assessments/assessment-choice.php**

It has also been argued that we need to remember that students from under-represented groups tend to suffer significantly (and more so than those from 'traditional' groups) from a lack of academic self-confidence, generally underestimating their abilities, overestim-ating what is required, and enduring significant assessment-related anxiety and stress (see Keane 2011b; Percy 2014). This is another area where explicitness about processes, practices and requirements plays an important role; clarity and explicitness can go a long way towards allaying the fears of our students. While this should feature throughout the learning and teaching process, clarity and explicitness should also be the aim in the provi-sion of formative feedback.

Clarity with respect to our *language* in, and of, assessment is also vital for students whose first language is other than the language of instruction. Unless we are careful, we may end up assessing linguistic competency rather than disciplinary knowledge and under-standing. We need to work to ensure all our students (but especially those whose first language is other than the language of instruction) are familiar with, and understand, key terms used in assessment items and related instructions.

Biggs (in conversation with Buckridge and Guest 2007) pointed to the need to create an environment with 'optimal degrees of freedom' in learning and assessment; a learning environment which is open enough to allow different students to reach for and attain different levels alongside the provision of appropriate levels of initial support.

Reflective Activity 15.6 Considering our assessment approach

Identify one module for which you are responsible or to which you contribute. List all assessment items pertaining to the module, in terms of mode/format, weighting, and any other relevant details. Identify any choices the students may have with regard to assessment. Reflect on general student performance on this module in the past, and note any issues which frequently arise or which you notice. For each item, consider whether any students may be consistently privileged or disadvantaged by its nature. Examine your learning outcomes, and consider the extent to which your assessment is congruent or aligned with these outcomes. What have you noticed? What assumptions may you have made in the design of assessment for this module? What could you do at overall module level to build in more (equivalent) assessment options, ensure greater clarity and explicitness, to be more flexible?

In the various sections on implementing inclusive teaching, we have examined issues relating to course design and preparation, curriculum and resources, learning and teaching methodologies and assessment. Having engaged with these areas, look again at your responses to **Reflective Activity 15.3**. Redo the exercise, the frame of which is copied below, drawing on what you have learned from this chapter.

Reflective Activity 15.7 Opportunities for inclusivity – revisited

Aspect of Professional Practice	Opportunity/ies for Inclusive Practice	Potential Constraints/ Considerations
Module Design		
Preparation and Planning		
Learning Outcomes		
Curriculum, Content and Resources		
Learning and Teaching Methodologies		
Assessment		
Relationships		
Student Support		
Other?		

CONCLUSION

In this chapter, we have considered the rationale for inclusive teaching, and what is involved in developing and implementing such an approach to teaching at a number of levels. Many examples of effective and innovative practices in the area of inclusion at institutional level can be found in May and Bridger (2010), and Thomas and May (2010). In addition, Liz Thomas (2019) outlines three approaches that institutions may adopt when responding to the challenge of widening participation: the academic, the utilitarian and the transformative. However, as we have seen, there is much that we, as teachers in higher education, can do to model a perspective that normalizes diversity and assists social integration, to promote positive attitudes to diversity amongst students and colleagues, and to develop and embed inclusion in our approach to teaching.

So much of what is suggested as 'good teaching for diversity and inclusion' is simply good teaching – for example, clarity, explicitness, careful planning, careful language use, maintaining and demonstrating high expectations, involving students, listening to students, offering choice, varying teaching and assessment methods, offering guidance and support, and carefully choosing/designing resources. Whilst this approach may initially take more time than do some traditional teaching approaches, the bulk of the additional work can be completed at the initial redesign phase through the application of Universal Design principles. Nonetheless, there is a danger that it will be seen as too labour-intensive a task for individual academics in institutions which may not require or adequately support or reward this work, particularly relative to research outcomes. Additionally, in a context of declining resources and simultaneously, in some countries, rising student numbers, it is understandable that this area is regarded as challenging.

Simply taking the time to familiarize ourselves with the rationale for an approach to teaching of this kind and becoming more conscious of being inclusive in our everyday professional practice is a start. To return to the United Nations' key pillars of *access, equality and inclusion*, it is incumbent upon us all to recognize the centrality of equity and inclusivity to scholarly activity.

KEY READINGS

For the UN Sustainable Development Goal for Education, see:

un.org/sustainabledevelopment/education

For a synthesis of research of inclusive learning and teaching in higher education, see:

Hockings, C. (2010) *Inclusive Learning and Teaching in Higher Education: A Synthesis of Research*. York: Higher Education Academy. Available at: **heacademy. ac.uk/system/files/inclusive_teaching_and_learning_in_he_synthesis_200410_0.pdf**

For help to develop an inclusive approach to teaching, including examples of inclusive practice at a number of levels and stages and in a range of subjects in higher education, see:

Thomas, L. and May, H. (2010) *Inclusive Learning and Teaching in Higher Education*. York: The Higher Education Academy. Available at: heacademy.ac.uk/ system/files/inclusivelearningandteaching_finalreport.pdf

For information on developing and embedding inclusivity at both policy and practice levels within higher education institutions, see:

May, H. and Bridger, K. (2010) *Developing and Embedding Inclusive Policy and Practice in Higher Education*. York: The Higher Education Academy. Available at: heacademy.ac.uk/system/files/developingembeddinginclusivepp_report.pdf

For guidelines on accessible online education, see:

Rogers-Shaw, C., Carr-Chellman, D. and Choi, J. (2018) 'Universal design for learning: Guidelines for accessible online instruction'. *Adult Learning*, 29(1), 20–31.

Part five

Deepening understanding

Part 5 is the final, synoptic part of the book. It integrates major themes through an examination of teacher expertise and professionalism. 'Expertise' (Chapter 16) focuses on how we can bring together reflective teaching and the scholarship of teaching and learning in order to develop expert teaching. The chapter returns to the ten principles outlined in Chapter 4 and considers how we might develop these through our teaching. Chapter 17 on 'Professionalism' considers the role that teaching in higher education plays within our societies and suggests how it might contribute to societal change.

Chapter 16
Expertise

How do we develop a career-long engagement with teaching?

INTRODUCTION

In this chapter, we examine how we can deepen our understanding and expertise as higher education teachers through ongoing personal and professional development. This builds on our discussions of Reflection in Chapter 3. The chapter begins with an overview of what it means to develop our 'expertise' in higher education teaching and puts this in relation to the notion of scholarship of teaching and learning. We look at the importance of informal learning and the influence of the collegial workplace in relation to our engagement and professional development. This chapter considers some of the ways in which universities are trying to appraise and reward engagement with teaching through a variety of reward mechanisms and promotion policies that focus on recognizing teaching excellence, scholarship of teaching and learning, and leadership in learning and teaching as key performance areas. Finally, we consider some of the milestones that might typically characterize an academic career and how we can engage with respect to our career trajectory and promotion opportunities, as well as what to consider when putting together a teaching portfolio.

See Chapter 4

TLRP Principles

Two principles are of particular relevance to this chapter on expertise in teaching and learning in higher education:

Principle 2: Effective teaching and learning depends on the scholarship and learning of all those educators who teach and research to support the learning of others. The need for lecturers, teachers and trainers to learn through engaging with research to improve their knowledge, expertise and skills for teaching should be recognized and supported.

Principle 3: Effective teaching and learning recognizes the significance of informal learning to developing specific expertise. Learning with friends, families, peer groups and professionals should be recognized as significant, and be valued and used in formal processes in higher education

WHAT DOES IT MEAN TO BE AN EXPERT TEACHER IN HIGHER EDUCATION?

Are we born to teach or is this an ability that can be developed? In this book we believe in the latter. As we discussed in Chapter 1, who we are as university teachers is shaped by our previous and current experience as well as where we see ourselves going in the future. This means that our sense of our teaching careers is dynamic and changing rather than something that is fixed. Or, as Boyer (1990, p. 24) puts it: 'good teaching means that faculty, as scholars, are also learners'.

This is a central underpinning assumption of this book. As we gradually engage with teaching, building a bank of experiences, perhaps participating in various teaching contexts, meeting a diversity of students, we have the opportunity to constantly reflect upon those experiences, engage in conversations and interactions with others and thereby engage with our own professional development. As Peter Kugel highlights in a classic essay (1993), 'How professors develop as teachers', the gradual, progressive and yet iterative focus on ourselves, our subjects, and on our students changes with experience as well as with every new teaching opportunity. When we are new to teaching, it is common to start focusing on ourselves, perhaps standing in front of a group of students, being a bit nervous and wondering whether we'll be able to answer their questions. We put efforts into preparing by reading and structuring the subject, so that we'll be able to present it to students in a coherent manner. With experience, Kugel describes, it becomes easier to focus on who the students are, what they already know and to think about activities that will engage students with learning the subject, with less focus on ourselves as teachers. However, whatever our level of teaching expertise, it is important to consider how we plan to develop this expertise further in a systematic and principled way. Thus this chapter will be relevant for both those new to teaching and those with many years of experience, although they are likely to take different things from it.

Teaching expertise

An expert is defined as one who has extensive skill or knowledge in a particular field; a novice, on the other hand, is someone new to a certain task or situation, and who demonstrates rudimentary rather than advanced, sophisticated capabilities in the field (*Collins English Dictionary*, 1979). A key characteristic of expert performance is continuous learning and development through a process of *deliberate practice* (Ericsson et al. 1993).

There is a substantial literature in the area of expertise development and many models have been proposed to depict the ways in which individuals progress from novice to expert status (see Forde and McMahon 2019 for a review of literature on expertise in teaching, and Tagg 2019 for a discussion of the nature of expertise in higher education). The model of Dreyfus and Dreyfus (1986) is one of the more widely known models. While its focus was originally on clinical skills development, it has been acknowledged as having wider applications across discipline areas. This model comprises five levels of proficiency, from novice to advanced beginner, followed by competent, then proficient and finally expert status. These levels reflect changes in three aspects of skilled performance. The first involves transition from reliance on abstract rules and principles to the use of personal, lived experience as the basis for making informed decisions. A second characteristic of the movement from novice to expert status reflects a changing view in one's perception of a situation. A novice tends to view a situation as a compilation of equally relevant parts; whereas an expert is more likely to perceive a situation more holistically with some parts more relevant and significant than others. A third characteristic of the shift from novice to expert status involves the capacity to move from being a 'detached observer' to an 'involved performer' who is actively engaged in a situation (Manley and Garbett 2000).

This model highlights the fact that an expert is characterized by the capacity to learn from experience, tacit knowledge and intuition, as opposed to rigid adherence to the rules and guidelines of others. This often-referenced model of expertise has been criticized, though, mainly for its lack of including systematized, documented, generalizable knowledge as part of the expert role (Dall'Alba and Sandberg 2006). We will return to this issue further when we later in this chapter reflect upon the relationship between reflective teaching and scholarship of teaching and learning.

Extending the thinking of Dreyfus and Dreyfus, Hattie (2003) contends that, in the domain of teaching, teacher expertise makes a difference to the quality of student learning. He posits that students who are taught by expert teachers demonstrate a more integrated and coherent understanding of concepts; thus, teacher expertise in turn fosters a higher level of abstraction among students. Hattie proposes five key attributes of expert teachers. They can:

1 identify essential representations of their subject;
2 guide learning through classroom interactions;
3 monitor learning and provide feedback;
4 attend to emotional attributes; and
5 influence student outcomes.

Kenny et al. (2017) offer a developmental framework for teaching expertise that involves 'multiple facets, habits of mind (or ways of knowing and being), and possible development activities'. The framework introduces three foundational habits of mind – inclusive, learning-centred and collaborative ways of knowing and being – that in turn make up the ground for five interwoven and non-hierarchical facets of teaching expertise: (1) teaching and supporting learning; (2) professional learning and development; (3) mentorship; (4) research, scholarship, and inquiry; and (5) educational leadership. This framework resonates well with the points that will be made towards the end of this chapter relating to collating a teaching portfolio. Kenny et al. (2017) also highlight that within each of the above-mentioned facets of teaching there is a 'developmental continuum from explore, to engage, to expand, demonstrating a shift from the growth of oneself within a local context toward contributing to the growth of others'.

Kreber (2002) defines three levels of teaching competence, which can be viewed as an expansion of the concept of expertise. Her three-tiered model also highlights the importance of making knowledge about teaching and learning explicit, systematically observed and documented as part of professional development. Her model defines *excellent teachers* as those who know how to motivate their students, how to convey concepts, and how to help students overcome difficulties in their learning. Teaching *expertise* is characterized also by theoretical knowledge about teaching and learning, and would define those teachers who read literature and engage with research about teaching and student learning. The third level, *scholarship of teaching and learning*, in her model contains dimensions of making systematic observations and inquiries into teaching and student learning, relating this to previous public knowledge, and some dimension of documenting and going public with the findings. We will return to this later in this chapter.

Reflective Activity 16.1 Reflecting on teaching expertise

Consider Hattie's (2003) five dimensions of teaching expertise listed above. Identify at least one experienced, expert teacher in your institution and ask them if you can spend time observing one or more of their classes. Arrange a time to meet for coffee to talk through their views of the following five dimensions.

Questions for reflection:

1 Can you see evidence of one or more of these five dimensions in their teaching? And/or in their approach to curriculum design?
2 Ask your expert colleague(s) whether they would add or remove anything from the five dimensions above. Why? Why not?
3 Use this discussion as the basis for considering your own journey from novice to expert teacher in higher education. Where would you place yourself on the novice–expert spectrum?
4 Identify at least one area in which you would like to develop further expertise and discuss with your colleague(s) strategies for developing expertise in this area.

Content, pedagogical and curricular knowledge

Is it sufficient to be an expert in your discipline in order to be an expert teacher? Most research in this area would say no. No doubt, disciplinary expertise is central and internationally, student surveys highlight the fact that students identify subject expertise and up-to-date knowledge among their lecturers as central to a valuable university experience (QAA 2012). However, subject knowledge in combination with Shulman's (1987, p. 8) 'pedagogical content knowledge' that we discussed in Chapters 4 and 11 (i.e. knowing what you teach and how to best teach it), together better represent the facets of an expert teacher. Ideally, Shulman's suggested 'curricular knowledge', knowing where our own piece of teaching (session, module, unit) fits in the course or the programme in question. In other words, we need not only know what to teach our students but also how to best teach this content in a discipline- and context-sensitive way, as well as being able to set your part in the bigger, curricular picture.

Informal learning and the collegial influence

What influences us in your teaching roles? What about our students, our colleagues, our disciplinary ways of thinking and practising, our leaders? As we examined in Chapter 5, how do social contexts *structure action*, and how do people, agency and interactions *enable our actions*? In what ways do institutional and disciplinary cultures impact on our teaching and our students' learning? The concept of teaching and learning regimes (Trowler 2020) might be useful as a way to understand how we in our works-groups, over time, develop norms, habits and traditions, in relation to teaching and learning that define for instance how we talk about our students, about teaching and learning, how we practise teaching and assessment in our courses. Much of this is implicit and taken-for-granted, and is related to 'the way we do things around here'. The norms and traditions may be most obvious to someone who is a new colleague, meeting our assumptions and practices for the first time (see Fanghanel 2009 for a concrete account of how this might appear). Critical reflection can assist us to stop for a while and scrutinise our own assumptions, preferably together with our colleagues. Do we talk to our colleagues about teaching? Handal (1999) has argued that teaching is, or at least has been, a rather 'private act', and instead suggests that it needs to be thought of in the same way as our research practice, through collegial consultations with 'critical friends'. A critical friendship includes a personal relationship of confidence; belief in the professional competence of the critical friend; expectation of personal integrity, and basic trust in the good intentions of the critical friend.

RESEARCH BRIEFING 16.1 Informal learning and collegial context

Roxå and Mårtensson (2009) have empirically established that academic teachers have a 'significant network' consisting of a handful of people, where informal, private conversations about teaching take place, characterized by mutual trust. The significant networks can stretch across and beyond organizational boundaries, and are related to how we perceive our local collegial culture, in terms of support for serious conversations about teaching. Van Waes et al. (2015) analysed academics' network in relation to different career stages, and demonstrate that over time the size, the strength, and the diversity of the networks change. Experienced expert teachers had larger, stronger, and more diverse networks compared with experienced non-experts. Furthermore, Thomson (2015) studied informal conversations in academic departments in Australia, with a focus on early- and mid-career academics and conclude that the conversations have a developmental role and a number of different purposes: seeking information, mentoring, generating ideas, as well as venting frustrations.

Elsewhere we have already discussed teaching and learning regimes (Trowler 2020) as one way to understand how different groups develop certain ways of thinking and practising. In a South-African context, Jawitz (2009) has also shown how the local collegial context exercises a strong influence on how we learn to assess and grade student learning. Jawitz studied different disciplinary groups within the same university, and hence the same institutional and policy-context, and demonstrates completely different ways for new academics to develop competence related to assessment. He concludes that there are informal learning processes where the individual habitus aligns with the collective habitus. Related to Jawitz' (2009) findings, Roxå and Mårtensson (2011/2013) studied five so-called microcultures in a research-intensive university. Microcultures were defined as local work contexts where the members over time develop traditions and habits in a similar way to that described above. Over time, the members collaboratively form versions of the overall academic culture in their respective institution. A microculture can be a department, a workgroup, a disciplinary community or something similar. It doesn't necessarily follow the formally designed organizational boundaries. In Roxå and Mårtensson's study, the microcultures, strong in both research and teaching, were characterized by high internal trust; intense interaction, communication and collegial support; high demands on students paired with active support for learning; and rich collaborations external to the microculture. Some of the teachers involved would, for instance, teach in pairs, share all teaching material with each other, act as critical friends to each other, or initiate a readers' club across disciplines in relation to their challenge of forming a joint international Masters programme. Not all microcultures were the same; each microculture was significantly influenced by their own story about themselves and who they were, but they also had a clear idea of where they were going, and what the purpose of their existence was. These future-oriented visions could be about changing the society, improving the industry, or developing the profession. In later work, Mårtensson and Roxå (2016) identified the role of competence, autonomy and social solidarity as important features of developing a sense of collegial engagement within a micro-culture.

Reflective Activity 16.2 Reflecting on informal learning and collegial influence

Consider the discussion and aspects of your teaching context outlined above.

Questions for reflection:

1 Who do you talk to about your teaching? How would you characterize your conversations? How has that changed over time?
2 Do you have a 'critical friend' to whom you can turn for advice and support in your teacher role?
3 How do you think a new colleague would perceive of your workplace? What norms and traditions are part of 'the way we do things around here'?
4 If you were to engage with critical reflections about your social teaching context – how would you go about it? What are potential enablers and barriers for you?

REFLECTIVE TEACHING, THE SCHOLARSHIP OF TEACHING AND LEARNING, AND YOUR CAREER PATH

The time has come to move beyond the tired old teaching versus research debate and give the familiar and honourable term scholarship a broader and more capacious meaning, one that brings legitimacy to the full scope of academic work.
(Boyer 1990, 16)

In 1990, Boyer argued that a full range of scholarly activity needed to be recognized, including the scholarship of: discovery, integration, application and teaching. This placed teaching alongside other scholarly endeavours. The scholarship of teaching and learning (SoTL) – as it has come to be known – involves critically reflecting and reporting on practice with a view to improving the quality of student learning and teaching (Prosser

2008). Internationally there are now institutes, conferences, societies, and peer-reviewed journals that support SoTL. Poole (2018) suggested that a starting point for engaging in SoTL is to take our intuitive and anecdotal experiences of teaching and student learning as an object for observations and basis for critical reflections. The notion of SoTL is, in this view, strongly congruent with the notion of reflective teaching, and the crucial role of evidence that we explored in Chapter 3.

Views about the purpose and nature of the scholarship of teaching vary. Andresen (2000, p. 147) describes SoTL as comprising evaluation of all aspects of teaching quality – preparation, objectives, curriculum design and delivery, assessment materials, and student learning outcomes. Kreber (2005) contends that SoTL should be conceived as a critical and intellectual activity, emphasizing the need to examine the 'forms of knowledge, skills and attitudes that are promoted in our curricula and ask why these are pursued and not others' (p. 396). Trigwell and Shale (2004) identify three core aims for the pursuit of scholarship of teaching as follows. It can, first, be a means through which the status of teaching may be raised. Second, it can be a means through which teachers may come to teach more knowledgeably and, third, it can provide a means through which the quality of teaching may be assessed and, in the long run, improved.

In summary, a useful working definition of the scholarship of teaching and learning is as follows: 'the systematic study of teaching and learning, using established or validated criteria of scholarship, to understand how teaching beliefs, behaviours, attitudes, and values can maximize learning, and/or develop a more accurate understanding of learning, resulting in products that are publicly shared for critique and use by an appropriate community' (Potter and Kustra 2011, p. 2). Fanghanel (2013) further claims that: 'SoTL provides a space for dialogic critique of singular investigations into practice that contribute to advancing individual and collective knowledge of the field of higher education.'

Kreber and Cranton (2000) argued that SoTL also includes formal educational research that should be recognized as equivalent to discipline-based research in its rigour and impact. Some higher education institutions have therefore used SoTL to raise the status of teaching, as well as to increase the research output. For instance, Vithal (2018) analyses an ambitious example at the University of KwaZulu-Natal in Durban, South Africa. Vithal (2018) highlights four inter-related activity areas which can be used to grow SoTL institutionally: (1) research and innovation; (2) recognition, rewards and academic promotions; (3) professional development and practice; and (4) policy review and development. One of the key features of this initiative was that the institution tied processes and products of SoTL to research, and that many different activities to support this development were inter-related at various institutional levels.

However, in some research-intensive institutions, concerns are raised from academics who are already engaged in disciplinary research. Where would they find time to engage in SoTL as educational research? Furthermore, some scholars raise concerns about the quality of such research if people are not sufficiently trained in educational research methods (Kanuka 2011). One way of thinking about SoTL in this tension is to focus on the purpose of investigation. Ashwin and Trigwell (2004) proposed a three-level matrix model in order to illustrate different aims and scope of investigation. The first level was 'the personal', with the intention to build knowledge to inform myself. The second level was 'the local', with the intention to inform and build knowledge in a local context. The third level was 'the public', with the intention to contribute to knowledge at a more global scale, across contexts. Thinking about the 'going public' aspect of SoTL, one might consider this not only as an outcome of research in terms of a publication in an international journal but also, and as valid, going public at the more local level, in campus conferences, newsletters, seminars etc. This is the approach deliberately taken at Lund University in Sweden, described in **Case Study 16.1**. This approach reflects, as we discussed in Chapter 3, the importance of articulating our ideas to others in developing an open, critical perspective on our teaching. If we are to develop sustained and sustainable approaches to teaching for understanding, then we need to do so in partnership with others. This strengthens the argument to go public about our teaching in our local contexts.

Given that SoTL can be interpreted and enacted in different ways, it can be useful to consider the relations between our reflective teaching, research and the scholarship of teaching and learning. D'Andrea and Gosling (2005) emphasize the connections between the teaching and research domains of academic work showing that scholarship is an activity that may span a range of activities that connect disciplinary and pedagogic research with teaching and the development of teaching. Both reflective teaching and SoTL connect teaching development with pedagogical research which 'simply means finding out more about how learning takes place so that we, as teachers, can direct our energies into approaches which are more likely to be successful' (Reid 2006, p. 1).

As we deepen our understanding of higher education teaching and learning and develop expertise in this field, we can consider the role of SoTL in our practices as reflective teacher in higher education. Bearing in mind the range of conceptions outlined in this section, in what ways can you commit to reflective teaching and the scholarship of teaching and learning? What evidence could you use to demonstrate this? What support would you need to engage further? What support could you give to others to engage?

If you think about the spectrum of activities incorporating reflective teaching, discipline-based research and SoTL activities, where would you plot your current academic activities and achievements? Are you conducting discipline-based research? Is there any overlap between your research and your reflective teaching that might shift your research closer to the SoTL/pedagogical research end of the spectrum? Projecting into the future, which areas would you like to develop further? What would it take to do so? Do you have evidence of developing expertise in SoTL? How will you demonstrate this evidence? Do any of your local colleagues engage in SoTL that you could respond to?

The scholarship of teaching and learning and institutional structures

Over the past decade a number of institutions in various geographical locations have developed support for and structures to embed SoTL into institutional culture and structures (Fanghanel et al. 2016). Equally, many higher education institutions have developed strategies, policies and structures to support, acknowledge and reward teaching excellence. However, Fanghanel et al. (2016), in a sector-wide study, point out that 'the recognition and reward of teaching excellence is a significant and yet under-utilized tool for institutions' (p. 16) and that '[G]aining a clear picture of progress in this area is difficult due to the variation in implementation of policies and difficulty in gaining data from institutions about promotions' (p. 19). Whether or not we plan to feature scholarship of teaching and learning achievements in our academic career trajectory, it is a good idea to become acquainted with our university's promotion policy and guidelines as early as possible. These documents provide us with an outline of the demonstrated skills and achievements required to progress from one academic level to the next. One of the most common errors made by academic staff is to leave their thinking and planning for promotion to the year in which they plan to submit their application. This is far too late. It is preferable to use the promotion framework to guide your professional development activities and priorities over time. Wherever possible, we can learn by talking with more senior colleagues about their strategies for developing their career achievements. Learning from fellow travellers is one of the best ways to progress in academia. In many institutions there are staff development units that support academics and it can be helpful to talk to them too.

Studies of academics' perceptions of the reward and recognition of teaching in higher education tend to find that the majority of academics agree that teaching excellence should be rewarded through the promotion system (HEA 2009; Tagg 2019), although it is important that the criteria for promotion are carefully developed (Subbaye and Vithal 2017). Whilst there has been progress with developing such reward systems for academics who research and teach, the career pathways for academics who focus on 'teaching-only roles' are less certain (Bennett et al. 2018). Institutional schemes such as teaching awards can also contribute to recognition and raising the status of teaching and learning, although these again need to be carefully designed if they are not to have dysfunctional outcomes (Seppala and Smith 2019). The ways in which teaching awards are acknowledged by the institution can play an important role in changing and embedding the culture, as can the way in which national initiatives are rated and recognized. There is also evidence that whilst institutions have policies that teaching contributions should be recognized as equally important as research contributions, these are not always effectively implemented (HEA 2009; Subbaye and Vithal 2017).

These findings resonate with the results from Chalmers (2011), concluding that although not always embedded in practice, a number of positive changes have taken place and many institutions are paying increased attention to the rewards and promotions related to teaching excellence, not least through the embedment of scholarship of teaching and learning. Williams et al. (2013) suggest an institutional framework based on a social network approach for weaving the scholarship of teaching and learning into institutional culture, and highlight the importance of 'providing tangible incentives and support for SoTL' and these are 'key to ensuring it becomes woven into institutional cultures' (p. 53). Williams et al. (2013) argue that 'for SoTL to take root in organizational cultures, there must be: (1) effective communication and dissemination of SoTL activity across all [institutional] levels, (2) well established social networks and links between these levels (nodes), and (3) sustained support by senior administration'.

Indeed, embedding SoTL in a higher education institution requires commitment, leadership, time and cultural change. Mårtensson et al. (2011) document a suite of strategies adopted at Lund University in Sweden over a period of years. In reading Case Study 16.1, we can consider what role we and our colleagues might play in shaping the institutional culture in relation to SoTL at our institutions. How might we demonstrate a leadership role in introducing SoTL or further embedding SoTL in our institution? What steps might we take to inform a review of the promotion policy at our institutions to ensure that the scholarly aspects of teaching and learning are effectively recognized and rewarded, in policies as well as in practice?

Case Study 16.1 Embedding the scholarship of teaching

This case study (Mårtensson 2014; Mårtensson, Roxå and Olsson 2011) is drawn from Lund University, located in the southern part of Sweden. Lund University, founded in 1666, one of the oldest and largest universities in Scandinavia, is ranked among the world's top 100 universities. It is research intensive and has (2017) about 800 full professors, and 4,100 academic staff and research students. It has 40,000 under-graduate and Masters-level students in eight autonomous faculties.

The overall objective of the development strategy is to support the emergence of a quality culture in relation to teaching and learning, where teaching develops slowly but constantly by the active involvement of academic teachers and leaders. Underpinning the strategy is an assumption that development will follow if *who* we talk to, *what* we talk about and *how* we talk about it changes. Therefore, a number of coordinated and interrelated activities have gradually been launched with careful timing in order to promote the embedding of scholarship of teaching and learning, and to cultivate cultural change. Increased engagement on the part of teachers, among other things, forms evidence of a cultural shift in relation to teaching and learning.

A summary of the Lund University strategy is outlined below. It comprises several parts.

1 *Pedagogical courses*. The recommended ten weeks of teacher training are modularized in order to support progression of knowledge and skills in relation to teaching and learning in higher education, as well as to support an increased sophistication of scholarship of teaching and learning (Roxå et al. 2008). Most courses range from 40 to 200 hours total participant working time, and include a written, scholarly assignment on a relevant teaching and learning issue.

2 *Scholarly papers*. Within the pedagogical courses, participants (academic teachers) reflect upon their own teaching experience, their students' learning and or their course design, and work on self-chosen projects directly related to their practice and their disciplinary context. Projects are reported in writing, underpinned by literature on teaching and learning in higher education, and peer-reviewed. These papers are disseminated across course cohorts, as locally produced scholarly knowledge and sources of inspiration.

3   *Critical friends.* A model based on the idea of critical friends (Handal 1999) is used in order to build bridges between what is addressed in pedagogical courses and the socio-cultural context in which the teachers have their day-to-day practice.

4   *Departmental seminars.* As a result of the critical friends model, departmental seminars have been initiated in some places where teachers present their development projects to their departmental colleagues.

5   *Campus conferences on teaching and learning.* The high number of documented and peer-reviewed projects has contributed to the fact that several faculties organize biennial campus conferences on teaching and learning. The alternate years a university-wide conference is organized, with all contributions collected in a documented and publicly available proceeding.

6   *Reward schemes.* Some faculties at Lund University have introduced voluntary reward schemes, so-called Pedagogical Academies, for scholarly teaching. Rewarded teachers focus their teaching practice on student learning, they show an advanced capability for scholarly reflection on their teaching practice and they demonstrate a striving to make their practice more public by engaging in scholarly discussions, conferences and publications (Olsson and Roxå 2013). The reward scheme is not an alternative career path; on the contrary, all teachers are encouraged to engage and show excellence in research as well as in teaching.

7   *Tenure and promotion.* The model underpinning the reward schemes described above, has gradually been introduced and used also as a model to consider assessment of teaching qualifications for appointments and promotion.

8   *Evidence of cultural change.* Levels of engagement by individual teachers, educational leaders *and* accounts about responses among colleagues after participation in educational development activities indicate effects on professional identity as well as on institutional culture.

The strategy described here generates personal commitment to teaching and student learning by nurturing significant networks with the scholarly reflected accounts of colleagues' teaching and learning experiences. This is achieved through careful introduction of documented accounts from university teachers and/or findings from educational research.

The teachers also 'go public' during discussions and interactions and thereby foster new significant relations. Because the conversations from within the courses are reified in written reports they can reach beyond the private domains. They can impact on the next generation of participants and the local culture within the department or faculty.

Drawing on the teaching and learning research programme concepts of effective teaching and learning

Throughout this book we have drawn up ten principles of teaching and learning to explore how to develop our approaches to reflective teaching in higher education. In Reflective Activity 16.3, we consider how we can use these ten principles to develop a coherent narrative around our continuing professional development.

Reflective Activity 16.3 Reflecting on teaching and learning principles

In Chapter 4 and at the start of each chapter, we have introduced teaching and learning principles from the Teaching and Learning Research Programme, funded by the UK Economic and Social Research Council, the UK's biggest-ever initiative in education research.

The idea of these principles is to help us to develop a language to talk about reflective teaching. You can see how this has been developed into a conceptual framework on the Reflective Teaching website: reflectiveteaching.co.uk/deepening-expertise/conceptual-framework

The ten principles are outlined again below. As you consider each principle, think about its application to your own work. Do all these principles apply to your teaching in some way? If so, how? Are there any disciplinary differences or institutional differences that need to be taken into account? How might you use the principles as the basis for developing your expertise as a reflective teacher in higher education?

Effective higher education teaching and learning:

1 Demands consistent policy frameworks, with support for learning for diverse students as their main focus. Policies at government, system, institutional and organizational level need to recognize the fundamental importance of learning for individual, team, organizational, institutional, national and system success. Policies should be designed to create effective and equitable learning environments for all students to benefit socially and economically.

2 Depends on the scholarship and learning of all those educators who teach and research to support the learning of others. The need for lecturers, teachers and trainers to learn through doing research to improve their knowledge, expertise and skills for teaching should be recognized and supported.

3 Recognizes the significance of informal learning to developing specific expertise. Learning with friends, families, peer groups and professionals should be recognized as significant, and be valued and used in formal processes in higher education.

4 Fosters both individual and social processes and outcomes. Students should be encouraged to build relationships and communication with others to assist the mutual construction of knowledge and enhance the achievements of individuals and groups. Consulting or collaborating with students as learners about their learning makes this happen.

5 Promotes the active engagement of the student as learner. A key aim of higher learning should be to develop students' independence and autonomy as learners. This involves engaging students actively in their own learning, and ensuring that they acquire a repertoire of learning strategies and practices, develop positive learning dispositions, and build the confidence to become agents in their own learning.

6 Needs assessment to be congruent with learning. Assessment should be designed for maximum validity in terms of learning outcomes and learning processes, and also should be specific to the type of subject or discipline involved, even if it is

interdisciplinary. It should help to advance learning as well as determine whether learning has occurred.

7   Requires learning to be systematically developed. Teachers, trainers, lecturers, researchers and all who support the learning of others should provide intellectual, social and emotional support which helps learners to develop expertise in their learning for it to be effective and secure.

8   Recognizes the importance of prior or concurrent experience and learning. Teaching and learning should take account of what the student as learner knows already to plan strategies for the future. This includes building on prior learning but also taking account of the emerging concurrent learning in context, and the personal and cultural experiences of different groups of students as learners.

9   Engages with expertise and valued forms of knowledge in disciplines and subjects. Teaching and learning should engage students with the concepts, key skills and processes, modes of discourse, ways of thinking and practising, and attitudes and relationships which are most valued in their subject. Students need to understand what constitutes quality, standards and expertise in different settings and subjects.

10 Equips learners for life in its broadest sense. Learning should help individuals develop the intellectual, personal and social resources that will enable them to participate as active citizens, contribute to economic, social or community development, and flourish as individuals in a diverse and changing society. This means adopting a broad conception of worthwhile learning outcomes and taking seriously issues of equity and social justice for all.

MANAGING YOUR ACADEMIC CAREER: MILESTONES, PLANNING AND DOCUMENTATION

In this section, we address various strategies for planning your own development as an academic teacher. As we work towards developing greater expertise in our academic work, it is important to be purposeful about managing our academic careers, particularly when planning how to balance our research, teaching and administrative, governance and/or service-related activities. The focus of this chapter is on developing and evidencing expertise and engagement in the teaching dimension of our work, but this needs to be seen in the context of our broader academic work responsibilities. We will introduce two different models of teaching competence, one UK-originated and one Nordic model, which can guide our reflections and considerations as we engage in professional development.

The development of academics as teachers is a relatively recent phenomenon. It is only in the past forty years that governments and universities in Australasia, the UK, USA and Canada, and the Scandinavian countries have formalized their support for academic staff development in the area of teaching (Ling 2009). Prior to this, the emphasis was on appointing staff on their academic merits, based on the assumption that they would 'pick up' the skills of teaching their discipline to their students (Prebble et al. 2004, p. 12). As the nature of academic work changes in response to shifts in the international higher education landscape (Krause 2009), so interest has grown in how individuals shape their career paths in academia. These paths may look quite different depending on such factors as our disciplines (Krause 2014), our particular academic micro-culture (Roxå and Mårtensson 2015) or our institution's policies on academic workload configurations. Key to managing our academic career successfully is the skill of deliberate planning and being aware, as early as possible, of the many opportunities available to develop our professional expertise.

Many institutions have a dedicated academic development unit, a teaching and learning centre, which offers an induction to university teaching. In some institutions this may comprise a compulsory short course. In other institutions it might be a longer module that all new academic staff to the institution are expected to complete within their first year or two of appointment. Typically, such induction programmes or compulsory introductory modules function as a useful foundation for early career academics and/or for those transitioning from one university to another. It is a good idea to make contact with the local academic development unit (or equivalent) as early as possible for they will invariably have a range of professional development offerings to support learning and teaching.

The key to success in establishing and working towards formal milestones in your academic career is the capacity to provide evidence of substantive developments in your impact on and contribution to student learning, to the broader institution and to your discipline. A useful starting point for determining these milestones is your institutional promotion policy, along with national frameworks like the UK Professional Standards Framework (UKPSF) or the like, which outline the typical indicators expected of academic staff as they progress from the early career phase to more experienced academic roles.

Reflective Activity 16.4 Identifying your level of expertise

The following descriptors from the UK Professional Standards Framework (UKPSF 2011, see: **heacademy.ac.uk/UKPSF**) demonstrate the qualitative differences in demonstrated levels of understanding and expertise required of an academic who progresses through four stages:

- Stage 1: 'Demonstrate *an understanding* of specific aspects of effective teaching, learning support methods and student learning.'
- Stage 2: 'Demonstrate *a broad understanding* of effective approaches to teaching and learning support as key contributions to high quality learning.'
- Stage 3: 'Demonstrate *a thorough understanding* of effective approaches to teaching and learning support as a key contribution to high-quality student learning.'
- Stage 4: 'Demonstrate *a sustained record of effective strategic leadership* in academic practice and academic development as a key contribution to high quality student learning.'

Questions for reflection:

1 Which stage am I at?
2 What sources of evidence am I able to provide to demonstrate that I am at this stage?
3 What strategies do I have in place to assist me to progress to the next stage?
4 Whom might I consult to seek advice on the most effective ways of putting these strategies into practice?
5 In what ways does this framework align with my institution's promotion policy? How might the PSF assist me in preparing for promotion?

Another model of teaching excellence (see Figure 16.1), not unlike Pollard's model of reflective teaching that was introduced in Chapter 3, has been developed at Lund University, Sweden, and gradually adopted in Sweden and other Nordic countries (Ryegård et al. 2010). This model highlights the broad scope of being a good teacher, not only with students in the classroom. It therefore differentiates *pedagogical competence* from *teaching skills*, where the latter is one part of the former (Olsson and Roxå 2013). The model has at its core the teaching practice, i.e. various ways to support student learning. However, in this model, pedagogical competence also includes making observations in the classroom and of student learning, interpreting these observations through knowledge about teaching and student learning, and finally planning further teaching, and development thereof, based on systematic, underpinned and interpreted observations. This

Figure 16.1
A model of pedagogical competence (adapted from Olsson et al., 2010)

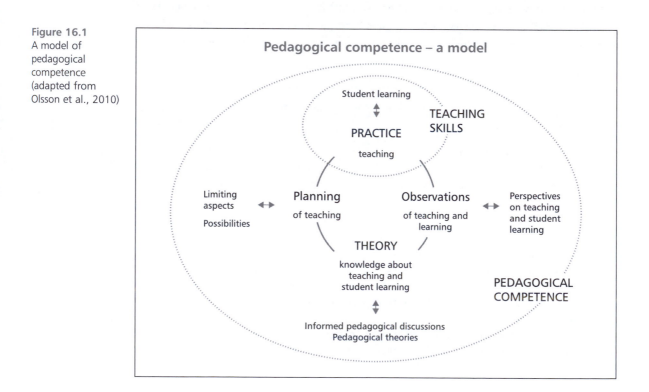

model does not differentiate between levels of expertise or experience, but is thought of as an iterative process, where the observations made might change over time depending on teaching experience and responsibilities. As a new teacher, for instance, you may observe what happens in a laboratory exercise, a lecture or a seminar and reflect upon how your observation, in relation to knowledge about student learning in such settings can help develop and improve students' learning. As a more experienced teacher, you may make observations about the relationship between intended learning outcomes and assessment results, or general course design, or how students' generic attributes are developed across the curriculum.

The two models have similar traits, although the UKPSF appears more of a stage model, related to an academic career trajectory. The Nordic model, being organically developed from within institutions rather than a national framework, is more iterative and circular. It is focused on the process of continuously reflecting upon teaching and student learning, at all stages of the academic career. One main difference in the two models therefore is their somewhat different understandings of expertise, stage-based or circular. The Nordic model is used across many institutions in Sweden and Norway, for instance, in relation to promotion, assessment of pedagogical competence and reward schemes (Olsson and Roxå 2013). The following criteria are commonly used together with the model, in portfolio- and evidence-based processes, to identify and assess pedagogical competence:

- a focus on student learning;
- clear development over time; and
- a scholarly approach.

As indicated by theses criteria, one important aspect in the use of this model is the development dimension. It is a common requirement in teaching portfolios composed in accordance with this model to reflect critically upon one's own development over time as a teacher, and one's own attempts to improve teaching with a focus on student learning.

Reflective Activity 16.5 Your pedagogical competence

Think about your own teaching experience so far.

1 What observations have you made in relation to student learning that might be worthwhile inquiring?
2 What do you know, or what do you need to understand better, in order to analyse and interpret these observations? What can you learn from searching literature and research related to this issue? What can you learn from engaging in conversations with colleagues?
3 How might you make a systematic inquiry into this issue?
4 How will your inquiries and deepened understanding potentially affect your future teaching, and the students' learning?

It is helpful to be aware of the need to be active and deliberate in developing our capabilities as we progress through our academic careers. We need to look for opportunities to develop our expertise as a higher education academic by making the most of mentoring and continuing professional development opportunities. Blackmore and Castley (2006, p. 3) outline some of the dimensions of capability development for academic staff in universities. These include:

- staff skills development, for example in our use of information and communications technologies;
- educational development, including how we develop curricula and assessment; and
- academic development, how we develop our expertise. This might include expertise in leading programme development teams or in matters relating to quality assurance and enhancement strategies within our institutions.

As we develop these capabilities, we need to ensure that we document them. We can seek advice from mentors, supervisors, leaders, trusted colleagues and academic development units within and beyond our institutions regarding areas of development so that we can plan ahead. We can also look for opportunities to engage in the scholarship of teaching and learning and to take on leadership roles in learning and teaching. These might include leadership at the academic programme level. We might also consider leadership of curriculum innovations in our department or faculty, or perhaps whole-of-institution leadership in learning and teaching initiatives such as peer review of teaching. Leadership through contribution to learning and teaching committees in our discipline or across the institution is another possible area to pursue.

As we discussed in Chapter 14, it is a good idea to keep a portfolio of achievements (see Reflective Activity 16.6) that includes a history of all the professional development programmes that you attend and, where possible, the impact these have had on your developing career. In many institutions, attendance at professional development events is centrally recorded as part of the institution's career development and performance review process. It can be very helpful to develop a reflective narrative that links these career development activities to demonstrate the significant milestones and 'step changes' in your career.

Reflective Activity 16.6 Developing a portfolio of your teaching achievements

Look at the following strategies for presenting a summary of your teaching achievements adapted from Krause 2012. Would this work for you? Consider how you might use or adapt this list of ideas to: (a) summarize your achievements, and (b) include in your teaching portfolio (or equivalent).

The following six areas are designed to give you ideas for documenting evidence in relation to your teaching practice. The relevance of these strategies for individual academic staff will vary according to such contextual factors as career stage and discipline as well as institutional policies.

Strategies for success

1 Articulate your teaching philosophy:
   - Develop a brief introductory statement of your intentions and main principles as a teacher in higher education. This statement may evolve over time as you teach in different contexts and develop greater expertise. Simple examples of a 'philosophy' statement include:
     a 'The degree to which students are engaged with the subject material is fundamental to their effective learning. Participation and interactivity are principal agents in stimulating this engagement . . . In my teaching I seek to . . .'
     b 'For the past decade my primary teaching goal has been to capture the educational potential of new technologies . . .'

2 Keep systematic records of your teaching, course reviews, leadership and service:
   - Keep a record of courses taught and of learning and teaching materials developed. This list should include details such as student numbers and teaching mode in order to establish context and to provide evidence of the breadth of your experience. When you design resources such as course notes, student workbooks or problem sheets, make a note of these, and save some documented examples.
   - Systematically collect and respond to student evaluations of courses and teaching. Keep electronic copies of evaluations for future purposes. For each set of evaluations, document (even briefly) what you have done in response to feedback. What improvements have you made? How has your teaching and curriculum design developed as a result of student feedback?
   - Comment on the currency of your curriculum content and learning objectives.
   - How and when do you review content and learning objectives? What are your sources for benchmarking and keeping up to date with developments in the field?

3 Describe how you implement a student-centred approach to teaching:
   - Reflect on your availability to students and strategies for connecting with students. Document the strategies you employed to facilitate student contact and advising.
   - Keep a record of your students' accomplishments beyond the classroom. Make a note of students' professional or research achievements, awards and publications.
   - Document your strategies for working with individual students or special student groups. How do you cater for international students, students with disabilities or students from diverse cultural backgrounds?
   - Document approaches to providing student feedback. When and how do you provide feedback to students and what is the impact of this approach? Save documented examples of formative and summative feedback to students.

4 List examples of scholarship in your discipline and in learning and teaching:
   - Argue for your scholarly approach to teaching. This may include your own research into learning and teaching or perhaps evidence-based approaches that inform curriculum design.

- Document professional development you have undertaken. This may include courses completed, conferences attended, or online professional development.
- Demonstrate how you address the learning and teaching priority areas of the University. This could include scholarly approaches to the implementation of work-integrated learning, research-based learning, blended learning, internationalizing the curriculum, public scholarship, community engagement, etc.
- Articulate how and why you use technology in your teaching. What impact has the use of ICTs had on student learning, attitudes and outcomes?
- List your conference papers and research publications related to learning and teaching. Outline these in such a way as to include reference to formal feedback and recognition from peers.
- Keep track of all awards, citations and invitations to speak on teaching, e.g. 'My national reputation as a teacher is evident in the regular invitations I receive to . . .'
- Include findings from evaluations and comment on actions taken in response to these. This could include student surveys, peer review, observations, self-review, e.g. 'Evidence of the high standard of my face-to-face teaching is as follows . . .'

5 Outline innovations you have developed in your teaching:
- Document innovations in teaching or grants received for innovation, e.g. 'I have been active and successful in applying for funds to address the following issues in relation to student learning in my discipline . . .'
- Comment on how you achieve teaching–research linkages in your practice, e.g. 'I have introduced the following strategies to ensure that my first-year students benefit from my disciplinary research programme . . .'
- Outline ways in which you have adapted curriculum to address the learning and teaching priority areas of the University as appropriate. What adaptations have you made to include international perspectives? How have you modified the curriculum in your discipline and courses to include blended learning approaches?

6 Describe examples of your leadership in learning and teaching:
- Identify your leadership in teaching in the discipline. Provide details of any textbooks you have written or to which you have contributed (especially those in widespread use – Who uses them? How many universities? International distribution?).
- Document your influence on the departmental context (and beyond), e.g. 'As a direct result of my influence/input on . . .'
- Document courses and programmes designed, reviewed and revised. To provide evidence of your leadership in teaching, it is worthwhile documenting your role in developing new courses or programmes in your discipline.
- Look for opportunities to demonstrate leadership. Outline any strategies you have for identifying opportunities to initiate change in teaching, curriculum design, and culture in relation to approaches to learning and teaching in your department.
- Document your postgraduate supervision responsibilities. List the number of students you have supervised and the outcomes of their research in terms of completions, publications, etc. Final suggestions for presenting evidence of good teaching practice.

- View your documentary evidence as an argument and a narrative – tell the story of your teaching and its development. Provide compelling, objective evidence and remain self-critically reflective.
- With regard to your contribution to teaching, focus not only on the scope, quality and effectiveness of your work, but also on the increasing sophistication of your contribution. Trace the increasing complexity of the tasks, document the leadership demonstrated, identify the growing knowledge base required.
- Keep returning to your main theme/organizing principle – aim to bring coherence to your argument. If possible, make sure you underpin your organizing principle/s with research and public knowledge about teaching and student learning.
- Strategically select supporting evidence and examples and be sure to keep documenting your evidence in a methodical, easy-to-access way each semester.

Key milestones in your academic career include annual performance review meetings which you should use to set objectives and goals with your supervisor. Where possible, it is a good idea to ask for a mentor in the early weeks or months of a new position, though it is never too late to request support from a mentor, or use your significant network to discuss your personal and professional development. As you progress through your academic career from one level to the next, mentoring and collegial support should be seen as an invaluable part of the journey. You may ask to be involved in a formal mentoring programme at your institution; alternatively, you may establish a more informal arrangement with a trusted colleague, a 'critical friend', with whom you meet to discuss your progress and to ask questions that will help you to continue to develop as an expert teacher.

CONCLUSION

In this chapter, we have explored the complex nature of expertise in higher education and the role of ongoing personal and professional development in deepening our approaches to reflective teaching in higher education. We have considered the role of informal learning and collegial contexts in shaping the way in which we think about and practise teaching. While many academic staff continue to express concern about the relative lack of professional reward and recognition for teaching in higher education, several positive developments have been highlighted, particularly in relation to the growing institutional and international recognition of scholarship of teaching and learning. We have considered some of the milestones that might characterize our academic careers and the value of engaging deliberately with respect to personal and professional development, to our career trajectories and promotion opportunities, particularly in relation to reflective teaching. One of the most important messages in this is the importance of ensuring that evidence to demonstrate engagement, expertise and excellence in teaching is characterized by a critically reflective and scholarly approach, robust indicators and rigorous evidence.

The ten principles emerging from the UK's Teaching and Learning Research Programme provide another useful framework for developing our expertise as reflective teachers. Maintaining a thoughtful and critically reflective engagement with our teaching, and engaging in intellectually intriguing conversations with our colleagues will provide avenues to continue to find teaching rewarding and meaningful over the course of our academic careers.

KEY READINGS

For explorations of the 'scholarship of learning and teaching in higher education', see:

Booth, S. and Woollacott, L. (2018) 'On the constitution of SoTL: Its domains and contexts', *Higher Education: The International Journal of Higher Education Research*, 75(3), 537–51.

Hutchings, P., Huber, M. and Ciccone, A. (2011) 'Getting there: An integrative vision of the scholarship of learning and teaching', *International Journal for the Scholarship of Teaching and Learning*, 5(1) Article 31.

For a practical account of SoTL in action, its rationales, methods, and implications, see:

Chick, N. (2018) *SoTL in Action. Illuminating Critical Moments of Practice*. Sterling, VA: Stylus Publishing.

For an examination of the different ways in which academic staff approach their growth and development as a university teacher, see:

Akerlind, G. (2007) 'Constraints on academics' potential for developing as a teacher', *Studies in Higher Education*, 32(1), 21–37.

For key readings about the importance of social networks and informal learning in professional development, see *International Journal for Academic Development*, special issue, 20(2), 2015.

For websites which include a number of practical resources to assist you with developing evidence for promotion, along with guidelines for ways to gather and document evidence about your teaching, see: University of Wollongong Focus on Teaching resource site: **focusonteaching.uow.edu.au/UOW066988** and University of Calgary, Taylor Institute for Teaching and Learning resource site: **taylorinstitute.ucalgary.ca**

INTRODUCTION

What is the purpose of higher education in society? In what ways does this purpose align – or conflict – with our own beliefs and values as university teachers? To what extent does higher education contribute to the transformation of people's lives? What role do we, as teachers, contribute to that transformation? In this chapter, we will examine these questions by exploring the relations among higher education, teachers and society, reflecting on the larger purpose of higher education and our roles within it.

Reflective teaching is a key part of our professionalism as academics in higher education. Being a reflective teacher in higher education necessarily involves an active and critical questioning of the nature of the relationship between education and society generally, and higher education and society specifically. Higher education plays a role in both reproducing and transforming our societies and economies.

Over the past few decades, there has been significant and far-reaching development and change in higher education. The values underpinning the philosophy of neo-liberalism, which emphasizes free-market economics, entrepreneurialism, individualism and competition, are increasingly evident in higher education worldwide. The effects are seen in the increased regulation of higher education systems with much greater emphasis on quality and accountability (for example, see Black et al. 2015). Greater attention has been devoted to embedding 'employability' in higher education curricula, through a focus on graduate 'attributes', 'transferable skills', and, increasingly, 'competencies'. As reflective teachers, we are faced with questions about the purposes and processes of higher education, how we as university teachers fit into the current system, and the extent to which we can transform it.

In this chapter, we will first examine the broad relationship between higher education and society, and how the purposes of higher education have shifted over time. We will then examine the concepts of 'graduateness' and employability, transferable skills, capabilities and competencies, reflecting on their pedagogical implications. Finally, we will explore the potential transformative and reproductive contributions of higher education in society, while noting the tensions associated with widening access and participation.

See Chapter 4

TLRP Principles

There are two particularly relevant underlying principles related to professionalism in higher education:

Principle 1: Effective teaching and learning demands consistent policy frameworks, with support for learning for diverse students as their main focus.
Policies at government, system, institutional and organizational level need to recognize the fundamental importance of learning for individual, team, organizational, institutional, national and system success. Policies should be designed to create effective and equitable learning environments for all students to benefit socially and economically.

> **Principle 10: Effective teaching and learning equips learners for life in its broadest sense.** Learning should help individuals develop the intellectual, personal and social resources that will enable them to participate as active citizens, contribute to economic, social or community development, and flourish as individuals in a diverse and changing society. This means adopting a broad conception of worthwhile learning outcomes and taking seriously issues of equity and social justice for all, across the full ethnic, racial, social, economic and gender spectrum.

HIGHER EDUCATION AND SOCIETY

In this section, we consider the relations between higher education and society. In doing so, we focus on two aspects of this relationship: how higher education contributes to the economy through producing employable graduates and how it contributes to equity, inclusion and social justice by increasing access to higher education. There is a long history of thought on the purposes and goals of higher education, and generally these relate to economic development, cultural reproduction, the creation of an informed citizenry, the discovery of new knowledge and social justice. These goals also reveal a central tension – Is higher education a private enterprise, designed to help particular groups of individual prosper, or a public good designed to help society more broadly?

When the first European universities were established in the late middle ages, their main goal was to educate a select group of individuals (usually men of the 'middling' or noble classes) around the teachings and wisdoms of classic Greek, Roman, early Christian and, later, Arabic scholars. These scholars, representing only a small portion of society, were entrusted with this knowledge in order to carefully preserve it for future scholars, providing commentary, learned thought, and the application of teachings to professional contexts (e.g. in law and medicine). Collectively, these students became Europe's professionals – clergymen, lawyers, physicians and tutors – and the expectation was that their work was godly in nature and expected to benefit society and civilization in the broadest sense. By the time of the Enlightenment in the seventeenth century though, many European universities were viewed as out of date, and the value of this social good lessened, given their focus on a 'moribund' medieval curriculum (Perkin 2007).

However, with the founding of the first colonial colleges in North America, most notably Harvard College in 1636, higher education was regarded as a different sort of social good, often viewed as a 'civilizing influence' in a disorderly world. Over the next two hundred or so years, as more institutions of higher education were founded worldwide, there were different social goods ascribed to the enterprise. Accompanying the Industrial Revolution, for example, there was an ongoing debate about whether colleges should provide vocational education and practical skills ('on-the-job training', as it were), or continue the tradition of a liberal arts education – with 'learning how to think' as a central component. Both models posited higher education as a means to promote economic growth and 'civilization'. The emergence of the German research university in the nineteenth century added nuance to this question, positing the role of discovery and the creation of new knowledge as a central goal of higher education.

Yet, it is essential to note that the questions surrounding the purpose of higher education, as well as who should go to college and why, were focused on a very small percentage of the overall population and generally excluded women and people of colour. It was not until the mid-twentieth century, following the passing of the G.I. Bill (1944) in the United States, and the Robbins Report (1963) in the UK, did participation and access to higher education increase substantially. True 'massification' of higher education did not occur until the 1960s.

Despite this widening access, as we saw in Chapter 15 on Inclusion, there is significant evidence that educational access is not equally distributed amongst all social groups. From the perspective of conflict theory, society is based on conflict between groups who are competing for power and are looking after their own interests. It argues that education socializes people to believe that society is meritocratic, while in reality factors such as socio-economic status, among others, actually determine success. Thus, education is seen as reproducing and maintaining social class and other inequalities (for example, as argued in the classic studies of Bowles and Gintis, 1976 and Bourdieu and Passeron, 1979. See Boliver 2017 for a more recent review).

While higher education has long been assumed to contribute socially and economically to society, recent years have seen increasing demands on higher education systems internationally to demonstrate their social and, particularly, economic relevance, usefulness and contribution. How we, as higher education teachers, think about these issues is of great relevance here and help to shape how we understand our academic identities (Macfarlane 2016; Beach 2018).

The role of higher education can be understood in 'universalist' or locally social embedded terms (for example, see Paterson 2003; Bertolin 2016; Cantwell et al. 2018). 'Universalist' approaches entail a detached stance, focused on the unfettered pursuit of knowledge for its own sake and a loyalty towards one's academic discipline and international peers. There is an emphasis on intellectual autonomy, with little emphasis on responsibility towards wider society. In contrast, locally/socially-embedded approaches focus on the importance of the contribution of higher education to society through educating future leaders, maintaining culture, developing people's expertise to contribute to the economy and civic engagement through contributing to public debate and policy-making, preparing students for important roles in society and being committed to the notion that knowledge generated should be socially useful.

Rather than being in direct opposition, there is evidence that academics can hold both approaches (Paterson and Bond 2005). The socially embedded critique of the universalist view of the purposes of higher education played a role in the emergence of service learning, community-based learning, work-based learning, and new thinking associated with the deliberate cultivation of transferable skills, 'graduateness' and employability, discussed more fully in the next section. Before we consider these, as reflective teachers, it is useful to explore our own beliefs about the purpose of higher education. This is the focus of Reflective Activity 17.1.

Reflective Activity 17.1 The relationship between higher education and society

Reflect on your views about the relationship between higher education and society.

- Consider these questions: What does 'education' mean? What does it mean to be educated? How does education function in society, and for what purpose? For example, does education only encompass the formal systems in place, i.e. schooling, higher education, etc., or is it something broader?
- Now consider the constructs of teaching and learning. What does it mean to teach? To learn? What is the purpose and value of each?
- Consider, now, higher education. In your view: what is the purpose and goal of higher education? Is it similar or different to how you view education more broadly? What might account for that difference?
- Finally, reflect on how your institution and/or unit (school, department, programme, etc.) describes its relationship to society. (You might, for example, consult mission statements, strategic plans and similar, etc.). From your own professional experiences, consider the extent to which stated policy/commitments align to actual practice.

While completing this exercise, you may have identified a range of purposes of education, and higher education, in society. How do these relate to the ideas presented above?

Employability, 'graduateness' and the rise of 'competency-based education'

In recent years, the increased focus on the contribution of higher education to the economy has led to much discussion about the sorts of graduates that higher education produces and how this impacts their 'employability'. The formal recognition and embedding of employability policy and practice in higher education systems differs internationally. For example, while it has developed as a very visible aspect of contemporary higher education policy and practice in the UK, it has not been as formally embedded in some other countries (for example, in the United States), although it has been visible in less formal ways worldwide.

Discussions about 'graduateness' tend to highlight issues around the skills and attributes of graduates. Two types are generally emphasized: 'hard' skills, which are subject/discipline-specific, and 'soft' skills and dispositions, which are regarded as being more generic and transferable in nature (Barrie 2006). 'Graduateness' has become inextricably linked with the concept of 'employability' (Walsh and Kotzee 2010), which Yorke (2004, p. 8) defines as:

A set of achievements – skills, understandings and personal attributes – that makes graduates more likely to gain employment and be successful in their chosen occupations, which benefit themselves, the workforce, the community and the economy.

At the same time, numerous studies have been conducted over the past twenty years that reveal a fundamental disconnect between how universities might understand 'job preparedness' or 'graduateness,' and how employers understand the term. While for some employers, disciplinary knowledge and skills are vital, others are satisfied with 'general graduateness' (Yorke 2004). Further, employers tend to focus on the ability to apply employability skills, such as literacy and numeracy, as opposed to just possessing them, and emphasize the need for them to be underpinned by a positive attitude (Pegg et al. 2012). In contrast, most higher education teachers' conceptions of 'graduateness' remain very much related to specific academic disciplines (Walsh and Kotzee 2010), and views about the appropriateness of 'employability' and related skills concerns are contested. In particular, concerns around problem-solving, creativity and communication have long been cited by employers and industry professionals (Moore and Morton 2017).

Those who argue in favour of embedding employability in higher education hold that it will positively impact public and private outcomes. For example, HEFCE (2011) emphasizes the private and public benefit of embedding employability in higher education. Pegg et al. (2012) argue that employability concerns can be complementary to the traditional academic goals of higher education, often with only minor adjustments. The recommended approach is to integrate, and thus contextualize, employability and the development of graduate attributes into the disciplines rather than offer extra-curricular sessions on these themes (Barrie 2006).

However, Bozalek (2013) argues that in the language of graduate attributes, there is little or no acknowledgement that students are 'differentially positioned', having diverse prior experiences, preparation for higher education, and learning and social needs, and also that higher education institutions are 'differently able to accommodate diverse students' social and learning needs' (p. 72). Bozalek (2013) argues that the capabilities approach, the focus of which is human 'flourishing' (see below), can inform existing graduate attributes approaches through its focus on the differential positioning of students in relation to the outcomes of a higher education, including graduate attributes. She argues that this is an institutional task, and that the barriers at individual institutional level need to be identified and addressed to enable all of our students to achieve the relevant required outcomes.

Responses from universities and academics to expectations about embedding employability in higher education curricula vary from aligning their programmes and teaching to employability outcomes, to being unwilling, or unable, to do so. What might be behind the unevenness of this response? Walsh and Kotzee (2010, p. 40) argue that this tension assumes that an academic education and vocational training are mutually exclusive, and that only the former is of relevance to universities. This is a highly charged and complex issue, and relates back to our earlier discussion about the fundamental purposes and goals of higher education, and their contribution to society.

Moore and Morton (2017) also posit another explanation, suggesting that universities may face significant challenges in bridging the gap between the two domains when designing the curriculum, finding it difficult to 'find similarities in tasks and content' in regards to academic learning and workplace application (p. 604). In their study, which focuses on written communication, they recommend that exposing students to 'a range of experiences and tasks . . . will help them to learn how to "shape" their acquired disciplinary knowledge in distinctive and communicatively appropriate ways' (p. 604). For example, Engineering students might write up lab results as a report to a simulated client, rather than as a traditional academically-oriented lab report. Political science students might write up an analysis of a political event in the form of an op-ed or think piece intended for public consumption (e.g. in a newspaper or podcast) rather than as an academic essay.

While we may recognize that both subject/discipline-specific knowledge and skills for the workplace are necessary in contemporary higher education programmes, it may be that we sense that that there is something important being lost in the drive towards skills development. Macfarlane (2004) suggests that this something important might be related to values. He claims that:

> While it is now widely recognized that a higher education must develop students with both subject knowledge and skills for the workplace, the role of values remains a neglected or largely lost dimension of the curriculum . . . [V]alues and affective aims are being quietly airbrushed out of the curriculum of higher education. (p. 28)

It is this sense of the 'airbrushing' out of values and affective aims that is particularly disturbing to university teachers, as opposed to the addition of skills-based objectives to traditional discipline-specific knowledge in higher education programmes. Macfarlane makes the point that rather than teaching about values, as university teachers, we can endeavour to teach through values. As he explains:

> Intellectual integrity, seeking the truth and tolerance of others are expectations that teachers in higher education have of their students. They are in no sense discipline-specific or demand that lecturers preach about values. Thus, teaching does not necessarily have to be explicitly *about* values. Rather, teaching *through* values means that certain principles and norms of behaviour are embedded into our expectations of students and, crucially, our own practice. (p. 30; emphasis in original)

Reflective Activity 17.2 Reflecting on our values

What are our values as higher education teachers? The UK Professional Standards Framework for Teaching and Supporting Learning in Higher Education includes specific areas of activity, core knowledge and professional values. The professional values ask teachers to:

- respect individual learners and diverse learning communities;
- promote participation in higher education and equality of opportunity for learners;
- use evidence-informed approaches and the outcomes from research, scholarship and continuing professional development; and
- acknowledge the wider context in which higher education operates, recognizing the implications for professional practice.

What are your views on the above stated professional values for teachers in higher education? How do you feel these relate to the employability agenda?

Thus, as reflective university teachers, can we find a way to reconcile our professional views and values with national policy expectations, particularly where we may have significant concerns about aspects of the agenda in question? We should seek to critically examine what is being asked of us as educators. For example, many higher education programmes already foster the development of student behaviours, skills and attitudes which are directly, or indirectly, aligned to employability attributes, competencies and transferable skills.

Where this is the case, it is suggested that we 'make the tacit explicit' (Knight et al. 2003) in relation to graduate and employability skills and attributes, in course documentation, in learning outcomes, stated competencies and in what we communicate to students. This involves being explicit and transparent to students about 'where, how and why they are developing graduate attributes' (Pegg et al. 2012, p. 42) in their specific areas, so that they can more readily identify this learning. Active and experiential methodologies, including work-based placements, are advocated in supporting students' development of employability attributes, as they seem to require critical and reflective student engagement and self-evaluation. Indeed, building in structured opportunities for students to reflect on their learning with respect to relevant skills and attributes is a central plank of what is advocated in this approach.

In recent years, many universities have responded to these questions by developing different programmes around community-based learning, service learning and workplace-based learning, which – while different in scope, location and function – are collectively designed to situate the learner within real-world contexts in order to not only learn and employ key 'real world' and transferable academic skills, but also to think about their work in the context of a broader social good and commitment to the community around them.

While there will be different opportunities in different subject areas for engagement in these sorts of activities, we should critically examine our programmes and our practice to investigate where opportunities for our students to develop discipline-related graduate attributes and employability skills, might naturally arise during their academic programmes.

Reflective Activity 17.3 'Graduateness' and 'employability' in your discipline

Select one programme in your discipline or professional area (choose one to which you contribute a module, or part of a module) and examine it with the following questions in mind (you may find it useful to do this with colleagues):

- What do 'graduateness' and 'employability' mean in this area?
- What learning outcomes in your curriculum currently relate to 'graduate attributes' and employability? Are there certain skills, competencies or attributes which are relevant but implicit in current learning outcomes? Could these be made more explicit? What ones might be adjusted or extended to include this focus? Might additional ones be added?
- What learning, teaching and assessment approaches might be adjusted or included to include a focus on graduate attributes and employability?

Next, consider the above questions in relation to the module, or part of the module, that you teach.

As university teachers, we may be limited in our ability to influence national policies, such as those regarding employability. However, as reflective teachers, we should consider how these policies may impact our course design and teaching, and ultimately student learning and outcomes, as well as the wider student experience.

Widening participation and access

In **Reflective Activity 17.2**, we considered the professional values identified in the UK Professional Standards Framework for Teaching and Supporting Learning in Higher Education. One of the values clearly relates to widening participation and access. As reflective university teachers, we are all involved in widening participation to some extent, and this area is an important part of the way our teaching contributes to wider society and to the transformative goals of higher education in society.

At first glance, it may seem that the rationale for *widening participation* is premised – at least mostly – on social justice concerns, as widening participation is recognized as a means of tackling inequality, redressing social exclusion and fostering human development. It is argued that increasing the higher education participation of students from under-represented groups, particularly for those from lower socio-economic groups, makes for a more egalitarian society, as higher education has traditionally acted as a type of 'gatekeeper' to the professions. Higher education is also increasingly viewed as a means of strengthening civic engagement and social inclusion more broadly. In the United States, for example, these aspirations have been made more explicit, particularly amongst those institutions that highlight the importance of service learning, community-based learning, and workplace learning.

However, Burke (2002) has argued that the emphasis on individualism and rights and responsibilities constructs widening participation as a means of supplying the economy with necessary human capital: 'upskilling' individuals enables them to improve their potential contribution to the economy through employment. As a result, discussion of the benefits of a higher education has tended to focus primarily on the labour market, in the terms we discussed in the previous section, rather than other benefits such as social engagement and transformation (Thomas and Quinn 2007; McArthur 2011).

Certainly, widening participation policies alone do not directly lead to upward social mobility for those concerned. Despite the significant progress noted internationally in the increase and widening of higher education opportunities (Cantwell et al. 2018), inequities remain in general, and in particular in relation to more selective institutions. While widening participation policies have resulted in increased learning opportunities for an increasingly diverse student population, they have not led to fair and equal access to equal types of higher education or equal outcomes in the labour market (David 2010; Cantwell et al. 2018).

Moreover, students from various under-represented groups tend to be over-represented in what are perceived to be 'lower status' institutions and programmes. Parry (2010, p. 39) points out the growth in 'lower-rank' institutions (including community, vocational and further education) at the pre-higher education entry stage and questions whether such a development should be regarded 'as a process of democratization or diversion'. If the former, then students qualifying for, or entering into, higher education from these establishments share in some of the opportunities made available to individuals on other pathways. If the latter, then the less-advantaged and non-traditional students (who commonly populate these institutions) find themselves steered into lower-status programmes, routes and outcomes. Rather than bringing new populations into higher education, the effect of expansion is diversion, so reducing the recruitment pressures on elite establishments and relieving them of responsibilities for widening participation (Parry 2010, pp. 39–40).

There is evidence to support concerns about the lack of students from under-represented groups in the most selective or 'prestigious' higher education institutions. Studies that have investigated the extent of 'fair' access to prestigious research-led universities in the UK have found that those from lower social class and state schools were far less likely to apply to these universities relative to their similarly qualified peers from higher class and private school backgrounds (Boliver 2013, 2015, 2016; Siddiqui et al. 2019). Overly-simplistic notions of student 'choice', in explaining the differential socio-demographic composition of the student body in different 'types' of institutions, and the related issue of students' decision-making with respect to applications, ought to be avoided. For example, these studies consistently show that applicants from state schools and Black and Asian backgrounds were far less likely to be offered a place at a prestigious university than were their comparably qualified peers from White backgrounds and private schools. Research also suggests that the core widening participation issue of students desiring to 'fit in' may impact on 'choices' in this regard; how 'hospitable', welcoming and comfortable will a potential student from an under-represented group perceive an institution to be when the majority of students in that institution are 'not like us'? (Wilson-Strydom, 2015; Bathmaker et al. 2016; Hanley 2016; Calitz 2018).

Widening participation is not just about getting students from under-represented groups into higher education, or into certain 'types' of higher education institutions. It is very much also about their success and progression. Stuart (2012) contends that the debate about higher education and social mobility has moved from a focus on widening participation to outcomes for graduates:

> While widening participation may be a precursor to upward social mobility, it does not automatically create it. For first generation students in higher education who come from lower socio-economic groups what matters most is not just getting into university but succeeding there and being able to gain employment that moves them beyond their family background. (Stuart 2012, p. 7)

However, as reflective university teachers, we must also question the assumption that 'upward' social mobility is always a straightforwardly good thing. For example, whereas no one could question the importance of being adequately resourced to live a healthy, happy and productive life, the assumption that movement to a 'higher' social group is intrinsically good stigmatizes those in other social groups. A key theme from Stuart's (2012) life-history study of 150 first-generation higher education students now working in higher education is that of 'movement', particularly *away* from their working-class roots. Similar studies conducted in the United States have described similar challenges and areas of concern, particularly among first generation college students (Hinz 2016).

As we discussed in Chapter 1, this raises questions about the extent to which individual students from, for example, a working-class background have to leave behind, or reject, their original familial and community background. Stuart (2012), drawing on a wide range of studies and evidence, acknowledges the growth in opportunities in both education and wider social mobility in the UK over the past few decades, but notes that access to the professions has become less socially representative over time. Of course, higher education is not the only influencing factor here: employers' recruitment policies also play a crucial role (Iannelli and Paterson 2006) and, as we saw earlier, so does the type of institution in which the degree was completed, as well as ethnicity and social class (Lessard-Phillips et al. 2018; Friedman and Laurison 2019).

What do these issues mean for us as reflective teachers in higher education? How we conceive of the relationship between higher education and social mobility, and how we conceive of widening participation, impacts upon our everyday practice with students and colleagues alike. As we discussed in Chapter 15, traditional conceptualizations of access and widening participation are generally regarded as being 'deficit' in nature, in that those from under-represented groups have been constructed variably as 'lacking' 'appropriate' motivation, aspirations, skills, qualifications, preparation and means to enter higher education. These individuals are therefore targeted and their entrance to higher education facilitated and supported. Such a conceptualization remains firmly focused on individual rather than structural barriers: the student is seen as being in deficit and must adapt in order to fit in with the system (see Younger et al. 2019 for a systematic review of different strategies for supporting widening participation).

As university teachers, if we subscribe to this sort of perspective, we do not perceive any need to challenge or adapt our practices. In contrast, a more 'transformative' (Jones and Thomas 2005; Thomas 2019) conceptualization recognizes and appreciates differences between groups and emphasizes the need for *institutional adaptation*, in terms of structures and processes (including curricula and teaching) as well as larger institutional programmes (e.g. mentoring networks, bridge programmes etc.) in order to respond to the diverse needs of students. From this perspective, the core values and assumptions underpinning traditional higher education teaching are questioned, and institutional and teacher development and adaptation, in terms of the need to develop a more inclusive approach, is promoted. These issues are examined further in Research Briefing 17.1.

RESEARCH BRIEFING 17.1 Learning and teaching for social diversity and difference in higher education

Hockings et al. (2010) examined the understandings and practices of eight university teachers in an old and a new university in the UK, focusing on how they approached increasing student diversity with their first-year undergraduates. Adopting an interpretive approach, their central research question related to how teachers academically engage all students in a diverse classroom, through student questionnaires, interviews and focus groups, teacher interviews, observation and recording of classes, and meetings between the teachers of specific subjects in the two institutions. The researchers took a complex and multi-faceted view of student diversity, which extended beyond class, ethnic and gender categorizations to include considerations relating to prior learning, entry route to higher education, living and family contexts, and approaches to learning, among others.

The students in their study reported a strong desire to 'fit in', often feeling that other students were 'cleverer' than them and, as such, being drawn to other students with whom the shared a common ground. They wanted to be viewed by their teachers as individuals, with particular needs and interests, as they had experienced before entry to the university. They felt that their university teachers did not have the time to know them in this way. They came to understand that the learning approaches they had employed at the pre-entry level were not sufficient at university, and that they needed to be more independent in their learning at university. In terms of 'ways of knowing', some students came to know by trying to make connections between what they were learning at university and their own lives, while many others focused on the knowledge presented by their teacher or textbooks. There were some disciplinary differences in this regard.

The teachers in the study knew little about their students' lives, backgrounds and interests but distanced themselves from deficit views of the 'non-traditional' student. All eight teachers espoused a student-centred approach to teaching, implementing small strategies designed to build rapport, to make content relevant and draw on prior knowledge, and, over time, create a learning environment in which students felt comfortable to share their beliefs and actively and collaboratively participate. Overall, students were most engaged when the activities and subject matter were relevant to their own lives and identities, when ground rules were firmly established at the outset, when examples were relevant and culturally sensitive, which was particularly noted in subjects with a professional orientation.

As discussed in other chapters, as teachers, we would do well to reflect on our identities, and critically examine our ideas around power, positionality and privilege. Awareness of one's own assumptions and biases is critical for creating inclusive learning environments. Despite the significant constraints faced by university teachers (e.g. increasing student numbers, decreasing resources), David et al. (2010) argue that inclusive learning environments can be created and they identify four ways of doing so:

1 **Creating individual and inclusive learning environments.** By making time to get to know students as individuals and by setting ground rules for, and modelling, collaborative learning behaviour.

2 **Using student-centred strategies.** By creating open, flexible, student-centred activities in which students can apply their own (and others') knowledge and experience.

3 **Connecting with students' lives.** By selecting and negotiating topics and activities relevant to students' lives, backgrounds and identities.

4 **Being aware of and taking account of cultural differences within the group.** By using resources, materials, humour, examples and anecdotes that are sensitive to the social and cultural diversity of the group. (Adapted from David et al. 2010, p. 196)

Additionally, we might add several points that we would do well to keep in mind. First, the notion of inclusion should not mean 'welcoming others into the classroom', or 'being aware that some students are different'. Those notions, no matter how well-intentioned, set up a palpable distinction that suggests that the classroom is rightfully inhabited by some people (e.g. white people) who are inviting others in as guests or as people who otherwise 'would not belong'. Second, we should think carefully about team and group activities – sometimes the default is to separate affinity groups (e.g. students from an under-represented group), so that there is one member of each under-represented group in every pairing. Such breakdowns generally benefit members of the dominant group, but can hurt members of the under-represented group (Ambrose et al. 2010).

These strategies are helpful to us as reflective university teachers at course development, planning and teaching levels. It is important to remember that such strategies can be developed and implemented in manageable ways, depending on the nature and demands of our individual institutional and discipline contexts.

Reflective Activity 17.4 Widening participation, your rationale and practice

- Does your institution have a policy with respect to widening participation? If so, what is the stated rationale? What have you observed about the way in which this policy has been implemented?
- From your perspective as a university teacher in your subject discipline, what impact, if any, has widening participation had on you, in terms of the various aspects of your professional role?
- How might your 'inclusive pedagogy' (see Chapter 15) be further informed and developed by the discussions earlier In in this chapter?

THE CONTRIBUTION OF REFLECTIVE TEACHING TO SOCIETY

One way of thinking about how higher education teaching contributes to society is by considering 'critical pedagogy', which we discussed in Chapter 12. A related body of work has examined human development and capabilities in the higher education context (for example, see McLean 2006; Walker 2006; Boni and Walker 2013; Calitz 2018). We examined some of this work in **Research Briefing 4.1**, when we discussed Walker and McLean's (2013) work on developing public good professionals in South Africa. This body of work emphasizes the emancipatory and transformative purposes of higher education, relating to the promotion of citizenship, democracy, equality, human development and sustainability, over reproductive and economy-based conceptualizations.

Our earlier discussion and critique of the employability and skills agenda in higher education is relevant here. McLean (2006), for example, argues that higher education's economic purposes are over-emphasized, relative to its intellectual and emancipatory purposes, and that the university 'lifeworld' has been 'colonized' by the values and norms of the marketplace. While noting the importance of students' skills development in the context of preparing citizens technically and professionally, McLean (2006) is clear that university teaching must also prepare citizens culturally and socially. Boni and Walker (2013, pp. 9–10) sum up this position:

> Universities, we think, are well positioned to help face local and global challenges regarding human and social development. They ought to be oriented to human and social challenges and be spaces for critical thought, reflection, action, unraveling complexity, and robust but respectful argument. At stake here is by doing particular kinds of educational things universities educate particular kinds of graduates who are both professionals and citizens. We suggest that the 'particular kinds of things' ought to be to educate people who act responsibly towards others, who contribute in different ways to creating and securing capabilities to all in society, and who value the building of a society which works in this way, faced as we are with staggering inequalities, poverty and vulnerability.

The human development and capabilities approach is explicitly oriented towards human well-being, plurality, flourishing and freedom. Walker (2010) suggests that universities adopt (and be evaluated on) four related dimensions: well-being, participation and empowerment, equity and diversity, and sustainability. A 'good' university would, thus, lead to the formation of graduates with the knowledge, capacities, capabilities and skills to actively contribute to social justice, as well as to the economy. This sort of graduate is a 'graduate citizen' (Walker 2010, p. 494), a 'self-knowing agent[s] capable of purposeful action for individual and collective change', who can make 'a positive difference in the everyday lives of the people with whom they come into contact' (Walker 2010, p. 487). These are the sorts of skills and capacities that McLean (2006, p. 79) identifies as being part of the 'communicatively reasonable' graduate: 'an analytic, critical and imaginative thinker who is committed to working with others for the public good.'

Walker and Boni (2013, pp. 24–25) emphasize the potential of teaching as a contributor to advancing the public and social good:

> In all this it may be that university teaching is one sure way to reinstate the public good and to advance the social good – to once again understand the hugely transformative potential of good teaching on undergraduates and postgraduates alike. This is the space in which we might educate, form and shape engaged public citizens, as critical reasoners and democratic citizens who understand their obligations to others, who are equipped to ask what the public implications of their actions are, and are morally prepared to ask of their actions and those of others, is it right?

As reflective university teachers, we understand the power of the curriculum in shaping student outcomes. The curriculum is also a potentially powerful transformative site in terms of what is selected as 'valid' knowledge and what is seen to be important for students to learn (as we have already seen in Chapter 9). For Walker and Boni (2013), the curriculum may also offer the potential for more sustainable change, than might teaching and learning processes, which often depend on the individual university teachers involved. Walker (2012) considers a curriculum with outcomes aligned to human development and capabilities outcomes.

Being a strong subject-expert is crucial but not sufficient; as we discussed in relation to Shulman's (1987) notion of 'pedagogical content knowledge' in Chapter 11, teachers must also understand how best to enable students to learn in their discipline. This involves engaging meaningfully in critical self-reflection, professional conversations, and 'applying pedagogic theory to teaching and learning as it is experienced' (Shulman 1987, p. 145). As part of this, McLean argues that we need to conceptualize teaching as promoting our students' intellectual growth and interrogate the overly simplistic, and often problematic, learning outcomes and skills discourses. We need to also ensure that we conceptualize learning as a complex process of interpretation and attempts at meaning-making, as opposed to a process of transmission of knowledge from the teacher to the student.

Hence, in this approach, the emphasis is on active and inclusive participation and engagement, and student-led learning. We try to develop our students' capacity for thinking 'beyond everyday concerns' (McLean 2006, p. 79) and for connecting their academic knowledge to culture and society. The sort of learning environment required for this to happen is one in which we provide formative feedback, make connections, exhibit high expectations and focus on the potential of all of our students, and include opportunities for discussion and active participation. These are all aspects of good teaching more generally. Deprez and Wood (2013) also emphasize the need to be actively aware of the varied and diverse capacities and prior learning that students bring to the classroom and learning experience, and the need to appropriately scaffold learning for all of our students, in terms of the necessary supports.

Through a critical pedagogical approach we, as reflective and engaged university teachers, can influence our students to become active citizens engaged with social justice issues. What might such a pedagogical approach look like? Similar to the argument in Chapter 15 with respect to teaching for inclusion, we must resist the urge here to seek quick-fix answers. We must instead reflect on whether our pedagogies 'humanize' or 'dehumanize' our students. As Martinez et al. (2016) suggest, 'dehumanizing pedagogies' are those methods and activities that oppress students, marginalize their sense of identity, or otherwise diminish their voices or ability to act. Dehumanizing pedagogies might include the traditional lecture, in which most students are never actively invited to express themselves. A dehumanizing pedagogy might also occur when learning tasks that privilege certain types of students (e.g. timed in-class exams) are emphasized.

On the other hand, Salazar (2013) notes five principles associated with humanizing pedagogy:

1 *The full development of the person is essential for humanization.* Students must engage in a *process of becoming fully human.* Educators must foster their students'

well-being by demonstrating compassion, by sharing themselves and allowing students to share themselves in return, and by helping students develop positive relationships with their peers (pp. 128–29).

2 *To deny someone else's humanization is also to deny one's own.* The denial of humanness arises from Freire's (1970) banking model of education which, as Salazar explains, 'transforms students into receiving objects by perpetuating practices such as rote memorization and skill-and-drill that encourage students to receive, file, and store deposits of knowledge transmitted by educators' (pp. 129–30). When students are viewed as objects, without agency, they are effectively dehumanized. When students lose the ability to act, speak, and perhaps even think for themselves, they may also internalize failure and denigrate themselves. As such, educators who dehumanize students are, in effect, also dehumanizing themselves.

3 *The journey for humanization is an individual and collective endeavour toward critical consciousness.* Drawing on Friere, Salazar explains that students and teachers must strive for 'mutual humanization' by developing critical consciousness, which only occurs through a process of transformative dialogue where teachers and students become 'subjects' rather than objects (pp. 131–33). Such dialogue is grounded in lived experience, and allows students and teachers to probe structural inequities and oppression, so that they make personal connections to learning, reflect on their own potential and the contributions they may make, and ultimately internalize their own sense of humanity.

4 *Critical reflection and action can transform structures that impede our own and others' humanness, thus facilitating liberation for all* (p. 128). Here, educators and students examine their own power and privilege within social and political hierarchies considering how those structural inequities and constructs impact others. Salazar (2013, p. 137) draws on Freire's (1970) argument that 'to exist humanely is to name the world, to change it'. Essentially, humanizing pedagogies are deeply connected with the notion of social change, and would include service-based learning, inquiry and/or problem-based learning that probes and challenges oppression and structural inequities, or social justice education more broadly.

5 *Educators are responsible for promoting a more fully human world through their pedagogical principles and practices.* Ultimately, as Salazar suggests, such principles and practices hold that:
- the reality of the learner is crucial;
- critical consciousness is imperative for students and educators;
- students' sociocultural resources are valued and extended;
- content is meaningful and relevant to students' lives;
- students' prior knowledge is linked to new learning;
- trusting and caring relationships advance the pursuit of humanization;
- mainstream knowledge and discourse styles matter;
- students will achieve through their academic, intellectual and social abilities;
- student empowerment requires the use of learning strategies; and
- challenging inequity in the educational system can promote transformation.

Dehumanizing pedagogies can have a significant negative impact on students. In a recent study of sixty Latinx and immigrant youths age 16–26, Martinez et al. (2016) found that participants had experienced a range of dehumanizing pedagogies, including 'feelings of isolation, negative peer influences, teachers' low expectations, and the lack of resources and other support programs for college-bound students. Even the college prep programs, meant to support high-achieving students, served to aggregate and alienate them from other students of color, and required them to shed cultural and familial ties' (p. 137). Others experienced more humanizing experiences, where teachers spent time getting to know students, or when teachers 'incorporated students' histories, cultures, and values as part of their pedagogy' (p. 141).

Ultimately, it is crucial for us to reflect deeply on the structural inequities that we may be reinforcing or confirming within our teaching contexts (considering too, the extent to which we might have benefited from such inequities ourselves), and helping students transform themselves by engaging in humanizing pedagogies.

Reflective Activity 17.5 Employing humanizing pedagogies

Consider the discussion of humanizing and dehumanizing pedagogies described above in light of the different contexts in which you teach, as well as in your larger professional practice. In what ways do you use and/or promote pedagogies that help humanize your students – that is, help them develop fully as humans – and in what ways might you be silencing or taking away the agency of your students? How can you rethink existing pedagogies to help students become transformed as learners and as humans?

Examples of critical pedagogy in higher education

In the context of an English-language teaching higher education classroom in Ireland, Crosbie (2013) describes her critical pedagogical approach to teaching a module for international students at upper intermediate level. Along with English-language outcomes, she aimed to develop her students' understanding of the processes of globalization, to facilitate group work, and to increase her students' learning autonomy through self-assessment and goal-setting exercises. Assessment was through interactive peer-teaching sessions, written reflective reports, and group oral reflective discussion on the learning process and outcomes. When describing the classroom activities, she explains (pp. 183–84):

During the course of the module the roles of teacher and learner changed substantially. I commenced practice in the traditional model of instigator and, to some extent, controller of course content, classroom dynamics and learning. When it was the students' turn to take over for the presentations and peer-teaching sessions, our positions reversed in that I sat at the back or to the side of the class and participated in learning events of their making. Thus, the balance of power shifted back and forth, both between tutor and students and at peer level. . . . I began teaching the course from the students' perspective, encouraging them to observe how globalization was affecting them on a personal level in terms of their quality of life, what they had in common as well as how they differed from each other, and how their lives compared with other economic, social, political and cultural groups across the world. This engagement with self and other was linked to studies and activities connected with ethnicity and identity and branched further into intercultural studies, with a focus on in-group/out-group theory. On the socio-economic front, we studied 'free' versus 'fair' trade and Developing World poverty, drawing on readings, videos and classroom debates to raise critical consciousness. I also gave a lecture on key aspects of globalization, including economic, social, political and technological dimensions. Students were then given a list of global bodies to choose from and in groups prepare short presentations for the class . . . and were encouraged to develop critical lateral thinking by highlighting positive, negative and interesting points related to their chosen topic.

For the peer-teaching sessions, eight groups were created from the class list and they self-selected the following themes: child labour, drugs, ethnicity, fair trade, McDonaldization, sport, and world music. It was interesting to note the level of creativity and dedication that many of them brought to the planning and execution of these themes. Those with technical abilities created their own videos with soundtracks and credits, others recorded interviews which they played in class, and most of them designed quizzes and other tasks to check comprehension, knowledge retention and vocabulary acquisition. They engaged well, for the most part, within a critical pedagogical framework, seeking to present different perspectives on topical issues in a bid to uncover and make sense of inequalities in the context of globalization.

In this example, we can see an acknowledgement of the changing power relations in terms of the student and teacher roles, the way in which changed roles afford the lecturer an opportunity to reflect on her own teaching, the important links to everyday life and their immediate environment, and the peer-teaching classroom approach employed by Crosbie. This kind of approach would be more challenging with a very large class grouping. However, Chapter 12 presents some ideas for how this might be done, for example through the use of 'textwalls'. It would be worth considering how this sort of critical pedagogical approach might be used in your own subject area and the sorts of learning outcomes you might help your students to achieve. A clear question here is whether these approaches are more applicable in some subjects than others. The work we have discussed already in terms of public-good professionals gives a sense of how these ideas could work beyond the social sciences, but it is true that there are less examples of this kind of approach in the natural sciences. The issue is the extent to which this is to do with the knowledge of these disciplines and the extent to which it is more about the ways in which these disciplines have been traditionally taught.

A small-scale example of a critical pedagogy in higher education can be found in Boland and Keane (2012). In their chapter, they discuss their (elective) service learning module ('Learning to Teach for Social Justice') in a teacher education programme, through which student teachers provide academic support for young people from disadvantaged and minority groups in a community context, whilst engaging in critical reflection and support sessions on campus. Alongside working in the community, critical reflection and open discussion form key parts of the pedagogical approach, and students are actively encouraged to make connections between theory and research examined as part of their study of their 'Education, Diversity and Social Justice' module, and their practical, on-the-ground experiences in the non-formal educational context of the service learning site. Potentially transformative outcomes were identified at the level of participating (school) students (in terms of improved engagement and achievement in education), the student teachers (particularly with regard to capacity for insight and empathy) and for the participating community and non-governmental organizations. One of the service learning sites was a Traveller-specific homework club. The student teachers involved in the initiative reported very positive experiences, emphasizing how much they valued the opportunity to meet members of the Travelling community:

> What I liked best was getting the opportunity to experience diversity and in particular to meet the children and their parents. Prior to being involved in the Pavee Study, I had little or no chance to meet with Travellers. It was also great to work with a small number of students. (Boland and Keane 2012, p. 148)

They also explained how the experience impacted on their own approach to learning and teaching in schools.

> because I have gained an insight into their culture, I have more patience and more under-standing when they become distracted or unmotivated. But I know that they need as much encouragement and as much motivation as students that have high expectations of themselves. (Boland and Keane 2012, p. 148)

Boland and Keane (2012) report that through their service learning experience, their student teachers learned about the centrality of relationship-building to teaching and learning, grew in confidence in terms of teaching for cultural diversity in their schools and classrooms, and came to a more critical understanding of the role of the key role played by the student–teacher relationship in the context of educational disadvantage. The authors argue that there was 'clear evidence of transformative outcomes for students, for example in terms of enhanced capacity for insight and empathy'. They contend that service learning offers significant transformative potential as a critical pedagogy in higher education, for all involved in the process, and in myriad ways:

> In the context of initial teacher education, S/CBL [Service/community-based learning] offers transformative potential both for student teachers and for the partners to the process. It can lead to significant change in student teachers' beliefs about diversity and enhance their confidence and competence in catering for diversity within their classrooms . . . It is our view that experiential learning of this nature also offers the poten-tial to enhance student teachers' sense of agency, giving them a deeper appreciation of how they can serve as agents of change in the schools in which they work. For minority and marginalized pupils, their involvement in homework club settings with student

teachers can enhance their engagement and achievement in education, ultimately contributing to equality in education. (Boland and Keane 2012, p. 151)

Certainly, this sort of approach to teaching may be more challenging than conventional approaches. However, there is some evidence to suggest that under-represented students who participate in service learning can positively influence retention and overall persistence rates at University (Song et al. 2017).

As well as the resource issues we have already discussed, McLean (2006) argues that many of the processes and practices inherent in the current approach to higher education are not conducive to the development of a critical pedagogy. The current 'new managerialism' approach (see Lynch et al. 2012) – marked by audit regimes in which 'quality' and 'standards' are ill-defined and their measurement is ill-conceived – results in a sense of constantly being 'under surveillance' and having to 'engage in relentless competition' with colleagues, which negatively impacts staff solidarity and interactions and leads to stress, work overload, disenchantment, mistrust and inauthenticity (McLean 2006). In this context, McLean argues that individual university teachers are 'unlikely to mobilize their communicative reason in relation to teaching' (McLean 2006, p. 51). Westheimer (2010) suggests that this is because our ability to constitute a vital critical democratic voice, and to be intellectually independent, is very much constrained in such an environment.

Notwithstanding the above, there are reasons to be optimistic about the transformative potential of higher education teaching in society. While Walker (2010) asks: 'Will producing different kinds of graduates even be possible and if it will, will they really bring about human development transformations?' (p. 492), she is pragmatic and emphasizes the possibility of contributing to inequality and injustice *reduction*, as opposed to elimination, as a perfectly valid and worthy goal.

Finally, as university teachers, we can also contribute to society through participation in the democratic process more broadly. Through our work, we contribute to society in myriad ways, both directly and indirectly, and at local, national and international levels. It is the normal way of the university to conduct research at the frontiers of knowledge, to lead and host discussions on challenging and sometimes controversial societal issues, and many individual university teachers get involved in local and national campaigns to redress social injustices. While the work of those in some disciplines (e.g. Social Sciences) may be very significantly aligned to participating in the democratic process, doing so is by no means limited to university teachers in such areas of academic enquiry. Reflective teachers in higher education are simultaneously citizens, and have a responsibility to use their knowledge and (potential) influence to inform decision-making and policy making in a democracy, particularly as we have privileged access to, and are creators of, knowledge. Where relevant, we can draw on important societal issues in their everyday teaching. We can also get more involved in debates and policy formation regarding education, including higher education, through various professional associations, through research about higher education, and through various pressure groups, campaigns and collective action more generally.

Reflective Activity 17.6 Higher education, teaching, and social justice

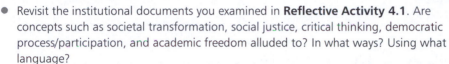

- Revisit the institutional documents you examined in **Reflective Activity 4.1**. Are concepts such as societal transformation, social justice, critical thinking, democratic process/participation, and academic freedom alluded to? In what ways? Using what language?
- Reflect on the everyday institutional and teaching practices and processes which you witness and in which you engage: to what extent do you feel your (or others') actual experiences and practices of institutional life are aligned to the stated ethos/mission?
- In the context of your own discipline, consider how the higher education experience, and teaching, can contribute to your students' capacity to positively influence the 'urgencies of our time'.

CONCLUSION

In this chapter, we explored how reflective teaching can contribute to our professionalism as academics through raising questions about the ways in which higher education contributes to society. A central consideration has been the relative contribution of higher education to the public/social good and economic development. While a dual role along these lines is not necessarily problematic, it is argued there has been an excessive focus on higher education's economic role. However, we did explore ways of focusing more on higher education teaching's humanizing and emancipatory power, through the consideration of critical pedagogy and the capabilities approach.

As university teachers, it is interesting to observe that a common theme in all the suggested approaches to teaching in this book is that of active student engagement. Helping students to make their learning deeper and more meaningful to their lives, exhibiting high expectations, and getting to know our students, are all part of student-centred approaches and are core parts of good teaching. There are certainly constraints upon our practice, but being reflective about our work, and being committed to the development of our practice, can enable us to manage many of these, in our quest to contribute to a more transformative higher education. The primary aim of this book is to support this important, inspiring and challenging quest.

KEY READINGS

For a guide targeted at the university teacher that considers both possibilities and constraints in embedding a teaching for employability and includes case studies from a range of learning and teaching contexts, see:

Pegg, A., Waldock, J., Hendy-Isaac, S. and Lawton, R. (2012) *Pedagogy for Employability*. York: The Higher Education Academy. Available online at: heacademy.ac.uk/system/files/pedagogy_for_employability_update_2012.pdf

For a consideration of how higher education institutions might advance equality and contribute to a sustainable and democratic society, see:

Boni, A. and Walker, M. (eds) (2013) *Human Development and Capabilities: Re-imagining the University of the Twenty-first Century*. London: Routledge.

For a helpful discussion of humanizing pedagogies, see

Salazar, M. (2013) 'A humanizing pedagogy: Reinventing the principles and practice of education as a journey toward liberation', *Review of Research in Education*, 37(1), 121–48.

For systematic review of approaches to widening participation, see:

Younger, K., Gascoine, L., Menzies, V. and Torgerson, C. (2019) 'A systematic review of evidence on the effectiveness of interventions and strategies for widening participation in higher education', *Journal of Further and Higher Education*, 43(6), 742–73.

On the relationship between increased access to higher education and equality, see:

Cantwell, B., Marginson, S. and Smolentseva, A. (eds) (2018) *High Participation Systems of Higher Education*. Oxford: Oxford University Press.

For an examination of the journey to and through higher education from the perspective of 150 first-generation higher education students over the past half century, using a life-history approach, see:

Stuart, M. (2012) *Social Mobility and Higher Education: The Life Experiences of First Generation Entrants in Higher Education*. Stoke-on-Trent: Trentham Books.

For an account of how social privilege supports success in the labour market after graduation, see:

Friedman, S. and Laurison, D. (2019) *The Class Ceiling: Why it Pays to be Privileged*. Bristol: Policy Press.

The Reflective Teaching in Higher Education Team

Paul Ashwin is Professor of Higher Education and Head of Department in the Department of Educational Research, Lancaster University, UK. Paul's research focuses on teaching, learning and curriculum practices in higher education and how they are shaped by higher education policies. Paul is a researcher in the Economic and Social Research Council, Office for Students and Research England funded 'Centre for Global Higher Education', a coordinating editor for the international journal *Higher Education*, and co-editor of the Bloomsbury book series 'Understanding Student Experiences of Higher Education'. Paul's recent books include *Higher Education Pathways: South African Undergraduate Education and the Public Good* (African Minds 2018) with Jenni Case, and *How Powerful Knowledge Disrupts Inequality: Reconceptualising Quality in Undergraduate Education* (Bloomsbury 2018) with Monica McLean and Andrea Abbas.

David Boud is Alfred Deakin Professor and Foundation Director of the Centre for Research in Assessment and Digital Learning, Deakin University; Professor in the Work and Learning Research Centre Middlesex University; and Emeritus Professor at the University of Technology Sydney. He is an Australian Learning and Teaching Senior Fellow and has published extensively on teaching, learning and assessment in adult, higher and professional education. He has also held various positions including Dean of the University Graduate School, Head of School and Associate Dean (Research and Development). His current areas of interest are in assessment in higher education and learning in the workplace. In the area of assessment, he has been a pioneer in learning-centred approaches to assessment, particularly through student self-assessment and building assessment skills for long-term learning. His most recent books are *Developing Evaluative Judgement in Higher Education: Assessment for Knowing and Producing Quality Work* (Routledge 2018) and *Re-imagining University Assessment in a Digital World* (Springer forthcoming) each with various others.

Susanna Calkins directs faculty initiatives at the Searle Center for Advancing Learning and Teaching at Northwestern University. She is the co-author of *Learning and Teaching* *in Higher Education: The Reflective Professional* (Sage 2009) and has published over twenty-five articles in areas related to learning and teaching, mentoring, teaching with technology and the history of higher education. Holding a PhD in History, she currently teaches in the Masters of Higher Education Administration Program at Northwestern.

Kelly Coate is the Pro Vice Chancellor for Education and Students, and Co-Director of the Centre for Higher Education and Equity Research, at the University of Sussex. Prior to joining Sussex, she was Vice Dean Education in the Faculty of Social Science and Public Policy at King's College London, and spent four years as Director of the King's Learning Institute. She has also worked at the National University of Ireland, Galway, and the Institute of Education at UCL. Her publications are in the areas of internationalization in higher education, the higher education curriculum, senior professional leadership in higher education, and gender and prestige in academic careers.

Fiona Hallett is a Professor in Education at Edge Hill University (UK) and Joint Editor of the *British Journal of Special Education*. She is interested in inclusive educational practices and has researched the lived experiences of marginalised learners across a range of national contexts. She is also interested in the ways in which research methodologies position the researcher and the researched and is currently using Visual Methodologies for an international project on learner voice.

Gregory Light is Professor of Learning Sciences (retired) and was the Director of the Searle Center for Advancing Learning and Teaching at Northwestern University from 2001–15. He has taught graduate courses in higher and professional education, and consulted across the higher and professional education sector in North and South America, Europe, Africa and Asia. Prior to Northwestern, he was deputy head and interim head of the department of Life-Long Learning at the Institute of Education, University College London. His research and scholarship are focused on student learning and the professional development of teaching in higher education. He has authored and co-authored more than sixty peer-reviewed papers and is the first author of the books *Learning and Teaching in Higher Education: The Reflective Professional* (Sage 2001, 2009) and *Making Scientists: Six Principles for Effective College Teaching* (Harvard University Press 2013).

Kathy Luckett is the Director of the Humanities Education Development Unit and Associate Professor in the Department of Sociology, University of Cape Town. She teaches and supervises on the School of Education's Masters in Higher Education Studies and supervises for the Department of Sociology. Her research interests are: higher education policy around equity, access and language; sociology of knowledge and curriculum studies with a focus on the Humanities, Africana, decolonial and postcolonial studies; discourse analysis using Systemic Functional Linguistics and Legitimation Code Theory; and research methods that apply social/critical realism to educational evaluation.

Iain MacLaren is the Director of the Centre for Excellence in Learning & Teaching at NUI Galway, where he has responsibility for academic staff development, curricular innovation, policy, learning technologies and civic engagement. He is also a member of the board of Ireland's National Forum for the Enhancement of Teaching & Learning and has many years' prior experience in teaching at undergraduate and postgraduate levels and in research in his original discipline (Physics) and higher education. He has worked in a number of universities in Scotland, England and Ireland, is a graduate of Edinburgh and Durham universities, and is a Principal Fellow of Higher Education Academy and a Fellow of the Royal Society of the Arts.

Katarina Mårtensson is senior lecturer and academic developer at Lund University, Sweden. Her work includes supporting organizational development through academic development, scholarship of teaching and learning, and leadership. Her research and publishing focuses on informal social networks, professional development, academic microcultures and academic leadership. Her PhD Thesis, published in 2014, was titled 'Influencing teaching and learning microcultures: Academic development in a research-intensive university'. She is co-editor of *Teaching & Learning Inquiry*, former co-president of ISSOTL, the International Society for Scholarship of Teaching and Learning, and former co-editor of *IJAD*, the *International Journal for Academic Development*. She received the 2019 Distinguished Service Award from ISSOTL.

Jan McArthur is Senior Lecturer in Education and Social Justice in the Department of Educational Research, Lancaster University, UK. Her research focuses on the nature of higher education and how this relates to practices of teaching, learning and assessment. She has a particular interest in critical theory. Her published work explores the ideas of Theodor Adorno, Max Horkheimer and Axel Honneth, applying these to higher education. She has published a book exploring how Adorno's critical theory can inform our understanding of knowledge in higher education for the purposes of greater social justice: *Rethinking Knowledge within Higher Education* (Bloomsbury 2012). Her most recent book uses Honneth's conceptualization of mutual recognition to rethink the nature of assessment in higher education: *Assessment for Social Justice* (Bloomsbury 2018). Jan is a researcher in the Economic and Social Research Council, Office for Students and Research England funded 'Centre for Global Higher Education', and Editor of the journal *Arts and Humanities in Higher Education*.

Velda McCune is Senior Lecturer and Deputy Director at the Institute for Academic Development at the University of Edinburgh. In her current role she leads a team who undertake development work with staff and students relating to university learning and teaching. Her research focuses on teaching–learning environments and students' experiences of learning in higher education. Currently she is doing research into how best to teach about 'wicked' problems such as climate change, health inequality and conflict.

Monica McLean is Professor of Higher Education in the School of Education at the University of Nottingham. Her main area of expertise is university curriculum and pedagogy as it relates to social justice. Recent research projects, both funded by the Economic and Social Research Council, have investigated the relevance of the capability approach to university-based professional education for the public good in South Africa; and quality and inequality in social science departments in UK universities of different reputation. She is currently a co-investigator for a ESRC/DfID-funded project focused on raising the learning outcomes of rural and township youth in South Africa. Her books are: *Pedagogy and the University: Critical Theory and Practice* (Continuum 2008); *Professional Education, Capabilities and the Public Good* (Routledge 2013); and *How Powerful Knowledge Disrupts Inequality: Reconceptualising Quality in Undergraduate Education* (Bloomsbury 2017).

Michelle Tooher is an Educational Developer in the Centre for Excellence in Learning & Teaching at the National University of Ireland, Galway. At NUI Galway, she contributes to their popular professional development teaching and learning programmes at Certificate, Diploma and Masters levels. Since 2008, she has worked on supporting curricular reform within the university and nationally through her involvement in local and national level groups and committees. More recently, Michelle has led a project across four higher education institutions to help improve their approaches to Continuing Professional Development for the enhancement of teaching and learning at the levels of middle to senior management.

ACKNOWLEDGEMENTS

In the second edition, Velda McCune led the rewriting of Chapter 1 on Identity adding more ideas about identities and values as well as discussing student mental health. Gregory Light and Susanna Calkins led the work on revising Chapter 2 on Learning, which now has discussions of the implications of recent work on learning gain. David Boud led the revisions to Chapter 3 on Reflection, further developing the model of reflection used in the chapter. Paul Ashwin led the amendment of Chapter 4 on Principles, as well as bringing the book together as a whole in his role as lead author. Kathy Luckett led the rewriting of Chapter 5 on Contexts adding new discussions of issues around the decolonizing of higher education and Chapter 9 on Curriculum, where we now discuss different models of curriculum and consider how knowledge from the global South impacts on our ideas about curriculum. Monica McLean led the further development of Chapter 6 on Relationships, which includes greater discussions of the emotional dimensions of relationships and Chapter 11 on Teaching, introducing a new focus on the bases underpinning our thinking about teaching. Kelly Coate led the amendment of Chapter 7 on Engagement, where we now have a greater focus on how we engage with students and Chapter 14 on Quality, which now discusses how recent developments in ideas and policies related teaching excellence impact on how we think about quality. Iain MacLaren led the rewriting of Chapter 8 on Spaces, which now has a much greater discussion of online spaces and social media as forms of educational space. Jan McArthur led the further development of Chapter 10 on Planning, which now has a greater focus on how we involve students in planning, and Chapter 13 on Assessment, which discusses the implications of ideas around assessment for social justice for our assessment practices. Michelle Tooher further developed Chapter 12 on Communication and this chapter now examines how we communicate about our teaching to our colleagues and students. Fiona Hallet led the further development of Chapter 15 on Inclusion, which is now organized around the UN

Sustainable Goals for Education. Katarina Mårtensson led the further development of Chapter 16 on Expertise and developed a greater focus on the Scholarship of Teaching and Learning and the impact of informal contexts on the development of expertise. Susanna Calkins and Gregory Light led the further development of Chapter 17 on Professionalism, which now includes a new focus on humanizing pedagogies. The author and publisher gratefully acknowledge the permission granted to reproduce the copyright material in this book:

Case Study 8.1 is reproduced with kind permission of Niall Ó Dochartaigh
Reflective Activity 14.1 is reproduced with kind permission of Elaine Keane
Figure 11.1 is reproduced with kind permission of the Teaching and Learning Research Programme
Figure 14.3 is reproduced with kind permission of Achievement Matters achievementmatters.com.au

Every effort has been made to trace copyright holders and to obtain their permission for the use of copyright material. The publisher apologizes for any errors or omissions in copyright acknowledgement and would be grateful if notified of any corrections that should be incorporated in future reprints or editions of this book.

Bibliography

Aamodt, P., Frølich, N. and Stensaker, B. (2018) 'Learning outcomes – a useful tool in quality assurance? Views from academic staff', *Studies in Higher Education*, 43(4), 614–24.

Abes, E. and Wallace, M. (2018) '"People see me, but they don't see me": An intersectional study of college students with physical disabilities', *Journal of College Student Development*, 59(5), 545–62.

Adkins, B. (2009) 'PhD pedagogy and the changing knowledge landscapes of universities', *Higher Education Research and Development*, 28, 165–77.

Adorno, T. and Becker, H. (1999) 'Education for maturity and responsibility', *History of the Human Sciences*, 12(3), 21–34.

Agarwal, P. (2019) 'Retrieval practice and Blooms taxonomy: Do students need fact knowledge before higher order learning?' *Journal of Educational Psychology*, 111(2), 189–209.

Ahern, L., Feller, J. and Nagle, T. (2016) 'Social media as a support for learning in universities: An empirical study of Facebook Groups', *Journal of Decision Systems*, 25(sup. 1), 35–49.

Airey, J. and Larsson, J. (2018) 'Developing students disciplinary literacy? The case of University Physics.' In K.-S. Tang and K. Danielsson (eds), *Global Developments in Literacy Research for Science Education*. Cham: Springer, 357–76.

Airey, J. and Linder, C. (2009) 'A disciplinary discourse perspective on university science learning, achieving fluency in a critical constellation of modes', *Journal of Research in Science Teaching*, 46(1), 27–49.

Ajjawi, R. and Boud, D. (2018) 'Examining the nature and effects of feedback dialogue', *Assessment & Evaluation in Higher Education*, 43, 1106–19.

Åkerlind, G. (2007) 'Constraints on academics' potential for developing as a teacher', *Studies in Higher Education*, 32(1), 21–37.

Åkerlind, G. (2008) 'A phenomenographic approach to developing academics' understanding of the nature of teaching and learning', *Teaching in Higher Education*, 13, 633–44.

Åkerlind, G. (2011) 'Separating the teaching from the academic, possible unintended consequences', *Teaching in Higher Education*, 16, 183–95.

Alcoff, L. (2011) 'An epistemology for the next revolution', *TRANSMODERNITY: Journal of Peripheral Cultural Production of the Luso-Hispanic World*, 1(2), 68–78.

Alexander, R. (2004) *Towards Dialogic Teaching: Rethinking Classroom Talk*. Cambridge: Dialogos.

Aloisi, C. and Callaghan, A. (2018) 'Threats to the validity of the Collegiate Learning Assessment (CLA+) as a measure of critical thinking skills and implications for Learning Gain', *Higher Education Pedagogies*, 3, 57–82.

Ambrose, S., Bridges, M., DiPietro, M., Lovett, M. and Norman, M. (2010) *How Learning Works: Seven Research-Based Principles for Smart Teaching*. San Francisco: John Wiley and Sons.

Anderson, C. and McCune, V. (2013) 'Fostering meaning, fostering community', *Higher Education*, 66, 283–96.

Anderson, C. and Hounsell, D. (2007) 'Knowledge practices, doing the subject in undergraduate courses', *Curriculum Journal*, 18, 463–78.

Anderson, G. (2006) 'Assuring quality/resisting Quality Assurance: Academics responses to quality in some Australian universities', *Quality in Higher Education*, 12, 161–73.

Anderson, L., Krathwohl, D., Airasian, P., Cruikshank, K., Mayer, R., Pintrich, P., Raths, J. and Wittrock, M. (2001) *A Taxonomy for Learning, Teaching and Assessing: A Revision of Blooms Taxonomy of Educational Objectives*. New York: Longman.

Andresen, L. (2000) 'A useable, trans-disciplinary conception of scholarship', *Higher Education Research and Development*, 19, 137–58.

Andrews, J., Garriso, D. and Magnusson, K. (1996) 'The teaching and learning transaction in Higher Education: A study of excellent professors and their students', *Teaching in Higher Education*, 1, 81–103.

Ankrah, S. and Omar, A. (2015) 'Universities–industry collaboration: A systematic review', *Scandinavian Journal of Management*, 31, 387–408.

Archer, M. (2000) *Being Human: The Problem of Agency*. Cambridge: Cambridge University Press.

Archer, M. (2003) *Structure, Agency and the Internal Conversation*. Cambridge: Cambridge University Press.

Arday, J. and Mirza, H. (eds) (2018) *Dismantling Race in Higher Education: Racism, Whiteness and Decolonising the Academy*. London: Palgrave Macmillan.

Armbruster, B. (2000) 'Taking notes from lectures.' In R. Flippo and D. Caverly (eds), *Handbook of College Reading and Study Strategy Research*. Mahwah, NJ: Lawrence Erlbaum Associates Publishers, 175–99.

Arthur, M. (2016) *Student Activism and Curricular Change in Higher Education*. London: Routledge.

Ashwin, P. (2003) 'Peer support, relations between the context, process and outcomes for the students who are supported', *Instructional Science*, 31, 159–73.

Ashwin, P. (2005) 'Variation in students' experiences of the Oxford Tutorial', *Higher Education*, 50, 631–44.

Ashwin, P. (2006) 'Variation in academics accounts of tutorials', *Studies in Higher Education*, 31, 651–65.

Ashwin, P. (2009) *Analysing Teaching-Learning Interactions in Higher Education: Accounting for Structure and Agency*. London: Continuum.

Ashwin, P. (2014) 'Knowledge, curriculum and student understanding in higher education', *Higher Education*, 67, 123–6.

Ashwin, P. (2015) 'Missionary zeal: some problems with the rhetoric, vision and approach of the AHELO project', *European Journal of Higher Education*, 5(4), 437–44.

Ashwin, P. (2017) 'What is the Teaching Excellence Framework in the United Kingdom, and will it work?' *International Higher Education*, (88), 10–11.

Ashwin, P. and Case, J. (eds) (2018) *Higher Education Pathways: South African Undergraduate Education and the Public Good*. Cape Town: African Minds.

Ashwin, P. and Komljenovic, J. (2018) 'The conceptualisation of students' personal transformation through their engagement in South African undergraduate education.' In P. Ashwin and J. Case (eds), *Higher Education Pathways: South African Undergraduate Education and the Public Good*. Cape Town: African Minds.

Ashwin, P. and McVitty, D. (2015) 'The meanings of student engagement: Implications for policies and practices.' In A. Curaj, L. Matei, R. Pricopie, J. Salmi, and P. Scott (eds), *The European Higher Education Area*. Springer International Publishing, 343–59.

Ashwin, P. and Trigwell, K. (2004) 'Investigating staff and educational development.' In D. Baume and P. Kahn (eds), *Enhancing Staff and Educational Development*. London: RoutledgeFalmer, 117–32.

Ashwin, P., Abbas, A. and McLean, M. (2012a) *Quality and Inequality in Undergraduate Courses: A Guide for National and Institutional Policy Makers*. Nottingham: University of Nottingham

(Available from: http://www.research.lancs.ac.uk/portal/services/downloadRegister/15790610/Education_brochure_21.03.12.pdf, last accessed 24 May 2019.)

Ashwin, P., Abbas, A. and McLean, M. (2012b) 'The pedagogic device, sociology, knowledge practices and teaching-learning processes.' In P. Trowler, M. Saunders and V. Bamber (eds), *Tribes and Territories in the 21st-Century, Rethinking the Significance of Disciplines in Higher Education*. Abingdon: Routledge, 118–29.

Ashwin, P., Abbas, A. and McLean, M. (2014) 'How do students accounts of sociology change over the course of their undergraduate degrees?', *Higher Education*, 67, 219–34.

Ashwin, P., Abbas, A. and McLean, M. (2015) 'Representations of a high-quality system of undergraduate education in English higher education policy documents', *Studies in Higher Education*, 40, 610–23.

Ashwin, P., Abbas, A. and McLean, M. (2016) 'Conceptualising transformative undergraduate experiences: A phenomenographic exploration of students' personal projects', *British Educational Research Journal*, 42(6), 962–77.

Ashwin, P., Abbas, A. and McLean, M. (2017) 'How does completing a dissertation transform undergraduate students understandings of disciplinary knowledge?' *Assessment and Evaluation in Higher Education*, 42(4), 517–30.

Astin, A. (1984) 'Student involvement: A developmental theory for Higher Education', *Journal of College Student Personnel*, 26, 297–308.

Atkinson, T. and Claxton, G. (eds) (2000) *The Intuitive Practitioner, on the Value of Not Always Knowing What One is Doing*. Buckingham: Open University Press.

Ausubel, D., Novak, J. and Hanesian, H. (1978) *Educational Psychology: A Cognitive View*. 2nd edn. New York: Holt, Rinehart and Winston.

Bach, S. Haynes, P. and Lewis-Smith, J. (2007) *Online Learning and Teaching in Higher Education*. Maidenhead: Open University Press

Baillie, C., Bowden, J. and Meyer, J. (2013) 'Threshold capabilities, threshold concepts and knowledge capability linked through variation theory', *Higher Education*, 65, 227–46.

Bakhtin, M. (1981) *The Dialogic Imagination: Four Essays by M. M. Bakhtin*. Austin, TX: University of Texas Press.

Ball, D. and Bass, H. (2000) 'Interweaving content and pedagogy in teaching and learning to teach, knowing and using mathematics.' In J. Boaler (ed.), *Multiple Perspectives on Mathematics Teaching and Learning*. Westport, CT: Ablex, 83–104.

Bamber, V. and Anderson, S. (2012) 'Evaluating learning and teaching: Institutional needs and individual practices', *International Journal for Academic Development*, 17, 5–18.

Bangeni, B. and Kapp, R. (eds) (2017) *Negotiating Learning and Identity in Higher Education: Access, Persistence and Retention*. London: Bloomsbury Academic.

Banks, J. (2002) *An Introduction to Multicultural Education*. 3rd edn. Boston, MA: Allyn and Bacon.

Barnacle, R. and Dall'Alba, G. (2017) 'Committed to learn: student engagement and care in higher education', *Higher Education Research and Development*, 36(7), 1326–8.

Barnett, R. (1997) *Higher Education: A Critical Business*. Buckingham: Open University Press and Society for Research into Higher Education.

Barnett, R. (2003) *Beyond All Reason: Living with Ideology in the University*. Buckingham: SRHE and OUP.

Barnett, R. and Coate, K. (2005) *Engaging the Curriculum in Higher Education*. Maidenhead: Open University Press and McGraw-Hill Education.

Barradell, S., Barrie, S. and Peseta, T. (2018) 'Ways of thinking and practising: Highlighting the complexities of higher education curriculum', *Innovations in Education and Teaching International*, 55(3), 266–75.

Barrett, T. and Moore, S. (2010) *New Approaches to Problem-based Learning: Revitalising Your Practice in Higher Education*. London: Routledge.

Barrie, S. (2006) 'Understanding what we mean by the generic attributes of graduates', *Higher Education*, 51, 215–41.

Barrie, S., Bucat, R., Buntine, M., Burke da Silva, K., Crisp, G., George, A., Jamie, I., Kable, S., Lim, K., Pyke, S. and Read, J. (2015) 'Development, evaluation and use of a student experience survey in undergraduate science laboratories: The advancing science by enhancing learning in the laboratory student laboratory learning experience survey', *International Journal of Science Education*, 37(11), 1795–814.

Bartley, K. (2010) 'Preface.' In A. Pollard (ed.), *Professionalism and Pedagogy: A Contemporary Opportunity*. London: Teaching and Learning Research Programme.

Bartolomé, L. (1994) 'Beyond the methods fetish: Toward a humanizing pedagogy', *Harvard Educational Review*, 64, 173–95.

Bass, R. (2012) 'Disrupting ourselves: The problem of learning in Higher Education', *EDUCAUSE Review*, 47(2), 23–33.

Bastalich, W. (2017) 'Content and context in knowledge production: A critical review of doctoral supervision literature', *Studies in Higher Education*, 42, 1145–57.

Bathmaker, A-M., Ingram, N., Abrahams, J., Hoare, A., Waller R. and Bradley H (2016) *Higher Education, Social Class and Social Mobility: The Degree Generation*. London: Palgrave MacMillan.

Baxter Magolda, M. (2004a) *Learning Partnerships: Theory and Models of Practice to Educate for Self-Authorship*. Sterling, VA: Stylus.

Baxter Magolda, M. (2004b) 'Evolution of a constructivist conceptualization of epistemological reflection', *Educational Psychologist*, 19, 31–42.

Baxter Magolda, M. (2016) 'Remaking Self-In-World.' In K. Quinlan' (ed.), *How Higher Education Feels*. Rotterdam: Sense Publishers, 53–77.

Beach, D. (2018) *Structural Injustices in Swedish Education*. London: Palgrave Macmillan.

Beaty, L., Gibbs, G. and Morgan, A. (1997) 'Learning orientations and study contracts.' In F. Marton, D. Hounsell and N. Entwistle (eds), *The Experience of Learning*. 2nd edn. Edinburgh: Scottish Academic Press, 72–86.

Beauchamp, C. and Thomas, L. (2009) 'Understanding teacher identity: An overview of issues in the literature and implications for Teacher Education', *Cambridge Journal of Education*, 39(2), 175–89.

Becher, T. (1989) *Academic Tribes and Territories, Intellectual Enquiry and the Cultures of Disciplines*. Buckingham: Society for Research into Higher Education and Open University Press.

Becher, T. and Trowler, P. (2001) *Academic Tribes and Territories, Intellectual Enquiry and the Cultures of Disciplines*. 2nd edn. Buckingham: Society for Research into Higher Education and Open University Press.

Beck, U. (1992) *Risk Society*. London: Sage.

Bedggood, R. and Donovan, J. (2012) 'University performance evaluations: What are we really measuring?', *Studies in Higher Education*, 37, 825–42.

Beetham, H. (2015) 'Thriving in a connected age: Digital capability and digital wellbeing', JISC Blog: https://www.jisc.ac.uk/blog/thriving-in-a-connected-age-digital-capability-and-digital-wellbeing-25-jun-2015

Behari-Leak, K. (2017) 'New academics, new higher education contexts: A critical perspective on professional development', *Teaching in Higher Education*, 22, 485–500.

Bell, L. and Adams, M. (2016) 'Theoretical foundations for social justice education.' In L. Bell and M. Adams (eds), *Teaching for Diversity and Social Justice*. London: Routledge, 21–44.

Bell, L., Washington, S., Weinstein, G. and Love, B. (2003) 'Knowing ourselves as instructors.' In A. Darder, M. Baltodano and R. Torres (eds), *The Critical Pedagogy Reader*. New York: Routledge Falmer, 464–78.

Bender, C., Daniels, P., Lazarus, J., Naude, L. and Sattar, K. (2006) *Service-Learning in the Curriculum, A Resource for Higher Education Institutions*. Pretoria: Council on Higher Education. (Available from: http://www.che.ac.za/media_and_publications/research/service-learning-curriculum-resource-higher-education-institutions, last accessed 24 May 2019.)

Bennett, D., Roberts, L., Ananthram, S. and Broughton, M. (2018) 'What is required to develop career pathways for teaching academics?', *Higher Education*, 75, 271–86.

Bennett, R. and Kottasz, R. (2006) 'Widening participation and student expectations of higher education', *International Journal of Management Education*, 5(2), 47–65.

Berghmans, I., Neckebroeck, F., Dochy, F. and Struyven, K. (2013) 'A typology of approaches to peer tutoring: Unraveling peer tutors behavioural strategies', *European Journal of Psychology of Education*, 28, 703–23.

Bernstein, B. (1970) 'Education cannot compensate for society', *New Society*, 15(387), 344–47.

Bernstein, B. (2000) *Pedagogy, Symbolic Control and Identity: Theory, Research and Critique.* Revised edn. Oxford: Rowman and Littlefield Publishers.

Bertolin, J. (2016) 'Ideologies and perceptions of quality in higher education: From the dichotomy between social and economic aspects to the "middle way"', *Policy Futures in Education*, 14, 971–87.

Bhambra, G., Gebrial, D. and Nisancioglu, K. (2018) *Decolonising the University.* London: Pluto Press.

Bhopal, K. (2002) 'Teaching womens studies: the effects of race and gender', *Journal of Further and Higher Education*, 26(2), 109–18.

Biesta, G., Field, J., Goodson, I., Hodkinson, P. and Macleod, F. (2010) *Improving Learning through the Lifecourse.* London: Routledge.

Biggs, J. (2003) *Teaching for Quality in Higher Education.* 2nd edn. Buckingham: Open University Press and Society for Research into Higher Education.

Biggs, J. (2014) 'Constructive alignment in university teaching', *HERDSA Review of Higher Education*, 1, 6–22.

Biggs, J. and Tang, C. (2011) *Teaching for Quality Learning at University: What the Student Does.* 4th edn. Maidenhead: Open University Press and Society for Research into Higher Education.

Black, J., Boggs, A., Fry, H., Hillman, N., Jackson, S., King, R., Lodge, M. and Underwood, S. (2015) *The Regulation of Higher Education.* Discussion Paper 77. London: Centre for Analysis of Risk and Regulation, School of Economics and Political Science.

Black, P. and Wiliam, D. (1998) 'Assessment and classroom learning', *Assessment in Education*, 5, 7–74.

Blackmore, J. (2009) 'Academic pedagogies, quality logics and performative universities: Evaluating teaching and what students want', *Studies in Higher Education*, 34, 857–72.

Blackmore, P. and Castley, A. (2006) *Capability Development in Universities.* London: Leadership Foundation for Higher Education.

Blackmore, P. and Kandiko, C. (eds) (2012) *Strategic Curriculum Change: Global Trends in Universities.* Abingdon: Routledge and SRHE.

Bligh, B. and Crook, C. (2017) 'Learning spaces.' In E. Duval, M. Sharples and R. Sutherland (eds), *Technology Enhanced Learning.* Cham: Springer, 69–87.

Bligh, D. (2000) *Whats the Use of Lectures?* Bristol: Intellect Books.

Bloom, B. (1956) *Taxonomy of Educational Objectives. Vol. 1: Cognitive Domain.* New York: McKay.

Bloxham, S. and Boyd, P. (2007) *Developing Assessment in Higher Education: A Practical Guide.* Buckingham: Open University Press.

Bloxham, S., Hudson, J., den Outer, B. and Price, M. (2015) 'External peer review of assessment: An effective approach to verifying standards?', *Higher Education Research and Development*, 34, 1069–82.

Boland, J. and Keane, E. (2012) 'The transformative potential of service/community-based learning as a pedagogy for diversity and social justice in teacher education: A case study from Ireland.' In T. Murphy and J. Tan (eds), *Service Learning and Educating in Challenging Context: International Perspectives.* London: Continuum Books.

Boler, M. (1999) *Feeling Power: Emotion and Education.* New York: Routledge.

Boliver, V. (2013) 'How fair is access to more prestigious UK Universities?' *British Journal of Sociology*, 64, 344–64.

Boliver, V. (2015) 'Lies, damned lies, and statistics on widening access to Russell Group universities', *Radical Statistics*, 113, 29–38.

Boliver, V. (2016) 'Exploring ethnic inequalities in admission to Russell Group universities', *Sociology*, 50, 247–66.

Boliver, V. (2017) 'Misplaced optimism: How higher education reproduces rather than reduces social inequality', *British Journal of Sociology of Education*, 38, 423–32.

Bologna Declaration (1999) 'The European higher education area', *Joint Declaration of the European Ministers of Education*, 19.

Bolton, G. (2014) *Reflective Practice: Writing and Professional Development*. 4th edn. London: Sage Publications.

Boni, A. and Walker, M. (eds) (2013) *Human Development and Capabilities: Re-imagining the University of the Twenty-First Century*. London: Routledge.

Booth, A. and Ludvigsson, D. (2017) 'Tuning history', *Arts and Humanities in Higher Education*, 16, 333–6.

Booth, S. and Woollacott, L. (2018) 'On the constitution of SoTL: Its domains and contexts', *Higher Education: The International Journal of Higher Education Research*, 75(3), 537–51.

Boring, A., Ottoboni, K. and Stark, P. (2016) 'Student evaluations of teaching (mostly) do not measure teaching effectiveness', *Science Open Research–EDU*, doi: 10.14293/S2199-1006.1. *SOR-EDU. AETBZC. v1*.

Boud, D. (2000) 'Sustainable assessment: Rethinking assessment for the learning society', *Studies in Continuing Education*, 22, 151–67.

Boud, D. (2010) 'Relocating reflection in the context of practice.' In H. Bradbury, N. Frost, S. Kilminster and M. Zukas (eds), *Beyond Reflective Practice: New Approaches to Professional Lifelong Learning*. Abingdon: Routledge, 25–37.

Boud, D. (2018) 'Assessment could demonstrate learning gains, but what is required for it to do so?' *Higher Education Pedagogies,* 3, 54–56.

Boud D. and Falchikov N. (2007) 'Introduction: Assessment for the longer term.' In D. Boud and N. Falchkov (eds), *Rethinking Assessment in Higher Education*. Abingdon: Routledge, 3–25.

Boud, D. and Lee, A. (2005) 'Peer learning as pedagogic discourse for research education', *Studies in Higher Education*, 30, 501–16.

Boud, D. and Molloy, E. (2013a) 'Rethinking models of feedback for learning: The challenge of design', *Assessment and Evaluation in Higher Education*, 38, 698–712.

Boud, D. and Molloy, E. (2013b) 'Decision-making for feedback.' In D. Boud and E. Molloy, (eds), *Feedback in Higher and Professional Education, Understanding It and Doing It Well*. London: Routledge, 202–18.

Boud, D. and Soler, R. (2016) 'Sustainable assessment revisited', *Assessment and Evaluation in Higher Education*, 41(3), 400–13.

Boud, D. and Walker, D. (1990) 'Making the most of experience', *Studies in Continuing Education*, 12(2), 61–80.

Boud, D. and Walker, D. (1998) 'Promoting reflection in professional courses: The challenge of context', *Studies in Higher Education,* 23, 191–206.

Boud, D., Keogh, R. and Walker, D. (1985) 'Promoting reflection in learning: A model.' In D. Boud, R. Keogh and D. Walker (eds), *Reflection: Turning Experience into Learning*. London: Kogan Page, 18–40.

Bourdieu, P. and Passeron, J. (1979) *The Inheritors: French Students and their Relation to Culture*. Chicago, IL: University of Chicago Press.

Bovill, C. and Woolmer, C. (2019) 'How conceptualisations of curriculum in higher education influence student-staff co-creation in and of the curriculum', *Higher Education*, 78(3), 407–22.

Bovill, C., Cook-Sather, A. and Felten, P. (2011) 'Students as co-creators of teaching approaches, course design, and curricula: Implications for academic developers', *International Journal for Academic Development*, 16(2), 133–45.

Bovill, C., Cook-Sather, A., Felten, P., Millard, L. and Moore-Cherry, N. (2016) 'Addressing potential challenges in co-creating learning and teaching: Overcoming resistance, navigating institutional norms and ensuring inclusivity in student–staff partnerships', *Higher Education*, 71(2), 195–208.

Bowden, J. and Marton, F. (1998) *The University of Learning: Beyond Quality and Competence in Higher Education*. London: Kogan Page.

Bower, M., Lee, M. and Dalgarno, B. (2017) 'Collaborative learning across physical and virtual worlds: Factors supporting and constraining learners in a blended reality environment', *British Journal of Educational Technology*, 48(2), 407–30.

Bowl, M. (2005) 'Valuing diversity in the social sciences curriculum', *Learning and Teaching in the Social Sciences*, 2(2), 121–36.

Bowles, S. and Gintis, H. (1976) *Schooling in Capitalist America: Education Reform and the Contradictions of Economic Life*. London: Routledge and Kegan Paul.

Boyer, E. (1990) *Scholarship Reconsidered, Priorities of the Professoriate*. Stanford, CA: Carnegie Foundation for the Advancement of Teaching.

boyd, d. (2014) *It's Complicated: The Social Lives of Networked Teens*. New Haven, CT: Yale University Press.

Boyd, M. and Markarian, W. (2011) 'Dialogic teaching: Talk in service of a dialogic stance', *Language and Education*, 25, 515–34.

Boyle, A., Maguire, S., Martin, A., Milsom, C., Nash, R., Rawlinson, A., Wurthmann, S. and Conchie, S. (2007) 'Fieldwork is good: The student perception and the affective domain', *Journal of Geography in Higher Education*, 31, 299–317.

Bozalek, V. (2013) 'Equity and graduate attributes.' In A. Boni and M. Walker (eds), *Human Development and Capabilities: Re-imagining the University of the Twenty-First Century*. London: Routledge, 69–81.

Bozalek, V. (2017) 'Participatory parity and emerging technologies.' In M. Walker and M. Wilson-Strydom (eds), *Socially Just Pedagogies, Capabilities and Quality in Higher Education*. London: Palgrave MacMillan.

Brennan, J., Edmunds, R., Houston, M., Jary, D., Lebeau, Y., Little, B., Osborne, M., Richardson, J. and Shah, T. (2010) *Improving What is Learned at University*. London: Routledge.

Brew, A. (2008) 'Disciplinary and interdisciplinary affiliations of experienced researchers', *Higher Education*, 56, 423–38.

Brew, A., Boud, D., Lucas, L. and Crawford, K. (2018) 'Academic artisans in the research university', *Higher Education*, 76(1), 115–27.

Brink, C. (2018) *The Soul of a University: Why Excellence is Not Enough*. Bristol: Policy Press.

Broadbent, J. and Poon, W. (2015) 'Self-regulated learning strategies and academic achievement in online higher education learning environments: A systematic review', *The Internet and Higher Education*, 27, 1–13.

Brookfield, S. (1987) *Developing Critical Thinkers: Challenging Adults to Explore Alternative Ways of Thinking and Acting*. San Francisco: Jossey-Bass.

Brookfield, S. (1990) *The Skilful Teacher*. San Francisco: Jossey-Bass.

Brookfield, S. (2017) *Becoming a Critically Reflective Teacher*. 2nd edn. John Wiley and Sons.

Brookfield, S. and Preskill, S. (2005) *Discussion as a Way of Teaching: Tools and Techniques for University Teachers*. 2nd edn. San Francisco: Jossey Bass.

Brookfield, S. and Preskill, S. (2016) *The Discussion Book: 50 Great Ways to get People Talking*. San Francisco: Jossey Bass.

Broucker, B., De Wit, K. and Verhoeven, J. (2018) 'Higher education for public value: Taking the debate beyond New Public Management', *Higher Education Research and Development*, 37(2), 227–40.

Brown, J. and Duguid, P. (2000) *The Social Life of Information*. Boston, MA: Harvard Business School Press.

Brown, M. and Long, P. (2006) 'Trends in Learning Space Design.' In D. Oblinger and J. Lippincott (eds), *Learning Spaces*. Washington, DC: Educause.

Bruno, A. and Dell'Aversana, G. (2017) 'Reflective practice for psychology students: The use of reflective journal feedback in higher education', *Psychology Learning and Teaching*, 16, 248–60.

Bryan, C. and Clegg, K. (eds) (2019) *Innovative Assessment in Higher Education: A Handbook for Academic Practitioners*. London: Routledge.

Buckridge, M. and Guest, R. (2007) 'A conversation about pedagogical responses to increased diversity in university classrooms', *Higher Education Research & Development*, 26, 133–46.

Bunbury, S. (2018) Disability in higher education – do reasonable adjustments contribute to an inclusive curriculum? *International Journal of Inclusive Education*, 1–16.

Buntine, M., Read, J., Barrie, S., Bucat, R., Crisp, G., George, A., Jamie, I. and Kable, S. (2007) 'Advancing Chemistry by Enhancing Learning in the Laboratory (ACELL): A model for providing professional and personal development and facilitating improved student laboratory learning outcomes', *Chemistry Education Research and Practice*, 8, 232–54.

Burbules, N. (1993) *Dialogue in Teaching: Theory and Practice (Advances in Contemporary Educational Thought)*. New York: Teachers College Press.

Burgess, A., Senior, C. and Moores, E. (2018) 'A 10-year case study on the changing determinants of university student satisfaction in the UK', *PloS one*, 13(2), e0192976.

Burgstahler, S. (2010) 'Universal design in higher education.' In S. Burgstahler and R. Cory (eds), *Universal Design in Higher Education: From Principles to Practice*. Cambridge, MA: Harvard Education Press, 3–20.

Burke, P. (2002) *Accessing Education: Effectively Widening Participation*. Stoke-on-Trent: Trentham Books.

Burke, P. (2012) *The Right to Higher Education: Beyond Widening Participation*. London: Routledge.

Burke, P., Crozier, G. and Misiaszek, L. (2017) *Changing Pedagogical Spaces in Higher Education*. London and New York: Routledge.

Burke, P., Hayton, A. and Stevenson, J. (eds) (2018) *Evaluating Equity and Widening Participation in Higher Education*. London: Trentham Books Limited.

Butin, D. (2006) 'The limits of service-learning in higher education', *The Review of Higher Education*, 29, 473–98.

Butin, D. (2010) *Service-Learning in Theory and Practice: The Future of Community Engagement in Higher Education*. New York: Palgrave MacMillan.

Buyl, E. (2017) 'Knowledge recontextualization in academic development: An empirical exploration on an emerging academic region', *Teaching in Higher Education*, 22, 78–91.

Calitz, T. (2018) *Enhancing the Freedom to Flourish in Higher Education: Participation, Equality and Capabilities*. London: Routledge.

Callaghan, A. (2018) 'Threats to the validity of the Collegiate Learning Assessment (CLA+) as a measure of critical thinking skills and implications for Learning Gain', *Higher Education Pedagogies*, 3(1), 57–82.

Callender, C. and Dougherty, K. (2018) 'Student choice in higher education – reducing or reproducing social inequalities?', *Social Sciences*, 7(10), 189.

Cantwell, B., Marginson, S. and Smolentseva, A. (eds) (2018) *High Participation Systems of Higher Education*. Oxford: Oxford University Press.

Capp, M. (2017) 'The effectiveness of universal design for learning: A meta-analysis of literature between 2013 and 2016', *International Journal of Inclusive Education*, 21, 791–807.

Carless, D. (2011) *From Testing to Productive Student Learning: Implementing Formative Assessment in Confucian-Heritage Settings*. New York: Routledge.

Carless, D. (2013) 'Sustainable feedback and the development of student self-evaluative capacities.' In S. Merry, M. Price, D. Carless and M. Taras (eds), *Reconceptualising Feedback in Higher Education: Developing Dialogue with Students*. Abingdon: Routledge, 113–22.

Carless, D. and Boud, D. (2018) 'The development of student feedback literacy: Enabling uptake of feedback', *Assessment and Evaluation in Higher Education*, 43, 1315–25.

Carless, D., Chan, K., To, J., Lo, M. and E. Barrett (2018) 'Developing students capacities for evaluative judgement through analysing exemplars.' In D. Boud, R. Ajjawi, P. Dawson and J. Tai (eds), *Developing Evaluative Judgement in Higher Education: Assessment for Knowing and Producing Quality Work.* London: Routledge.

Carnoy, M., Froumin, I., Loyalka, P. and Tilak, J. (2014) 'The concept of public goods, the state, and higher education finance: A view from the BRICs', *Higher Education*, 68, 359–78.

Carvalho, T. and Diogo, S. (2018) 'Exploring the relationship between institutional and professional autonomy: A comparative study between Portugal and Finland', *Journal of Higher Education Policy and Management*, 40(1), 18–33.

Case, A. (2010) 'We are all cyborgs now', TEDWomen 2010. Available online at: https://www.ted.com/talks/amber_case_we_are_all_cyborgs_now.

Case, J. (2013) *Researching Student Learning in Higher Education: A Social Realist Account.* London: Routledge.

Case, J., Marshall, D., McKenna, S. and Mogashana, D. (2018) *Going to University: The Influence of Higher Education on the Lives of Young South Africans*. Cape Town: African Minds.

Cassidy, S. (2011) 'Self-regulated learning in higher education, identifying key component processes', *Studies in Higher Education*, 36, 989–1000.

Cassidy, S. (2012) 'Exploring individual differences as determining factors in student academic achievement in higher education', *Studies in Higher Education*, 37, 793–810.

Chalmers, D. (2011) 'Progress and challenges to the recognition and reward of the scholarship of teaching in higher education', *Higher Education Research and Development*, 30, 25–38.

Chang, C., Wu, B., Seow, T. and Irvine, K. (eds) (2018) *Learning Geography Beyond the Traditional Classroom*. Singapore: Springer.

Chanock, K. (2010) 'The right to reticence', *Teaching in Higher Education*, 15, 543–52.

Cheng, L. and Yang, H. (2015) 'Learning about gender on campus: An analysis of the hidden curriculum for medical students', *Medical Education*, 49, 321–31.

Chick, N. (ed.) (2018) *SoTL in Action. Illuminating Critical Moments of Practice*. Stirling, VA: Stylus Publishing.

Chickering, A. and Gamson, Z. (1987) 'Seven principles for good practice in undergraduate education', *American Association for Higher Education Bulletin*, March 1987, 3–7.

Christie, H., Tett, L., Cree, V., Hounsell, J. and McCune, V. (2008) 'A real rollercoaster of confidence and emotions: Learning to be a university student', *Studies in Higher Education*, 33, 567–81.

Clarence, S. and McKenna, S. (2017) 'Developing academic literacies through understanding the nature of disciplinary knowledge', *London Review of Education*, 15(1), 38–49.

Clegg, S. (2009) 'Forms of knowing and academic development practice', *Studies in Higher Education*, 34, 403–16.

Clegg, S. and Rowland, S. (2010) 'Kindness in pedagogical practice and academic life', *British Journal of Sociology of Education*, 31, 719–35.

Coate, K., Barnett, R. and Williams, G. (2001) 'Relationships between Teaching and Research in English Higher Education', *Higher Education Quarterly*, 55(2), 158–74.

Cole, M. (1996) *Cultural Psychology: A Once and Future Discipline.* Cambridge, MA: The Belknapp Press of Harvard University.

Collini, S. (2012) *What are Universities For?* London: Penguin Books.

Connell, R., Pearse, R., Collyer, F., Maia, J. and Morrell, R. (2018) 'Negotiating with the North: How Southern-tier intellectual workers deal with the global economy of knowledge', *The Sociological Review*, 66, 41–57.

Cook-Sather, A. (2015) 'Dialogue across differences of position, perspective, and identity: Reflective practice in/on a student-faculty pedagogical partnership program', *Teachers College Record*, 117, 2.

Cook-Sather, A. and Des-Ogugua, C. (2019) 'Lessons we still need to learn on creating more inclusive and responsive classrooms: Recommendations from one student-faculty partnership programme', *International Journal of Inclusive Education*, 23(6), 594–608.

Cook-Sather, A., Bovill, C. and Felten, P. (2014) *Engaging Students as Partners in Teaching & Learning: A Guide for Faculty*. San Francisco, CA: Jossey-Bass.

Cotton, D., Joyner, M., George, R. and Cotton, P. (2016) 'Understanding the gender and ethnicity attainment gap in UK higher education', *Innovations in Education and Teaching International*, 53, 475–86.

Craig, C. (2019) 'Sustaining self and others in the teaching profession: A personal perspective.' In J. Murray, Swennen, A. and Kosnik, C. (eds), *International Research, Policy and Practice in Teacher Education*. Cham: Springer, 79–91.

Cressey, P., Boud, D. and Docherty, P. (2006) 'The emergence of productive reflection.' In D. Boud, P. Cressey and P. Docherty (eds), *Productive Reflection at Work*. Abingdon: Routledge, 11–26.

Crosbie, V. (2013) 'Capabilities and a pedagogy for global identities.' In A. Boni and M. Walker (eds), *Human Development and Capabilities: Re-imagining the University of the Twenty-First Century*. London: Routledge, 178–91.

Crouch, C., Watkins, J., Fagen, A. and Mazur, E. (2007) 'Peer instruction: Engaging students one-on-one, all at once.' In E. Redish and P. Cooney (eds), *Research-Based Reform of University Physics*. College Park, MD: American Association of Physics Teachers. (Available from: http://www.per-central.org/document/ServeFile.cfm?ID=4990, last accessed 24 May 2019.)

Croy, S. (2018) 'Development of a group work assessment pedagogy using constructive alignment theory', *Nurse Education Today,* 61, 49–53.

Crozier, G., Reay, D. and Clayton, J. (2010) 'The socio-cultural and learning experiences of working-class students in higher education.' In M. David, (ed.), *Improving Learning by Widening Participation*. London: Routledge.

Crozier, G., Reay, D., Clayton, J., Colliander, L. and Grinstead, J. (2008) 'Different strokes for different folks: Diverse students in diverse institutions – experiences of higher education', *Research Papers in Education*, 23, 167–77.

Daddow, A. (2016) 'Curricula and pedagogic potentials when educating diverse students in higher education: Students Funds of Knowledge as a bridge to disciplinary learning', *Teaching in Higher Education*, 21(7), 741–58.

Dall'Alba, G. and Sandberg, J. (2006) 'Unveiling professional development: A critical review of stage models, *Review of Educational Research*, 76, 383–412.

D'Andrea, V. and Gosling D. (2005) *Improving Teaching and Learning in Higher Education*. Maidenhead: Society for Research into Higher Education and Open University Press.

Darling-Hammond, L. (2007) *Testimony before the House Education and Labor Committee on the Re-Authorization of the NCLB legislation*. September 10.

David, M. (2009) *Effective Learning and Teaching in UK Higher Education: A Commentary by the Teaching and Learning Research Programme*. London: Teaching and Learning Research Programme.

David, M. (ed.) (2010) *Improving Learning by Widening Participation in Higher Education*. London: Routledge.

David, M. (with contributions from Crozier, G., Hayward, G., Ertl, H., Williams, J. and Hockings, C.) (2010) 'How do we improve learning by widening participation in higher education? Institutional practices and pedagogies for social diversity.' In M. David (ed.), *Improving Learning by Widening Participation in Higher Education*. London: Routledge, 180–201.

Davis, B. and Renert, M. (2013) 'Profound understanding of emergent mathematics: Broadening the construct of teachers disciplinary knowledge', *Educational Studies in Mathematics*, 82, 245–65.

Davis, J. and Jurgenson, N. (2014) 'Context collapse: *Theorizing* context collusions and colli-
sions', *Information, Communication and Society*, 17, 476–85.

Deane, E. and Krause, K. (2013) *Towards a learning standards framework. Learning and teaching
standards (LaTS) project: Peer review and moderation in the disciplines*. Learning Standards
Discussion Paper.

De Backer, L., Van Keer, H. and Valcke, M. (2012) 'Exploring the potential impact of reciprocal
peer tutoring on higher education students metacognitive knowledge and regulation',
Instructional Science, 40, 559–88.

Delaney, L., Harmon, C. and Redmond, C. (2010) *Parental Education, Grade Attainment and
Earnings: Expectations among University Students*. Dublin, UCD Geary Institute Discussion
Paper Series; WP 10 35. (Available from: http://ideas.repec.org/p/ucd/wpaper/201035.html, last
accessed: 24 May 2019.)

Deprez, L. and Wood, D. (2013) 'Teaching for well-being: Pedagogical strategies for meaning,
value, relevance and justice.' In A. Boni and M. Walker, (eds), *Human Development and
Capabilities: Re-imagining the University of the Twenty-First Century*. London: Routledge,
145–61.

Dewey, J. (1933) *How We Think: A Restatement of the Relation of Reflective Thinking to the
Educative Process*. Chicago, IL: Henry Regnery.

Dickeson, R. (2010) *Prioritizing Academic Programs and Services*. San Francisco, CA: J. Wiley
and Sons.

Dillenbourg, P. (2013) 'Design for classroom orchestration', *Computers and Education*, 69,
485–92.

Dolgon, C., Mitchell, T. and Eatman, T. (eds) (2017) *The Cambridge Handbook of Service
Learning and Community Engagement*. Cambridge: Cambridge University Press.

Domin D (1999) 'A review of laboratory instruction styles', *Journal of Chemical Education*, 76,
543–7.

Drane, D., Micari, M. and Light, G. (2014) 'Students as teachers: Effectiveness of a peer-led
STEM learning programme over 10 years', *Educational Research and Evaluation*, 20(3),
210–30.

Dreyfus, H. and Dreyfus, S. (1986) *Mind Over Machine: The Power of Human Intuition and
Expertise in the Age of the Computer*. Oxford: Basil Blackwell.

Dubet, F. (2000) 'The sociology of pupils', *Journal of Education Policy*, 15, 93–104.

Duggan, F. (2011) 'Some models for re-shaping learning spaces.' In A. Boddington and J. Boys
(eds), *Re-Shaping Learning: A Critical Reader*. Rotterdam: Sense Publishers, 147–54.

Dunne, L. and Zandstra, D. (2011) *Students as Change Agents: New Ways of Engaging with
Learning and Teaching in Higher Education*. Bristol: ESCalate, HEA Subject Centre for
Education. (Available from: https://dera.ioe.ac.uk/13078/7/8189.pdf, last accessed 24 May
2019.)

Dweck, C. S. (2013) *Self-theories: Their Role in Motivation, Personality, and Development*. New
York: Psychology Press.

Edward, N. (2002) 'The role of laboratory work in engineering education: Student and staff
perceptions', *International Journal of Electrical Engineering Education* 39: 11–19.

Ellis, R. and Goodyear, P. (2016) 'Models of learning space: Integrating research on space, place
and learning in higher education', *Review of Education*, 4, 149–91.

Engelhardt, R. (2016) 'From fragmentation to congruence-designing an interdisciplinary project
course.' In *Improving University Science Teaching and Learning*. Department of Science
Education, Faculty of Science, University of Copenhagen, 297–304.

Engeström, Y. (2018) *Expertise in Transition: Expansive Learning in Medical Work*. Cambridge:
Cambridge University Press.

Entwistle, N. (2009) *Teaching for Understanding at University: Deep Approaches and Distinctive
Ways of Thinking*. Basingstoke: Palgrave Macmillan.

Entwistle, N. (2018) *Student Learning and Academic Understanding: A Research Perspective with Implications for Teaching*. London: Academic Press.

Entwistle N. and Hounsell, D. (2007) 'Learning and teaching at university: The influence of subjects and settings', *Teaching and Learning Research Briefing*, 31 December 2007. London: Teaching and Learning Research Programme.

Entwistle, N. and McCune, V. (2013) 'The disposition to understand for oneself at university: Integrating learning processes with motivation and metacognition', *British Journal of Educational Psychology*, 83, 267–79.

Ericsson, K., Krampe, R. and Tesch-Romer, C. (1993) 'The role of deliberate practice in the acquisition of expert performance', *Psychological Review*, 100, 363–406.

Evans, C. (1993) *English People: The Experience of Teaching and Learning in British Universities*. Buckingham: Open University Press.

Evans, C. (2013) 'Making sense of assessment feedback in Higher Education', *Review of Educational Research*, 83, 70–120.

Evans, L. and Nixon, J. (eds) (2015) *Academic Identities in Higher Education: The Changing European Landscape*. London: Bloomsbury Publishing.

Exeter, D., Ameratunga, S., Ratima, M., Morton, S., Dickson, M. and Hsu, D. (2010) 'Student engagement in very large classes: The teachers perspective', *Studies in Higher Education*, 35, 761–75.

Falchikov, N. (2005) *Improving Assessment through Student Involvement: Practical Solutions for Aiding Learning in Higher and Further Education*. Abingdon: RoutledgeFalmer.

Fanghanel, J. (2004) 'Capturing dissonance in university teacher education environments', *Studies in Higher Education*, 29, 575–90.

Fanghanel, J. (2009) 'Exploring teaching and learning regimes in higher education settings.' In C. Kreber (ed.), *The University and Its Disciplines – Within and Beyond Disciplinary Boundaries*. London: Routledge, 196–208.

Fanghanel, J. (2013) 'Going public with pedagogical inquiries: SoTL as a methodology for faculty professional development', *Teaching and Learning Inquiry*, 1(1), 59–70.

Fanghanel, J., Potter, J., Pritchard, J. and Wisker, G. (2016) *Defining and Supporting the Scholarship of Teaching and Learning: A Sector-Wide Study*. York: Higher Education Academy.

Fataar, A. (2015) *Engaging Schooling Subjectivities Across Postapartheid Spaces*. Stellenbosch: SUN Media.

Fletcher, J. (2018) 'Peer observation of teaching: A practical tool in higher education', *The Journal of Faculty Development*, 32, 51–64.

Florian, L. (2015) Conceptualising inclusive pedagogy. In. C. Forlin (ed.), *International Perspectives on Inclusive Education: Inclusive Pedagogy Across the Curriculum*. Bingley: Emerald.

Forde, C. and McMahon, M. (2019) *Teacher Quality, Professional Learning and Policy*. London: Palgrave Macmillan.

Fraser, S. and Bosanquet, A. (2006) 'The curriculum? That's just a unit outline, isnt it?', *Studies in Higher Education*, 31, 269–84.

Freire, P. (1970) *Pedagogy of the Oppressed*. Translated by M. B. Ramos. New York: Continuum.

Freire, P. (1996) *Pedagogy of the Oppressed*. London: Penguin.

Friedman, S. and Laurison, D. (2019) *The Class Ceiling: Why it Pays to be Privileged*. Bristol: Policy Press.

Fuller, M., Georgeson, J., Healey, M., Hurst, A., Kelly, K., Riddell, S., Roberts, H. and Weedon, E. (2009) *Improving Disabled Students Learning*. London: Routledge.

Fung, D. and Gordon, C. (2016) *Rewarding Educators and Education Leaders in Research-Intensive Universities*. York: Higher Education Academy.

Furedi, F. (2013) 'University students – are they toddlers or young adults?' *Independent*, 7 March 2013.

Gallagher, G. (2017) 'Aligning for learning: Including feedback in the constructive alignment model', *AISHE-J: The All Ireland Journal of Teaching and Learning in Higher Education*, 9(1).

Game, A. and Metcalfe, A. (2009) 'Dialogue and team teaching', *Higher Education Research and Development*, 28, 45–57.

Gee, J. (2017) *Teaching, Learning, Literacy in Our High-Risk High-Tech World: A Framework for Becoming Human*. New York: Teachers College Press.

Georgiou, H. (2016) 'Putting physics knowledge in the hot seat: The semantics of student understandings of thermodynamics.' In K. Maton, S. Hood and S. Shay (eds), *Knowledge-Building: Educational Studies in Legitimation Code Theory*. Abingdon and New York: Routledge, 176–92.

Ghaye, T. (2010) *Teaching and Learning through Reflective Practice: A Practical Guide for Positive Action*. London: Routledge.

Gibbs, G. (2006) 'How assessment frames student learning.' In C. Bryan and K. Clegg (eds), *Innovative Assessment in Higher Education*. London: Routledge, 23–36.

Gibbs, G. (2010) *Dimensions of Quality*. Higher Education Academy. (Available from: https://www.heacademy.ac.uk/system/files/dimensions_of_quality.pdf, last accessed 7 November 2018.)

Gibbs, G. (2012) *Implications of 'Dimensions of Quality' in a Market Environment*. York: Higher Education Academy.

Giddens, A. (1990) *The Consequences of Modernity*. Cambridge: Polity Press.

Gillborn, D. (2008) *Racism and Education: Co-incidence or Conspiracy?* London: Routledge.

Goldman, S., Britt, M., Brown, W., Cribb, G., George, M., Greenleaf, C., Lee, C., Shanahan, C. and Project READI (2016) 'Disciplinary literacies and learning to read for understanding: A conceptual framework for disciplinary literacy', *Educational Psychologist*, 51(2), 219–46.

Goos, M. and Salomons, A. (2017) Measuring teaching quality in higher education: Assessing selection bias in course evaluations, *Research in Higher Education*, 58, 341–64.

Gordon, L. (2014) 'Disciplinary decadence and the decolonisation of knowledge', *Africa Development*, 39(1), 81–92.

Gordon, P. (2005) 'Not a mormon: Confessions of a dangerous nomo', *Cultural Studies*, 19, 423–9.

Gosling, D. and Moon, J. (2003) *How to Use Learning Outcomes and Assessment Criteria*. 3rd edn. London: SEEC.

Gourley, L. (2015) 'Student engagement and the tyranny of participation', *Teaching in Higher Education*, 20, 402–11.

Graff. G. (2003) *Clueless in Academe: How Schooling Obscures the Life of the Mind*. New Haven, CT, and London: Yale University Press.

Grant, B. (2003) 'Mapping the pleasures and risks of supervision', *Discourse: Studies in the Cultural Politics of Education,* 24(2), 175–90.

Grant, B. (2008) 'Agonistic struggle: Master–slave dialogues in humanities supervision', *Arts and Humanities in Higher Education*, 7(1), 9–27.

Grant, B. (2010) The limits of "teaching and learning": Indigenous students and doctoral supervision. *Teaching in Higher Education*, 15, 505–17.

Griffiths, S. (2010) *Teaching for Inclusion in Higher Education: A Guide to Practice*. Dublin: All Ireland Society for Higher Education (AISHE). (Available from: https://www.qub.ac.uk/directorates/AcademicStudentAffairs/CentreforEducationalDevelopment/UsefulInformation/Inclusion/, last accessed 24 May 2019.)

Grosfoguel, R. (2013) 'The structure of knowledge in Westernized universities: Epistemic racism/sexism and the four genocides of the long 16th Century', *Human Architecture: Journal of the Sociology of Self-Knowledge*, 11, 73–90.

Gunn, A. (2018) 'Metrics and methodologies for measuring teaching quality in higher education: Developing the Teaching Excellence Framework (TEF)', *Educational Review*, 70(2), 129–48.

Gurung, R., Chick, N. and Haynie (eds) (2009) *Exploring Signature Pedaogies: Approaches to Teaching Disciplinary Habits of Mind*. Stirling, VA: Stylus Publishing.

Habermas, J. (1987) *The Theory of Communicative Reason, Volume 2: Lifeworld and System: A Critique of Functionalist Reason*, trans. T. McCarthy. Boston, MA: Beacon Press.

Habermas, J. and Blazek, J. (1987) 'The idea of the university: Learning processes', *New German Critique*, 41, 3–22.

Haggis, T. (2006) 'Pedagogies for diversity: Retaining critical challenge amidst fears of dumbing down', *Studies in Higher Education*, 31, 521–35.

Halliday, M. (1994) *An Introduction to Functional Grammar*. 2nd edn. London: Edward Arnold.

Hammersley-Fletcher, L. and Orsmond, P. (2005) 'Reflecting on reflective practices within peer observation', *Studies in Higher Education*, 30, 213–24.

Handal, G. (1999) 'Consultation using critical friends', *New Directions for Teaching and Learning*, 79, 59–70.

Hanley, L. (2016) *Respectable: The Experience of Class*. London: Penguin, Random House.

Hanson, J., Trolian, T., Paulsen, M. and Pascarella, E. (2016) 'Evaluating the influence of peer learning on psychological well-being', *Teaching in Higher Education*, 21, 191–206.

Hardarson, A. (2017) 'Aims of education: How to resist the temptation of technocratic models, *Journal of Philosophy of Education*, 51, 59–72.

Harrison, N. (2018) 'Using the lens of possible selves to explore access to higher education: A new conceptual model for practice, policy, and research', *Social Sciences*, 7, 209.

Hartog, P. and Rhodes, E. (1935) *An Examination of Examinations*. London: Macmillan.

Hartog, P. and Rhodes, E. (1936) *The Marks of Examiners*. London: Macmillan.

Hathaway, J. (2015) 'Developing that voice: Locating academic writing tuition in the mainstream of higher education', *Teaching in Higher Education*, 20, 506–17.

Hattie, J. (2003) *Teachers Make a Difference: What is the Research Evidence?* Paper presented at the Australian Council for Educational Research Annual Conference. (Available from: https://research.acer.edu.au/cgi/viewcontent.cgi?article=1003&context=research_conference_2003, last accessed 24 May 2019.)

Hattie, J. (2015) 'The applicability of Visible Learning to higher education', *Scholarship of Teaching and Learning in Psychology*, 1(1), 79.

Hattie, J. and Donoghue, G. (2016) 'Learning strategies: A synthesis and conceptual model', *npj Science of Learning*, 1, 16013.

Hattie, J. and Timperley, H. (2007) 'The power of feedback', *Review of Educational Research*, 77, 81–112.

Hay, D., Williams, D., Stahl, D. and Wingate, R. (2013) 'Using drawings of the brain cell to exhibit expertise in neuroscience: Exploring the boundaries of experimental culture', *Science Education*, 97, 468–91.

Haynes, A., Lisic, E., Harris, K., Leming, K., Shanks, K. and Stein B. (2015) 'Using the critical thinking assessment test (CAT) as a model for designing within-course assessments', *Inquiry: Critical Thinking Across the Disciplines*, 30(3), 38–48.

Healey, M. (2005) 'Linking research and teaching: Exploring disciplinary spaces and the role of inquiry-based learning.' In R. Barnett (ed.), *Reshaping the University: New Relationships between Research, Scholarship and Teaching*. Maidenhead: Open University Press.

Healey, M. and Jenkins, A. (2009) *Developing Undergraduate Research and Inquiry*. York: The Higher Education Academy.

Healey, M., Bradford, M., Roberts, C. and Knight, Y. (2013) 'Collaborative discipline-based curriculum change: Applying Change Academy processes at departmental level', *International Journal for Academic Development,* 18, 31–44.

Healey, M., Jenkins, A. and Lea, J. (2014) *Developing Research-Based Curricula in College-Based Higher Education*. York: Higher Education Academy.

Heijstra, T., Einarsdóttir, T., Pétursdóttir, G. and Steinþórsdóttir, F. (2017) 'Testing the concept of academic housework in a European setting: Part of academic career-making or gendered barrier to the top?' *European Education Research Journal*, 16(2–3), 200–14.

Heilbronn, R. (2010) 'The nature of practice-based knowledge and understanding.' In R. Heilbronn and J. Yandell (eds), *Critical Practice in Teacher Education: A Study of Professional Learning*. London: Institute of Education.

Henard, F. and Roseveare, D. (2012) *Fostering Quality Teaching in Higher Education. Policies and Practices – An IMHE Guide for Higher Education Institutions*. Paris: OECD. (Available from: http://www.oecd.org/edu/imhe/QT%20policies%20and%20practices.pdf, last accessed 24 May 2019.)

Hendersen, E. (2018) 'Anticipating doctoral supervision: (Not) bridging the transition from super-visee to supervisor', *Teaching in Higher Education*, 23, 403–18.

Henkel, M. (2000) *Academic Identities and Policy Change in Higher Education*. London: Jessica Kingsley Publishers.

Heron, M. (2019) 'Pedagogic practices to support international students in seminar discussions', *Higher Education Research and Development*, 38, 266–79.

Herrington, J., Reeves, T. and Oliver, R. (2014) 'Authentic learning environments.' In J. Spector, M. Merrill, J. Elen and M. Bishop (eds), *Handbook of Research on Educational Communications and Technology*. New York: Springer, 401–12.

Higgins, R., Hogg, P. and Robinson, L. (2017) 'Constructive alignment of a research-informed teaching activity within an undergraduate diagnostic radiography curriculum: A reflection', *Radiography*, 23, S30–S36.

Higher Education Academy (2009) *Reward and Recognition in Higher Education Institutional Policies and their Implementation*. York: Higher Education Academy

Higher Education Academy (2012) *A Handbook for External Examining*. Higher Education Academy: York. (Available from: https://www.heacademy.ac.uk/project-section/external-examining-handbook, last accessed 24 May 2019.)

Higher Education Funding Council for England (2011) *Opportunity, Choice and Excellence in Higher Education*. Bristol: HEFCE.

Hildebrand, M. (1973) 'The character and skills of the effective professor', *Journal of Higher Education*, 44, 41–50.

Hinz, S. (2016) 'Upwardly mobile: attitudes toward the class transition among first-generation college students', *Journal of College Student Development*, 57, 285–99.

Hockings, C. (2010) *Inclusive Learning and Teaching in Higher Education: A Synthesis of Research*. York: Higher Education Academy. (Available from: https://www.heacademy.ac.uk/system/files/inclusive_teaching_and_learning_in_he_synthesis_200410_0.pdf, last accessed 24 May 2019.)

Hockings, C., Cooke, S. and Bowl, M. (2010) 'Learning and teaching in two universities within the context of increasing student diversity: Complexity, contradictions and challenges.' In M. David (ed.). *Improving Learning by Widening Participation*. London: Routledge, 95–108.

Hockings, C., Thomas, L., Ottaway, J. and Jones, R. (2018) 'Independent learning – what we do when you're not there', *Teaching in Higher Education*, 23, 145–61.

Hodgson, V. and McConnell, D. (2019) 'Networked learning and postdigital education', *Postdigital Science and Education*, 1, 43–64.

Hofer, B. and Pintrich, P. (2002) *Personal Epistemology: The Psychology of Beliefs about Knowledge and Knowing*. New York: Routledge.

Hofer, B. and Sinatra, G. (2010) 'Epistemology, metacognition, and self-regulation: Musings on an emerging field', *Metacognition and Learning*, 5(1), 113–20.

Hofstein, A. and Lunetta, V. (2004) 'The laboratory in science education: Foundations for the twenty-first century', *Science Education*, 88, 28–54.

Hoidn, S. (2016) *Student-Centered Learning Environments in Higher Education Classrooms*. London: Palgrave Macmillan.

Holmgren, R. (2010) 'Learning commons: A learning-centered library design', *College and Undergraduate Libraries*, 17, 177–91.

hooks, b. (2003) 'Confronting class in the classroom.' In A. Darder, M. Baltodano and R. Torres, *The Critical Pedagogy Reader*. New York: Routledge Falmer, 142–50.

Hounsell, D. (1997) 'Contrasting conceptions of essay-writing.' In F. Marton, D. Hounsell and N. Entwistle (eds), *The Experience of Learning, Implications for Teaching and Studying in Higher Education*. 2nd edn. Edinburgh: Scottish Academic Press, 106–25.

Hounsell, D. (2007) 'Towards more sustainable feedback to students.' In D. Boud and N. Falchikov (eds), *Rethinking Assessment for Higher Education: Learning for the Longer Term*. London: Routledge.

Hounsell, D. and Anderson, C. (2009) 'Ways of thinking and practicing in biology and history: Disciplinary aspects of teaching and learning environments.' In C. Kreber (ed.), *The University and its Disciplines, Teaching and Learning Within and Beyond Disciplinary Boundaries*. New York: Routledge, 71–83.

Hounsell, D. and Hounsell, J. (2007) 'Teaching–learning environments in contemporary mass higher education.' In N. Entwistle and P. Tomlinson (eds), *Student Learning and University Teaching*. Leicester: British Psychological Society, 91–111.

Hountondji, P. (1997) 'Introduction: Recentring Africa.' In P. Hountondji (ed.), *Endogenous Knowledge: Research Trails*. Dakar, Senegal: CODESRIA, 1–39.

Howell, C. (2018) 'Participation of students with disabilities in South African higher education: Contesting the uncontested.' In N. Singal, P. Lynch and S. Johansson (eds), *Education and Disability in the Global South: New Perspectives from Africa and Asia*. London: Bloomsbury, 127–43.

Hubbard, J. and Couch, B. (2018) 'The positive effect of in-class clicker questions on later exams depends on initial student performance level but not question format', *Computers and Education*, 120, 1–12.

Hutchings, C. (2014) 'Referencing and identity, voice and agency: Adult learners transformations within literacy practices', *Higher Education Research and Development*, 33, 312–24.

Hutchings, P., Huber, M. and Ciccone, A. (2011) 'Getting there: An integrative vision of the scholarship of learning and teaching', *International Journal for the Scholarship of Teaching and Learning*, 5(1), Article 31.

Huxham, M., Hunter, M., McIntyre, A., Shilland, R. and McArthur, J. (2015) 'Student and teacher co-navigation of a course: Following the natural lines of academic enquiry', *Teaching in Higher Education*, 1–12.

Iannelli, C. and Paterson, L. (2006) 'Social mobility in Scotland since the middle of the twentieth century', *The Sociological Review*, 54, 520–45.

Ivanič, R., Edwards, R., Barton, D., Martin-Jones, M., Fowler, Z., Hughes, B., Mannion, G., Miller, K., Satchwell, C. and Smith, J. (2009) *Improving Learning in College: Rethinking Literacies Across the Curriculum*. London: Routledge.

Jaarsma, A., De Grave, W., Muijtjens, A., Scherpbier, A. and van Beukelen, P. (2008) 'Perceptions of learning as a function of seminar group factors', *Medical Education*, 42, 1178–84.

Jääskelä, P., Poikkeus, A-M., Vasalampi, K., Valleal, U. and Rasku-Puttonen, H. (2017) 'Assessing agency of university students: Validation of the AUS Scale', *Studies in Higher Education*, 42(11), 2061–79.

James, M. (2005) Insights on teacher learning from the Teaching and Learning Research Programme (TLRP). *Research Papers in Education*, 20(2), 105–8.

James, M. and Pollard, A. (2012) *Principles for Effective Pedagogy: International Responses to Evidence from the UK Teaching and Learning Research Programme*. London: Routledge.

Jamieson, P. (2003) 'Designing more effective on-campus teaching and learning spaces: A role for academic developers', *International Journal for Academic Development*, 8, 119–33.

Jamieson, P., Fisher, K., Gilding, T., Taylor, P. and Trevitt, A. (2000) 'Place and space in the design of new learning environments', *Higher Education Research & Development*, 19, 221–36.

Janice, E., Yeo, M. and Manarin, K. (2018) 'Challenges to disciplinary knowing and identity: Experiences of scholars in a SoTL development program', *International Journal for the Scholarship of Teaching and Learning*, 12(1), 3.

Jary, D. and Lebeau, Y. (2009) 'The student experience and subject engagement in UK sociology: A proposed typology', *British Journal of Sociology of Education*, 30, 697–712.

Jauhiainen, A., Jauhiainen, A. and Laiho, A. (2009) 'The dilemmas of the efficiency university policy and the everyday life of university teachers', *Teaching in Higher Education*, 14, 417–28.

Jawitz, J. (2009) 'Learning in the academic workplace: The harmonization of the collective and the individual habitus', *Studies in Higher Education*, 34, 601–14.

Jenkins, A., Healey, M. and Zetter, R. (2007) *Linking Teaching and Research in Disciplines and Departments*. York: Higher Education Academy.

Jenkins, C., Barnes, C., McLean, M., Abbas, A. and Ashwin, P. (2017) 'Sociological knowledge and transformation.' In M. Walker and M. Wilson-Strydom (eds), *Socially Just Pedagogies, Capabilities and Quality in Higher Education*. London: Palgrave Macmillan.

Jervis, L. and Jervis, L. (2005) 'What is the constructivism in constructive alignment?' *Bioscience Education*, 6(1), 1–14.

Jester, N. (2018) 'Representation within higher education curricula: Contextualising and advocating for feminist digital activism', *Teaching in Higher Education*, 23, 606–18.

Johnston, B., Mitchell, R., Myles F. and Ford, P. (2012) *Developing Student Criticality in Higher Education: Undergraduate Learning in the Arts and Social Sciences*. London: Bloomsbury.

Jones, A. (2011) 'Seeing the messiness of academic practice: Exploring the work of academics through narrative', *International Journal for Academic Development*, 16(2), 109–18.

Jones, E. (2017) 'Problematising and reimagining the notion of international student experience', *Studies in Higher Education*, 42(5), 933–43.

Jones, S. (2018) 'Expectation vs experience: Might transition gaps predict undergraduate students outcome gaps?' *Journal of Further and Higher Education*, 42, 908–21.

Jones, R. and Thomas, L. (2005) 'The 2003 UK Government higher education White paper: A critical assessment of the implications for the access and widening participation agenda', *Journal of Education Policy*, 20, 615–30.

Jungblut, J., Vukasovic, M. and Stensaker, B. (2015) 'Student perspectives on quality in higher education', *European Journal of Higher Education*, 5(2), 157–80.

Kahn, P. (2009) 'Contexts for teaching and the exercise of agency in early-career academics: Perspectives from realist social theory', *International Journal for Academic Development*, 14(3), 197–207.

Kahu, E. and Nelson, K. (2018) 'Student engagement in the educational interface: Understanding the mechanisms of student success', *Higher Education Research and Development*, 37(1), 58–71.

Kalman, C. (ed.) (2017) *Successful Science and Engineering Teaching in Colleges and Universities*. 2nd edn. Charlotte, NC: Information Age Publishing.

Kandiko Howson, C. (2018) *Evaluation of HEFCEs Learning Gain Pilot Projects Year 2*. London: Office for Students.

Kandiko Howson, C., Coate, K. and de St Croix, T. (2018) 'Mid-career academic women and the prestige economy', *Higher Education Research and Development*, 37(3), 533–48.

Kane, R., Sandretto, S. and Heath, C. (2004) 'An investigation into excellent tertiary teaching: Emphasising reflective practice', *Higher Education*, 47, 283–310.

Kanuka, H. (2011) 'Keeping the scholarship in the scholarship of teaching and learning', *International Journal for the Scholarship of Teaching and Learning*, 5(1), 3.

Kay, J., Dunne, L. and Hutchinson, J. (2010) *Rethinking the Values of Higher Education: Students as Change Agents?* Gloucester: Quality Assurance Agency. http://dera.ioe.ac.uk/1193/

Keane, E. (2011a) 'Distancing to self-protect: The perpetuation of inequality in higher education through socio-relational dis/engagement', *British Journal of Sociology of Education*, 32, 449–66.

Keane, E. (2011b) 'Dependence-deconstruction: Widening participation and traditional-entry students transitioning from school to higher education in Ireland', *Teaching in Higher Education*, 16, 707–18.

Keane, E. (2012) 'Differential prioritising: Orientations to higher education and widening participation', *International Journal of Educational Research*, 53, 150–59.

Keane, E. (2013) *International Review of the Effectiveness of Widening Participation, Ireland Report*. Bristol: Higher Education Funding Council for England.

Kelly-Laubscher, R. and Luckett, K. (2016) 'Differences in curriculum structure between high school and university Biology: The implications for epistemological access', *Journal of Biological Education*, 50(4), 425–41.

Kent, M., Gilbertson, D. and Hunt, C. (1997) 'Fieldwork in geography teaching: A critical review of the literature and approaches', *Journal of Geography in Higher Education*, 21, 313–32.

Kenny, A., Fleming, T., Loxley, A. and Finnegan, F. (2010) *Where Next? A Study of Work and Life Experiences of Mature Students in Three Higher Education Institutions*. Dublin: Combat Poverty Agency.

Kenny, J. (2017) 'Academic work and performativity', *Higher Education*, 74(5), 897–913.

Kenny, N., Berenson, C., Chick, N., Johnson, C., Keegan, D., Read, E. and Reid, L. (2017) A developmental framework for teaching expertise in postsecondary education. *Poster presented at the International Society for the Scholarship of Teaching and Learning Conference, Calgary, Alberta, Canada*. Retrieved from http://connections.ucalgaryblogs.ca/files/2017/11/CC4_Teaching-Expertise-Framework-Fall-2017.pdf

Kent, M., Gilbertson, D. and Hunt, C. (1997) 'Fieldwork in geography teaching: A critical review of the literature and approaches', *Journal of Geography in Higher Education*, 21, 313–32.

Kilgo, C., Sheets, J. and Pascarella, E. (2015) 'The link between high-impact practices and student learning: Some longitudinal evidence', *Higher Education*, 69, 509–25.

Kincaid, S. and Pecorino, P. (2004) *The Profession of Education: Responsibilities, Ethics and Pedagogic Experimentation*. (Available from: http://www.qcc.cuny.edu/socialsciences/ppecorino/Profession-Education-ch-4-Professional-Responsibilities.html, last accessed 21 October 2018.)

Kivinen, O. and Ristela, P. (2003) 'From constructivism to a pragmatist conception of learning', *Oxford Review of Education*, 29, 363–75.

Klemenčič, M. and Chirikov, I. (2015) 'How do we know how students experience higher education? On the use of student surveys.' In R. Pricopie, P. Scott, J. Salmi and A. Curaj (eds), *The European Higher Education Area: Between Critical Reflection and Future Policies*. Dordrecht: Springer, 367–86.

Knight, P. (1995) 'Introduction.' In P. Knight (ed.), *Assessment for Learning in Higher Education*. London: Kogan Page, 13–23.

Knight, P. and ESECT colleagues (2003) *Briefings on Employability 3: The Contribution of LTA and Other Curriculum Projects to Student Employability*. York: Higher Education Academy.

Knowles, M. (1975) *Self-Directed Learning*. Englewood Cliffs, CA: Prentice Hall.

Krathwohl, D. (2002) 'A revision of Blooms Taxonomy: An overview', *Theory into Practice*, 41(4), 212–18.

Krause, K. (2009) 'Interpreting changing academic roles and identities in higher education.' In M. Tight (ed.), *International Handbook of Higher Education*. London: Routledge, 413–26.

Krause, K. (2011) 'Using student survey data to shape academic priorities and approaches.' In L. Stefani (ed.), *Evaluating the Effectiveness of Academic Development*. New York: Routledge, 59–72.

Krause, K. (2012) 'A quality approach to university teaching.' In L. Hunt and D. Chalmers (eds), *University Teaching in Focus: A Learning-Centred Approach*. Camberwell: ACER Press, 235–52.

Krause, K. (2014) 'Challenging perspectives on learning and teaching in the disciplines: The academic voice', *Studies in Higher Education*, 39, 2–19.

Kreber, C. (2001) 'Learning experientially through case studies? A conceptual analysis', *Teaching in Higher Education*, 6, 217–28.

Kreber, C. (2002) 'Teaching excellence, teaching expertise and the scholarship of teaching', *Innovative Higher Education*, 27, 5–23.

Kreber, C. (2004) 'An analysis of two models of reflection and their implications for educational development', *International Journal of Academic Development*, 9, 29–49.

Kreber, C. (2005) 'Charting a critical course on the scholarship of university teaching movement', *Studies in Higher Education*, 30, 389–407.

Kreber, C. (ed.) (2009) *The University and its Disciplines: Teaching and Learning Within and Beyond Disciplinary Boundaries*. New York: Routledge.

Kreber, C. and Cranton, P. (2000) 'Exploring the scholarship of teaching', *The Journal of Higher Education*, 71, 476–95.

Kricsfalusy, V., George, C. and Reed, M. (2018) 'Integrating problem- and project-based learning opportunities: Assessing outcomes of a field course in environment and sustainability', *Environmental Education Research*, 24(4), 593–610.

Kugel, P. (1993) 'How professors develop as teachers', *Studies in Higher Education*, 18, 315–28.

Kuh, G. (2008) *High-Impact Educational Practices: What They Are, Who has Access to Them, and Why They Matter*. Washington, DC: Association of American Colleges and Universities.

Lamb, G. and Shraiky, J. (2013) 'Designing for competence: Spaces that enhance collaboration readiness in healthcare', *Journal of Interprofessional Care*, 27, 14–23.

Land, R. (2011) 'There could be trouble ahead: Using threshold concepts as a tool of analysis', *International Journal for Academic Development*, 16(2), 175–78.

Land, R. and Gordon, G. (2013) 'To see ourselves as others see us: The Scottish approach to quality enhancement.' In R. Land and G. Gordon (eds), *Enhancing Quality in Higher Education, International Perspectives*. London: Routledge, 81–93.

Land, R., Meyer, J. and Flanagan, M. (eds) (2016) *Threshold Concepts in Practice*. Rotterdam: Sense Publications.

Lang, R. (2006) 'Crafting a Teaching Persona', *The Higher Education Chronicle*, 6 February. (Available from: https://www.chronicle.com/article/Crafting-a-Teaching-Persona/46671.)

Langan, A. and Harris, W. (2019). 'National student survey metrics: Where is the room for improvement?' *Higher Education*, 1–15.

Lange, L. (2018) 'Institutional curriculum, pedagogy and the decolonisation of the South African university.' In J. Jansen (ed.), *Fallism and Curriculum in South African Universities*. Stellenbosch: SUN Media.

Lanterman, C. (2010) 'Reframing disability: Social justice through universal and inclusive design', *ALERT Newsletter*, Association on Higher Education and Disability.

Laurillard, D. (1997) 'Styles and approaches in problem-solving.' In F. Marton, D. Hounsell and N. Entwistle (eds), *The Experience of Learning, Implications for Teaching and Studying in Higher Education*. 2nd edn. Edinburgh: Scottish Academic Press, 126–44.

Laurillard, D. (2002) 'Rethinking teaching for the knowledge society', *Educause Review*, January/February, 16–25.

Laurillard, D. (2012) *Teaching as a Design Science: Building Pedagogical Patterns for Learning and Technology*. Abingdon: Routledge.

Lave, J. and Wenger, E. (1991) *Situated Learning: Legitimate Peripheral Participation*. Cambridge: Cambridge University Press.

Lee, A. (2008) 'How are doctoral students supervised? Concepts of doctoral research supervision', *Studies in Higher Education*, 33, 267–81

Leibowitz, B. (2017) 'Cognitive Justice and the Higher Education Curriculum', *Journal of Education*, 68, 93–111.

Leibowitz, B. and Holgate, D. (2012) 'Critical Professionalism: A lecturer attribute for troubled times.' In B. Leibowitz (ed.), *Higher Education for the Public Good: Views from the South.* Stoke-on-Trent and Stellenbosch: Trentham Book Ltd. and SUN Media, 165–78.

Leibowitz, B., van Schalkwyk, S., van der Merwe, A., Herman, H. and Young, G. (2009) 'What makes a "Good" first year lecturer?' In B. Leibowitz, A. van der Merwe and S. van Schalkwyk (eds), *Focus on First Year Success: Perspectives Emerging from South Africa and Beyond.* Stellenbosch, South Africa: Sun Press.

Leibowitz, B., Bozalek, V., Carolissen, R., Nicholls, L., Rohleder, P. and Swartz, L. (2010) 'Bringing the social into pedagogy: Unsafe learning in an uncertain world', *Teaching in Higher Education*, 15, 123–33.

Leibowitz, B., van Schalkwyk, S., Ruiters, J., Farmer, J. and Adendorff, H. (2012) '"It's been a wonderful life": Accounts of the interplay between structure and agency by a "good" university teacher', *Higher Education*, 63, 353–65.

Leibowitz, B., Bozalek, V., Van Schalkwyk, S. and Winberg, C. (2015) 'Institutional context matters: The professional development of academics as teachers in South African higher education', *Higher Education*, 69(2), 315–30.

Lessard-Phillips, L., Boliver, V., Pampaka, M. and Swain, D. (2018) 'Exploring ethnic differences in the post-university destinations of Russell Group graduates', *Ethnicities*, 18, 496–517.

Lewin, K. (1951) *Field Theory in Social Science: Selected Theoretical Papers*. New York: Harper and Row.

Leydon, J. and Turner, S. (2013) 'The challenges and rewards of introducing field trips into a large introductory geography class', *Journal of Geography*, 112, 248–61.

Light, G. and Calkins, S. (2015) 'The experience of academic learning: Uneven conceptions of learning across research and teaching', *Higher Education*, 69(3), 345–59.

Light, G. and Micari, M. (2013) *Making Scientists: Six Principles for Effective College Teaching.* Cambridge, MA: Harvard University Press.

Light, G., Calkins, S. and Cox, R. (2009) *Learning and Teaching in Higher Education: The Reflective Professional*. London: Sage.

Lillis, T. (2003) 'Student writing as academic literacies: Drawing on Bakhtin to move from critique to design', *Language and Education*, 17(3), 192–207.

Lillis, T. and Tuck, T. (2016) 'Academic literacies: A critical lens on writing and reading in the academy.' In K. Hyland and P. Shaw (eds), *The Routledge Handbook of English for Academic Purposes.* London: Routledge, 30–43.

Lillis, T., Harrington, K., Lea, M. and Mitchell, S. (eds) (2016) *Working with Academic Literacies: Case Studies Towards Transformative Practice. Perspectives on Writing.* Fort Collins, CO: The WAC Clearinghouse/Parlor Press.

Lindblom-Ylänne, S. and Pihlajamaki, H. (2003) 'Can a collaborative network environment enhance essay-writing processes?' *British Journal of Educational Technology*, 34(1), 17–30.

Lindblom-Ylänne, S., Trigwell, K., Nevgi, A. and Ashwin, P. (2006) 'How approaches to teaching are affected by discipline and teaching context', *Studies in Higher Education,* 31, 285–98.

Ling, P. (2009) *Development of Academics and Higher Education Futures: Volume 1.* Strawberry Hills, NSW: Australian Learning and Teaching Council. (Available from: http://hdl.voced.edu. au/10707/328585, last accessed 24 May 2019.)

Lomas, C. and Oblinger, D. (2006) 'Student practices and their impact on learning spaces.' In D. Oblinger (ed.), *Learning Spaces*. EDUCAUSE. (Available from: https://www.educause.edu/ research-and-publications/books/learning-spaces/chapter-5-student-practices-and-their-impact-learning-spaces, last accessed 24 May 2019.)

Lowe, H. and Cook, A. (2003) 'Mind the gap: Are students prepared for higher education?' *Journal of Further and Higher Education*, 27, 53–76.

Luckett, K. (2009) 'The relationship between knowledge structure and curriculum: A case study in sociology', *Studies in Higher Education*, 34, 441–53.

Luckett, K. (2019) 'Gazes in the post-colony: An analysis of African philosophies using Legitimation Code Theory', *Teaching in Higher Education*, 24(2), 197–211.

Luckett, K., Morreira, S. and Baijnath, M. (2019) 'Decolonising the curriculum: Recontextualisation, identity and self-critique in a post-apartheid university.' In L. Quinn. (ed.), *Reimagining Curriculum: Spaces for Disruption*. Stellenbosch: African Sun Media.

Lygo-Baker, S. (2017) 'The role of values in higher education.' In I Kinchin and N. Winstone (eds), *Pedagogic Frailty and Resilience in the University*. Rotterdam: Sense Publishers, 79–91.

Lynch, K., Baker, J. and Lyons, M. (2009) *Affective Equality: Love, Care and Injustice*. Basingstoke: Palgrave Macmillan,

Lynch, K., Grummell, B. and Devine, D. (2012) *New Managerialism in Education: Commercialization, Carelessness and Gender*. London: Palgrave Macmillan.

Macfarlane, B. (2004) *Teaching with Integrity: The Ethics of Higher Education Practice*. London: RoutledgeFalmer.

Macfarlane, B. (2016) 'From identity to identities: A story of fragmentation', *Higher Education Research and Development*, 35, 1083–5.

Mackh, B. (2018) *Higher Education by Design: Best Practices for Curricular Planning and Instruction*. London: Routledge.

MacMillan, J. and McLean, M. (2005) 'Making first-year tutorials count: Operationalizing the assessment-learning connection', *Active Learning in Higher Education*, 6(2), 94–105.

MacNell, L., Driscoll, A. and Hunt, A. (2015) 'What's in a name: Exposing gender bias in student ratings of teaching', *Innovative Higher Education*, 40, 291–303.

Malesky, L. and Peters, C. (2012) 'Defining appropriate professional behavior for faculty and university students on social networking websites', *Higher Education*, 63, 135–51.

Mälkki, K. and Lindblom-Ylänne, S. (2012) 'From reflection to action? Barriers and bridges between higher education teachers thoughts and actions', *Studies in Higher Education*, 37, 33–50.

Mamdani, M. (2012) *Reading Ibn Khaldun in Kampala*. Paper presented at the After Bandung: Non-Western Modernities and the International Order, Makerere.

Manley, K. and Garbett, R. (2000) 'Paying Peter and Paul: Reconciling concepts of expertise with competency for a clinical career structure', *Journal of Clinical Nursing*, 9, 347–59.

Mann, S. (2000) 'The students experience of reading', *Higher Education*, 39, 297–317.

Mann, S. (2001) 'Alternative perspectives on the student experience: Alienation and engagement', *Studies in Higher Education*, 26, 7–19.

Mann, S. (2003) 'Inquiring into a higher education classroom: Insights into the different perspective of teacher and students.' In C. Rust (ed.), *Improving Student Learning: Theory and Practice 10 years On*. Oxford: The Oxford Centre for Staff and Learning Development, 215–24.

Mann, S. (2008) *Study, Power and the University*. Buckinghamshire: Open University Press.

Mann, S. and Robinson, A. (2009) 'Boredom in the lecture theatre: An investigation into the contributors, moderators and outcomes of boredom amongst university students', *British Educational Research Journal*, 35(2), 243–58.

Marsh, H. (2007) 'Students' evaluations of university teaching: Dimensionality, reliability, validity, potential biases and usefulness.' In R. Perry and J. Smart (ed.), *The Scholarship of Teaching and Learning in Higher Education: An Evidence-Based Perspective*. Dordrecht: Springer, 319–83.

Mårtensson, K. (2014) *Influencing Teaching and Learning Microcultures. Academic Development in a Research-intensive University*. PhD thesis. Lund University Press, Lund, Sweden. (Available at: http://portal.research.lu.se/ws/files/3403041/4438677.pdf.)

Mårtensson, K. and Roxå, T. (2016) 'Collegial engagement for teaching and learning: Competence, autonomy and social solidarity in academic microcultures', *Uniped*, 39, 131–43.

Mårtensson, K., Roxå, T. and Olsson, T. (2011) 'Developing a quality culture through the Scholarship of Teaching and Learning', *Higher Education Research & Development*, 30, 51–62.

Martin, F., Wang, C. and Sadaf, A. (2018) 'Student perception of helpfulness of facilitation strategies that enhance instructor presence, connectedness, engagement and learning in online courses', *The Internet and Higher Education*, 37, 52–65.

Martinez, L., Salazar, M. and Ortega, D. (2016) 'Dehumanizing and humanizing pedagogies: Lessons from U.S. Latin@ and undocumented youth through the P-16 Pipeline.' In F. Tuitt, C. Haynes and S. Stewart (eds), *Race, Equity, and the Learning Environment: The Global Relevance of Critical and Inclusive Pedagogies in Higher Education*. Sterling, VA: Stylus.

Martínez-Fernández, J. and Vermunt, J. (2013) 'A cross-cultural analysis of the patterns of learning and academic performance of Spanish and Latin-American undergraduates', *Studies in Higher Education*, 40(2), 278–95.

Marton, F. (2014) *Necessary Conditions of Learning*. New York: Routledge.

Marton, F. and Säljö, R. (1997) 'Approaches to learning.' In F. Marton, D. Hounsell and N. Entwistle (eds), *The Experience of Learning*. 2nd edn. Edinburgh: Scottish Academic Press, 39–58.

Marton, F., DallAlba, G. and Beaty, E. (1993) 'Conceptions of learning', *International Journal of Educational Research*, 19, 277–300.

Marzetti, H. (2018) 'Proudly proactive: Celebrating and supporting LGBT+ students in Scotland', *Teaching in Higher Education*, 23(6), 701–17.

Mason, R. and Rennie, F. (2006) *E-Learning: The Key Concepts*. London: Routledge.

Maton, K. (2014) *Knowledge and Knowers: Towards a Realist Sociology of Education*. London, Routledge.

Maton, K., Hood, S. and Shay, S. (eds) (2016) *Knowledge-building: Educational Studies in Legitimation Code Theory*. Abingdon and New York: Routledge.

Matthews, K., Cook-Sather, A., Acai, A., Dvorakova, S., Felten, P., Marquis, E. and Mercer-Mapstone, L. (2019) 'Toward theories of partnership praxis: An analysis of interpretive framing in literature on students as partners in teaching and learning', *Higher Education Research and Development*, 38, 280–93.

May, H. and Bridger, K. (2010) *Developing and Embedding Inclusive Policy and Practice in Higher Education*. York: The Higher Education Academy. (Available from: www.heacademy. ac.uk/system/files/developingembeddinginclusivepp_report.pdf, last accessed 24 May 2019.)

Mayhew, M., Pascarella, E., Bowman, N., Rockenbach, A., Seifert, T., Terenzini, P. and Wolniak, G. (2016) *How College Affects Students: 21st Century Evidence that Higher Education Works* (Vol. 3). San Francisco, CA: Jossey-Bass.

Mazur, E. (1997) *Peer instruction: A users manual*. Englewood Cliffs, CA: Prentice Hall.

Mazur, E. (2009) 'Farewell lecture?', *Science*, 323, 50–51.

Mbembe, A. (2016) 'Decolonizing the university: New directions', *Arts and Humanities in Higher Education*, 15(1), 29–45.

McAlpine, L. and Amundsen, C. (2018) *Identity-Trajectories of Early Career Researchers*. London: Palgrave Macmillan.

McAlpine, L. and Harris, R. (2002) 'Evaluating teaching effectiveness and teaching improvement: A language for institutional policies and academic development practices', *International Journal for Academic Development*, 7(1), 7–17.

McAlpine, L. and Weston, C. (2000) 'Reflection: Issues related to improving professors' teaching and students' learning', *Instructional Science*, 28, 363–85.

McArthur, J. (2009) 'Diverse student voices in disciplinary discourses.' In C. Kreber (ed.), *The University and its Disciplines*. New York: Routledge, 119–28.

McArthur, J. (2010) 'Time to look anew: Critical pedagogy and disciplines within higher education', *Studies in Higher Education*, 35, 301–15.

McArthur, J. (2011) 'Reconsidering the social and economic purposes of higher education', *Higher Education Research & Development*, 30, 737–49.

McArthur, J. (2013) *Rethinking Knowledge in Higher Education: Adorno and Social Justice*. London: Bloomsbury.

McArthur, J. (2016) 'Assessment for social justice: the role of assessment in achieving social justice', *Assessment & Evaluation in Higher Education*, 41(7), 967–81.

McArthur, J. (2018) *Assessment for Social Justice*. London: Bloomsbury.

McArthur, J. and Huxham, M. (2011) *Sharing control: A partnership approach to curriculum design and delivery.* York: Higher Education Academy. (Available from http://eprints.lancs.ac.uk/73157/1/Sharing_Control_2011.pdf, last accessed 24 May 2019.)

McArthur, J. and Huxham, M. (2013) 'Feedback unbound: From master to usher.' In S. Merry, D. Carless, M. Price and M. Tara (eds), *Reconceptualising Feedback in Higher Education*. London: Routledge.

McArthur, J., Land, R., Earl, S., Elvidge, L., Juwah, C. and Ross, D. (2004) *PROMOTE: Alternative Ways of Fostering Educational Development.* Edinburgh: Napier University.

McArthur, J., Huxham, M., Hounsell, J. and Warsop, C. (2011) *Tipping out the Boot Grit: The Use of On-Going Feedback Devices to Enhance Feedback Dialogue.* York: Higher Education Academy. (Available from: https://www.heacademy.ac.uk/knowledge-hub/tipping-out-boot-grit-use-going-feedback-devices-enhance-feedback-dialogue, last accessed 24 May 2019.)

McConnell, D. (2006) *E-Learning Groups and Communities*. Maidenhead: Society for Research into Higher Education and Open University Press.

McCowan, T. (2017) 'Higher education, unbundling and the end of the university as we know it', *Oxford Review of Education*, 43(6), 733–48.

McCune, V. (2009) 'Final year biosciences students' willingness to engage: Teaching-learning environments, authentic learning experiences and identities', *Studies in Higher Education*, 34, 347–61.

McCune, V. and Hounsell, D. (2005) 'The development of students' ways of thinking and practising in three final-year biology courses', *Higher Education*, 49, 255–89.

McGrath, C., Guerin, B., Harte, E., Frearson, M. and Manville, C. (2015) *Learning Gain in Higher Education*. Santa Monica, CA: RAND Corporation.

McGregor, R. and Park, M. (2019) 'Towards a deconstructed curriculum: Rethinking higher education in the global North', *Teaching in Higher Education*, 24, 332–45.

McInnis, C. (2010) 'Traditions of academic professionalism and shifting identities.' In G. Gordon and C. Whitchurch (eds), *Academic and Professional Identities in Higher Education: The Challenges of a Diversifying Workforce*. London: Routledge.

McLean, M. (2006) *Pedagogy and the University*. London: Continuum.

McLean, M. and Ashwin, P. (2016) 'The quality of learning, teaching, and curriculum.' In P. Scott, J. Gallacher and G. Parry (eds), *New Languages and Landscapes of Higher Education*. Oxford: Oxford University Press, 84–102.

McLean, M., Abbas, A. and Ashwin, P. (2018) *How Powerful Knowledge Disrupts Inequality: Reconceptualising Quality in Undergraduate Education*. London: Bloomsbury.

Mead, N. (2019) *Values and Professional Knowledge in Teacher Education*. London.

Merry, S. and Orsmond, P. (2018) 'Peer assessment: The role of relational learning through communities of practice', *Studies in Higher Education*.

Meschitti, V. (2019) 'Can peer learning support doctoral education? Evidence from an ethnography of a research team', *Studies in Higher Education*, 44(7), 1209–21.

Meyer, J. and Land, R. (2003) 'Threshold concepts and troublesome knowledge: Linkages to ways of thinking and practising.' In C. Rust (ed.), *Improving Student Learning: Theory and Practice Ten Years On.* Oxford: Oxford Centre for Staff and Learning Development, 412–24.

Meyer, J. and Land, R. (2005) 'Threshold concepts and troublesome knowledge (2): Epistemological considerations and a conceptual framework for teaching and learning', *Higher Education*, 49, 373–88.

Mezirow, J. (1991) *Fostering Critical Reflection in Adulthood: A Guide to Transformative and Emancipatory Learning*. San Francisco, CA: Jossey-Bass.

Mezirow, J. (ed.) (2009) *Transformative Learning in Practice: Insights from Community, Workplace and Higher Education*. San Francisco, CA: Jossey Bass.

Middendorf, J. and Pace, D. (2004) 'Decoding the disciplines: A model for helping students learn disciplinary ways of thinking', *New Directions for Teaching and Learning*, 98: 1–12.

Mignolo, W. (2010) 'Introduction: Coloniality of power and de-colonial thinking.' In W. Mignolo and A. Escobar (eds), *Globalization and the Decolonial Option*, Abingdon: Routledge, 1–21.

Mignolo, W. and Escobar, A. (eds) (2010) *Globalization and the Decolonial Option*. New York: Routledge.

Mitchell, K. and Martin, J. (2018) 'Gender bias in student evaluations', *PS: Political Science & Politics*, 51(3), 648–52.

Molloy, E. and Boud, D. (2013) 'Changing conceptions of feedback.' In D. Boud and E. Molloy (eds), *Feedback in Higher and Professional Education: Understanding It and Doing It Well*. London: Routledge, 11–33.

Molloy, E., Borrell-Carrió, F. and Epstein, R. (2013) 'The impact of emotions in feedback.' In D. Boud and E. Molloy (eds), *Feedback in Higher and Professional Education: Understanding It and Doing It Well*. London: Routledge, 50–71.

Moore, R. (2000) 'For knowledge: Tradition, progressivism and progress in education – reconstructing the curriculum debate', *Cambridge Journal of Education*, 30, 17–36.

Moore, R. and Young, M. (2001) 'Knowledge and the curriculum in the sociology of education: Towards a reconceptualisation', *British Journal of Sociology of Education,* 22, 445–61.

Moore, T. and Morton, J. (2017) 'The myth of job readiness? Written communication, employability, and the skills gap in higher education', *Studies in Higher Education*, 42, 591–609.

Morley, D. (ed.) (2018) *Enhancing Employability in Higher Education through Work-Based Learning*. Cham: Springer.

Morley, L. (2016) 'Troubling intra-actions: Gender, neo-liberalism and research in the global academy', *Journal of Education Policy*, 31(1), 28–45.

Morrissey, J., Clavin, A. and Reilly, K. (2013) 'Field-based learning: The challenge of practising participatory knowledge', *Journal of Geography in Higher Education*, 37, 619–27.

Morrow, W. (2009) *The Bounds of Democracy: Epistemological Access in Higher Education*. Cape Town: HSRC Press.

Mountford-Zimdars, A., Sanders, J., Jones, S., Sabri, D. and Moore, J. (2015) *Causes of Differences in Student Outcomes*. Bristol: Higher Education Funding Council for England.

Mueller, J. and O'Connor, C. (2007) 'Telling and retelling about self and others: How pre-service teachers (re)interpret privilege and disadvantage in one college classroom', *Teaching and Teacher Education*, 23, 840–56.

Muller, J. (2009) 'Forms of knowledge and curriculum coherence', *Journal of Education and Work*, 22, 205–26.

Murray, N. and Nalaya, S. (2016) 'Embedding academic literacies in university programme curricula: A case study', *Studies in Higher Education*, 41, 1296–312.

Naidoo, R. and Williams, J. (2015) 'The neoliberal regime in English higher education: Charters, consumers and the erosion of the public good', *Critical Studies in Education*, 56(2), 208–23.

Narey, M. (2019) 'Who stands for what is right? Teachers creative capacity and change agency in the struggle for educational quality.' In C. Mullen (ed.), *Creativity Under Duress in Education?* New York: Springer, 313–37.

National Forum for the Enhancement of Teaching and Learning in Higher Education (2016) *National Professional Development Framework for All Staff Who Teach in Higher Education*. (Accessible from https://www.teachingandlearning.ie/wp-content/uploads/2016/09/PD-Framework-FINAL.pdf, last accessed October 2018.)

Natriello, G. (2005) 'Modest changes, revolutionary possibilities: Distance learning and the future of education', *Teachers College Record*, 107, 1885–904.

Ndlovu-Gatsheni, S. (2013) *Empire, Global Coloniality and African Subjectivity*. New York: Berghahn Books.

Nespor, J. (1994) *Knowledge in Motion: Space, Time and Curriculum in Undergraduate Physics and Management*. London: RoutledgeFalmer.

Neuman, R (2017) 'Charting the future of U.S. higher education: A look at the Spellings Report ten years later', *Liberal Education*, 103, 1.

Ngabaza, S., Shefer, T. and Clowes, L. (2018) 'Students' narratives on gender and sexuality in the project of social justice and belonging in higher education', *South African Journal of Higher Education*, 32(3): 139–53.

Nicholson, D. (2011) 'Embedding research in a field-based module through peer review and assessment for learning', *Journal of Geography in Higher Education*, 35, 529–49.

Nicol, D. (2009) 'Assessment for learner self-regulation: Enhancing achievement in the first year using learning technologies', *Assessment & Evaluation in Higher Education*, 34, 335–52.

Nicol, D. (2010) 'From monologue to dialogue: Improving written feedback processes in mass higher education', *Assessment & Evaluation in Higher Education*, 35(5), 501–17.

Nicol, D. and Macfarlane-Dick, D. (2006) 'Formative assessment and self-regulated learning: A model and seven principles of good feedback practice', *Studies in Higher Education*, 31, 199–218.

Nicol, D., Thomson, A. and Breslin, C. (2014) 'Rethinking feedback practices in higher education: A peer review perspective', *Assessment & Evaluation in Higher Education*, 39(1), 102–22.

Nixon, J. (2001) 'Not without dust and heat. The moral bases of the new academic profession-alism: A manifesto of hope', *British Journal of Educational Studies*, 49(2): 173–86.

Nixon, J. (2008) *Towards the Virtuous University.* New York and London: Routledge.

Norodien-Fataar, N. (2018) 'First generation disadvantaged students mediation practices in the uneven field of a South African university.' In A. Fataar (ed.), *The Educational Practices and Pathways of South African Students across Power-marginalised Spaces*. Stellenbosch: SUN Media.

Northedge, A. (2003a) 'Enabling participation in academic discourse', *Teaching in Higher Education*, 8, 169–80.

Northedge, A. (2003b) 'Rethinking teaching in the context of diversity', *Teaching in Higher Education*, 8, 17–32.

Northedge, A. and McArthur J. (2009) 'Guiding students into a discipline – the significance of the teacher.' In C. Kreber (ed.), *The University and its Disciplines*, New York: Routledge, 107–18.

Nystrand, M. (1997) *Opening Dialogue: Understanding the Dynamics of Language and Learning in the English Classroom.* New York: Teachers College Press.

O'Donoghue, T., Chapman, A., Pyvis, D., Aspland, T. and Melville, I. (2010) *Enhancing Frameworks for Assuring the Quality of Learning and Teaching in University Offshore Education Programs.* Sydney: Australian Learning and Teaching Council.

O'Donovan, B., Price, M. and Rust, C. (2008) 'Developing student understanding of assessment standards: A nested hierarchy of approaches', *Teaching in Higher Education*, 13, 205–17.

O'Donovan, B., Rust, C. and Price, M. (2016) 'A scholarly approach to solving the feedback dilemma in practice', *Assessment and Evaluation in Higher Education*, 41, 938–49.

Oberst, U., Gallifa, J., Farriols, N. and Vilaregut, A. (2009) 'Training emotional and social compet-ences in higher education: The seminar methodology', *European Journal of Higher Education*, 34, 523–35.

OECD (2011) *The Nature of Learning. Using Research to Inspire Practice.* Paris: OECD.

Olsson, T. and Roxå, T. (2013) 'Assessing and rewarding excellent academic teachers for the benfit of an organization', *European Journal of Higher Education*, 3, 40–60.

Olsson, T., Mårtensson, K. and Roxå, T. (2010) 'Pedagogical competence – a development perspective from Lund University.' In Å. Ryegård, Olsson T. and K. Apelgren (eds), *A Swedish Perspective on Pedagogical Competence*. Upssala: Division for Development of Teaching and Learning, Uppsala University, 121–32.

O'Neill, G. (2015) *Curriculum Design in Higher Education: Theory to Practice,* Dublin: UCD Teaching and Learning. https://researchrepository.ucd.ie/handle/10197/7137

Pai, H., Sears, D. and Maeda, Y. (2015) 'Effects of small-group learning on transfer: A meta-analysis', *Educational Psychology Review*, 27(1), 79–102.

Parini, J. (2005) *The Art of Teaching*. Oxford: Oxford University Press.

Parry, G. (2010) 'Policy contexts, differentiation, competition and policies for widening participation.' In M. David (ed.), (2010) *Improving Learning by Widening Participation in Higher Education*. London: Routledge, 31–46.

Paterson, L. (2003) 'The survival of the democratic intellect: Academic values in Scotland and England', *Higher Education Quarterly*, 57, 67–93.

Paterson, L. and Bond, R. (2005) 'Higher education and critical citizenship: A survey of academics' views in Scotland and England', *Pedagogy, Culture and Society*, 13, 205–31.

Paul, A., Gilbert, K. and Remedios, L. (2013) 'Socio-cultural considerations in feedback.' In D. Boud and E. Molloy (eds), *Feedback in Higher and Professional Education: Understanding It and Doing It Well*. London: Routledge, 72–89.

Peelo, M. (2011) *Understanding Supervision and the PhD*. London: Continuum.

Pegg, A., Waldock, J., Hendy-Isaac, S. and Lawton, R. (2012) *Pedagogy for Employability*. York: The Higher Education Academy. (Available from: https://www.heacademy.ac.uk/system/files/pedagogy_for_employability_update_2012.pdf, last accessed 24 May 2019.)

Percy, A. (2014) 'Re-integrating academic development and academic language and learning: A call to reason', *Higher Education Research and Development*, 33, 1194–207.

Perkin, H. (2007) 'History of universities.' In J. Forest and P. Altbach (eds), *International Handbook of Higher Education*. Dordrecht: Springer, 159–205.

Perkins, D. (2006) 'Constructivism and troublesome knowledge.' In J. Meyer and R. Land (eds), *Overcoming Barriers to Student Learning: Threshold Concepts and Troublesome Knowledge*. New York: Routledge, 33–47.

Perry, W. (1999) *Forms of Intellectual and Ethical Development in the College Years: A Scheme. Jossey-Bass Higher and Adult Education Series*. San Francisco, CA: Jossey-Bass Publishers.

Petersen, E. (2007) 'Negotiating academicity: Postgraduate research supervision as category boundary work', *Studies in Higher Education*, 32: 475–87.

Phipps, A. and Young, I. (2015) 'Neoliberalisation and lad cultures in higher education', *Sociology*, 49, 305–22.

Pollard, A. (1982) 'A model of classroom coping strategies', *British Journal of Sociology of Education*, 3: 19–37.

Pollard, A. (2007) 'The UK's Teaching and Learning Research Programme: Findings and significance', *British Educational Research Journal*, 33(5), 639–46.

Pollard, A. (2018) *Reflective Teaching in Schools*. 5th edn. London: Bloomsbury.

Poole, G. (2018) 'Using intuition, anecdote, and observation.' In N. Chick (ed.), *SoTL in Action: Illuminating Critical Moments of Practice*. Sterling, VA: Stylus Publishing.

Porter, S. and Swing, R. (2006) 'Understanding how first year seminars affect persistence', *Research in Higher Education*, 47, 89–110.

Potter, M. and Kustra, E. (2011) 'The relationship between scholarly teaching and SoTL: Models, distinctions, and clarifications', *International Journal for the Scholarship of Teaching and Learning*, 5(1), 1–18.

Prebble, T., Hargraves, H., Leach, L., Naidoo, K., Suddaby, G. and Zepke, N. (2004) *Impact of Student Support Services and Academic Development Programmes on Student Outcomes in Undergraduate Tertiary Study: A Synthesis of the Research*. Wellington: Ministry of Education

Pring, R. (2001) 'Education as a Moral Practice', *Journal of Moral Education*, 30, 101–12.

Pring, R. (2008) 'Blooms taxonomy: A philosophical critique.' In N. Norris (ed.), *Curriculum and the Teacher: 35 Years of the Cambridge Journal of Education*. London: Routledge, 36–43.

Pritchard, D. (2010) 'Where learning starts? A framework for thinking about lectures in university mathematics', *International Journal of Mathematical Education in Science and Technology*, 41, 609–23.

Prosser, M. (2008) 'The Scholarship of Teaching and Learning: What is it? A personal view', *International Journal for the Scholarship of Teaching and Learning*, 2(2), 1–4.

Prosser, M. and Trigwell, K. (1999) *Understanding Learning and Teaching: The Experience in Higher Education*. Buckingham: Society for Research into Higher Education and Open University Press.

Quality Assurance Agency (2011) *UK Quality Code for Higher Education*. Gloucester: Quality Assurance Agency.

Quality Assurance Agency (2012) *Student Experience Research 2012: Part 1, Teaching and Learning*. Gloucester: Quality Assurance Agency.

Quinlan, K. (2016) *How Higher Education Feels: Commentaries on Poems That Illuminate Emotions in Learning and Teaching*. Rotterdam: Sense Publishers.

Ramsden, P. (1991) 'A performance indicator of teaching quality in higher education: The Course Experience Questionnaire', *Studies in Higher Education*, 16, 129–50.

Ramsden, P. (2003) *Learning to Teach in Higher Education*. 2nd edn. London: RoutledgeFalmer.

Randall, V., Brooks, R., Montgomery, A. and McNally, L. (2018) 'Threshold concepts in medical education', *MedEdPublish*, 7.

Read, B., Archer, L. and Leathwood, C. (2003) 'Challenging cultures? Student conceptions of belonging and isolation at a post-1992 university', *Studies in Higher Education*, 28, 261–77.

Read, B., Francis, B. and Robson, J. (2005) 'Gender bias, assessment and feedback: Analyzing the written assessment of undergraduate history essays', *Assessment & Evaluation in Higher Education*, 30, 241–60.

Reay, D. (2005) 'Beyond consciousness? The psychic landscape of social class', *Sociology*, 39, 911–28.

Reay, D., David, M. and Ball, S. (2005) *Degrees of Choice: Social Class, Race, and Gender in Higher Education*. Stoke-on-Trent: Trentham Books.

Reay, D., Crozier, G. and Clayton, J. (2009) 'Strangers in paradise? Working-class students in elite universities', *Sociology*, 43, 1103–21.

Reid, N. (2006) *Getting Started in Pedagogical Research in the Physical Sciences*. Hull: UK Physical Sciences Centre. (Available from: https://www.heacademy.ac.uk/system/files/getting_started_ped_research.pdf. Last accessed 24 May 2019.)

Reinholz, D. (2016) 'The assessment cycle: A model for learning through peer assessment', *Assessment and Evaluation in Higher Education*, 41(2), 301–15.

Reports from the Department of Education, University of Göteborg, No. 76. Göteborg: University of Göteborg.

Reyna, J., Hanham, J. and Meier, P. (2018) 'A framework for digital media literacies for teaching and learning in higher education', *E-Learning and Digital Media*, 15(4), 176–90.

Rhodes Must Fall (RMF) Movement. (2015) 'UCT Rhodes Must Fall Mission Statement', *The Salon*, 9, 6–8.

Richardson, J. (2015) 'The under-attainment of ethnic minority students in UK higher education: What we know and what we don't know', *Journal of Further and Higher Education*, 39, 278–91.

Richardson, R. and Skinner, E. (1991) *Achieving Quality and Diversity: Universities in a Multicultural Society*. New York: American Council on Education and Macmillan Publishing Company.

Rizvi, F. (2006) 'Imagination and the globalisation of educational policy research', *Globalisation, Societies and Education*, 4(2), 193–205.

Rogers, R. (2001) 'Reflection in higher education: A concept analysis', *Innovative Higher Education*, 26, 37–57.

Rogers-Shaw, C., Carr-Chellman, D. and Choi, J. (2018) 'Universal design for learning: Guidelines for accessible online instruction', *Adult Learning*, 29, 20–31.

Rooney, D., Hopwood, N., Boud, D. and Kelly, M. (2015) 'The role of simulation in pedagogies of higher education for the health professions: Through a practice-based lens', *Vocations and Learning*, 8(3), 269–85.

Rourke, L., Anderson, T., Garrison, D. and Archer, W. (2001) 'Assessing social presence in asynchronous text-based computer conferencing', *Journal of Distance Education*, 14(3), 51–71.

Rowland, S. (2000) *The Enquiring University Teacher*. Buckingham: Open University Press and Society for Research into Higher Education.

Rowland, S. (2003) 'Learning to comply: Learning to contest.' In J. Satterthwaite, E. Atkinson and K. Gale (eds), *Discourses, Power and Resistance*. Stoke-on-Trent: Trentham Books, 13–25.

Rowland, S. (2005) 'Intellectual love and the link between teaching and research.' In R. Barnett (ed.), *Reshaping the University*. Maidenhead: Society for Research into Higher Education and Open University Press, 92–101.

Rowland, S., Byron, C., Furedi, F., Padfield, N. and Smyth, T. (1998) 'Turning academics into teachers?' *Teaching in Higher Education*, 3, 133–41.

Roxå, T. and Mårtensson, K. (2009) 'Significant conversations and significant networks: Exploring the backstage of the teaching arena', *Studies in Higher Education,* 34, 547–59.

Roxå, T. and Mårtensson, K. (2011/2013) *Understanding Strong Academic Microcultures – An Exploratory Study*. Report from a pilot-project. Lund: Lund University.

Roxå, T. and Mårtensson, K. (2009) 'Significant conversations and significant networks – exploring the backstage of the teaching arena', *Studies in Higher Education*, 34: 547–59.

Roxå, T., Olsson, T. and Mårtensson, K. (2008) 'Appropriate use of theory in the scholarship of teaching and learning as a strategy for institutional development', *Arts and Humanities in Higher Education*, 7(3), 276–94.

Roxå, T. and Mårtensson, K. (2015) 'Microcultures and informal learning: A heuristic guiding analysis of conditions for informal learning in local higher education workplaces', *International Journal for Academic Development*, 20(2), 193–205.

Rust, C. (2007) 'Towards a scholarship of assessment', *Assessment & Evaluation in Higher Education*, 32, 229–37.

Ryan, J. and Viete, R. (2009) 'Respectful interactions: Learning with international students in the English-speaking academy', *Teaching in Higher Education*, 14, 303–14.

Ryegård, Å., Apelgren, K. and Olsson, T. (eds) (2010) *A Swedish Perspective on Pedagogical Competence*. Uppsala, Sweden: Uppsala University Division for Development of Teaching and Learning.

Sadler, D. (1987) 'Specifying and promulgating achievement standards', *Oxford Review of Education*, 13, 191–209.

Sadler, D. (2009) 'Indeterminacy in the use of preset criteria for assessment and grading', *Assessment & Evaluation in Higher Education*, 34, 159–79.

Sadler, D. (2010) 'Beyond feedback: Developing student capability in complex appraisal', *Assessment and Evaluation in Higher Education*, 35(5), 535–50.

Sadler, D. (2012) 'Assuring academic achievement standards: From moderation to calibration', *Assessment in Education: Principles, Policy and Practice*, 1–15

Salazar, M. (2013) 'A humanizing pedagogy: Reinventing the principles and practice of education as a journey toward liberation', *Review of Research in Education*, 37: 121–48.

Säljö, R. (1979) *Learning in the Learners Perspective I: Some Common-Sense Conceptions*.

Salzberger-Wittenberg, I., Henry G. and Osborne, E. (1983) *The Emotional Experience of Learning and Teaching*. London: Routledge and Kegan Paul.

Samball, K., McDowell, E. and Montgomery, C. (2012) *Assessment for Learning in Higher Education*. London: Routledge.

Saunders, M. (2014) 'Quality enhancement: An overview of lessons from the Scottish experience.' In M. Rosa and A. Amaral (eds), *Quality Assurance in Higher Education*. Palgrave Macmillan: London, 117–31.

Saunders, M., Bonamy, J. and Charlier, B. (2005) 'Using evaluation to create provisional stabilities: Bridging innovation in Higher Education change processes', *Evaluation*, 11(2), 37–55.

Savin-Baden, M. (2003) *Facilitating Problem-Based Learning: Illuminating Perspectives*. Maidenhead: Society for Research into Higher Education and Open University Press.

Savin-Baden, M. (2008) *Learning Spaces: Creating Opportunities for Knowledge Creation in Academic Life*. Maidenhead: Society for Research into Higher Education and Open University Press.

Sawyer, R. (2011) *Structure and Improvisation in Creative Teaching*. Cambridge: Cambridge University Press.

Schell, J. and Butler, A. (2018) 'Insights from the science of learning: Understanding why peer instruction is effective can inform implementation', *Frontiers in Education*, 3, 33.

Schoepp, K. (2019) 'The state of course learning outcomes at leading universities', *Studies in Higher Education*, 44, 615–27.

Schön, D. (1983) *The Reflective Practitioner: How Professionals Think in Action*. London: Temple Smith.

Schön, D. (1987) *Educating the Reflective Practitioner*. San Francisco, CA: Jossey-Bass.

Scott, J. (2006) The mission of the university: Medieval to postmodern transformations. *The Journal of Higher Education*, 77, 1–39.

Seery, M. (2015) 'Flipped learning in higher education chemistry: Emerging trends and potential directions', *Chemistry Education Research and Practice*, 16, 758–68.

Selwyn, N. (2013) *Distrusting Educational Technology: Critical Questions for Changing Times*. London: Routledge.

Seppala, N. and Smith, C. (2019) 'Teaching awards in higher education: A qualitative study of motivation and outcomes', *Studies in Higher Education*, 1–15.

Sfard, A. (2009) 'Moving between discourses: From learning as acquisition to learning as participation', *American Institute of Physics, Physics Education Research Conference Proceedings*, 1179, 55–58.

Sfard A. (2015) 'Metaphors for learning.' In R. Gunstone (eds), *Encyclopedia of Science Education*. Dordrecht: Springer.

Sfard, A. and Prusak, A. (2005) 'Telling identities: In search of an analytic tool for investigating learning as a culturally shaped activity', *Educational Researcher*, 34(4), 14–22.

Share, M. and Carroll, C. (2013) *Ripples of Hope: The Family and Community Impact of Trinity College Dublin Access Graduates*, Dublin: Children's Research Centre, Trinity College Dublin.

Sharpe, R., Beetham, H., De Freitas, S. and Conole, G. (2013) 'Introduction to rethinking learning for a digital age.' In R. Sharpe, H. Beetham and S. De Freitas (eds), *Rethinking Learning for a Digital Age: How Learners are Shaping Their Own Experiences*. Abingdon: Routledge, 1–12.

Shaw, L., Carey, P. and Mair, M. (2008) 'Studying interaction in undergraduate tutorials: Results from a small-scale evaluation', *Teaching in Higher Education*, 13, 703–14.

Shay, S. and Steyn, D. (2016) 'Enabling knowledge progression in vocational curricula: Design as a case study.' In K. Maton, S. Hood and S. Shay (eds), *Knowledge-Building: Educational Studies in Legitimation Code Theory*. Abingdon and New York: Routledge, 138–57.

Shay, S., Wolff, K. and Clarence-Fincham, J. (2016) 'Curriculum reform in South Africa: More time for what?' *Critical Studies in Teaching and Learning*, 4, 74–88.

Sheridan, V. (2011) 'A holistic approach to international students: Institutional habitus and academic literacies in an Irish third level institution', *Higher Education*, 62, 129–40.

Shor, I. (1996) *When Students Have Power*. Chicago, IL: University of Chicago Press.

Shor, I. and Freire, P. (1987) 'What is the dialogical method of teaching?' *Journal of Education*, 169(3), 11–31.

Shulman, L. (1987) 'Knowledge and teaching: Foundations of the new reform', *Harvard Educational Review*, 57, 1–23.

Siddiqui, N., Boliver, V. and Gorard, S. (2019) 'Reliability of longitudinal social surveys of access to higher education: The case of next steps in England', *Social Inclusion*, 7, 80–89.

Siemens, G. (2004) Connectivism: A learning theory for the digital age. (Available from: http://citeseerx.ist.psu.edu/viewdoc/download?doi=10.1.1.87.3793andrep=rep1andtype=pdf, last accessed 21 October 2018.)

Skidmore, D. (2006) 'Pedagogy and dialogue', *Cambridge Journal of Education*, 36(4), 503–14.

Skidmore, D. and Murakami, K. (eds) (2016) *Dialogic Pedagogy: The Importance of Dialogue in Teaching and Learning*. Bristol: Channel View Publications.

Skinner, K., Hyde, S. and McPherson, K. (2016) 'Improving students interpersonal skills through experiential small group learning', *Journal of Learning Design*, 9, 21–36.

Smith, J. (2017) 'Target-setting, early-career academic identities and the measurement culture of UK higher education', *Higher Education Research and Development*, 36(3), 597–611.

Smith, J., Rattray, J., Peseta, T. and Loads, D. (eds) (2016) *Identity Work in the Contemporary University: Exploring an Uneasy Profession*. Rotterdam: Sense Publishers.

Soilemetzidis, I., Bennett, P., Buckley, A., Hillman, N. and Stoakes, G. (2014) *The 2014 Student Academic Experience Survey*. York: Higher Education Academy.

Solbrekke, T. and Helstad, K. (2016) 'Student formation in higher education: Teachers approaches matter', *Teaching in Higher Education*, 21, 962–77.

Song, W., Furco, A., Lopez, I. and Maruyama, G. (2017) 'Examining the relationship between service-learning participation and the educational success of underrepresented students', *Michigan Journal of Community Service Learning*, 24, 23–37.

Soudien, C. (2012) 'The promise of the university: What it's become and where it could go.' In B. Leibowitz (ed.), *Higher Education for the Public Good: Views from the South* Stoke-on-Trent and Stellenbosch: Trentham Books Ltd. and SUN Media, 31–43.

Spellings, M. (2006) *A Test of Leadership. Charting the Future of U.S. Higher Education: A Report of the Commission*. Washington: U.S. Department of Education.

Spence, C. (2019) 'Judgement versus metrics in higher education management', *Higher Education*, 77(5), 761–75.

Stein, B., Haynes, A. and Reading, M. (2006) Project CAT: Assessing critical thinking skills. *Proceedings of the National STEM Assessment Conference*. Hosted by the National Science Foundation and Drury University. 19–21 October, 290–99.

Stein, B., Haynes, A., Redding, M., Ennis, T. and Cecil, M. (2007) 'Assessing critical thinking in STEM and beyond.' In M. Iskander (ed.), *E-learning, Instruction Technology, Assessment and Engineering Education*. Cham: Springer, 79–82.

Stenhouse, L. (1975) *An Introduction to Curriculum Research and Development*. London: Heinemann.

Stevenson, E. (2011) 'Public engagement with science: Ways of thinking and practicing', *New Directions*, 7, 45–51.

Strang, L., Bélanger, J., Manville, C. and Meads, C. (2016) *Review of the Research Literature on Defining and Demonstrating Quality Teaching and Impact in Higher Education*. York: Higher Education Academy.

Stuart, M. (2012) *Social Mobility and Higher Education: The Life Experiences of First Generation Entrants in Higher Education*. Stoke-on-Trent: Trentham Books.

Subbaye, R. and Vithal, R. (2017) 'Teaching criteria that matter in university academic promotions', *Assessment and Evaluation in Higher Education*, 42, 37–60.

Subreenduth, S. (2012) 'Disrupting mainstream discourse in teacher education through decolonising strategies.' In B. Leibowitz (ed.), *Higher Education for the Public Good: Views from the South*. Stoke-on-Trent and Stellenbosch: Trentham Books Ltd. and SUN Media, 127–38.

Summerlee, A. (2018) 'Inquiry-based learning: A socially just approach to higher education', *Journal of Human Behavior in the Social Environment*, 28: 406–18.

Sun, A. and Chen, X. (2016) 'Online education and its effective practice: A research review', *Journal of Information Technology Education*, 15.

Swan, E. and Bailey, A. (2004) 'Thinking with feeling: The emotions of reflection.' In M. Reynolds and R. Vince (eds), *Organizing Reflection*. Aldershort, Ashgate, 105–25.

Swanson, E., McCulley, L., Osman, D., Scammacca Lewis, N. and Solis, M. (2019) 'The effect of team-based learning on content knowledge: A meta-analysis', *Active Learning in Higher Education*, 20(1), 39–50.

Sweetman, R. (2019) 'Incompatible enactments of learning outcomes? Leader, teacher and student experiences of an ambiguous policy object', *Teaching in Higher Education*, 24, 141–56.

Tagg, J. (2019) *The Instruction Myth: Why Higher Education is Hard to Change, and How to Change it*. New Brunswick, NJ: Rutgers University Press.

Tai, J., Canny, B., Haines, T. and Molloy, E. (2016) 'The role of peer-assisted learning in building evaluative judgement: Opportunities in clinical medical education', *Advances in Health Sciences Education*, 21(3), 659–76.

Tapp, J. (2015) 'Framing the curriculum for participation: A Bernsteinian perspective on academic literacies', *Teaching in Higher Education*, 20, 711–22.

Taylor, P. (2008) 'Being an academic today.' In R. Barnett and R. Di Napoli (eds), *Changing Identities in Higher Education: Voicing Perspectives*. Oxford: Routledge, 27–39.

Temple, P. (2008) 'Learning spaces in higher education: An under-researched topic', *London Review of Education*, 6, 229–41.

Thesen, L. (2009) 'Researching ideological becoming in lectures: Challenges for knowing differently', *Studies in Higher Education*, 34, 391–402.

Thomas, G. and Thorpe, S. (2019) 'Enhancing the facilitation of online groups in higher education: A review of the literature on face-to-face and online group-facilitation', *Interactive Learning Environments*, 27(1), 62–71.

Thomas, L. (2002) 'Student retention in higher education: The role of institutional habitus', *Journal of Education Policy*, 17, 423–32.

Thomas, L. (2005) 'Diversity, access and success: Learning, teaching and curriculum development to improve student retention', Enhancing the Student Experience: The First Annual Higher Education Academy Conference, Edinburgh, 29 June–1 July.

Thomas, L. (2012) *Building Student Engagement and Belonging in Higher Education at a Time of Change: Final Report from the What Works? Student Retention & Success Programme*. London: Paul Hamlyn Foundation. (Available from: https://www.heacademy.ac.uk/system/files/what_works_final_report.pdf, last accessed 24 May 2019.)

Thomas, L. (2014) 'Developing a curriculum for diversity: Raising awareness, increasing understanding and changing practice.' In B. Cunningham (ed.), *Professional Life in Modern British Higher Education: The Death of the Don?* London: Institute of Education.

Thomas, L. (2019) 'Governing access and recruitment in higher education.' In P. Teixeira, J. Shin, A. Amaral, A. Bernasconi, A. Magalhaes, B. Kehm, B. Stensaker, E. Choi, E. Balbachevsky, F. Hunter, G. Goastellec, G. Mohamedbhai, H. de Wit, J. Välimaa, L. Rumbley, L. Unangst, M. Klemencic, P. Langa, R. Yang, and T. Nokkala (eds) (2019) *Encyclopedia of International Higher Education Systems and Institutions*. Springer.

Thomas, L. and May, H. (2010) *Inclusive Learning and Teaching in Higher Education*, York: The Higher Education Academy. (Available from: http://www.heacademy.ac.uk/assets/documents/inclusion/InclusiveLearningandTeaching_FinalReport.pdf, last accessed 17 July 2014.)

Thomas, L. and Quinn, J. (2007) *First Generation Entry into Higher Education: An International Study*. Maidenhead: Open University Press.

Thompson, S. and Thompson, N. (2018) *The Critically Reflective Practitioner*. London: Macmillan.

Thomson, K. (2015) 'Informal conversations about teaching and their relationship to a formal development program: Learning opportunities for novice and mid-career academics', *International Journal for Academic Development*, 20, 137–49.

Thomson, K. and Trigwell, K. (2018) 'The role of informal conversations in developing university teaching?' *Studies in Higher Education*, 43, 1536–47.

Tierney, W. (1988) 'Organizational culture in higher education: Defining the essentials', *The Journal of Higher Education*, 59, 2–21.

Tight, M. (2013) 'Discipline and methodology in higher education research', *Higher Education Research and Development*, 32, 136–51.

Tight, M. (2015) 'Theory application in higher education research: The case of communities of practice', *European Journal of Higher Education*, 5(2), 111–26.

Tight, M. (2015a) 'Theory development and application in higher education research: Tribes and territories', *Higher Education Policy*, 28(3), 277–93.

Tight, M. (2016) 'Phenomenography: The development and application of an innovative research design in higher education research', *International Journal of Social Research Methodology*, 19, 319–38.

To, J. and Panadero, E. (2019) 'Peer assessment effects on the self-assessment process of first-year undergraduates', *Assessment and Evaluation in Higher Education*, 44, 920–32.

Tomlinson, M. (2017) 'Student perceptions of themselves as "consumers" of higher education', *British Journal of Sociology of Education*, 38(4), 450–67.

Tooher, M. and MacLaren, I. (2019) Collaborative Knowledge Exchange for Learning Impact Project Report. National Forum for the Enhancement of Learning & Teaching, Ireland. Available online: https://www.teachingandlearning.ie/project/collaborative-knowledge-exchange-for-learning-impact/, accessed July 2019.

Tormey, R. and Henchy, D. (2008) 'Re-imagining the traditional lecture: An action research approach to teaching student teachers to do philosophy', *Teaching in Higher Education*, 13, 303–14.

Trigwell, K. (2001) 'Judging university teaching', *The International Journal for Academic Development*, 6, 65–73.

Trigwell, K. and Shale, S. (2004) 'Student learning and the scholarship of university teaching', *Studies in Higher Education*, 29, 523–36.

Trigwell, K., Ashwin, P. and Millan, E. (2013) 'Evoked prior learning experience and approach to learning as predictors of academic achievement', *British Journal of Educational Psychology*, 83, 363–78.

Tronto, J. (2010) 'Creating caring institutions: Policy, plurality and purpose', *Ethics and Social Welfare*, 4, 158–71.

Trowler, P. (2020) *Accomplishing Change in Teaching and Learning Regimes: Higher Education and the Practice Sensibility.* Oxford: Oxford University Press.

Trowler, P. and Cooper, A. (2002) 'Teaching and learning regimes: Implicit theories and recurrent practices in the enhancement of teaching and learning through educational development programmes', *Higher Education Research and Development*, 21, 221–40.

Trowler, P., Ashwin, P. and Saunders, M. (2014) *The Role of HEFCE in Teaching and Learning Enhancement: A Review of Evaluative Evidence.* York: Higher Education Academy.

Trowler, P., Saunders, M. and Bamber, V. (eds) (2012) *Tribes and Territories in the 21st Century: Rethinking the Significance of Disciplines in Higher Education.* London: Routledge.

Trowler, V. (2010) *Student Engagement Literature Review.* York: Higher Education Academy.

Trowler, V. (2019) 'Transit and transition: Student identity and the contested landscape of Higher Education'. In S. Habib and M. Ward, *Identities, Youth and Belonging.* London: Palgrave Macmillan, 87–104.

Trowler, V., Trowler, P. and Saunders, M. (2018) *Responding to Student Voice: Insights into International Practice.* Glasgow: QAA Scotland.

UCC PLUS+ (2011) *Gateway to sUCCess: The Destination of UCC PLUS+ Graduates.* Cork: University College Cork.

UK Professional Standards Framework (2011) *UK Professional Standards Framework for Teaching and Supporting Learning in Higher Education.* York: Higher Education Academy.

United Nations (2015) Transforming our world: the 2030 agenda for sustainable development. *Resolution Adopted by the General Assembly.* Available at: http://www.un.org/en/development/desa/population/migration/generalassembly/docs/globalcompact/A_RES_70_1_E.pdf

University of Brighton (2012) *Module Design.* Brighton: Centre for Learning and Teaching, University of Brighton.

University of Cape Town (2018) *Curriculum Change Framework.* Cape Town: University of Cape Town.

Ursin, J., Vähäsantanen, K., McAlpine, L. and Hökkä, P. (2018) 'Emotionally loaded identity and agency in Finnish academic work', *Journal of Further and Higher Education*, 1–15.

Van Beveren, L., Roets, G., Buysse, A. and Rutten, K. (2018) 'We all reflect, but why? A systematic review of the purposes of reflection in higher education in social and behavioral sciences', *Educational Research Review*, 24, 1–9.

Van Lankveld, T., Schoonenboom, J., Volman, M., Croiset, G. and Beishuizen, J. (2017) 'Developing a teacher identity in the university context: A systematic review of the literature', *Higher Education Research and Development*, 36(2), 325–42.

van Rossum, E., and Hamer, R. (2010) *The Meaning of Learning and Knowing*. Rotterdam: Sense Publishers.

Vansteenkiste, M., Aelterman, N., De Muynck, G., Haerens, L., Patall, E. and Reeve, J. (2018) 'Fostering personal meaning and self-relevance: A self-determination theory perspective on internalization', *The Journal of Experimental Education*, 86(1), 30–49.

Van Waes, S., Van den Bossche, P., Moolenaar, N. M., De Maeyer, S. and Van Petegem, P. (2015) 'Know-who? Linking faculty's networks to stages of instructional development', *Higher Education*, 70, 807–26.

Vermunt, J. (2007) 'The power of teaching-learning environments to influence student learning.' In N. Entwistle and P. Tomlinson (eds), *Student Learning and University Teaching*. Leicester: British Psychological Society, 73–90.

Vermunt, J. and Donche, V. (2017) 'A learning patterns perspective on student learning in higher education: State of the art and moving forward', *Educational Psychology Review*, 29(2), 269–99.

Vermunt, J. and Verloop, N. (1999) 'Congruence and friction between learning and teaching', *Learning and Instruction*, 9, 257–80.

Vithal, R. (2018) 'Growing a scholarship of teaching and learning institutionally', *Studies in Higher Education*, 43, 468–83.

Waghid, Y. (2010) *Education, Democracy and Citizenship Revisited: Pedagogical Encounters*. Stellenbosch: Sun Press.

Wainwright, E. and Watts, M. (2019) 'Social mobility in the slipstream: First-generation students narratives of university participation and family', *Educational Review*, 1–17.

Walker, M. (2001) *Reconstructing Professionalism in University Teaching: Teachers and Learners in Action*. London: Society for Research in Higher Education.

Walker, M. (2006) *Higher Education Pedagogies*. Maidenhead: Society for Research into Higher Education and Open University Press.

Walker, M. (2010) 'A human development and capabilities prospective analysis of global higher education policy', *Journal of Education Policy*, 25, 485–501.

Walker, M. (2012) 'Universities and human development ethics: A capabilities approach to curriculum', *European Journal of Education*, 47, 448–61.

Walker, M. (2018) 'Aspirations and equality in higher education: Gender in a South African University', *Cambridge Journal of Education*, 48(1), 123–39.

Walker, M. and McLean, M. (2013) *Professional Education Capabilities and Contributions to the Public Good: The Role of Universities in Promoting Human Development*. London: Routledge.

Walker, M. and Thomson, P. (eds) (2010) *The Routledge Doctoral Supervisors Companion: Supporting Effective Research in Education and the Social Sciences*. Abingdon: Routledge.

Walker, M. and Wilson-Strydom, M. (eds) (2017) *Socially Just Pedagogies, Capabilities and Quality in Higher Education*. London: Palgrave Macmillan.

Waller, R., Ingram, N. and Ward, M. (eds) (2017) *Higher Education and Social Inequalities: University Admissions, Experiences, and Outcomes*. London: Routledge.

Walsh, A. and Kotzee, B. (2010) 'Reconciling graduateness and work-based learning', *Learning and Teaching in Higher Education*, 4(1), 36–50.

Walvoord, B. and Anderson, V. (2009) *Effective Grading: A Tool for Learning and Assessment in College*. 2nd edn. San Fransico, CA: Jossey-Bass

Watkins, J. and Mazur, E. (2013) 'Retaining students in Science, Technology, Engineering, and Mathematics (STEM) majors', *Journal of College Science Teaching*, 42(5), 36–41.

Watson, C. (2006) 'Narratives of practice and the construction of identity in teaching', *Teachers and Teaching: Theory and Practice*, 12(5), 509–26.

Watson, D. (2014) *The Question of Conscience: Higher Education and Personal Responsibility*. London: Institute of Education Press.

Webster, R. (2012) 'Challenging student satisfaction through the education of desires', *Australian Journal of Teacher Education*, 37(9), 81–92.

Weller, S. (2012) 'Achieving curriculum coherence: Curriculum design and delivery as social practice.' In P. Blackmore and C. Kandiko (eds), *Strategic Curriculum Change: Global Trends in Universities*. Abingdon and London: Routledge and SRHE.

Wells, G. (2001) 'The case for dialogic inquiry.' In G. Wells (ed.), *Action, Talk and Text: Learning and Teaching through Inquiry.* New York: Teachers College Press, 171–94.

Wenger E. (2010) 'Communities of practice and social learning systems: The Career of a Concept.' In C. Blackmore (eds), *Social Learning Systems and Communities of Practice*. London: Springer, 179–98.

Wenger, E., McDermott, R. and Snyder, W. (2002) *Cultivating Communities of Practice: A Guide to Managing Knowledge.* Boston, MA: Harvard Business School Press.

Wenger, E. White, N. and Smith, J. (2009) *Digital Habitats: Stewarding Technology for Communities*. Portland, OR: CPsquare.

Westheimer, J. (2010) 'Higher education or education for hire? Corporatization and the threat to democratic thinking', *Academic Matters*, April–May Issue. (Available from: http://www.academicmatters.ca/2010/04/higher-education-or-education-for-hire-corporatization-and-the-threat-to-democratic-thinking/, last accessed 24 May 2019.)

Weston, C. and McAlpine, L. (1998) 'How six outstanding math professors view teaching and learning: The importance of caring', *International Journal for Academic Development*, 3, 146–55.

Wheelahan, L. (2010) *Why Knowledge Matters in Curriculum: A Social Realist Argument.* Abingdon: Routledge.

Whitchurch, C. and Gordon, G. (2017) *Reconstructing Relationships in Higher Education: Challenging Agendas*. London: Routledge.

White, D. and Le Cornu, A. (2011) 'Visitors and residents: A new typology for online engagement', *First Monday*, 16, 9: http://firstmonday.org/ojs/index.php/fm/article/view/3171/3049

Wieman, C. (2017) *Improving How Universities Teach Science: Lessons from the Science Education Initiative*. Harvard, CT: Harvard University Press.

Wilcox, S. (1996) 'Fostering self-directed learning in the university setting', *Studies in Higher Education*, 21, 165–76.

Wilhelm, A. (2000) *Democracy in the Digital Age: Challenges to Political Life in Cyberspace* London: Routledge.

Williams, A., Verwoord, R., Beery, T., Dalton, H., McKinnon, J., Strickland, K., Pace, J. and Poole, G. (2013) 'The power of social networks: A model for weaving the scholarship of teaching and learning into institutional culture', *Teaching and Learning Inquiry*, 1, 49–62.

Wilson-Strydom, M. (2015) *University Access and Success: Capabilities, Diversity and Social Justice*. London: Routledge.

Wingate, U. (2007) 'A framework for transition: Supporting learning to learn in higher education', *Higher Education Quarterly*, 61, 391–405.

Wingate, U. (2012) 'Argument! Helping students understand what essay writing is about', *Journal of English for Academic Purposes*, 11, 145–54.

Wingrove, D., Hammersley-Fletcher, L., Clarke, A. and Chester, A. (2018) 'Leading developmental peer observation of teaching in higher education: Perspectives from Australia and England', *British Journal of Educational Studies*, 66, 365–81.

Winstone, N., Nash, R., Rowntree, J. and Parker, M. (2017) '"It'd be useful, but I wouldn't use it": Barriers to university students' feedback seeking and recipience', *Studies in Higher Education*, 42, 2026–41.

Wisker, G. (2012) *The Good Supervisor: Supervising Postgraduate and Undergraduate Research for Doctoral Theses and Dissertations*. 2nd edn. Basingstoke: Palgrave Macmillan.

Wolff, K. (2017) 'Engineering problem-solving knowledge: The impact of context', *Journal of Education and Work*, 30(8), 840–53.

Wolff, K. and Luckett, K. (2013) 'Integrating multidisciplinary engineering knowledge', *Teaching in Higher Education*, 18(1), 78–92.

Wolmarans, N. (2016) 'Inferential reasoning in design: Relations between material product and specialised disciplinary knowledge', *Design Studies*, 45, 92–115.

Wood, L. and Harding, A. (2007) 'Can you show you are a good lecturer?', *International Journal of Mathematical Education in Science and Technology*, 38, 939–47.

Woodward-Kron, R. (2008) 'More than just jargon: The nature and role of specialist language in learning disciplinary knowledge', *Journal of English for Academic Purposes*, 7, 234–49.

Yan, L. (2013) *Class Engagement of the Silent Asian Students in UK: New Perspectives on Engagement, Silence and Education*. Unpublished Masters thesis. University of Edinburgh.

Yeung, A., Cornish, S., Kable, S. and Sharma, M. (2019) 'What can instructors focus on when improving undergraduate science experiments? Supporting a cross-disciplinary approach', *International Journal of Innovation in Science and Mathematics Education (formerly CAL-laborate International)*, 27(3).

Yorke, M. (1998) 'The management of assessment in higher education', *Assessment & Evaluation in Higher Education*, 23, 101–16.

Yorke, M. (2004) 'Employability in the undergraduate curriculum: Some students perspectives', *European Journal of Education*, 39, 409–27.

Yorke, M. (2008) *Grading Student Achievement in Higher Education: Signals and Shortcomings*. London: Routledge.

Yosso, T. and Burciaga, R. (2016) Reclaiming our histories: Recovering community cultural wealth. *Center for Critical Race Studies at UCLA R*, 5. (Available from: https://issuu.com/almaiflores/docs/ty___rb_research_brief_final_versio.)

Young, M. (ed.) (1971) *Knowledge and Control: New Directions for the Sociology of Education*. London: Collier Mcmillan.

Young, M. (2008) *Bringing Knowledge Back In: From Social Constructivism to Social Realism in the Sociology of Education*. Abingdon: Routledge.

Younger, K., Gascoine, L., Menzies, V. and Torgerson, C. (2019) 'A systematic review of evidence on the effectiveness of interventions and strategies for widening participation in higher education, *Journal of Further and Higher Education*, 43(6), 742–73.

Zeichner, K. and Liston, D. (1996) *Reflective Teaching: An Introduction*. Mahwah, NJ: Lawrence Erlbaum Associates.

Zembylas, M. (2008) *The Politics of Trauma in Education*. New York: Palgrave Macmillan.

Zepke, N. (2018) 'Student engagement in neo-liberal times: What is missing?' *Higher Education Research and Development*, 37(2), 433–46.

Zhang, P., Ding, L. and Mazur, E. (2017) 'Peer instruction in introductory physics: A method to bring about positive changes in students' attitudes and beliefs', *Physical Review Physics Education Research*, 13(1), 010104.

Zipin, L., Fataar, A. and Brennan, M. (2015) 'Can social realism do social justice? Debating the warrants for curriculum knowledge selection', *Education as Change*, 19, 9–36.

Zuber-Skerritt, O., Fletcher, M. and Kearney, J. (2015) *Professional Learning in Higher Education and Communities: Towards a New Vision for Action Research*. London: Palgrave Macmillan.

Zusho, A. (2017) 'Toward an integrated model of student learning in the college classroom', *Educational Psychology Review*, 29(2), 301–24.

Zusho, A. and Edwards, K. (2011) 'Self-regulation and achievement goals in the college classroom', *New Directions for Teaching and Learning*, 126, 21–31.

Index

This index covers Chapters 1–17 but not the Introduction, summary pages at the start of each chapter or reading lists. Selected significant proper names are indexed. The index covers topics in case studies and reflective activities; an 'f' after a page number indicates a figure; an '(RA)' indicates a reflective activity (in boxed text); an '(RB)' indicates a figure in a research briefing; a '(CS)' indicates a case study; bold type indicates TLRP principles (in boxed text); underlined type indicates principal coverage of these principles (Chapter 4).